Patriarchs and Prophets

Ellen G. White

1890

LS Company

ISBN:978-1-0879-0764-2

Copyright © 2021

Preface

The publishers send out this work from a conviction that it throws light upon a subject of paramount importance and universal interest, and one on which light is to be greatly desired; that it presents truths too little known or too widely ignored. The great controversy between truth and error, between light and darkness, between the power of God and the attempted usurpations of the enemy of all righteousness, is the one great spectacle which it is reasonable to suppose must engage the attention of all worlds. That such a controversy exists as the result of sin, that it is to pass through various stages of progress, and end at last in a manner to redound to the glory of God and the higher exaltation of His loyal servants, is as certain as that the Bible is a revelation from God to men. That word reveals the great features of this controversy, a conflict which embraces the redemption of a world; and there are special epochs when these questions assume unwonted interest, and it becomes a matter of the first importance to understand our relation thereto.

Such a time is the present, for all things indicate that we may now confidently cherish the hope that this long controversy is drawing near its close. Yet many now seem disposed to relegate to the realm of fable that portion of the record opening to our view the steps by which our world became involved in this great issue; and others, though avoiding this extreme view, seem nevertheless inclined to regard it as obsolete and unimportant, and are thus led to treat it with neglect.

But who would not wish to look into the secret causes of so strange a defection; to discern its spirit, to mark its consequences, and to learn how to avoid its results? With such themes this volume deals. It tends to foster a living interest in those portions of God's word most often neglected. It clothes with new meaning the promises and prophecies of the sacred record, vindicates the ways of God in dealing with rebellion, and shows forth the wonderful grace of God in devising a way of salvation for sinful man. Thus we are taken down in the history of this work to a time when the plans and purposes of God had been clearly unfolded to the chosen people.

Though dealing with themes so exalted, themes that stir the heart to its depths and awaken the liveliest emotions of the mind, the style of the book is lucid, and the language plain and direct. We commend this volume to all who take pleasure in studying the divine plan of human redemption and who feel any interest in the relation of their own souls to Christ's atoning work; and to all others we commend it, that it may awaken in them an interest in these things.

Introduction

[19]

This volume treats upon the themes of Bible history, themes not in themselves new, yet here so presented as to give them a new significance, revealing springs of action, showing the important bearing of certain movements, and bringing into stronger light some features that are but briefly mentioned in the Bible. Thus the scenes have a vividness and importance that tend to make new and lasting impressions. Such a light is shed upon the Scripture record as to reveal more fully the character and purposes of God; to make manifest the wiles of Satan and the means by which his power will be finally overthrown; to bring to view the weakness of the human heart, and show how the grace of God has enabled men to conquer in the battle with evil. All this is in harmony with what God has shown to be His purpose in unfolding to men the truths of His word. The agency by which these revelations have been given is seen—when tested by the Scriptures—to be one of the methods God still employs to impart instruction to the children of men.

While it is not now as it was in the beginning, when man in his holiness and innocence had personal instruction from his Maker, still man is not left without a divine teacher which God has provided in His representative, the Holy Spirit. So we hear the apostle Paul declaring that a certain divine "illumination" is the privilege of the followers of Christ; and that they are "enlightened" by being made "partakers of the Holy Ghost." Hebrews 10:32; 6:4. John also says, "Ye have an unction from the Holy One." 1 John 2:20. And Christ promised the disciples, as He was about to leave them, that He would send them the Holy Spirit as a comforter and guide to lead them into all truth. John 14:16, 26.

To show how this promise was to be fulfilled to the church, the apostle Paul, in two of his epistles, presents formal declaration that certain gifts of the Spirit have been placed in the Church for its edification and instruction to the end of time. 1 Corinthians 12; Ephesians 4:8-13; Matthew 28:20 Nor is this all: a number of clear

[20]

v

and explicit prophecies declare that in the last days there will be a special outpouring of the Holy Spirit, and that the church at the time of Christ's appearing will have had, during its closing experience, "the testimony of Jesus," which is the spirit of prophecy. Acts 2:17-20, 39; 1 Corinthians 1:7; Revelation 12:17; Revelation 19:10. In these facts we see an evidence of God's care and love for His people; for the presence of the Holy Spirit as a comforter, teacher, and guide, not only in its ordinary, but in its extraordinary, methods of operation, certainly is needed by the church as it enters the perils of the last days, more than in any other part of its experience.

The Scriptures point out various channels through which the Holy Spirit would operate on the hearts and minds of men to enlighten their understanding and guide their steps. Among these were visions and dreams. In this way God would still communicate with the children of men. Here is His promise on this point: "Hear now my words: If there be a prophet among you, I the Lord will make Myself known unto him in a vision, and will speak unto him in a dream." Numbers 12:6. By this means supernatural knowledge was communicated to Balaam. Thus He says: "Balaam the son of Beor hath said, and the man whose eyes are open hath said: he hath said, which heard the words of God, and knew the knowledge of the Most High, which saw the vision of the almighty, falling into a trance, but having his eyes open." Numbers 24:15, 16.

It thus becomes a matter of great interest to investigate the testimony of the Scriptures concerning the extent to which the Lord designed that the Spirit should manifest itself in the church during the period of human probation.

[21] After the plan of salvation had been devised, God, as we have seen, could still, through the ministry of His Son and the holy angels, communicate with men across the gulf which sin had made. Sometimes He spoke face to face with them, as in the case of Moses, but more frequently by dreams and visions. Instances of such communication are everywhere prominent upon the sacred record, covering all dispensations. Enoch the seventh from Adam looked forward in the spirit of prophecy to the second advent of Christ in power and glory, and exclaimed, "Behold, the Lord cometh with ten thousands of His saints." Jude 14. "Holy men of God spake as they were moved by the Holy Ghost." 2 Peter 1:21. If the operation of the spirit of

prophecy has at times seemed almost to disappear, as the spirituality of the people waned, it has nevertheless marked all the great crises in the experience of the church, and the epochs which witnessed the change from one dispensation to another. When the era marked by the incarnation of Christ was reached, the father of John the Baptist was filled with the Holy Spirit, and prophesied. Luke 1:67. To Simeon it was revealed that he should not see death till he had seen the Lord; and when the parents of Jesus brought Him into the temple that He might be dedicated, Simeon came by the Spirit into the temple, took Him into his arms, and blessed Him while he prophesied concerning Him. And Anna, a prophetess, coming in the same instant, spake of Him to all them that looked for redemption in Jerusalem. Luke 2:26, 36.

The outpouring of the Holy Spirit which was to attend the preaching of the gospel by the followers of Christ was announced by the prophet in these words: "And it shall come to pass afterward, that I will pour out My Spirit upon all flesh; and your sons and your daughters shall prophesy, and your old men shall dream dreams, your young men shall see visions: And also upon the servants and upon the handmaids in those days will I pour out My Spirit. And I will show wonders in the heavens and in the earth, blood, and fire, and pillars of smoke. The sun shall be turned into darkness, and the moon into blood, before the great and the terrible day of the Lord come." Joel 2:28-31.

Peter, on the Day of Pentecost, quoted this prophecy in explanation of the wonderful scene which then occurred. Cloven tongues like as of fire sat upon each of the disciples; they were filled with the holy spirit, and spake with other tongues. And when the mockers charged that they were filled with new wine, Peter answered, "These are not drunken, as ye suppose, seeing it is but the third hour of the day. But this is that which was spoken by the prophet Joel." Then he quotes the prophecy substantially as found in Joel (quoted above), only he puts the words "in the last days," in the place of "Afterward," making it read, "and it shall come to pass in the last days, saith God, I will pour out of My Spirit," etc.

It is evident that it was that part of the prophecy only which relates to the outpouring of the Spirit, that began to be fulfilled on that day; for there were no old men there dreaming dreams, nor young men and maidens seeing visions and prophesying; and no wonders of blood and fire and pillars of smoke then appeared; and the sun was not darkened and the moon was not turned to blood at that time; and yet what was there witnessed was in fulfillment of the prophecy of Joel. It is equally evident that this part of the prophecy concerning the outpouring of the Spirit was not exhausted in that one manifestation; for the prophecy covers all days from that time on to the coming of the great day of the Lord.

But the Day of Pentecost was in fulfillment of other prophecies besides that of Joel. It fulfilled the words of Christ Himself as well. In His last discourse to His disciples before His crucifixion, He said to them: "I will pray the Father, and He shall give you another Comforter, ... Even the Spirit of truth." John 14:16, 17. "But the Comforter, which is the Holy Ghost, whom the Father will send in My name, He shall teach you all things." Verse 26. "Howbeit when He, the Spirit of truth, is come, He will guide you into all truth." Chapter 16:13. And after Christ had risen from the dead, He said to the disciples, "Behold, I send the promise of my Father upon you: But tarry ye in the city of Jerusalem, until ye be endued with power from on high." Luke 24:49.

On the Day of Pentecost the disciples were thus endued with power from on high. But this promise of Christ's was not, any more than the prophecy of Joel, confined to that occasion. For He gave them the same promise in another form by assuring them that He would be with them always, even to the end of the world. Matthew 28:20. Mark tells us in what sense and what manner the Lord was to be with them. He says, "And they went forth, and preached everywhere, the Lord working with them, and confirming the word with signs following." Mark 16:20. And Peter, on the Day of Pentecost, testified concerning the perpetuity of this operation of the Spirit which they had witnessed. When the convicted Jews said unto the apostles, "What shall we do?" Peter answered, "Repent, and be baptized every one of you in the name of Jesus Christ for the remission of sins, and ye shall receive the gift of the Holy Ghost. For the promise is unto you, and to your children, and to all that are afar off, even as many as the Lord our God shall call." Acts 2:37-39. This certainly provides for the operation of the Holy Spirit in the church, even in its special manifestations, to all coming time, as long as mercy shall invite men to accept the pardoning love of Christ.

Twenty-eight years later in his letter to the Corinthians, Paul set before that church a formal argument on the question. He says (1 Corinthians 12:1), "Now concerning spiritual gifts, brethren, I would not have you ignorant"—so important did he deem it that this subject should be understood in the Christian church. After stating that though the Spirit is one it has diversities of operation, and explaining what those diversities are, he introduces the figure of the human body, with its various members, to show how the church is constituted with its different offices and gifts. And as the body has its various members, each having its particular office to fill, and all working together in unity of purpose to constitute one harmonious whole, so the Spirit was to operate through various channels in the church to constitute a perfect religious body. Paul then continues in these words: "And God hath set some in the church, first apostles, secondarily prophets, thirdly teachers, after that miracles, then gifts of healing, helps, governments, diversities of tongues."

The declaration that God *hath set* some in the church, etc., implies something more than that the way was left open for the gifts to appear if circumstances should chance to favor. It rather signifies that they were to be permanent parts of the true spiritual constitution of the church, and that if these were not in active operation the church would be in the condition of a human body, some of whose members had, through accident or disease, become crippled and helpless. Having once been set in the church, there these gifts must remain until they are formally removed. But there is no record that they ever have been removed.

Five years later the same apostle writes to the Ephesians relative to the same gifts, plainly stating their object, and thus showing indirectly that they must continue till that object is accomplished. He says (Ephesians 4:8, 11-13): "Wherefore He saith, when He ascended up on high, He led captivity captive, and gave gifts unto men.... And He gave some, apostles; and some, prophets; and some, evangelists; and some, pastors and teachers; for the perfecting of the saints, for the work of the ministry, for the edifying of the body of Christ: Till we all come in the unity of the faith, and of the knowledge of the Son of God, unto a perfect man, unto the measure of the stature of the fullness of Christ."

The church did not reach the state of unity here contemplated, in the apostolic age; and very soon after that age, the gloom of the great spiritual apostasy began to overshadow the church; and certainly during the state of declension, this fullness of Christ, and unity of faith, was not reached. Nor will it be reached till the last message of mercy shall have gathered out of every kindred and people, every class of society, and every organization of error, a people complete in all gospel reforms, waiting for the coming of the Son of man. And truly, if ever in her experience the church would need the benefit of every agency ordained for her comfort and guidance, encouragement and protection, it would be amid the perils of the last days, when the powers of evil, well-nigh perfected by experience and training for their nefarious work, would, by their masterpieces of imposture, deceive if it were possible even the elect. Very appropriately, therefore, come in the special prophecies of the outpouring of the Spirit for the benefit of the church in the last days.

It is, however, usually taught, in the current literature of the Christian world, that the gifts of the Spirit were only for the apostolic age; that they were given simply for the planting of the gospel; and that the gospel being once established, the gifts were no longer needed, and consequently were suffered soon to disappear from the church. But the apostle Paul warned the Christians of his day that the "mystery of iniquity" was already at work, and that after his departure, grievous wolves would enter in among them, not sparing the flock, and that also of their own selves men would arise, speaking perverse things to draw away disciples after them. Acts 20:29, 30. It cannot therefore be that the gifts, placed in the church to guard against these very evils, were ready, when that time came, to pass away as having accomplished their object; for their presence and help would be needed under these conditions more than when the apostles themselves were on the stage of action.

We find another statement in Paul's letter to the Corinthian church, which shows that the popular conception of the temporary continuance of the gifts cannot be correct. It is his contrast between the present, imperfect state, and the glorious, immortal condition to which the Christian will finally arrive. 1 Corinthians 13. He says

(Verses 9, 10). "For we know in part, and we prophesy in part. But when that which is perfect is come, then that which is in part shall be done away." He further illustrates this present state by comparing it to the period of childhood with its weakness and immaturity of thought and action; and the perfect state, to the condition of manhood with its clearer vision, maturity, and strength. And he classes the gifts among those things which are needed in this present, imperfect condition, but which we shall have no occasion for when the perfect state is come. "Now," he says (Verse 12), "we see through a glass, darkly; but then face to face: Now I know in part; but then shall I know even as also I am known." Then he states what graces are adapted to the eternal state, and will there exist, namely, faith, hope, and charity, or love, "these three; but the greatest of these is charity."

This explains the language of Verse 8: "Charity never faileth;" that is, charity, the heavenly grace of love, will endure forever; it is the crowning glory of man's future, immortal condition; but "whether there be prophecies, they shall fail;" that is, the time will come when prophecies will be no longer needed, and the gift of prophecy, as one of the helps in the church, will no longer be exercised; "whether there be tongues, they shall cease;" that is, the gift of tongues will no longer be of service; "whether there be knowledge, it shall vanish away;" that is, knowledge, not in the abstract, but as one of the special gifts of the Spirit, will be rendered unnecessary by the perfect knowledge with which we shall be endowed in the eternal world.

Now, if we take the position that the gifts ceased with the apostolic age, because no longer needed, we commit ourselves to the position that the apostolic age was the weak and childish age of the church, when everything was seen through a glass, darkly; but the age that followed, when grievous wolves were to enter in, not sparing the flock, and men were to arise, even in the church, speaking perverse things to draw away disciples after them, was an age of perfect light and knowledge, in which the imperfect and childish and darkened knowledge of apostolic times had passed away! For, be it remembered, the gifts cease only when a perfect state is reached, and because that state is reached, which renders them no longer necessary. But no one, on sober thought, can for a moment seek to maintain the position that the apostolic age was inferior in spiritual elevation to any age which has succeeded it. And if the gifts were needed then, they certainly are needed now.

Among the agencies which the apostle in his letters to both the Corinthians and Ephesians enumerates as "gifts" *set* in the church, we find "pastors," "teachers," "helps," and "governments;" and all these are acknowledged, on every hand, as still continuing in the church. Why not, then, the others also, including faith, healing, prophecy, etc.? Who is competent to draw the line, and say what gifts have been "set out" of the church, when all were, in the beginning, equally "set" therein?

Revelation 12:17 has been referred to as a prophecy that the gifts would be restored in the last days. An examination of its testimony will confirm this view. The text speaks of the remnant of the woman's seed. The woman being a symbol of the church, her seed would be the individual members composing the church at any one time; and the "remnant" of her seed would be the last generation of Christians, or those living on the earth at the second coming of Christ. The text further declares that these "keep the commandments of God, and have the testimony of Jesus Christ;" and the "testimony of Jesus" is explained in chapter 19:10 to be "the spirit of prophecy," which must be understood as that which among the gifts is called "the gift of prophecy." 1 Corinthians 12:9, 10.

The setting of the gifts in the church does not imply that every individual was to have them in exercise. On this point the apostle (1 Corinthians 12:29) says, "Are all apostles? Are all prophets? Are all teachers?" etc. the implied answer is no; not all are; but the gifts are divided among the members as it pleases God. 1 Corinthians 12:7, 11. Yet these gifts are said to be "set in the *church*," and if a gift is bestowed upon even one member of the church, it may be said that that gift is "in the church," or that the church "has" it. So the last generation was to have, and it is believed does now have, the testimony of Jesus, or the gift of prophecy.

Another portion of Scripture evidently written with reference to the last days, brings the same fact plainly to view. 1 Thessalonians 5. The apostle opens the chapter with these words: "But of the times and the seasons, brethren, you have no need that I write unto you. For yourselves know perfectly that the day of the Lord so cometh as a thief in the night." In Verse 4 he adds, "But ye, brethren, are not in darkness, that that day should overtake you as a thief." Then he gives them sundry admonitions in view of that event, among which are these (verses 19-21): "Quench not the Spirit. Despise not prophesyings. Prove all things; hold fast that which is good." And in verse 23 he prays that these very ones who were thus to have to do with "prophesyings" may be preserved blameless unto the *coming of the Lord*.

On the strength of these considerations are we not justified in believing that the gift of prophecy will be manifested in the church in the last days, and that through it much light will be imparted, and much timely instruction given?

All things are to be treated according to the apostle's rule: "Prove all things; hold fast that which is good;" and to be tested by the Saviour's standard: "By their fruits ye shall know them." Appealing to this standard in behalf of what claims to be a manifestation of the gift of prophecy, we commend this volume to the consideration of those who believe that the Bible is the word of God, and that the church is the body of which Christ is head.

U. Smith.

Contents

Preface	iii
Introduction	v
Chapter 1—Why was Sin Permitted?	17
Chapter 2—The Creation	28
Chapter 3—The Temptation and Fall	36
Chapter 4—The Plan of Redemption	47
Chapter 5—Cain and Abel Tested	55
Chapter 6—Seth and Enoch	62
Chapter 7—The Flood	72
Chapter 8—After the Flood	85
Chapter 9—The Literal Week	91
Chapter 10—The Tower of Babel	97
Chapter 11—The Call of Abraham	103
Chapter 12—Abraham in Canaan	110
Chapter 13—The Test of Faith	123
Chapter 14—Destruction of Sodom	132
Chapter 15—The Marriage of Isaac	145
Chapter 16—Jacob and Esau	151
Chapter 17—Jacob's Flight and Exile	157
Chapter 18—The Night of Wrestling	167
Chapter 19—The Return to Canaan	174
Chapter 20—Joseph in Egypt	183
Chapter 21—Joseph and His Brothers	192
Chapter 22—Moses	210
Chapter 23—The Plagues of Egypt	224
Chapter 24—The Passover	239
Chapter 25—The Exodus	245
Chapter 26—From the Red Sea to Sinai	254
Chapter 27—The Law Given to Israel	266
Chapter 28—Idolatry at Sinai	278
Chapter 29—Satan's Enmity Against the Law	292
Chapter 30—The Tabernacle and Its Services	304
Chapter 31—The Sin of Nadab and Abihu	318

Chapter 32—The Law and the Covenants 322
Chapter 33—From Sinai to Kadesh...................... 333
Chapter 34—The Twelve Spies 346
Chapter 35—The Rebellion of Korah 354
Chapter 36—In the Wilderness 366
Chapter 37—The Smitten Rock......................... 371
Chapter 38—The Journey Around Edom 380
Chapter 39—The Conquest of Bashan 391
Chapter 40—Balaam.................................. 396
Chapter 41—Apostasy at the Jordan 410
Chapter 42—The Law Repeated 419
Chapter 43—The Death of Moses 426
Chapter 44—Crossing the Jordan 436
Chapter 45—The Fall of Jericho 442
Chapter 46—The Blessings and the Curses 452
Chapter 47—League With the Gibeonites 456
Chapter 48—The Division of Canaan 461
Chapter 49—The Last Words of Joshua 472
Chapter 50—Tithes and Offerings....................... 476
Chapter 51—God's Care for the Poor 481
Chapter 52—The Annual Feasts 488
Chapter 53—The Earlier Judges 495
Chapter 54—Samson 510
Chapter 55—The Child Samuel......................... 519
Chapter 56—Eli and His Sons 525
Chapter 57—The Ark Taken by the Philistines 531
Chapter 58—The Schools of the Prophets 542
Chapter 59—The First King of Israel 551
Chapter 60—The Presumption of Saul 564
Chapter 61—Saul Rejected 573
Chapter 62—The Anointing of David.................... 583
Chapter 63—David and Goliath 587
Chapter 64—David a Fugitive 593
Chapter 65—The Magnanimity of David 604
Chapter 66—The Death of Saul......................... 617
Chapter 67—Ancient and Modern Sorcery 623
Chapter 68—David at Ziklag 630
Chapter 69—David Called to the Throne 637

Chapter 70—The Reign of David 643
Chapter 71—David's Sin and Repentance 656
Chapter 72—The Rebellion of Absalom................... 667
Chapter 73—The Last Years of David 684
Appendix 694

Chapter 1—Why was Sin Permitted?

"God is love." 1 John 4:16. His nature, His law, is love. It ever has been; it ever will be. "The high and lofty One that inhabiteth eternity," whose "ways are everlasting," changeth not. With Him "is no variableness, neither shadow of turning." Isaiah 57:15; Habakkuk 3:6; James 1:17.

Every manifestation of creative power is an expression of infinite love. The sovereignty of God involves fullness of blessing to all created beings. The psalmist says:

"Strong is Thy hand, and high is Thy right hand.
  Righteousness and judgment are the foundation of Thy throne:
Mercy and truth go before Thy face.
  Blessed is the people that know the joyful sound:
They walk, O Lord, in the light of Thy countenance.
  In Thy name do they rejoice all the day:
And in Thy righteousness are they exalted.
  For Thou art the glory of their strength: ...
For our shield belongeth unto Jehovah,
  And our king to the Holy One."

Psalm 89:13-18, R.V. [Note: In this text and in some other Bible quotations used in this book the word "Jehovah" is employed instead of "Lord," as rendered in the American Supplement to the Revised Version.]

The history of the great conflict between good and evil, from the time it first began in heaven to the final overthrow of rebellion and the total eradication of sin, is also a demonstration of God's unchanging love.

The Sovereign of the universe was not alone in His work of beneficence. He had an associate—a co-worker who could appreciate His purposes, and could share His joy in giving happiness to created beings. "In the beginning was the Word, and the Word was with God, and the Word was God. The same was in the beginning with God." John 1:1, 2. Christ, the Word, the only begotten of God, was one with the eternal Father—one in nature, in character, in purpose—the only being that could enter into all the counsels and purposes of God. "His name shall be called Wonderful, Counselor, The mighty God, The everlasting Father, The Prince of Peace." Isaiah 9:6. His "goings forth have been from of old, from everlasting." Micah 5:2. And the Son of God declares concerning Himself: "The Lord possessed Me in the beginning of His way, before His works of old. I was set up from everlasting.... When He appointed the foundations of the earth: then I was by Him, as one brought up with Him: and I was daily His delight, rejoicing always before Him." Proverbs 8:22-30.

The Father wrought by His Son in the creation of all heavenly beings. "By Him were all things created, ... whether they be thrones, or dominions, or principalities, or powers: all things were created by Him, and for Him." Colossians 1:16. Angels are God's ministers, radiant with the light ever flowing from His presence and speeding on rapid wing to execute His will. But the Son, the anointed of God, the "express image of His person," "the brightness of His glory," "upholding all things by the word of His power," holds supremacy over them all. Hebrews 1:3. "A glorious high throne from the beginning," was the place of His sanctuary (Jeremiah 17:12); "a scepter of righteousness," the scepter of His kingdom. Hebrews 1:8. "Honor and majesty are before Him: strength and beauty are in His sanctuary." Psalm 96:6. Mercy and truth go before His face. Psalm 89:14.

The law of love being the foundation of the government of God, the happiness of all intelligent beings depends upon their perfect accord with its great principles of righteousness. God desires from all His creatures the service of love—service that springs from an appreciation of His character. He takes no pleasure in a forced obedience; and to all He grants freedom of will, that they may render Him voluntary service.

So long as all created beings acknowledged the allegiance of love, there was perfect harmony throughout the universe of God. It was the joy of the heavenly host to fulfill the purpose of their Creator. They delighted in reflecting His glory and showing forth His praise. And while love to God was supreme, love for one another was confiding and unselfish. There was no note of discord to mar the celestial harmonies. But a change came over this happy state. There was one who perverted the freedom that God had granted to His creatures. Sin originated with him who, next to Christ, had been most honored of God and was highest in power and glory among the inhabitants of heaven. Lucifer, "son of the morning," was first of the covering cherubs, holy and undefiled. He stood in the presence of the great Creator, and the ceaseless beams of glory enshrouding the eternal God rested upon him. "Thus saith the Lord God; Thou sealest up the sum, full of wisdom, and perfect in beauty. Thou hast been in Eden the garden of God; every precious stone was thy covering.... Thou art the anointed cherub that covereth; and I have set thee so: thou wast upon the holy mountain of God; thou hast walked up and down in the midst of the stones of fire. Thou wast perfect in thy ways from the day that thou wast created, till iniquity was found in thee." Ezekiel 28:12-15.

Little by little Lucifer came to indulge the desire for self-exaltation. The Scripture says, "Thine heart was lifted up because of thy beauty, thou hast corrupted thy wisdom by reason of thy brightness." Ezekiel 28:17. "Thou hast said in thine heart, ...I will exalt my throne above the stars of God.... I will be like the Most High." Isaiah 14:13, 14. Though all his glory was from God, this mighty angel came to regard it as pertaining to himself. Not content with his position, though honored above the heavenly host, he ventured to covet homage due alone to the Creator. Instead of seeking to make God supreme in the affections and allegiance of all created beings, it was his endeavor to secure their service and loyalty to himself. And coveting the glory with which the infinite Father had invested His Son, this prince of angels aspired to power that was the prerogative of Christ alone.

Now the perfect harmony of heaven was broken. Lucifer's disposition to serve himself instead of his Creator aroused a feeling of apprehension when observed by those who considered that the glory of God should be supreme. In heavenly council the angels pleaded with Lucifer. The Son of God presented before him the greatness, the goodness, and the justice of the Creator, and the sacred, unchanging nature of His law. God Himself had established the order of heaven; and in departing from it, Lucifer would dishonor his Maker and bring ruin upon himself. But the warning, given in infinite love and mercy, only aroused a spirit of resistance. Lucifer allowed his jealousy of Christ to prevail, and became the more determined.

To dispute the supremacy of the Son of God, thus impeaching the wisdom and love of the Creator, had become the purpose of this prince of angels. To this object he was about to bend the energies of that master mind, which, next to Christ's, was first among the hosts of God. But He who would have the will of all His creatures free, left none unguarded to the bewildering sophistry by which rebellion would seek to justify itself. Before the great contest should open, all were to have a clear presentation of His will, whose wisdom and goodness were the spring of all their joy.

The King of the universe summoned the heavenly hosts before Him, that in their presence He might set forth the true position of His Son and show the relation He sustained to all created beings. The Son of God shared the Father's throne, and the glory of the eternal, self-existent One encircled both. About the throne gathered the holy angels, a vast, unnumbered throng—"ten thousand times ten thousand, and thousands of thousands" (Revelation 5:11.), the most exalted angels, as ministers and subjects, rejoicing in the light that fell upon them from the presence of the Deity. Before the assembled inhabitants of heaven the King declared that none but Christ, the Only Begotten of God, could fully enter into His purposes, and to Him it was committed to execute the mighty counsels of His will. The Son of God had wrought the Father's will in the creation of all the hosts of heaven; and to Him, as well as to God, their homage and allegiance were due. Christ was still to exercise divine power, in the creation of the earth and its inhabitants. But in all this He would not seek power or exaltation for Himself contrary to God's plan, but would exalt the Father's glory and execute His purposes of beneficence and love.

The angels joyfully acknowledged the supremacy of Christ, and prostrating themselves before Him, poured out their love and adoration. Lucifer bowed with them, but in his heart there was a strange, fierce conflict. Truth, justice, and loyalty were struggling against envy and jealousy. The influence of the holy angels seemed for a time to carry him with them. As songs of praise ascended in melodious strains, swelled by thousands of glad voices, the spirit of evil seemed vanquished; unutterable love thrilled his entire being; his soul went out, in harmony with the sinless worshippers, in love to the Father and the Son. But again he was filled with pride in his own glory. His desire for supremacy returned, and envy of Christ was once more indulged. The high honors conferred upon Lucifer were not appreciated as God's special gift, and therefore, called forth no gratitude to his Creator. He gloried in his brightness and exaltation and aspired to be equal with God. He was beloved and reverenced by the heavenly host, angels delighted to execute his commands, and he was clothed with wisdom and glory above them all. Yet the Son of God was exalted above him, as one in power and authority with the Father. He shared the Father's counsels, while Lucifer did not thus enter into the purposes of God. "Why," questioned this mighty angel, "should Christ have the supremacy? Why is He honored above Lucifer?"

Leaving his place in the immediate presence of the Father, Lucifer went forth to diffuse the spirit of discontent among the angels. He worked with mysterious secrecy, and for a time concealed his real purpose under an appearance of reverence for God. He began to insinuate doubts concerning the laws that governed heavenly beings, intimating that though laws might be necessary for the inhabitants of the worlds, angels, being more exalted, needed no such restraint, for their own wisdom was a sufficient guide. They were not beings that could bring dishonor to God; all their thoughts were holy; it was no more possible for them than for God Himself to err. The exaltation of the Son of God as equal with the Father was represented as an injustice to Lucifer, who, it was claimed, was also entitled to reverence and honor. If this prince of angels could but attain to his true, exalted position, great good would accrue to the entire host of heaven; for it was his object to secure freedom for all. But now even the liberty which they had hitherto enjoyed was at an end; for an absolute Ruler had been appointed them, and to His authority all

[37]

must pay homage. Such were the subtle deceptions that through the wiles of Lucifer were fast obtaining in the heavenly courts.

There had been no change in the position or authority of Christ. Lucifer's envy and misrepresentation and his claims to equality with Christ had made necessary a statement of the true position of the Son of God; but this had been the same from the beginning. Many of the angels were, however, blinded by Lucifer's deceptions.

Taking advantage of the loving, loyal trust reposed in him by the holy beings under his command, he had so artfully instilled into their minds his own distrust and discontent that his agency was not discerned. Lucifer had presented the purposes of God in a false light—misconstruing and distorting them to excite dissent and dissatisfaction. He cunningly drew his hearers on to give utterance to their feelings; then these expressions were repeated by him when it would serve his purpose, as evidence that the angels were not fully in harmony with the government of God. While claiming for himself perfect loyalty to God, he urged that changes in the order and laws of heaven were necessary for the stability of the divine government. Thus while working to excite opposition to the law of God and to instill his own discontent into the minds of the angels under him, he was ostensibly seeking to remove dissatisfaction and to reconcile disaffected angels to the order of heaven. While secretly fomenting discord and rebellion, he with consummate craft caused it to appear as his sole purpose to promote loyalty and to preserve harmony and peace.

The spirit of dissatisfaction thus kindled was doing its baleful work. While there was no open outbreak, division of feeling imperceptibly grew up among the angels. There were some who looked with favor upon Lucifer's insinuations against the government of God. Although they had heretofore been in perfect harmony with the order which God had established, they were now discontented and unhappy because they could not penetrate His unsearchable counsels; they were dissatisfied with His purpose in exalting Christ. These stood ready to second Lucifer's demand for equal authority with the Son of God. But angels who were loyal and true maintained the wisdom and justice of the divine decree and endeavored to reconcile this disaffected being to the will of God. Christ was the Son of God; He had been one with Him before the angels were called into existence. He had ever stood at the right hand of the Father; His supremacy, so full of blessing to all who came under its benignant control, had not heretofore been questioned. The harmony of heaven had never been interrupted; wherefore should there now be discord? The loyal angels could see only terrible consequences from this dissension, and with earnest entreaty they counseled the disaffected ones to renounce their purpose and prove themselves loyal to God by fidelity to His government.

In great mercy, according to His divine character, God bore long with Lucifer. The spirit of discontent and disaffection had never before been known in heaven. It was a new element, strange, mysterious, unaccountable. Lucifer himself had not at first been acquainted with the real nature of his feelings; for a time he had feared to express the workings and imaginings of his mind; yet he did not dismiss them. He did not see whither he was drifting. But such efforts as infinite love and wisdom only could devise, were made to convince him of his error. His disaffection was proved to be without cause, and he was made to see what would be the result of persisting in revolt. Lucifer was convinced that he was in the wrong. He saw that "the Lord is righteous in all His ways, and holy in all His works" (Psalm 145:17); that the divine statutes are just, and that he ought to acknowledge them as such before all heaven. Had he done this, he might have saved himself and many angels. He had not at that time fully cast off his allegiance to God. Though he had left his position as covering cherub, yet if he had been willing to return to God, acknowledging the Creator's wisdom, and satisfied to fill the place appointed him in God's great plan, he would have been reinstated in his office. The time had come for a final decision; he must fully yield to the divine sovereignty or place himself in open rebellion. He nearly reached the decision to return, but pride forbade him. It was too great a sacrifice for one who had been so highly honored to confess that he had been in error, that his imaginings were false, and to yield to the authority which he had been working to prove unjust.

A compassionate Creator, in yearning pity for Lucifer and his followers, was seeking to draw them back from the abyss of ruin into which they were about to plunge. But His mercy was misinterpreted. Lucifer pointed to the long-suffering of God as an evidence of his

[39]

[40] own superiority, an indication that the King of the universe would yet accede to his terms. If the angels would stand firmly with him, he declared, they could yet gain all that they desired. He persistently defended his own course, and fully committed himself to the great controversy against his Maker. Thus it was that Lucifer, "the light bearer," the sharer of God's glory, the attendant of His throne, by transgression became Satan, "the adversary" of God and holy beings and the destroyer of those whom Heaven had committed to his guidance and guardianship.

Rejecting with disdain the arguments and entreaties of the loyal angels, he denounced them as deluded slaves. The preference shown to Christ he declared an act of injustice both to himself and to all the heavenly host, and announced that he would no longer submit to this invasion of his rights and theirs. He would never again acknowledge the supremacy of Christ. He had determined to claim the honor which should have been given him, and take command of all who would become his followers; and he promised those who would enter his ranks a new and better government, under which all would enjoy freedom. Great numbers of the angels signified their purpose to accept him as their leader. Flattered by the favor with which his advances were received, he hoped to win all the angels to his side, to become equal with God Himself, and to be obeyed by the entire host of heaven.

Still the loyal angels urged him and his sympathizers to submit to God; and they set before them the inevitable result should they refuse: He who had created them could overthrow their power and signally punish their rebellious daring. No angel could successfully oppose the law of God, which was as sacred as Himself. They warned all to close their ears against Lucifer's deceptive reasoning, and urged him and his followers to seek the presence of God without delay and confess the error of questioning His wisdom and authority.

Many were disposed to heed this counsel, to repent of their disaffection, and seek to be again received into favor with the Father and His Son. But Lucifer had another deception ready. The mighty revolter now declared that the angels who had united with him had gone too far to return; that he was acquainted with the divine law, and knew that God would not forgive. He declared that all who should submit to the authority of Heaven would be stripped of their honor, degraded from their position. For himself, he was determined never again to acknowledge the authority of Christ. The only course remaining for him and his followers, he said, was to assert their liberty, and gain by force the rights which had not been willingly accorded them.

[41]

So far as Satan himself was concerned, it was true that he had now gone too far to return. But not so with those who had been blinded by his deceptions. To them the counsel and entreaties of the loyal angels opened a door of hope; and had they heeded the warning, they might have broken away from the snare of Satan. But pride, love for their leader, and the desire for unrestricted freedom were permitted to bear sway, and the pleadings of divine love and mercy were finally rejected.

God permitted Satan to carry forward his work until the spirit of disaffection ripened into active revolt. It was necessary for his plans to be fully developed, that their true nature and tendency might be seen by all. Lucifer, as the anointed cherub, had been highly exalted; he was greatly loved by the heavenly beings, and his influence over them was strong. God's government included not only the inhabitants of heaven, but of all the worlds that He had created; and Lucifer had concluded that if he could carry the angels of heaven with him in rebellion, he could carry also all the worlds. He had artfully presented his side of the question, employing sophistry and fraud to secure his objects. His power to deceive was very great. By disguising himself in a cloak of falsehood, he had gained an advantage. All his acts were so clothed with mystery that it was difficult to disclose to the angels the true nature of his work. Until fully developed, it could not be made to appear the evil thing it was; his disaffection would not be seen to be rebellion. Even the loyal angels could not fully discern his character or see to what his work was leading.

Lucifer had at first so conducted his temptations that he himself stood uncommitted. The angels whom he could not bring fully to his side, he accused of indifference to the interests of heavenly beings. The very work which he himself was doing, he charged upon the loyal angels. It was his policy to perplex with subtle arguments concerning the purposes of God. Everything that was simple he shrouded in mystery, and by artful perversion cast doubt upon the plainest statements of Jehovah. And his high position, so closely connected with the divine government, gave greater force to his representations.

God could employ only such means as were consistent with truth and righteousness. Satan could use what God could not—flattery and deceit. He had sought to falsify the word of God and had misrepresented His plan of government, claiming that God was not just in imposing laws upon the angels; that in requiring submission and obedience from His creatures, He was seeking merely the exaltation of Himself. It was therefore necessary to demonstrate before the inhabitants of heaven, and of all the worlds, that God's government is just, His law perfect. Satan had made it appear that he himself was seeking to promote the good of the universe. The true character of the usurper and his real object must be understood by all. He must have time to manifest himself by his wicked works.

The discord which his own course had caused in heaven, Satan charged upon the government of God. All evil he declared to be the result of the divine administration. He claimed that it was his own object to improve upon the statutes of Jehovah. Therefore God permitted him to demonstrate the nature of his claims, to show the working out of his proposed changes in the divine law. His own work must condemn him. Satan had claimed from the first that he was not in rebellion. The whole universe must see the deceiver unmasked.

Even when he was cast out of heaven, Infinite Wisdom did not destroy Satan. Since only the service of love can be acceptable to God, the allegiance of His creatures must rest upon a conviction of His justice and benevolence. The inhabitants of heaven and of the worlds, being unprepared to comprehend the nature or consequences of sin, could not then have seen the justice of God in the destruction of Satan. Had he been immediately blotted out of existence, some would have served God from fear rather than from love. The influence of the deceiver would not have been fully destroyed, nor would the spirit of rebellion have been utterly eradicated. For the good of the entire universe through ceaseless ages, he must more fully develop his principles, that his charges against the divine government might be seen in their true light by all created beings, and that the justice and mercy of God and the immutability of His law might be forever placed beyond all question.

Satan's rebellion was to be a lesson to the universe through all coming ages—a perpetual testimony to the nature of sin and its terrible results. The working out of Satan's rule, its effects upon both men and angels, would show what must be the fruit of setting aside the divine authority. It would testify that with the existence of God's government is bound up the well-being of all the creatures He has made. Thus the history of this terrible experiment of rebellion was to be a perpetual safeguard to all holy beings, to prevent them from being deceived as to the nature of transgression, to save them from committing sin, and suffering its penalty.

He that ruleth in the heavens is the one who sees the end from the beginning—the one before whom the mysteries of the past and the future are alike outspread, and who, beyond the woe and darkness and ruin that sin has wrought, beholds the accomplishment of His own purposes of love and blessing. Though "clouds and darkness are round about Him: righteousness and judgment are the foundation of His throne." Psalm 97:2, R.V. And this the inhabitants of the universe, both loyal and disloyal, will one day understand. "His work is perfect: for all His ways are judgment: a God of truth and without iniquity, just and right is He." Deuteronomy 32:4.

Chapter 2—The Creation

This chapter is based on Genesis 1 and 2.

"By the word of the Lord were the heavens made; and all the host of them by the breath of His mouth." "For He spake, and it was;" "He commanded, and it stood fast." Psalm 33:6, 9. He "laid the foundations of the earth, that it should not be removed forever." Psalm 104:5.

As the earth came forth from the hand of its Maker, it was exceedingly beautiful. Its surface was diversified with mountains, hills, and plains, interspersed with noble rivers and lovely lakes; but the hills and mountains were not abrupt and rugged, abounding in terrific steeps and frightful chasms, as they now do; the sharp, ragged edges of earth's rocky framework were buried beneath the fruitful soil, which everywhere produced a luxuriant growth of verdure. There were no loathsome swamps or barren deserts. Graceful shrubs and delicate flowers greeted the eye at every turn. The heights were crowned with trees more majestic than any that now exist. The air, untainted by foul miasma, was clear and healthful. The entire landscape outvied in beauty the decorated grounds of the proudest palace. The angelic host viewed the scene with delight, and rejoiced at the wonderful works of God.

After the earth with its teeming animal and vegetable life had been called into existence, man, the crowning work of the Creator, and the one for whom the beautiful earth had been fitted up, was brought upon the stage of action. To him was given dominion over all that his eye could behold; for "God said, Let Us make man in Our image, after Our likeness: and let them have dominion over ...all the earth.... So God created man in His own image; ...male and female created He them." Here is clearly set forth the origin of the human race; and the divine record is so plainly stated that there is no occasion for erroneous conclusions. God created man in His own image. Here is no mystery. There is no ground for the supposition that man was evolved by slow degrees of development from the lower forms of animal or vegetable life. Such teaching lowers the great work of the Creator to the level of man's narrow, earthly conceptions. Men are so intent upon excluding God from the sovereignty of the universe that they degrade man and defraud him of the dignity of his origin. He who set the starry worlds on high and tinted with delicate skill the flowers of the field, who filled the earth and the heavens with the wonders of His power, when He came to crown His glorious work, to place one in the midst to stand as ruler of the fair earth, did not fail to create a being worthy of the hand that gave him life. The genealogy of our race, as given by inspiration, traces back its origin, not to a line of developing germs, mollusks, and quadrupeds, but to the great Creator. Though formed from the dust, Adam was "the son of God."

He was placed, as God's representative, over the lower orders of being. They cannot understand or acknowledge the sovereignty of God, yet they were made capable of loving and serving man. The psalmist says, "Thou madest him to have dominion over the works of Thy hands; Thou hast put all things under his feet: ... the beasts of the field; the fowl of the air, ... and whatsoever passeth through the paths of the seas." Psalm 8:6-8.

Man was to bear God's image, both in outward resemblance and in character. Christ alone is "the express image" (Hebrews 1:3) of the Father; but man was formed in the likeness of God. His nature was in harmony with the will of God. His mind was capable of comprehending divine things. His affections were pure; his appetites and passions were under the control of reason. He was holy and happy in bearing the image of God and in perfect obedience to His will.

As man came forth from the hand of his Creator, he was of lofty stature and perfect symmetry. His countenance bore the ruddy tint of health and glowed with the light of life and joy. Adam's height was much greater than that of men who now inhabit the earth. Eve was somewhat less in stature; yet her form was noble, and full of beauty. The sinless pair wore no artificial garments; they were clothed with a covering of light and glory, such as the angels wear. So long as they lived in obedience to God, this robe of light continued to enshroud them.

[46] After the creation of Adam every living creature was brought before him to receive its name; he saw that to each had been given a companion, but among them "there was not found an help meet for him." Among all the creatures that God had made on the earth, there was not one equal to man. And God said, "It is not good that the man should be alone; I will make him an help meet for him." Man was not made to dwell in solitude; he was to be a social being. Without companionship the beautiful scenes and delightful employments of Eden would have failed to yield perfect happiness. Even communion with angels could not have satisfied his desire for sympathy and companionship. There was none of the same nature to love and to be loved.

God Himself gave Adam a companion. He provided "an help meet for him"—a helper corresponding to him—one who was fitted to be his companion, and who could be one with him in love and sympathy. Eve was created from a rib taken from the side of Adam, signifying that she was not to control him as the head, nor to be trampled under his feet as an inferior, but to stand by his side as an equal, to be loved and protected by him. A part of man, bone of his bone, and flesh of his flesh, she was his second self, showing the close union and the affectionate attachment that should exist in this relation. "For no man ever yet hated his own flesh; but nourisheth and cherisheth it." Ephesians 5:29. "Therefore shall a man leave his father and his mother, and shall cleave unto his wife; and they shall be one."

God celebrated the first marriage. Thus the institution has for its originator the Creator of the universe. "Marriage is honorable" (Hebrews 13:4); it was one of the first gifts of God to man, and it is one of the two institutions that, after the Fall, Adam brought with him beyond the gates of Paradise. When the divine principles are recognized and obeyed in this relation, marriage is a blessing; it guards the purity and happiness of the race, it provides for man's social needs, it elevates the physical, the intellectual, and the moral nature.

"And the Lord God planted a garden eastward in Eden; and there He put the man whom He had formed." Everything that God had made was the perfection of beauty, and nothing seemed wanting that [47] could contribute to the happiness of the holy pair; yet the Creator gave them still another token of His love, by preparing a garden especially for their home. In this garden were trees of every variety, many of them laden with fragrant and delicious fruit. There were lovely vines, growing upright, yet presenting a most graceful appearance, with their branches drooping under their load of tempting fruit of the richest and most varied hues. It was the work of Adam and Eve to train the branches of the vine to form bowers, thus making for themselves a dwelling from living trees covered with foliage and fruit. There were fragrant flowers of every hue in rich profusion. In the midst of the garden stood the tree of life, surpassing in glory all other trees. Its fruit appeared like apples of gold and silver, and had the power to perpetuate life.

The creation was now complete. "The heavens and the earth were finished, and all the host of them." "And God saw everything that He had made, and, behold, it was very good." Eden bloomed on earth. Adam and Eve had free access to the tree of life. No taint of sin or shadow of death marred the fair creation. "The morning stars sang together, and all the sons of God shouted for joy." Job 38:7.

The great Jehovah had laid the foundations of the earth; He had dressed the whole world in the garb of beauty and had filled it with things useful to man; He had created all the wonders of the land and of the sea. In six days the great work of creation had been accomplished. And God "rested on the seventh day from all His work which He had made. And God blessed the seventh day, and sanctified it: because that in it He had rested from all His work which God created and made." God looked with satisfaction upon the work of His hands. All was perfect, worthy of its divine Author, and He rested, not as one weary, but as well pleased with the fruits of His wisdom and goodness and the manifestations of His glory.

After resting upon the seventh day, God sanctified it, or set it apart, as a day of rest for man. Following the example of the Creator, man was to rest upon this sacred day, that as he should look upon the heavens and the earth, he might reflect upon God's great work of creation; and that as he should behold the evidences of God's wisdom and goodness, his heart might be filled with love and reverence for his Maker.

In Eden, God set up the memorial of His work of creation, in placing His blessing upon the seventh day. The Sabbath was com-

[48]

mitted to Adam, the father and representative of the whole human family. Its observance was to be an act of grateful acknowledgment, on the part of all who should dwell upon the earth, that God was their Creator and their rightful Sovereign; that they were the work of His hands and the subjects of His authority. Thus the institution was wholly commemorative, and given to all mankind. There was nothing in it shadowy or of restricted application to any people.

God saw that a Sabbath was essential for man, even in Paradise. He needed to lay aside his own interests and pursuits for one day of the seven, that he might more fully contemplate the works of God and meditate upon His power and goodness. He needed a Sabbath to remind him more vividly of God and to awaken gratitude because all that he enjoyed and possessed came from the beneficent hand of the Creator.

God designs that the Sabbath shall direct the minds of men to the contemplation of His created works. Nature speaks to their senses, declaring that there is a living God, the Creator, the Supreme Ruler of all. "The heavens declare the glory of God; and the firmament showeth His handiwork. Day unto day uttereth speech, and night unto night showeth knowledge." Psalm 19:1, 2. The beauty that clothes the earth is a token of God's love. We may behold it in the everlasting hills, in the lofty trees, in the opening buds and the delicate flowers. All speak to us of God. The Sabbath, ever pointing to Him who made them all, bids men open the great book of nature and trace therein the wisdom, the power, and the love of the Creator.

Our first parents, though created innocent and holy, were not placed beyond the possibility of wrongdoing. God made them free moral agents, capable of appreciating the wisdom and benevolence of His character and the justice of His requirements, and with full liberty to yield or to withhold obedience. They were to enjoy communion with God and with holy angels; but before they could be rendered eternally secure, their loyalty must be tested. At the very beginning of man's existence a check was placed upon the desire for self-indulgence, the fatal passion that lay at the foundation of Satan's fall. The tree of knowledge, which stood near the tree of life in the midst of the garden, was to be a test of the obedience, faith, and love of our parents. While permitted to eat freely of every other tree, they were forbidden to taste of this, on pain of death.

They were also to be exposed to the temptations of Satan; but if they endured the trial, they would finally be placed beyond his power, to enjoy perpetual favor with God.

God placed man under law, as an indispensable condition of his very existence. He was a subject of the divine government, and there can be no government without law. God might have created man without the power to transgress His law; He might have withheld the hand of Adam from touching the forbidden fruit; but in that case man would have been, not a free moral agent, but a mere automaton. Without freedom of choice, his obedience would not have been voluntary, but forced. There could have been no development of character. Such a course would have been contrary to God's plan in dealing with the inhabitants of other worlds. It would have been unworthy of man as an intelligent being, and would have sustained Satan's charge of God's arbitrary rule.

God made man upright; He gave him noble traits of character, with no bias toward evil. He endowed him with high intellectual powers, and presented before him the strongest possible inducements to be true to his allegiance. Obedience, perfect and perpetual, was the condition of eternal happiness. On this condition he was to have access to the tree of life.

The home of our first parents was to be a pattern for other homes as their children should go forth to occupy the earth. That home, beautified by the hand of God Himself, was not a gorgeous palace. Men, in their pride, delight in magnificent and costly edifices and glory in the works of their own hands; but God placed Adam in a garden. This was his dwelling. The blue heavens were its dome; the earth, with its delicate flowers and carpet of living green, was its floor; and the leafy branches of the goodly trees were its canopy. Its walls were hung with the most magnificent adornings—the handiwork of the great Master Artist. In the surroundings of the holy pair was a lesson for all time—that true happiness is found, not in the indulgence of pride and luxury, but in communion with God through His created works. If men would give less attention to the artificial, and would cultivate greater simplicity, they would come far nearer to answering the purpose of God in their creation. Pride and ambition are never satisfied, but those who are truly wise will

[50]

find substantial and elevating pleasure in the sources of enjoyment that God has placed within the reach of all.

To the dwellers in Eden was committed the care of the garden, "to dress it and to keep it." Their occupation was not wearisome, but pleasant and invigorating. God appointed labor as a blessing to man, to occupy his mind, to strengthen his body, and to develop his faculties. In mental and physical activity Adam found one of the highest pleasures of his holy existence. And when, as a result of his disobedience, he was driven from his beautiful home, and forced to struggle with a stubborn soil to gain his daily bread, that very labor, although widely different from his pleasant occupation in the garden, was a safeguard against temptation and a source of happiness. Those who regard work as a curse, attended though it be with weariness and pain, are cherishing an error. The rich often look down with contempt upon the working classes, but this is wholly at variance with God's purpose in creating man. What are the possessions of even the most wealthy in comparison with the heritage given to the lordly Adam? Yet Adam was not to be idle. Our Creator, who understands what is for man's happiness, appointed Adam his work. The true joy of life is found only by the working men and women. The angels are diligent workers; they are the ministers of God to the children of men. The Creator has prepared no place for the stagnating practice of indolence.

While they remained true to God, Adam and his companion were to bear rule over the earth. Unlimited control was given them over every living thing. The lion and the lamb sported peacefully around them or lay down together at their feet. The happy birds flitted about them without fear; and as their glad songs ascended to the praise of their Creator, Adam and Eve united with them in thanksgiving to the Father and the Son.

The holy pair were not only children under the fatherly care of God but students receiving instruction from the all-wise Creator. They were visited by angels, and were granted communion with their Maker, with no obscuring veil between. They were full of the vigor imparted by the tree of life, and their intellectual power was but little less than that of the angels. The mysteries of the visible universe—"the wondrous works of Him which is perfect in knowledge" (Job 37:16)—afforded them an exhaustless source of instruction and delight. The laws and operations of nature, which have engaged men's study for six thousand years, were opened to their minds by the infinite Framer and Upholder of all. They held converse with leaf and flower and tree, gathering from each the secrets of its life. With every living creature, from the mighty leviathan that playeth among the waters to the insect mote that floats in the sunbeam, Adam was familiar. He had given to each its name, and he was acquainted with the nature and habits of all. God's glory in the heavens, the innumerable worlds in their orderly revolutions, "the balancings of the clouds," the mysteries of light and sound, of day and night—all were open to the study of our first parents. On every leaf of the forest or stone of the mountains, in every shining star, in earth and air and sky, God's name was written. The order and harmony of creation spoke to them of infinite wisdom and power. They were ever discovering some attraction that filled their hearts with deeper love and called forth fresh expressions of gratitude.

So long as they remained loyal to the divine law, their capacity to know, to enjoy, and to love would continually increase. They would be constantly gaining new treasures of knowledge, discovering fresh springs of happiness, and obtaining clearer and yet clearer conceptions of the immeasurable, unfailing love of God.

Chapter 3—The Temptation and Fall

This chapter is based on Genesis 3.

No longer free to stir up rebellion in heaven, Satan's enmity against God found a new field in plotting the ruin of the human race. In the happiness and peace of the holy pair in Eden he beheld a vision of the bliss that to him was forever lost. Moved by envy, he determined to incite them to disobedience, and bring upon them the guilt and penalty of sin. He would change their love to distrust and their songs of praise to reproaches against their Maker. Thus he would not only plunge these innocent beings into the same misery which he was himself enduring, but would cast dishonor upon God, and cause grief in heaven.

Our first parents were not left without a warning of the danger that threatened them. Heavenly messengers opened to them the history of Satan's fall and his plots for their destruction, unfolding more fully the nature of the divine government, which the prince of evil was trying to overthrow. It was by disobedience to the just commands of God that Satan and his host had fallen. How important, then, that Adam and Eve should honor that law by which alone it was possible for order and equity to be maintained.

The law of God is as sacred as God Himself. It is a revelation of His will, a transcript of His character, the expression of divine love and wisdom. The harmony of creation depends upon the perfect conformity of all beings, of everything, animate and inanimate, to the law of the Creator. God has ordained laws for the government, not only of living beings, but of all the operations of nature. Everything is under fixed laws, which cannot be disregarded. But while everything in nature is governed by natural laws, man alone, of all that inhabits the earth, is amenable to moral law. To man, the crowning work of creation, God has given power to understand His requirements, to comprehend the justice and beneficence of His law, and its sacred claims upon him; and of man unswerving obedience is required.

Like the angels, the dwellers in Eden had been placed upon probation; their happy estate could be retained only on condition of fidelity to the Creator's law. They could obey and live, or disobey and perish. God had made them the recipients of rich blessings; but should they disregard His will, He who spared not the angels that sinned, could not spare them; transgression would forfeit His gifts and bring upon them misery and ruin.

The angels warned them to be on their guard against the devices of Satan, for his efforts to ensnare them would be unwearied. While they were obedient to God the evil one could not harm them; for, if need be, every angel in heaven would be sent to their help. If they steadfastly repelled his first insinuations, they would be as secure as the heavenly messengers. But should they once yield to temptation, their nature would become so depraved that in themselves they would have no power and no disposition to resist Satan.

The tree of knowledge had been made a test of their obedience and their love to God. The Lord had seen fit to lay upon them but one prohibition as to the use of all that was in the garden; but if they should disregard His will in this particular, they would incur the guilt of transgression. Satan was not to follow them with continual temptations; he could have access to them only at the forbidden tree. Should they attempt to investigate its nature, they would be exposed to his wiles. They were admonished to give careful heed to the warning which God had sent them and to be content with the instruction which He had seen fit to impart.

In order to accomplish his work unperceived, Satan chose to employ as his medium the serpent—a disguise well adapted for his purpose of deception. The serpent was then one of the wisest and most beautiful creatures on the earth. It had wings, and while flying through the air presented an appearance of dazzling brightness, having the color and brilliancy of burnished gold. Resting in the rich-laden branches of the forbidden tree and regaling itself with the delicious fruit, it was an object to arrest the attention and delight the eye of the beholder. Thus in the garden of peace lurked the destroyer, watching for his prey.

The angels had cautioned Eve to beware of separating herself from her husband while occupied in their daily labor in the garden; with him she would be in less danger from temptation than if she were alone. But absorbed in her pleasing task, she unconsciously wandered from his side. On perceiving that she was alone, she felt an apprehension of danger, but dismissed her fears, deciding that she had sufficient wisdom and strength to discern evil and to withstand it. Unmindful of the angels' caution, she soon found herself gazing with mingled curiosity and admiration upon the forbidden tree. The fruit was very beautiful, and she questioned with herself why God had withheld it from them. Now was the tempter's opportunity. As if he were able to discern the workings of her mind, he addressed her: "Yea, hath God said, Ye shall not eat of every tree of the garden?" Eve was surprised and startled as she thus seemed to hear the echo of her thoughts. But the serpent continued, in a musical voice, with subtle praise of her surpassing loveliness; and his words were not displeasing. Instead of fleeing from the spot she lingered wonderingly to hear a serpent speak. Had she been addressed by a being like the angels, her fears would have been excited; but she had no thought that the fascinating serpent could become the medium of the fallen foe.

To the tempter's ensnaring question she replied: "We may eat of the fruit of the trees of the garden: but of the fruit of the tree which is in the midst of the garden, God hath said, Ye shall not eat of it, neither shall ye touch it, lest ye die. And the serpent said unto the woman, Ye shall not surely die: for God doth know that in the day ye eat thereof, then your eyes shall be opened, and ye shall be as gods, knowing good and evil."

By partaking of this tree, he declared, they would attain to a more exalted sphere of existence and enter a broader field of knowledge. He himself had eaten of the forbidden fruit, and as a result had acquired the power of speech. And he insinuated that the Lord jealously desired to withhold it from them, lest they should be exalted to equality with Himself. It was because of its wonderful properties, imparting wisdom and power, that He had prohibited them from tasting or even touching it. The tempter intimated that the divine warning was not to be actually fulfilled; it was designed merely to intimidate them. How could it be possible for them to die? Had they not eaten of the tree of life? God had been seeking to prevent them from reaching a nobler development and finding greater happiness.

Such has been Satan's work from the days of Adam to the present, and he has pursued it with great success. He tempts men to distrust God's love and to doubt His wisdom. He is constantly seeking to excite a spirit of irreverent curiosity, a restless, inquisitive desire to penetrate the secrets of divine wisdom and power. In their efforts to search out what God has been pleased to withhold, multitudes overlook the truths which He has revealed, and which are essential to salvation. Satan tempts men to disobedience by leading them to believe they are entering a wonderful field of knowledge. But this is all a deception. Elated with their ideas of progression, they are, by trampling on God's requirements, setting their feet in the path that leads to degradation and death.

[55]

Satan represented to the holy pair that they would be gainers by breaking the law of God. Do we not today hear similar reasoning? Many talk of the narrowness of those who obey God's commandments, while they themselves claim to have broader ideas and to enjoy greater liberty. What is this but an echo of the voice from Eden, "In the day ye eat thereof"—transgress the divine requirement—"ye shall be as gods"? Satan claimed to have received great good by eating of the forbidden fruit, but he did not let it appear that by transgression he had become an outcast from heaven. Though he had found sin to result in infinite loss, he concealed his own misery in order to draw others into the same position. So now the transgressor seeks to disguise his true character; he may claim to be holy; but his exalted profession only makes him the more dangerous as a deceiver. He is on the side of Satan, trampling upon the law of God, and leading others to do the same, to their eternal ruin.

Eve really believed the words of Satan, but her belief did not save her from the penalty of sin. She disbelieved the words of God, and this was what led to her fall. In the judgment men will not be condemned because they conscientiously believed a lie, but because they did not believe the truth, because they neglected the opportunity of learning what is truth. Notwithstanding the sophistry of Satan to the contrary, it is always disastrous to disobey God. We must set our hearts to know what is truth. All the lessons which God has caused to be placed on record in His word are for our warning and instruction. They are given to save us from deception. Their neglect will result in ruin to ourselves. Whatever contradicts God's word, we may be sure proceeds from Satan.

The serpent plucked the fruit of the forbidden tree and placed it in the hands of the half-reluctant Eve. Then he reminded her of her own words, that God had forbidden them to touch it, lest they die. She would receive no more harm from eating the fruit, he declared, than from touching it. Perceiving no evil results from what she had done, Eve grew bolder. When she "saw that the tree was good for food, and that it was pleasant to the eyes, and a tree to be desired to make one wise, she took of the fruit thereof, and did eat." It was grateful to the taste, and as she ate, she seemed to feel a vivifying power, and imagined herself entering upon a higher state of existence. Without a fear she plucked and ate. And now, having herself transgressed, she became the agent of Satan in working the ruin of her husband. In a state of strange, unnatural excitement, with her hands filled with the forbidden fruit, she sought his presence, and related all that had occurred.

An expression of sadness came over the face of Adam. He appeared astonished and alarmed. To the words of Eve he replied that this must be the foe against whom they had been warned; and by the divine sentence she must die. In answer she urged him to eat, repeating the words of the serpent, that they should not surely die. She reasoned that this must be true, for she felt no evidence of God's displeasure, but on the contrary realized a delicious, exhilarating influence, thrilling every faculty with new life, such, she imagined, as inspired the heavenly messengers.

Adam understood that his companion had transgressed the command of God, disregarded the only prohibition laid upon them as a test of their fidelity and love. There was a terrible struggle in his mind. He mourned that he had permitted Eve to wander from his side. But now the deed was done; he must be separated from her whose society had been his joy. How could he have it thus? Adam had enjoyed the companionship of God and of holy angels. He had looked upon the glory of the Creator. He understood the high destiny opened to the human race should they remain faithful to God. Yet all these blessings were lost sight of in the fear of losing that one gift which in his eyes outvalued every other. Love, gratitude, loyalty to the Creator—all were overborne by love to Eve. She was a part of himself, and he could not endure the thought of separation. He did not realize that the same Infinite Power who had from the dust of the earth created him, a living, beautiful form, and had in love given him a companion, could supply her place. He resolved to share her fate; if she must die, he would die with her. After all, he reasoned, might not the words of the wise serpent be true? Eve was before him, as beautiful and apparently as innocent as before this act of disobedience. She expressed greater love for him than before. No sign of death appeared in her, and he decided to brave the consequences. He seized the fruit and quickly ate. [57]

After his transgression Adam at first imagined himself entering upon a higher state of existence. But soon the thought of his sin filled him with terror. The air, which had hitherto been of a mild and uniform temperature, seemed to chill the guilty pair. The love and peace which had been theirs was gone, and in its place they felt a sense of sin, a dread of the future, a nakedness of soul. The robe of light which had enshrouded them, now disappeared, and to supply its place they endeavored to fashion for themselves a covering; for they could not, while unclothed, meet the eye of God and holy angels.

They now began to see the true character of their sin. Adam reproached his companion for her folly in leaving his side and permitting herself to be deceived by the serpent; but they both flattered themselves that He who had given them so many evidences of His love, would pardon this one transgression, or that they would not be subjected to so dire a punishment as they had feared.

Satan exulted in his success. He had tempted the woman to distrust God's love, to doubt His wisdom, and to transgress His law, and through her he had caused the overthrow of Adam.

But the great Lawgiver was about to make known to Adam and Eve the consequences of their transgression. The divine presence was manifested in the garden. In their innocence and holiness they had joyfully welcomed the approach of their Creator; but now they fled in terror, and sought to hide in the deepest recesses of the garden. But "the Lord God called unto Adam, and said unto him, Where art thou? And he said, I heard Thy voice in the garden, and I was afraid, because I was naked; and I hid myself. And He said, Who told thee that thou wast naked? Hast thou eaten of the tree, whereof I commanded thee that thou shouldest not eat?"

Adam could neither deny nor excuse his sin; but instead of manifesting penitence, he endeavored to cast the blame upon his wife, and thus upon God Himself: "The woman whom *Thou gavest* to be with me, she gave me of the tree, and I did eat." He who, from love to Eve, had deliberately chosen to forfeit the approval of God, his home in Paradise, and an eternal life of joy, could now, after his fall, endeavor to make his companion, and even the Creator Himself, responsible for the transgression. So terrible is the power of sin.

When the woman was asked, "What is this that thou hast done?" she answered, "The serpent beguiled me, and I did eat." "Why didst Thou create the serpent? Why didst Thou suffer him to enter Eden?"—these were the questions implied in her excuse for her sin. Thus, like Adam, she charged God with the responsibility of their fall. The spirit of self-justification originated in the father of lies; it was indulged by our first parents as soon as they yielded to the influence of Satan, and has been exhibited by all the sons and daughters of Adam. Instead of humbly confessing their sins, they try to shield themselves by casting the blame upon others, upon circumstances, or upon God—making even His blessings an occasion of murmuring against Him.

The Lord then passed sentence upon the serpent: "Because thou hast done this, thou art cursed above all cattle, and above every beast of the field; upon thy belly shalt thou go, and dust shalt thou eat all the days of thy life." Since it had been employed as Satan's medium, the serpent was to share the visitation of divine judgment. From the most beautiful and admired of the creatures of the field, it was to become the most groveling and detested of them all, feared and hated by both man and beast. The words next addressed to the serpent applied directly to Satan himself, pointing forward to his ultimate defeat and destruction: "I will put enmity between thee and the woman, and between thy seed and her seed; it shall bruise thy head, and thou shalt bruise his heel."

Eve was told of the sorrow and pain that must henceforth be her portion. And the Lord said, "Thy desire shall be to thy husband, and he shall rule over thee." In the creation God had made her the equal of Adam. Had they remained obedient to God—in harmony with His great law of love—they would ever have been in harmony with each other; but sin had brought discord, and now their union could be maintained and harmony preserved only by submission on the part of the one or the other. Eve had been the first in transgression; and she had fallen into temptation by separating from her companion, contrary to the divine direction. It was by her solicitation that Adam sinned, and she was now placed in subjection to her husband. Had the principles enjoined in the law of God been cherished by the fallen race, this sentence, though growing out of the results of sin, would have proved a blessing to them; but man's abuse of the supremacy thus given him has too often rendered the lot of woman very bitter and made her life a burden.

[59]

Eve had been perfectly happy by her husband's side in her Eden home; but, like restless modern Eves, she was flattered with the hope of entering a higher sphere than that which God had assigned her. In attempting to rise above her original position, she fell far below it. A similar result will be reached by all who are unwilling to take up cheerfully their life duties in accordance with God's plan. In their efforts to reach positions for which He has not fitted them, many are leaving vacant the place where they might be a blessing. In their desire for a higher sphere, many have sacrificed true womanly dignity and nobility of character, and have left undone the very work that Heaven appointed them.

To Adam the Lord declared: "Because thou hast hearkened unto the voice of thy wife, and hast eaten of the tree, of which I commanded thee, saying, Thou shalt not eat of it: cursed is the ground for thy sake; in sorrow shalt thou eat of it all the days of thy life; thorns also and thistles shall it bring forth to thee; and thou shalt eat the herb of the field; in the sweat of thy face shalt thou eat bread, till thou return unto the ground; for out of it wast thou taken: for dust thou art, and unto dust shalt thou return."

It was not the will of God that the sinless pair should know aught of evil. He had freely given them the good, and had withheld the evil. But, contrary to His command, they had eaten of the forbidden tree, and now they would continue to eat of it—they would have the knowledge of evil—all the days of their life. From that time the race would be afflicted by Satan's temptations. Instead of the happy labor heretofore appointed them, anxiety and toil were to be their lot. They would be subject to disappointment, grief, and pain, and finally to death.

Under the curse of sin all nature was to witness to man of the character and results of rebellion against God. When God made man He made him rule over the earth and all living creatures. So long as Adam remained loyal to Heaven, all nature was in subjection to him. But when he rebelled against the divine law, the inferior creatures were in rebellion against his rule. Thus the Lord, in His great mercy, would show men the sacredness of His law, and lead them, by their own experience, to see the danger of setting it aside, even in the slightest degree.

And the life of toil and care which was henceforth to be man's lot was appointed in love. It was a discipline rendered needful by his sin, to place a check upon the indulgence of appetite and passion, to develop habits of self-control. It was a part of God's great plan of man's recovery from the ruin and degradation of sin.

The warning given to our first parents—"In the day that thou eatest thereof thou shalt surely die" (Genesis 2:17)—did not imply that they were to die on the very day when they partook of the forbidden fruit. But on that day the irrevocable sentence would be pronounced. Immortality was promised them on condition of obedience; by transgression they would forfeit eternal life. That very day they would be doomed to death.

In order to possess an endless existence, man must continue to partake of the tree of life. Deprived of this, his vitality would gradually diminish until life should become extinct. It was Satan's plan that Adam and Eve should by disobedience incur God's displeasure; and then, if they failed to obtain forgiveness, he hoped that they would eat of the tree of life, and thus perpetuate an existence of sin and misery. But after man's fall, holy angels were immediately commissioned to guard the tree of life. Around these angels flashed beams of light having the appearance of a glittering sword. None of the family of Adam were permitted to pass the barrier to partake of the life-giving fruit; hence there is not an immortal sinner.

The tide of woe that flowed from the transgression of our first parents is regarded by many as too awful a consequence for so small a sin, and they impeach the wisdom and justice of God in His dealings with man. But if they would look more deeply into this question, they might discern their error. God created man after His own likeness, free from sin. The earth was to be peopled with beings only a little lower than the angels; but their obedience must be tested; for God would not permit the world to be filled with those who would disregard His law. Yet, in His great mercy, He appointed Adam no severe test. And the very lightness of the prohibition made the sin exceedingly great. If Adam could not bear the smallest of tests, he could not have endured a greater trial had he been entrusted with higher responsibilities.

[61]

Had some great test been appointed Adam, then those whose hearts incline to evil would have excused themselves by saying, "This is a trivial matter, and God is not so particular about little things." And there would be continual transgression in things looked upon as small, and which pass unrebuked among men. But the Lord has made it evident that sin in any degree is offensive to Him.

To Eve it seemed a small thing to disobey God by tasting the fruit of the forbidden tree, and to tempt her husband also to transgress; but their sin opened the floodgates of woe upon the world. Who can know, in the moment of temptation, the terrible consequences that will result from one wrong step?

Many who teach that the law of God is not binding upon man, urge that it is impossible for him to obey its precepts. But if this were true, why did Adam suffer the penalty of transgression? The sin of our first parents brought guilt and sorrow upon the world, and had it not been for the goodness and mercy of God, would have plunged the race into hopeless despair. Let none deceive themselves. "The wages of sin is death." Romans 6:23. The law of God can no more be transgressed with impunity now than when sentence was pronounced upon the father of mankind.

After their sin Adam and Eve were no longer to dwell in Eden. They earnestly entreated that they might remain in the home of their innocence and joy. They confessed that they had forfeited all right to that happy abode, but pledged themselves for the future to yield strict obedience to God. But they were told that their nature had become depraved by sin; they had lessened their strength to resist evil and had opened the way for Satan to gain more ready access to them. In their innocence they had yielded to temptation; and now, in a state of conscious guilt, they would have less power to maintain their integrity.

In humility and unutterable sadness they bade farewell to their beautiful home and went forth to dwell upon the earth, where rested the curse of sin. The atmosphere, once so mild and uniform in temperature, was now subject to marked changes, and the Lord mercifully provided them with a garment of skins as a protection from the extremes of heat and cold.

As they witnessed in drooping flower and falling leaf the first signs of decay, Adam and his companion mourned more deeply than men now mourn over their dead. The death of the frail, delicate flowers was indeed a cause of sorrow; but when the goodly trees cast off their leaves, the scene brought vividly to mind the stern fact that death is the portion of every living thing.

The Garden of Eden remained upon the earth long after man had become an outcast from its pleasant paths. The fallen race were long permitted to gaze upon the home of innocence, their entrance barred only by the watching angels. At the cherubim-guarded gate of Paradise the divine glory was revealed. Hither came Adam and his sons to worship God. Here they renewed their vows of obedience to that law the transgression of which had banished them from Eden. When the tide of iniquity overspread the world, and the wickedness of men determined their destruction by a flood of waters, the hand that had planted Eden withdrew it from the earth. But in the final restitution, when there shall be "a new heaven and a new earth" (Revelation 21:1), it is to be restored more gloriously adorned than at the beginning.

Then they that have kept God's commandments shall breathe in immortal vigor beneath the tree of life; and through unending ages the inhabitants of sinless worlds shall behold, in that garden of delight, a sample of the perfect work of God's creation, untouched by the curse of sin—a sample of what the whole earth would have become, had man but fulfilled the Creator's glorious plan.

Chapter 4—The Plan of Redemption

The fall of man filled all heaven with sorrow. The world that God had made was blighted with the curse of sin and inhabited by beings doomed to misery and death. There appeared no escape for those who had transgressed the law. Angels ceased their songs of praise. Throughout the heavenly courts there was mourning for the ruin that sin had wrought.

The Son of God, heaven's glorious Commander, was touched with pity for the fallen race. His heart was moved with infinite compassion as the woes of the lost world rose up before Him. But divine love had conceived a plan whereby man might be redeemed. The broken law of God demanded the life of the sinner. In all the universe there was but one who could, in behalf of man, satisfy its claims. Since the divine law is as sacred as God Himself, only one equal with God could make atonement for its transgression. None but Christ could redeem fallen man from the curse of the law and bring him again into harmony with Heaven. Christ would take upon Himself the guilt and shame of sin—sin so offensive to a holy God that it must separate the Father and His Son. Christ would reach to the depths of misery to rescue the ruined race.

Before the Father He pleaded in the sinner's behalf, while the host of heaven awaited the result with an intensity of interest that words cannot express. Long continued was that mysterious communing—"the counsel of peace" (Zechariah 6:13) for the fallen sons of men. The plan of salvation had been laid before the creation of the earth; for Christ is "the Lamb slain from the foundation of the world" (Revelation 13:8); yet it was a struggle, even with the King of the universe, to yield up His Son to die for the guilty race. But "God so loved the world, that He gave His only-begotten Son, that whosoever believeth in Him should not perish, but have everlasting life." John 3:16. Oh, the mystery of redemption! the love of God for a world that did not love Him! Who can know the depths of that love which "passeth knowledge"? Through endless ages immortal minds, seeking to comprehend the mystery of that incomprehensible love, will wonder and adore.

God was to be manifest in Christ, "reconciling the world unto Himself." 2 Corinthians 5:19. Man had become so degraded by sin that it was impossible for him, in himself, to come into harmony with Him whose nature is purity and goodness. But Christ, after having redeemed man from the condemnation of the law, could impart divine power to unite with human effort. Thus by repentance toward God and faith in Christ the fallen children of Adam might once more become "sons of God." 1 John 3:2.

The plan by which alone man's salvation could be secured, involved all heaven in its infinite sacrifice. The angels could not rejoice as Christ opened before them the plan of redemption, for they saw that man's salvation must cost their loved Commander unutterable woe. In grief and wonder they listened to His words as He told them how He must descend from heaven's purity and peace, its joy and glory and immortal life, and come in contact with the degradation of earth, to endure its sorrow, shame, and death. He was to stand between the sinner and the penalty of sin; yet few would receive Him as the Son of God. He would leave His high position as the Majesty of heaven, appear upon earth and humble Himself as a man, and by His own experience become acquainted with the sorrows and temptations which man would have to endure. All this would be necessary in order that He might be able to succor them that should be tempted. Hebrews 2:18. When His mission as a teacher should be ended, He must be delivered into the hands of wicked men and be subjected to every insult and torture that Satan could inspire them to inflict. He must die the cruelest of deaths, lifted up between the heavens and the earth as a guilty sinner. He must pass long hours of agony so terrible that angels could not look upon it, but would veil their faces from the sight. He must endure anguish of soul, the hiding of His Father's face, while the guilt of transgression—the weight of the sins of the whole world—should be upon Him.

The angels prostrated themselves at the feet of their Commander and offered to become a sacrifice for man. But an angel's life could not pay the debt; only He who created man had power to redeem him. Yet the angels were to have a part to act in the plan of redemption. Christ was to be made "a little lower than the angels for the suffering of death." Hebrews 2:9. As He should take human nature upon Him, His strength would not be equal to theirs, and they were to minister to Him, to strengthen and soothe Him under His sufferings. They were also to be ministering spirits, sent forth to minister for them who should be heirs of salvation. Hebrews 1:14. They would guard the subjects of grace from the power of evil angels and from the darkness constantly thrown around them by Satan.

When the angels should witness the agony and humiliation of their Lord, they would be filled with grief and indignation and would wish to deliver Him from His murderers; but they were not to interpose in order to prevent anything which they should behold. It was a part of the plan of redemption that Christ should suffer the scorn and abuse of wicked men, and He consented to all this when He became the Redeemer of man.

Christ assured the angels that by His death He would ransom many, and would destroy him who had the power of death. He would recover the kingdom which man had lost by transgression, and the redeemed were to inherit it with Him, and dwell therein forever. Sin and sinners would be blotted out, nevermore to disturb the peace of heaven or earth. He bade the angelic host to be in accord with the plan that His Father had accepted, and rejoice that, through His death, fallen man could be reconciled to God.

Then joy, inexpressible joy, filled heaven. The glory and blessedness of a world redeemed, outmeasured even the anguish and sacrifice of the Prince of life. Through the celestial courts echoed the first strains of that song which was to ring out above the hills of Bethlehem—"Glory to God in the highest, and on earth peace, good will toward men." Luke 2:14. With a deeper gladness now than in the rapture of the new creation, "the morning stars sang together, and all the sons of God shouted for joy." Job 38:7.

To man the first intimation of redemption was communicated in the sentence pronounced upon Satan in the garden. The Lord declared, "I will put enmity between thee and the woman, and between thy seed and her seed; it shall bruise thy head, and thou shalt bruise his heel." Genesis 3:15. This sentence, uttered in the hearing of our first parents, was to them a promise. While it foretold war between man and Satan, it declared that the power of the great adversary would finally be broken. Adam and Eve stood as criminals before the righteous Judge, awaiting the sentence which transgression had incurred; but before they heard of the life of toil and sorrow which must be their portion, or of the decree that they must return to dust, they listened to words that could not fail to give them hope. Though they must suffer from the power of their mighty foe, they could look forward to final victory.

When Satan heard that enmity should exist between himself and the woman, and between his seed and her seed, he knew that his work of depraving human nature would be interrupted; that by some means man would be enabled to resist his power. Yet as the plan of salvation was more fully unfolded, Satan rejoiced with his angels that, having caused man's fall, he could bring down the Son of God from His exalted position. He declared that his plans had thus far been successful upon the earth, and that when Christ should take upon Himself human nature, He also might be overcome, and thus the redemption of the fallen race might be prevented.

Heavenly angels more fully opened to our first parents the plan that had been devised for their salvation. Adam and his companion were assured that notwithstanding their great sin, they were not to be abandoned to the control of Satan. The Son of God had offered to atone, with His own life, for their transgression. A period of probation would be granted them, and through repentance and faith in Christ they might again become the children of God.

The sacrifice demanded by their transgression revealed to Adam and Eve the sacred character of the law of God; and they saw, as they had never seen before, the guilt of sin and its dire results. In their remorse and anguish they pleaded that the penalty might not fall upon Him whose love had been the source of all their joy; rather let it descend upon them and their posterity.

They were told that since the law of Jehovah is the foundation of His government in heaven as well as upon the earth, even the life of an angel could not be accepted as a sacrifice for its transgression. Not one of its precepts could be abrogated or changed to meet man in his fallen condition; but the Son of God, who had created man, could make an atonement for him. As Adam's transgression had brought wretchedness and death, so the sacrifice of Christ would bring life and immortality.

Not only man but the earth had by sin come under the power of the wicked one, and was to be restored by the plan of redemption. At his creation Adam was placed in dominion over the earth. But by yielding to temptation, he was brought under the power of Satan. "Of whom a man is overcome, of the same is he brought in bondage." 2 Peter 2:19. When man became Satan's captive, the dominion which he held, passed to his conqueror. Thus Satan became "the god of this world." 2 Corinthians 4:4. He had usurped that dominion over the earth which had been originally given to Adam. But Christ, by His sacrifice paying the penalty of sin, would not only redeem man, but recover the dominion which he had forfeited. All that was lost by the first Adam will be restored by the second. Says the prophet, "O tower of the flock, the stronghold of the daughter of Zion, unto thee shall it come, even the first dominion." Micah 4:8. And the apostle Paul points forward to the "redemption of the purchased possession." Ephesians 1:14. God created the earth to be the abode of holy, happy beings. The Lord "formed the earth and made it; He hath established it, He created it not in vain, He formed it to be inhabited." Isaiah 45:18. That purpose will be fulfilled, when, renewed by the power of God, and freed from sin and sorrow, it shall become the eternal abode of the redeemed. "The righteous shall inherit the land, and dwell therein forever." "And there shall be no more curse: but the throne of God and of the Lamb shall be in it; and His servants shall serve Him." Psalm 37:29; Revelation 22:3.

Adam, in his innocence, had enjoyed open communion with his Maker; but sin brought separation between God and man, and the atonement of Christ alone could span the abyss and make possible the communication of blessing or salvation from heaven to earth. Man was still cut off from direct approach to his Creator, but God would communicate with him through Christ and angels.

Thus were revealed to Adam important events in the history of mankind, from the time when the divine sentence was pronounced in Eden, to the Flood, and onward to the first advent of the Son of God. He was shown that while the sacrifice of Christ would be of sufficient value to save the whole world, many would choose a life of sin rather than of repentance and obedience. Crime would increase through successive generations, and the curse of sin would rest more and more heavily upon the human race, upon the beasts, and upon the earth. The days of man would be shortened by his own course of sin; he would deteriorate in physical stature and endurance and in moral and intellectual power, until the world would be filled with misery of every type. Through the indulgence of appetite and passion men would become incapable of appreciating the great truths of the plan of redemption. Yet Christ, true to the purpose for which He left heaven, would continue His interest in men, and still invite them to hide their weakness and deficiencies in Him. He would supply the needs of all who would come unto Him in faith. And there would ever be a few who would preserve the knowledge of God and would remain unsullied amid the prevailing iniquity.

The sacrificial offerings were ordained by God to be to man a perpetual reminder and a penitential acknowledgment of his sin and a confession of his faith in the promised Redeemer. They were intended to impress upon the fallen race the solemn truth that it was sin that caused death. To Adam, the offering of the first sacrifice was a most painful ceremony. His hand must be raised to take life, which only God could give. It was the first time he had ever witnessed death, and he knew that had he been obedient to God, there would have been no death of man or beast. As he slew the innocent victim, he trembled at the thought that his sin must shed the blood of the spotless Lamb of God. This scene gave him a deeper and more vivid sense of the greatness of his transgression, which nothing but the death of God's dear Son could expiate. And he marveled at the infinite goodness that would give such a ransom to save the guilty. A star of hope illumined the dark and terrible future and relieved it of its utter desolation.

But the plan of redemption had a yet broader and deeper purpose than the salvation of man. It was not for this alone that Christ came to the earth; it was not merely that the inhabitants of this little world might regard the law of God as it should be regarded; but it was to vindicate the character of God before the universe. To this result of His great sacrifice—its influence upon the intelligences of other worlds, as well as upon man—the Saviour looked forward when just before His crucifixion He said: "Now is the judgment of this world: now shall the prince of this world be cast out. And I, if I be lifted up from the earth, will draw all unto Me." John 12:31, 32. The act of Christ in dying for the salvation of man would not only make heaven accessible to men, but before all the universe it would justify God and His Son in their dealing with the rebellion of Satan. It would establish the perpetuity of the law of God and would reveal the nature and the results of sin.

From the first the great controversy had been upon the law of God. Satan had sought to prove that God was unjust, that His law was faulty, and that the good of the universe required it to be changed. In attacking the law he aimed to overthrow the authority of its Author. In the controversy it was to be shown whether the divine statutes were defective and subject to change, or perfect and immutable.

When Satan was thrust out of heaven, he determined to make the earth his kingdom. When he tempted and overcame Adam and Eve, he thought that he had gained possession of this world; "because," said he, "they have chosen me as their ruler." He claimed that it was impossible that forgiveness should be granted to the sinner, and therefore the fallen race were his rightful subjects, and the world was his. But God gave His own dear Son—one equal with Himself—to bear the penalty of transgression, and thus He provided a way by which they might be restored to His favor, and brought back to their Eden home. Christ undertook to redeem man and to rescue the world from the grasp of Satan. The great controversy begun in heaven was to be decided in the very world, on the very same field, that Satan claimed as his.

It was the marvel of all the universe that Christ should humble Himself to save fallen man. That He who had passed from star to star, from world to world, superintending all, by His providence supplying the needs of every order of being in His vast creation—that He should consent to leave His glory and take upon Himself human nature, was a mystery which the sinless intelligences of other worlds desired to understand. When Christ came to our world in the form of humanity, all were intensely interested in following Him as He traversed, step by step, the bloodstained path from the manger to Calvary. Heaven marked the insult and mockery that He received, and knew that it was at Satan's instigation. They marked the work of counteragencies going forward; Satan constantly pressing darkness, sorrow, and suffering upon the race, and Christ counteracting it. They watched the battle between light and darkness as it waxed stronger. And as Christ in His expiring agony upon the cross cried out, "It is finished" (John 19:30), a shout of triumph rang through every world and through heaven itself. The great contest that had been so long in progress in this world was now decided, and Christ was conqueror. His death had answered the question whether the Father and the Son had sufficient love for man to exercise self-denial and a spirit of sacrifice. Satan had revealed his true character as a liar and a murderer. It was seen that the very same spirit with which he had ruled the children of men who were under his power, he would have manifested if permitted to control the intelligences of heaven. With one voice the loyal universe united in extolling the divine administration.

If the law could be changed, man might have been saved without the sacrifice of Christ; but the fact that it was necessary for Christ to give His life for the fallen race, proves that the law of God will not release the sinner from its claims upon him. It is demonstrated that the wages of sin is death. When Christ died, the destruction of Satan was made certain. But if the law was abolished at the cross, as many claim, then the agony and death of God's dear Son were endured only to give to Satan just what he asked; then the prince of evil triumphed, his charges against the divine government were sustained. The very fact that Christ bore the penalty of man's transgression is a mighty argument to all created intelligences that the law is changeless; that God is righteous, merciful, and self-denying; and that infinite justice and mercy unite in the administration of His government.

Chapter 5—Cain and Abel Tested

This chapter is based on Genesis 4:1-15.

Cain and Abel, the sons of Adam, differed widely in character. Abel had a spirit of loyalty to God; he saw justice and mercy in the Creator's dealings with the fallen race, and gratefully accepted the hope of redemption. But Cain cherished feelings of rebellion, and murmured against God because of the curse pronounced upon the earth and upon the human race for Adam's sin. He permitted his mind to run in the same channel that led to Satan's fall—indulging the desire for self-exaltation and questioning the divine justice and authority.

These brothers were tested, as Adam had been tested before them, to prove whether they would believe and obey the word of God. They were acquainted with the provision made for the salvation of man, and understood the system of offerings which God had ordained. They knew that in these offerings they were to express faith in the Saviour whom the offerings typified, and at the same time to acknowledge their total dependence on Him for pardon; and they knew that by thus conforming to the divine plan for their redemption, they were giving proof of their obedience to the will of God. Without the shedding of blood there could be no remission of sin; and they were to show their faith in the blood of Christ as the promised atonement by offering the firstlings of the flock in sacrifice. Besides this, the first fruits of the earth were to be presented before the Lord as a thank offering.

The two brothers erected their altars alike, and each brought an offering. Abel presented a sacrifice from the flock, in accordance with the Lord's directions. "And the Lord had respect unto Abel and to his offering." Fire flashed from heaven and consumed the sacrifice. But Cain, disregarding the Lord's direct and explicit command, presented only an offering of fruit. There was no token from heaven to show that it was accepted. Abel pleaded with his brother to approach God in the divinely prescribed way, but his entreaties only made Cain the more determined to follow his own will. As the eldest, he felt above being admonished by his brother, and despised his counsel.

Cain came before God with murmuring and infidelity in his heart in regard to the promised sacrifice and the necessity of the sacrificial offerings. His gift expressed no penitence for sin. He felt, as many now feel, that it would be an acknowledgment of weakness to follow the exact plan marked out by God, of trusting his salvation wholly to the atonement of the promised Saviour. He chose the course of self-dependence. He would come in his own merits. He would not bring the lamb, and mingle its blood with his offering, but would present *his* fruits, the products of *his* labor. He presented his offering as a favor done to God, through which he expected to secure the divine approval. Cain obeyed in building an altar, obeyed in bringing a sacrifice; but he rendered only a partial obedience. The essential part, the recognition of the need of a Redeemer, was left out.

So far as birth and religious instruction were concerned, these brothers were equal. Both were sinners, and both acknowledged the claims of God to reverence and worship. To outward appearance their religion was the same up to a certain point, but beyond this the difference between the two was great.

"By faith Abel offered unto God a more excellent sacrifice than Cain." Hebrews 11:4. Abel grasped the great principles of redemption. He saw himself a sinner, and he saw sin and its penalty, death, standing between his soul and communion with God. He brought the slain victim, the sacrificed life, thus acknowledging the claims of the law that had been transgressed. Through the shed blood he looked to the future sacrifice, Christ dying on the cross of Calvary; and trusting in the atonement that was there to be made, he had the witness that he was righteous, and his offering accepted.

Cain had the same opportunity of learning and accepting these truths as had Abel. He was not the victim of an arbitrary purpose. One brother was not elected to be accepted of God, and the other to be rejected. Abel chose faith and obedience; Cain, unbelief and rebellion. Here the whole matter rested.

Cain and Abel represent two classes that will exist in the world till the close of time. One class avail themselves of the appointed sacrifice for sin; the other venture to depend upon their own merits; theirs is a sacrifice without the virtue of divine mediation, and thus it is not able to bring man into favor with God. It is only through the merits of Jesus that our transgressions can be pardoned. Those who feel no need of the blood of Christ, who feel that without divine grace they can by their own works secure the approval of God, are making the same mistake as did Cain. If they do not accept the cleansing blood, they are under condemnation. There is no other provision made whereby they can be released from the thralldom of sin.

The class of worshipers who follow the example of Cain includes by far the greater portion of the world; for nearly every false religion has been based on the same principle—that man can depend upon his own efforts for salvation. It is claimed by some that the human race is in need, not of redemption, but of development—that it can refine, elevate, and regenerate itself. As Cain thought to secure the divine favor by an offering that lacked the blood of a sacrifice, so do these expect to exalt humanity to the divine standard, independent of the atonement. The history of Cain shows what must be the results. It shows what man will become apart from Christ. Humanity has no power to regenerate itself. It does not tend upward, toward the divine, but downward, toward the satanic. Christ is our only hope. "There is none other name under heaven given among men, whereby we must be saved." "Neither is there salvation in any other." Acts 4:12.

True faith, which relies wholly upon Christ, will be manifested by obedience to all the requirements of God. From Adam's day to the present time the great controversy has been concerning obedience to God's law. In all ages there have been those who claimed a right to the favor of God even while they were disregarding some of His commands. But the Scriptures declare that by works is "faith made perfect;" and that, without the works of obedience, faith "is dead." James 2:22, 17. He that professes to know God, "and keepeth not His commandments, is a liar, and the truth is not in him." 1 John 2:4.

When Cain saw that his offering was rejected, he was angry with the Lord and with Abel; he was angry that God did not accept man's substitute in place of the sacrifice divinely ordained, and angry with his brother for choosing to obey God instead of joining in rebellion against Him. Notwithstanding Cain's disregard of the divine command, God did not leave him to himself; but He condescended to reason with the man who had shown himself so unreasonable. And the Lord said unto Cain, "Why art thou wroth? and why is thy countenance fallen?" Through an angel messenger the divine warning was conveyed: "If thou doest well, shalt thou not be accepted? And if thou doest not well, sin lieth at the door." The choice lay with Cain himself. If he would trust to the merits of the promised Saviour, and would obey God's requirements, he would enjoy His favor. But should he persist in unbelief and transgression, he would have no ground for complaint because he was rejected by the Lord.

But instead of acknowledging his sin, Cain continued to complain of the injustice of God and to cherish jealousy and hatred of Abel. He angrily reproached his brother, and attempted to draw him into controversy concerning God's dealings with them. In meekness, yet fearlessly and firmly, Abel defended the justice and goodness of God. He pointed out Cain's error, and tried to convince him that the wrong was in himself. He pointed to the compassion of God in sparing the life of their parents when He might have punished them with instant death, and urged that God loved them, or He would not have given His Son, innocent and holy, to suffer the penalty which they had incurred. All this caused Cain's anger to burn the hotter. Reason and conscience told him that Abel was in the right; but he was enraged that one who had been wont to heed his counsel should now presume to disagree with him, and that he could gain no sympathy in his rebellion. In the fury of his passion he slew his brother.

Cain hated and killed his brother, not for any wrong that Abel had done, but "because his own works were evil, and his brother's righteous." 1 John 3:12. So in all ages the wicked have hated those who were better than themselves. Abel's life of obedience and unswerving faith was to Cain a perpetual reproof. "Everyone that doeth evil hateth the light, neither cometh to the light, lest his deeds should be reproved." John 3:20. The brighter the heavenly light that is reflected from the character of God's faithful servants, the more clearly the sins of the ungodly are revealed, and the more determined will be their efforts to destroy those who disturb their peace.

The murder of Abel was the first example of the enmity that

God had declared would exist between the serpent and the seed of the woman—between Satan and his subjects and Christ and His followers. Through man's sin, Satan had gained control of the human race, but Christ would enable them to cast off his yoke. Whenever, through faith in the Lamb of God, a soul renounces the service of sin, Satan's wrath is kindled. The holy life of Abel testified against Satan's claim that it is impossible for man to keep God's law. When Cain, moved by the spirit of the wicked one, saw that he could not control Abel, he was so enraged that he destroyed his life. And wherever there are any who will stand in vindication of the righteousness of the law of God, the same spirit will be manifested against them. It is the spirit that through all the ages has set up the stake and kindled the burning pile for the disciples of Christ. But the cruelties heaped upon the follower of Jesus are instigated by Satan and his hosts because they cannot force him to submit to their control. It is the rage of a vanquished foe. Every martyr of Jesus has died a conqueror. Says the prophet, "They overcame him ["that old serpent, called the devil, and Satan"] by the blood of the Lamb, and by the word of their testimony; and they loved not their lives unto the death." Revelation 12:11, 9.

Cain the murderer was soon called to answer for his crime. "The Lord said unto Cain, Where is Abel thy brother? And he said, I know not: Am I my brother's keeper?" Cain had gone so far in sin that he had lost a sense of the continual presence of God and of His greatness and omniscience. So he resorted to falsehood to conceal his guilt.

Again the Lord said to Cain, "What hast thou done? The voice of thy brother's blood crieth unto Me from the ground." God had given Cain an opportunity to confess his sin. He had had time to reflect. He knew the enormity of the deed he had done, and of the falsehood he had uttered to conceal it; but he was rebellious still, and sentence was no longer deferred. The divine voice that had been heard in entreaty and admonition pronounced the terrible words: "And now art thou cursed from the earth, which hath opened her mouth to receive thy brother's blood from thy hand. When thou tillest the ground, it shall not henceforth yield unto thee her strength; a fugitive and a vagabond shalt thou be in the earth."

Notwithstanding that Cain had by his crimes merited the sentence of death, a merciful Creator still spared his life, and granted him opportunity for repentance. But Cain lived only to harden his heart, to encourage rebellion against the divine authority, and to become the head of a line of bold, abandoned sinners. This one apostate, led on by Satan, became a tempter to others; and his example and influence exerted their demoralizing power, until the earth became so corrupt and filled with violence as to call for its destruction.

In sparing the life of the first murderer, God presented before the whole universe a lesson bearing upon the great controversy. The dark history of Cain and his descendants was an illustration of what would have been the result of permitting the sinner to live on forever, to carry out his rebellion against God. The forbearance of God only rendered the wicked more bold and defiant in their iniquity. Fifteen centuries after the sentence pronounced upon Cain, the universe witnessed the fruition of his influence and example, in the crime and pollution that flooded the earth. It was made manifest that the sentence of death pronounced upon the fallen race for the transgression of God's law was both just and merciful. The longer men lived in sin, the more abandoned they became. The divine sentence cutting short a career of unbridled iniquity, and freeing the world from the influence of those who had become hardened in rebellion, was a blessing rather than a curse.

Satan is constantly at work, with intense energy and under a thousand disguises, to misrepresent the character and government of God. With extensive, well-organized plans and marvelous power, he is working to hold the inhabitants of the world under his deceptions. God, the One infinite and all-wise, sees the end from the beginning, and in dealing with evil His plans were far-reaching and comprehensive. It was His purpose, not merely to put down the rebellion, but to demonstrate to all the universe the nature of the rebellion. God's plan was unfolding, showing both His justice and His mercy, and fully vindicating His wisdom and righteousness in His dealings with evil.

The holy inhabitants of other worlds were watching with the deepest interest the events taking place on the earth. In the condition of the world that existed before the Flood they saw illustrated the results of the administration which Lucifer had endeavored to establish in heaven, in rejecting the authority of Christ and casting aside the law of God. In those high-handed sinners of the antediluvian world they saw the subjects over whom Satan held sway. The thoughts of men's hearts were only evil continually. Genesis 6:5. Every emotion, every impulse and imagination, was at war with the divine principles of purity and peace and love. It was an example of the awful depravity resulting from Satan's policy to remove from God's creatures the restraint of His holy law.

By the facts unfolded in the progress of the great controversy, God will demonstrate the principles of His rules of government, which have been falsified by Satan and by all whom he has deceived. His justice will finally be acknowledged by the whole world, though the acknowledgment will be made too late to save the rebellious. God carries with Him the sympathy and approval of the whole universe as step by step His great plan advances to its complete fulfillment. He will carry it with Him in the final eradication of rebellion. It will be seen that all who have forsaken the divine precepts have placed themselves on the side of Satan, in warfare against Christ. When the prince of this world shall be judged, and all who have united with him shall share his fate, the whole universe as witnesses to the sentence will declare, "Just and true are Thy ways, Thou King of saints." Revelation 15:3.

Chapter 6—Seth and Enoch

This chapter is based on Genesis 4:25 to 6:2.

To Adam was given another son, to be the inheritor of the divine promise, the heir of the spiritual birthright. The name Seth, given to this son, signified "appointed," or "compensation;" "for," said the mother, "God hath appointed me another seed instead of Abel, whom Cain slew." Seth was of more noble stature than Cain or Abel, and resembled Adam more closely than did his other sons. He was a worthy character, following in the steps of Abel. Yet he inherited no more natural goodness than did Cain. Concerning the creation of Adam it is said, "In the likeness of God made He him;" but man, after the Fall, "begat a son in his *own* likeness, after *his* image." While Adam was created sinless, in the likeness of God, Seth, like Cain, inherited the fallen nature of his parents. But he received also the knowledge of the Redeemer and instruction in righteousness. By divine grace he served and honored God; and he labored, as Abel would have done, had he lived, to turn the minds of sinful men to revere and obey their Creator.

"To Seth, to him also there was born a son; and he called his name Enos: then began men to call upon the name of Jehovah." The faithful had worshiped God before; but as men increased, the distinction between the two classes became more marked. There was an open profession of loyalty to God on the part of one, as there was of contempt and disobedience on the part of the other.

Before the Fall our first parents had kept the Sabbath, which was instituted in Eden; and after their expulsion from Paradise they continued its observance. They had tasted the bitter fruits of disobedience, and had learned what every one that tramples upon God's commandments will sooner or later learn—that the divine precepts are sacred and immutable, and that the penalty of transgression will surely be inflicted. The Sabbath was honored by all the children of Adam that remained loyal to God. But Cain and his descendants did not respect the day upon which God had rested. They chose their own time for labor and for rest, regardless of Jehovah's express command.

Upon receiving the curse of God, Cain had withdrawn from his father's household. He had first chosen his occupation as a tiller of the soil, and he now founded a city, calling it after the name of his eldest son. He had gone out from the presence of the Lord, cast away the promise of the restored Eden, to seek his possessions and enjoyment in the earth under the curse of sin, thus standing at the head of that great class of men who worship the god of this world. In that which pertains to mere earthly and material progress, his descendants became distinguished. But they were regardless of God, and in opposition to His purposes for man. To the crime of murder, in which Cain had led the way, Lamech, the fifth in descent, added polygamy, and, boastfully defiant, he acknowledged God, only to draw from the avenging of Cain an assurance of his own safety. Abel had led a pastoral life, dwelling in tents or booths, and the descendants of Seth followed the same course, counting themselves "strangers and pilgrims on the earth," seeking "a better country, that is, an heavenly." Hebrews 11:13, 16.

For some time the two classes remained separate. The race of Cain, spreading from the place of their first settlement, dispersed over the plains and valleys where the children of Seth had dwelt; and the latter, in order to escape from their contaminating influence, withdrew to the mountains, and there made their home. So long as this separation continued, they maintained the worship of God in its purity. But in the lapse of time they ventured, little by little, to mingle with the inhabitants of the valleys. This association was productive of the worst results. "The sons of God saw the daughters of men that they were fair." The children of Seth, attracted by the beauty of the daughters of Cain's descendants, displeased the Lord by intermarrying with them. Many of the worshipers of God were beguiled into sin by the allurements that were now constantly before them, and they lost their peculiar, holy character. Mingling with the depraved, they became like them in spirit and in deeds; the restrictions of the seventh commandment were disregarded, "and they took them wives of all which they chose." The children of Seth went "in the way of Cain" (Jude 11); they fixed their minds upon worldly prosperity and enjoyment and neglected the commandments of the Lord. Men "did not like to retain God in their knowledge;" they "became vain in their imaginations, and their foolish heart was darkened." Romans 1:21. Therefore "God gave them over to a mind void of judgment." Verse 28, margin. Sin spread abroad in the earth like a deadly leprosy.

For nearly a thousand years Adam lived among men, a witness to the results of sin. Faithfully he sought to stem the tide of evil. He had been commanded to instruct his posterity in the way of the Lord; and he carefully treasured what God had revealed to him, and repeated it to succeeding generations. To his children and children's children, to the ninth generation, he described man's holy and happy estate in Paradise, and repeated the history of his fall, telling them of the sufferings by which God had taught him the necessity of strict adherence to His law, and explaining to them the merciful provisions for their salvation. Yet there were but few who gave heed to his words. Often he was met with bitter reproaches for the sin that had brought such woe upon his posterity.

Adam's life was one of sorrow, humility, and contrition. When he left Eden, the thought that he must die thrilled him with horror. He was first made acquainted with the reality of death in the human family when Cain, his first-born son, became the murderer of his brother. Filled with the keenest remorse for his own sin, and doubly bereaved in the death of Abel and the rejection of Cain, Adam was bowed down with anguish. He witnessed the wide-spreading corruption that was finally to cause the destruction of the world by a flood; and though the sentence of death pronounced upon him by his Maker had at first appeared terrible, yet after beholding for nearly a thousand years the results of sin, he felt that it was merciful in God to bring to an end a life of suffering and sorrow.

Notwithstanding the wickedness of the antediluvian world, that age was not, as has often been supposed, an era of ignorance and barbarism. The people were granted the opportunity of reaching a high standard of moral and intellectual attainment. They possessed great physical and mental strength, and their advantages for acquiring both religious and scientific knowledge were unrivaled. It is a mistake to suppose that because they lived to a great age their minds matured late; their mental powers were early developed, and those who cherished the fear of God and lived in harmony with His will continued to increase in knowledge and wisdom throughout their life. Could illustrious scholars of our time be placed in contrast with men of the same age who lived before the Flood, they would appear as greatly inferior in mental as in physical strength. As the years of man have decreased, and his physical strength has diminished, so his mental capacities have lessened. There are men who now apply themselves to study during a period of from twenty to fifty years, and the world is filled with admiration of their attainments. But how limited are these acquirements in comparison with those of men whose mental and physical powers were developing for centuries!

It is true that the people of modern times have the benefit of the attainments of their predecessors. The men of masterly minds, who planned and studied and wrote, have left their work for those who follow. But even in this respect, and so far as merely human knowledge is concerned, how much greater the advantages of the men of that olden time! They had among them for hundreds of years him who was formed in God's image, whom the Creator Himself pronounced "good"—the man whom God had instructed in all the wisdom pertaining to the material world. Adam had learned from the Creator the history of creation; he himself witnessed the events of nine centuries; and he imparted his knowledge to his descendants. The antediluvians were without books, they had no written records; but with their great physical and mental vigor, they had strong memories, able to grasp and to retain that which was communicated to them, and in turn to transmit it unimpaired to their posterity. And for hundreds of years there were seven generations living upon the earth contemporaneously, having the opportunity of consulting together and profiting each by the knowledge and experience of all.

The advantages enjoyed by men of that age to gain a knowledge of God through His works have never been equaled since. And so far from being an era of religious darkness, that was an age of great light. All the world had opportunity to receive instruction from Adam, and those who feared the Lord had also Christ and angels for their teachers. And they had a silent witness to the truth, in the garden of God, which for so many centuries remained among men. At the cherubim-guarded gate of Paradise the glory of God was revealed, and hither came the first worshipers. Here their altars were reared, and their offerings presented. It was here that Cain and Abel had brought their sacrifices, and God had condescended to communicate with them.

Skepticism could not deny the existence of Eden while it stood just in sight, its entrance barred by watching angels. The order of creation, the object of the garden, the history of its two trees so closely connected with man's destiny, were undisputed facts. And the existence and supreme authority of God, the obligation of His law, were truths which men were slow to question while Adam was among them.

Notwithstanding the prevailing iniquity, there was a line of holy men who, elevated and ennobled by communion with God, lived as in the companionship of heaven. They were men of massive intellect, of wonderful attainments. They had a great and holy mission—to develop a character of righteousness, to teach a lesson of godliness, not only to the men of their time, but for future generations. Only a few of the most prominent are mentioned in the Scriptures; but all through the ages God had faithful witnesses, truehearted worshipers.

Of Enoch it is written that he lived sixty-five years, and begat a son. After that he walked with God three hundred years. During these earlier years Enoch had loved and feared God and had kept His commandments. He was one of the holy line, the preservers of the true faith, the progenitors of the promised seed. From the lips of Adam he had learned the dark story of the Fall, and the cheering one of God's grace as seen in the promise; and he relied upon the Redeemer to come. But after the birth of his first son, Enoch reached a higher experience; he was drawn into a closer relationship with God. He realized more fully his own obligations and responsibility as a son of God. And as he saw the child's love for its father, its simple trust in his protection; as he felt the deep, yearning tenderness of his own heart for that first-born son, he learned a precious lesson of the wonderful love of God to men in the gift of His Son, and the confidence which the children of God may repose in their heavenly Father. The infinite, unfathomable love of God through Christ became the subject of his meditations day and night; and with all the fervor of his soul he sought to reveal that love to the people among whom he dwelt.

Enoch's walk with God was not in a trance or vision, but in all the duties of his daily life. He did not become a hermit, shutting himself entirely from the world; for he had a work to do for God in the world. In the family and in his intercourse with men, as a husband and father, a friend, a citizen, he was the steadfast, unwavering servant of the Lord.

His heart was in harmony with God's will; for "can two walk together, except they be agreed?" Amos 3:3. And this holy walk was continued for three hundred years. There are few Christians who would not be far more earnest and devoted if they knew that they had but a short time to live, or that the coming of Christ was about to take place. But Enoch's faith waxed the stronger, his love became more ardent, with the lapse of centuries.

Enoch was a man of strong and highly cultivated mind and extensive knowledge; he was honored with special revelations from God; yet being in constant communion with Heaven, with a sense of the divine greatness and perfection ever before him, he was one of the humblest of men. The closer the connection with God, the deeper was the sense of his own weakness and imperfection.

Distressed by the increasing wickedness of the ungodly, and fearing that their infidelity might lessen his reverence for God, Enoch avoided constant association with them, and spent much time in solitude, giving himself to meditation and prayer. Thus he waited before the Lord, seeking a clearer knowledge of His will, that he might perform it. To him prayer was as the breath of the soul; he lived in the very atmosphere of heaven.

Through holy angels God revealed to Enoch His purpose to destroy the world by a flood, and He also opened more fully to him the plan of redemption. By the spirit of prophecy He carried him down through the generations that should live after the Flood, and showed him the great events connected with the second coming of Christ and the end of the world.

Enoch had been troubled in regard to the dead. It had seemed to him that the righteous and the wicked would go to the dust together, and that this would be their end. He could not see the life of the just beyond the grave. In prophetic vision he was instructed concerning the death of Christ, and was shown His coming in glory, attended by all the holy angels, to ransom His people from the grave. He also saw the corrupt state of the world when Christ should appear the second time—that there would be a boastful, presumptuous, self-willed generation, denying the only God and the Lord Jesus Christ, trampling upon the law, and despising the atonement. He saw the righteous crowned with glory and honor, and the wicked banished from the presence of the Lord, and destroyed by fire.

Enoch became a preacher of righteousness, making known to the people what God had revealed to him. Those who feared the Lord sought out this holy man, to share his instruction and his prayers. He labored publicly also, bearing God's messages to all who would hear the words of warning. His labors were not restricted to the Sethites. In the land where Cain had sought to flee from the divine Presence, the prophet of God made known the wonderful scenes that had passed before his vision. "Behold," he declared, "the Lord cometh with ten thousands of His saints, to execute judgment upon all, and to convince all that are ungodly among them of all their ungodly deeds." Jude 14, 15.

He was a fearless reprover of sin. While he preached the love of God in Christ to the people of his time, and pleaded with them to forsake their evil ways, he rebuked the prevailing iniquity and warned the men of his generation that judgment would surely be visited upon the transgressor. It was the Spirit of Christ that spoke through Enoch; that Spirit is manifested, not alone in utterances of love, compassion, and entreaty; it is not smooth things only that are spoken by holy men. God puts into the heart and lips of His messengers truths to utter that are keen and cutting as a two-edged sword.

The power of God that wrought with His servant was felt by those who heard. Some gave heed to the warning, and renounced their sins; but the multitudes mocked at the solemn message, and went on more boldly in their evil ways. The servants of God are to bear a similar message to the world in the last days, and it will also be received with unbelief and mockery. The antediluvian world rejected the warning words of him who walked with God. So will the last generation make light of the warnings of the Lord's messengers.

In the midst of a life of active labor, Enoch steadfastly maintained his communion with God. The greater and more pressing his labors, the more constant and earnest were his prayers. He continued to exclude himself, at certain periods, from all society. After remaining for a time among the people, laboring to benefit them by instruction and example, he would withdraw, to spend a season in solitude, hungering and thirsting for that divine knowledge which God alone can impart. Communing thus with God, Enoch came more and more to reflect the divine image. His face was radiant with a holy light, even the light that shineth in the face of Jesus. As he came forth from these divine communings, even the ungodly beheld with awe the impress of heaven upon his countenance.

The wickedness of men had reached such a height that destruction was pronounced against them. As year after year passed on, deeper and deeper grew the tide of human guilt, darker and darker gathered the clouds of divine judgment. Yet Enoch, the witness of faith, held on his way, warning, pleading, entreating, striving to turn back the tide of guilt and to stay the bolts of vengeance. Though his warnings were disregarded by a sinful, pleasure-loving people, he had the testimony that God approved, and he continued to battle faithfully against the prevailing evil, until God removed him from a world of sin to the pure joys of heaven.

The men of that generation had mocked the folly of him who sought not to gather gold or silver or to build up possessions here. But Enoch's heart was upon eternal treasures. He had looked upon the celestial city. He had seen the King in His glory in the midst of Zion. His mind, his heart, his conversation, were in heaven. The greater the existing iniquity, the more earnest was his longing for the home of God. While still on earth, he dwelt, by faith, in the realms of light.

"Blessed are the pure in heart: for they shall see God." Matthew 5:8. For three hundred years Enoch had been seeking purity of soul, that he might be in harmony with Heaven. For three centuries he had walked with God. Day by day he had longed for a closer union; nearer and nearer had grown the communion, until God took him to Himself. He had stood at the threshold of the eternal world, only a step between him and the land of the blest; and now the portals opened, the walk with God, so long pursued on earth, continued, and he passed through the gates of the Holy City—the first from among men to enter there.

His loss was felt on earth. The voice that had been heard day after day in warning and instruction was missed. There were some, both of the righteous and the wicked, who had witnessed his departure; and hoping that he might have been conveyed to some one of his places of retirement, those who loved him made diligent search, as afterward the sons of the prophets searched for Elijah; but without avail. They reported that he was not, for God had taken him.

By the translation of Enoch the Lord designed to teach an important lesson. There was danger that men would yield to discouragement, because of the fearful results of Adam's sin. Many were ready to exclaim, "What profit is it that we have feared the Lord and have kept His ordinances, since a heavy curse is resting upon the race, and death is the portion of us all?" But the instructions which God gave to Adam, and which were repeated by Seth, and exemplified by Enoch, swept away the gloom and darkness, and gave hope to man, that as through Adam came death, so through the promised Redeemer would come life and immortality. Satan was urging upon men the belief that there was no reward for the righteous or punishment for the wicked, and that it was impossible for men to obey the divine statutes. But in the case of Enoch, God declares "that He is, and that He is a rewarder of them that diligently seek Him." Hebrews 11:6. He shows what He will do for those who keep His commandments. Men were taught that it is possible to obey the law of God; that even while living in the midst of the sinful and corrupt, they were able, by the grace of God, to resist temptation, and become pure and holy. They saw in his example the blessedness of such a life; and his translation was an evidence of the truth of his prophecy concerning the hereafter, with its award of joy and glory and immortal life to the obedient, and of condemnation, woe, and death to the transgressor.

By faith Enoch "was translated that he should not see death; ... for before his translation he had this testimony, that he pleased God." Hebrews 11:5. In the midst of a world by its iniquity doomed to destruction, Enoch lived a life of such close communion with God that he was not permitted to fall under the power of death. The godly character of this prophet represents the state of holiness which must be attained by those who shall be "redeemed from the earth" (Revelation 14:3) at the time of Christ's second advent. Then, as in the world before the Flood, iniquity will prevail. Following the promptings of their corrupt hearts and the teachings of a deceptive philosophy, men will rebel against the authority of Heaven. But like Enoch, God's people will seek for purity of heart and conformity to His will, until they shall reflect the likeness of Christ. Like Enoch, they will warn the world of the Lord's second coming and of the judgments to be visited upon transgression, and by their holy conversation and example they will condemn the sins of the ungodly. As Enoch was translated to heaven before the destruction of the world by water, so the living righteous will be translated from the earth before its destruction by fire. Says the apostle: "We shall not all sleep, but we shall all be changed, in a moment, in the twinkling of an eye, at the last trump." "For the Lord Himself shall descend from heaven with a shout, with the voice of the Archangel, and with the trump of God;" "the trumpet shall sound, and the dead shall be raised incorruptible, and we shall be changed." "The dead in Christ shall rise first: then we which are alive and remain shall be caught up together with them in the clouds, to meet the Lord in the air: and so shall we ever be with the Lord. Wherefore comfort one another with these words." 1 Corinthians 15:51, 52; 1 Thessalonians 4:16-18.

Chapter 7—The Flood

This chapter is based on Genesis 6 and 7.

In the days of Noah a double curse was resting upon the earth in consequence of Adam's transgression and of the murder committed by Cain. Yet this had not greatly changed the face of nature. There were evident tokens of decay, but the earth was still rich and beautiful in the gifts of God's providence. The hills were crowned with majestic trees supporting the fruit-laden branches of the vine. The vast, gardenlike plains were clothed with verdure, and sweet with the fragrance of a thousand flowers. The fruits of the earth were in great variety, and almost without limit. The trees far surpassed in size, beauty, and perfect proportion any now to be found; their wood was of fine grain and hard substance, closely resembling stone, and hardly less enduring. Gold, silver, and precious stones existed in abundance.

The human race yet retained much of its early vigor. But a few generations had passed since Adam had access to the tree which was to prolong life; and man's existence was still measured by centuries. Had that long-lived people, with their rare powers to plan and execute, devoted themselves to the service of God, they would have made their Creator's name a praise in the earth, and would have answered the purpose for which He gave them life. But they failed to do this. There were many giants, men of great stature and strength, renowned for wisdom, skillful in devising the most cunning and wonderful works; but their guilt in giving loose rein to iniquity was in proportion to their skill and mental ability.

God bestowed upon these antediluvians many and rich gifts; but they used His bounties to glorify themselves, and turned them into a curse by fixing their affections upon the gifts instead of the Giver. They employed the gold and silver, the precious stones and the choice wood, in the construction of habitations for themselves, and endeavored to excel one another in beautifying their dwellings with the most skillful workmanship. They sought only to gratify the desires of their own proud hearts, and reveled in scenes of pleasure and wickedness. Not desiring to retain God in their knowledge, they soon came to deny His existence. They adored nature in place of the God of nature. They glorified human genius, worshiped the works of their own hands, and taught their children to bow down to graven images.

In the green fields and under the shadow of the goodly trees they set up the altars of their idols. Extensive groves, that retained their foliage throughout the year, were dedicated to the worship of false gods. With these groves were connected beautiful gardens, their long, winding avenues overhung with fruit-bearing trees of all descriptions, adorned with statuary, and furnished with all that could delight the senses or minister to the voluptuous desires of the people, and thus allure them to participate in the idolatrous worship.

Men put God out of their knowledge and worshiped the creatures of their own imagination; and as the result, they became more and more debased. The psalmist describes the effect produced upon the worshiper by the adoration of idols. He says, "They that make them are like unto them; so is every one that trusteth in them." Psalm 115:8. It is a law of the human mind that by beholding we become changed. Man will rise no higher than his conceptions of truth, purity, and holiness. If the mind is never exalted above the level of humanity, if it is not uplifted by faith to contemplate infinite wisdom and love, the man will be constantly sinking lower and lower. The worshipers of false gods clothed their deities with human attributes and passions, and thus their standard of character was degraded to the likeness of sinful humanity. They were defiled in consequence. "God saw that the wickedness of man was great in the earth, and that every imagination of the thoughts of his heart was only evil continually.... The earth also was corrupt before God; and the earth was filled with violence." God had given men His commandments as a rule of life, but His law was transgressed, and every conceivable sin was the result. The wickedness of men was open and daring, justice was trampled in the dust, and the cries of the oppressed reached unto heaven.

Polygamy had been early introduced, contrary to the divine arrangement at the beginning. The Lord gave to Adam one wife, showing His order in that respect. But after the Fall, men chose to follow their own sinful desires; and as the result, crime and wretchedness rapidly increased. Neither the marriage relation nor the rights of property were respected. Whoever coveted the wives or the possessions of his neighbor, took them by force, and men exulted in their deeds of violence. They delighted in destroying the life of animals; and the use of flesh for food rendered them still more cruel and bloodthirsty, until they came to regard human life with astonishing indifference.

The world was in its infancy; yet iniquity had become so deep and widespread that God could no longer bear with it; and He said, "I will destroy man whom I have created from the face of the earth." He declared that His Spirit should not always strive with the guilty race. If they did not cease to pollute with their sins the world and its rich treasures, He would blot them from His creation, and would destroy the things with which He had delighted to bless them; He would sweep away the beasts of the field, and the vegetation which furnished such an abundant supply of food, and would transform the fair earth into one vast scene of desolation and ruin.

Amid the prevailing corruption, Methuselah, Noah, and many others labored to keep alive the knowledge of the true God and to stay the tide of moral evil. A hundred and twenty years before the Flood, the Lord by a holy angel declared to Noah His purpose, and directed him to build an ark. While building the ark he was to preach that God would bring a flood of water upon the earth to destroy the wicked. Those who would believe the message, and would prepare for that event by repentance and reformation, should find pardon and be saved. Enoch had repeated to his children what God had shown him in regard to the Flood, and Methuselah and his sons, who lived to hear the preaching of Noah, assisted in building the ark.

God gave Noah the exact dimensions of the ark and explicit directions in regard to its construction in every particular. Human wisdom could not have devised a structure of so great strength and durability. God was the designer, and Noah the master builder. It was constructed like the hull of a ship, that it might float upon the water, but in some respects it more nearly resembled a house. It was three stories high, with but one door, which was in the side. The light was admitted at the top, and the different apartments were so arranged that all were lighted. The material employed in the construction of the ark was the cypress, or gopher wood, which would be untouched by decay for hundreds of years. The building of this immense structure was a slow and laborious process. On account of the great size of the trees and the nature of the wood, much more labor was required then than now to prepare timber, even with the greater strength which men then possessed. All that man could do was done to render the work perfect, yet the ark could not of itself have withstood the storm which was to come upon the earth. God alone could preserve His servants upon the tempestuous waters.

"By faith Noah, being warned of God of things not seen as yet, moved with fear, prepared an ark to the saving of his house; by the which he condemned the world, and became heir of the righteousness which is by faith." Hebrews 11:7. While Noah was giving his warning message to the world, his works testified of his sincerity. It was thus that his faith was perfected and made evident. He gave the world an example of believing just what God says. All that he possessed, he invested in the ark. As he began to construct that immense boat on dry ground, multitudes came from every direction to see the strange sight and to hear the earnest, fervent words of the singular preacher. Every blow struck upon the ark was a witness to the people.

Many at first appeared to receive the warning; yet they did not turn to God with true repentance. They were unwilling to renounce their sins. During the time that elapsed before the coming of the Flood, their faith was tested, and they failed to endure the trial. Overcome by the prevailing unbelief, they finally joined their former associates in rejecting the solemn message. Some were deeply convicted, and would have heeded the words of warning; but there were so many to jest and ridicule, that they partook of the same spirit, resisted the invitations of mercy, and were soon among the boldest and most defiant scoffers; for none are so reckless and go to such lengths in sin as do those who have once had light, but have resisted the convicting Spirit of God.

The men of that generation were not all, in the fullest acceptation of the term, idolaters. Many professed to be worshipers of God. They claimed that their idols were representations of the Deity, and that through them the people could obtain a clearer conception of the divine Being. This class were foremost in rejecting the preaching of Noah. As they endeavored to represent God by material objects, their minds were blinded to His majesty and power; they ceased to realize the holiness of His character, or the sacred, unchanging nature of His requirements. As sin became general, it appeared less and less sinful, and they finally declared that the divine law was no longer in force; that it was contrary to the character of God to punish transgression; and they denied that His judgments were to be visited upon the earth. Had the men of that generation obeyed the divine law, they would have recognized the voice of God in the warning of His servant; but their minds had become so blinded by rejection of light that they really believed Noah's message to be a delusion.

It was not multitudes or majorities that were on the side of right. The world was arrayed against God's justice and His laws, and Noah was regarded as a fanatic. Satan, when tempting Eve to disobey God, said to her, "Ye shall not surely die." Genesis 3:4. Great men, worldly, honored, and wise men, repeated the same. "The threatenings of God," they said, "are for the purpose of intimidating, and will never be verified. You need not be alarmed. Such an event as the destruction of the world by the God who made it, and the punishment of the beings He has created, will never take place. Be at peace; fear not. Noah is a wild fanatic." The world made merry at the folly of the deluded old man. Instead of humbling the heart before God, they continued their disobedience and wickedness, the same as though God had not spoken to them through His servant.

But Noah stood like a rock amid the tempest. Surrounded by popular contempt and ridicule, he distinguished himself by his holy integrity and unwavering faithfulness. A power attended his words, for it was the voice of God to man through His servant. Connection with God made him strong in the strength of infinite power, while for one hundred and twenty years his solemn voice fell upon the ears of that generation in regard to events, which, so far as human wisdom could judge, were impossible.

The world before the Flood reasoned that for centuries the laws of nature had been fixed. The recurring seasons had come in their order. Heretofore rain had never fallen; the earth had been watered by a mist or dew. The rivers had never yet passed their boundaries, but had borne their waters safely to the sea. Fixed decrees had kept the waters from overflowing their banks. But these reasoners did not recognize the hand of Him who had stayed the waters, saying, "Hitherto shalt thou come, but no further." Job 38:11.

As time passed on, with no apparent change in nature, men whose hearts had at times trembled with fear, began to be reassured. They reasoned, as many reason now, that nature is above the God of nature, and that her laws are so firmly established that God Himself could not change them. Reasoning that if the message of Noah were correct, nature would be turned out of her course, they made that message, in the minds of the world, a delusion—a grand deception. They manifested their contempt for the warning of God by doing just as they had done before the warning was given. They continued their festivities and their gluttonous feasts; they ate and drank, planted and built, laying their plans in reference to advantages they hoped to gain in the future; and they went to greater lengths in wickedness, and in defiant disregard of God's requirements, to testify that they had no fear of the Infinite One. They asserted that if there were any truth in what Noah had said, the men of renown—the wise, the prudent, the great men—would understand the matter.

Had the antediluvians believed the warning, and repented of their evil deeds, the Lord would have turned aside His wrath, as he afterward did from Nineveh. But by their obstinate resistance to the reproofs of conscience and the warnings of God's prophet, that generation filled up the measure of their iniquity, and became ripe for destruction.

The period of their probation was about to expire. Noah had faithfully followed the instructions which he had received from God. The ark was finished in every part as the Lord had directed, and was stored with food for man and beast. And now the servant of God made his last solemn appeal to the people. With an agony of desire that words cannot express, he entreated them to seek a refuge while it might be found. Again they rejected his words, and raised their voices in jest and scoffing. Suddenly a silence fell upon the mocking throng. Beasts of every description, the fiercest as well as the most gentle, were seen coming from mountain and forest and quietly making their way toward the ark. A noise as of a rushing wind was heard, and lo, birds were flocking from all directions, their numbers darkening the heavens, and in perfect order they passed to the ark. Animals obeyed the command of God, while men were disobedient. Guided by holy angels, they "went in two and two unto Noah into the ark," and the clean beasts by sevens. The world looked on in wonder, some in fear. Philosophers were called upon to account for the singular occurrence, but in vain. It was a mystery which they could not fathom. But men had become so hardened by their persistent rejection of light that even this scene produced but a momentary impression. As the doomed race beheld the sun shining in its glory, and the earth clad in almost Eden beauty, they banished their rising fears by boisterous merriment, and by their deeds of violence they seemed to invite upon themselves the visitation of the already awakened wrath of God.

God commanded Noah, "Come thou and all thy house into the ark; for thee have I seen righteous before Me in this generation." Noah's warnings had been rejected by the world, but his influence and example resulted in blessings to his family. As a reward for his faithfulness and integrity, God saved all the members of his family with him. What encouragement to parental fidelity!

Mercy had ceased its pleadings for the guilty race. The beasts of the field and the birds of the air had entered the place of refuge. Noah and his household were within the ark, "and the Lord shut him in." A flash of dazzling light was seen, and a cloud of glory more vivid than the lightning descended from heaven and hovered before the entrance of the ark. The massive door, which it was impossible for those within to close, was slowly swung to its place by unseen hands. Noah was shut in, and the rejecters of God's mercy were shut out. The seal of Heaven was on that door; God had shut it, and God alone could open it. So when Christ shall cease His intercession for guilty men, before His coming in the clouds of heaven, the door of mercy will be shut. Then divine grace will no longer restrain the wicked, and Satan will have full control of those who have rejected mercy. They will endeavor to destroy God's people; but as Noah was shut into the ark, so the righteous will be shielded by divine power.

For seven days after Noah and his family entered the ark, there appeared no sign of the coming storm. During this period their faith was tested. It was a time of triumph to the world without. The apparent delay confirmed them in the belief that Noah's message was a delusion, and that the Flood would never come. Notwithstanding the solemn scenes which they had witnessed—the beasts and birds entering the ark, and the angel of God closing the door—they still continued their sport and revelry, even making a jest of these signal manifestations of God's power. They gathered in crowds about the ark, deriding its inmates with a daring violence which they had never ventured upon before.

But upon the eighth day dark clouds overspread the heavens. There followed the muttering of thunder and the flash of lightning. Soon large drops of rain began to fall. The world had never witnessed anything like this, and the hearts of men were struck with fear. All were secretly inquiring, "Can it be that Noah was in the right, and that the world is doomed to destruction?" Darker and darker grew the heavens, and faster came the falling rain. The beasts were roaming about in the wildest terror, and their discordant cries seemed to moan out their own destiny and the fate of man. Then "the fountains of the great deep" were "broken up, and the windows of heaven were opened." Water appeared to come from the clouds in mighty cataracts. Rivers broke away from their boundaries, and overflowed the valleys. Jets of water burst from the earth with indescribable force, throwing massive rocks hundreds of feet into the air, and these, in falling, buried themselves deep in the ground.

The people first beheld the destruction of the works of their own hands. Their splendid buildings, and the beautiful gardens and groves where they had placed their idols, were destroyed by lightning from heaven, and the ruins were scattered far and wide. The altars on which human sacrifices had been offered were torn down, and the worshipers were made to tremble at the power of the living God, and to know that it was their corruption and idolatry which had called down their destruction.

As the violence of the storm increased, trees, buildings, rocks, and earth were hurled in every direction. The terror of man and beast was beyond description. Above the roar of the tempest was heard the wailing of a people that had despised the authority of God. Satan himself, who was compelled to remain in the midst of the warring elements, feared for his own existence. He had delighted to control so powerful a race, and desired them to live to practice their abominations and continue their rebellion against the Ruler of heaven. He now uttered imprecations against God, charging Him with injustice and cruelty. Many of the people, like Satan, blasphemed God, and had they been able, they would have torn Him from the throne of power. Others were frantic with fear, stretching their hands toward the ark and pleading for admittance. But their entreaties were in vain. Conscience was at last aroused to know that there is a God who ruleth in the heavens. They called upon Him earnestly, but His ear was not open to their cry. In that terrible hour they saw that the transgression of God's law had caused their ruin. Yet while, through fear of punishment, they acknowledged their sin, they felt no true contrition, no abhorrence of evil. They would have returned to their defiance of Heaven, had the judgment been removed. So when God's judgments shall fall upon the earth before its deluge by fire, the impenitent will know just where and what their sin is—the despising of His holy law. Yet they will have no more true repentance than did the old-world sinners.

Some in their desperation endeavored to break into the ark, but the firm-made structure withstood their efforts. Some clung to the ark until they were borne away by the surging waters, or their hold was broken by collision with rocks and trees. The massive ark trembled in every fiber as it was beaten by the merciless winds and flung from billow to billow. The cries of the beasts within expressed their fear and pain. But amid the warring elements it continued to ride safely. Angels that excel in strength were commissioned to preserve it.

The beasts, exposed to the tempest, rushed toward man, as though expecting help from him. Some of the people bound their children and themselves upon powerful animals, knowing that these were tenacious of life, and would climb to the highest points to escape the rising waters. Some fastened themselves to lofty trees on the summit of hills or mountains; but the trees were uprooted, and with their burden of living beings were hurled into the seething billows. One spot after another that promised safety was abandoned. As the waters rose higher and higher, the people fled for refuge to the loftiest mountains. Often man and beast would struggle together for a foothold, until both were swept away.

From the highest peaks men looked abroad upon a shoreless ocean. The solemn warnings of God's servant no longer seemed a subject for ridicule and scorning. How those doomed sinners longed for the opportunities which they had slighted! How they pleaded for one hour's probation, one more privilege of mercy, one call from the lips of Noah! But the sweet voice of mercy was no more to be heard by them. Love, no less than justice, demanded that God's judgments should put a check on sin. The avenging waters swept over the last retreat, and the despisers of God perished in the black depths.

"By the word of God ... the world that then was, being overflowed with water, perished: but the heavens and the earth, which are now, by the same word are kept in store, reserved unto fire against the day of judgment and perdition of ungodly men." 2 Peter 3:5-7. Another storm is coming. The earth will again be swept by the desolating wrath of God, and sin and sinners will be destroyed.

The sins that called for vengeance upon the antediluvian world exist today. The fear of God is banished from the hearts of men, and His law is treated with indifference and contempt. The intense worldliness of that generation is equaled by that of the generation now living. Said Christ, "As in the days that were before the Flood they were eating and drinking, marrying and giving in marriage, until the day that Noah entered into the ark, and knew not until the Flood came, and took them all away; so shall also the coming of the Son of man be." Matthew 24:38, 39. God did not condemn the antediluvians for eating and drinking; He had given them the fruits of the earth in great abundance to supply their physical wants. Their sin consisted in taking these gifts without gratitude to the Giver, and debasing themselves by indulging appetite without restraint. It was lawful for them to marry. Marriage was in God's order; it was one of the first institutions which He established. He gave special directions concerning this ordinance, clothing it with sanctity and beauty; but these directions were forgotten, and marriage was perverted and made to minister to passion.

A similar condition of things exists now. That which is lawful in itself is carried to excess. Appetite is indulged without restraint. Professed followers of Christ are today eating and drinking with the drunken, while their names stand in honored church records. Intemperance benumbs the moral and spiritual powers and prepares the way for indulgence of the lower passions. Multitudes feel under no moral obligation to curb their sensual desires, and they become

[102] the slaves of lust. Men are living for the pleasures of sense; for this world and this life alone. Extravagance pervades all circles of society. Integrity is sacrificed for luxury and display. They that make haste to be rich pervert justice and oppress the poor, and "slaves and souls of men" are still bought and sold. Fraud and bribery and theft stalk unrebuked in high places and in low. The issues of the press teem with records of murder—crimes so cold-blooded and causeless that it seems as though every instinct of humanity were blotted out. And these atrocities have become of so common occurrence that they hardly elicit a comment or awaken surprise. The spirit of anarchy is permeating all nations, and the outbreaks that from time to time excite the horror of the world are but indications of the pent-up fires of passion and lawlessness that, having once escaped control, will fill the earth with woe and desolation. The picture which Inspiration has given of the antediluvian world represents too truly the condition to which modern society is fast hastening. Even now, in the present century, and in professedly Christian lands, there are crimes daily perpetrated as black and terrible as those for which the old-world sinners were destroyed.

Before the Flood God sent Noah to warn the world, that the people might be led to repentance, and thus escape the threatened destruction. As the time of Christ's second appearing draws near, the Lord sends His servants with a warning to the world to prepare for that great event. Multitudes have been living in transgression of God's law, and now He in mercy calls them to obey its sacred precepts. All who will put away their sins by repentance toward God and faith in Christ are offered pardon. But many feel that it requires too great a sacrifice to put away sin. Because their life does not harmonize with the pure principles of God's moral government, they reject His warnings and deny the authority of His law.

Of the vast population of the earth before the Flood, only eight souls believed and obeyed God's word through Noah. For a hundred and twenty years the preacher of righteousness warned the world of the coming destruction, but his message was rejected and despised. So it will be now. Before the Lawgiver shall come to punish the disobedient, transgressors are warned to repent, and return to their allegiance; but with the majority these warnings will be in vain. Says the apostle Peter, "There shall come in the last days scoffers, walking after their own lusts, and saying, Where is the promise of His coming? for since the fathers fell asleep, all things continue as they were from the beginning." 2 Peter 3:3, 4. Do we not hear these very words repeated, not merely by the openly ungodly, but by many who occupy the pulpits of our land? "There is no cause for alarm," they cry. "Before Christ shall come, all the world is to be converted, and righteousness is to reign for a thousand years. Peace, peace! all things continue as they were from the beginning. Let none be disturbed by the exciting message of these alarmists." But this doctrine of the millennium does not harmonize with the teachings of Christ and His apostles. Jesus asked the significant question, "When the Son of man cometh, shall He find faith on the earth?" Luke 18:8. And, as we have seen, He declares that the state of the world will be as in the days of Noah. Paul warns us that we may look for wickedness to increase as the end draws near: "The Spirit speaketh expressly, that in the latter times some shall depart from the faith, giving heed to seducing spirits, and doctrines of devils." 1 Timothy 4:1. The apostle says that "in the last days perilous times shall come." 2 Timothy 3:1. And he gives a startling list of sins that will be found among those who have a form of godliness.

As the time of their probation was closing, the antediluvians gave themselves up to exciting amusements and festivities. Those who possessed influence and power were bent on keeping the minds of the people engrossed with mirth and pleasure, lest any should be impressed by the last solemn warning. Do we not see the same repeated in our day? While God's servants are giving the message that the end of all things is at hand, the world is absorbed in amusements and pleasure seeking. There is a constant round of excitement that causes indifference to God and prevents the people from being impressed by the truths which alone can save them from the coming destruction.

In Noah's day philosophers declared that it was impossible for the world to be destroyed by water; so now there are men of science who endeavor to show that the world cannot be destroyed by fire—that this would be inconsistent with the laws of nature. But the God of nature, the Maker and Controller of her laws, can use the works of His hands to serve His own purpose.

When great and wise men had proved to their satisfaction that it was impossible for the world to be destroyed by water, when the fears of the people were quieted, when all regarded Noah's prophecy as a delusion, and looked upon him as a fanatic—then it was that God's time had come. "The fountains of the great deep" were "broken up, and the windows of heaven were opened," and the scoffers were overwhelmed in the waters of the Flood. With all their boasted philosophy, men found too late that their wisdom was foolishness, that the Lawgiver is greater than the laws of nature, and that Omnipotence is at no loss for means to accomplish His purposes. "As it was in the days of Noah," "even thus shall it be in the days when the Son of man is revealed." Luke 17:26, 30. "The day of the Lord will come as a thief in the night; in the which the heavens shall pass away with a great noise, and the elements shall melt with fervent heat, the earth also and the works that are therein shall be burned up." 2 Peter 3:10. When the reasoning of philosophy has banished the fear of God's judgments; when religious teachers are pointing forward to long ages of peace and prosperity, and the world are absorbed in their rounds of business and pleasure, planting and building, feasting and merrymaking, rejecting God's warnings and mocking His messengers—then it is that sudden destruction cometh upon them, and they shall not escape. 1 Thessalonians 5:3.

Chapter 8—After the Flood

The waters rose fifteen cubits above the highest mountains. It often seemed to the family within the ark that they must perish, as for five long months their boat was tossed about, apparently at the mercy of wind and wave. It was a trying ordeal; but Noah's faith did not waver, for he had the assurance that the divine hand was upon the helm.

As the waters began to subside, the Lord caused the ark to drift into a spot protected by a group of mountains that had been preserved by His power. These mountains were but a little distance apart, and the ark moved about in this quiet haven, and was no longer driven upon the boundless ocean. This gave great relief to the weary, tempest-tossed voyagers.

Noah and his family anxiously waited for the decrease of the waters, for they longed to go forth again upon the earth. Forty days after the tops of the mountains became visible, they sent out a raven, a bird of quick scent, to discover whether the earth had become dry. This bird, finding nothing but water, continued to fly to and from the ark. Seven days later a dove was sent forth, which, finding no footing, returned to the ark. Noah waited seven days longer, and again sent forth the dove. When she returned at evening with an olive leaf in her mouth, there was great rejoicing. Later "Noah removed the covering of the ark, and looked, and, behold, the face of the ground was dry." Still he waited patiently within the ark. As he had entered at God's command, he waited for special directions to depart.

At last an angel descended from heaven, opened the massive door, and bade the patriarch and his household go forth upon the earth and take with them every living thing. In the joy of their release Noah did not forget Him by whose gracious care they had been preserved. His first act after leaving the ark was to build an altar and offer from every kind of clean beast and fowl a sacrifice, thus manifesting his gratitude to God for deliverance and his faith in

Christ, the great sacrifice. This offering was pleasing to the Lord; and a blessing resulted, not only to the patriarch and his family, but to all who should live upon the earth. "The Lord smelled a sweet savor; and the Lord said in His heart, I will not again curse the ground any more for man's sake.... While the earth remaineth, seedtime and harvest, and cold and heat, and summer and winter, and day and night shall not cease." Here was a lesson for all succeeding generations. Noah had come forth upon a desolate earth, but before preparing a house for himself he built an altar to God. His stock of cattle was small, and had been preserved at great expense; yet he cheerfully gave a part to the Lord as an acknowledgment that all was His. In like manner it should be our first care to render our freewill offerings to God. Every manifestation of His mercy and love toward us should be gratefully acknowledged, both by acts of devotion and by gifts to His cause.

Lest the gathering clouds and falling rain should fill men with constant terror, from fear of another flood, the Lord encouraged the family of Noah by a promise: "I will establish My covenant with you; ... neither shall there any more be a flood to destroy the earth.... I do set My bow in the cloud, and it shall be for a token of a covenant between Me and the earth. And it shall come to pass, when I bring a cloud over the earth, that the bow shall be seen in the cloud.... And I will look upon it, that I may remember the everlasting covenant between God and every living creature."

How great the condescension of God and His compassion for His erring creatures in thus placing the beautiful rainbow in the clouds as a token of His covenant with men! The Lord declares that when He looks upon the bow, He will remember His covenant. This does not imply that He would ever forget; but He speaks to us in our own language, that we may better understand Him. It was God's purpose that as the children of after generations should ask the meaning of the glorious arch which spans the heavens, their parents should repeat the story of the Flood, and tell them that the Most High had bended the bow and placed it in the clouds as an assurance that the waters should never again overflow the earth. Thus from generation to generation it would testify of divine love to man and would strengthen his confidence in God.

In heaven the semblance of a rainbow encircles the throne and overarches the head of Christ. The prophet says, "As the appearance of the bow that is in the cloud in the day of rain, so was the appearance of the brightness round about [the throne]. This was the appearance of the likeness of the glory of Jehovah." Ezekiel 1:28. The revelator declares, "Behold, a throne was set in heaven, and one sat on the throne.... There was a rainbow round about the throne, in sight like unto an emerald." Revelation 4:2, 3. When man by his great wickedness invites the divine judgments, the Saviour, interceding with the Father in his behalf, points to the bow in the clouds, to the rainbow around the throne and above His own head, as a token of the mercy of God toward the repentant sinner.

With the assurance given to Noah concerning the Flood, God Himself has linked one of the most precious promises of His grace: "As I have sworn that the waters of Noah should no more go over the earth; so have I sworn that I would not be wroth with thee, nor rebuke thee. For the mountains shall depart, and the hills be removed; but My kindness shall not depart from thee, neither shall the covenant of My peace be removed, saith Jehovah that hath mercy on thee." Isaiah 54:9, 10.

As Noah looked upon the powerful beasts of prey that came forth with him from the ark, he feared that his family, numbering only eight persons, would be destroyed by them. But the Lord sent an angel to His servant with the assuring message: "The fear of you and the dread of you shall be upon every beast of the earth, and upon every fowl of the air, upon all that moveth upon the earth, and upon all the fishes of the sea; into your hand are they delivered. Every moving thing that liveth shall be meat for you; even as the green herb have I given you all things." Before this time God had given man no permission to eat animal food; He intended that the race should subsist wholly upon the productions of the earth; but now that every green thing had been destroyed, He allowed them to eat the flesh of the clean beasts that had been preserved in the ark.

The entire surface of the earth was changed at the Flood. A third dreadful curse rested upon it in consequence of sin. As the water began to subside, the hills and mountains were surrounded by a vast, turbid sea, Everywhere were strewn the dead bodies of men and beasts. The Lord would not permit these to remain to decompose and pollute the air, therefore He made of the earth a vast burial ground. A violent wind which was caused to blow for the purpose of drying up the waters, moved them with great force, in some instances even carrying away the tops of the mountains and heaping up trees, rocks, and earth above the bodies of the dead. By the same means the silver and gold, the choice wood and precious stones, which had enriched and adorned the world before the Flood, and which the inhabitants had idolized, were concealed from the sight and search of men, the violent action of the waters piling earth and rocks upon these treasures, and in some cases even forming mountains above them. God saw that the more He enriched and prospered sinful men, the more they would corrupt their ways before Him. The treasures that should have led them to glorify the bountiful Giver had been worshiped, while God had been dishonored and despised.

The earth presented an appearance of confusion and desolation impossible to describe. The mountains, once so beautiful in their perfect symmetry, had become broken and irregular. Stones, ledges, and ragged rocks were now scattered upon the surface of the earth. In many places hills and mountains had disappeared, leaving no trace where they once stood; and plains had given place to mountain ranges. These changes were more marked in some places than in others. Where once had been earth's richest treasures of gold, silver, and precious stones, were seen the heaviest marks of the curse. And upon countries that were not inhabited, and those where there had been the least crime, the curse rested more lightly.

At this time immense forests were buried. These have since been changed to coal, forming the extensive coal beds that now exist, and also yielding large quantities of oil. The coal and oil frequently ignite and burn beneath the surface of the earth. Thus rocks are heated, limestone is burned, and iron ore melted. The action of the water upon the lime adds fury to the intense heat, and causes earthquakes, volcanoes, and fiery issues. As the fire and water come in contact with ledges of rock and ore, there are heavy explosions underground, which sound like muffled thunder. The air is hot and suffocating. Volcanic eruptions follow; and these often failing to give sufficient vent to the heated elements, the earth itself is convulsed, the ground heaves and swells like the waves of the sea, great fissures appear, and sometimes cities, villages, and burning mountains are swallowed up.

These wonderful manifestations will be more and more frequent and terrible just before the second coming of Christ and the end of the world, as signs of its speedy destruction.

The depths of the earth are the Lord's arsenal, whence were drawn weapons to be employed in the destruction of the old world. Waters gushing from the earth united with the waters from heaven to accomplish the work of desolation. Since the Flood, fire as well as water has been God's agent to destroy very wicked cities. These judgments are sent that those who lightly regard God's law and trample upon His authority may be led to tremble before His power and to confess His just sovereignty. As men have beheld burning mountains pouring forth fire and flames and torrents of melted ore, drying up rivers, overwhelming populous cities, and everywhere spreading ruin and desolation, the stoutest heart has been filled with terror and infidels and blasphemers have been constrained to acknowledge the infinite power of God.

Said the prophets of old, referring to scenes like these: "Oh that Thou wouldest rend the heavens, that Thou wouldest come down, that the mountains might flow down at Thy presence, as when the melting fire burneth, the fire causeth the waters to boil, to make Thy name known to Thine adversaries, that the nations may tremble at Thy presence! When Thou didst terrible things which we looked not for, Thou camest down, the mountains flowed down at Thy presence." Isaiah 64:1-3. "The Lord hath His way in the whirlwind and in the storm, and the clouds are the dust of His feet. He rebuketh the sea, and maketh it dry, and drieth up all the rivers." Nahum 1:3, 4.

More terrible manifestations than the world has ever yet beheld, will be witnessed at the second advent of Christ. "The mountains quake at Him, and the hills melt, and the earth is burned at His presence, yea, the world, and all that dwell therein. Who can stand before His indignation? and who can abide in the fierceness of His anger?" Nahum 1:5, 6. "Bow Thy heavens, O Lord, and come down: touch the mountains, and they shall smoke. Cast forth lightning, and scatter them: shoot out Thine arrows, and destroy them." Psalm 144:5, 6.

"I will show wonders in heaven above, and signs in the earth beneath; blood, and fire, and vapor of smoke." Acts 2:19. "And there were voices, and thunders, and lightnings; and there was a great earthquake, such as was not since men were upon the earth, so mighty an earthquake, and so great." "And every island fled away, and the mountains were not found. And there fell upon men a great hail out of heaven, every stone about the weight of a talent." Revelation 16:18, 20, 21.

As lightnings from heaven unite with the fire in the earth, the mountains will burn like a furnace, and will pour forth terrific streams of lava, overwhelming gardens and fields, villages and cities. Seething molten masses thrown into the rivers will cause the waters to boil, sending forth massive rocks with indescribable violence and scattering their broken fragments upon the land. Rivers will be dried up. The earth will be convulsed; everywhere there will be dreadful earthquakes and eruptions.

Thus God will destroy the wicked from off the earth. But the righteous will be preserved in the midst of these commotions, as Noah was preserved in the ark. God will be their refuge, and under His wings shall they trust. Says the psalmist: "Because thou hast made the Lord, which is my refuge, even the Most High, thy habitation; there shall no evil befall thee." Psalm 91:9, 10. "In the time of trouble He shall hide me in His pavilion: in the secret of His tabernacle shall He hide me." Psalm 27:5. God's promise is, "Because he hath set his love upon Me, therefore will I deliver him: I will set him on high, because he hath known My name." Psalm 91:14.

Chapter 9—The Literal Week

Like the Sabbath, the week originated at creation, and it has been preserved and brought down to us through Bible history. God Himself measured off the first week as a sample for successive weeks to the close of time. Like every other, it consisted of seven literal days. Six days were employed in the work of creation; upon the seventh, God rested, and He then blessed this day and set it apart as a day of rest for man.

In the law given from Sinai, God recognized the week, and the facts upon which it is based. After giving the command, "Remember the Sabbath day, to keep it holy," and specifying what shall be done on the six days, and what shall not be done on the seventh, He states the reason for thus observing the week, by pointing back to His own example: "For in six days the Lord made heaven and earth, the sea, and all that in them is, and rested the seventh day: wherefore the Lord blessed the Sabbath day, and hallowed it." Exodus 20:8-11. This reason appears beautiful and forcible when we understand the days of creation to be literal. The first six days of each week are given to man for labor, because God employed the same period of the first week in the work of creation. On the seventh day man is to refrain from labor, in commemoration of the Creator's rest.

But the assumption that the events of the first week required thousands upon thousands of years, strikes directly at the foundation of the fourth commandment. It represents the Creator as commanding men to observe the week of literal days in commemoration of vast, indefinite periods. This is unlike His method of dealing with His creatures. It makes indefinite and obscure that which He has made very plain. It is infidelity in its most insidious and hence most dangerous form; its real character is so disguised that it is held and taught by many who profess to believe the Bible.

"By the word of the Lord were the heavens made; and all the host of them by the breath of His mouth." "For He spake, and it was done; He commanded, and it stood fast." Psalm 33:6, 9. The Bible recognizes no long ages in which the earth was slowly evolved from chaos. Of each successive day of creation, the sacred record declares that it consisted of the evening and the morning, like all other days that have followed. At the close of each day is given the result of the Creator's work. The statement is made at the close of the first week's record, "These are the generations of the heavens and of the earth when they were created." Genesis 2:4. But this does not convey the idea that the days of creation were other than literal days. Each day was called a generation, because that in it God generated, or produced, some new portion of His work.

Geologists claim to find evidence from the earth itself that it is very much older than the Mosaic record teaches. Bones of men and animals, as well as instruments of warfare, petrified trees, et cetera, much larger than any that now exist, or that have existed for thousands of years, have been discovered, and from this it is inferred that the earth was populated long before the time brought to view in the record of creation, and by a race of beings vastly superior in size to any men now living. Such reasoning has led many professed Bible believers to adopt the position that the days of creation were vast, indefinite periods.

But apart from Bible history, geology can prove nothing. Those who reason so confidently upon its discoveries have no adequate conception of the size of men, animals, and trees before the Flood, or of the great changes which then took place. Relics found in the earth do give evidence of conditions differing in many respects from the present, but the time when these conditions existed can be learned only from the Inspired Record. In the history of the Flood, inspiration has explained that which geology alone could never fathom. In the days of Noah, men, animals, and trees, many times larger than now exist, were buried, and thus preserved as an evidence to later generations that the antediluvians perished by a flood. God designed that the discovery of these things should establish faith in inspired history; but men, with their vain reasoning, fall into the same error as did the people before the Flood—the things which God gave them as a benefit, they turn into a curse by making a wrong use of them.

It is one of Satan's devices to lead the people to accept the fables of infidelity; for he can thus obscure the law of God, in itself very plain, and embolden men to rebel against the divine government. His efforts are especially directed against the fourth commandment, because it so clearly points to the living God, the Maker of the heavens and the earth.

There is a constant effort made to explain the work of creation as the result of natural causes; and human reasoning is accepted even by professed Christians, in opposition to plain Scripture facts. There are many who oppose the investigation of the prophecies, especially those of Daniel and the Revelation, declaring them to be so obscure that we cannot understand them; yet these very persons eagerly receive the suppositions of geologists, in contradiction of the Mosaic record. But if that which God has revealed is so difficult to understand, how inconsistent it is to accept mere suppositions in regard to that which He has not revealed!

"The secret things belong unto the Lord our God: but those things which are revealed belong unto us and to our children forever." Deuteronomy 29:29. Just how God accomplished the work of creation He has never revealed to men; human science cannot search out the secrets of the Most High. His creative power is as incomprehensible as His existence.

God has permitted a flood of light to be poured upon the world in both science and art; but when professedly scientific men treat upon these subjects from a merely human point of view, they will assuredly come to wrong conclusions. It may be innocent to speculate beyond what God's word has revealed, if our theories do not contradict facts found in the Scriptures; but those who leave the word of God, and seek to account for His created works upon scientific principles, are drifting without chart or compass upon an unknown ocean. The greatest minds, if not guided by the word of God in their research, become bewildered in their attempts to trace the relations of science and revelation. Because the Creator and His works are so far beyond their comprehension that they are unable to explain them by natural laws, they regard Bible history as unreliable. Those who doubt the reliability of the records of the Old and New Testaments, will be led to go a step further, and doubt the existence of God; and then, having lost their anchor, they are left to beat about upon the rocks of infidelity.

These persons have lost the simplicity of faith. There should be a settled belief in the divine authority of God's Holy Word. The Bible is not to be tested by men's ideas of science. Human knowledge is an unreliable guide. Skeptics who read the Bible for the sake of caviling, may, through an imperfect comprehension of either science or revelation, claim to find contradictions between them; but rightly understood, they are in perfect harmony. Moses wrote under the guidance of the Spirit of God, and a correct theory of geology will never claim discoveries that cannot be reconciled with his statements. All truth, whether in nature or in revelation, is consistent with itself in all its manifestations.

In the word of God many queries are raised that the most profound scholars can never answer. Attention is called to these subjects to show us how much there is, even among the common things of everyday life, that finite minds, with all their boasted wisdom, can never fully understand.

Yet men of science think that they can comprehend the wisdom of God, that which He has done or can do. The idea largely prevails that He is restricted by His own laws. Men either deny or ignore His existence, or think to explain everything, even the operation of His Spirit upon the human heart; and they no longer reverence His name or fear His power. They do not believe in the supernatural, not understanding God's laws or His infinite power to work His will through them. As commonly used, the term "laws of nature" comprises what men have been able to discover with regard to the laws that govern the physical world; but how limited is their knowledge, and how vast the field in which the Creator can work in harmony with His own laws and yet wholly beyond the comprehension of finite beings!

Many teach that matter possesses vital power—that certain properties are imparted to matter, and it is then left to act through its own inherent energy; and that the operations of nature are conducted in harmony with fixed laws, with which God Himself cannot interfere. This is false science, and is not sustained by the word of God. Nature is the servant of her Creator. God does not annul His laws or work contrary to them, but He is continually using them as His instruments. Nature testifies of an intelligence, a presence, an active energy, that works in and through her laws. There is in nature the continual working of the Father and the Son. Christ says, "My Father worketh hitherto, and I work." John 5:17.

The Levites, in their hymn recorded by Nehemiah, sang, "Thou, even Thou, art Lord alone; Thou hast made heaven, the heaven of heavens, with all their host, the earth, and all things therein, ... and Thou *preservest* them all." Nehemiah 9:6. As regards this world, God's work of creation is completed. For "the works were finished from the foundation of the world." Hebrews 4:3. But His energy is still exerted in upholding the objects of His creation. It is not because the mechanism that has once been set in motion continues to act by its own inherent energy that the pulse beats and breath follows breath; but every breath, every pulsation of the heart, is an evidence of the all-pervading care of Him in whom "we live, and move, and have our being." Acts 17:28. It is not because of inherent power that year by year the earth produces her bounties and continues her motion around the sun. The hand of God guides the planets and keeps them in position in their orderly march through the heavens. He "bringeth out their host by number: He calleth them all by names by the greatness of His might, for that He is strong in power; not one faileth." Isaiah 40:26. It is through His power that vegetation flourishes, that the leaves appear and the flowers bloom. He "maketh grass to grow upon the mountains" (Psalm 147:8), and by Him the valleys are made fruitful. "All the beasts of the forest ... seek their meat from God," and every living creature, from the smallest insect up to man, is daily dependent upon His providential care. In the beautiful words of the psalmist, "These wait all upon Thee.... That Thou givest them they gather: Thou openest Thine hand, they are filled with good." Psalm 104:20, 21, 27, 28. His word controls the elements; He covers the heavens with clouds and prepares rain for the earth. "He giveth snow like wool: He scattereth the hoarfrost like ashes." Psalm 147:16. "When He uttereth His voice, there is a multitude of waters in the heavens, and He causeth the vapors to ascend from the ends of the earth; He maketh lightnings with rain, and bringeth forth the wind out of His treasuries." Jeremiah 10:13.

God is the foundation of everything. All true science is in harmony with His works; all true education leads to obedience to His government. Science opens new wonders to our view; she soars high, and explores new depths; but she brings nothing from her

[115]

research that conflicts with divine revelation. Ignorance may seek to support false views of God by appeals to science, but the book of nature and the written word shed light upon each other. We are thus led to adore the Creator and to have an intelligent trust in His word.

No finite mind can fully comprehend the existence, the power, the wisdom, or the works of the Infinite One. Says the sacred writer: "Canst thou by searching find out God? canst thou find out the Almighty unto perfection? It is as high as heaven; what canst thou do? deeper than hell; what canst thou know? The measure thereof is longer than the earth, and broader than the sea." Job 11:7-9. The mightiest intellects of earth cannot comprehend God. Men may be ever searching, ever learning, and still there is an infinity beyond.

Yet the works of creation testify of God's power and greatness. "The heavens declare the glory of God; and the firmament showeth His handiwork." Psalm 19:1. Those who take the written word as their counselor will find in science an aid to understand God. "The invisible things of Him from the creation of the world are clearly seen, being understood by the things that are made, even His eternal power and Godhead." Romans 1:20.

Chapter 10—The Tower of Babel

To repeople the desolate earth, which the Flood had so lately swept from its moral corruption, God had preserved but one family, the household of Noah, to whom He had declared, "Thee have I seen righteous before Me in this generation." Genesis 7:1. Yet in the three sons of Noah was speedily developed the same great distinction seen in the world before the Flood. In Shem, Ham, and Japheth, who were to be the founders of the human race, was foreshadowed the character of their posterity.

Noah, speaking by divine inspiration, foretold the history of the three great races to spring from these fathers of mankind. Tracing the descendants of Ham, through the son rather than the father, he declared, "Cursed be Canaan; a servant of servants shall he be unto his brethren." The unnatural crime of Ham declared that filial reverence had long before been cast from his soul, and it revealed the impiety and vileness of his character. These evil characteristics were perpetuated in Canaan and his posterity, whose continued guilt called upon them the judgments of God.

On the other hand, the reverence manifested by Shem and Japheth for their father, and thus for the divine statutes, promised a brighter future for their descendants. Concerning these sons it was declared: "Blessed be Jehovah, God of Shem; and Canaan shall be his servant. God shall enlarge Japheth, and he shall dwell in the tents of Shem; and Canaan shall be his servant." The line of Shem was to be that of the chosen people, of God's covenant, of the promised Redeemer. Jehovah was the God of Shem. From him would descend Abraham, and the people of Israel, through whom Christ was to come. "Happy is that people, whose God is the Lord." Psalm 144:15. And Japheth "shall dwell in the tents of Shem." In the blessings of the gospel the descendants of Japheth were especially to share.

The posterity of Canaan descended to the most degrading forms of heathenism. Though the prophetic curse had doomed them to slavery, the doom was withheld for centuries. God bore with their impiety and corruption until they passed the limits of divine forbearance. Then they were dispossessed, and became bondmen to the descendants of Shem and Japheth.

The prophecy of Noah was no arbitrary denunciation of wrath or declaration of favor. It did not fix the character and destiny of his sons. But it showed what would be the result of the course of life they had severally chosen and the character they had developed. It was an expression of God's purpose toward them and their posterity in view of their own character and conduct. As a rule, children inherit the dispositions and tendencies of their parents, and imitate their example; so that the sins of the parents are practiced by the children from generation to generation. Thus the vileness and irreverence of Ham were reproduced in his posterity, bringing a curse upon them for many generations. "One sinner destroyeth much good." Ecclesiastes 9:18.

On the other hand, how richly rewarded was Shem's respect for his father; and what an illustrious line of holy men appears in his posterity! "The Lord knoweth the days of the upright," "and his seed is blessed." Psalm 37:18, 26. "Know therefore that the Lord thy God He is God, the faithful God, which keepeth covenant and mercy with them that love Him and keep His commandments to a thousand generations." Deuteronomy 7:9.

For a time the descendants of Noah continued to dwell among the mountains where the ark had rested. As their numbers increased, apostasy soon led to division. Those who desired to forget their Creator and to cast off the restraint of His law felt a constant annoyance from the teaching and example of their God-fearing associates, and after a time they decided to separate from the worshipers of God. Accordingly they journeyed to the plain of Shinar, on the banks of the river Euphrates. They were attracted by the beauty of the situation and the fertility of the soil, and upon this plain they determined to make their home.

Here they decided to build a city, and in it a tower of such stupendous height as should render it the wonder of the world. These enterprises were designed to prevent the people from scattering abroad in colonies. God had directed men to disperse throughout the earth, to replenish and subdue it; but these Babel builders determined to keep their community united in one body, and to found a monarchy that should eventually embrace the whole earth. Thus their city would become the metropolis of a universal empire; its glory would command the admiration and homage of the world and render the founders illustrious. The magnificent tower, reaching to the heavens, was intended to stand as a monument of the power and wisdom of its builders, perpetuating their fame to the latest generations.

The dwellers on the plain of Shinar disbelieved God's covenant that He would not again bring a flood upon the earth. Many of them denied the existence of God and attributed the Flood to the operation of natural causes. Others believed in a Supreme Being, and that it was He who had destroyed the antediluvian world; and their hearts, like that of Cain, rose up in rebellion against Him. One object before them in the erection of the tower was to secure their own safety in case of another deluge. By carrying the structure to a much greater height than was reached by the waters of the Flood, they thought to place themselves beyond all possibility of danger. And as they would be able to ascend to the region of the clouds, they hoped to ascertain the cause of the Flood. The whole undertaking was designed to exalt still further the pride of its projectors and to turn the minds of future generations away from God and lead them into idolatry.

When the tower had been partially completed, a portion of it was occupied as a dwelling place for the builders; other apartments, splendidly furnished and adorned, were devoted to their idols. The people rejoiced in their success, and praised the gods of silver and gold, and set themselves against the Ruler of heaven and earth. Suddenly the work that had been advancing so prosperously was checked. Angels were sent to bring to naught the purpose of the builders. The tower had reached a lofty height, and it was impossible for the workmen at the top to communicate directly with those at the base; therefore men were stationed at different points, each to receive and report to the one next below him the orders for needed material or other directions concerning the work. As messages were thus passing from one to another the language was confounded, so that material was called for which was not needed, and the directions delivered were often the reverse of those that had been given. Confusion and dismay followed. All work came to a standstill. There could be no further harmony or co-operation. The builders were wholly unable to account for the strange misunderstandings among them, and in their rage and disappointment they reproached one another. Their confederacy ended in strife and bloodshed. Lightnings from heaven, as an evidence of God's displeasure, broke off the upper portion of the tower and cast it to the ground. Men were made to feel that there is a God who ruleth in the heavens.

Up to this time all men had spoken the same language; now those that could understand one another's speech united in companies; some went one way, and some another. "The Lord scattered them abroad from thence upon the face of all the earth." This dispersion was the means of peopling the earth, and thus the Lord's purpose was accomplished through the very means that men had employed to prevent its fulfillment.

But at what a loss to those who had set themselves against God! It was His purpose that as men should go forth to found nations in different parts of the earth they should carry with them a knowledge of His will, that the light of truth might shine undimmed to succeeding generations. Noah, the faithful preacher of righteousness, lived for three hundred and fifty years after the Flood, Shem for five hundred years, and thus their descendants had an opportunity to become acquainted with the requirements of God and the history of His dealings with their fathers. But they were unwilling to listen to these unpalatable truths; they had no desire to retain God in their knowledge; and by the confusion of tongues they were, in a great measure, shut out from intercourse with those who might have given them light.

The Babel builders had indulged the spirit of murmuring against God. Instead of gratefully remembering His mercy to Adam and His gracious covenant with Noah, they had complained of His severity in expelling the first pair from Eden and destroying the world by a flood. But while they murmured against God as arbitrary and severe, they were accepting the rule of the cruelest of tyrants. Satan was seeking to bring contempt upon the sacrificial offerings that prefigured the death of Christ; and as the minds of the people were darkened by idolatry, he led them to counterfeit these offerings and sacrifice their own children upon the altars of their gods. As men turned away from God, the divine attributes—justice, purity, and love—were supplanted by oppression, violence, and brutality.

The men of Babel had determined to establish a government that should be independent of God. There were some among them, however, who feared the Lord, but who had been deceived by the pretensions of the ungodly and drawn into their schemes. For the sake of these faithful ones the Lord delayed His judgments and gave the people time to reveal their true character. As this was developed, the sons of God labored to turn them from their purpose; but the people were fully united in their Heaven-daring undertaking. Had they gone on unchecked, they would have demoralized the world in its infancy. Their confederacy was founded in rebellion; a kingdom established for self-exaltation, but in which God was to have no rule or honor. Had this confederacy been permitted, a mighty power would have borne sway to banish righteousness—and with it peace, happiness, and security—from the earth. For the divine statutes, which are "holy and just and good" (Romans 7:12), men were endeavoring to substitute laws to suit the purpose of their own selfish and cruel hearts.

Those that feared the Lord cried unto Him to interpose. "And the Lord came down to see the city and the tower, which the children of men builded." In mercy to the world He defeated the purpose of the tower builders and overthrew the memorial of their daring. In mercy He confounded their speech, thus putting a check on their purposes of rebellion. God bears long with the perversity of men, giving them ample opportunity for repentance; but He marks all their devices to resist the authority of His just and holy law. From time to time the unseen hand that holds the scepter of government is stretched out to restrain iniquity. Unmistakable evidence is given that the Creator of the universe, the One infinite in wisdom and love and truth, is the Supreme Ruler of heaven and earth, and that none can with impunity defy His power.

The schemes of the Babel builders ended in shame and defeat. The monument to their pride became the memorial of their folly. Yet men are continually pursuing the same course—depending upon self, and rejecting God's law. It is the principle that Satan tried to carry out in heaven; the same that governed Cain in presenting his offering.

There are tower builders in our time. Infidels construct their theories from the supposed deductions of sciences, and reject the revealed word of God. They presume to pass sentence upon God's moral government; they despise His law and boast of the sufficiency of human reason. Then, "because sentence against an evil work is not executed speedily, therefore the heart of the sons of men is fully set in them to do evil." Ecclesiastes 8:11.

In the professedly Christian world many turn away from the plain teachings of the Bible and build up a creed from human speculations and pleasing fables, and they point to their tower as a way to climb up to heaven. Men hang with admiration upon the lips of eloquence while it teaches that the transgressor shall not die, that salvation may be secured without obedience to the law of God. If the professed followers of Christ would accept God's standard, it would bring them into unity; but so long as human wisdom is exalted above His Holy Word, there will be divisions and dissension. The existing confusion of conflicting creeds and sects is fitly represented by the term "Babylon," which prophecy (Revelation 14:8; 18:2) applies to the world-loving churches of the last days.

Many seek to make a heaven for themselves by obtaining riches and power. They "speak wickedly concerning oppression: they speak loftily" (Psalm 73:8), trampling upon human rights and disregarding divine authority. The proud may be for a time in great power, and may see success in all that they undertake; but in the end they will find only disappointment and wretchedness.

The time of God's investigation is at hand. The Most High will come down to see that which the children of men have builded. His sovereign power will be revealed; the works of human pride will be laid low. "The Lord looketh from heaven; He beholdeth all the sons of men. From the place of His habitation He looketh upon all the inhabitants of the earth." "The Lord bringeth the counsel of the heathen to nought: He maketh the devices of the people of none effect. The counsel of the Lord standeth forever, the thoughts of His heart to all generations." Psalm 33:13, 14, 10, 11.

Chapter 11—The Call of Abraham [125]

After the dispersion from Babel idolatry again became well-nigh universal, and the Lord finally left the hardened transgressors to follow their evil ways, while He chose Abraham, of the line of Shem, and made him the keeper of His law for future generations. Abraham had grown up in the midst of superstition and heathenism. Even his father's household, by whom the knowledge of God had been preserved, were yielding to the seductive influences surrounding them, and they "served other gods" than Jehovah. But the true faith was not to become extinct. God has ever preserved a remnant to serve Him. Adam, Seth, Enoch, Methuselah, Noah, Shem, in unbroken line, had preserved from age to age the precious revealings of His will. The son of Terah became the inheritor of this holy trust. Idolatry invited him on every side, but in vain. Faithful among the faithless, uncorrupted by the prevailing apostasy, he steadfastly adhered to the worship of the one true God. "The Lord is nigh unto all them that call upon Him, to all that call upon Him in truth." Psalm 145:18. He communicated His will to Abraham, and gave him a distinct knowledge of the requirements of His law and of the salvation that would be accomplished through Christ.

There was given to Abraham the promise, especially dear to the people of that age, of a numerous posterity and of national greatness: "I will make of thee a great nation, and I will bless thee, and make thy name great; and thou shalt be a blessing." And to this was added the assurance, precious above every other to the inheritor of faith, that of his line the Redeemer of the world should come: "In thee shall all families of the earth be blessed." Yet, as the first condition of fulfillment, there was to be a test of faith; a sacrifice was demanded.

The message of God came to Abraham, "Get thee out of thy [126] country, and from thy kindred, and from thy father's house, unto a land that I will show thee." In order that God might qualify him for his great work as the keeper of the sacred oracles, Abraham must be separated from the associations of his early life. The influence of kindred and friends would interfere with the training which the Lord purposed to give His servant. Now that Abraham was, in a special sense, connected with heaven, he must dwell among strangers. His character must be peculiar, differing from all the world. He could not even explain his course of action so as to be understood by his friends. Spiritual things are spiritually discerned, and his motives and actions were not comprehended by his idolatrous kindred.

"By faith Abraham, when he was called to go out into a place which he should after receive for an inheritance, obeyed; and he went out, not knowing whither he went." Hebrews 11:8. Abraham's unquestioning obedience is one of the most striking evidences of faith to be found in all the Bible. To him, faith was "the substance of things hoped for, the evidence of things not seen." Verse 1. Relying upon the divine promise, without the least outward assurance of its fulfillment, he abandoned home and kindred and native land, and went forth, he knew not whither, to follow where God should lead. "By faith he became a sojourner in the land of promise, as in a land not his own, dwelling in tents, with Isaac and Jacob, the heirs with him of the same promise." Hebrews 11:9, R.V.

It was no light test that was thus brought upon Abraham, no small sacrifice that was required of him. There were strong ties to bind him to his country, his kindred, and his home. But he did not hesitate to obey the call. He had no question to ask concerning the land of promise—whether the soil was fertile and the climate healthful; whether the country afforded agreeable surroundings and would afford opportunities for amassing wealth. God has spoken, and His servant must obey; the happiest place on earth for him was the place where God would have him to be.

Many are still tested as was Abraham. They do not hear the voice of God speaking directly from the heavens, but He calls them by the teachings of His word and the events of His providence. They may be required to abandon a career that promises wealth and honor, to leave congenial and profitable associations and separate from kindred, to enter upon what appears to be only a path of self-denial, hardship, and sacrifice. God has a work for them to do; but a life of ease and the influence of friends and kindred would hinder the development of the very traits essential for its accomplishment. He calls them away from human influences and aid, and leads them to feel the need of His help, and to depend upon Him alone, that He may reveal Himself to them. Who is ready at the call of Providence to renounce cherished plans and familiar associations? Who will accept new duties and enter untried fields, doing God's work with firm and willing heart, for Christ's sake counting his losses gain? He who will do this has the faith of Abraham, and will share with him that "far more exceeding and eternal weight of glory," with which "the sufferings of this present time are not worthy to be compared." 2 Corinthians 4:17; Romans 8:18.

The call from heaven first came to Abraham while he dwelt in "Ur of the Chaldees" and in obedience to it he removed to Haran. Thus far his father's family accompanied him, for with their idolatry they united the worship of the true God. Here Abraham remained till the death of Terah. But from his father's grave the divine Voice bade him go forward. His brother Nahor with his household clung to their home and their idols. Besides Sarah, the wife of Abraham, only Lot, the son of Haran long since dead, chose to share the patriarch's, pilgrim life. Yet it was a large company that set out from Mesopotamia. Abraham already possessed extensive flocks and herds, the riches of the East, and he was surrounded by a numerous body of servants and retainers. He was departing from the land of his fathers, never to return, and he took with him all that he had, "their substance that they had gathered, and the souls that they had gotten in Haran." Among these were many led by higher considerations than those of service and self-interest. During their stay in Haran, both Abraham and Sarah had led others to the worship and service of the true God. These attached themselves to the patriarch's household, and accompanied him to the land of promise. "And they went forth to go into the land of Canaan; and into the land of Canaan they came."

The place where they first tarried was Shechem. Under the shade of the oaks of Moreh, in a wide, grassy valley, with its olive groves and gushing springs, between Mount Ebal on the one side and Mount Gerizim on the other, Abraham made his encampment. It was a fair and goodly country that the patriarch had entered—"a land of brooks of water, of fountains and depths that spring out of valleys and hills; a land of wheat, and barley, and vines, and fig trees, and pomegranates; a land of oil olive, and honey." Deuteronomy

[128]

8:7, 8. But to the worshiper of Jehovah, a heavy shadow rested upon wooded hill and fruitful plain. "The Canaanite was then in the land." Abraham had reached the goal of his hopes to find a country occupied by an alien race and overspread with idolatry. In the groves were set up the altars of false gods, and human sacrifices were offered upon the neighboring heights. While he clung to the divine promise, it was not without distressful forebodings that he pitched his tent. Then "the Lord appeared unto Abram, and said, Unto thy seed will I give this land." His faith was strengthened by this assurance that the divine presence was with him, that he was not left to the mercy of the wicked. "And there builded he an altar unto the Lord, who appeared unto him." Still a wayfarer, he soon removed to a spot near Bethel, and again erected an altar, and called upon the name of the Lord.

Abraham, "the friend of God," set us a worthy example. His was a life of prayer. Wherever he pitched his tent, close beside it was set up his altar, calling all within his encampment to the morning and evening sacrifice. When his tent was removed, the altar remained. In following years, there were those among the roving Canaanites who received instruction from Abraham; and whenever one of these came to that altar, he knew who had been there before him; and when he had pitched his tent, he repaired the altar, and there worshiped the living God.

Abraham continued to journey southward, and again his faith was tested. The heavens withheld their rain, the brooks ceased to flow in the valleys, and the grass withered on the plains. The flocks and herds found no pasture, and starvation threatened the whole encampment. Did not the patriarch now question the leadings of Providence? Did he not look back with longing to the plenty of the Chaldean plains? All were eagerly watching to see what Abraham would do, as trouble after trouble came upon him. So long as his confidence appeared unshaken, they felt that there was hope; they were assured that God was his Friend, and that He was still guiding him.

Abraham could not explain the leadings of Providence; he had not realized his expectations; but he held fast the promise, "I will bless thee, and make thy name great; and thou shalt be a blessing." With earnest prayer he considered how to preserve the life of his people and his flocks, but he would not allow circumstances to shake his faith in God's word. To escape the famine he went down into Egypt. He did not forsake Canaan, or in his extremity turn back to the Chaldean land from which he came, where there was no scarcity of bread; but he sought a temporary refuge as near as possible to the Land of Promise, intending shortly to return where God had placed him.

The Lord in His providence had brought this trial upon Abraham to teach him lessons of submission, patience, and faith—lessons that were to be placed on record for the benefit of all who should afterward be called to endure affliction. God leads His children by a way that they know not, but He does not forget or cast off those who put their trust in Him. He permitted affliction to come upon Job, but He did not forsake him. He allowed the beloved John to be exiled to lonely Patmos, but the Son of God met him there, and his vision was filled with scenes of immortal glory. God permits trials to assail His people, that by their constancy and obedience they themselves may be spiritually enriched, and that their example may be a source of strength to others. "I know the thoughts that I think toward you, saith the Lord, thoughts of peace, and not of evil." Jeremiah 29:11. The very trials that task our faith most severely and make it seem that God has forsaken us, are to lead us closer to Christ, that we may lay all our burdens at His feet and experience the peace which He will give us in exchange.

God has always tried His people in the furnace of affliction. It is in the heat of the furnace that the dross is separated from the true gold of the Christian character. Jesus watches the test; He knows what is needed to purify the precious metal, that it may reflect the radiance of His love. It is by close, testing trials that God disciplines His servants. He sees that some have powers which may be used in the advancement of His work, and He puts these persons upon trial; in His providence He brings them into positions that test their character and reveal defects and weaknesses that have been hidden from their own knowledge. He gives them opportunity to correct these defects and to fit themselves for His service. He shows them their own weakness, and teaches them to lean upon Him; for He is their only help and safeguard. Thus His object is attained. They are educated, trained, and disciplined, prepared to fulfill the grand purpose for which their powers were given them. When God calls them to action, they are ready, and heavenly angels can unite with them in the work to be accomplished on the earth.

During his stay in Egypt, Abraham gave evidence that he was not free from human weakness and imperfection. In concealing the fact that Sarah was his wife, he betrayed a distrust of the divine care, a lack of that lofty faith and courage so often and nobly exemplified in his life. Sarah was fair to look upon, and he doubted not that the dusky Egyptians would covet the beautiful stranger, and that in order to secure her, they would not scruple to slay her husband. He reasoned that he was not guilty of falsehood in representing Sarah as his sister, for she was the daughter of his father, though not of his mother. But this concealment of the real relation between them was deception. No deviation from strict integrity can meet God's approval. Through Abraham's lack of faith, Sarah was placed in great peril. The king of Egypt, being informed of her beauty, caused her to be taken to his palace, intending to make her his wife. But the Lord, in His great mercy, protected Sarah by sending judgments upon the royal household. By this means the monarch learned the truth in the matter, and, indignant at the deception practiced upon him, he reproved Abraham and restored to him his wife, saying, "What is this that thou hast done unto me? ... Why saidst thou, She is my sister? So I might have taken her to me to wife. Now therefore behold thy wife, take her, and go thy way."

Abraham had been greatly favored by the king; even now Pharaoh would permit no harm to be done him or his company, but ordered a guard to conduct them in safety out of his dominions. At this time laws were made prohibiting the Egyptians from intercourse with foreign shepherds in any such familiarity as eating or drinking with them. Pharaoh's dismissal of Abraham was kind and generous; but he bade him leave Egypt, for he dared not permit him to remain. He had ignorantly been about to do him a serious injury, but God had interposed, and saved the monarch from committing so great a sin. Pharaoh saw in this stranger a man whom the God of heaven honored, and he feared to have in his kingdom one who was so evidently under divine favor. Should Abraham remain in Egypt, his increasing wealth and honor would be likely to excite the envy or covetousness of the Egyptians, and some injury might be done him, for which the monarch would be held responsible, and which might again bring judgments upon the royal house.

The warning that had been given to Pharaoh proved a protection to Abraham in his after-intercourse with heathen peoples; for the matter could not be kept secret, and it was seen that the God whom Abraham worshiped would protect His servant, and that any injury done him would be avenged. It is a dangerous thing to wrong one of the children of the King of heaven. The psalmist refers to this chapter in Abraham's experience when he says, in speaking of the chosen people, that God "reproved kings for their sakes; saying, Touch not Mine anointed, and do My prophets no harm." Psalm 105:14, 15.

There is an interesting similarity between Abraham's experience in Egypt and that of his posterity, centuries later. Both went down into Egypt on account of a famine, and both sojourned there. Through the manifestation of divine judgments in their behalf, the fear of them fell upon the Egyptians; and, enriched by the gifts of the heathen, they went out with great substance.

Chapter 12—Abraham in Canaan

This chapter is based on Genesis 13; to 15;; 17: 1-16; 18.

Abraham returned to Canaan "very rich in cattle, in silver, and in gold." Lot was still with him, and again they came to Bethel, and pitched their tents by the altar which they had before erected. They soon found that increased possessions brought increased trouble. In the midst of hardships and trials they had dwelt together in harmony, but in their prosperity there was danger of strife between them. The pasturage was not sufficient for the flocks and herds of both, and the frequent disputes among the herdsmen were brought for settlement to their masters. It was evident that they must separate. Abraham was Lot's senior in years, and his superior in relation, in wealth, and in position; yet he was the first to propose plans for preserving peace. Although the whole land had been given him by God Himself, he courteously waived this right.

"Let there be no strife," he said, "between me and thee, and between my herdmen and thy herdmen; for we be brethren. Is not the whole land before thee? separate thyself, I pray thee, from me: if thou wilt take the left hand, then I will go to the right; or if thou depart to the right hand, then I will go to the left."

Here the noble, unselfish spirit of Abraham was displayed. How many under similar circumstances would, at all hazards, cling to their individual rights and preferences! How many households have thus been rent asunder! How many churches have been divided, making the cause of truth a byword and a reproach among the wicked! "Let there be no strife between me and thee," said Abraham, "for we be brethren;" not only by natural relationship, but as worshipers of the true God. The children of God the world over are one family, and the same spirit of love and conciliation should govern them. "Be kindly affectioned one to another with brotherly love; in honor preferring one another" (Romans 12:10), is the teaching of our Saviour. The cultivation of a uniform courtesy, a willingness to do to others as we would wish them to do to us, would annihilate half the ills of life. The spirit of self-aggrandizement is the spirit of Satan; but the heart in which the love of Christ is cherished, will possess that charity which seeketh not her own. Such will heed the divine injunction, "Look not every man on his own things, but every man also on the things of others." Philippians 2:4.

Although Lot owed his prosperity to his connection with Abraham, he manifested no gratitude to his benefactor. Courtesy would have dictated that he yield the choice to Abraham, but instead of this he selfishly endeavored to grasp all its advantages. He "lifted up his eyes, and beheld all the plain of Jordan, that it was well watered everywhere, ... even as the garden of the Lord, like the land of Egypt, as thou comest unto Zoar." The most fertile region in all Palestine was the Jordan Valley, reminding the beholders of the lost Paradise and equaling the beauty and productiveness of the Nile-enriched plains they had so lately left. There were cities also, wealthy and beautiful, inviting to profitable traffic in their crowded marts. Dazzled with visions of worldly gain, Lot overlooked the moral and spiritual evils that would be encountered there. The inhabitants of the plain were "sinners before the Lord exceedingly;" but of this he was ignorant, or, knowing, gave it but little weight. He "chose him all the plain of Jordan," and "pitched his tent toward Sodom." How little did he foresee the terrible results of that selfish choice!

After the separation from Lot, Abraham again received from the Lord a promise of the whole country. Soon after this he removed to Hebron, pitching his tent under the oaks of Mamre and erecting beside it an altar to the Lord. In the free air of those upland plains, with their olive groves and vineyards, their fields of waving grain, and the wide pasture grounds of the encircling hills, he dwelt, well content with his simple, patriarchal life, and leaving to Lot the perilous luxury of the vale of Sodom.

Abraham was honored by the surrounding nations as a mighty prince and a wise and able chief. He did not shut away his influence from his neighbors. His life and character, in their marked contrast with those of the worshipers of idols, exerted a telling influence in favor of the true faith. His allegiance to God was unswerving, while his affability and benevolence inspired confidence and friendship and his unaffected greatness commanded respect and honor.

His religion was not held as a precious treasure to be jealously guarded and enjoyed solely by the possessor. True religion cannot be thus held, for such a spirit is contrary to the principles of the gospel. While Christ is dwelling in the heart it is impossible to conceal the light of His presence, or for that light to grow dim. On the contrary, it will grow brighter and brighter as day by day the mists of selfishness and sin that envelop the soul are dispelled by the bright beams of the Sun of Righteousness.

The people of God are His representatives upon the earth, and He intends that they shall be lights in the moral darkness of this world. Scattered all over the country, in the towns, cities, and villages, they are God's witnesses, the channels through which He will communicate to an unbelieving world the knowledge of His will and the wonders of His grace. It is His plan that all who are partakers of the great salvation shall be missionaries for Him. The piety of the Christian constitutes the standard by which worldlings judge the gospel. Trials patiently borne, blessings gratefully received, meekness, kindness, mercy, and love, habitually exhibited, are the lights that shine forth in the character before the world, revealing the contrast with the darkness that comes of the selfishness of the natural heart.

Rich in faith, noble in generosity, unfaltering in obedience, and humble in the simplicity of his pilgrim life, Abraham was also wise in diplomacy and brave and skillful in war. Notwithstanding he was known as the teacher of a new religion, three royal brothers, rulers of the Amorite plains in which he dwelt, manifested their friendship by inviting him to enter into an alliance with them for greater security; for the country was filled with violence and oppression. An occasion soon arose for him to avail himself of this alliance.

Chedorlaomer, king of Elam, had invaded Canaan fourteen years before, and made it tributary to him. Several of the princes now revolted, and the Elamite king, with four allies, again marched into the country to reduce them to submission. Five kings of Canaan joined their forces and met the invaders in the vale of Siddim, but only to be completely overthrown. A large part of the army was cut to pieces, and those who escaped fled for safety to the mountains. The victors plundered the cities of the plain and departed with rich spoil and many captives, among whom were Lot and his family.

Abraham, dwelling in peace in the oak groves at Mamre, learned from one of the fugitives the story of the battle and the calamity that had befallen his nephew. He had cherished no unkind memory of Lot's ingratitude. All his affection for him was awakened, and he determined that he should be rescued. Seeking, first of all, divine counsel, Abraham prepared for war. From his own encampment he summoned three hundred and eighteen trained servants, men trained in the fear of God, in the service of their master, and in the practice of arms. His confederates, Mamre, Eschol, and Aner, joined him with their bands, and together they started in pursuit of the invaders. The Elamites and their allies had encamped at Dan, on the northern border of Canaan. Flushed with victory, and having no fear of an assault from their vanquished foes, they had given themselves up to reveling. The patriarch divided his force so as to approach from different directions, and came upon the encampment by night. His attack, so vigorous and unexpected, resulted in speedy victory. The king of Elam was slain and his panic-stricken forces were utterly routed. Lot and his family, with all the prisoners and their goods, were recovered, and a rich booty fell into the hands of the victors. To Abraham, under God, the triumph was due. The worshiper of Jehovah had not only rendered a great service to the country, but had proved himself a man of valor. It was seen that righteousness is not cowardice, and that Abraham's religion made him courageous in maintaining the right and defending the oppressed. His heroic act gave him a widespread influence among the surrounding tribes. On his return, the king of Sodom came out with his retinue to honor the conqueror. He bade him take the goods, begging only that the prisoners should be restored. By the usage of war, the spoils belonged to the conquerors; but Abraham had undertaken this expedition with no purpose of gain, and he refused to take advantage of the unfortunate, only stipulating that his confederates should receive the portion to which they were entitled.

Few, if subjected to such a test, would have shown themselves as noble as did Abraham. Few would have resisted the temptation to secure so rich a booty. His example is a rebuke to self-seeking, mercenary spirits. Abraham regarded the claims of justice and humanity. His conduct illustrates the inspired maxim, "Thou shalt love thy neighbor as thyself." Leviticus 19:18. "I have lifted up my hand," he said, "unto the Lord, the most high God, the possessor of heaven and earth, that I will not take from a thread even to a shoe latchet, and that I will not take anything that is thine, lest thou shouldest say, I have made Abram rich." He would give them no occasion to think that he had engaged in warfare for the sake of gain, or to attribute his prosperity to their gifts or favor. God had promised to bless Abraham, and to Him the glory should be ascribed.

Another who came out to welcome the victorious patriarch was Melchizedek, king of Salem, who brought forth bread and wine for the refreshment of his army. As "priest of the most high God," he pronounced a blessing upon Abraham, and gave thanks to the Lord, who had wrought so great a deliverance by His servant. And Abraham "gave him tithes of all."

Abraham gladly returned to his tents and his flocks, but his mind was disturbed by harassing thoughts. He had been a man of peace, so far as possible shunning enmity and strife; and with horror he recalled the scene of carnage he had witnessed. But the nations whose forces he had defeated would doubtless renew the invasion of Canaan, and make him the special object of their vengeance. Becoming thus involved in national quarrels, the peaceful quiet of his life would be broken. Furthermore, he had not entered upon the possession of Canaan, nor could he now hope for an heir, to whom the promise might be fulfilled.

In a vision of the night the divine Voice was again heard. "Fear not, Abram," were the words of the Prince of princes; "I am thy shield, and thy exceeding great reward." But his mind was so oppressed by forebodings that he could not now grasp the promise with unquestioning confidence as heretofore. He prayed for some tangible evidence that it would be fulfilled. And how was the covenant promise to be realized, while the gift of a son was withheld? "What wilt Thou give me," he said, "seeing I go childless?" "And, lo, one born in my house is mine heir." He proposed to make his trusty servant Eliezer his son by adoption, and the inheritor of his possessions. But he was assured that a child of his own was to be his heir. Then he was led outside his tent, and told to look up to the unnumbered stars glittering in the heavens; and as he did so, the words were spoken, "So shall thy seed be." "Abraham believed God, and it was counted unto him for righteousness." Romans 4:3.

Still the patriarch begged for some visible token as a confirmation of his faith and as an evidence to after-generations that God's gracious purposes toward them would be accomplished. The Lord condescended to enter into a covenant with His servant, employing such forms as were customary among men for the ratification of a solemn engagement. By divine direction, Abraham sacrificed a heifer, a she-goat, and a ram, each three years old, dividing the bodies and laying the pieces a little distance apart. To these he added a turtledove and a young pigeon, which, however, were not divided. This being done, he reverently passed between the parts of the sacrifice, making a solemn vow to God of perpetual obedience. Watchful and steadfast, he remained beside the carcasses till the going down of the sun, to guard them from being defiled or devoured by birds of prey. About sunset he sank into a deep sleep; and, "lo, a horror of great darkness fell upon him." And the voice of God was heard, bidding him not to expect immediate possession of the Promised Land, and pointing forward to the sufferings of his posterity before their establishment in Canaan. The plan of redemption was here opened to him, in the death of Christ, the great sacrifice, and His coming in glory. Abraham saw also the earth restored to its Eden beauty, to be given him for an everlasting possession, as the final and complete fulfillment of the promise.

As a pledge of this covenant of God with men, a smoking furnace and a burning lamp, symbols of the divine presence, passed between the severed victims, totally consuming them. And again a voice was heard by Abraham, confirming the gift of the land of Canaan to his descendants, "from the river of Egypt unto the great river, the river Euphrates."

When Abraham had been nearly twenty-five years in Canaan, the Lord appeared unto him, and said, "I am the Almighty God; walk before Me, and be thou perfect." In awe, the patriarch fell upon his face, and the message continued: "Behold, My covenant is with thee, and thou shalt be a father of many nations." In token of the fulfillment of this covenant, his name, heretofore called Abram, was changed to Abraham, which signifies, "father of a great multitude." Sarai's name became Sarah—"princess;" for, said the divine Voice, "she shall be a mother of nations; kings of people shall be of her."

[138]

At this time the rite of circumcision was given to Abraham as "a seal of the righteousness of the faith which he had yet being uncircumcised." Romans 4:11. It was to be observed by the patriarch and his descendants as a token that they were devoted to the service of God and thus separated from idolaters, and that God accepted them as His peculiar treasure. By this rite they were pledged to fulfill, on their part, the conditions of the covenant made with Abraham. They were not to contract marriages with the heathen; for by so doing they would lose their reverence for God and His holy law; they would be tempted to engage in the sinful practices of other nations, and would be seduced into idolatry.

God conferred great honor upon Abraham. Angels of heaven walked and talked with him as friend with friend. When judgments were about to be visited upon Sodom, the fact was not hidden from him, and he became an intercessor with God for sinners. His interview with the angels presents also a beautiful example of hospitality.

In the hot summer noontide the patriarch was sitting in his tent door, looking out over the quiet landscape, when he saw in the distance three travelers approaching. Before reaching his tent, the strangers halted, as if consulting as to their course. Without waiting for them to solicit favors, Abraham rose quickly, and as they were apparently turning in another direction, he hastened after them, and with the utmost courtesy urged them to honor him by tarrying for refreshment. With his own hands he brought water that they might wash the dust of travel from their feet. He himself selected their food, and while they were at rest under the cooling shade, an entertainment was made ready, and he stood respectfully beside them while they partook of his hospitality. This act of courtesy God regarded of sufficient importance to record in His word; and a thousand years later it was referred to by an inspired apostle: "Be not forgetful to entertain strangers: for thereby some have entertained angels unawares." Hebrews 13:2.

Abraham had seen in his guests only three tired wayfarers, little thinking that among them was One whom he might worship without sin. But the true character of the heavenly messengers was now revealed. Though they were on their way as ministers of wrath, yet to Abraham, the man of faith, they spoke first of blessings. Though God is strict to mark iniquity and to punish transgression, He takes no delight in vengeance. The work of destruction is a "strange work" to Him who is infinite in love.

"The secret of the Lord is with them that fear Him." Psalm 25:14. Abraham had honored God, and the Lord honored him, taking him into His counsels, and revealing to him His purposes. "Shall I hide from Abraham that thing which I do?" said the Lord. "The cry of Sodom and Gomorrah is great, and because their sin is very grievous, I will go down now, and see whether they have done altogether according to the cry of it, which is come unto me; and if not, I will know." God knew well the measure of Sodom's guilt; but He expressed Himself after the manner of men, that the justice of His dealings might be understood. Before bringing judgment upon the transgressors He would go Himself, to institute an examination of their course; if they had not passed the limits of divine mercy, He would still grant them space for repentance.

Two of the heavenly messengers departed, leaving Abraham alone with Him whom he now knew to be the Son of God. And the man of faith pleaded for the inhabitants of Sodom. Once he had saved them by his sword, now he endeavored to save them by prayer. Lot and his household were still dwellers there; and the unselfish love that prompted Abraham to their rescue from the Elamites, now sought to save them, if it were God's will, from the storm of divine judgment.

With deep reverence and humility he urged his plea: "I have taken upon me to speak unto the Lord, which am but dust and ashes." There was no self-confidence, no boasting of his own righteousness. He did not claim favor on the ground of his obedience, or of the sacrifices he had made in doing God's will. Himself a sinner, he pleaded in the sinner's behalf. Such a spirit all who approach God should possess. Yet Abraham manifested the confidence of a child pleading with a loved father. He came close to the heavenly Messenger, and fervently urged his petition. Though Lot had become a dweller in Sodom, he did not partake in the iniquity of its inhabitants. Abraham thought that in that populous city there must be other worshipers of the true God. And in view of this he pleaded, "That be far from Thee, to do after this manner, to slay the righteous with the wicked: ... that be far from Thee: Shall not the Judge of all the earth do right?" Abraham asked not once merely, but many times. Waxing bolder as his requests were granted, he continued until he gained the assurance that if even ten righteous persons could be found in it, the city would be spared.

Love for perishing souls inspired Abraham's prayer. While he loathed the sins of that corrupt city, he desired that the sinners might be saved. His deep interest for Sodom shows the anxiety that we should feel for the impenitent. We should cherish hatred of sin, but pity and love for the sinner. All around us are souls going down to ruin as hopeless, as terrible, as that which befell Sodom. Every day the probation of some is closing. Every hour some are passing beyond the reach of mercy. And where are the voices of warning and entreaty to bid the sinner flee from this fearful doom? Where are the hands stretched out to draw him back from death? Where are those who with humility and persevering faith are pleading with God for him?

The spirit of Abraham was the spirit of Christ. The Son of God is Himself the great Intercessor in the sinner's behalf. He who has paid the price for its redemption knows the worth of the human soul. With an antagonism to evil such as can exist only in a nature spotlessly pure, Christ manifested toward the sinner a love which infinite goodness alone could conceive. In the agonies of the crucifixion, Himself burdened with the awful weight of the sins of the whole world, He prayed for His revilers and murderers, "Father, forgive them; for they know not what they do." Luke 23:34.

Of Abraham it is written that "he was called the friend of God," "the father of all them that believe." James 2:23; Romans 4:11. The testimony of God concerning this faithful patriarch is, "Abraham obeyed My voice, and kept My charge, My commandments, My statutes, and My laws." And again, "I know him, that he will command his children and his household after him, and they shall keep the way of the Lord, to do justice and judgment; that the Lord may bring upon Abraham that which he hath spoken of him." It was a high honor to which Abraham was called, that of being the father of the people who for centuries were the guardians and preservers of the truth of God for the world—of that people through whom all the nations of the earth should be blessed in the advent of the promised Messiah. But He who called the patriarch judged him worthy. It is God that speaks. He who understands the thoughts afar off, and places the right estimate upon men, says, "I know him." There would be on the part of Abraham no betraying of the truth for selfish purposes. He would keep the law and deal justly and righteously. And he would not only fear the Lord himself, but would cultivate religion in his home. He would instruct his family in righteousness. The law of God would be the rule in his household.

Abraham's household comprised more than a thousand souls. Those who were led by his teachings to worship the one God, found a home in his encampment; and here, as in a school, they received such instruction as would prepare them to be representatives of the true faith. Thus a great responsibility rested upon him. He was training heads of families, and his methods of government would be carried out in the households over which they should preside.

In early times the father was the ruler and priest of his own family, and he exercised authority over his children, even after they had families of their own. His descendants were taught to look up to him as their head, in both religious and secular matters. This patriarchal system of government Abraham endeavored to perpetuate, as it tended to preserve the knowledge of God. It was necessary to bind the members of the household together, in order to build up a barrier against the idolatry that had become so widespread and so deep-seated. Abraham sought by every means in his power to guard the inmates of his encampment against mingling with the heathen and witnessing their idolatrous practices, for he knew that familiarity with evil would insensibly corrupt the principles. The greatest care was exercised to shut out every form of false religion and to impress the mind with the majesty and glory of the living God as the true object of worship.

It was a wise arrangement, which God Himself had made, to cut off His people, so far as possible, from connection with the heathen, making them a people dwelling alone, and not reckoned among the nations. He had separated Abraham from his idolatrous kindred, that the patriarch might train and educate his family apart from the seductive influences which would have surrounded them in Mesopotamia, and that the true faith might be preserved in its purity by his descendants from generation to generation.

Abraham's affection for his children and his household led him to guard their religious faith, to impart to them a knowledge of the divine statutes, as the most precious legacy he could transmit to them, and through them to the world. All were taught that they were under the rule of the God of heaven. There was to be no oppression on the part of parents and no disobedience on the part of children. God's law had appointed to each his duties, and only in obedience to it could any secure happiness or prosperity.

His own example, the silent influence of his daily life, was a constant lesson. The unswerving integrity, the benevolence and unselfish courtesy, which had won the admiration of kings, were displayed in the home. There was a fragrance about the life, a nobility and loveliness of character, which revealed to all that he was connected with Heaven. He did not neglect the soul of the humblest servant. In his household there was not one law for the master and another for the servant; a royal way for the rich and another for the poor. All were treated with justice and compassion, as inheritors with him of the grace of life.

"He will command his ... household." There would be no sinful neglect to restrain the evil propensities of his children, no weak, unwise, indulgent favoritism; no yielding of his conviction of duty to the claims of mistaken affection. Abraham would not only give right instruction, but he would maintain the authority of just and righteous laws.

How few there are in our day who follow this example! On the part of too many parents there is a blind and selfish sentimentalism, miscalled love, which is manifested in leaving children, with their unformed judgment and undisciplined passions, to the control of their own will. This is the veriest cruelty to the youth and a great wrong to the world. Parental indulgence causes disorder in families and in society. It confirms in the young the desire to follow inclination, instead of submitting to the divine requirements. Thus they grow up with a heart averse to doing God's will, and they transmit their irreligious, insubordinate spirit to their children and children's children. Like Abraham, parents should command their households after them. Let obedience to parental authority be taught and enforced as the first step in obedience to the authority of God.

The light esteem in which the law of God is held, even by religious leaders, has been productive of great evil. The teaching which has become so widespread, that the divine statutes are no longer binding upon men, is the same as idolatry in its effect upon the morals of the people. Those who seek to lessen the claims of God's holy law are striking directly at the foundation of the government of families and nations. Religious parents, failing to walk in His statutes, do not command their household to keep the way of the Lord. The law of God is not made the rule of life. The children, as they make homes of their own, feel under no obligation to teach their children what they themselves have never been taught. And this is why there are so many godless families; this is why depravity is so deep and widespread.

Not until parents themselves walk in the law of the Lord with perfect hearts will they be prepared to command their children after them. A reformation in this respect is needed—a reformation which shall be deep and broad. Parents need to reform; ministers need to reform; they need God in their households. If they would see a different state of things, they must bring His word into their families and must make it their counselor. They must teach their children that it is the voice of God addressed to them, and is to be implicitly obeyed. They should patiently instruct their children, kindly and untiringly teach them how to live in order to please God. The children of such a household are prepared to meet the sophistries of infidelity. They have accepted the Bible as the basis of their faith, and they have a foundation that cannot be swept away by the incoming tide of skepticism.

In too many households prayer is neglected. Parents feel that they have no time for morning and evening worship. They cannot spare a few moments to be spent in thanksgiving to God for His abundant mercies—for the blessed sunshine and the showers of rain, which cause vegetation to flourish, and for the guardianship of holy angels. They have no time to offer prayer for divine help and guidance and for the abiding presence of Jesus in the household. They go forth to labor as the ox or the horse goes, without one thought of God or heaven. They have souls so precious that rather than permit them to be hopelessly lost, the Son of God gave His life to ransom them; but they have little more appreciation of His great goodness than have the beasts that perish.

[144]

Like the patriarchs of old, those who profess to love God should erect an altar to the Lord wherever they pitch their tent. If ever there was a time when every house should be a house of prayer, it is now. Fathers and mothers should often lift up their hearts to God in humble supplication for themselves and their children. Let the father, as priest of the household, lay upon the altar of God the morning and evening sacrifice, while the wife and children unite in prayer and praise. In such a household Jesus will love to tarry.

From every Christian home a holy light should shine forth. Love should be revealed in action. It should flow out in all home intercourse, showing itself in thoughtful kindness, in gentle, unselfish courtesy. There are homes where this principle is carried out—homes where God is worshiped and truest love reigns. From these homes morning and evening prayer ascends to God as sweet incense, and His mercies and blessings descend upon the suppliants like the morning dew.

A well-ordered Christian household is a powerful argument in favor of the reality of the Christian religion—an argument that the infidel cannot gainsay. All can see that there is an influence at work in the family that affects the children, and that the God of Abraham is with them. If the homes of professed Christians had a right religious mold, they would exert a mighty influence for good. They would indeed be the "light of the world." The God of heaven speaks to every faithful parent in the words addressed to Abraham: "I know him, that he will command his children and his household after him, and they shall keep the way of the Lord, to do justice and judgment; that the Lord may bring upon Abraham that which He hath spoken of him."

Chapter 13—The Test of Faith

This chapter is based on Genesis 16; 17:18-20; 21:1-14; 22:1-19.

Abraham had accepted without question the promise of a son, but he did not wait for God to fulfill His word in His own time and way. A delay was permitted, to test his faith in the power of God; but he failed to endure the trial. Thinking it impossible that a child should be given her in her old age, Sarah suggested, as a plan by which the divine purpose might be fulfilled, that one of her handmaidens should be taken by Abraham as a secondary wife. Polygamy had become so widespread that it had ceased to be regarded as a sin, but it was no less a violation of the law of God, and was fatal to the sacredness and peace of the family relation. Abraham's marriage with Hagar resulted in evil, not only to his own household, but to future generations.

Flattered with the honor of her new position as Abraham's wife, and hoping to be the mother of the great nation to descend from him, Hagar became proud and boastful, and treated her mistress with contempt. Mutual jealousies disturbed the peace of the once happy home. Forced to listen to the complaints of both, Abraham vainly endeavored to restore harmony. Though it was at Sarah's earnest entreaty that he had married Hagar, she now reproached him as the one at fault. She desired to banish her rival; but Abraham refused to permit this; for Hagar was to be the mother of his child, as he fondly hoped, the son of promise. She was Sarah's servant, however, and he still left her to the control of her mistress. Hagar's haughty spirit would not brook the harshness which her insolence had provoked. "When Sarai dealt hardly with her, she fled from her face."

She made her way to the desert, and as she rested beside a fountain, lonely and friendless, an angel of the Lord, in human form, appeared to her. Addressing her as "Hagar, Sarai's maid," to remind her of her position and her duty, he bade her, "Return to thy mistress, and submit thyself under her hands." Yet with the reproof there were mingled words of comfort. "The Lord hath heard thy affliction." "I will multiply thy seed exceedingly, that it shall not be numbered for multitude." And as a perpetual reminder of His mercy, she was bidden to call her child Ishmael, "God shall hear."

When Abraham was nearly one hundred years old, the promise of a son was repeated to him, with the assurance that the future heir should be the child of Sarah. But Abraham did not yet understand the promise. His mind at once turned to Ishmael, clinging to the belief that through him God's gracious purposes were to be accomplished. In his affection for his son he exclaimed, "O that Ishmael might live before Thee!" Again the promise was given, in words that could not be mistaken: "Sarah thy wife shall bear thee a son indeed; and thou shalt call his name Isaac: and I will establish My covenant with him." Yet God was not unmindful of the father's prayer. "As for Ishmael," He said, "I have heard thee: Behold, I have blessed him, ... and I will make him a great nation."

The birth of Isaac, bringing, after a lifelong waiting, the fulfillment of their dearest hopes, filled the tents of Abraham and Sarah with gladness. But to Hagar this event was the overthrow of her fondly cherished ambitions. Ishmael, now a youth, had been regarded by all in the encampment as the heir of Abraham's wealth and the inheritor of the blessings promised to his descendants. Now he was suddenly set aside; and in their disappointment, mother and son hated the child of Sarah. The general rejoicing increased their jealousy, until Ishmael dared openly to mock the heir of God's promise. Sarah saw in Ishmael's turbulent disposition a perpetual source of discord, and she appealed to Abraham, urging that Hagar and Ishmael be sent away from the encampment. The patriarch was thrown into great distress. How could he banish Ishmael his son, still dearly beloved? In his perplexity he pleaded for divine guidance. The Lord, through a holy angel, directed him to grant Sarah's desire; his love for Ishmael or Hagar ought not to stand in the way, for only thus could he restore harmony and happiness to his family. And the angel gave him the consoling promise that though separated from his father's home, Ishmael should not be forsaken by God; his life should be preserved, and he should become the father of a great nation. Abraham obeyed the angel's word, but it was not without keen suffering. The father's heart was heavy with unspoken grief as he sent away Hagar and his son.

The instruction given to Abraham touching the sacredness of the marriage relation was to be a lesson for all ages. It declares that the rights and happiness of this relation are to be carefully guarded, even at a great sacrifice. Sarah was the only true wife of Abraham. Her rights as a wife and mother no other person was entitled to share. She reverenced her husband, and in this she is presented in the New Testament as a worthy example. But she was unwilling that Abraham's affections should be given to another, and the Lord did not reprove her for requiring the banishment of her rival. Both Abraham and Sarah distrusted the power of God, and it was this error that led to the marriage with Hagar.

God had called Abraham to be the father of the faithful, and his life was to stand as an example of faith to succeeding generations. But his faith had not been perfect. He had shown distrust of God in concealing the fact that Sarah was his wife, and again in his marriage with Hagar. That he might reach the highest standard, God subjected him to another test, the closest which man was ever called to endure. In a vision of the night he was directed to repair to the land of Moriah, and there offer up his son as a burnt offering upon a mountain that should be shown him.

At the time of receiving this command, Abraham had reached the age of a hundred and twenty years. He was regarded as an old man, even in his generation. In his earlier years he had been strong to endure hardship and to brave danger, but now the ardor of his youth had passed away. One in the vigor of manhood may with courage meet difficulties and afflictions that would cause his heart to fail later in life, when his feet are faltering toward the grave. But God had reserved His last, most trying test for Abraham until the burden of years was heavy upon him, and he longed for rest from anxiety and toil.

The patriarch was dwelling at Beersheba, surrounded by prosperity and honor. He was very rich, and was honored as a mighty prince by the rulers of the land. Thousands of sheep and cattle covered the plains that spread out beyond his encampment. On every side were the tents of his retainers, the home of hundreds of faithful servants. The son of promise had grown up to manhood by his side. Heaven seemed to have crowned with its blessing a life of sacrifice in patient endurance of hope deferred.

In the obedience of faith, Abraham had forsaken his native country—had turned away from the graves of his fathers and the home of his kindred. He had wandered as a stranger in the land of his inheritance. He had waited long for the birth of the promised heir. At the command of God he had sent away his son Ishmael. And now, when the child so long desired was entering upon manhood, and the patriarch seemed able to discern the fruition of his hopes, a trial greater than all others was before him.

The command was expressed in words that must have wrung with anguish that father's heart: "Take now thy son, thine only son Isaac, whom thou lovest, ... and offer him there for a burnt offering." Isaac was the light of his home, the solace of his old age, above all else the inheritor of the promised blessing. The loss of such a son by accident or disease would have been heart rending to the fond father; it would have bowed down his whitened head with grief; but he was commanded to shed the blood of that son with his own hand. It seemed to him a fearful impossibility.

Satan was at hand to suggest that he must be deceived, for the divine law commands, "Thou shalt not kill," and God would not require what He had once forbidden. Going outside his tent, Abraham looked up to the calm brightness of the unclouded heavens, and recalled the promise made nearly fifty years before, that his seed should be innumerable as the stars. If this promise was to be fulfilled through Isaac, how could he be put to death? Abraham was tempted to believe that he might be under a delusion. In his doubt and anguish he bowed upon the earth, and prayed, as he had never prayed before, for some confirmation of the command if he must perform this terrible duty. He remembered the angels sent to reveal to him God's purpose to destroy Sodom, and who bore to him the promise of this same son Isaac, and he went to the place where he had several times met the heavenly messengers, hoping to meet them again, and receive some further direction; but none came to his relief. Darkness seemed to shut him in; but the command of God was sounding in his ears, "Take now thy son, thine only son Isaac, whom thou lovest." That command must be obeyed, and he dared not delay. Day was approaching, and he must be on his journey.

Returning to his tent, he went to the place where Isaac lay sleeping the deep, untroubled sleep of youth and innocence. For a moment the father looked upon the dear face of his son, then turned tremblingly away. He went to the side of Sarah, who was also sleeping. Should he awaken her, that she might once more embrace her child? Should he tell her of God's requirement? He longed to unburden his heart to her, and share with her this terrible responsibility; but he was restrained by the fear that she might hinder him. Isaac was her joy and pride; her life was bound up in him, and the mother's love might refuse the sacrifice.

Abraham at last summoned his son, telling him of the command to offer sacrifice upon a distant mountain. Isaac had often gone with his father to worship at some one of the various altars that marked his wanderings, and this summons excited no surprise. The preparations for the journey were quickly completed. The wood was made ready and put upon the ass, and with two menservants they set forth.

Side by side the father and the son journeyed in silence. The patriarch, pondering his heavy secret, had no heart for words. His thoughts were of the proud, fond mother, and the day when he should return to her alone. Well he knew that the knife would pierce her heart when it took the life of her son.

That day—the longest that Abraham had ever experienced—dragged slowly to its close. While his son and the young men were sleeping, he spent the night in prayer, still hoping that some heavenly messenger might come to say that the trial was enough, that the youth might return unharmed to his mother. But no relief came to his tortured soul. Another long day, another night of humiliation and prayer, while ever the command that was to leave him childless was ringing in his ears. Satan was near to whisper doubts and unbelief, but Abraham resisted his suggestions. As they were about to begin the journey of the third day, the patriarch, looking northward, saw the promised sign, a cloud of glory hovering over Mount Moriah, and he knew that the voice which had spoken to him was from heaven.

Even now he did not murmur against God, but strengthened his soul by dwelling upon the evidences of the Lord's goodness and faithfulness. This son had been unexpectedly given; and had not He who bestowed the precious gift a right to recall His own? Then faith repeated the promise, "In Isaac shall thy seed be called"—a seed numberless as the grains of sand upon the shore. Isaac was the child of a miracle, and could not the power that gave him life restore it? Looking beyond that which was seen, Abraham grasped the divine word, "accounting that God was able to raise him up, even from the dead." Hebrews 11:19.

Yet none but God could understand how great was the father's sacrifice in yielding up his son to death; Abraham desired that none but God should witness the parting scene. He bade his servants remain behind, saying, "I and the lad will go yonder and worship, and come again to you." The wood was laid upon Isaac, the one to be offered, the father took the knife and the fire, and together they ascended toward the mountain summit, the young man silently wondering whence, so far from folds and flocks, the offering was to come. At last he spoke, "My father," "behold the fire and the wood: but where is the lamb for a burnt offering?" Oh, what a test was this! How the endearing words, "my father," pierced Abraham's heart! Not yet—he could not tell him now. "My son," he said, "God will provide Himself a lamb for a burnt offering."

At the appointed place they built the altar and laid the wood upon it. Then, with trembling voice, Abraham unfolded to his son the divine message. It was with terror and amazement that Isaac learned his fate, but he offered no resistance. He could have escaped his doom, had he chosen to do so; the grief-stricken old man, exhausted with the struggle of those three terrible days, could not have opposed the will of the vigorous youth. But Isaac had been trained from childhood to ready, trusting obedience, and as the purpose of God was opened before him, he yielded a willing submission. He was a sharer in Abraham's faith, and he felt that he was honored in being called to give his life as an offering to God. He tenderly seeks to lighten the father's grief, and encourages his nerveless hands to bind the cords that confine him to the altar.

And now the last words of love are spoken, the last tears are shed, the last embrace is given. The father lifts the knife to slay his son, when suddenly his arm is stayed. An angel of God calls to the patriarch out of heaven, "Abraham, Abraham!" He quickly answers, "Here am I," And again the voice is heard, "Lay not thine hand upon the lad, neither do thou any thing unto him: for now I know that thou fearest God, seeing thou hast not withheld thy son, thine only son, from Me."

Then Abraham saw "a ram caught in a thicket," and quickly bringing the new victim, he offered it "in the stead of his son." In his joy and gratitude Abraham gave a new name to the sacred spot—"Jehovah-jireh," "the Lord will provide."

[153]

On Mount Moriah, God again renewed His covenant, confirming with a solemn oath the blessing to Abraham and to his seed through all coming generations: "By myself have I sworn, saith Jehovah, for because thou hast done this thing, and hast not withheld thy son, thine only son, that in blessing I will bless thee, and in multiplying I will multiply thy seed as the stars of the heaven, and as the sand which is upon the seashore; and thy seed shall possess the gate of his enemies; and in thy seed shall all the nations of the earth be blessed; because thou hast obeyed My voice."

Abraham's great act of faith stands like a pillar of light, illuminating the pathway of God's servants in all succeeding ages. Abraham did not seek to excuse himself from doing the will of God. During that three days' journey he had sufficient time to reason, and to doubt God, if he was disposed to doubt. He might have reasoned that the slaying of his son would cause him to be looked upon as a murderer, a second Cain; that it would cause his teaching to be rejected and despised; and thus destroy his power to do good to his fellow men. He might have pleaded that age should excuse him from obedience. But the patriarch did not take refuge in any of these excuses. Abraham was human; his passions and attachments were like ours; but he did not stop to question how the promise could be fulfilled if Isaac should be slain. He did not stay to reason with his aching heart. He knew that God is just and righteous in all His requirements, and he obeyed the command to the very letter.

"Abraham believed God, and it was imputed unto him for righteousness: and he was called the friend of God." James 2:23. And Paul says, "They which are of faith, the same are the children of Abraham." Galatians 3:7. But Abraham's faith was made manifest by his works. "Was not Abraham our father justified by works, when he had offered Isaac his son upon the altar? Seest thou how faith wrought with his works, and by works was faith made perfect?" James 2:21, 22. There are many who fail to understand the relation of faith and works. They say, "Only believe in Christ, and you are safe. You have nothing to do with keeping the law." But genuine faith will be manifest in obedience. Said Christ to the unbelieving Jews, "If ye were Abraham's children, ye would do the works of Abraham." John 8:39. And concerning the father of the faithful the Lord declares, "Abraham obeyed My voice, and kept My charge, My commandments, My statutes, and My laws." Genesis 26:5. Says the apostle James, "Faith, if it hath not works, is dead, being alone." James 2:17. And John, who dwells so fully upon love, tells us, "This is the love of God, that we keep His commandments." 1 John 5:3.

Through type and promise God "preached before the gospel unto Abraham." Galatians 3:8. And the patriarch's faith was fixed upon the Redeemer to come. Said Christ to the Jews. "Your father Abraham rejoiced that he should see My day; and he saw it, and was glad." John 8:56, R.V., margin. The ram offered in the place of Isaac represented the Son of God, who was to be sacrificed in our stead. When man was doomed to death by transgression of the law of God, the Father, looking upon His Son, said to the sinner, "Live: I have found a ransom."

It was to impress Abraham's mind with the reality of the gospel, as well as to test his faith, that God commanded him to slay his son. The agony which he endured during the dark days of that fearful trial was permitted that he might understand from his own experience something of the greatness of the sacrifice made by the infinite God for man's redemption. No other test could have caused Abraham such torture of soul as did the offering of his son. God gave His Son to a death of agony and shame. The angels who witnessed the humiliation and soul anguish of the Son of God were not permitted to interpose, as in the case of Isaac. There was no voice to cry, "It is enough." To save the fallen race, the King of glory yielded up His life. What stronger proof can be given of the infinite compassion and love of God? "He that spared not His own Son, but delivered Him up for us all, how shall He not with Him also freely give us all things?" Romans 8:32.

The sacrifice required of Abraham was not alone for his own good, nor solely for the benefit of succeeding generations; but it was also for the instruction of the sinless intelligences of heaven and of other worlds. The field of the controversy between Christ and

Satan—the field on which the plan of redemption is wrought out—is the lesson book of the universe. Because Abraham had shown a lack of faith in God's promises, Satan had accused him before the angels and before God of having failed to comply with the conditions of the covenant, and as unworthy of its blessings. God desired to prove the loyalty of His servant before all heaven, to demonstrate that nothing less than perfect obedience can be accepted, and to open more fully before them the plan of salvation.

Heavenly beings were witnesses of the scene as the faith of Abraham and the submission of Isaac were tested. The trial was far more severe than that which had been brought upon Adam. Compliance with the prohibition laid upon our first parents involved no suffering, but the command to Abraham demanded the most agonizing sacrifice. All heaven beheld with wonder and admiration Abraham's unfaltering obedience. All heaven applauded his fidelity. Satan's accusations were shown to be false. God declared to His servant, "Now I know that thou fearest God [notwithstanding Satan's charges], seeing thou hast not withheld thy son, thine only son from Me." God's covenant, confirmed to Abraham by an oath before the intelligences of other worlds, testified that obedience will be rewarded.

It had been difficult even for the angels to grasp the mystery of redemption—to comprehend that the Commander of heaven, the Son of God, must die for guilty man. When the command was given to Abraham to offer up his son, the interest of all heavenly beings was enlisted. With intense earnestness they watched each step in the fulfillment of this command. When to Isaac's question, "Where is the lamb for a burnt offering?" Abraham made answer, "God will provide Himself a lamb;" and when the father's hand was stayed as he was about to slay his son, and the ram which God had provided was offered in the place of Isaac—then light was shed upon the mystery of redemption, and even the angels understood more clearly the wonderful provision that God had made for man's salvation. 1 Peter 1:12.

Chapter 14—Destruction of Sodom

This chapter is based on Genesis 19.

Fairest among the cities of the Jordan Valley was Sodom, set in a plain which was "as the garden of the Lord" in its fertility and beauty. Here the luxuriant vegetation of the tropics flourished. Here was the home of the palm tree, the olive, and the vine; and flowers shed their fragrance throughout the year. Rich harvests clothed the fields, and flocks and herds covered the encircling hills. Art and commerce contributed to enrich the proud city of the plain. The treasures of the East adorned her palaces, and the caravans of the desert brought their stores of precious things to supply her marts of trade. With little thought or labor, every want of life could be supplied, and the whole year seemed one round of festivity.

The profusion reigning everywhere gave birth to luxury and pride. Idleness and riches make the heart hard that has never been oppressed by want or burdened by sorrow. The love of pleasure was fostered by wealth and leisure, and the people gave themselves up to sensual indulgence. "Behold," says the prophet, "this was the iniquity of thy sister Sodom, pride, fullness of bread, and abundance of idleness was in her and in her daughters, neither did she strengthen the hand of the poor and needy. And they were haughty, and committed abomination before Me: therefore I took them away as I saw good." Ezekiel 16:49, 50. There is nothing more desired among men than riches and leisure, and yet these gave birth to the sins that brought destruction upon the cities of the plain. Their useless, idle life made them a prey to Satan's temptations, and they defaced the image of God, and became satanic rather than divine. Idleness is the greatest curse that can fall upon man, for vice and crime follow in its train. It enfeebles the mind, perverts the understanding, and debases the soul. Satan lies in ambush, ready to destroy those who are unguarded, whose leisure gives him opportunity to insinuate himself under some attractive disguise. He is never more successful than when he comes to men in their idle hours.

In Sodom there was mirth and revelry, feasting and drunkenness. The vilest and most brutal passions were unrestrained. The people openly defied God and His law and delighted in deeds of violence. Though they had before them the example of the antediluvian world, and knew how the wrath of God had been manifested in their destruction, yet they followed the same course of wickedness.

At the time of Lot's removal to Sodom, corruption had not become universal, and God in His mercy permitted rays of light to shine amid the moral darkness. When Abraham rescued the captives from the Elamites, the attention of the people was called to the true faith. Abraham was not a stranger to the people of Sodom, and his worship of the unseen God had been a matter of ridicule among them; but his victory over greatly superior forces, and his magnanimous disposition of the prisoners and spoil, excited wonder and admiration. While his skill and valor were extolled, none could avoid the conviction that a divine power had made him conqueror. And his noble and unselfish spirit, so foreign to the self-seeking inhabitants of Sodom, was another evidence of the superiority of the religion which he had honored by his courage and fidelity.

Melchizedek, in bestowing the benediction upon Abraham, had acknowledged Jehovah as the source of his strength and the author of the victory: "Blessed be Abram of the most high God, possessor of heaven and earth: and blessed be the most high God, which hath delivered thine enemies into thy hand." Genesis 14:19, 20. God was speaking to that people by His providence, but the last ray of light was rejected as all before had been.

And now the last night of Sodom was approaching. Already the clouds of vengeance cast their shadows over the devoted city. But men perceived it not. While angels drew near on their mission of destruction, men were dreaming of prosperity and pleasure. The last day was like every other that had come and gone. Evening fell upon a scene of loveliness and security. A landscape of unrivaled beauty was bathed in the rays of the declining sun. The coolness of eventide had called forth the inhabitants of the city, and the pleasure-seeking throngs were passing to and fro, intent upon the enjoyment of the hour.

[158]

In the twilight two strangers drew near to the city gate. They were apparently travelers coming in to tarry for the night. None could discern in those humble wayfarers the mighty heralds of divine judgment, and little dreamed the gay, careless multitude that in their treatment of these heavenly messengers that very night they would reach the climax of the guilt which doomed their proud city. But there was one man who manifested kindly attention toward the strangers and invited them to his home. Lot did not know their true character, but politeness and hospitality were habitual with him; they were a part of his religion—lessons that he had learned from the example of Abraham. Had he not cultivated a spirit of courtesy, he might have been left to perish with the rest of Sodom. Many a household, in closing its doors against a stranger, has shut out God's messenger, who would have brought blessing and hope and peace.

Every act of life, however small, has its bearing for good or for evil. Faithfulness or neglect in what are apparently the smallest duties may open the door for life's richest blessings or its greatest calamities. It is little things that test the character. It is the unpretending acts of daily self-denial, performed with a cheerful, willing heart, that God smiles upon. We are not to live for self, but for others. And it is only by self-forgetfulness, by cherishing a loving, helpful spirit, that we can make our life a blessing. The little attentions, the small, simple courtesies, go far to make up the sum of life's happiness, and the neglect of these constitutes no small share of human wretchedness.

Seeing the abuse to which strangers were exposed in Sodom, Lot made it one of his duties to guard them at their entrance, by offering them entertainment at his own house. He was sitting at the gate as the travelers approached, and upon observing them, he rose from his place to meet them, and bowing courteously, said, "Behold now, my lords, turn in, I pray you, into your servant's house, and tarry all night." They seemed to decline his hospitality, saying, "Nay; but we will abide in the street." Their object in this answer was twofold—to test the sincerity of Lot and also to appear ignorant of the character of the men of Sodom, as if they supposed it safe to remain in the street at night. Their answer made Lot the more determined not to leave them to the mercy of the rabble. He pressed his invitation until they yielded, and accompanied him to his house.

Destruction of Sodom

He had hoped to conceal his intention from the idlers at the gate by bringing the strangers to his home by a circuitous route; but their hesitation and delay, and his persistent urging, caused them to be observed, and before they had retired for the night, a lawless crowd gathered about the house. It was an immense company, youth and aged men alike inflamed by the vilest passions. The strangers had been making inquiry in regard to the character of the city, and Lot had warned them not to venture out of his door that night, when the hooting and jeers of the mob were heard, demanding that the men be brought out to them.

Knowing that if provoked to violence they could easily break into his house, Lot went out to try the effect of persuasion upon them. "I pray you, brethren," he said, "do not so wickedly," using the term "brethren" in the sense of neighbors, and hoping to conciliate them and make them ashamed of their vile purposes. But his words were like oil upon the flames. Their rage became like the roaring of a tempest. They mocked Lot as making himself a judge over them, and threatened to deal worse with him than they had purposed toward his guests. They rushed upon him, and would have torn him in pieces had he not been rescued by the angels of God. The heavenly messengers "put forth their hand, and pulled Lot into the house to them, and shut to the door." The events that followed, revealed the character of the guests he had entertained. "They smote the men that were at the door of the house with blindness, both small and great: so that they wearied themselves to find the door." Had they not been visited with double blindness, being given up to hardness of heart, the stroke of God upon them would have caused them to fear, and to desist from their evil work. That last night was marked by no greater sins than many others before it; but mercy, so long slighted, had at last ceased its pleading. The inhabitants of Sodom had passed the limits of divine forbearance—"the hidden boundary between God's patience and His wrath." The fires of His vengeance were about to be kindled in the vale of Siddim.

The angels revealed to Lot the object of their mission: "We will destroy this place, because the cry of them is waxen great before the face of the Lord; and the Lord hath sent us to destroy it." The strangers whom Lot had endeavored to protect, now promised to protect him, and to save also all the members of his family who

[160]

would flee with him from the wicked city. The mob had wearied themselves out and departed, and Lot went out to warn his children. He repeated the words of the angels, "Up, get you out of this place; for the Lord will destroy this city." But he seemed to them as one that mocked. They laughed at what they called his superstitious fears. His daughters were influenced by their husbands. They were well enough off where they were. They could see no evidence of danger. Everything was just as it had been. They had great possessions, and they could not believe it possible that beautiful Sodom would be destroyed.

Lot returned sorrowfully to his home and told the story of his failure. Then the angels bade him arise and take his wife and the two daughters who were yet in his house and leave the city. But Lot delayed. Though daily distressed at beholding deeds of violence, he had no true conception of the debasing and abominable iniquity practiced in that vile city. He did not realize the terrible necessity for God's judgments to put a check on sin. Some of his children clung to Sodom, and his wife refused to depart without them. The thought of leaving those whom he held dearest on earth seemed more than he could bear. It was hard to forsake his luxurious home and all the wealth acquired by the labors of his whole life, to go forth a destitute wanderer. Stupefied with sorrow, he lingered, loath to depart. But for the angels of God, they would all have perished in the ruin of Sodom. The heavenly messengers took him and his wife and daughters by the hand and led them out of the city.

Here the angels left them, and turned back to Sodom to accomplish their work of destruction. Another—He with whom Abraham had pleaded—drew near to Lot. In all the cities of the plain, even ten righteous persons had not been found; but in answer to the patriarch's prayer, the one man who feared God was snatched from destruction. The command was given with startling vehemence: "Escape for thy life; look not behind thee, neither stay thou in all the plain; escape to the mountain, lest thou be consumed." Hesitancy or delay now would be fatal. To cast one lingering look upon the devoted city, to tarry for one moment from regret to leave so beautiful a home, would have cost their life. The storm of divine judgment was only waiting that these poor fugitives might make their escape.

But Lot, confused and terrified, pleaded that he could not do as he was required lest some evil should overtake him and he should die. Living in that wicked city, in the midst of unbelief, his faith had grown dim. The Prince of heaven was by his side, yet he pleaded for his own life as though God, who had manifested such care and love for him, would not still preserve him. He should have trusted himself wholly to the divine Messenger, giving his will and his life into the Lord's hands without a doubt or a question. But like so many others, he endeavored to plan for himself: "Behold now, this city is near to flee unto, and it is a little one: O, let me escape thither, (is it not a little one?) and my soul shall live." The city here mentioned was Bela, afterward called Zoar. It was but a few miles from Sodom, and, like it, was corrupt and doomed to destruction. But Lot asked that it might be spared, urging that this was but a small request; and his desire was granted. The Lord assured him, "I have accepted thee concerning this thing also, that I will not overthrow this city, for the which thou hast spoken." Oh, how great the mercy of God toward His erring creatures!

Again the solemn command was given to hasten, for the fiery storm would be delayed but little longer. But one of the fugitives ventured to cast a look backward to the doomed city, and she became a monument of God's judgment. If Lot himself had manifested no hesitancy to obey the angels' warning, but had earnestly fled toward the mountains, without one word of pleading or remonstrance, his wife also would have made her escape. The influence of his example would have saved her from the sin that sealed her doom. But his hesitancy and delay caused her to lightly regard the divine warning. While her body was upon the plain, her heart clung to Sodom, and she perished with it. She rebelled against God because His judgments involved her possessions and her children in the ruin. Although so greatly favored in being called out from the wicked city, she felt that she was severely dealt with, because the wealth that it had taken years to accumulate must be left to destruction. Instead of thankfully accepting deliverance, she presumptuously looked back to desire the life of those who had rejected the divine warning. Her sin showed her to be unworthy of life, for the preservation of which she felt so little gratitude.

We should beware of treating lightly God's gracious provisions for our salvation. There are Christians who say, "I do not care to be saved unless my companion and children are saved with me." They feel that heaven would not be heaven to them without the presence of those who are so dear. But have those who cherish this feeling a right conception of their own relation to God, in view of His great goodness and mercy toward them? Have they forgotten that they are bound by the strongest ties of love and honor and loyalty to the service of their Creator and Redeemer? The invitations of mercy are addressed to all; and because our friends reject the Saviour's pleading love, shall we also turn away? The redemption of the soul is precious. Christ has paid an infinite price for our salvation, and no one who appreciates the value of this great sacrifice or the worth of the soul will despise God's offered mercy because others choose to do so. The very fact that others are ignoring His just claims should arouse us to greater diligence, that we may honor God ourselves, and lead all whom we can influence, to accept His love.

"The sun was risen upon the earth when Lot entered into Zoar." The bright rays of the morning seemed to speak only prosperity and peace to the cities of the plain. The stir of active life began in the streets; men were going their various ways, intent on the business or the pleasures of the day. The sons-in-law of Lot were making merry at the fears and warnings of the weak-minded old man. Suddenly and unexpectedly as would be a thunder peal from an unclouded sky, the tempest broke. The Lord rained brimstone and fire out of heaven upon the cities and the fruitful plain; its palaces and temples, costly dwellings, gardens and vineyards, and the gay, pleasure-seeking throngs that only the night before had insulted the messengers of heaven—all were consumed. The smoke of the conflagration went up like the smoke of a great furnace. And the fair vale of Siddim became a desolation, a place never to be built up or inhabited—a witness to all generations of the certainty of God's judgments upon transgression.

The flames that consumed the cities of the plain shed their warning light down even to our time. We are taught the fearful and solemn lesson that while God's mercy bears long with the transgressor, there is a limit beyond which men may not go on in sin. When that limit is reached, then the offers of mercy are withdrawn, and the ministration of judgment begins.

The Redeemer of the world declares that there are greater sins than that for which Sodom and Gomorrah were destroyed. Those who hear the gospel invitation calling sinners to repentance, and heed it not, are more guilty before God than were the dwellers in the vale of Siddim. And still greater sin is theirs who profess to know God and to keep His commandments, yet who deny Christ in their character and their daily life. In the light of the Saviour's warning, the fate of Sodom is a solemn admonition, not merely to those who are guilty of outbreaking sin, but to all who are trifling with Heaven-sent light and privileges.

Said the True Witness to the church at Ephesus: "I have somewhat against thee, because thou hast left thy first love. Remember therefore from whence thou art fallen, and repent, and do the first works; or else I will come unto thee quickly, and will remove thy candlestick out of his place, except thou repent." Revelation 2:4, 5. The Saviour watches for a response to His offers of love and forgiveness, with a more tender compassion than that which moves the heart of an earthly parent to forgive a wayward, suffering son. He cries after the wanderer, "Return unto Me, and I will return unto you." Malachi 3:7. But if the erring one persistently refuses to heed the voice that calls him with pitying, tender love, he will at last be left in darkness. The heart that has long slighted God's mercy, becomes hardened in sin, and is no longer susceptible to the influence of the grace of God. Fearful will be the doom of that soul of whom the pleading Saviour shall finally declare, he "is joined to idols: let him alone." Hosea 4:17. It will be more tolerable in the day of judgment for the cities of the plain than for those who have known the love of Christ, and yet have turned away to choose the pleasures of a world of sin.

You who are slighting the offers of mercy, think of the long array of figures accumulating against you in the books of heaven; for there is a record kept of the impieties of nations, of families, of individuals. God may bear long while the account goes on, and calls to repentance and offers of pardon may be given; yet a time will come when the account will be full; when the soul's decision has been made; when by his own choice man's destiny has been fixed. Then the signal will be given for judgment to be executed.

There is cause for alarm in the condition of the religious world today. God's mercy has been trifled with. The multitudes make void the law of Jehovah, "teaching for doctrines the commandments of men." Matthew 15:9. Infidelity prevails in many of the churches in our land; not infidelity in its broadest sense—an open denial of the Bible—but an infidelity that is robed in the garb of Christianity, while it is undermining faith in the Bible as a revelation from God. Fervent devotion and vital piety have given place to hollow formalism. As the result, apostasy and sensualism prevail. Christ declared, "As it was in the days of Lot, ... even thus shall it be in the day when the Son of man is revealed." Luke 17:28, 30. The daily record of passing events testifies to the fulfillment of His words. The world is fast becoming ripe for destruction. Soon the judgments of God are to be poured out, and sin and sinners are to be consumed.

Said our Saviour: "Take heed to yourselves, lest at any time your hearts be overcharged with surfeiting, and drunkenness, and cares of this life, and so that day come upon you unawares. For as a snare shall it come on all them that dwell on the face of the whole earth"—upon all whose interests are centered in this world. "Watch ye therefore, and pray always, that ye may be accounted worthy to escape all these things that shall come to pass, and to stand before the Son of man." Luke 21:34-36.

Before the destruction of Sodom, God sent a message to Lot, "Escape for thy life; look not behind thee, neither stay thou in all the plain; escape to the mountain, lest thou be consumed." The same voice of warning was heard by the disciples of Christ before the destruction of Jerusalem: "When ye shall see Jerusalem compassed with armies, then know that the desolation thereof is nigh. Then let them which are in Judea flee to the mountains." Luke 21:20, 21. They must not tarry to secure anything from their possessions, but must make the most of the opportunity to escape.

There was a coming out, a decided separation from the wicked, an escape for life. So it was in the days of Noah; so with Lot; so with the disciples prior to the destruction of Jerusalem; and so it will be in the last days. Again the voice of God is heard in a message of warning, bidding His people separate themselves from the prevailing iniquity.

The state of corruption and apostasy that in the last days would exist in the religious world, was presented to the prophet John in the vision of Babylon, "that great city, which reigneth over the kings of the earth." Revelation 17:18. Before its destruction the call is to be given from heaven, "Come out of her, My people, that ye be not partakers of her sins, and that ye receive not of her plagues." Revelation 18:4. As in the days of Noah and Lot, there must be a marked separation from sin and sinners. There can be no compromise between God and the world, no turning back to secure earthly treasures. "Ye cannot serve God and mammon." Matthew 6:24.

Like the dwellers in the vale of Siddim, the people are dreaming of prosperity and peace. "Escape for thy life," is the warning from the angels of God; but other voices are heard saying, "Be not excited; there is no cause for alarm." The multitudes cry, "Peace and safety," while Heaven declares that swift destruction is about to come upon the transgressor. On the night prior to their destruction, the cities of the plain rioted in pleasure and derided the fears and warnings of the messenger of God; but those scoffers perished in the flames; that very night the door of mercy was forever closed to the wicked, careless inhabitants of Sodom. God will not always be mocked; He will not long be trifled with. "Behold, the day of the Lord cometh, cruel both with wrath and fierce anger, to lay the land desolate: and He shall destroy the sinners thereof out of it." Isaiah 13:9. The great mass of the world will reject God's mercy, and will be overwhelmed in swift and irretrievable ruin. But those who heed the warning shall dwell "in the secret place of the Most High," and "abide under the shadow of the Almighty." His truth shall be their shield and buckler. For them is the promise, "With long life will I satisfy him, and show him My salvation." Psalm 91:1, 4, 16.

Lot dwelt but a short time in Zoar. Iniquity prevailed there as in Sodom, and he feared to remain, lest the city should be destroyed. Not long after, Zoar was consumed, as God had purposed. Lot made his way to the mountains, and abode in a cave, stripped of all for which he had dared to subject his family to the influences of a wicked city. But the curse of Sodom followed him even here. The sinful conduct of his daughters was the result of the evil associations of that vile place. Its moral corruption had become so interwoven with their character that they could not distinguish between good and evil. Lot's only posterity, the Moabites and Ammonites, were vile, idolatrous tribes, rebels against God and bitter enemies of His people.

In how wide contrast to the life of Abraham was that of Lot! Once they had been companions, worshiping at one altar, dwelling side by side in their pilgrim tents; but how widely separated now! Lot had chosen Sodom for its pleasure and profit. Leaving Abraham's altar and its daily sacrifice to the living God, he had permitted his children to mingle with a corrupt and idolatrous people; yet he had retained in his heart the fear of God, for he is declared in the Scriptures to have been a "just" man; his righteous soul was vexed with the vile conversation that greeted his ears daily and the violence and crime he was powerless to prevent. He was saved at last as "a brand plucked out of the fire" (Zechariah 3:2), yet stripped of his possessions, bereaved of his wife and children, dwelling in caves, like the wild beasts, covered with infamy in his old age; and he gave to the world, not a race of righteous men, but two idolatrous nations, at enmity with God and warring upon His people, until, their cup of iniquity being full, they were appointed to destruction. How terrible were the results that followed one unwise step!

Says the wise man, "Labor not to be rich: cease from thine own wisdom." "He that is greedy of gain troubleth his own house; but he that hateth gifts shall live." Proverbs 23:4; 15:27. And the apostle Paul declares, "They that will be rich fall into temptation and a snare, and into many foolish and hurtful lusts, which drown men in destruction and perdition." 1 Timothy 6:9.

When Lot entered Sodom he fully intended to keep himself free from iniquity and to command his household after him. But he signally failed. The corrupting influences about him had an effect upon his own faith, and his children's connection with the inhabitants of Sodom bound up his interest in a measure with theirs. The result is before us.

Many are still making a similar mistake. In selecting a home they look more to the temporal advantages they may gain than to the moral and social influences that will surround themselves and their families. They choose a beautiful and fertile country, or remove to some flourishing city, in the hope of securing greater prosperity; but their children are surrounded by temptation, and too often they form associations that are unfavorable to the development of piety and the formation of a right character. The atmosphere of lax morality, of unbelief, of indifference to religious things, has a tendency to counteract the influence of the parents. Examples of rebellion against parental and divine authority are ever before the youth; many form attachments for infidels and unbelievers, and cast in their lot with the enemies of God.

In choosing a home, God would have us consider, first of all, the moral and religious influences that will surround us and our families. We may be placed in trying positions, for many cannot have their surroundings what they would; and whenever duty calls us, God will enable us to stand uncorrupted, if we watch and pray, trusting in the grace of Christ. But we should not needlessly expose ourselves to influences that are unfavorable to the formation of Christian character. When we voluntarily place ourselves in an atmosphere of worldliness and unbelief, we displease God and drive holy angels from our homes.

Those who secure for their children worldly wealth and honor at the expense of their eternal interests, will find in the end that these advantages are a terrible loss. Like Lot, many see their children ruined, and barely save their own souls. Their lifework is lost; their life is a sad failure. Had they exercised true wisdom, their children might have had less of worldly prosperity, but they would have made sure of a title to the immortal inheritance.

The heritage that God has promised to His people is not in this world. Abraham had no possession in the earth, "no, not so much as to set his foot on." Acts 7:5. He possessed great substance, and he used it to the glory of God and the good of his fellow men; but he did not look upon this world as his home. The Lord had called him to leave his idolatrous countrymen, with the promise of the land of Canaan as an everlasting possession; yet neither he nor his son nor his son's son received it. When Abraham desired a burial place for his dead, he had to buy it of the Canaanites. His sole possession in the Land of Promise was that rock-hewn tomb in the cave of Machpelah.

But the word of God had not failed; neither did it meet its final accomplishment in the occupation of Canaan by the Jewish people. "To Abraham and his seed were the promises made." Galatians 3:16. Abraham himself was to share the inheritance. The fulfillment of God's promise may seem to be long delayed—for "one day is with the Lord as a thousand years, and a thousand years as one day" (2 Peter 3:8); it may appear to tarry; but at the appointed time "it will surely come, it will not tarry." Habakkuk 2:3. The gift to Abraham and his seed included not merely the land of Canaan, but the whole earth. So says the apostle, "The promise, that he should be the *heir of the world*, was not to Abraham, or to his seed, through the law, but through the righteousness of faith." Romans 4:13. And the Bible plainly teaches that the promises made to Abraham are to be fulfilled through Christ. All that are Christ's are "Abraham's seed, and heirs according to the promise"—heirs to "an inheritance incorruptible, and undefiled, and that fadeth not away"—the earth freed from the curse of sin. Galatians 3:29; 1 Peter 1:4. For "the kingdom and dominion, and the greatness of the kingdom under the whole heaven, shall be given to the people of the saints of the Most High;" and "the meek shall inherit the earth; and shall delight themselves in the abundance of peace." Daniel 7:27; Psalm 37:11.

God gave to Abraham a view of this immortal inheritance, and with this hope he was content. "By faith he sojourned in the Land of Promise, as in a strange country, dwelling in tabernacles with Isaac and Jacob, the heirs with him of the same promise: for he looked for a city which hath foundations, whose builder and maker is God." Hebrews 11:9, 10.

Of the posterity of Abraham it is written, "These all died in faith, not having received the promises, but having seen them afar off, and were persuaded of them, and embraced them, and confessed that they were strangers and pilgrims on the earth." Verse 13. We must dwell as pilgrims and strangers here if we would gain "a better country, that is, an heavenly." Verse 16. Those who are children of Abraham will be seeking the city which he looked for, "whose builder and maker is God."

Chapter 15—The Marriage of Isaac [171]

This chapter is based on Genesis 24.

Abraham had become an old man, and expected soon to die; yet one act remained for him to do in securing the fulfillment of the promise to his posterity. Isaac was the one divinely appointed to succeed him as the keeper of the law of God and the father of the chosen people, but he was yet unmarried. The inhabitants of Canaan were given to idolatry, and God had forbidden intermarriage between His people and them, knowing that such marriages would lead to apostasy. The patriarch feared the effect of the corrupting influences surrounding his son. Abraham's habitual faith in God and submission to His will were reflected in the character of Isaac; but the young man's affections were strong, and he was gentle and yielding in disposition. If united with one who did not fear God, he would be in danger of sacrificing principle for the sake of harmony. In the mind of Abraham the choice of a wife for his son was a matter of grave importance; he was anxious to have him marry one who would not lead him from God.

In ancient times marriage engagements were generally made by the parents, and this was the custom among those who worshiped God. None were required to marry those whom they could not love; but in the bestowal of their affections the youth were guided by the judgment of their experienced, God-fearing parents. It was regarded as a dishonor to parents, and even a crime, to pursue a course contrary to this.

Isaac, trusting to his father's wisdom and affection, was satisfied to commit the matter to him, believing also that God Himself would direct in the choice made. The patriarch's thoughts turned to his father's kindred in the land of Mesopotamia. Though not free from idolatry, they cherished the knowledge and the worship of the true God. Isaac must not leave Canaan to go to them, but it might be that among them could be found one who would leave her home and

[172] unite with him in maintaining the pure worship of the living God. Abraham committed the important matter to "his eldest servant," a man of piety, experience, and sound judgment, who had rendered him long and faithful service. He required this servant to make a solemn oath before the Lord, that he would not take a wife for Isaac of the Canaanites, but would choose a maiden from the family of Nahor in Mesopotamia. He charged him not to take Isaac thither. If a damsel could not be found who would leave her kindred, then the messenger would be released from his oath. The patriarch encouraged him in his difficult and delicate undertaking with the assurance that God would crown his mission with success. "The Lord God of heaven," he said, "which took me from my father's house, and from the land of my kindred, ... He shall send His angel before thee."

The messenger set out without delay. Taking with him ten camels for the use of his own company and the bridal party that might return with him, provided also with gifts for the intended wife and her friends, he made the long journey beyond Damascus, and onward to the rich plains that border on the great river of the East. Arrived at Haran, "the city of Nahor," he halted outside the walls, near the well to which the women of the place came at evening for water. It was a time of anxious thought with him. Important results, not only to his master's household, but to future generations, might follow from the choice he made; and how was he to choose wisely among entire strangers? Remembering the words of Abraham, that God would send His angel with him, he prayed earnestly for positive guidance. In the family of his master he was accustomed to the constant exercise of kindness and hospitality, and he now asked that an act of courtesy might indicate the maiden whom God had chosen.

Hardly was the prayer uttered before the answer was given. Among the women who were gathered at the well, the courteous manners of one attracted his attention. As she came from the well, the stranger went to meet her, asking for some water from the pitcher upon her shoulder. The request received a kindly answer, with an offer to draw water for the camels also, a service which it was customary even for the daughters of princes to perform for their fathers' flocks and herds. Thus the desired sign was given. The maiden "was very fair to look upon," and her ready courtesy gave

[173] evidence of a kind heart and an active, energetic nature. Thus far the

divine hand had been with him. After acknowledging her kindness by rich gifts, the messengers asked her parentage, and on learning that she was the daughter of Bethuel, Abraham's nephew, he "bowed down his head, and worshiped the Lord."

The man had asked for entertainment at her father's house, and in his expressions of thanksgiving had revealed the fact of his connection with Abraham. Returning home, the maiden told what had happened, and Laban, her brother, at once hastened to bring the stranger and his attendants to share their hospitality.

Eliezer would not partake of food until he had told his errand, his prayer at the well, with all the circumstances attending it. Then he said, "And now, if ye will deal kindly and truly with my master, tell me: and if not, tell me; that I may turn to the right hand, or to the left." The answer was, "The thing proceedeth from the Lord: we cannot speak unto thee bad or good. Behold, Rebekah is before thee; take her, and go, and let her be thy master's son's wife, as the Lord hath spoken."

After the consent of the family had been obtained, Rebekah herself was consulted as to whether she would go to so great a distance from her father's house, to marry the son of Abraham. She believed, from what had taken place, that God had selected her to be Isaac's wife, and she said, "I will go."

The servant, anticipating his master's joy at the success of his mission, was impatient to be gone; and with the morning they set out on the homeward journey. Abraham dwelt at Beersheba, and Isaac, who had been attending to the flocks in the adjoining country, had returned to his father's tent to await the arrival of the messenger from Haran. "And Isaac went out to meditate in the field at the eventide: and he lifted up his eyes, and saw, and, behold, the camels were coming. And Rebekah lifted up her eyes, and when she saw Isaac, she lighted off the camel. For she had said unto the servant, What man is that that walketh in the field to meet us? And the servant had said, It is my master: therefore she took a veil, and covered herself. And the servant told Isaac all things that he had done. And Isaac brought her into his mother Sarah's tent, and took Rebekah, and she became his wife; and he loved her: and Isaac was comforted after his mother's death."

[174] Abraham had marked the result of the intermarriage of those who feared God and those who feared Him not, from the days of Cain to his own time. The consequences of his own marriage with Hagar, and of the marriage connections of Ishmael and Lot, were before him. The lack of faith on the part of Abraham and Sarah had resulted in the birth of Ishmael, the mingling of the righteous seed with the ungodly. The father's influence upon his son was counteracted by that of the mother's idolatrous kindred and by Ishmael's connection with heathen wives. The jealousy of Hagar, and of the wives whom she chose for Ishmael, surrounded his family with a barrier that Abraham endeavored in vain to overcome.

Abraham's early teachings had not been without effect upon Ishmael, but the influence of his wives resulted in establishing idolatry in his family. Separated from his father, and embittered by the strife and contention of a home destitute of the love and fear of God, Ishmael was driven to choose the wild, marauding life of the desert chief, "his hand" "against every man, and every man's hand against him." Genesis 16:12. In his latter days he repented of his evil ways and returned to his father's God, but the stamp of character given to his posterity remained. The powerful nation descended from him were a turbulent, heathen people, who were ever an annoyance and affliction to the descendants of Isaac.

The wife of Lot was a selfish, irreligious woman, and her influence was exerted to separate her husband from Abraham. But for her, Lot would not have remained in Sodom, deprived of the counsel of the wise, God-fearing patriarch. The influence of his wife and the associations of that wicked city would have led him to apostatize from God had it not been for the faithful instruction he had early received from Abraham. The marriage of Lot and his choice of Sodom for a home were the first links in a chain of events fraught with evil to the world for many generations.

No one who fears God can without danger connect himself with one who fears Him not. "Can two walk together, except they be agreed?" Amos 3:3. The happiness and prosperity of the marriage relation depends upon the unity of the parties; but between the believer and the unbeliever there is a radical difference of tastes, inclinations, and purposes. They are serving two masters, between whom there can be no concord. However pure and correct one's principles may be, the influence of an unbelieving companion will have a tendency to lead away from God.

He who has entered the marriage relation while unconverted, is by his conversion placed under stronger obligation to be faithful to his companion, however widely they may differ in regard to religious faith; yet the claims of God should be placed above every earthly relationship, even though trials and persecution may be the result. With the spirit of love and meekness, this fidelity may have an influence to win the unbelieving one. But the marriage of Christians with the ungodly is forbidden in the Bible. The Lord's direction is, "Be ye not unequally yoked together with unbelievers." 2 Corinthians 6:14, 17, 18.

Isaac was highly honored by God in being made inheritor of the promises through which the world was to be blessed; yet when he was forty years of age he submitted to his father's judgment in appointing his experienced, God-fearing servant to choose a wife for him. And the result of that marriage, as presented in the Scriptures, is a tender and beautiful picture of domestic happiness: "Isaac brought her into his mother Sarah's tent, and took Rebekah, and she became his wife; and he loved her: and Isaac was comforted after his mother's death."

What a contrast between the course of Isaac and that pursued by the youth of our time, even among professed Christians! Young people too often feel that the bestowal of their affections is a matter in which self alone should be consulted—a matter that neither God nor their parents should in any wise control. Long before they have reached manhood or womanhood they think themselves competent to make their own choice, without the aid of their parents. A few years of married life are usually sufficient to show them their error, but often too late to prevent its baleful results. For the same lack of wisdom and self-control that dictated the hasty choice is permitted to aggravate the evil, until the marriage relation becomes a galling yoke. Many have thus wrecked their happiness in this life and their hope of the life to come.

If there is any subject which should be carefully considered and in which the counsel of older and more experienced persons should be sought, it is the subject of marriage; if ever the Bible was needed

[175]

as a counselor, if ever divine guidance should be sought in prayer, it is before taking a step that binds persons together for life.

[176] Parents should never lose sight of their own responsibility for the future happiness of their children. Isaac's deference to his father's judgment was the result of the training that had taught him to love a life of obedience. While Abraham required his children to respect parental authority, his daily life testified that that authority was not a selfish or arbitrary control, but was founded in love, and had their welfare and happiness in view.

Fathers and mothers should feel that a duty devolves upon them to guide the affections of the youth, that they may be placed upon those who will be suitable companions. They should feel it a duty, by their own teaching and example, with the assisting grace of God, to so mold the character of the children from their earliest years that they will be pure and noble and will be attracted to the good and true. Like attracts like; like appreciates like. Let the love for truth and purity and goodness be early implanted in the soul, and the youth will seek the society of those who possess these characteristics.

Let parents seek, in their own character and in their home life, to exemplify the love and beneficence of the heavenly Father. Let the home be full of sunshine. This will be worth far more to your children than lands or money. Let the home love be kept alive in their hearts, that they may look back upon the home of their childhood as a place of peace and happiness next to heaven. The members of the family do not all have the same stamp of character, and there will be frequent occasion for the exercise of patience and forbearance; but through love and self-discipline all may be bound together in the closest union.

True love is a high and holy principle, altogether different in character from that love which is awakened by impulse and which suddenly dies when severely tested. It is by faithfulness to duty in the parental home that the youth are to prepare themselves for homes of their own. Let them here practice self-denial and manifest kindness, courtesy, and Christian sympathy. Thus love will be kept warm in the heart, and he who goes out from such a household to stand at the head of a family of his own will know how to promote the happiness of her whom he has chosen as a companion for life. Marriage, instead of being the end of love, will be only its beginning.

Chapter 16—Jacob and Esau

This chapter is based on Genesis 25:19-24; 27.

Jacob and Esau, the twin sons of Isaac, present a striking contrast, both in character and in life. This unlikeness was foretold by the angel of God before their birth. When in answer to Rebekah's troubled prayer he declared that two sons would be given her, he opened to her their future history, that each would become the head of a mighty nation, but that one would be greater than the other, and that the younger would have the pre-eminence.

Esau grew up loving self-gratification and centering all his interest in the present. Impatient of restraint, he delighted in the wild freedom of the chase, and early chose the life of a hunter. Yet he was the father's favorite. The quiet, peace-loving shepherd was attracted by the daring and vigor of this elder son, who fearlessly ranged over mountain and desert, returning home with game for his father and with exciting accounts of his adventurous life. Jacob, thoughtful, diligent, and care-taking, ever thinking more of the future than the present, was content to dwell at home, occupied in the care of the flocks and the tillage of the soil. His patient perseverance, thrift, and foresight were valued by the mother. His affections were deep and strong, and his gentle, unremitting attentions added far more to her happiness than did the boisterous and occasional kindnesses of Esau. To Rebekah, Jacob was the dearer son.

The promises made to Abraham and confirmed to his son were held by Isaac and Rebekah as the great object of their desires and hopes. With these promises Esau and Jacob were familiar. They were taught to regard the birthright as a matter of great importance, for it included not only an inheritance of worldly wealth but spiritual pre-eminence. He who received it was to be the priest of his family, and in the line of his posterity the Redeemer of the world would come. On the other hand, there were obligations resting upon the possessor of the birthright. He who should inherit its blessings must devote his life to the service of God. Like Abraham, he must be obedient to the divine requirements. In marriage, in his family relations, in public life, he must consult the will of God.

Isaac made known to his sons these privileges and conditions, and plainly stated that Esau, as the eldest, was the one entitled to the birthright. But Esau had no love for devotion, no inclination to a religious life. The requirements that accompanied the spiritual birthright were an unwelcome and even hateful restraint to him. The law of God, which was the condition of the divine covenant with Abraham, was regarded by Esau as a yoke of bondage. Bent on self-indulgence, he desired nothing so much as liberty to do as he pleased. To him power and riches, feasting and reveling, were happiness. He gloried in the unrestrained freedom of his wild, roving life. Rebekah remembered the words of the angel, and she read with clearer insight than did her husband the character of their sons. She was convinced that the heritage of divine promise was intended for Jacob. She repeated to Isaac the angel's words; but the father's affections were centered upon the elder son, and he was unshaken in his purpose.

Jacob had learned from his mother of the divine intimation that the birthright should fall to him, and he was filled with an unspeakable desire for the privileges which it would confer. It was not the possession of his father's wealth that he craved; the spiritual birthright was the object of his longing. To commune with God as did righteous Abraham, to offer the sacrifice of atonement for his family, to be the progenitor of the chosen people and of the promised Messiah, and to inherit the immortal possessions embraced in the blessings of the covenant—here were the privileges and honors that kindled his most ardent desires. His mind was ever reaching forward to the future, and seeking to grasp its unseen blessings.

With secret longing he listened to all that his father told concerning the spiritual birthright; he carefully treasured what he had learned from his mother. Day and night the subject occupied his thoughts, until it became the absorbing interest of his life. But while he thus esteemed eternal above temporal blessings, Jacob had not an experimental knowledge of the God whom he revered. His heart had not been renewed by divine grace. He believed that the promise concerning himself could not be fulfilled so long as Esau retained the rights of the first-born, and he constantly studied to devise some way whereby he might secure the blessing which his brother held so lightly, but which was so precious to himself.

When Esau, coming home one day faint and weary from the chase, asked for the food that Jacob was preparing, the latter, with whom one thought was ever uppermost, seized upon his advantage, and offered to satisfy his brother's hunger at the price of the birthright. "Behold, I am at the point to die," cried the reckless, self-indulgent hunter, "and what profit shall this birthright do to me?" And for a dish of red pottage he parted with his birthright, and confirmed the transaction by an oath. A short time at most would have secured him food in his father's tents, but to satisfy the desire of the moment he carelessly bartered the glorious heritage that God Himself had promised to his fathers. His whole interest was in the present. He was ready to sacrifice the heavenly to the earthly, to exchange a future good for a momentary indulgence.

"Thus Esau despised his birthright." In disposing of it he felt a sense of relief. Now his way was unobstructed; he could do as he liked. For this wild pleasure, miscalled freedom, how many are still selling their birthright to an inheritance pure and undefiled, eternal in the heavens!

Ever subject to mere outward and earthly attractions, Esau took two wives of the daughters of Heth. They were worshipers of false gods, and their idolatry was a bitter grief to Isaac and Rebekah. Esau had violated one of the conditions of the covenant, which forbade intermarriage between the chosen people and the heathen; yet Isaac was still unshaken in his determination to bestow upon him the birthright. The reasoning of Rebekah, Jacob's strong desire for the blessing, and Esau's indifference to its obligations had no effect to change the father's purpose.

Years passed on, until Isaac, old and blind, and expecting soon to die, determined no longer to delay the bestowal of the blessing upon his elder son. But knowing the opposition of Rebekah and Jacob, he decided to perform the solemn ceremony in secret. In accordance with the custom of making a feast upon such occasions, the patriarch bade Esau, "Go out to the field, and take me some venison; and make me savory meat, ... that my soul may bless thee before I die."

Rebekah divined his purpose. She was confident that it was

[180]

contrary to what God had revealed as His will. Isaac was in danger of incurring the divine displeasure and of debarring his younger son from the position to which God had called him. She had in vain tried the effect of reasoning with Isaac, and she determined to resort to stratagem.

No sooner had Esau departed on his errand than Rebekah set about the accomplishment of her purpose. She told Jacob what had taken place, urging the necessity of immediate action to prevent the bestowal of the blessing, finally and irrevocably, upon Esau. And she assured her son that if he would follow her directions, he might obtain it as God had promised. Jacob did not readily consent to the plan that she proposed. The thought of deceiving his father caused him great distress. He felt that such a sin would bring a curse rather than a blessing. But his scruples were overborne, and he proceeded to carry out his mother's suggestions. It was not his intention to utter a direct falsehood, but once in the presence of his father he seemed to have gone too far to retreat, and he obtained by fraud the coveted blessing.

Jacob and Rebekah succeeded in their purpose, but they gained only trouble and sorrow by their deception. God had declared that Jacob should receive the birthright, and His word would have been fulfilled in His own time had they waited in faith for Him to work for them. But like many who now profess to be children of God, they were unwilling to leave the matter in His hands. Rebekah bitterly repented the wrong counsel she had given her son; it was the means of separating him from her, and she never saw his face again. From the hour when he received the birthright, Jacob was weighed down with self-condemnation. He had sinned against his father, his brother, his own soul, and against God. In one short hour he had made work for a lifelong repentance. This scene was vivid before him in afteryears, when the wicked course of his sons oppressed his soul.

No sooner had Jacob left his father's tent than Esau entered. Though he had sold his birthright, and confirmed the transfer by a solemn oath, he was now determined to secure its blessings, regardless of his brother's claim. With the spiritual was connected the temporal birthright, which would give him the headship of the family and possession of a double portion of his father's wealth.

These were blessings that he could value. "Let my father arise," he said, "and eat of his son's venison, that thy soul may bless me."

Trembling with astonishment and distress, the blind old father learned the deception that had been practiced upon him. His long and fondly cherished hopes had been thwarted, and he keenly felt the disappointment that must come upon his elder son. Yet the conviction flashed upon him that it was God's providence which had defeated his purpose and brought about the very thing he had determined to prevent. He remembered the words of the angel to Rebekah, and notwithstanding the sin of which Jacob was now guilty, he saw in him the one best fitted to accomplish the purposes of God. While the words of blessing were upon his lips, he had felt the Spirit of inspiration upon him; and now, knowing all the circumstances, he ratified the benediction unwittingly pronounced upon Jacob: "I have blessed him; yea, and he shall be blessed."

Esau had lightly valued the blessing while it seemed within his reach, but he desired to possess it now that it was gone from him forever. All the strength of his impulsive, passionate nature was aroused, and his grief and rage were terrible. He cried with an exceeding bitter cry, "Bless me, even me also, O my father!" "Hast thou not reserved a blessing for me?" But the promise given was not to be recalled. The birthright which he had so carelessly bartered he could not now regain. "For one morsel of meat," for a momentary gratification of appetite that had never been restrained, Esau sold his inheritance; but when he saw his folly, it was too late to recover the blessing. "He found no place of repentance, though he sought it carefully with tears." Hebrews 12:16, 17. Esau was not shut out from the privilege of seeking God's favor by repentance, but he could find no means of recovering the birthright. His grief did not spring from conviction of sin; he did not desire to be reconciled to God. He sorrowed because of the results of his sin, but not for the sin itself.

Because of his indifference to the divine blessings and requirements, Esau is called in Scripture "a profane person." Verse 16. He represents those who lightly value the redemption purchased for them by Christ, and are ready to sacrifice their heirship to heaven for the perishable things of earth. Multitudes live for the present, with no thought or care for the future. Like Esau they cry, "Let us eat and drink; for tomorrow we die." 1 Corinthians 15:32. They are controlled by inclination; and rather than practice self-denial, they will forgo the most valuable considerations. If one must be relinquished, the gratification of a depraved appetite or the heavenly blessings promised only to the self-denying and God-fearing, the claims of appetite prevail, and God and heaven are virtually despised. How many, even of professed Christians, cling to indulgences that are injurious to health and that benumb the sensibilities of the soul. When the duty is presented of cleansing themselves from all filthiness of the flesh and spirit, perfecting holiness in the fear of God, they are offended. They see that they cannot retain these hurtful gratifications and yet secure heaven, and they conclude that since the way to eternal life is so strait, they will no longer walk therein.

Multitudes are selling their birthright for sensual indulgence. Health is sacrificed, the mental faculties are enfeebled, and heaven is forfeited; and all for a mere temporary pleasure—an indulgence at once both weakening and debasing in its character. As Esau awoke to see the folly of his rash exchange when it was too late to recover his loss, so it will be in the day of God with those who have bartered their heirship to heaven for selfish gratifications.

Chapter 17—Jacob's Flight and Exile

This chapter is based on Genesis 28 to 31.

Threatened with death by the wrath of Esau, Jacob went out from his father's home a fugitive; but he carried with him the father's blessing; Isaac had renewed to him the covenant promise, and had bidden him, as its inheritor, to seek a wife of his mother's family in Mesopotamia. Yet it was with a deeply troubled heart that Jacob set out on his lonely journey. With only his staff in his hand he must travel hundreds of miles through a country inhabited by wild, roving tribes. In his remorse and timidity he sought to avoid men, lest he should be traced by his angry brother. He feared that he had lost forever the blessing that God had purposed to give him; and Satan was at hand to press temptations upon him.

The evening of the second day found him far away from his father's tents. He felt that he was an outcast, and he knew that all this trouble had been brought upon him by his own wrong course. The darkness of despair pressed upon his soul, and he hardly dared to pray. But he was so utterly lonely that he felt the need of protection from God as he had never felt it before. With weeping and deep humiliation he confessed his sin, and entreated for some evidence that he was not utterly forsaken. Still his burdened heart found no relief. He had lost all confidence in himself, and he feared that the God of his fathers had cast him off.

But God did not forsake Jacob. His mercy was still extended to His erring, distrustful servant. The Lord compassionately revealed just what Jacob needed—a Saviour. He had sinned, but his heart was filled with gratitude as he saw revealed a way by which he could be restored to the favor of God.

Wearied with his journey, the wanderer lay down upon the ground, with a stone for his pillow. As he slept he beheld a ladder, bright and shining, whose base rested upon the earth, while the top reached to heaven. Upon this ladder angels were ascending and descending; above it was the Lord of glory, and from the heavens His voice was heard: "I am the Lord God of Abraham thy father, and the God of Isaac." The land whereon he lay as an exile and fugitive was promised to him and to his posterity, with the assurance, "In thee and in thy seed shall all the families of the earth be blessed." This promise had been given to Abraham and to Isaac, and now it was renewed to Jacob. Then in special regard to his present loneliness and distress, the words of comfort and encouragement were spoken: "Behold, I am with thee, and will keep thee in all places whither thou goest, and will bring thee again into this land; for I will not leave thee, until I have done that which I have spoken to thee of."

The Lord knew the evil influences that would surround Jacob, and the perils to which he would be exposed. In mercy He opened up the future before the repentant fugitive, that he might understand the divine purpose with reference to himself, and be prepared to resist the temptations that would surely come to him when alone amid idolaters and scheming men. There would be ever before him the high standard at which he must aim; and the knowledge that through him the purpose of God was reaching its accomplishment, would constantly prompt him to faithfulness.

In the vision the plan of redemption was presented to Jacob, not fully, but in such parts as were essential to him at that time. The mystic ladder revealed to him in his dream was the same to which Christ referred in His conversation with Nathanael. Said He, "Ye shall see heaven open, and the angels of God ascending and descending upon the Son of man." John 1:51. Up to the time of man's rebellion against the government of God, there had been free communion between God and man. But the sin of Adam and Eve separated earth from heaven, so that man could not have communion with his Maker. Yet the world was not left in solitary hopelessness. The ladder represents Jesus, the appointed medium of communication. Had He not with His own merits bridged the gulf that sin had made, the ministering angels could have held no communion with fallen man. Christ connects man in his weakness and helplessness with the source of infinite power.

All this was revealed to Jacob in his dream. Although his mind at once grasped a part of the revelation, its great and mysterious truths were the study of his lifetime, and unfolded to his understanding more and more.

Jacob awoke from his sleep in the deep stillness of night. The shining forms of his vision had disappeared. Only the dim outline of the lonely hills, and above them the heavens bright with stars, now met his gaze. But he had a solemn sense that God was with him. An unseen presence filled the solitude. "Surely the Lord is in this place," he said, "and I knew it not.... This is none other but the house of God, and this is the gate of heaven."

"And Jacob rose up early in the morning, and took the stone that he had put for his pillows, and set it up for a pillar, and poured oil upon the top of it." In accordance with the custom of commemorating important events, Jacob set up a memorial of God's mercy, that whenever he should pass that way he might tarry at this sacred spot to worship the Lord. And he called the place Bethel, or the "house of God." With deep gratitude he repeated the promise that God's presence would be with him; and then he made the solemn vow, "If God will be with me, and will keep me in this way that I go, and will give me bread to eat, and raiment to put on, so that I come again to my father's house in peace; then shall the Lord be my God: and this stone, which I have set for a pillar, shall be God's house: and of all that Thou shalt give me I will surely give the tenth unto Thee."

Jacob was not here seeking to make terms with God. The Lord had already promised him prosperity, and this vow was the outflow of a heart filled with gratitude for the assurance of God's love and mercy. Jacob felt that God had claims upon him which he must acknowledge, and that the special tokens of divine favor granted him demanded a return. So does every blessing bestowed upon us call for a response to the Author of all our mercies. The Christian should often review his past life and recall with gratitude the precious deliverances that God has wrought for him, supporting him in trial, opening ways before him when all seemed dark and forbidding, refreshing him when ready to faint. He should recognize all of them as evidences of the watchcare of heavenly angels. In view of these innumerable blessings he should often ask, with subdued and grateful heart, "What shall I render unto the Lord for all His benefits toward me?" Psalm 116:12.

[185]
[186]
[187]

Our time, our talents, our property, should be sacredly devoted to Him who has given us these blessings in trust. Whenever a special deliverance is wrought in our behalf, or new and unexpected favors are granted us, we should acknowledge God's goodness, not only by expressing our gratitude in words, but, like Jacob, by gifts and offerings to His cause. As we are continually receiving the blessings of God, so we are to be continually giving.

"Of all that Thou shalt give me," said Jacob, "I will surely give the tenth unto Thee." Shall we who enjoy the full light and privileges of the gospel be content to give less to God than was given by those who lived in the former, less favored dispensation? Nay, as the blessings we enjoy are greater, are not our obligations correspondingly increased? But how small the estimate; how vain the endeavor to measure with mathematical rules, time, money, and love, against a love so immeasurable and a gift of such inconceivable worth. Tithes for Christ! Oh, meager pittance, shameful recompense for that which cost so much! From the cross of Calvary, Christ calls for an unreserved consecration. All that we have, all that we are, should be devoted to God.

With a new and abiding faith in the divine promises, and assured of the presence and guardianship of heavenly angels, Jacob pursued his journey to "the land of the children of the East." Genesis 29:1, margin. But how different his arrival from that of Abraham's messenger nearly a hundred years before! The servant had come with a train of attendants riding upon camels, and with rich gifts of gold and silver; the son was a lonely, footsore traveler, with no possession save his staff. Like Abraham's servant, Jacob tarried beside a well, and it was here that he met Rachel, Laban's younger daughter. It was Jacob now who rendered service, rolling the stone from the well and watering the flocks. On making known his kinship, he was welcomed to the home of Laban. Though he came portionless and unattended, a few weeks showed the worth of his diligence and skill, and he was urged to tarry. It was arranged that he should render Laban seven years' service for the hand of Rachel.

In early times custom required the bridegroom, before the ratification of a marriage engagement, to pay a sum of money or its equivalent in other property, according to his circumstances, to the father of his wife. This was regarded as a safeguard to the marriage relation. Fathers did not think it safe to trust the happiness of their daughters to men who had not made provision for the support of a family. If they had not sufficient thrift and energy to manage business and acquire cattle or lands, it was feared that their life would prove worthless. But provision was made to test those who had nothing to pay for a wife. They were permitted to labor for the father whose daughter they loved, the length of time being regulated by the value of the dowry required. When the suitor was faithful in his services, and proved in other respects worthy, he obtained the daughter as his wife; and generally the dowry which the father had received was given her at her marriage. In the case of both Rachel and Leah, however, Laban selfishly retained the dowry that should have been given them; they referred to this when they said, just before the removal from Mesopotamia, "He hath sold us, and hath quite devoured also our money."

The ancient custom, though sometimes abused, as by Laban, was productive of good results. When the suitor was required to render service to secure his bride, a hasty marriage was prevented, and there was opportunity to test the depth of his affections, as well as his ability to provide for a family. In our time many evils result from pursuing an opposite course. It is often the case that persons before marriage have little opportunity to become acquainted with each other's habits and disposition, and, so far as everyday life is concerned, they are virtually strangers when they unite their interests at the altar. Many find, too late, that they are not adapted to each other, and lifelong wretchedness is the result of their union. Often the wife and children suffer from the indolence and inefficiency or the vicious habits of the husband and father. If the character of the suitor had been tested before marriage, according to the ancient custom, great unhappiness might have been prevented.

Seven years of faithful service Jacob gave for Rachel, and the years that he served "seemed unto him but a few days, for the love he had to her." But the selfish and grasping Laban, desiring to retain so valuable a helper, practiced a cruel deception in substituting Leah for Rachel. The fact that Leah herself was a party to the cheat, caused Jacob to feel that he could not love her. His indignant rebuke to Laban was met with the offer of Rachel for another seven years' service. But the father insisted that Leah should not be discarded, since this would bring disgrace upon the family. Jacob was thus placed in a most painful and trying position; he finally decided to retain Leah and marry Rachel. Rachel was ever the one best loved; but his preference for her excited envy and jealousy, and his life was embittered by the rivalry between the sister-wives.

For twenty years Jacob remained in Mesopotamia, laboring in the service of Laban, who, disregarding the ties of kinship, was bent upon securing to himself all the benefits of their connection. Fourteen years of toil he demanded for his two daughters; and during the remaining period, Jacob's wages were ten times changed. Yet Jacob's service was diligent and faithful. His words to Laban in their last interview vividly describe the untiring vigilance which he had given to the interests of his exacting master: "This twenty years have I been with thee; thy ewes and thy she-goats have not cast their young, and the rams of thy flock have I not eaten. That which was torn of beasts I brought not unto thee; I bare the loss of it; of my hand didst thou require it, whether stolen by day, or stolen by night. Thus I was; in the day the drought consumed me, and the frost by night; and my sleep departed from mine eyes."

It was necessary for the shepherd to watch his flocks day and night. They were in danger from robbers, and also from wild beasts, which were numerous and bold, often committing great havoc in flocks that were not faithfully guarded. Jacob had many assistants in caring for the extensive flocks of Laban, but he himself was held responsible for them all. During some portions of the year it was necessary for him to be constantly with the flocks in person, to guard them in the dry season against perishing from thirst, and during the coldest months from becoming chilled with the heavy night frosts. Jacob was the chief shepherd; the servants in his employ were the undershepherds. If any of the sheep were missing, the chief shepherd suffered the loss; and he called the servants to whom he entrusted the care of the flock to a strict account if it was not found in a flourishing condition.

The shepherd's life of diligence and care-taking, and his tender compassion for the helpless creatures entrusted to his charge, have been employed by the inspired writers to illustrate some of the most precious truths of the gospel. Christ, in His relation to His people, is compared to a shepherd. After the Fall He saw His sheep doomed to

Jacob's Flight and Exile

perish in the dark ways of sin. To save these wandering ones He left the honors and glories of His Father's house. He says, "I will seek that which was lost, and bring again that which was driven away, and will bind up that which was broken, and will strengthen that which was sick." I will "save My flock, and they shall no more be a prey." "Neither shall the beast of the land devour them." Ezekiel 34:16, 22, 28. His voice is heard calling them to His fold, "a shadow in the daytime from the heat, and for a place of refuge, and for a covert from storm and from rain." Isaiah 4:6. His care for the flock is unwearied. He strengthens the weak, relieves the suffering, gathers the lambs in His arms, and carries them in His bosom. His sheep love Him. "And a stranger will they not follow, but will flee from him; for they know not the voice of strangers." John 10:5.

Christ says, "The good shepherd giveth his life for the sheep. But he that is an hireling, and not the shepherd, whose own the sheep are not, seeth the wolf coming, and leaveth the sheep, and fleeth; and the wolf catcheth them, and scattereth the sheep. The hireling fleeth, because he is an hireling, and careth not for the sheep. I am the Good Shepherd, and know My sheep, and am known of Mine." Verses 11-14.

Christ, the Chief Shepherd, has entrusted the care of His flock to His ministers as undershepherds; and He bids them have the same interest that He has manifested, and feel the sacred responsibility of the charge He has entrusted to them. He has solemnly commanded them to be faithful, to feed the flock, to strengthen the weak, to revive the fainting, and to shield them from devouring wolves.

To save His sheep, Christ laid down His own life; and He points His shepherds to the love thus manifested, as their example. But "he that is an hireling, ... whose own the sheep are not," has no real interest in the flock. He is laboring merely for gain, and he cares only for himself. He studies his own profit instead of the interest of his charge; and in time of peril or danger he will flee, and leave the flock.

The apostle Peter admonishes the undershepherds: "Feed the flock of God which is among you, taking the oversight thereof, not by constraint, but willingly; not for filthy lucre, but of a ready mind; neither as being lords over God's heritage, but being ensamples to the flock." 1 Peter 5:2, 3. Paul says, "Take heed therefore unto

[191]

yourselves, and to all the flock, over the which the Holy Ghost hath made you overseers, to feed the church of God, which He hath purchased with His own blood. For I know this, that after my departing shall grievous wolves enter in among you, not sparing the flock." Acts 20:28, 29.

All who regard as an unwelcome task the care and burdens that fall to the lot of the faithful shepherd, are reproved by the apostle: "Not by constraint, but willingly; not for filthy lucre, but of a ready mind." 1 Peter 5:2. All such unfaithful servants the Chief Shepherd would willingly release. The church of Christ has been purchased with His blood, and every shepherd should realize that the sheep under his care cost an infinite sacrifice. He should regard them each as of priceless worth, and should be unwearied in his efforts to keep them in a healthy, flourishing condition. The shepherd who is imbued with the spirit of Christ will imitate His self-denying example, constantly laboring for the welfare of his charge; and the flock will prosper under his care.

All will be called to render a strict account of their ministry. The Master will demand of every shepherd, "Where is the flock that was given thee, thy beautiful flock?" Jeremiah 13:20. He that is found faithful, will receive a rich reward. "When the Chief Shepherd shall appear," says the apostle, "ye shall receive a crown of glory that fadeth not away." 1 Peter 5:4.

When Jacob, growing weary of Laban's service, proposed to return to Canaan, he said to his father-in-law, "Send me away, that I may go unto mine own place, and to my country. Give me my wives and my children, for whom I have served thee, and let me go: for thou knowest my service which I have done thee." But Laban urged him to remain, declaring, "I have learned by experience that the Lord hath blessed me for thy sake." He saw that his property was increasing under the care of his son-in-law.

Said Jacob, "It was little which thou hadst before I came, and it is now increased unto a multitude." But as time passed on, Laban became envious of the greater prosperity of Jacob, who "increased exceedingly, and had much cattle, and maidservants, and menservants, and camels, and asses." Laban's sons shared their father's jealousy, and their malicious speeches came to Jacob's ears: He "hath taken away all that was our father's, and of that which was our father's hath he gotten all this glory. And Jacob beheld the countenance of Laban, and, behold, it was not toward him as before."

Jacob would have left his crafty kinsman long before but for the fear of encountering Esau. Now he felt that he was in danger from the sons of Laban, who, looking upon his wealth as their own, might endeavor to secure it by violence. He was in great perplexity and distress, not knowing which way to turn. But mindful of the gracious Bethel promise, he carried his case to God, and sought direction from Him. In a dream his prayer was answered: "Return unto the land of thy fathers, and to thy kindred; and I will be with thee."

Laban's absence afforded opportunity for departure. The flocks and herds were speedily gathered and sent forward, and with his wives, children, and servants, Jacob crossed the Euphrates, urging his way toward Gilead, on the borders of Canaan. After three days Laban learned of their flight, and set forth in pursuit, overtaking the company on the seventh day of their journey. He was hot with anger, and bent on forcing them to return, which he doubted not he could do, since his band was much the stronger. The fugitives were indeed in great peril.

That he did not carry out his hostile purpose was due to the fact that God Himself had interposed for the protection of His servant. "It is in the power of my hand to do you hurt," said Laban, "but the God of your father spake unto me yesternight, saying, Take thou heed that thou speak not to Jacob either good or bad;" that is, he should not force him to return, or urge him by flattering inducements.

Laban had withheld the marriage dowry of his daughters and had ever treated Jacob with craft and harshness; but with characteristic dissimulation he now reproached him for his secret departure, which had given the father no opportunity to make a parting feast or even to bid farewell to his daughters and their children.

In reply Jacob plainly set forth Laban's selfish and grasping policy, and appealed to him as a witness to his own faithfulness and honesty. "Except the God of my father, the God of Abraham, and the fear of Isaac, had been with me," said Jacob, "surely thou hadst sent me away now empty. God hath seen mine affliction, and the labor of my hands, and rebuked thee yesternight."

Laban could not deny the facts brought forward, and he now proposed to enter into a covenant of peace. Jacob consented to the proposal, and a pile of stones was erected as a token of the compact. To this pillar Laban gave the name Mizpah, "watchtower," saying, "The Lord watch between me and thee, when we are absent one from another."

"And Laban said to Jacob, Behold this heap, and behold this pillar, which I have cast betwixt me and thee; this heap be witness, and this pillar be witness, that I will not pass over this heap to thee, and that thou shalt not pass over this heap and this pillar unto me, for harm. The God of Abraham, and the God of Nahor, the God of their father, judge betwixt us. And Jacob sware by the fear of his father Isaac." To confirm the treaty, the parties held a feast. The night was spent in friendly communing; and at the dawn of day, Laban and his company departed. With this separation ceased all trace of connection between the children of Abraham and the dwellers in Mesopotamia.

Chapter 18—The Night of Wrestling [195]

This chapter is based on Genesis 32 and 33.

Though Jacob had left Padan-aram in obedience to the divine direction, it was not without many misgivings that he retraced the road which he had trodden as a fugitive twenty years before. His sin in the deception of his father was ever before him. He knew that his long exile was the direct result of that sin, and he pondered over these things day and night, the reproaches of an accusing conscience making his journey very sad. As the hills of his native land appeared before him in the distance, the heart of the patriarch was deeply moved. All the past rose vividly before him. With the memory of his sin came also the thought of God's favor toward him, and the promises of divine help and guidance.

As he drew nearer his journey's end, the thought of Esau brought many a troubled foreboding. After the flight of Jacob, Esau had regarded himself as the sole heir of their father's possessions. The news of Jacob's return would excite the fear that he was coming to claim the inheritance. Esau was now able to do his brother great injury, if so disposed, and he might be moved to violence against him, not only by the desire for revenge, but in order to secure undisturbed possession of the wealth which he had so long looked upon as his own.

Again the Lord granted Jacob a token of the divine care. As he traveled southward from Mount Gilead, two hosts of heavenly angels seemed to encompass him behind and before, advancing with his company, as if for their protection. Jacob remembered the vision at Bethel so long before, and his burdened heart grew lighter at this evidence that the divine messengers who had brought him hope and courage at his flight from Canaan were to be the guardians of his return. And he said, "This is God's host: and he called the name of that place Mahanaim"—"two hosts, or, camps."

Yet Jacob felt that he had something to do to secure his own safety. He therefore dispatched messengers with a conciliatory greeting to his brother. He instructed them as to the exact words in which they were to address Esau. It had been foretold before the birth of the two brothers that the elder should serve the younger, and, lest the memory of this should be a cause of bitterness, Jacob told the servants they were sent to "my lord Esau;" when brought before him, they were to refer to their master as "thy servant Jacob;" and to remove the fear that he was returning, a destitute wanderer, to claim the paternal inheritance, Jacob was careful to state in his message, "I have oxen, and asses, flocks, and menservants, and womenservants: and I have sent to tell my lord, that I may find grace in thy sight."

But the servants returned with the tidings that Esau was approaching with four hundred men, and no response was sent to the friendly message. It appeared certain that he was coming to seek revenge. Terror pervaded the camp. "Jacob was greatly afraid and distressed." He could not go back, and he feared to advance. His company, unarmed and defenseless, were wholly unprepared for a hostile encounter. He accordingly divided them into two bands, so that if one should be attacked, the other might have an opportunity to escape. He sent from his vast flocks generous presents to Esau, with a friendly message. He did all in his power to atone for the wrong to his brother and to avert the threatened danger, and then in humiliation and repentance he pleaded for divine protection: Thou "saidst unto me, Return unto thy country, and to thy kindred, and I will deal well with thee: I am not worthy of the least of all the mercies, and of all the truth, which Thou hast showed unto Thy servant; for with my staff I passed over this Jordan; and now I am become two bands. Deliver me, I pray Thee, from the hand of my brother, from the hand of Esau: for I fear him, lest he will come and smite me, and the mother with the children."

They had now reached the river Jabbok, and as night came on, Jacob sent his family across the ford of the river, while he alone remained behind. He had decided to spend the night in prayer, and he desired to be alone with God. God could soften the heart of Esau. In Him was the patriarch's only hope.

It was in a lonely, mountainous region, the haunt of wild beasts and the lurking place of robbers and murderers. Solitary and unprotected, Jacob bowed in deep distress upon the earth. It was midnight. All that made life dear to him were at a distance, exposed to danger and death. Bitterest of all was the thought that it was his own sin which had brought this peril upon the innocent. With earnest cries and tears he made his prayer before God. Suddenly a strong hand was laid upon him. He thought that an enemy was seeking his life, and he endeavored to wrest himself from the grasp of his assailant. In the darkness the two struggled for the mastery. Not a word was spoken, but Jacob put forth all his strength, and did not relax his efforts for a moment. While he was thus battling for his life, the sense of his guilt pressed upon his soul; his sins rose up before him, to shut him out from God. But in his terrible extremity he remembered God's promises, and his whole heart went out in entreaty for His mercy. The struggle continued until near the break of day, when the stranger placed his finger upon Jacob's thigh, and he was crippled instantly. The patriarch now discerned the character of his antagonist. He knew that he had been in conflict with a heavenly messenger, and this was why his almost superhuman effort had not gained the victory. It was Christ, "the Angel of the covenant," who had revealed Himself to Jacob. The patriarch was now disabled and suffering the keenest pain, but he would not loosen his hold. All penitent and broken, he clung to the Angel; "he wept, and made supplication" (Hosea 12:4), pleading for a blessing. He must have the assurance that his sin was pardoned. Physical pain was not sufficient to divert his mind from this object. His determination grew stronger, his faith more earnest and persevering, until the very last. The Angel tried to release Himself; He urged, "Let Me go, for the day breaketh;" but Jacob answered, "I will not let Thee go, except Thou bless me." Had this been a boastful, presumptuous confidence, Jacob would have been instantly destroyed; but his was the assurance of one who confesses his own unworthiness, yet trusts the faithfulness of a covenant-keeping God.

Jacob "had power over the Angel, and prevailed." Hosea 12:4. Through humiliation, repentance, and self-surrender, this sinful, erring mortal prevailed with the Majesty of heaven. He had fastened his trembling grasp upon the promises of God, and the heart of Infinite Love could not turn away the sinner's plea.

The error that had led to Jacob's sin in obtaining the birthright by fraud was now clearly set before him. He had not trusted God's promises, but had sought by his own efforts to bring about that which God would have accomplished in His own time and way. As an evidence that he had been forgiven, his name was changed from one that was a reminder of his sin, to one that commemorated his victory. "Thy name," said the Angel, "shall be called no more Jacob [the supplanter], but Israel: for as a prince hast thou power with God and with men, and hast prevailed."

Jacob had received the blessing for which his soul had longed. His sin as a supplanter and deceiver had been pardoned. The crisis in his life was past. Doubt, perplexity, and remorse had embittered his existence, but now all was changed; and sweet was the peace of reconciliation with God. Jacob no longer feared to meet his brother. God, who had forgiven his sin, could move the heart of Esau also to accept his humiliation and repentance.

While Jacob was wrestling with the Angel, another heavenly messenger was sent to Esau. In a dream, Esau beheld his brother for twenty years an exile from his father's house; he witnessed his grief at finding his mother dead; he saw him encompassed by the hosts of God. This dream was related by Esau to his soldiers, with the charge not to harm Jacob, for the God of his father was with him.

The two companies at last approached each other, the desert chief leading his men of war, and Jacob with his wives and children, attended by shepherds and handmaidens, and followed by long lines of flocks and herds. Leaning upon his staff, the patriarch went forward to meet the band of soldiers. He was pale and disabled from his recent conflict, and he walked slowly and painfully, halting at every step; but his countenance was lighted up with joy and peace.

At sight of that crippled sufferer, "Esau ran to meet him, and embraced him, and fell on his neck, and kissed him: and they wept." As they looked upon the scene, even the hearts of Esau's rude soldiers were touched. Notwithstanding he had told them of his dream, they could not account for the change that had come over their captain. Though they beheld the patriarch's infirmity, they little thought that this his weakness had been made his strength.

In his night of anguish beside the Jabbok, when destruction seemed just before him, Jacob had been taught how vain is the help of man, how groundless is all trust in human power. He saw that his only help must come from Him against whom he had so grievously sinned. Helpless and unworthy, he pleaded God's promise of mercy to the repentant sinner. That promise was his assurance that God would pardon and accept him. Sooner might heaven and earth pass than that word could fail; and it was this that sustained him through that fearful conflict.

Jacob's experience during that night of wrestling and anguish represents the trial through which the people of God must pass just before Christ's second coming. The prophet Jeremiah, in holy vision looking down to this time, said, "We have heard a voice of trembling, of fear, and not of peace.... All faces are turned into paleness. Alas! for that day is great, so that none is like it: it is even the time of Jacob's trouble; but he shall be saved out of it." Jeremiah 30:5-7.

When Christ shall cease His work as mediator in man's behalf, then this time of trouble will begin. Then the case of every soul will have been decided, and there will be no atoning blood to cleanse from sin. When Jesus leaves His position as man's intercessor before God, the solemn announcement is made, "He that is unjust, let him be unjust still: and he which is filthy, let him be filthy still: and he that is righteous, let him be righteous still: and he that is holy, let him be holy still." Revelation 22:11. Then the restraining Spirit of God is withdrawn from the earth. As Jacob was threatened with death by his angry brother, so the people of God will be in peril from the wicked who are seeking to destroy them. And as the patriarch wrestled all night for deliverance from the hand of Esau, so the righteous will cry to God day and night for deliverance from the enemies that surround them.

Satan had accused Jacob before the angels of God, claiming the right to destroy him because of his sin; he had moved upon Esau to march against him; and during the patriarch's long night of wrestling, Satan endeavored to force upon him a sense of his guilt, in order to discourage him, and break his hold upon God. When in his distress Jacob laid hold of the Angel, and made supplication with tears, the heavenly Messenger, in order to try his faith, also reminded him of his sin, and endeavored to escape from him. But Jacob would not be turned away. He had learned that God is merciful, and he cast himself upon His mercy. He pointed back to his repentance for his sin, and pleaded for deliverance. As he reviewed his life, he was driven almost to despair; but he held fast the Angel, and with earnest, agonizing cries urged his petition until he prevailed.

Such will be the experience of God's people in their final struggle with the powers of evil. God will test their faith, their perseverance, their confidence in His power to deliver them. Satan will endeavor to terrify them with the thought that their cases are hopeless; that their sins have been too great to receive pardon. They will have a deep sense of their shortcomings, and as they review their lives their hopes will sink. But remembering the greatness of God's mercy, and their own sincere repentance, they will plead His promises made through Christ to helpless, repenting sinners. Their faith will not fail because their prayers are not immediately answered. They will lay hold of the strength of God, as Jacob laid hold of the Angel, and the language of their souls will be, "I will not let Thee go, except Thou bless me."

Had not Jacob previously repented of his sin in obtaining the birthright by fraud, God could not have heard his prayer and mercifully preserved his life. So in the time of trouble, if the people of God had unconfessed sins to appear before them while tortured with fear and anguish, they would be overwhelmed; despair would cut off their faith, and they could not have confidence to plead with God for deliverance. But while they have a deep sense of their unworthiness, they will have no concealed wrongs to reveal. Their sins will have been blotted out by the atoning blood of Christ, and they cannot bring them to remembrance.

Satan leads many to believe that God will overlook their unfaithfulness in the minor affairs of life; but the Lord shows in His dealing with Jacob that He can in no wise sanction or tolerate evil. All who endeavor to excuse or conceal their sins, and permit them to remain upon the books of heaven, unconfessed and unforgiven, will be overcome by Satan. The more exalted their profession, and the more honorable the position which they hold, the more grievous is their course in the sight of God, and the more certain the triumph of the great adversary.

Yet Jacob's history is an assurance that God will not cast off those who have been betrayed into sin, but who have returned unto Him with true repentance. It was by self-surrender and confiding faith that Jacob gained what he had failed to gain by conflict in his own strength. God thus taught His servant that divine power and grace alone could give him the blessing he craved. Thus it will be with those who live in the last days. As dangers surround them, and despair seizes upon the soul, they must depend solely upon the merits of the atonement. We can do nothing of ourselves. In all our helpless unworthiness we must trust in the merits of the crucified and risen Saviour. None will ever perish while they do this. The long, black catalogue of our delinquencies is before the eye of the Infinite. The register is complete; none of our offenses are forgotten. But He who listened to the cries of His servants of old, will hear the prayer of faith and pardon our transgressions. He has promised, and He will fulfill His word.

Jacob prevailed because he was persevering and determined. His experience testifies to the power of importunate prayer. It is now that we are to learn this lesson of prevailing prayer, of unyielding faith. The greatest victories to the church of Christ or to the individual Christian are not those that are gained by talent or education, by wealth or the favor of men. They are those victories that are gained in the audience chamber with God, when earnest, agonizing faith lays hold upon the mighty arm of power.

Those who are unwilling to forsake every sin and to seek earnestly for God's blessing, will not obtain it. But all who will lay hold of God's promises as did Jacob, and be as earnest and persevering as he was, will succeed as he succeeded. "Shall not God avenge His own elect, which cry day and night unto Him, though He bear long with them? I tell you that He will avenge them speedily." Luke 18:7, 8.

Chapter 19—The Return to Canaan

This chapter is based on Genesis 34; 35; 37.

Crossing the Jordan, "Jacob came in peace to the city of Shechem, which is in the land of Canaan." Genesis 33:18, R.V. Thus the patriarch's prayer at Bethel, that God would bring him again in peace to his own land, had been granted. For a time he dwelt in the vale of Shechem. It was here that Abraham, more than a hundred years before, had made his first encampment and erected his first altar in the Land of Promise. Here Jacob "bought the parcel of ground where he had spread his tent, at the hand of the children of Hamor, Shechem's father, for a hundred pieces of money. And he erected there an altar, and called it El-elohe-Israel" (verses 19, 20)—"God, the God of Israel." Like Abraham, Jacob set up beside his tent an altar unto the Lord, calling the members of his household to the morning and the evening sacrifice. It was here also that he dug the well to which, seventeen centuries later, came Jacob's Son and Saviour, and beside which, resting during the noontide heat, He told His wondering hearers of that "well of water springing up into everlasting life." John 4:14.

The tarry of Jacob and his sons at Shechem ended in violence and bloodshed. The one daughter of the household had been brought to shame and sorrow, two brothers were involved in the guilt of murder, a whole city had been given to ruin and slaughter, in retaliation for the lawless deed of one rash youth. The beginning that led to results so terrible was the act of Jacob's daughter, who "went out to see the daughters of the land," thus venturing into association with the ungodly. He who seeks pleasure among those that fear not God is placing himself on Satan's ground and inviting his temptations.

The treacherous cruelty of Simeon and Levi was not unprovoked; yet in their course toward the Shechemites they committed a grievous sin. They had carefully concealed from Jacob their intentions, and the tidings of their revenge filled him with horror. Heartsick at the deceit and violence of his sons, he only said, "Ye have troubled me to make me to stink among the inhabitants of the land: ... and I being few in number, they shall gather themselves together against me, and slay me; and I shall be destroyed, I and my house." But the grief and abhorrence with which he regarded their bloody deed is shown by the words in which, nearly fifty years later, he referred to it, as he lay upon his deathbed in Egypt: "Simeon and Levi are brethren; instruments of cruelty are in their habitations. O my soul, come not thou into their secret; unto their assembly, mine honor, be not thou united.... Cursed be their anger, for it was fierce; and their wrath, for it was cruel." Genesis 49:5-7.

Jacob felt that there was cause for deep humiliation. Cruelty and falsehood were manifest in the character of his sons. There were false gods in the camp, and idolatry had to some extent gained a foothold even in his household. Should the Lord deal with them according to their deserts, would He not leave them to the vengeance of the surrounding nations?

While Jacob was thus bowed down with trouble, the Lord directed him to journey southward to Bethel. The thought of this place reminded the patriarch not only of his vision of the angels and of God's promises of mercy, but also of the vow which he had made there, that the Lord should be his God. He determined that before going to this sacred spot his household should be freed from the defilement of idolatry. He therefore gave direction to all in the encampment, "Put away the strange gods that are among you, and be clean, and change your garments: and let us arise, and go up to Bethel; and I will make there an altar unto God, who answered me in the day of my distress, and was with me in the way which I went."

With deep emotion Jacob repeated the story of his first visit to Bethel, when he left his father's tent a lonely wanderer, fleeing for his life, and how the Lord had appeared to him in the night vision. As he reviewed the wonderful dealings of God with him, his own heart was softened, his children also were touched by a subduing power; he had taken the most effectual way to prepare them to join in the worship of God when they should arrive at Bethel. "And they gave unto Jacob all the strange gods which were in their hand, and all their earrings which were in their ears; and Jacob hid them under the oak which was by Shechem."

God caused a fear to rest upon the inhabitants of the land, so that they made no attempt to avenge the slaughter at Shechem. The travelers reached Bethel unmolested. Here the Lord again appeared to Jacob and renewed to him the covenant promise. "And Jacob set up a pillar in the place where He talked with him, even a pillar of stone."

At Bethel, Jacob was called to mourn the loss of one who had long been an honored member of his father's family—Rebekah's nurse, Deborah, who had accompanied her mistress from Mesopotamia to the land of Canaan. The presence of this aged woman had been to Jacob a precious tie that bound him to his early life, and especially to the mother whose love for him had been so strong and tender. Deborah was buried with expressions of so great sorrow that the oak under which her grave was made, was called "the oak of weeping." It should not be passed unnoticed that the memory of her life of faithful service and of the mourning over this household friend has been accounted worthy to be preserved in the word of God.

From Bethel it was only a two days' journey to Hebron, but it brought to Jacob a heavy grief in the death of Rachel. Twice seven years' service he had rendered for her sake, and his love had made the toil but light. How deep and abiding that love had been, was shown when long afterward, as Jacob in Egypt lay near his death, Joseph came to visit his father, and the aged patriarch, glancing back upon his own life, said, "As for me, when I came from Padan, Rachel died by me in the land of Canaan in the way, when yet there was but a little way to come unto Ephrath: and I buried her there in the way of Ephrath." Genesis 48:7. In the family history of his long and troubled life the loss of Rachel was alone recalled.

Before her death Rachel gave birth to a second son. With her parting breath she named the child Benoni, "son of my sorrow." But his father called him Benjamin, "son of my right hand," or "my strength." Rachel was buried where she died, and a pillar was raised upon the spot to perpetuate her memory.

On the way to Ephrath another dark crime stained the family of Jacob, causing Reuben, the first-born son, to be denied the privileges and honors of the birthright.

At last Jacob came to his journey's end, "unto Isaac his father unto Mamre, ... which is Hebron, where Abraham and Isaac sojourned." Here he remained during the closing years of his father's life. To Isaac, infirm and blind, the kind attentions of this long-absent son were a comfort during years of loneliness and bereavement.

Jacob and Esau met at the deathbed of their father. Once the elder brother had looked forward to this event as an opportunity for revenge, but his feelings had since greatly changed. And Jacob, well content with the spiritual blessings of the birthright, resigned to the elder brother the inheritance of their father's wealth—the only inheritance that Esau sought or valued. They were no longer estranged by jealousy or hatred, yet they parted, Esau removing to Mount Seir. God, who is rich in blessing, had granted to Jacob worldly wealth, in addition to the higher good that he had sought. The possessions of the two brothers "were more than that they might dwell together; and the land wherein they were strangers could not bear them because of their cattle." This separation was in accordance with the divine purpose concerning Jacob. Since the brothers differed so greatly in regard to religious faith, it was better for them to dwell apart.

Esau and Jacob had alike been instructed in the knowledge of God, and both were free to walk in His commandments and to receive His favor; but they had not both chosen to do this. The two brothers had walked in different ways, and their paths would continue to diverge more and more widely.

There was no arbitrary choice on the part of God by which Esau was shut out from the blessings of salvation. The gifts of His grace through Christ are free to all. There is no election but one's own by which any may perish. God has set forth in His word the conditions upon which every soul will be elected to eternal life—obedience to His commandments, through faith in Christ. God has elected a character in harmony with His law, and anyone who shall reach the standard of His requirement will have an entrance into the kingdom of glory. Christ Himself said, "He that believeth on the Son hath everlasting life: and he that believeth not the Son shall not see life." John 3:36. "Not everyone that saith unto Me, Lord, Lord, shall enter into the kingdom of heaven; but he that *doeth the will of My Father* which is in heaven." Matthew 7:21. And in the Revelation He declares, "Blessed are they that do His commandments, that they may have right to the tree of life, and may enter in through the gates into the city." Revelation 22:14. As regards man's final salvation, this is the only election brought to view in the word of God.

Every soul is elected who will work out his own salvation with fear and trembling. He is elected who will put on the armor and fight the good fight of faith. He is elected who will watch unto prayer, who will search the Scriptures, and flee from temptation. He is elected who will have faith continually, and who will be obedient to every word that proceedeth out of the mouth of God. The *provisions* of redemption are free to all; the *results* of redemption will be enjoyed by those who have complied with the conditions.

Esau had despised the blessings of the covenant. He had valued temporal above spiritual good, and he had received that which he desired. It was by his own deliberate choice that he was separated from the people of God. Jacob had chosen the inheritance of faith. He had endeavored to obtain it by craft, treachery, and falsehood; but God had permitted his sin to work out its correction. Yet through all the bitter experience of his later years, Jacob had never swerved from his purpose or renounced his choice. He had learned that in resorting to human skill and craft to secure the blessing, he had been warring against God. From that night of wrestling beside the Jabbok, Jacob had come forth a different man. Self-confidence had been uprooted. Henceforth the early cunning was no longer seen. In place of craft and deception, his life was marked by simplicity and truth. He had learned the lesson of simple reliance upon the Almighty Arm, and amid trial and affliction he bowed in humble submission to the will of God. The baser elements of character were consumed in the furnace fire, the true gold was refined, until the faith of Abraham and Isaac appeared undimmed in Jacob.

The sin of Jacob, and the train of events to which it led, had not failed to exert an influence for evil—an influence that revealed its bitter fruit in the character and life of his sons. As these sons arrived at manhood they developed serious faults. The results of polygamy were manifest in the household. This terrible evil tends to dry up the very springs of love, and its influence weakens the most sacred ties. The jealousy of the several mothers had embittered the family relation, the children had grown up contentious and impatient of control, and the father's life was darkened with anxiety and grief.

There was one, however, of a widely different character—the elder son of Rachel, Joseph, whose rare personal beauty seemed but to reflect an inward beauty of mind and heart. Pure, active, and joyous, the lad gave evidence also of moral earnestness and firmness. He listened to his father's instructions, and loved to obey God. The qualities that afterward distinguished him in Egypt—gentleness, fidelity, and truthfulness—were already manifest in his daily life. His mother being dead, his affections clung the more closely to the father, and Jacob's heart was bound up in this child of his old age. He "loved Joseph more than all his children."

But even this affection was to become a cause of trouble and sorrow. Jacob unwisely manifested his preference for Joseph, and this excited the jealousy of his other sons. As Joseph witnessed the evil conduct of his brothers, he was greatly troubled; he ventured gently to remonstrate with them, but only aroused still further their hatred and resentment. He could not endure to see them sinning against God, and he laid the matter before his father, hoping that his authority might lead them to reform.

Jacob carefully avoided exciting their anger by harshness or severity. With deep emotion he expressed his solicitude for his children, and implored them to have respect for his gray hairs, and not to bring reproach upon his name, and above all not to dishonor God by such disregard of His precepts. Ashamed that their wickedness was known, the young men seemed to be repentant, but they only concealed their real feelings, which were rendered more bitter by this exposure.

The father's injudicious gift to Joseph of a costly coat, or tunic, such as was usually worn by persons of distinction, seemed to them another evidence of his partiality, and excited a suspicion that he intended to pass by his elder children, to bestow the birthright upon the son of Rachel. Their malice was still further increased as the boy one day told them of a dream that he had had. "Behold," he said, "we were binding sheaves in the field, and, lo, my sheaf arose, and also stood upright; and, behold, your sheaves stood round about, and made obeisance to my sheaf."

"Shalt thou indeed reign over us? or shalt thou indeed have dominion over us?" exclaimed his brothers in envious anger.

[210]

Soon he had another dream, of similar import, which he also related: "Behold, the sun and the moon and the eleven stars made obeisance to me." This dream was interpreted as readily as the first. The father, who was present, spoke reprovingly—"What is this dream that thou hast dreamed? Shall I and thy mother and thy brethren indeed come to bow down ourselves to thee to the earth?" Notwithstanding the apparent severity of his words, Jacob believed that the Lord was revealing the future to Joseph.

As the lad stood before his brothers, his beautiful countenance lighted up with the Spirit of inspiration, they could not withhold their admiration; but they did not choose to renounce their evil ways, and they hated the purity that reproved their sins. The same spirit that actuated Cain was kindling in their hearts.

The brothers were obliged to move from place to place to secure pasturage for their flocks, and frequently they were absent from home for months together. After the circumstances just related, they went to the place which their father had bought at Shechem. Some time passed, bringing no tidings from them, and the father began to fear for their safety, on account of their former cruelty toward the Shechemites. He therefore sent Joseph to find them, and bring him words as to their welfare. Had Jacob known the real feeling of his sons toward Joseph, he would not have trusted him alone with them; but this they had carefully concealed.

With a joyful heart, Joseph parted from his father, neither the aged man nor the youth dreaming of what would happen before they should meet again. When, after his long and solitary journey, Joseph arrived at Shechem, his brothers and their flocks were not to be found. Upon inquiring for them, he was directed to Dothan. He had already traveled more than fifty miles, and now an additional distance of fifteen lay before him, but he hastened on, forgetting his weariness in the thought of relieving the anxiety of his father, and meeting the brothers, whom, despite their unkindness, he still loved.

His brothers saw him approaching; but no thought of the long journey he had made to meet them, of his weariness and hunger, of his claims upon their hospitality and brotherly love, softened the bitterness of their hatred. The sight of the coat, the token of their father's love, filled them with frenzy. "Behold, this dreamer cometh," they cried in mockery. Envy and revenge, long secretly cherished, now controlled them. "Let us slay him," they said, "and cast him into some pit, and we will say, Some evil beast hath devoured him; and we shall see what will become of his dreams."

They would have executed their purpose but for Reuben. He shrank from participating in the murder of his brother, and proposed that Joseph be cast alive into a pit, and left there to perish; secretly intending, however, to rescue him and return him to his father. Having persuaded all to consent to this plan, Reuben left the company, fearing that he might fail to control his feelings, and that his real intentions would be discovered.

Joseph came on, unsuspicious of danger, and glad that the object of his long search was accomplished; but instead of the expected greeting, he was terrified by the angry and revengeful glances which he met. He was seized and his coat stripped from him. Taunts and threats revealed a deadly purpose. His entreaties were unheeded. He was wholly in the power of those maddened men. Rudely dragging him to a deep pit, they thrust him in, and having made sure that there was no possibility of his escape, they left him there to perish from hunger, while they "sat down to eat bread."

But some of them were ill at ease; they did not feel the satisfaction they had anticipated from their revenge. Soon a company of travelers was seen approaching. It was a caravan of Ishmaelites from beyond Jordan, on their way to Egypt with spices and other merchandise. Judah now proposed to sell their brother to these heathen traders instead of leaving him to die. While he would be effectually put out of their way, they would remain clear of his blood; "for," he urged, "he is our brother and our flesh." To this proposition all agreed, and Joseph was quickly drawn out of the pit.

As he saw the merchants the dreadful truth flashed upon him. To become a slave was a fate more to be feared than death. In an agony of terror he appealed to one and another of his brothers, but in vain. Some were moved with pity, but fear of derision kept them silent; all felt that they had now gone too far to retreat. If Joseph were spared, he would doubtless report them to the father, who would not overlook their cruelty toward his favorite son. Steeling their hearts against his entreaties, they delivered him into the hands of the heathen traders. The caravan moved on, and was soon lost to view.

[212]

Reuben returned to the pit, but Joseph was not there. In alarm and self-reproach he rent his garments, and sought his brothers, exclaiming, "The child is not; and I, whither shall I go?" Upon learning the fate of Joseph, and that it would now be impossible to recover him, Reuben was induced to unite with the rest in the attempt to conceal their guilt. Having killed a kid, they dipped Joseph's coat in its blood, and took it to their father, telling him that they had found it in the fields, and that they feared it was their brother's. "Know now," they said, "whether it be thy son's coat or no." They had looked forward to this scene with dread, but they were not prepared for the heart-rending anguish, the utter abandonment of grief, which they were compelled to witness. "It is my son's coat," said Jacob; "an evil beast hath devoured him. Joseph is without doubt rent in pieces." Vainly his sons and daughters attempted to comfort him. He "rent his clothes, and put sackcloth upon his loins, and mourned for his son many days." Time seemed to bring no alleviation of his grief. "I will go down into the grave unto my son mourning," was his despairing cry. The young men, terrified at what they had done, yet dreading their father's reproaches, still hid in their own hearts the knowledge of their guilt, which even to themselves seemed very great.

Chapter 20—Joseph in Egypt

This chapter is based on Genesis 39 to 41.

Meanwhile, Joseph with his captors was on the way to Egypt. As the caravan journeyed southward toward the borders of Canaan, the boy could discern in the distance the hills among which lay his father's tents. Bitterly he wept at thought of that loving father in his loneliness and affliction. Again the scene at Dothan came up before him. He saw his angry brothers and felt their fierce glances bent upon him. The stinging, insulting words that had met his agonized entreaties were ringing in his ears. With a trembling heart he looked forward to the future. What a change in situation—from the tenderly cherished son to the despised and helpless slave! Alone and friendless, what would be his lot in the strange land to which he was going? For a time Joseph gave himself up to uncontrolled grief and terror.

But, in the providence of God, even this experience was to be a blessing to him. He had learned in a few hours that which years might not otherwise have taught him. His father, strong and tender as his love had been, had done him wrong by his partiality and indulgence. This unwise preference had angered his brothers and provoked them to the cruel deed that had separated him from his home. Its effects were manifest also in his own character. Faults had been encouraged that were now to be corrected. He was becoming self-sufficient and exacting. Accustomed to the tenderness of his father's care, he felt that he was unprepared to cope with the difficulties before him, in the bitter, uncared-for life of a stranger and a slave.

Then his thoughts turned to his father's God. In his childhood he had been taught to love and fear Him. Often in his father's tent he had listened to the story of the vision that Jacob saw as he fled from his home an exile and a fugitive. He had been told of the Lord's promises to Jacob, and how they had been fulfilled—how, in the hour of need, the angels of God had come to instruct, comfort, and protect him. And he had learned of the love of God in providing for men a Redeemer. Now all these precious lessons came vividly before him. Joseph believed that the God of his fathers would be his God. He then and there gave himself fully to the Lord, and he prayed that the Keeper of Israel would be with him in the land of his exile.

His soul thrilled with the high resolve to prove himself true to God—under all circumstances to act as became a subject of the King of heaven. He would serve the Lord with undivided heart; he would meet the trials of his lot with fortitude and perform every duty with fidelity. One day's experience had been the turning point in Joseph's life. Its terrible calamity had transformed him from a petted child to a man, thoughtful, courageous, and self-possessed.

Arriving in Egypt, Joseph was sold to Potiphar, captain of the king's guard, in whose service he remained for ten years. He was here exposed to temptations of no ordinary character. He was in the midst of idolatry. The worship of false gods was surrounded by all the pomp of royalty, supported by the wealth and culture of the most highly civilized nation then in existence. Yet Joseph preserved his simplicity and his fidelity to God. The sights and sounds of vice were all about him, but he was as one who saw and heard not. His thoughts were not permitted to linger upon forbidden subjects. The desire to gain the favor of the Egyptians could not cause him to conceal his principles. Had he attempted to do this, he would have been overcome by temptation; but he was not ashamed of the religion of his fathers, and he made no effort to hide the fact that he was a worshiper of Jehovah.

"And the Lord was with Joseph, and he was a prosperous man.... And his master saw that the Lord was with him, and that the Lord made all that he did to prosper in his hand." Potiphar's confidence in Joseph increased daily, and he finally promoted him to be his steward, with full control over all his possessions. "And he left all that he had in Joseph's hand; and he knew not aught he had, save the bread which he did eat."

The marked prosperity which attended everything placed under Joseph's care was not the result of a direct miracle; but his industry, care, and energy were crowned with the divine blessing. Joseph attributed his success to the favor of God, and even his idolatrous master accepted this as the secret of his unparalleled prosperity. Without steadfast, well-directed effort, however, success could never have been attained. God was glorified by the faithfulness of His servant. It was His purpose that in purity and uprightness the believer in God should appear in marked contrast to the worshipers of idols—that thus the light of heavenly grace might shine forth amid the darkness of heathenism.

Joseph's gentleness and fidelity won the heart of the chief captain, who came to regard him as a son rather than a slave. The youth was brought in contact with men of rank and learning, and he acquired a knowledge of science, of languages, and of affairs—an education needful to the future prime minister of Egypt.

But Joseph's faith and integrity were to be tested by fiery trials. His master's wife endeavored to entice the young man to transgress the law of God. Heretofore he had remained untainted by the corruption teeming in that heathen land; but this temptation, so sudden, so strong, so seductive—how should it be met? Joseph knew well what would be the consequence of resistance. On the one hand were concealment, favor, and rewards; on the other, disgrace, imprisonment, perhaps death. His whole future life depended upon the decision of the moment. Would principle triumph? Would Joseph still be true to God? With inexpressible anxiety, angels looked upon the scene.

Joseph's answer reveals the power of religious principle. He would not betray the confidence of his master on earth, and, whatever the consequences, he would be true to his Master in heaven. Under the inspecting eye of God and holy angels many take liberties of which they would not be guilty in the presence of their fellow men, but Joseph's first thought was of God. "How ... can I do this great wickedness, and sin against God?" he said.

If we were to cherish an habitual impression that God sees and hears all that we do and say and keeps a faithful record of our words and actions, and that we must meet it all, we would fear to sin. Let the young ever remember that wherever they are, and whatever they do, they are in the presence of God. No part of our conduct escapes observation. We cannot hide our ways from the Most High. Human laws, though sometimes severe, are often transgressed without detection, and hence with impunity. But not so with the law of God. The deepest midnight is no cover for the guilty one. He may think himself alone, but to every deed there is an unseen witness. The very motives of his heart are open to divine inspection. Every act, every word, every thought, is as distinctly marked as though there were only one person in the whole world, and the attention of heaven were centered upon him.

Joseph suffered for his integrity, for his tempter revenged herself by accusing him of a foul crime, and causing him to be thrust into prison. Had Potiphar believed his wife's charge against Joseph, the young Hebrew would have lost his life; but the modesty and uprightness that had uniformly characterized his conduct were proof of his innocence; and yet, to save the reputation of his master's house, he was abandoned to disgrace and bondage.

At the first Joseph was treated with great severity by his jailers. The psalmist says, "His feet they hurt with fetters; he was laid in chains of iron: until the time that his word came to pass; the word of the Lord tried him." Psalm 105:18, 19, R.V. But Joseph's real character shines out, even in the darkness of the dungeon. He held fast his faith and patience; his years of faithful service had been most cruelly repaid, yet this did not render him morose or distrustful. He had the peace that comes from conscious innocence, and he trusted his case with God. He did not brood upon his own wrongs, but forgot his sorrow in trying to lighten the sorrows of others. He found a work to do, even in the prison. God was preparing him in the school of affliction for greater usefulness, and he did not refuse the needful discipline. In the prison, witnessing the results of oppression and tyranny and the effects of crime, he learned lessons of justice, sympathy, and mercy, that prepared him to exercise power with wisdom and compassion.

Joseph gradually gained the confidence of the keeper of the prison, and was finally entrusted with the charge of all the prisoners. It was the part he acted in the prison—the integrity of his daily life and his sympathy for those who were in trouble and distress—that opened the way for his future prosperity and honor. Every ray of light that we shed upon others is reflected upon ourselves. Every kind and sympathizing word spoken to the sorrowful, every act to relieve the oppressed, and every gift to the needy, if prompted by a right motive, will result in blessings to the giver.

The chief baker and chief butler of the king had been cast into prison for some offense, and they came under Joseph's charge. One morning, observing that they appeared very sad, he kindly inquired the cause and was told that each had had a remarkable dream, of which they were anxious to learn the significance. "Do not interpretations belong to God?" said Joseph, "tell me them, I pray you." As each related his dream, Joseph made known its import: In three days the butler was to be reinstated in his position, and give the cup into Pharaoh's hand as before, but the chief baker would be put to death by the king's command. In both cases the event occurred as foretold.

The king's cupbearer had professed the deepest gratitude to Joseph, both for the cheering interpretation of his dream and for many acts of kind attention; and in return the latter, referring in a most touching manner to his own unjust captivity, entreated that his case be brought before the king. "Think on me," he said, "when it shall be well with thee, and show kindness, I pray thee, unto me, and make mention of me unto Pharaoh, and bring me out of this house: for indeed I was stolen away out of the land of the Hebrews: and here also have I done nothing that they should put me into the dungeon." The chief butler saw the dream fulfilled in every particular; but when restored to royal favor, he thought no more of his benefactor. For two years longer Joseph remained a prisoner. The hope that had been kindled in his heart gradually died out, and to all other trials was added the bitter sting of ingratitude.

But a divine hand was about to open the prison gates. The king of Egypt had in one night two dreams, apparently pointing to the same event and seeming to foreshadow some great calamity. He could not determine their significance, yet they continued to trouble his mind. The magicians and wise men of his realm could give no interpretation. The king's perplexity and distress increased, and terror spread throughout his palace. The general agitation recalled to the chief butler's mind the circumstances of his own dream; with it came the memory of Joseph, and a pang of remorse for his forgetfulness and ingratitude. He at once informed the king how his own dream and that of the chief baker had been interpreted by a Hebrew captive, and how the predictions had been fulfilled.

It was humiliating to Pharaoh to turn away from the magicians and wise men of his kingdom to consult an alien and a slave, but he was ready to accept the lowliest service if his troubled mind might find relief. Joseph was immediately sent for; he put off his prison attire, and shaved himself, for his hair had grown long during the period of his disgrace and confinement. He was then conducted to the presence of the king.

"And Pharaoh said unto Joseph, I have dreamed a dream, and there is none that can interpret it: and I have heard say of thee, that thou canst understand a dream to interpret it. And Joseph answered Pharaoh, saying, It is not in me: God shall give Pharaoh an answer of peace." Joseph's reply to the king reveals his humility and his faith in God. He modestly disclaims the honor of possessing in himself superior wisdom. "It is not in me." God alone can explain these mysteries.

Pharaoh then proceeded to relate his dreams: "Behold, I stood upon the bank of the river: and, behold, there came up out of the river seven kine, fat-fleshed and well-favored; and they fed in a meadow: and, behold, seven other kine came up after them, poor and very ill-favored and lean-fleshed, such as I never saw in all the land of Egypt for badness: and the lean and the ill-favored kine did eat up the first seven fat kine: and when they had eaten them up, it could not be known that they had eaten them; but they were still ill-favored, as at the beginning. So I awoke. And I saw in my dream, and, behold, seven ears came up in one stalk, full and good: and, behold, seven ears, withered, thin, and blasted with the east wind, sprung up after them: and the thin ears devoured the seven good ears: and I told this unto the magicians; but there was none that could declare it to me."

"The dream of Pharaoh is one," said Joseph. "God hath showed Pharaoh what He is about to do." There were to be seven years of great plenty. Field and garden would yield more abundantly than ever before. And this period was to be followed by seven years of famine. "And the plenty shall not be known in the land by reason of that famine following; for it shall be very grievous." The repetition of the dream was evidence both of the certainty and nearness of the fulfillment. "Now therefore," he continued, "let Pharaoh look out a man discreet and wise, and set him over the land of Egypt. Let Pharaoh do this, and let him appoint officers over the land, and take up the fifth part of the land of Egypt in the seven plenteous years. And let them gather all the food of those good years that come, and lay up corn under the hand of Pharaoh, and let them keep food in the cities. And that food shall be for store to the land against the seven years of famine."

The interpretation was so reasonable and consistent, and the policy which it recommended was so sound and shrewd, that its correctness could not be doubted. But who was to be entrusted with the execution of the plan? Upon the wisdom of this choice depended the nation's preservation. The king was troubled. For some time the matter of the appointment was under consideration. Through the chief butler the monarch had learned of the wisdom and prudence displayed by Joseph in the management of the prison; it was evident that he possessed administrative ability in a pre-eminent degree. The cupbearer, now filled with self-reproach, endeavored to atone for his former ingratitude, by the warmest praise of his benefactor; and further inquiry by the king proved the correctness of his report. In all the realm Joseph was the only man gifted with wisdom to point out the danger that threatened the kingdom and the preparation necessary to meet it; and the king was convinced that he was the one best qualified to execute the plans which he had proposed. It was evident that a divine power was with him, and that there were none among the king's officers of state so well qualified to conduct the affairs of the nation at this crisis. The fact that he was a Hebrew and a slave was of little moment when weighed against his evident wisdom and sound judgment. "Can we find such a one as this is, a man in whom the Spirit of God is?" said the king to his counselors.

The appointment was decided upon, and to Joseph the astonishing announcement was made, "Forasmuch as God hath showed thee all this, there is none so discreet and wise as thou art: thou shalt be over my house, and according unto thy word shall all my people be ruled: only in the throne will I be greater than thou." The king proceeded to invest Joseph with the insignia of his high office. "And Pharaoh took off his ring from his hand, and put it upon Joseph's hand, and arrayed him in vestures of fine linen, and put a gold chain about his neck; and he made him to ride in the second chariot which he had; and they cried before him, Bow the knee."

"He made him lord of his house, and ruler of all his substance:

to bind his princes at his pleasure; and teach his senators wisdom." Psalm 105:21, 22. From the dungeon Joseph was exalted to be ruler over all the land of Egypt. It was a position of high honor, yet it was beset with difficulty and peril. One cannot stand upon a lofty height without danger. As the tempest leaves unharmed the lowly flower of the valley, while it uproots the stately tree upon the mountaintop, so those who have maintained their integrity in humble life may be dragged down to the pit by the temptations that assail worldly success and honor. But Joseph's character bore the test alike of adversity and prosperity. The same fidelity to God was manifest when he stood in the palace of the Pharaohs as when in a prisoner's cell. He was still a stranger in a heathen land, separated from his kindred, the worshipers of God; but he fully believed that the divine hand had directed his steps, and in constant reliance upon God he faithfully discharged the duties of his position. Through Joseph the attention of the king and great men of Egypt was directed to the true God; and though they adhered to their idolatry, they learned to respect the principles revealed in the life and character of the worshiper of Jehovah.

How was Joseph enabled to make such a record of firmness of character, uprightness, and wisdom?—In his early years he had consulted duty rather than inclination; and the integrity, the simple trust, the noble nature, of the youth bore fruit in the deeds of the man. A pure and simple life had favored the vigorous development of both physical and intellectual powers. Communion with God through His works and the contemplation of the grand truths entrusted to the inheritors of faith had elevated and ennobled his spiritual nature, broadening and strengthening the mind as no other study could do. Faithful attention to duty in every station, from the lowliest to the most exalted, had been training every power for its highest service. He who lives in accordance with the Creator's will is securing to himself the truest and noblest development of character. "The fear of the Lord, that is wisdom; and to depart from evil is understanding." Job 28:28.

There are few who realize the influence of the little things of life upon the development of character. Nothing with which we have to do is really small. The varied circumstances that we meet day by day are designed to test our faithfulness and to qualify us for greater trusts. By adherence to principle in the transactions of ordinary life, the mind becomes accustomed to hold the claims of duty above those of pleasure and inclination. Minds thus disciplined are not wavering between right and wrong, like the reed trembling in the wind; they are loyal to duty because they have trained themselves to habits of fidelity and truth. By faithfulness in that which is least they acquire strength to be faithful in greater matters.

An upright character is of greater worth than the gold of Ophir. Without it none can rise to an honorable eminence. But character is not inherited. It cannot be bought. Moral excellence and fine mental qualities are not the result of accident. The most precious gifts are of no value unless they are improved. The formation of a noble character is the work of a lifetime and must be the result of diligent and persevering effort. God gives opportunities; success depends upon the use made of them.

Chapter 21—Joseph and His Brothers

This chapter is based on Genesis 41:54-56; 42 to 50.

At the very opening of the fruitful years began the preparation for the approaching famine. Under the direction of Joseph, immense storehouses were erected in all the principal places throughout the land of Egypt, and ample arrangements were made for preserving the surplus of the expected harvest. The same policy was continued during the seven years of plenty, until the amount of grain laid in store was beyond computation.

And now the seven years of dearth began to come, according to Joseph's prediction. "And the dearth was in all lands; but in all the land of Egypt there was bread. And when all the land of Egypt was famished, the people cried to Pharaoh for bread: and Pharaoh said unto all the Egyptians, Go unto Joseph; what he saith to you, do. And the famine was over all the face of the earth: and Joseph opened all the storehouses, and sold unto the Egyptians."

The famine extended to the land of Canaan and was severely felt in that part of the country where Jacob dwelt. Hearing of the abundant provision made by the king of Egypt, ten of Jacob's sons journeyed thither to purchase grain. On their arrival they were directed to the king's deputy, and with other applicants they came to present themselves before the ruler of the land. And they "bowed down themselves before him with their faces to the earth." "Joseph knew his brethren, but they knew not him." His Hebrew name had been exchanged for the one bestowed upon him by the king, and there was little resemblance between the prime minister of Egypt and the stripling whom they had sold to the Ishmaelites. As Joseph saw his brothers stooping and making obeisance, his dreams came to his mind, and the scenes of the past rose vividly before him. His keen eye, surveying the group, discovered that Benjamin was not among them. Had he also fallen a victim to the treacherous cruelty of those savage men? He determined to learn the truth. "Ye are spies," he said sternly; "to see the nakedness of the land ye are come."

They answered, "Nay, my lord, but to buy food are thy servants come. We are all one man's sons; we are true men; thy servants are no spies." He wished to learn if they possessed the same haughty spirit as when he was with them, and also to draw from them some information in regard to their home; yet he well knew how deceptive their statements might be. He repeated the charge, and they replied, "Thy servants are twelve brethren, the sons of one man in the land of Canaan; and, behold, the youngest is this day with our father, and one is not."

Professing to doubt the truthfulness of their story, and to still look upon them as spies, the governor declared that he would prove them, by requiring them to remain in Egypt till one of their number should go and bring their youngest brother down. If they would not consent to this, they were to be treated as spies. But to such an arrangement the sons of Jacob could not agree, since the time required for carrying it out would cause their families to suffer for food; and who among them would undertake the journey alone, leaving his brothers in prison? How could he meet his father under such circumstances? It appeared probable that they were to be put to death or to be made slaves; and if Benjamin were brought, it might be only to share their fate. They decided to remain and suffer together, rather than bring additional sorrow upon their father by the loss of his only remaining son. They were accordingly cast into prison, where they remained three days.

During the years since Joseph had been separated from his brothers, these sons of Jacob had changed in character. Envious, turbulent, deceptive, cruel, and revengeful they had been; but now, when tested by adversity, they were shown to be unselfish, true to one another, devoted to their father, and, themselves middle-aged men, subject to his authority.

The three days in the Egyptian prison were days of bitter sorrow as the brothers reflected upon their past sins. Unless Benjamin could be produced their conviction as spies appeared certain, and they had little hope of gaining their father's consent to Benjamin's absence. On the third day Joseph caused the brothers to be brought before him. He dared not detain them longer. Already his father and the families with him might be suffering for food. "This do, and live," he said; "for I fear God; if ye be true men, let one of your brethren be bound in the house of your prison: go ye, carry corn for the famine of your houses: but bring your youngest brother unto me; so shall your words be verified, and ye shall not die." This proposition they agreed to accept, though expressing little hope that their father would let Benjamin return with them. Joseph had communicated with them through an interpreter, and having no thought that the governor understood them, they conversed freely with one another in his presence. They accused themselves in regard to their treatment of Joseph: "We are verily guilty concerning our brother, in that we saw the anguish of his soul, when he besought us, and we would not hear; therefore is this distress come upon us." Reuben, who had formed the plan for delivering him at Dothan, added, "Spake I not unto you, saying, Do not sin against the child; and ye would not hear? therefore, behold, also his blood is required." Joseph, listening, could not control his emotions, and he went out and wept. On his return he commanded that Simeon be bound before them and again committed to prison. In the cruel treatment of their brother, Simeon had been the instigator and chief actor, and it was for this reason that the choice fell upon him.

Before permitting his brothers to depart, Joseph gave directions that they should be supplied with grain, and also that each man's money should be secretly placed in the mouth of his sack. Provender for the beasts on the homeward journey was also supplied. On the way one of the company, opening his sack, was surprised to find his bag of silver. On his making known the fact to the others, they were alarmed and perplexed, and said one to another, "What is this that God hath done unto us?"—should they regard it as a token of good from the Lord, or had He suffered it to occur to punish them for their sins and plunge them still deeper in affliction? They acknowledged that God had seen their sins, and that He was now punishing them.

Jacob was anxiously awaiting the return of his sons, and on their arrival the whole encampment gathered eagerly around them as they related to their father all that had occurred. Alarm and apprehension filled every heart. The conduct of the Egyptian governor seemed to imply some evil design, and their fears were confirmed, when, as they opened their sacks, the owner's money was found in each. In his distress the aged father exclaimed, "Me have ye bereaved of my children: Joseph is not, and Simeon is not, and ye will take Benjamin away: all these things are against me." Reuben answered, "Slay my two sons, if I bring him not to thee: deliver him into my hand, and I will bring him to thee again." This rash speech did not relieve the mind of Jacob. His answer was, "My son shall not go down with you; for his brother is dead, and he is left alone: if mischief befall him by the way in the which ye go, then shall ye bring down my gray hairs with sorrow to the grave."

But the drought continued, and in process of time the supply of grain that had been brought from Egypt was nearly exhausted. The sons of Jacob well knew that it would be in vain to return to Egypt without Benjamin. They had little hope of changing their father's resolution, and they awaited the issue in silence. Deeper and deeper grew the shadow of approaching famine; in the anxious faces of all in the encampment the old man read their need; at last he said, "Go again, buy us a little food."

Judah answered, "The man did solemnly protest unto us, saying, Ye shall not see my face, except your brother be with you. If thou wilt send our brother with us, we will go down and buy thee food: but if thou wilt not send him, we will not go down: for the man said unto us, Ye shall not see my face, except your brother be with you." Seeing that his father's resolution began to waver, he added, "Send the lad with me, and we will arise and go; that we may live, and not die, both we, and thou, and also our little ones;" and he offered to be surety for his brother and to bear the blame forever if he failed to restore Benjamin to his father.

Jacob could no longer withhold his consent, and he directed his sons to prepare for the journey. He bade them also take to the ruler a present of such things as the famine-wasted country afforded—"a little balm, and a little honey, spices and myrrh, nuts and almonds," also a double quantity of money. "Take also your brother," he said, "and arise, go again unto the man." As his sons were about to depart on their doubtful journey the aged father arose, and raising his hands to heaven, uttered the prayer, "God Almighty give you mercy before the man, that he may send away your other brother, and Benjamin. If I be bereaved of my children, I am bereaved."

Again they journeyed to Egypt and presented themselves before

[228]

Joseph. As his eye fell upon Benjamin, his own mother's son, he was deeply moved. He concealed his emotion, however, but ordered that they be taken to his house, and that preparation be made for them to dine with him. Upon being conducted to the governor's palace, the brothers were greatly alarmed, fearing that they were to be called to account for the money found in their sacks. They thought that it might have been intentionally placed there, to furnish occasion for making them slaves. In their distress they consulted with the steward of the house, relating to him the circumstances of their visit to Egypt; and in proof of their innocence informed him that they had brought back the money found in their sacks, also other money to buy food; and they added, "We cannot tell who put our money in our sacks." The man replied, "Peace be to you, fear not: your God, and the God of your father, hath given you treasure in your sacks: I had your money." Their anxiety was relieved, and when Simeon, who had been released from prison, joined them, they felt that God was indeed gracious unto them.

When the governor again met them they presented their gifts and humbly "bowed themselves to him to the earth." Again his dreams came to his mind, and after saluting his guests he hastened to ask, "Is your father well, the old man of whom ye spake? Is he yet alive?" "Thy servant our father is in good health, he is yet alive," was the answer, as they again made obeisance. Then his eye rested upon Benjamin, and he said, "Is this your younger brother, of whom ye spake unto me?" "God be gracious unto thee, my son;" but, overpowered by feelings of tenderness, he could say no more. "He entered into his chamber, and wept there."

Having recovered his self-possession, he returned, and all proceeded to the feast. By the laws of caste the Egyptians were forbidden to eat with people of any other nation. The sons of Jacob had therefore a table by themselves, while the governor, on account of his high rank, ate by himself, and the Egyptians also had separate tables. When all were seated the brothers were surprised to see that they were arranged in exact order, according to their ages. Joseph "sent messes unto them from before him;" but Benjamin's was five times as much as any of theirs. By this token of favor to Benjamin he hoped to ascertain if the youngest brother was regarded with the envy and hatred that had been manifested toward himself. Still supposing that Joseph did not understand their language, the brothers freely conversed with one another; thus he had a good opportunity to learn their real feelings. Still he desired to test them further, and before their departure he ordered that his own drinking cup of silver should be concealed in the sack of the youngest.

Joyfully they set out on their return. Simeon and Benjamin were with them, their animals were laden with grain, and all felt that they had safely escaped the perils that had seemed to surround them. But they had only reached the outskirts of the city when they were overtaken by the governor's steward, who uttered the scathing inquiry, "Wherefore have ye rewarded evil for good? Is not this it in which my lord drinketh, and whereby indeed he divineth? ye have done evil in so doing." This cup was supposed to possess the power of detecting any poisonous substance placed therein. At that day cups of this kind were highly valued as a safeguard against murder by poisoning.

To the steward's accusation the travelers answered, "Wherefore saith my lord these words? God forbid that thy servants should do according to this thing: behold, the money, which we found in our sacks' mouths, we brought again unto thee out of the land of Canaan: how then should we steal out of thy lord's house silver or gold? With whomsoever of thy servants it be found, both let him die, and we also will be my lord's bondmen."

"Now also let it be according unto your words," said the steward; "he with whom it is found shall be my servant; and ye shall be blameless."

The search began immediately. "They speedily took down every man his sack to the ground," and the steward examined each, beginning with Reuben's, and taking them in order down to that of the youngest. In Benjamin's sack the cup was found.

The brothers rent their garments in token of utter wretchedness, and slowly returned to the city. By their own promise Benjamin was doomed to a life of slavery. They followed the steward to the palace, and finding the governor yet there, they prostrated themselves before him. "What deed is this that ye have done?" he said. "Wot ye not that such a man as I can certainly divine?" Joseph designed to draw from them an acknowledgment of their sin. He had never claimed the power of divination, but was willing to have them believe that he could read the secrets of their lives.

Judah answered, "What shall we say unto my lord? what shall we speak? or how shall we clear ourselves? God hath found out the iniquity of thy servants: behold, we are my lord's servants, both we, and he also with whom the cup is found."

"God forbid that I should do so," was the reply; "but the man in whose hand the cup is found, he shall be my servant; and as for you, get you up in peace unto your father."

In his deep distress Judah now drew near to the ruler and exclaimed, "O my lord, let thy servant, I pray thee, speak a word in my lord's ears, and let not thine anger burn against thy servant: for thou art even as Pharaoh." In words of touching eloquence he described his father's grief at the loss of Joseph and his reluctance to let Benjamin come with them to Egypt, as he was the only son left of his mother, Rachel, whom Jacob so dearly loved. "Now therefore," he said, "when I come to thy servant my father, and the lad be not with us; seeing that his life is bound up in the lad's life; it shall come to pass, when he seeth that the lad is not with us, that he will die: and thy servants shall bring down the gray hairs of thy servant our father with sorrow to the grave. For thy servant became surety for the lad unto my father, saying, If I bring him not unto thee, then I shall bear the blame to my father forever. Now therefore, I pray thee, let thy servant abide instead of the lad a bondman to my lord; and let the lad go up with his brethren. For how shall I go up to my father, and the lad be not with me? lest peradventure I see the evil that shall come on my father."

Joseph was satisfied. He had seen in his brothers the fruits of true repentance. Upon hearing Judah's noble offer he gave orders that all but these men should withdraw; then, weeping aloud, he cried, "I am Joseph; doth my father yet live?"

His brothers stood motionless, dumb with fear and amazement. The ruler of Egypt their brother Joseph, whom they had envied and would have murdered, and finally sold as a slave! All their ill treatment of him passed before them. They remembered how they had despised his dreams and had labored to prevent their fulfillment. Yet they had acted their part in fulfilling these dreams; and now that they were completely in his power he would, no doubt, avenge the wrong that he had suffered.

Seeing their confusion, he said kindly, "Come near to me, I pray you;" and as they came near, he continued, "I am Joseph your brother, whom ye sold into Egypt. Now therefore be not grieved, nor angry with yourselves, that ye sold me hither: for God did send me before you to preserve life." Feeling that they had already suffered enough for their cruelty toward him, he nobly sought to banish their fears and lessen the bitterness of their self-reproach.

[231]

"For these two years," he continued, "hath the famine been in the land: and yet there are five years, in the which there shall neither be earing nor harvest. And God sent me before you to preserve you a posterity in the earth, and to save your lives by a great deliverance. So now it was not you that sent me hither, but God: and He hath made me a father to Pharaoh, and lord of all his house, and a ruler throughout all the land of Egypt. Haste ye, and go up to my father, and say unto him, Thus saith thy son Joseph, God hath made me lord of all Egypt: come down unto me tarry not: and thou shalt dwell in the land of Goshen, and thou shalt be near unto me, thou, and thy children, and thy children's children, and thy flocks, and thy herds, and all that thou hast: and there will I nourish thee; for yet there are five years of famine; lest thou, and thy household, and all that thou hast, come to poverty. And, behold, your eyes see, and the eyes of my brother Benjamin, that it is my mouth that speaketh unto you." "And he fell upon his brother Benjamin's neck, and wept; and Benjamin wept upon his neck. Moreover he kissed all his brethren, and wept upon them: and after that his brethren talked with him." They humbly confessed their sin and entreated his forgiveness. They had long suffered anxiety and remorse, and now they rejoiced that he was still alive.

The news of what had taken place was quickly carried to the king, who, eager to manifest his gratitude to Joseph, confirmed the governor's invitation to his family, saying, "The good of all the land of Egypt is yours." The brothers were sent away abundantly supplied with provision and carriages and everything necessary for the removal of all their families and attendants to Egypt. On Benjamin, Joseph bestowed more valuable gifts than upon the others. Then, fearing that disputes would arise among them on the homeward journey, he gave them, as they were about to leave him, the charge, "See that ye fall not out by the way."

The sons of Jacob returned to their father with the joyful tidings, "Joseph is yet alive, and he is governor over all the land of Egypt." At first the aged man was overwhelmed; he could not believe what he heard; but when he saw the long train of wagons and loaded animals, and when Benjamin was with him once more, he was convinced, and in the fullness of his joy exclaimed, "It is enough; Joseph my son is yet alive: I will go and see him before I die."

Another act of humiliation remained for the ten brothers. They now confessed to their father the deceit and cruelty that for so many years had embittered his life and theirs. Jacob had not suspected them of so base a sin, but he saw that all had been overruled for good, and he forgave and blessed his erring children.

The father and his sons, with their families, their flocks and herds, and numerous attendants, were soon on the way to Egypt. With gladness of heart they pursued their journey, and when they came to Beersheba the patriarch offered grateful sacrifices and entreated the Lord to grant them an assurance that He would go with them. In a vision of the night the divine word came to him: "Fear not to go down into Egypt; for I will there make of thee a great nation. I will go down with thee into Egypt; and I will also surely bring thee up again."

The assurance, "Fear not to go down into Egypt; for I will *there* make of thee a great nation," was significant. The promise had been given to Abraham of a posterity numberless as the stars, but as yet the chosen people had increased but slowly. And the land of Canaan now offered no field for the development of such a nation as had been foretold. It was in the possession of powerful heathen tribes, that were not to be dispossessed until "the fourth generation." If the descendants of Israel were here to become a numerous people, they must either drive out the inhabitants of the land or disperse themselves among them. The former, according to the divine arrangement, they could not do; and should they mingle with the Canaanites, they would be in danger of being seduced into idolatry. Egypt, however, offered the conditions necessary to the fulfillment of the divine purpose. A section of country well-watered and fertile was open to them there, affording every advantage for their speedy increase. And the antipathy they must encounter in Egypt on account of their occupation—for every shepherd was "an abomination unto the Egyptians"—would enable them to remain a distinct and separate people and would thus serve to shut them out from participation in the idolatry of Egypt.

Upon reaching Egypt the company proceeded directly to the land of Goshen. Thither came Joseph in his chariot of state, attended by a princely retinue. The splendor of his surroundings and the dignity of his position were alike forgotten; one thought alone filled his mind, one longing thrilled his heart. As he beheld the travelers approaching, the love whose yearnings had for so many long years been repressed, would no longer be controlled. He sprang from his chariot and hastened forward to bid his father welcome. "And he fell on his neck, and wept on his neck a good while. And Israel said unto Joseph, Now let me die, since I have seen thy face, because thou art yet alive." [233]

Joseph took five of his brothers to present to Pharaoh and receive from him the grant of land for their future home. Gratitude to his prime minister would have led the monarch to honor them with appointments to offices of state; but Joseph, true to the worship of Jehovah, sought to save his brothers from the temptations to which they would be exposed at a heathen court; therefore he counseled them, when questioned by the king, to tell him frankly their occupation. The sons of Jacob followed this counsel, being careful also to state that they had come to sojourn in the land, not to become permanent dwellers there, thus reserving the right to depart if they chose. The king assigned them a home, as offered, in "the best of the land," the country of Goshen.

Not long after their arrival Joseph brought his father also to be presented to the king. The patriarch was a stranger in royal courts; but amid the sublime scenes of nature he had communed with a mightier Monarch; and now, in conscious superiority, he raised his hands and blessed Pharaoh.

In his first greeting to Joseph, Jacob had spoken as if, with this joyful ending to his long anxiety and sorrow, he was ready to die. But seventeen years were yet to be granted him in the peaceful retirement of Goshen. These years were in happy contrast to those that had preceded them. He saw in his sons evidence of true repentance;

he saw his family surrounded by all the conditions needful for the development of a great nation; and his faith grasped the sure promise of their future establishment in Canaan. He himself was surrounded with every token of love and favor that the prime minister of Egypt could bestow; and happy in the society of his long-lost son, he passed down gently and peacefully to the grave.

[234] As he felt death approaching, he sent for Joseph. Still holding fast the promise of God respecting the possession of Canaan, he said, "Bury me not, I pray thee, in Egypt: but I will lie with my fathers, and thou shalt carry me out of Egypt, and bury me in their burying place." Joseph promised to do so, but Jacob was not satisfied; he exacted a solemn oath to lay him beside his fathers in the cave of Machpelah.

Another important matter demanded attention; the sons of Joseph were to be formally instated among the children of Israel. Joseph, coming for a last interview with his father, brought with him Ephraim and Manasseh. These youths were connected, through their mother, with the highest order of the Egyptian priesthood; and the position of their father opened to them the avenues to wealth and distinction, should they choose to connect themselves with the Egyptians. It was Joseph's desire, however, that they should unite with their own people. He manifested his faith in the covenant promise, in behalf of his sons renouncing all the honors that the court of Egypt offered, for a place among the despised shepherd tribes, to whom had been entrusted the oracles of God.

Said Jacob, "Thy two sons, Ephraim, and Manasseh, which were born unto thee in the land of Egypt, before I came unto thee into Egypt, are mine; as Reuben and Simeon, they shall be mine." They were to be adopted as his own, and to become the heads of separate tribes. Thus one of the birthright privileges, which Reuben had forfeited, was to fall to Joseph—a double portion in Israel.

Jacob's eyes were dim with age, and he had not been aware of the presence of the young men; but now, catching the outline of their forms, he said, "Who are these?" On being told, he added, "Bring them, I pray thee, unto me, and I will bless them." As they came nearer, the patriarch embraced and kissed them, solemnly laying his hands upon their heads in benediction. Then he uttered the prayer, "God, before whom my fathers Abraham and Isaac did walk, the

God which fed me all my life long unto this day, the Angel which redeemed me from all evil, bless the lads." There was no spirit of self-dependence, no reliance upon human power or cunning now. God had been his preserver and support. There was no complaint of the evil days in the past. Its trials and sorrows were no longer regarded as things that were "against" him. Memory recalled only His mercy and loving-kindness who had been with him throughout his pilgrimage.

[235]

The blessing ended, Jacob gave his son the assurance—leaving for the generations to come, through long years of bondage and sorrow, this testimony to his faith—"Behold, I die; but God shall be with you, and bring you again unto the land of your fathers."

At the last all the sons of Jacob were gathered about his dying bed. And Jacob called unto his sons, and said, "Gather yourselves together, and hear, ye sons of Jacob; and hearken unto Israel your father," "that I may tell you that which shall befall you in the last days." Often and anxiously he had thought of their future, and had endeavored to picture to himself the history of the different tribes. Now as his children waited to receive his last blessing the Spirit of Inspiration rested upon him, and before him in prophetic vision the future of his descendants was unfolded. One after another the names of his sons were mentioned, the character of each was described, and the future history of the tribes was briefly foretold.

"Reuben, thou art my first-born,
   My might, and the beginning of my strength,
The excellency of dignity, and the excellency of power."

Thus the father pictured what should have been the position of Reuben as the first-born son; but his grievous sin at Edar had made him unworthy of the birthright blessing. Jacob continued—

"Unstable as water,
   Thou shalt not excel."

The priesthood was apportioned to Levi, the kingdom and the Messianic promise to Judah, and the double portion of the inheritance to Joseph. The tribe of Reuben never rose to any eminence in

Israel; it was not so numerous as Judah, Joseph, or Dan, and was among the first that were carried into captivity.

Next in age to Reuben were Simeon and Levi. They had been united in their cruelty toward the Shechemites, and they had also been the most guilty in the selling of Joseph. Concerning them it was declared—

"I will divide them in Jacob,
    And scatter them in Israel."

[236] At the numbering of Israel, just before their entrance to Canaan, Simeon was the smallest tribe. Moses, in his last blessing, made no reference to Simeon. In the settlement of Canaan this tribe had only a small portion of Judah's lot, and such families as afterward became powerful formed different colonies and settled in territory outside the borders of the Holy Land. Levi also received no inheritance except forty-eight cities scattered in different parts of the land. In the case of this tribe, however, their fidelity to Jehovah when the other tribes apostatized, secured their appointment to the sacred service of the sanctuary, and thus the curse was changed into a blessing.

The crowning blessings of the birthright were transferred to Judah. The significance of the name—which denotes praise,—is unfolded in the prophetic history of this tribe:

"Judah, thou art he whom thy brethren shall praise:
    Thy hand shall be in the neck of thine enemies;
Thy father's children shall bow down before thee.
    Judah is a lion's whelp:
From the prey, my son, thou art gone up:
    He stooped down, he couched as a lion,
And as an old lion: who shall rouse him up?
    The scepter shall not depart from Judah,
Nor a lawgiver from between his feet,
    Until Shiloh come;
And unto Him shall the gathering of the people be."

The lion, king of the forest, is a fitting symbol of this tribe, from which came David, and the Son of David, Shiloh, the true "Lion of the tribe of Judah," to whom all powers shall finally bow and all nations render homage.

For most of his children Jacob foretold a prosperous future. At last the name of Joseph was reached, and the father's heart overflowed as he invoked blessings upon "the head of him that was separate from his brethren":

"Joseph is a fruitful bough,
    Even a fruitful bough by a well;
Whose branches run over the wall:
    The archers have sorely grieved him,
And shot at him, and hated him:
    But his bow abode in strength,
And the arms of his hands were made strong
    By the hands of the mighty God of Jacob;
(From thence is the shepherd, the stone of Israel;).
    Even by the God of thy father, who shall help thee;
And by the Almighty, who shall bless thee
    With blessings of heaven above,
Blessings of the deep that lieth under,
    Blessings of the breasts, and of the womb:
The blessings of thy father have prevailed
    Above the blessings of my progenitors
Unto the utmost bound of the everlasting hills:
    They shall be on the head of Joseph,
And on the crown of the head of him that was separate from
    his brethren."

[237]

Jacob had ever been a man of deep and ardent affection; his love for his sons was strong and tender, and his dying testimony to them was not the utterance of partiality or resentment. He had forgiven them all, and he loved them to the last. His paternal tenderness would have found expression only in words of encouragement and hope; but the power of God rested upon him, and under the influence of Inspiration he was constrained to declare the truth, however painful.

The last blessings pronounced, Jacob repeated the charge concerning his burial place: "I am to be gathered unto my people: bury me with my fathers ... in the cave that is in the field of Machpelah."

"There they buried Abraham and Sarah his wife; there they buried Isaac and Rebekah his wife; and there I buried Leah." Thus the last act of his life was to manifest his faith in God's promise.

Jacob's last years brought an evening of tranquillity and repose after a troubled and weary day. Clouds had gathered dark above his path, yet his sun set clear, and the radiance of heaven illumined his parting hours. Says the Scripture, "At evening time it shall be light." Zechariah 14:7. "Mark the perfect man, and behold the upright: for the end of that man is peace." Psalm 37:37.

Jacob had sinned, and had deeply suffered. Many years of toil, care, and sorrow had been his since the day when his great sin caused him to flee from his father's tents. A homeless fugitive, separated from his mother, whom he never saw again; laboring seven years for her whom he loved, only to be basely cheated; toiling twenty years in the service of a covetous and grasping kinsman; seeing his wealth increasing, and sons rising around him, but finding little joy in the contentious and divided household; distressed by his daughter's shame, by her brothers' revenge, by the death of Rachel, by the unnatural crime of Reuben, by Judah's sin, by the cruel deception and malice practiced toward Joseph—how long and dark is the catalogue of evils spread out to view! Again and again he had reaped the fruit of that first wrong deed. Over and over he saw repeated among his sons the sins of which he himself had been guilty. But bitter as had been the discipline, it had accomplished its work. The chastening, though grievous, had yielded "the peaceable fruit of righteousness." Hebrews 12:11.

Inspiration faithfully records the faults of good men, those who were distinguished by the favor of God; indeed, their faults are more fully presented than their virtues. This has been a subject of wonder to many, and has given the infidel occasion to scoff at the Bible. But it is one of the strongest evidences of the truth of Scripture, that facts are not glossed over, nor the sins of its chief characters suppressed. The minds of men are so subject to prejudice that it is not possible for human histories to be absolutely impartial. Had the Bible been written by uninspired persons, it would no doubt have presented the character of its honored men in a more flattering light. But as it is, we have a correct record of their experiences.

Men whom God favored, and to whom He entrusted great responsibilities, were sometimes overcome by temptation and committed sin, even as we at the present day strive, waver, and frequently fall into error. Their lives, with all their faults and follies, are open before us, both for our encouragement and warning. If they had been represented as without fault, we, with our sinful nature, might despair at our own mistakes and failures. But seeing where others struggled through discouragements like our own, where they fell under temptations as we have done, and yet took heart again and conquered through the grace of God, we are encouraged in our striving after righteousness. As they, though sometimes beaten back, recovered their ground, and were blessed of God, so we too may be overcomers in the strength of Jesus. On the other hand, the record of their lives may serve as a warning to us. It shows that God will by no means clear the guilty. He sees sin in His most favored ones, and He deals with it in them even more strictly than in those who have less light and responsibility.

After the burial of Jacob fear again filled the hearts of Joseph's brothers. Notwithstanding his kindness toward them, conscious guilt made them distrustful and suspicious. It might be that he had but delayed his revenge, out of regard to their father, and that he would now visit upon them the long-deferred punishment for their crime. They dared not appear before him in person, but sent a message: "Thy father did command before he died, saying, So shall ye say unto Joseph, Forgive, I pray thee now, the trespass of thy brethren, and their sin; for they did unto thee evil: and now, we pray thee, forgive the trespass of the servants of the God of thy father." This message affected Joseph to tears, and, encouraged by this, his brothers came and fell down before him, with the words, "Behold, we be thy servants." Joseph's love for his brothers was deep and unselfish, and he was pained at the thought that they could regard him as cherishing a spirit of revenge toward them. "Fear not," he said; "for am I in the place of God? But as for you, ye thought evil against me; but God meant it unto good, to bring to pass, as it is this day, to save much people alive. Now therefore fear ye not: I will nourish you, and your little ones."

The life of Joseph illustrates the life of Christ. It was envy that moved the brothers of Joseph to sell him as a slave; they hoped to prevent him from becoming greater than themselves. And when he was carried to Egypt, they flattered themselves that they were to be no more troubled with his dreams, that they had removed all possibility of their fulfillment. But their own course was overruled by God to bring about the very event that they designed to hinder. So the Jewish priests and elders were jealous of Christ, fearing that He would attract the attention of the people from them. They put Him to death, to prevent Him from becoming king, but they were thus bringing about this very result.

Joseph, through his bondage in Egypt, became a savior to his father's family; yet this fact did not lessen the guilt of his brothers. So the crucifixion of Christ by His enemies made Him the Redeemer of mankind, the Saviour of the fallen race, and Ruler over the whole world; but the crime of His murderers was just as heinous as though God's providential hand had not controlled events for His own glory and the good of man.

As Joseph was sold to the heathen by his own brothers, so Christ was sold to His bitterest enemies by one of His disciples. Joseph was falsely accused and thrust into prison because of his virtue; so Christ was despised and rejected because His righteous, self-denying life was a rebuke to sin; and though guilty of no wrong, He was condemned upon the testimony of false witnesses. And Joseph's patience and meekness under injustice and oppression, his ready forgiveness and noble benevolence toward his unnatural brothers, represent the Saviour's uncomplaining endurance of the malice and abuse of wicked men, and His forgiveness, not only of His murderers, but of all who have come to Him confessing their sins and seeking pardon.

Joseph outlived his father fifty-four years. He lived to see "Ephraim's children of the third generation: the children also of Machir the son of Manasseh were brought up upon Joseph's knees." He witnessed the increase and prosperity of his people, and through all the years his faith in God's restoration of Israel to the Land of Promise was unshaken.

When he saw that his end was near, he summoned his kinsmen about him. Honored as he had been in the land of the Pharaohs, Egypt was to him but the place of his exile; his last act was to signify that his lot was cast with Israel. His last words were, "God will surely visit you, and bring you out of this land unto the land which He sware to Abraham, to Isaac, and to Jacob." And he took a solemn oath of the children of Israel that they would carry up his bones with them to the land of Canaan. "So Joseph died, being an hundred and ten years old: and they embalmed him, and he was put in a coffin in Egypt." And through the centuries of toil which followed, the coffin, a reminder of the dying words of Joseph, testified to Israel that they were only sojourners in Egypt, and bade them keep their hopes fixed upon the Land of Promise, for the time of deliverance would surely come.

Chapter 22—Moses

This chapter is based on Exodus 1 to Exodus 4.

The people of Egypt, in order to supply themselves with food during the famine, had sold to the crown their cattle and lands, and had finally bound themselves to perpetual serfdom. Joseph wisely provided for their release; he permitted them to become royal tenants, holding their lands of the king, and paying an annual tribute of one fifth of the products of their labor.

But the children of Jacob were not under the necessity of making such conditions. On account of the service that Joseph had rendered the Egyptian nation, they were not only granted a part of the country as a home, but were exempted from taxation, and liberally supplied with food during the continuance of the famine. The king publicly acknowledged that it was through the merciful interposition of the God of Joseph that Egypt enjoyed plenty while other nations were perishing from famine. He saw, too, that Joseph's management had greatly enriched the kingdom, and his gratitude surrounded the family of Jacob with royal favor.

But as time rolled on, the great man to whom Egypt owed so much, and the generation blessed by his labors, passed to the grave. And "there arose up a new king over Egypt, which knew not Joseph." Not that he was ignorant of Joseph's services to the nation, but he wished to make no recognition of them, and, so far as possible, to bury them in oblivion. "And he said unto his people, Behold, the people of the children of Israel are more and mightier than we: come on, let us deal wisely with them; lest they multiply, and it come to pass, that, when there falleth out any war, they join also unto our enemies, and fight against us, and so get them up out of the land."

The Israelites had already become very numerous; they "were fruitful, and increased abundantly, and multiplied, and waxed exceeding mighty; and the land was filled with them." Under Joseph's fostering care, and the favor of the king who was then ruling, they had spread rapidly over the land. But they had kept themselves a distinct race, having nothing in common with the Egyptians in customs or religion; and their increasing numbers now excited the fears of the king and his people, lest in case of war they should join themselves with the enemies of Egypt. Yet policy forbade their banishment from the country. Many of them were able and understanding workmen, and they added greatly to the wealth of the nation; the king needed such laborers for the erection of his magnificent palaces and temples. Accordingly he ranked them with the Egyptians who had sold themselves with their possessions to the kingdom. Soon taskmasters were set over them, and their slavery became complete. "And the Egyptians made the children of Israel to serve with rigor: and they made their lives bitter with hard bondage, in mortar, and in brick, and in all manner of service in the field: all their service, wherein they made them serve, was with rigor." "But the more they afflicted them, the more they multiplied and grew."

The king and his counselors had hoped to subdue the Israelites with hard labor, and thus decrease their numbers and crush out their independent spirit. Failing to accomplish their purpose, they proceeded to more cruel measures. Orders were issued to the women whose employment gave them opportunity for executing the command, to destroy the Hebrew male children at their birth. Satan was the mover in this matter. He knew that a deliverer was to be raised up among the Israelites; and by leading the king to destroy their children he hoped to defeat the divine purpose. But the women feared God, and dared not execute the cruel mandate. The Lord approved their course, and prospered them. The king, angry at the failure of his design, made the command more urgent and extensive. The whole nation was called upon to hunt out and slaughter his helpless victims. "And Pharaoh charged all his people, saying, Every son that is born ye shall cast into the river, and every daughter ye shall save alive."

While this decree was in full force a son was born to Amram and Jochebed, devout Israelites of the tribe of Levi. The babe was "a goodly child;" and the parents, believing that the time of Israel's release was drawing near, and that God would raise up a deliverer for His people, determined that their little one should not be sacrificed.

Faith in God strengthened their hearts, "and they were not afraid of the king's commandment." Hebrews 11:23.

The mother succeeded in concealing the child for three months. Then, finding that she could no longer keep him safely, she prepared a little ark of rushes, making it watertight by means of slime and pitch; and laying the babe therein, she placed it among the flags at the river's brink. She dared not remain to guard it, lest the child's life and her own should be forfeited; but his sister, Miriam, lingered near, apparently indifferent, but anxiously watching to see what would become of her little brother. And there were other watchers. The mother's earnest prayers had committed her child to the care of God; and angels, unseen, hovered above his lowly resting place. Angels directed Pharaoh's daughter thither. Her curiosity was excited by the little basket, and as she looked upon the beautiful child within, she read the story at a glance. The tears of the babe awakened her compassion, and her sympathies went out to the unknown mother who had resorted to this means to preserve the life of her precious little one. She determined that he should be saved; she would adopt him as her own.

Miriam had been secretly noting every movement; perceiving that the child was tenderly regarded, she ventured nearer, and at last said, "Shall I go and call thee a nurse of the Hebrew women, that she may nurse the child for thee?" And permission was given.

The sister hastened to her mother with the happy news, and without delay returned with her to the presence of Pharaoh's daughter. "Take this child away, and nurse it for me, and I will give thee thy wages," said the princess.

God had heard the mother's prayers; her faith had been rewarded. It was with deep gratitude that she entered upon her now safe and happy task. She faithfully improved her opportunity to educate her child for God. She felt confident that he had been preserved for some great work, and she knew that he must soon be given up to his royal mother, to be surrounded with influences that would tend to lead him away from God. All this rendered her more diligent and careful in his instruction than in that of her other children. She endeavored to imbue his mind with the fear of God and the love of truth and justice, and earnestly prayed that he might be preserved from every corrupting influence. She showed him the folly and sin of idolatry, and early taught him to bow down and pray to the living God, who alone could hear him and help him in every emergency.

She kept the boy as long as she could, but was obliged to give him up when he was about twelve years old. From his humble cabin home he was taken to the royal palace, to the daughter of Pharaoh, "and he became her son." Yet even here he did not lose the impressions received in childhood. The lessons learned at his mother's side could not be forgotten. They were a shield from the pride, the infidelity, and the vice that flourished amid the splendor of the court.

How far-reaching in its results was the influence of that one Hebrew woman, and she an exile and a slave! The whole future life of Moses, the great mission which he fulfilled as the leader of Israel, testifies to the importance of the work of the Christian mother. There is no other work that can equal this. To a very great extent the mother holds in her own hands the destiny of her children. She is dealing with developing minds and characters, working not alone for time, but for eternity. She is sowing seed that will spring up and bear fruit, either for good or for evil. She has not to paint a form of beauty upon canvas or to chisel it from marble, but to impress upon a human soul the image of the divine. Especially during their early years the responsibility rests upon her of forming the character of her children. The impressions now made upon their developing minds will remain with them all through life. Parents should direct the instruction and training of their children while very young, to the end that they may be Christians. They are placed in our care to be trained, not as heirs to the throne of an earthly empire, but as kings unto God, to reign through unending ages.

Let every mother feel that her moments are priceless; her work will be tested in the solemn day of accounts. Then it will be found that many of the failures and crimes of men and women have resulted from the ignorance and neglect of those whose duty it was to guide their childish feet in the right way. Then it will be found that many who have blessed the world with the light of genius and truth and holiness, owe the principles that were the mainspring of their influence and success to a praying, Christian mother.

At the court of Pharaoh, Moses received the highest civil and military training. The monarch had determined to make his adopted grandson his successor on the throne, and the youth was educated for his high station. "And Moses was learned in all the wisdom of the Egyptians, and was mighty in words and in deeds." Acts 7:22. His ability as a military leader made him a favorite with the armies of Egypt, and he was generally regarded as a remarkable character. Satan had been defeated in his purpose. The very decree condemning the Hebrew children to death had been overruled by God for the training and education of the future leader of His people.

The elders of Israel were taught by angels that the time for their deliverance was near, and that Moses was the man whom God would employ to accomplish this work. Angels instructed Moses also that Jehovah had chosen him to break the bondage of His people. He, supposing that they were to obtain their freedom by force of arms, expected to lead the Hebrew host against the armies of Egypt, and having this in view, he guarded his affections, lest in his attachment to his foster mother or to Pharaoh he would not be free to do the will of God.

By the laws of Egypt all who occupied the throne of the Pharaohs must become members of the priestly caste; and Moses, as the heir apparent, was to be initiated into the mysteries of the national religion. This duty was committed to the priests. But while he was an ardent and untiring student, he could not be induced to participate in the worship of the gods. He was threatened with the loss of the crown, and warned that he would be disowned by the princess should he persist in his adherence to the Hebrew faith. But he was unshaken in his determination to render homage to none save the one God, the Maker of heaven and earth. He reasoned with priests and worshipers, showing the folly of their superstitious veneration of senseless objects. None could refute his arguments or change his purpose, yet for the time his firmness was tolerated on account of his high position and the favor with which he was regarded by both the king and the people.

"By faith Moses, when he was come to years, refused to be called the son of Pharaoh's daughter; choosing rather to suffer affliction with the people of God, than to enjoy the pleasures of sin for a season; esteeming the reproach of Christ greater riches than the treasures in Egypt: for he had respect unto the recompense of the reward." Hebrews 11:24-26. Moses was fitted to take pre-eminence among the great of the earth, to shine in the courts of its most glorious kingdom, and to sway the scepter of its power. His intellectual greatness distinguishes him above the great men of all ages. As historian, poet, philosopher, general of armies, and legislator, he stands without a peer. Yet with the world before him, he had the moral strength to refuse the flattering prospects of wealth and greatness and fame, "choosing rather to suffer affliction with the people of God, than to enjoy the pleasures of sin for a season."

Moses had been instructed in regard to the final reward to be given to the humble and obedient servants of God, and worldly gain sank to its proper insignificance in comparison. The magnificent palace of Pharaoh and the monarch's throne were held out as an inducement to Moses; but he knew that the sinful pleasures that make men forget God were in its lordly courts. He looked beyond the gorgeous palace, beyond a monarch's crown, to the high honors that will be bestowed on the saints of the Most High in a kingdom untainted by sin. He saw by faith an imperishable crown that the King of heaven would place on the brow of the overcomer. This faith led him to turn away from the lordly ones of earth and join the humble, poor, despised nation that had chosen to obey God rather than to serve sin.

Moses remained at court until he was forty years of age. His thoughts often turned upon the abject condition of his people, and he visited his brethren in their servitude, and encouraged them with the assurance that God would work for their deliverance. Often, stung to resentment by the sight of injustice and oppression, he burned to avenge their wrongs. One day, while thus abroad, seeing an Egyptian smiting an Israelite, he sprang forward and slew the Egyptian. Except the Israelite, there had been no witness to the deed, and Moses immediately buried the body in the sand. He had now shown himself ready to maintain the cause of his people, and he hoped to see them rise to recover their liberty. "He supposed his brethren would have understood how that God by his hand would deliver them; but they understood not." Acts 7:25. They were not yet prepared for freedom. On the following day Moses saw two Hebrews striving together, one of them evidently at fault. Moses reproved the offender, who at once retaliated upon the reprover, denying his right to interfere, and basely accusing him of crime:

"Who made thee a prince and a judge over us?" he said. "Intendest thou to kill me, as thou killedst the Egyptian?"

The whole matter was quickly made known to the Egyptians, and, greatly exaggerated, soon reached the ears of Pharaoh. It was represented to the king that this act meant much; that Moses designed to lead his people against the Egyptians, to overthrow the government, and to seat himself upon the throne; and that there could be no security for the kingdom while he lived. It was at once determined by the monarch that he should die; but, becoming aware of his danger, he made his escape and fled toward Arabia.

The Lord directed his course, and he found a home with Jethro, the priest and prince of Midian, who was also a worshiper of God. After a time Moses married one of the daughters of Jethro; and here, in the service of his father-in-law, as keeper of his flocks, he remained forty years.

In slaying the Egyptian, Moses had fallen into the same error so often committed by his fathers, of taking into their own hands the work that God had promised to do. It was not God's will to deliver His people by warfare, as Moses thought, but by His own mighty power, that the glory might be ascribed to Him alone. Yet even this rash act was overruled by God to accomplish His purposes. Moses was not prepared for his great work. He had yet to learn the same lesson of faith that Abraham and Jacob had been taught—not to rely upon human strength or wisdom, but upon the power of God for the fulfillment of His promises. And there were other lessons that, amid the solitude of the mountains, Moses was to receive. In the school of self-denial and hardship he was to learn patience, to temper his passions. Before he could govern wisely, he must be trained to obey. His own heart must be fully in harmony with God before he could teach the knowledge of His will to Israel. By his own experience he must be prepared to exercise a fatherly care over all who needed his help.

Man would have dispensed with that long period of toil and obscurity, deeming it a great loss of time. But Infinite Wisdom called him who was to become the leader of his people to spend forty years in the humble work of a shepherd. The habits of caretaking, of self-forgetfulness and tender solicitude for his flock, thus developed, would prepare him to become the compassionate, longsuffering shepherd of Israel. No advantage that human training or culture could bestow, could be a substitute for this experience.

Moses had been learning much that he must unlearn. The influences that had surrounded him in Egypt—the love of his foster mother, his own high position as the king's grandson, the dissipation on every hand, the refinement, the subtlety, and the mysticism of a false religion, the splendor of idolatrous worship, the solemn grandeur of architecture and sculpture—all had left deep impressions upon his developing mind and had molded, to some extent, his habits and character. Time, change of surroundings, and communion with God could remove these impressions. It would require on the part of Moses himself a struggle as for life to renounce error and accept truth, but God would be his helper when the conflict should be too severe for human strength.

In all who have been chosen to accomplish a work for God the human element is seen. Yet they have not been men of stereotyped habits and character, who were satisfied to remain in that condition. They earnestly desired to obtain wisdom from God and to learn to work for Him. Says the apostle, "If any of you lack wisdom, let him ask of God, that giveth to all men liberally, and upbraideth not; and it shall be given him." James 1:5. But God will not impart to men divine light while they are content to remain in darkness. In order to receive God's help, man must realize his weakness and deficiency; he must apply his own mind to the great change to be wrought in himself; he must be aroused to earnest and persevering prayer and effort. Wrong habits and customs must be shaken off; and it is only by determined endeavor to correct these errors and to conform to right principles that the victory can be gained. Many never attain to the position that they might occupy, because they wait for God to do for them that which He has given them power to do for themselves. All who are fitted for usefulness must be trained by the severest mental and moral discipline, and God will assist them by uniting divine power with human effort.

Shut in by the bulwarks of the mountains, Moses was alone with God. The magnificent temples of Egypt no longer impressed his mind with their superstition and falsehood. In the solemn grandeur of the everlasting hills he beheld the majesty of the Most High, and in contrast realized how powerless and insignificant were the gods of

Egypt. Everywhere the Creator's name was written. Moses seemed to stand in His presence and to be over-shadowed by His power. Here his pride and self-sufficiency were swept away. In the stern simplicity of his wilderness life, the results of the ease and luxury of Egypt disappeared. Moses became patient, reverent, and humble, "very meek, above all the men which were upon the face of the earth" (Numbers 12:3), yet strong in faith in the mighty God of Jacob.

As the years rolled on, and he wandered with his flocks in solitary places, pondering upon the oppressed condition of his people, he recounted the dealings of God with his fathers and the promises that were the heritage of the chosen nation, and his prayers for Israel ascended by day and by night. Heavenly angels shed their light around him. Here, under the inspiration of the Holy Spirit, he wrote the book of Genesis. The long years spent amid the desert solitudes were rich in blessing, not alone to Moses and his people, but to the world in all succeeding ages.

"And it came to pass in process of time, that the king of Egypt died: and the children of Israel sighed by reason of the bondage, and they cried, and their cry came up unto God by reason of the bondage. And God heard their groaning, and God remembered His covenant with Abraham, with Isaac, and with Jacob. And God looked upon the children of Israel, and God had respect unto them." The time for Israel's deliverance had come. But God's purpose was to be accomplished in a manner to pour contempt on human pride. The deliverer was to go forth as a humble shepherd, with only a rod in his hand; but God would make that rod the symbol of His power. Leading his flocks one day near Horeb, "the mountain of God," Moses saw a bush in flames, branches, foliage, and trunk, all burning, yet seeming not to be consumed. He drew near to view the wonderful sight, when a voice from out of the flame called him by name. With trembling lips he answered, "Here am I." He was warned not to approach irreverently: "Put off thy shoes from off thy feet; for the place whereon thou standest is holy ground.... I am the God of thy father, the God of Abraham, the God of Isaac, and the God of Jacob." It was He who, as the Angel of the covenant, had revealed Himself to the fathers in ages past. "And Moses hid his face; for he was afraid to look upon God."

Humility and reverence should characterize the deportment of all who come into the presence of God. In the name of Jesus we may come before Him with confidence, but we must not approach Him with the boldness of presumption, as though He were on a level with ourselves. There are those who address the great and all-powerful and holy God, who dwelleth in light unapproachable, as they would address an equal, or even an inferior. There are those who conduct themselves in His house as they would not presume to do in the audience chamber of an earthly ruler. These should remember that they are in His sight whom seraphim adore, before whom angels veil their faces. God is greatly to be reverenced; all who truly realize His presence will bow in humility before Him, and, like Jacob beholding the vision of God, they will cry out, "How dreadful is this place! This is none other but the house of God, and this is the gate of heaven."

As Moses waited in reverent awe before God the words continued: "I have surely seen the affliction of My people which are in Egypt, and have heard their cry by reason of their taskmasters; for I know their sorrows; and I am come down to deliver them out of the hand of the Egyptians, and to bring them up out of that land unto a good land and a large, unto a land flowing with milk and honey.... Come now therefore, and I will send thee unto Pharaoh, that thou mayest bring forth My people the children of Israel out of Egypt."

Amazed and terrified at the command, Moses drew back, saying, "Who am I, that I should go unto Pharaoh, and that I should bring forth the children of Israel out of Egypt?" The reply was, "Certainly I will be with thee; and this shall be a token unto thee, that I have sent thee: When thou hast brought forth the people out of Egypt, ye shall serve God upon this mountain."

Moses thought of the difficulties to be encountered, of the blindness, ignorance, and unbelief of his people, many of whom were almost destitute of a knowledge of God. "Behold," he said, "when I come unto the children of Israel, and shall say unto them, The God of your fathers hath sent me unto you; and they shall say to me, What is His name? what shall I say unto them?" The answer was—

"I AM THAT I AM." "Thus shalt thou say unto the children of Israel, I AM hath sent me unto you."

Moses was commanded first to assemble the elders of Israel, the most noble and righteous among them, who had long grieved because of their bondage, and to declare to them a message from God, with a promise of deliverance. Then he was to go with the elders before the king, and say to him—

"The Lord God of the Hebrews hath met with us: and now let us go, we beseech thee, three days' journey into the wilderness, that we may sacrifice to the Lord our God."

Moses was forewarned that Pharaoh would resist the appeal to let Israel go. Yet the courage of God's servant must not fail; for the Lord would make this the occasion to manifest His power before the Egyptians and before His people. "And I will stretch out My hand, and smite Egypt with all My wonders which I will do in the midst thereof: and after that he will let you go."

Direction was also given concerning the provision they were to make for the journey. The Lord declared, "It shall come to pass, that, when ye go, ye shall not go empty: but every woman shall borrow of her neighbor, and of her that sojourneth in her house, jewels of silver, and jewels of gold, and raiment." The Egyptians had been enriched by the labor unjustly exacted from the Israelites, and as the latter were to start on the journey to their new home, it was right for them to claim the reward of their years of toil. They were to ask for articles of value, such as could be easily transported, and God would give them favor in the sight of the Egyptians. The mighty miracles wrought for their deliverance would strike terror to the oppressors, so that the requests of the bondmen would be granted.

Moses saw before him difficulties that seemed insurmountable. What proof could he give his people that God had indeed sent him? "Behold," he said, "they will not believe me, nor hearken unto my voice: for they will say, The Lord hath not appeared unto thee." Evidence that appealed to his own senses was now given. He was told to cast his rod upon the ground. As he did so, "it became a serpent; and Moses fled from before it." He was commanded to seize it, and in his hand it became a rod. He was bidden to put his hand into his bosom. He obeyed, and "when he took it out, behold, his hand was leprous as snow." Being told to put it again into his bosom, he found on withdrawing it that it had become like the other. By these signs the Lord assured Moses that His own people, as well as

Pharaoh, should be convinced that One mightier than the king of Egypt was manifest among them.

But the servant of God was still overwhelmed by the thought of the strange and wonderful work before him. In his distress and fear he now pleaded as an excuse a lack of ready speech: "O my Lord, I am not eloquent, neither heretofore, nor since Thou hast spoken unto Thy servant; but I am slow of speech, and of a slow tongue." He had been so long away from the Egyptians that he had not so clear knowledge and ready use of their language as when he was among them.

The Lord said unto him, "Who hath made man's mouth? or who maketh the dumb, or deaf, or the seeing, or the blind? have not I the Lord?" To this was added another assurance of divine aid: "Now therefore go, and I will be with thy mouth, and teach thee what thou shalt say." But Moses still entreated that a more competent person be selected. These excuses at first proceeded from humility and diffidence; but after the Lord had promised to remove all difficulties, and to give him final success, then any further shrinking back and complaining of his unfitness showed distrust of God. It implied a fear that God was unable to qualify him for the great work to which He had called him, or that He had made a mistake in the selection of the man.

Moses was now directed to Aaron, his elder brother, who, having been in daily use of the language of the Egyptians, was able to speak it perfectly. He was told that Aaron was coming to meet him. The next words from the Lord were an unqualified command:

"Thou shalt speak unto him, and put words in his mouth: and I will be with thy mouth, and with his mouth, and will teach you what ye shall do. And he shall be thy spokesman unto the people: and he shall be, even he shall be to thee instead of a mouth, and thou shalt be to him instead of God. And thou shalt take this rod in thine hand, wherewith thou shalt do signs." He could make no further resistance, for all ground for excuse was removed.

The divine command given to Moses found him self-distrustful, slow of speech, and timid. He was overwhelmed with a sense of his incapacity to be a mouthpiece for God to Israel. But having once accepted the work, he entered upon it with his whole heart, putting all his trust in the Lord. The greatness of his mission called

[255]

into exercise the best powers of his mind. God blessed his ready obedience, and he became eloquent, hopeful, self-possessed, and well fitted for the greatest work ever given to man. This is an example of what God does to strengthen the character of those who trust Him fully and give themselves unreservedly to His commands.

A man will gain power and efficiency as he accepts the responsibilities that God places upon him, and with his whole soul seeks to qualify himself to bear them aright. However humble his position or limited his ability, that man will attain true greatness who, trusting to divine strength, seeks to perform his work with fidelity. Had Moses relied upon his own strength and wisdom, and eagerly accepted the great charge, he would have evinced his entire unfitness for such a work. The fact that a man feels his weakness is at least some evidence that he realizes the magnitude of the work appointed him, and that he will make God his counselor and his strength.

Moses returned to his father-in-law and expressed his desire to visit his brethren in Egypt. Jethro's consent was given, with his blessing, "Go in peace." With his wife and children, Moses set forth on the journey. He had not dared to make known the object of his mission, lest they should not be allowed to accompany him. Before reaching Egypt, however, he himself thought it best for their own safety to send them back to the home in Midian.

A secret dread of Pharaoh and the Egyptians, whose anger had been kindled against him forty years before, had rendered Moses still more reluctant to return to Egypt; but after he had set out to obey the divine command, the Lord revealed to him that his enemies were dead.

On the way from Midian, Moses received a startling and terrible warning of the Lord's displeasure. An angel appeared to him in a threatening manner, as if he would immediately destroy him. No explanation was given; but Moses remembered that he had disregarded one of God's requirements; yielding to the persuasion of his wife, he had neglected to perform the rite of circumcision upon their youngest son. He had failed to comply with the condition by which his child could be entitled to the blessings of God's covenant with Israel; and such a neglect on the part of their chosen leader could not but lessen the force of the divine precepts upon the people. Zipporah, fearing that her husband would be slain, performed the rite herself, and the angel then permitted Moses to pursue his journey. In his mission to Pharaoh, Moses was to be placed in a position of great peril; his life could be preserved only through the protection of holy angels. But while living in neglect of a known duty, he would not be secure; for he could not be shielded by the angels of God.

In the time of trouble just before the coming of Christ, the righteous will be preserved through the ministration of heavenly angels; but there will be no security for the transgressor of God's law. Angels cannot then protect those who are disregarding one of the divine precepts.

Chapter 23—The Plagues of Egypt

This chapter is based on Exodus 5-10.

Aaron, being instructed by angels, went forth to meet his brother, from whom he had been so long separated; and they met amid the desert solitudes, near Horeb. Here they communed together, and Moses told Aaron "all the words of the Lord who had sent him, and all the signs which He had commanded him." Exodus 4:28. Together they journeyed to Egypt; and having reached the land of Goshen, they proceeded to assemble the elders of Israel. Aaron repeated to them all the dealings of God with Moses, and then the signs which God had given Moses were shown before the people. "The people believed: and when they heard that the Lord had visited the children of Israel, and that He had looked upon their affliction, then they bowed their heads and worshiped." Verse 31.

Moses had been charged also with a message for the king. The two brothers entered the palace of the Pharaohs as ambassadors from the King of kings, and they spoke in His name: "Thus saith Jehovah, God of Israel, Let My people go, that they may hold a feast unto Me in the wilderness."

"Who is Jehovah, that I should obey His voice to let Israel go?" demanded the monarch; "I know not Jehovah, neither will I let Israel go."

Their answer was, "The God of the Hebrews hath met with us: let us go, we pray thee, three days' journey into the desert, and sacrifice unto the Lord our God; lest He fall upon us with pestilence, or with the sword."

Tidings of them and of the interest they were exciting among the people had already reached the king. His anger was kindled. "Wherefore do ye, Moses and Aaron, let [hinder] the people from their works?" he said. "Get you unto your burdens." Already the kingdom had suffered loss by the interference of these strangers. At thought of this he added, "Behold, the people of the land now are many, and ye make them rest from their burdens."

In their bondage the Israelites had to some extent lost the knowledge of God's law, and they had departed from its precepts. The Sabbath had been generally disregarded, and the exactions of their taskmasters made its observance apparently impossible. But Moses had shown his people that obedience to God was the first condition of deliverance; and the efforts made to restore the observance of the Sabbath had come to the notice of their oppressors. [See Appendix, note 1.]

The king, thoroughly roused, suspected the Israelites of a design to revolt from his service. Disaffection was the result of idleness; he would see that no time was left them for dangerous scheming. And he at once adopted measures to tighten their bonds and crush out their independent spirit. The same day orders were issued that rendered their labor still more cruel and oppressive. The most common building material of that country was sun-dried brick; the walls of the finest edifices were made of this, and then faced with stone; and the manufacture of brick employed great numbers of the bondmen. Cut straw being intermixed with the clay, to hold it together, large quantities of straw were required for the work; the king now directed that no more straw be furnished; the laborers must find it for themselves, while the same amount of brick should be exacted.

This order produced great distress among the Israelites throughout the land. The Egyptian taskmasters had appointed Hebrew officers to oversee the work of the people, and these officers were responsible for the labor performed by those under their charge. When the requirement of the king was put in force, the people scattered themselves throughout the land, to gather stubble instead of straw; but they found it impossible to accomplish the usual amount of labor. For this failure the Hebrew officers were cruelly beaten.

These officers supposed that their oppression came from their taskmasters, and not from the king himself; and they went to him with their grievances. Their remonstrance was met by Pharaoh with a taunt: "Ye are idle, ye are idle: therefore ye say, Let us go and do sacrifice to the Lord." They were ordered back to their work, with the declaration that their burdens were in no case to be lightened. Returning, they met Moses and Aaron, and cried out to them, "The Lord look upon you, and judge; because ye have made our savor to be abhorred in the eyes of Pharaoh, and in the eyes of his servants, to put a sword in their hand to slay us."

As Moses listened to these reproaches he was greatly distressed. The sufferings of the people had been much increased. All over the land a cry of despair went up from old and young, and all united in charging upon him the disastrous change in their condition. In bitterness of soul he went before God, with the cry, "Lord, wherefore hast Thou so evil entreated this people? why is it that Thou hast sent me? For since I came to Pharaoh to speak in Thy name, he hath done evil to this people; neither hast Thou delivered Thy people at all." The answer was, "Now shalt thou see what I will do to Pharaoh: for with a strong hand shall he let them go, and with a strong hand shall he drive them out of his land." Again he was pointed back to the covenant which God had made with the fathers, and was assured that it would be fulfilled.

During all the years of servitude in Egypt there had been among the Israelites some who adhered to the worship of Jehovah. These were sorely troubled as they saw their children daily witnessing the abominations of the heathen, and even bowing down to their false gods. In their distress they cried unto the Lord for deliverance from the Egyptian yoke, that they might be freed from the corrupting influence of idolatry. They did not conceal their faith, but declared to the Egyptians that the object of their worship was the Maker of heaven and earth, the only true and living God. They rehearsed the evidences of His existence and power, from creation down to the days of Jacob. The Egyptians thus had an opportunity to become acquainted with the religion of the Hebrews; but disdaining to be instructed by their slaves, they tried to seduce the worshipers of God by promises of reward, and, this failing, by threats and cruelty.

The elders of Israel endeavored to sustain the sinking faith of their brethren by repeating the promises made to their fathers, and the prophetic words of Joseph before his death, foretelling their deliverance from Egypt. Some would listen and believe. Others, looking at the circumstances that surrounded them, refused to hope. The Egyptians, being informed of what was reported among their bondmen, derided their expectations and scornfully denied the power of their God. They pointed to their situation as a nation of slaves, and tauntingly said, "If your God is just and merciful, and possesses power above that of the Egyptian gods, why does He not make you a free people?" They called attention to their own condition. They worshiped deities termed by the Israelites false gods, yet they were a rich and powerful nation. They declared that their gods had blessed them with prosperity, and had given them the Israelites as servants, and they gloried in their power to oppress and destroy the worshipers of Jehovah. Pharaoh himself boasted that the God of the Hebrews could not deliver them from his hand.

Words like these destroyed the hopes of many of the Israelites. The case appeared to them very much as the Egyptians had represented. It was true that they were slaves, and must endure whatever their cruel taskmasters might choose to inflict. Their children had been hunted and slain, and their own lives were a burden. Yet they were worshiping the God of heaven. If Jehovah were indeed above all gods, surely He would not thus leave them in bondage to idolaters. But those who were true to God understood that it was because of Israel's departure from Him—because of their disposition to marry with heathen nations, thus being led into idolatry—that the Lord had permitted them to become bondmen; and they confidently assured their brethren that He would soon break the yoke of the oppressor.

The Hebrews had expected to obtain their freedom without any special trial of their faith or any real suffering or hardship. But they were not yet prepared for deliverance. They had little faith in God, and were unwilling patiently to endure their afflictions until He should see fit to work for them. Many were content to remain in bondage rather than meet the difficulties attending removal to a strange land; and the habits of some had become so much like those of the Egyptians that they preferred to dwell in Egypt. Therefore the Lord did not deliver them by the first manifestation of His power before Pharaoh. He overruled events more fully to develop the tyrannical spirit of the Egyptian king and also to reveal Himself to His people. Beholding His justice, His power, and His love, they would choose to leave Egypt and give themselves to His service. The task of Moses would have been much less difficult had not many of the Israelites become so corrupted that they were unwilling to leave Egypt.

The Lord directed Moses to go again to the people and repeat the promise of deliverance, with a fresh assurance of divine favor.

He went as he was commanded; but they would not listen. Says the Scripture, "They hearkened not ... for anguish of spirit, and for cruel bondage." Again the divine message came to Moses, "Go in, speak unto Pharaoh king of Egypt, that he let the children of Israel go out of his land." In discouragement he replied, "Behold, the children of Israel have not hearkened unto me; how then shall Pharaoh hear me?" He was told to take Aaron with him and go before Pharaoh, and again demand "that he send the children of Israel out of his land."

He was informed that the monarch would not yield until God should visit judgments upon Egypt and bring out Israel by the signal manifestation of His power. Before the infliction of each plague, Moses was to describe its nature and effects, that the king might save himself from it if he chose. Every punishment rejected would be followed by one more severe, until his proud heart would be humbled, and he would acknowledge the Maker of heaven and earth as the true and living God. The Lord would give the Egyptians an opportunity to see how vain was the wisdom of their mighty men, how feeble the power of their gods, when opposed to the commands of Jehovah. He would punish the people of Egypt for their idolatry and silence their boasting of the blessings received from their senseless deities. God would glorify His own name, that other nations might hear of His power and tremble at His mighty acts, and that His people might be led to turn from their idolatry and render Him pure worship.

Again Moses and Aaron entered the lordly halls of the king of Egypt. There, surrounded by lofty columns and glittering adornments, by the rich paintings and sculptured images of heathen gods, before the monarch of the most powerful kingdom then in existence, stood the two representatives of the enslaved race, to repeat the command from God for Israel's release. The king demanded a miracle, in evidence of their divine commission. Moses and Aaron had been directed how to act in case such a demand should be made, and Aaron now took the rod and cast it down before Pharaoh. It became a serpent. The monarch sent for his "wise men and the sorcerers," who "cast down every man his rod and they became serpents: but Aaron's rod swallowed up their rods." Then the king, more determined than before, declared his magicians equal in power with Moses and Aaron; he denounced the servants of the Lord as impostors, and felt himself secure in resisting their demands. Yet while he despised their message, he was restrained by divine power from doing them harm.

It was the hand of God, and no human influence or power possessed by Moses and Aaron, that wrought the miracles which they showed before Pharaoh. Those signs and wonders were designed to convince Pharaoh that the great "I AM" had sent Moses, and that it was the duty of the king to let Israel go, that they might serve the living God. The magicians also showed signs and wonders; for they wrought not by their own skill alone, but by the power of their god, Satan, who assisted them in counterfeiting the work of Jehovah.

The magicians did not really cause their rods to become serpents; but by magic, aided by the great deceiver, they were able to produce this appearance. It was beyond the power of Satan to change the rods to living serpents. The prince of evil, though possessing all the wisdom and might of an angel fallen, has not power to create, or to give life; this is the prerogative of God alone. But all that was in Satan's power to do, he did; he produced a counterfeit. To human sight the rods were changed to serpents. Such they were believed to be by Pharaoh and his court. There was nothing in their appearance to distinguish them from the serpent produced by Moses. Though the Lord caused the real serpent to swallow up the spurious ones, yet even this was regarded by Pharaoh, not as a work of God's power, but as the result of a kind of magic superior to that of his servants.

Pharaoh desired to justify his stubbornness in resisting the divine command, and hence he was seeking some pretext for disregarding the miracles that God had wrought through Moses. Satan gave him just what he wanted. By the work that he wrought through the magicians he made it appear to the Egyptians that Moses and Aaron were only magicians and sorcerers, and that the message they brought could not claim respect as coming from a superior being. Thus Satan's counterfeit accomplished its purpose of emboldening the Egyptians in their rebellion and causing Pharaoh to harden his heart against conviction. Satan hoped also to shake the faith of Moses and Aaron in the divine origin of their mission, that his instruments might prevail. He was unwilling that the children of Israel should be released from bondage to serve the living God.

But the prince of evil had a still deeper object in manifesting his wonders through the magicians. He well knew that Moses, in breaking the yoke of bondage from off the children of Israel, prefigured Christ, who was to break the reign of sin over the human family. He knew that when Christ should appear, mighty miracles would be wrought as an evidence to the world that God had sent Him. Satan trembled for his power. By counterfeiting the work of God through Moses, he hoped not only to prevent the deliverance of Israel, but to exert an influence through future ages to destroy faith in the miracles of Christ. Satan is constantly seeking to counterfeit the work of Christ and to establish his own power and claims. He leads men to account for the miracles of Christ by making them appear to be the result of human skill and power. In many minds he thus destroys faith in Christ as the Son of God, and leads them to reject the gracious offers of mercy through the plan of redemption.

Moses and Aaron were directed to visit the riverside next morning, where the king was accustomed to repair. The overflowing of the Nile being the source of food and wealth for all Egypt, the river was worshiped as a god, and the monarch came thither daily to pay his devotions. Here the two brothers again repeated the message to him, and then they stretched out the rod and smote upon the water. The sacred stream ran blood, the fish died, and the river became offensive to the smell. The water in the houses, the supply preserved in cisterns, was likewise changed to blood. But "the magicians of Egypt did so with their enchantments," and "Pharaoh turned and went into his house, neither did he set his heart to this also." For seven days the plague continued, but without effect.

Again the rod was stretched out over the waters, and frogs came up from the river and spread over the land. They overran the houses, took possession of the bed chambers, and even the ovens and kneading troughs. The frog was regarded as sacred by the Egyptians, and they would not destroy it; but the slimy pests had now become intolerable. They swarmed even in the palace of the Pharaohs, and the king was impatient to have them removed. The magicians had appeared to produce frogs, but they could not remove them. Upon seeing this, Pharaoh was somewhat humbled. He sent for Moses and Aaron, and said, "Entreat the Lord, that He may take away the frogs from me, and from my people; and I will let the people go, that they may do sacrifice unto the Lord." After reminding the king of his former boasting, they requested him to appoint a time when they should pray for the removal of the plague. He set the next day, secretly hoping that in the interval the frogs might disappear of themselves, and thus save him from the bitter humiliation of submitting to the God of Israel. The plague, however, continued till the time specified, when throughout all Egypt the frogs died, but their putrid bodies, which remained, polluted the atmosphere.

The Lord could have caused them to return to dust in a moment; but He did not do this lest after their removal the king and his people should pronounce it the result of sorcery or enchantment, like the work of the magicians. The frogs died, and were then gathered together in heaps. Here the king and all Egypt had evidence which their vain philosophy could not gainsay, that this work was not accomplished by magic, but was a judgment from the God of heaven.

"When Pharaoh saw that there was respite, he hardened his heart." At the command of God, Aaron stretched out his hand, and the dust of the earth became lice throughout all the land of Egypt. Pharaoh called upon the magicians to do the same, but they could not. The work of God was thus shown to be superior to that of Satan. The magicians themselves acknowledged, "This is the finger of God." But the king was still unmoved.

Appeal and warning were ineffectual, and another judgment was inflicted. The time of its occurrence was foretold, that it might not be said to have come by chance. Flies filled the houses and swarmed upon the ground, so that "the land was corrupted by reason of the swarms of flies." These flies were large and venomous, and their bite was extremely painful to man and beast. As had been foretold, this visitation did not extend to the land of Goshen.

Pharaoh now offered the Israelites permission to sacrifice in Egypt, but they refused to accept such conditions. "It is not meet," said Moses; "lo, shall we sacrifice the abomination of the Egyptians before their eyes, and will they not stone us?" The animals which the Hebrews would be required to sacrifice were among those regarded as sacred by the Egyptians; and such was the reverence in which these creatures were held, that to slay one, even accidentally, was a crime punishable with death. It would be impossible for the Hebrews to worship in Egypt without giving offense to their masters. Moses again proposed to go three days' journey into the wilderness. The monarch consented, and begged the servants of God to entreat that the plague might be removed. They promised to do this, but warned him against dealing deceitfully with them. The plague was stayed, but the king's heart had become hardened by persistent rebellion, and he still refused to yield.

A more terrible stroke followed—murrain upon all the Egyptian cattle that were in the field. Both the sacred animals and the beasts of burden—kine and oxen and sheep, horses and camels and asses—were destroyed. It had been distinctly stated that the Hebrews were to be exempt; and Pharaoh, on sending messengers to the home of the Israelites, proved the truth of this declaration of Moses. "Of the cattle of the children of Israel died not one." Still the king was obstinate.

Moses was next directed to take ashes of the furnace, and "sprinkle it toward heaven in the sight of Pharaoh." This act was deeply significant. Four hundred years before, God had shown to Abraham the future oppression of His people, under the figure of a smoking furnace and a burning lamp. He had declared that He would visit judgments upon their oppressors, and would bring forth the captives with great substance. In Egypt, Israel had long languished in the furnace of affliction. This act of Moses was an assurance to them that God was mindful of His covenant, and that the time for their deliverance had come.

As the ashes were sprinkled toward heaven, the fine particles spread over all the land of Egypt, and wherever they settled, produced boils "breaking forth with blains upon man, and upon beast." The priests and magicians had hitherto encouraged Pharaoh in his stubbornness, but now a judgment had come that reached even them. Smitten with a loathsome and painful disease, their vaunted power only making them contemptible, they were no longer able to contend against the God of Israel. The whole nation was made to see the folly of trusting in the magicians, when they were not able to protect even their own persons.

Still the heart of Pharaoh grew harder. And now the Lord sent a message to him, declaring, "I will at this time send all My plagues upon thy heart, and upon thy servants, and upon thy people; that thou mayest know that there is none like Me in all the earth.... And in very deed for this cause have I raised thee up, for to show in thee My power." Not that God had given him an existence for this purpose, but His providence had overruled events to place him upon the throne at the very time appointed for Israel's deliverance. Though this haughty tyrant had by his crimes forfeited the mercy of God, yet his life had been preserved that through his stubbornness the Lord might manifest His wonders in the land of Egypt. The disposing of events is of God's providence. He could have placed upon the throne a more merciful king, who would not have dared to withstand the mighty manifestations of divine power. But in that case the Lord's purposes would not have been accomplished. His people were permitted to experience the grinding cruelty of the Egyptians, that they might not be deceived concerning the debasing influence of idolatry. In His dealing with Pharaoh, the Lord manifested His hatred of idolatry and His determination to punish cruelty and oppression.

God had declared concerning Pharaoh, "I will harden his heart, that he shall not let the people go." Exodus 4:21. There was no exercise of supernatural power to harden the heart of the king. God gave to Pharaoh the most striking evidence of divine power, but the monarch stubbornly refused to heed the light. Every display of infinite power rejected by him, rendered him the more determined in his rebellion. The seeds of rebellion that he sowed when he rejected the first miracle, produced their harvest. As he continued to venture on in his own course, going from one degree of stubbornness to another, his heart became more and more hardened, until he was called to look upon the cold, dead faces of the first-born.

God speaks to men through His servants, giving cautions and warnings, and rebuking sin. He gives to each an opportunity to correct his errors before they become fixed in the character; but if one refuses to be corrected, divine power does not interpose to counteract the tendency of his own action. He finds it more easy to repeat the same course. He is hardening the heart against the influence of the Holy Spirit. A further rejection of light places him where a far stronger influence will be ineffectual to make an abiding impression.

He who has once yielded to temptation will yield more readily the second time. Every repetition of the sin lessens his power of resistance, blinds his eyes, and stifles conviction. Every seed of indulgence sown will bear fruit. God works no miracle to prevent the harvest. "Whatsoever a man soweth, that shall he also reap." Galatians 6:7. He who manifests an infidel hardihood, a stolid indifference to divine truth, is but reaping the harvest of that which he has himself sown. It is thus that multitudes come to listen with stoical indifference to the truths that once stirred their very souls. They sowed neglect and resistance to the truth, and such is the harvest which they reap.

Those who are quieting a guilty conscience with the thought that they can change a course of evil when they choose, that they can trifle with the invitations of mercy, and yet be again and again impressed, take this course at their peril. They think that after casting all their influence on the side of the great rebel, in a moment of utmost extremity, when danger compasses them about, they will change leaders. But this is not so easily done. The experience, the education, the discipline of a life of sinful indulgence, has so thoroughly molded the character that they cannot then receive the image of Jesus. Had no light shone upon their pathway, the case would have been different. Mercy might interpose, and give them an opportunity to accept her overtures; but after light has been long rejected and despised, it will be finally withdrawn.

A plague of hail was next threatened upon Pharaoh, with the warning, "Send therefore now, and gather thy cattle, and all that thou hast in the field; for upon every man and beast which shall be found in the field, and shall not be brought home, the hail shall come down upon them, and they shall die." Rain or hail was unusual in Egypt, and such a storm as was foretold had never been witnessed. The report spread rapidly, and all who believed the word of the Lord gathered in their cattle, while those who despised the warning left them in the field. Thus in the midst of judgment the mercy of God was displayed, the people were tested, and it was shown how many had been led to fear God by the manifestation of His power.

The storm came as predicted—thunder and hail, and fire mingled with it, "very grievous, such as there was none like it in all the land of Egypt since it became a nation. And the hail smote throughout all the land of Egypt all that was in the field, both man and beast; and the hail smote every herb of the field, and brake every tree of the field." Ruin and desolation marked the path of the destroying angel.

The land of Goshen alone was spared. It was demonstrated to the Egyptians that the earth is under the control of the living God, that the elements obey His voice, and that the only safety is in obedience to Him.

All Egypt trembled before the awful outpouring of divine judgment. Pharaoh hastily sent for the two brothers, and cried out, "I have sinned this time: the Lord is righteous, and I and my people are wicked. Entreat the Lord (for it is enough) that there be no more mighty thunderings and hail; and I will let you go, and ye shall stay no longer." The answer was, "As soon as I am gone out of the city, I will spread abroad my hands unto the Lord; and the thunder shall cease, neither shall there be any more hail; that thou mayest know how that the earth is the Lord's. But as for thee and thy servants, I know that ye will not yet fear the Lord God." [270]

Moses knew that the contest was not ended. Pharaoh's confessions and promises were not the effect of any radical change in his mind or heart, but were wrung from him by terror and anguish. Moses promised, however, to grant his request; for he would give him no occasion for further stubbornness. The prophet went forth, unheeding the fury of the tempest, and Pharaoh and all his host were witnesses to the power of Jehovah to preserve His messenger. Having passed without the city, Moses "spread abroad his hands unto the Lord: and the thunders and hail ceased, and the rain was not poured upon the earth." But no sooner had the king recovered from his fears than his heart returned to its perversity.

Then the Lord said unto Moses, "Go in unto Pharaoh: for I have hardened his heart, and the heart of his servants, that I might show these My signs before him; and that thou mayest tell in the ears of thy son, and of thy son's son, what things I have wrought in Egypt, and My signs which I have done among them; that ye may know how that I am Jehovah." The Lord was manifesting His power, to confirm the faith of Israel in Him as the only true and living God. He would give unmistakable evidence of the difference He placed between them and the Egyptians, and would cause all nations to know that the Hebrews, whom they had despised and oppressed, were under the protection of the God of heaven.

Moses warned the monarch that if he still remained obstinate, a plague of locusts would be sent, which would cover the face of the earth and eat up every green thing that remained; they would fill the houses, even the palace itself; such a scourge, he said, as "neither thy fathers, nor thy fathers' fathers have seen, since the day that they were upon the earth unto this day."

[271] The counselors of Pharaoh stood aghast. The nation had sustained great loss in the death of their cattle. Many of the people had been killed by the hail. The forests were broken down and the crops destroyed. They were fast losing all that had been gained by the labor of the Hebrews. The whole land was threatened with starvation. Princes and courtiers pressed about the king and angrily demanded, "How long shall this man be a snare unto us? let the men go, that they may serve the Lord their God: knowest thou not yet that Egypt is destroyed?"

Moses and Aaron were again summoned, and the monarch said to them, "Go, serve the Lord your God: but who are they that shall go?"

The answer was, "We will go with our young and with our old, with our sons and with our daughters, with our flocks and with our herds will we go; for we must hold a feast unto the Lord."

The king was filled with rage. "Let the Lord be so with you," he cried, "as I will let you go, and your little ones: look to it; for evil is before you. Not so: go now ye that are men, and serve the Lord; for that ye did desire. And they were driven out from Pharaoh's presence." Pharaoh had endeavored to destroy the Israelites by hard labor, but he now pretended to have a deep interest in their welfare and a tender care for their little ones. His real object was to keep the women and children as surety for the return of the men.

Moses now stretched forth his rod over the land, and an east wind blew, and brought locusts. "Very grievous were they; before them there were no such locusts as they, neither after them shall be such." They filled the sky till the land was darkened, and devoured every green thing remaining. Pharaoh sent for the prophets in haste, and said, "I have sinned against the Lord your God, and against you. Now therefore, forgive, I pray thee, my sin only this once, and entreat the Lord your God, that He may take away from me this death only." They did so, and a strong west wind carried away the locusts toward the Red Sea. Still the king persisted in his stubborn resolution.

The people of Egypt were ready to despair. The scourges that had already fallen upon them seemed almost beyond endurance, and they were filled with fear for the future. The nation had worshiped Pharaoh as a representative of their god, but many were now convinced that he was opposing himself to One who made all the powers of nature the ministers of His will. The Hebrew slaves, so miraculously favored, were becoming confident of deliverance. Their taskmasters dared not oppress them as heretofore. Throughout Egypt there was a secret fear that the enslaved race would rise and avenge their wrongs. Everywhere men were asking with bated breath, What will come next?

[272]

Suddenly a darkness settled upon the land, so thick and black that it seemed a "darkness which may be felt." Not only were the people deprived of light, but the atmosphere was very oppressive, so that breathing was difficult. "They saw not one another, neither rose any from his place for three days: but all the children of Israel had light in their dwellings." The sun and moon were objects of worship to the Egyptians; in this mysterious darkness the people and their gods alike were smitten by the power that had undertaken the cause of the bondmen. [See Appendix, note 2.] Yet fearful as it was, this judgment is an evidence of God's compassion and His unwillingness to destroy. He would give the people time for reflection and repentance before bringing upon them the last and most terrible of the plagues.

Fear at last wrung from Pharaoh a further concession. At the end of the third day of darkness he summoned Moses, and consented to the departure of the people, provided the flocks and herds were permitted to remain. "There shall not an hoof be left behind," replied the resolute Hebrew. "We know not with what we must serve the Lord, until we come thither." The king's anger burst forth beyond control. "Get thee from me," he cried, "take heed to thyself, see my face no more; for in that day thou seest my face thou shalt die."

The answer was, "Thou hast spoken well, I will see thy face again no more."

"The man Moses was very great in the land of Egypt, in the sight of Pharaoh's servants, and in the sight of the people." Moses was regarded with awe by the Egyptians. The king dared not harm him, for the people looked upon him as alone possessing power to remove the plagues. They desired that the Israelites might be permitted to leave Egypt. It was the king and the priests that opposed to the last the demands of Moses.

Chapter 24—The Passover

This chapter is based on Exodus 11; 12:1-32.

When the demand for Israel's release had been first presented to the king of Egypt, the warning of the most terrible of the plagues had been given. Moses was directed to say to Pharaoh, "Thus saith the Lord, Israel is My son, even My first-born: and I say unto thee, Let My son go, that he may serve Me: and if thou refuse to let him go, behold, I will slay thy son, even thy first-born." Exodus 4:22, 23. Though despised by the Egyptians, the Israelites had been honored by God, in that they were singled out to be the depositaries of His law. In the special blessings and privileges accorded them, they had pre-eminence among the nations, as the first-born son had among brothers.

The judgment of which Egypt had first been warned, was to be the last visited. God is long-suffering and plenteous in mercy. He has a tender care for the beings formed in His image. If the loss of their harvests and their flocks and herds had brought Egypt to repentance, the children would not have been smitten; but the nation had stubbornly resisted the divine command, and now the final blow was about to fall.

Moses had been forbidden, on pain of death, to appear again in Pharaoh's presence; but a last message from God was to be delivered to the rebellious monarch, and again Moses came before him, with the terrible announcement: "Thus saith the Lord, About midnight will I go out into the midst of Egypt: and all the first-born in the land of Egypt shall die, from the first-born of Pharaoh that sitteth upon his throne, even unto the first-born of the maidservant that is behind the mill; and all the first-born of beasts. And there shall be a great cry throughout all the land of Egypt, such as there was none like it, nor shall be like it any more. But against any of the children of Israel shall not a dog move his tongue, against man or beast: that ye may know how that the Lord doth put a difference between the

Egyptians and Israel. And all these thy servants shall come down unto me, and bow down themselves unto me, saying, Get thee out, and all the people that follow thee: and after that I will go out."

Before the execution of this sentence the Lord through Moses gave direction to the children of Israel concerning their departure from Egypt, and especially for their preservation from the coming judgment. Each family, alone or in connection with others, was to slay a lamb or a kid "without blemish," and with a bunch of hyssop sprinkle its blood on "the two side posts and on the upper doorpost" of the house, that the destroying angel, coming at midnight, might not enter that dwelling. They were to eat the flesh roasted, with unleavened bread and bitter herbs, at night, as Moses said, "with your loins girded, your shoes on your feet, and your staff in your hand; and ye shall eat it in haste: it is the Lord's Passover."

The Lord declared: "I will pass through the land of Egypt this night, and will smite all the first-born in the land of Egypt, both man and beast; and against all the gods of Egypt I will execute judgment.... And the blood shall be to you for a token upon the houses where ye are: and when I see the blood, I will pass over you, and the plague shall not be upon you to destroy you, when I smite the land of Egypt."

In commemoration of this great deliverance a feast was to be observed yearly by the people of Israel in all future generations. "This day shall be unto you for a memorial; and ye shall keep it a feast to the Lord throughout your generations: ye shall keep it a feast by an ordinance forever." As they should keep the feast in future years, they were to repeat to their children the story of this great deliverance, as Moses bade them: "Ye shall say, It is the sacrifice of the Lord's Passover, who passed over the houses of the children of Israel in Egypt, when He smote the Egyptians, and delivered our houses."

Furthermore, the first-born of both man and beast were to be the Lord's, to be bought back only by a ransom, in acknowledgment that when the first-born in Egypt perished, that of Israel, though graciously preserved, had been justly exposed to the same doom but for the atoning sacrifice. "All the first-born are Mine," the Lord declared; "for on the day that I smote all the first-born in the land of Egypt, I hallowed unto Me all the first-born in Israel, both man and beast: Mine they shall be," Numbers 3:13. After the institution of the tabernacle service the Lord chose unto Himself the tribe of Levi for the work of the sanctuary, instead of the first-born of the people. "They are wholly given unto Me from among the children of Israel," He said. "Instead of the first-born of all the children of Israel, have I taken them unto Me." Numbers 8:16. All the people were, however, still required, in acknowledgment of God's mercy, to pay a redemption price for the first-born son. Numbers 18:15, 16.

The Passover was to be both commemorative and typical, not only pointing back to the deliverance from Egypt, but forward to the greater deliverance which Christ was to accomplish in freeing His people from the bondage of sin. The sacrificial lamb represents "the Lamb of God," in whom is our only hope of salvation. Says the apostle, "Christ our Passover is sacrificed for us." 1 Corinthians 5:7. It was not enough that the paschal lamb be slain; its blood must be sprinkled upon the doorposts; so the merits of Christ's blood must be applied to the soul. We must believe, not only that He died for the world, but that He died for us individually. We must appropriate to ourselves the virtue of the atoning sacrifice.

The hyssop used in sprinkling the blood was the symbol of purification, being thus employed in the cleansing of the leper and of those defiled by contact with the dead. In the psalmist's prayer also its significance is seen: "Purge me with hyssop, and I shall be clean: wash me, and I shall be whiter than snow." Psalm 51:7.

The lamb was to be prepared whole, not a bone of it being broken: so not a bone was to be broken of the Lamb of God, who was to die for us. John 19:36. Thus was also represented the completeness of Christ's sacrifice.

The flesh was to be eaten. It is not enough even that we believe on Christ for the forgiveness of sin; we must by faith be constantly receiving spiritual strength and nourishment from Him through His word. Said Christ, "Except ye eat the flesh of the Son of man, and drink His blood, ye have no life in you. Whoso eateth My flesh, and drinketh My blood, hath eternal life." John 6:53, 54. And to explain His meaning He said, "The words that I speak unto you, they are spirit, and they are life." Verse 63. Jesus accepted His Father's law, wrought out its principles in His life, manifested its spirit, and showed its beneficent power in the heart. Says John, "The

Word was made flesh and dwelt among us, (and we beheld His glory, the glory as of the only begotten of the Father,) full of grace and truth." John 1:14. The followers of Christ must be partakers of His experience. They must receive and assimilate the word of God so that it shall become the motive power of life and action. By the power of Christ they must be changed into His likeness, and reflect the divine attributes. They must eat the flesh and drink the blood of the Son of God, or there is no life in them. The spirit and work of Christ must become the spirit and work of His disciples.

The lamb was to be eaten with bitter herbs, as pointing back to the bitterness of the bondage in Egypt. So when we feed upon Christ, it should be with contrition of heart, because of our sins. The use of unleavened bread also was significant. It was expressly enjoined in the law of the Passover, and as strictly observed by the Jews in their practice, that no leaven should be found in their houses during the feast. In like manner the leaven of sin must be put away from all who would receive life and nourishment from Christ. So Paul writes to the Corinthian church, "Purge out therefore the old leaven, that ye may be a new lump.... For even Christ our Passover is sacrificed for us: therefore let us keep the feast, not with old leaven, neither with the leaven of malice and wickedness; but with the unleavened bread of sincerity and truth." 1 Corinthians 5:7, 8.

Before obtaining freedom, the bondmen must show their faith in the great deliverance about to be accomplished. The token of blood must be placed upon their houses, and they must separate themselves and their families from the Egyptians, and gather within their own dwellings. Had the Israelites disregarded in any particular the directions given them, had they neglected to separate their children from the Egyptians, had they slain the lamb, but failed to strike the doorpost with blood, or had any gone out of their houses, they would not have been secure. They might have honestly believed that they had done all that was necessary, but their sincerity would not have saved them. All who failed to heed the Lord's directions would lose their first-born by the hand of the destroyer.

By obedience the people were to give evidence of their faith. So all who hope to be saved by the merits of the blood of Christ should realize that they themselves have something to do in securing their salvation. While it is Christ only that can redeem us from the penalty of transgression, we are to turn from sin to obedience. Man is to be saved by faith, not by works; yet his faith must be shown by his works. God has given His Son to die as a propitiation for sin, He has manifested the light of truth, the way of life, He has given facilities, ordinances, and privileges; and now man must co-operate with these saving agencies; he must appreciate and use the helps that God has provided—believe and obey all the divine requirements.

As Moses rehearsed to Israel the provisions of God for their deliverance, "the people bowed the head and worshiped." The glad hope of freedom, the awful knowledge of the impending judgment upon their oppressors, the cares and labors incident to their speedy departure—all were for the time swallowed up in gratitude to their gracious Deliverer. Many of the Egyptians had been led to acknowledge the God of the Hebrews as the only true God, and these now begged to be permitted to find shelter in the homes of Israel when the destroying angel should pass through the land. They were gladly welcomed, and they pledged themselves henceforth to serve the God of Jacob and to go forth from Egypt with His people.

The Israelites obeyed the directions that God had given. Swiftly and secretly they made their preparations for departure. Their families were gathered, the paschal lamb slain, the flesh roasted with fire, the unleavened bread and bitter herbs prepared. The father and priest of the household sprinkled the blood upon the doorpost, and joined his family within the dwelling. In haste and silence the paschal lamb was eaten. In awe the people prayed and watched, the heart of the eldest born, from the strong man down to the little child, throbbing with indefinable dread. Fathers and mothers clasped in their arms their loved first-born as they thought of the fearful stroke that was to fall that night. But no dwelling of Israel was visited by the death-dealing angel. The sign of blood—the sign of a Saviour's protection—was on their doors, and the destroyer entered not.

At midnight "there was a great cry in Egypt: for there was not a house where there was not one dead." All the first-born in the land, "from the firstborn of Pharaoh that sat on his throne unto the firstborn of the captive that was in the dungeon; and all the firstborn of cattle" had been smitten by the destroyer. Throughout the vast realm of Egypt the pride of every household had been laid low. The shrieks and wails of the mourners filled the air. King and

[280]

courtiers, with blanched faces and trembling limbs, stood aghast at the overmastering horror. Pharaoh remembered how he had once exclaimed, "Who is Jehovah, that I should obey His voice to let Israel go? I know not Jehovah, neither will I let Israel go." Now, his heaven-daring pride humbled in the dust, he "called for Moses and Aaron by night, and said, Rise up, and get you forth from among my people, both ye and the children of Israel; and go, serve the Lord, as ye have said. Also take your flocks and your herds, as ye have said.... And be gone; and bless me also." The royal counselors also and the people entreated the Israelites to depart "out of the land in haste; for they said, We be all dead men."

Chapter 25—The Exodus

This chapter is based on Exodus 12:34-51; 13-15.

With their loins girt, with sandaled feet, and staff in hand, the people of Israel had stood, hushed, awed, yet expectant, awaiting the royal mandate that should bid them go forth. Before the morning broke, they were on their way. During the plagues, as the manifestation of God's power had kindled faith in the hearts of the bondmen and had struck terror to their oppressors, the Israelites had gradually assembled themselves in Goshen; and notwithstanding the suddenness of their flight, some provision had already been made for the necessary organization and control of the moving multitudes, they being divided into companies, under appointed leaders.

And they went out, "about six hundred thousand on foot that were men, beside children. And a mixed multitude went up also with them." In this multitude were not only those who were actuated by faith in the God of Israel, but also a far greater number who desired only to escape from the plagues, or who followed in the wake of the moving multitudes merely from excitement and curiosity. This class were ever a hindrance and a snare to Israel.

The people took also with them "flocks, and herds, even very much cattle." These were the property of the Israelites, who had never sold their possessions to the king, as had the Egyptians. Jacob and his sons had brought their flocks and herds with them to Egypt, where they had greatly increased. Before leaving Egypt, the people, by the direction of Moses, claimed a recompense for their unpaid labor; and the Egyptians were too eager to be freed from their presence to refuse them. The bondmen went forth laden with the spoil of their oppressors.

That day completed the history revealed to Abraham in prophetic vision centuries before: "Thy seed shall be a stranger in a land that is not theirs, and shall serve them; and they shall afflict them four hundred years; and also that nation, whom they shall serve, will

I judge: and afterward shall they come out with great substance." Genesis 15:13, 14. [See Appendix, note 3.] The four hundred years had been fulfilled. "And it came to pass the selfsame day, that the Lord did bring the children of Israel out of the land of Egypt by their armies." In their departure from Egypt the Israelites bore with them a precious legacy, in the bones of Joseph, which had so long awaited the fulfillment of God's promise, and which, during the dark years of bondage, had been a reminder of Israel's deliverance.

Instead of pursuing the direct route to Canaan, which lay through the country of the Philistines, the Lord directed their course southward, toward the shores of the Red Sea. "For God said, Lest peradventure the people repent when they see war, and they return to Egypt." Had they attempted to pass through Philistia, their progress would have been opposed; for the Philistines, regarding them as slaves escaping from their masters, would not have hesitated to make war upon them. The Israelites were poorly prepared for an encounter with that powerful and warlike people. They had little knowledge of God and little faith in Him, and they would have become terrified and disheartened. They were unarmed and unaccustomed to war, their spirits were depressed by long bondage, and they were encumbered with women and children, flocks and herds. In leading them by the way of the Red Sea, the Lord revealed Himself as a God of compassion as well as of judgment.

"And they took their journey from Succoth, and encamped in Etham, in the edge of the wilderness. And the Lord went before them by day in a pillar of cloud, to lead them the way; and by night in a pillar of fire, to give them light; to go by day and night. He took not away the pillar of the cloud by day, nor the pillar of fire by night, from before the people." Says the psalmist, "He spread a cloud for a covering; and fire to give light in the night." Psalm 105:39. See also 1 Corinthians 10:1, 2. The standard of their invisible Leader was ever with them. By day the cloud directed their journeyings or spread as a canopy above the host. It served as a protection from the burning heat, and by its coolness and moisture afforded grateful refreshment in the parched, thirsty desert. By night it became a pillar of fire, illuminating their encampment and constantly assuring them of the divine presence.

In one of the most beautiful and comforting passages of Isaiah's prophecy, reference is made to the pillar of cloud and of fire to represent God's care for His people in the great final struggle with the powers of evil: "The Lord will create upon every dwelling place of Mount Zion, and upon her assemblies, a cloud and smoke by day, and the shining of a flaming fire by night: for above all the glory shall be a covering. And there shall be a tabernacle for a shadow in the daytime from the heat, and for a place of refuge, and for a covert from storm and from rain." Isaiah 4:5, 6, margin.

Across a dreary, desertlike expanse they journeyed. Already they began to wonder whither their course would lead; they were becoming weary with the toilsome way, and in some hearts began to arise a fear of pursuit by the Egyptians. But the cloud went forward, and they followed. And now the Lord directed Moses to turn aside into a rocky defile, and encamp beside the sea. It was revealed to him that Pharaoh would pursue them, but that God would be honored in their deliverance.

In Egypt the report was spread that the children of Israel, instead of tarrying to worship in the desert, were pressing on toward the Red Sea. Pharaoh's counselors declared to the king that their bondmen had fled, never to return. The people deplored their folly in attributing the death of the first-born to the power of God. Their great men, recovering from their fears, accounted for the plagues as the result of natural causes. "Why have we done this, that we have let Israel go from serving us?" was the bitter cry.

Pharaoh collected his forces, "six hundred chosen chariots, and all the chariots of Egypt," horsemen, captains, and foot soldiers. The king himself, attended by the great men of his realm, headed the attacking army. To secure the favor of the gods, and thus ensure the success of their undertaking, the priests also accompanied them. The king was resolved to intimidate the Israelites by a grand display of his power. The Egyptians feared lest their forced submission to the God of Israel should subject them to the derision of other nations; but if they should now go forth with a great show of power and bring back the fugitives, they would redeem their glory, as well as recover the services of their bondmen.

The Hebrews were encamped beside the sea, whose waters presented a seemingly impassable barrier before them, while on the south a rugged mountain obstructed their further progress. Suddenly they beheld in the distance the flashing armor and moving chariots betokening the advance guard of a great army. As the force drew nearer, the hosts of Egypt were seen in full pursuit. Terror filled the hearts of Israel. Some cried unto the Lord, but far the greater part hastened to Moses with their complaints: "Because there were no graves in Egypt, hast thou taken us away to die in the wilderness? wherefore hast thou dealt thus with us, to carry us forth out of Egypt? Is not this the word that we did tell thee in Egypt, saying, Let us alone, that we may serve the Egyptians? For it had been better for us to serve the Egyptians, than that we should die in the wilderness."

Moses was greatly troubled that his people should manifest so little faith in God, notwithstanding they had repeatedly witnessed the manifestation of His power in their behalf. How could they charge upon him the dangers and difficulties of their situation, when he had followed the express command of God? True, there was no possibility of deliverance unless God Himself should interpose for their release; but having been brought into this position in obedience to the divine direction, Moses felt no fear of the consequences. His calm and assuring reply to the people was, "Fear ye not, stand still, and see the salvation of the Lord, which He will show to you today: for the Egyptians whom ye have seen today, ye shall see them again no more forever. The Lord shall fight for you, and ye shall hold your peace."

It was not an easy thing to hold the hosts of Israel in waiting before the Lord. Lacking discipline and self-control, they became violent and unreasonable. They expected speedily to fall into the hands of their oppressors, and their wailings and lamentations were loud and deep. The wonderful pillar of cloud had been followed as the signal of God to go forward; but now they questioned among themselves if it might not foreshadow some great calamity; for had it not led them on the wrong side of the mountain, into an impassable way? Thus the angel of God appeared to their deluded minds as the harbinger of disaster.

But now, as the Egyptian host approached them, expecting to make them an easy prey, the cloudy column rose majestically into the heavens, passed over the Israelites, and descended between them and the armies of Egypt. A wall of darkness interposed between the pursued and their pursuers. The Egyptians could no longer discern the camp of the Hebrews, and were forced to halt. But as the darkness of night deepened, the wall of cloud became a great light to the Hebrews, flooding the entire encampment with the radiance of day.

Then hope returned to the hearts of Israel. And Moses lifted up his voice unto the Lord. "And the Lord said unto Moses, Wherefore criest thou unto Me? speak unto the children of Israel, that they go forward. But lift thou up thy rod, and stretch out thine hand over the sea, and divide it: and the children of Israel shall go on dry ground through the midst of the sea."

The psalmist, describing the passage of the sea by Israel, sang, "Thy way was in the sea, and Thy paths in the great waters, and Thy footsteps were not known. Thou leddest Thy people like a flock, by the hand of Moses and Aaron." Psalm 77:19, 20, R.V. As Moses stretched out his rod the waters parted, and Israel went into the midst of the sea, upon dry ground, while the waters stood like a wall upon each side. The light from God's pillar of fire shone upon the foam-capped billows, and lighted the road that was cut like a mighty furrow through the waters of the sea, and was lost in the obscurity of the farther shore.

"The Egyptians pursued, and went in after them to the midst of the sea, even all Pharaoh's horses, his chariots, and his horsemen. And it came to pass, that in the morning watch the Lord looked unto the host of the Egyptians through the pillar of fire and of the cloud, and troubled the host of the Egyptians." The mysterious cloud changed to a pillar of fire before their astonished eyes. The thunders pealed and the lightnings flashed. "The clouds poured out water; the skies sent out a sound: Thine arrows also went abroad. The voice of Thy thunder was in the whirlwind; the lightning lightened the world: the earth trembled and shook." Psalm 77:17, 18, R.V.

The Egyptians were seized with confusion and dismay. Amid the wrath of the elements, in which they heard the voice of an angry God, they endeavored to retrace their steps and flee to the shore they had quitted. But Moses stretched out his rod, and the piled-up waters, hissing, roaring, and eager for their prey, rushed together and swallowed the Egyptian army in their black depths.

As morning broke it revealed to the multitudes of Israel all that remained of their mighty foes—the mail-clad bodies cast upon the shore. From the most terrible peril, one night had brought complete deliverance. That vast, helpless throng—bondmen unused to battle, women, children, and cattle, with the sea before them, and the mighty armies of Egypt pressing behind—had seen their path opened through the waters and their enemies overwhelmed in the moment of expected triumph. Jehovah alone had brought them deliverance, and to Him their hearts were turned in gratitude and faith. Their emotion found utterance in songs of praise. The Spirit of God rested upon Moses, and he led the people in a triumphant anthem of thanksgiving, the earliest and one of the most sublime that are known to man.

> "I will sing unto Jehovah, for He hath triumphed gloriously;
>   The horse and his rider hath He thrown into the sea.
> The Lord is my strength and my song,
>   And He is become my salvation:
> This is my God, and I will praise Him;
>   My father's God, and I will exalt Him.
> The Lord is a man of war:
>   Jehovah is His name. Pharaoh's chariots and his host hath
>   He cast into the sea:
> And his chosen captains are sunk in the Red Sea.
>   The deeps cover them:
> They went down into the depths like a stone.
>   Thy right hand, O Lord, is glorious in power,
> Thy right hand, O Lord, dasheth in pieces the enemy....
>   Who is like unto Thee, O Lord, among the gods?
> Who is like Thee, glorious in holiness,
>   Fearful in praises, doing wonders? ...
> Thou in Thy mercy hast led the people which Thou has redeemed:
>
>   Thou hast guided them in Thy strength to Thy holy habitation.
>
> The peoples have heard, they tremble....
>   Terror and dread falleth upon them;
> By the greatness of Thine arm they are as still as a stone;
>   Till Thy people pass over, O Lord,
> Till the people pass over which Thou hast purchased.
>   Thou shalt bring them in, and plant them in the mountain of

Thine inheritance,
> The place, O Lord, which Thou hast made for Thee to dwell in."

Exodus 15:1-16, R.V.

Like the voice of the great deep, rose from the vast hosts of Israel that sublime ascription. It was taken up by the women of Israel, Miriam, the sister of Moses, leading the way, as they went forth with timbrel and dance. Far over desert and sea rang the joyous refrain, and the mountains re-echoed the words of their praise—"Sing ye to Jehovah, for He hath triumphed gloriously."

This song and the great deliverance which it commemorates, made an impression never to be effaced from the memory of the Hebrew people. From age to age it was echoed by the prophets and singers of Israel, testifying that Jehovah is the strength and deliverance of those who trust in Him. That song does not belong to the Jewish people alone. It points forward to the destruction of all the foes of righteousness and the final victory of the Israel of God. The prophet of Patmos beholds the white-robed multitude that have "gotten the victory," standing on the "sea of glass mingled with fire," having "the harps of God. And they sing the song of Moses the servant of God, and the song of the Lamb." Revelation 15:2, 3.

"Not unto us, O Lord, not unto us, but unto Thy name give glory, for Thy mercy, and for Thy truth's sake." Psalm 115:1. Such was the spirit that pervaded Israel's song of deliverance, and it is the spirit that should dwell in the hearts of all who love and fear God. In freeing our souls from the bondage of sin, God has wrought for us a deliverance greater than that of the Hebrews at the Red Sea. Like the Hebrew host, we should praise the Lord with heart and soul and voice for His "wonderful works to the children of men." Those who dwell upon God's great mercies, and are not unmindful of His lesser gifts, will put on the girdle of gladness and make melody in their hearts to the Lord. The daily blessings that we receive from the hand of God, and above all else the death of Jesus to bring happiness and heaven within our reach, should be a theme for constant gratitude. What compassion, what matchless love, has God shown to us, lost sinners, in connecting us with Himself, to be to Him a peculiar treasure! What a sacrifice has been made by our Redeemer, that we may be called children of God! We should praise God for the blessed hope held out before us in the great plan of redemption, we should praise Him for the heavenly inheritance and for His rich promises; praise Him that Jesus lives to intercede for us.

"Whoso offereth praise," says the Creator, "glorifieth Me." Psalm 50:23. All the inhabitants of heaven unite in praising God. Let us learn the song of the angels now, that we may sing it when we join their shining ranks. Let us say with the psalmist, "While I live will I praise the Lord: I will sing praises unto my God while I have any being." "Let the people praise Thee, O God; let all the people praise Thee." Psalm 146:2; 67:5.

God in His providence brought the Hebrews into the mountain fastnesses before the sea, that He might manifest His power in their deliverance and signally humble the pride of their oppressors. He might have saved them in any other way, but He chose this method in order to test their faith and strengthen their trust in Him. The people were weary and terrified, yet if they had held back when Moses bade them advance, God would never have opened the path for them. It was "by faith" that "they passed through the Red Sea as by dry land." Hebrews 11:29. In marching down to the very water, they showed that they believed the word of God as spoken by Moses. They did all that was in their power to do, and then the Mighty One of Israel divided the sea to make a path for their feet.

The great lesson here taught is for all time. Often the Christian life is beset by dangers, and duty seems hard to perform. The imagination pictures impending ruin before and bondage or death behind. Yet the voice of God speaks clearly, "Go forward." We should obey this command, even though our eyes cannot penetrate the darkness, and we feel the cold waves about our feet. The obstacles that hinder our progress will never disappear before a halting, doubting spirit. Those who defer obedience till every shadow of uncertainty disappears and there remains no risk of failure or defeat, will never obey at all. Unbelief whispers, "Let us wait till the obstructions are removed, and we can see our way clearly;" but faith courageously urges an advance, hoping all things, believing all things.

The cloud that was a wall of darkness to the Egyptians was to the Hebrews a great flood of light, illuminating the whole camp, and shedding brightness upon the path before them. So the dealings of

Providence bring to the unbelieving, darkness and despair, while to the trusting soul they are full of light and peace. The path where God leads the way may lie through the desert or the sea, but it is a safe path.

Chapter 26—From the Red Sea to Sinai

This chapter is based on Exodus 15:22-27; 16 to 18.

From the Red Sea the hosts of Israel again set forth on their journey, under the guidance of the pillar of cloud. The scene around them was most dreary—bare, desolate-looking mountains, barren plains, and the sea stretching far away, its shores strewn with the bodies of their enemies; yet they were full of joy in the consciousness of freedom, and every thought of discontent was hushed.

But for three days, as they journeyed, they could find no water. The supply which they had taken with them was exhausted. There was nothing to quench their burning thirst as they dragged wearily over the sun-burnt plains. Moses, who was familiar with this region, knew what the others did not, that at Marah, the nearest station where springs were to be found, the water was unfit for use. With intense anxiety he watched the guiding cloud. With a sinking heart he heard the glad shout. "Water! water!" echoed along the line. Men, women, and children in joyous haste crowded to the fountain, when, lo, a cry of anguish burst forth from the host—the water was bitter.

In their horror and despair they reproached Moses for having led them in such a way, not remembering that the divine presence in that mysterious cloud had been leading him as well as them. In his grief at their distress Moses did what they had forgotten to do; he cried earnestly to God for help. "And the Lord showed him a tree, which when he had cast into the waters, the waters were made sweet." Here the promise was given to Israel through Moses, "If thou wilt diligently hearken to the voice of the Lord thy God, and wilt do that which is right in His sight, and wilt give ear to His commandments, and keep all His statutes, I will put none of these diseases upon thee, which I have brought upon the Egyptians: for I am the Lord that healeth thee."

From Marah the people journeyed to Elim, where they found "twelve wells of water, and threescore and ten palm trees." Here they remained several days before entering the wilderness of Sin. When they had been a month absent from Egypt, they made their first encampment in the wilderness. Their store of provisions had now begun to fail. There was scanty herbage in the wilderness, and their flocks were diminishing. How was food to be supplied for these vast multitudes? Doubts filled their hearts, and again they murmured. Even the rulers and elders of the people joined in complaining against the leaders of God's appointment: "Would to God we had died by the hand of the Lord in the land of Egypt, when we sat by the fleshpots, and when we did eat bread to the full; for ye have brought us forth into this wilderness, to kill this whole assembly with hunger."

They had not as yet suffered from hunger; their present wants were supplied, but they feared for the future. They could not understand how these vast multitudes were to subsist in their travels through the wilderness, and in imagination they saw their children famishing. The Lord permitted difficulties to surround them, and their supply of food to be cut short, that their hearts might turn to Him who had hitherto been their Deliverer. If in their want they would call upon Him, He would still grant them manifest tokens of His love and care. He had promised that if they would obey His commandments, no disease should come upon them, and it was sinful unbelief on their part to anticipate that they or their children might die of hunger.

God had promised to be their God, to take them to Himself as a people, and to lead them to a large and good land; but they were ready to faint at every obstacle encountered in the way to that land. In a marvelous manner He had brought them out from their bondage in Egypt, that He might elevate and ennoble them and make them a praise in the earth. But it was necessary for them to encounter difficulties and to endure privations. God was bringing them from a state of degradation and fitting them to occupy an honorable place among the nations and to receive important and sacred trusts. Had they possessed faith in Him, in view of all that He had wrought for them, they would cheerfully have borne inconvenience, privation, and even real suffering; but they were unwilling to trust the Lord any further than they could witness the continual evidences of His power. They forgot their bitter service in Egypt. They forgot the goodness and power of God displayed in their behalf in their deliverance from bondage. They forgot how their children had been spared when the destroying angel slew all the first-born of Egypt. They forgot the grand exhibition of divine power at the Red Sea. They forgot that while they had crossed safely in the path that had been opened for them, the armies of their enemies, attempting to follow them, had been overwhelmed by the waters of the sea. They saw and felt only their present inconveniences and trials; and instead of saying, "God has done great things for us; whereas we were slaves, He is making of us a great nation," they talked of the hardness of the way, and wondered when their weary pilgrimage would end.

The history of the wilderness life of Israel was chronicled for the benefit of the Israel of God to the close of time. The record of God's dealings with the wanderers of the desert in all their marchings to and fro, in their exposure to hunger, thirst, and weariness, and in the striking manifestations of His power for their relief, is fraught with warning and instruction for His people in all ages. The varied experience of the Hebrews was a school of preparation for their promised home in Canaan. God would have His people in these days review with a humble heart and teachable spirit the trials through which ancient Israel passed, that they may be instructed in their preparation for the heavenly Canaan.

Many look back to the Israelites, and marvel at their unbelief and murmuring, feeling that they themselves would not have been so ungrateful; but when their faith is tested, even by little trials, they manifest no more faith or patience than did ancient Israel. When brought into strait places, they murmur at the process by which God has chosen to purify them. Though their present needs are supplied, many are unwilling to trust God for the future, and they are in constant anxiety lest poverty shall come upon them, and their children shall be left to suffer. Some are always anticipating evil or magnifying the difficulties that really exist, so that their eyes are blinded to the many blessings which demand their gratitude. The obstacles they encounter, instead of leading them to seek help from God, the only Source of strength, separate them from Him, because they awaken unrest and repining.

Do we well to be thus unbelieving? Why should we be ungrateful and distrustful? Jesus is our friend; all heaven is interested in our welfare; and our anxiety and fear grieve the Holy Spirit of God. We should not indulge in a solicitude that only frets and wears us, but does not help us to bear trials. No place should be given to that distrust of God which leads us to make a preparation against future want the chief pursuit of life, as though our happiness consisted in these earthly things. It is not the will of God that His people should be weighed down with care. But our Lord does not tell us that there are no dangers in our path. He does not propose to take His people out of the world of sin and evil, but He points us to a never-failing refuge. He invites the weary and care-laden, "Come unto Me, all ye that labor and are heavy-laden, and I will give you rest." Lay off the yoke of anxiety and worldly care that you have placed on your own neck, and "take My yoke upon you, and learn of Me; for I am meek and lowly in heart: and ye shall find rest unto your souls." Matthew 11:28, 29. We may find rest and peace in God, casting all our care upon Him; for He careth for us. See 1 Peter 5:7.

Says the apostle Paul, "Take heed, brethren, lest there be in any of you an evil heart of unbelief, in departing from the living God." Hebrews 3:12. In view of all that God has wrought for us, our faith should be strong, active, and enduring. Instead of murmuring and complaining, the language of our hearts should be, "Bless the Lord, O my soul: and all that is within me, bless His holy name. Bless the Lord, O my soul, and forget not all His benefits." Psalm 103:1, 2.

God was not unmindful of the wants of Israel. He said to their leader, "I will rain bread from heaven for you." And directions were given that the people gather a daily supply, with a double amount on the sixth day, that the sacred observance of the Sabbath might be maintained.

Moses assured the congregation that their wants were to be supplied: "The Lord shall give you in the evening flesh to eat, and in the morning bread to the full." And he added, "What are we? your murmurings are not against us, but against the Lord." He further bade Aaron say to them, "Come near before the Lord: for He hath heard your murmurings." While Aaron was speaking, "they looked toward the wilderness, and, behold, the glory of the Lord appeared in the cloud." A splendor such as they had never witnessed symbolized the divine Presence. Through manifestations addressed to their senses, they were to obtain a knowledge of God. They must be taught that

[295]

the Most High, and not merely the man Moses, was their leader, that they might fear His name and obey His voice.

At nightfall the camp was surrounded by vast flocks of quails, enough to supply the entire company. In the morning there lay upon the surface of the ground "a small round thing, as small as the hoarfrost." "It was like coriander seed, white." The people called it "manna." Moses said, "This is the bread which the Lord hath given you to eat." The people gathered the manna, and found that there was an abundant supply for all. They "ground it in mills, or beat it in a mortar, and baked it in pans, and made cakes of it." Numbers 11:8. "And the taste of it was like wafers made with honey." They were directed to gather daily an omer for every person; and they were not to leave of it until the morning. Some attempted to keep a supply until the next day, but it was then found to be unfit for food. The provision for the day must be gathered in the morning; for all that remained upon the ground was melted by the sun.

In the gathering of the manna it was found that some obtained more and some less than the stipulated amount; but "when they did mete it with an omer, he that gathered much had nothing over, and he that gathered little had no lack." An explanation of this scripture, as well as a practical lesson from it, is given by the apostle Paul in his second epistle to the Corinthians. He says, "I mean not that other men be eased, and ye burdened: but by an equality, that now at this time your abundance may be a supply for their want, that their abundance also may be a supply for your want: that there may be equality: as it is written, He that had gathered much had nothing over; and he that had gathered little had no lack." 2 Corinthians 8:13-15.

On the sixth day the people gathered two omers for every person. The rulers hastened to acquaint Moses with what had been done. His answer was, "This is that which the Lord hath said, Tomorrow is the rest of the holy Sabbath unto the Lord: bake that which ye will bake today, and seethe that ye will seethe; and that which remaineth over lay up for you to be kept until the morning." They did so, and found that it remained unchanged. "And Moses said, Eat that today; for today is a Sabbath unto the Lord: today ye shall not find it in the field. Six days ye shall gather it; but on the seventh day, which is the Sabbath, in it there shall be none."

God requires that His holy day be as sacredly observed now as in the time of Israel. The command given to the Hebrews should be regarded by all Christians as an injunction from Jehovah to them. The day before the Sabbath should be made a day of preparation, that everything may be in readiness for its sacred hours. In no case should our own business be allowed to encroach upon holy time. God has directed that the sick and suffering be cared for; the labor required to make them comfortable is a work of mercy, and no violation of the Sabbath; but all unnecessary work should be avoided. Many carelessly put off till the beginning of the Sabbath little things that might have been done on the day of preparation. This should not be. Work that is neglected until the beginning of the Sabbath should remain undone until it is past. This course might help the memory of these thoughtless ones, and make them careful to do their own work on the six working days.

Every week during their long sojourn in the wilderness the Israelites witnessed a threefold miracle, designed to impress their minds with the sacredness of the Sabbath: a double quantity of manna fell on the sixth day, none on the seventh, and the portion needed for the Sabbath was preserved sweet and pure, when if any were kept over at any other time it became unfit for use.

In the circumstances connected with the giving of the manna, we have conclusive evidence that the Sabbath was not instituted, as many claim, when the law was given at Sinai. Before the Israelites came to Sinai they understood the Sabbath to be obligatory upon them. In being obliged to gather every Friday a double portion of manna in preparation for the Sabbath, when none would fall, the sacred nature of the day of rest was continually impressed upon them. And when some of the people went out on the Sabbath to gather manna, the Lord asked, "How long *refuse ye* to keep My commandments and My laws?"

"The children of Israel did eat manna forty years, until they came to a land inhabited: they did eat manna, until they came unto the borders of the land of Canaan." For forty years they were daily reminded by this miraculous provision, of God's unfailing care and tender love. In the words of the psalmist, God gave them "of the corn of heaven. Man did eat angels' food" (Psalm 78:24, 25)—that is, food provided for them by the angels. Sustained by "the corn of heaven," they were daily taught that, having God's promise, they were as secure from want as if surrounded by fields of waving grain on the fertile plains of Canaan.

The manna, falling from heaven for the sustenance of Israel, was a type of Him who came from God to give life to the world. Said Jesus, "I am that Bread of life. Your fathers did eat manna in the wilderness, and are dead. This is the bread which cometh down from heaven.... If any man eat of this bread, he shall live forever: and the bread that I will give is My flesh, which I will give for the life of the world." John 6:48-51. And among the promises of blessing to God's people in the future life it is written, "To him that overcometh will I give to eat of the hidden manna." Revelation 2:17.

After leaving the wilderness of Sin, the Israelites encamped in Rephidim. Here there was no water, and again they distrusted the providence of God. In their blindness and presumption the people came to Moses with the demand, "Give us water that we may drink." But his patience failed not. "Why chide ye with me?" he said; "wherefore do ye tempt the Lord?" They cried in anger, "Wherefore is this, that thou hast brought us up out of Egypt, to kill us and our children and our cattle with thirst?" When they had been so abundantly supplied with food, they remembered with shame their unbelief and murmurings, and promised to trust the Lord in the future; but they soon forgot their promise, and failed at the first trial of their faith. The pillar of cloud that was leading them seemed to veil a fearful mystery. And Moses—who was he? they questioned, and what could be his object in bringing them from Egypt? Suspicion and distrust filled their hearts, and they boldly accused him of designing to kill them and their children by privations and hardships that he might enrich himself with their possessions. In the tumult of rage and indignation they were about to stone him.

In distress Moses cried to the Lord, "What shall I do unto this people?" He was directed to take the elders of Israel and the rod wherewith he had wrought wonders in Egypt, and to go on before the people. And the Lord said unto him, "Behold, I will stand before thee there upon the rock in Horeb; and thou shalt smite the rock, and there shall come water out of it, that the people may drink." He obeyed, and the waters burst forth in a living stream that abundantly supplied the encampment. Instead of commanding Moses to lift up his rod and call down some terrible plague, like those on Egypt, upon the leaders in this wicked murmuring, the Lord in His great mercy made the rod His instrument to work their deliverance.

"He clave the rocks in the wilderness, and gave them drink as out of the great depths. He brought streams also out of the rock, and caused waters to run down like rivers." Psalm 78:15, 16. Moses smote the rock, but it was the Son of God who, veiled in the cloudy pillar, stood beside Moses, and caused the life-giving water to flow. Not only Moses and the elders, but all the congregation who stood at a distance, beheld the glory of the Lord; but had the cloud been removed, they would have been slain by the terrible brightness of Him who abode therein.

In their thirst the people had tempted God, saying, "Is the Lord among us, or not?"—"If God has brought us here, why does He not give us water as well as bread?" The unbelief thus manifested was criminal, and Moses feared that the judgments of God would rest upon them. And he called the name of the place Massah, "temptation," and Meribah, "chiding," as a memorial of their sin.

A new danger now threatened them. Because of their murmuring against Him, the Lord suffered them to be attacked by their enemies. The Amalekites, a fierce, warlike tribe inhabiting that region, came out against them and smote those who, faint and weary, had fallen into the rear. Moses, knowing that the masses of the people were unprepared for battle, directed Joshua to choose from the different tribes a body of soldiers, and lead them on the morrow against the enemy, while he himself would stand on an eminence near by with the rod of God in his hand. Accordingly the next day Joshua and his company attacked the foe, while Moses and Aaron and Hur were stationed on a hill overlooking the battlefield. With arms outstretched toward heaven, and holding the rod of God in his right hand, Moses prayed for the success of the armies of Israel. As the battle progressed, it was observed that so long as his hands were reaching upward, Israel prevailed, but when they were lowered, the enemy was victorious. As Moses became weary, Aaron and Hur stayed up his hands until the going down of the sun, when the enemy was put to flight.

As Aaron and Hur supported the hands of Moses, they showed the people their duty to sustain him in his arduous work while he should receive the word from God to speak to them. And the act of Moses also was significant, showing that God held their destiny in His hands; while they made Him their trust, He would fight for them and subdue their enemies; but when they should let go their hold upon Him, and trust in their own power, they would be even weaker than those who had not the knowledge of God, and their foes would prevail against them.

As the Hebrews triumphed when Moses was reaching his hands toward heaven and interceding in their behalf, so the Israel of God prevail when they by faith take hold upon the strength of their mighty Helper. Yet divine strength is to be combined with human effort. Moses did not believe that God would overcome their foes while Israel remained inactive. While the great leader was pleading with the Lord, Joshua and his brave followers were putting forth their utmost efforts to repulse the enemies of Israel and of God.

After the defeat of the Amalekites, God directed Moses, "Write this for a memorial in a book, and rehearse it in the ears of Joshua: for I will utterly put out the remembrance of Amalek from under heaven." Just before his death the great leader delivered to his people the solemn charge: "Remember what Amalek did unto thee by the way, when ye were come forth out of Egypt; how he met thee by the way, and smote the hindmost of thee, even all that were feeble behind thee, when thou wast faint and weary; and he feared not God.... Thou shalt blot out the remembrance of Amalek from under heaven; thou shalt not forget it." Deuteronomy 25:17-19. Concerning this wicked people the Lord declared, "The hand of Amalek is against the throne of Jehovah." Exodus 17:16, margin.

The Amalekites were not ignorant of God's character or of His sovereignty, but instead of fearing before Him, they had set themselves to defy His power. The wonders wrought by Moses before the Egyptians were made a subject of mockery by the people of Amalek, and the fears of surrounding nations were ridiculed. They had taken oath by their gods that they would destroy the Hebrews, so that not one should escape, and they boasted that Israel's God would be powerless to resist them. They had not been injured or threatened by the Israelites. Their assault was wholly unprovoked. It was to manifest their hatred and defiance of God that they sought to destroy His people. The Amalekites had long been high-handed sinners, and their crimes had cried to God for vengeance, yet His mercy had still called them to repentance; but when the men of Amalek fell upon the wearied and defenseless ranks of Israel, they sealed their nation's doom. The care of God is over the weakest of His children. No act of cruelty or oppression toward them is unmarked by Heaven. Over all who love and fear Him, His hand extends as a shield; let men beware that they smite not that hand; for it wields the sword of justice.

Not far distant from where the Israelites were now encamped was the home of Jethro, the father-in-law of Moses. Jethro had heard of the deliverance of the Hebrews, and he now set out to visit them, and restore to Moses his wife and two sons. The great leader was informed by messengers of their approach, and he went out with joy to meet them, and, the first greetings over, conducted them to his tent. He had sent back his family when on his way to the perils of leading Israel from Egypt, but now he could again enjoy the relief and comfort of their society. To Jethro he recounted the wonderful dealings of God with Israel, and the patriarch rejoiced and blessed the Lord, and with Moses and the elders he united in offering sacrifice and holding a solemn feast in commemoration of God's mercy.

As Jethro remained in the camp, he soon saw how heavy were the burdens that rested upon Moses. To maintain order and discipline among that vast, ignorant, and untrained multitude was indeed a stupendous task. Moses was their recognized leader and magistrate, and not only the general interests and duties of the people, but the controversies that arose among them, were referred to him. He had permitted this, for it gave him an opportunity to instruct them; as he said, "I do make them know the statutes of God, and His laws." But Jethro remonstrated against this, saying, "This thing is too heavy for thee; thou art not able to perform it thyself alone." "Thou wilt surely wear away," and he counseled Moses to appoint proper persons as rulers of thousands, and others as rulers of hundreds, and others of tens. They should be "able men, such as fear God, men of truth, hating covetousness." These were to judge in all matters of minor consequence, while the most difficult and important cases should still be brought before Moses, who was to be to the people, said Jethro, "to God-ward, that thou mayest bring the causes unto God:

and thou shalt teach them ordinances and laws, and shalt show them the way wherein they must walk, and the work that they must do." This counsel was accepted, and it not only brought relief to Moses, but resulted in establishing more perfect order among the people.

The Lord had greatly honored Moses, and had wrought wonders by his hand; but the fact that he had been chosen to instruct others did not lead him to conclude that he himself needed no instruction. The chosen leader of Israel listened gladly to the suggestions of the godly priest of Midian, and adopted his plan as a wise arrangement.

From Rephidim the people continued their journey, following the movement of the cloudy pillar. Their route had led across barren plains, over steep ascents, and through rocky defiles. Often as they had traversed the sandy wastes, they had seen before them rugged mountains, like huge bulwarks, piled up directly across their course, and seeming to forbid all further progress. But as they approached, openings here and there appeared in the mountain wall, and beyond, another plain opened to view. Through one of the deep, gravelly passes they were now led. It was a grand and impressive scene. Between the rocky cliffs rising hundreds of feet on either side, flowed in a living tide, far as the eye could reach, the hosts of Israel with their flocks and herds. And now before them in solemn majesty Mount Sinai lifted its massive front. The cloudy pillar rested upon its summit, and the people spread their tents upon the plain beneath. Here was to be their home for nearly a year. At night the pillar of fire assured them of the divine protection, and while they were locked in slumber, the bread of heaven fell gently upon the encampment.

The dawn gilded the dark ridges of the mountains, and the sun's golden rays pierced the deep gorges, seeming to these weary travelers like beams of mercy from the throne of God. On every hand vast, rugged heights seemed in their solitary grandeur to speak of eternal endurance and majesty. Here the mind was impressed with solemnity and awe. Man was made to feel his ignorance and weakness in the presence of Him who "weighed the mountains in scales, and the hills in a balance." Isaiah 40:12. Here Israel was to receive the most wonderful revelation ever made by God to men. Here the Lord had gathered His people that He might impress upon them the sacredness of His requirements by declaring with His own voice His holy law. Great and radical changes were to be wrought in them; for the degrading influences of servitude and a long-continued association with idolatry had left their mark upon habits and character. God was working to lift them to a higher moral level by giving them a knowledge of Himself.

Chapter 27—The Law Given to Israel

This chapter is based on Exodus 19 to 24.

Soon after the encampment at Sinai, Moses was called up into the mountain to meet with God. Alone he climbed the steep and rugged path, and drew near to the cloud that marked the place of Jehovah's presence. Israel was now to be taken into a close and peculiar relation to the Most High—to be incorporated as a church and a nation under the government of God. The message to Moses for the people was:

"Ye have seen what I did unto the Egyptians, and how I bare you on eagles' wings, and brought you unto Myself. Now therefore, if ye will obey My voice indeed, and keep My covenant, then ye shall be a peculiar treasure unto Me above all people: for all the earth is Mine: and ye shall be unto Me a kingdom of priests, and an holy nation."

Moses returned to the camp, and having summoned the elders of Israel, he repeated to them the divine message. Their answer was, "All that the Lord hath spoken we will do." Thus they entered into a solemn covenant with God, pledging themselves to accept Him as their ruler, by which they became, in a special sense, the subjects of His authority.

Again their leader ascended the mountain, and the Lord said unto him, "Lo, I come unto thee in a thick cloud, that the people may hear when I speak with thee, and believe thee forever." When they met with difficulties in the way, they were disposed to murmur against Moses and Aaron, and accuse them of leading the hosts of Israel from Egypt to destroy them. The Lord would honor Moses before them, that they might be led to confide in his instructions.

God purposed to make the occasion of speaking His law a scene of awful grandeur, in keeping with its exalted character. The people were to be impressed that everything connected with the service of God must be regarded with the greatest reverence. The Lord said to

Moses, "Go unto the people, and sanctify them today and tomorrow, and let them wash their clothes, and be ready against the third day: for the third day the Lord will come down in the sight of all the people upon Mount Sinai." During these intervening days all were to occupy the time in solemn preparation to appear before God. Their person and their clothing must be freed from impurity. And as Moses should point out their sins, they were to devote themselves to humiliation, fasting, and prayer, that their hearts might be cleansed from iniquity.

The preparations were made, according to the command; and in obedience to a further injunction, Moses directed that a barrier be placed about the mount, that neither man nor beast might intrude upon the sacred precinct. If any ventured so much as to touch it, the penalty was instant death.

On the morning of the third day, as the eyes of all the people were turned toward the mount, its summit was covered with a thick cloud, which grew more black and dense, sweeping downward until the entire mountain was wrapped in darkness and awful mystery. Then a sound as of a trumpet was heard, summoning the people to meet with God; and Moses led them forth to the base of the mountain. From the thick darkness flashed vivid lightnings, while peals of thunder echoed and re-echoed among the surrounding heights. "And Mount Sinai was altogether on a smoke, because the Lord descended upon it in fire: and the smoke thereof ascended as the smoke of a furnace, and the whole mount quaked greatly." "The glory of the Lord was like devouring fire on the top of the mount" in the sight of the assembled multitude. And "the voice of the trumpet sounded long, and waxed louder and louder." So terrible were the tokens of Jehovah's presence that the hosts of Israel shook with fear, and fell upon their faces before the Lord. Even Moses exclaimed, "I exceedingly fear and quake." Hebrews 12:21.

And now the thunders ceased; the trumpet was no longer heard; the earth was still. There was a period of solemn silence, and then the voice of God was heard. Speaking out of the thick darkness that enshrouded Him, as He stood upon the mount, surrounded by a retinue of angels, the Lord made known His law. Moses, describing the scene, says: "The Lord came from Sinai, and rose up from Seir unto them; He shined forth from Mount Paran, and He came with ten thousands of saints: from His right hand went a fiery law for them. Yea, He loved the people; all His saints are in Thy hand: and they sat down at Thy feet; every one shall receive of Thy words." Deuteronomy 33:2, 3.

Jehovah revealed Himself, not alone in the awful majesty of the judge and lawgiver, but as the compassionate guardian of His people: "I am the Lord thy God, which have brought thee out of the land of Egypt, out of the house of bondage." He whom they had already known as their Guide and Deliverer, who had brought them forth from Egypt, making a way for them through the sea, and overthrowing Pharaoh and his hosts, who had thus shown Himself to be above all the gods of Egypt—He it was who now spoke His law.

The law was not spoken at this time exclusively for the benefit of the Hebrews. God honored them by making them the guardians and keepers of His law, but it was to be held as a sacred trust for the whole world. The precepts of the Decalogue are adapted to all mankind, and they were given for the instruction and government of all. Ten precepts, brief, comprehensive, and authoritative, cover the duty of man to God and to his fellow man; and all based upon the great fundamental principle of love. "Thou shalt love the Lord thy God with all thy heart, and with all thy soul, and with all thy strength, and with all thy mind; and thy neighbor as thyself." Luke 10:27. See also Deuteronomy 6:4, 5; Leviticus 19:18. In the Ten Commandments these principles are carried out in detail, and made applicable to the condition and circumstances of man.

"Thou shalt have no other gods before Me."

Jehovah, the eternal, self-existent, uncreated One, Himself the Source and Sustainer of all, is alone entitled to supreme reverence and worship. Man is forbidden to give to any other object the first place in his affections or his service. Whatever we cherish that tends to lessen our love for God or to interfere with the service due Him, of that do we make a god.

"Thou shalt not make unto thee any graven image, or any likeness of anything that is in heaven above, or that is in the earth beneath, or that is in the water under the earth: thou shalt not bow down thyself to them, nor serve them."

The second commandment forbids the worship of the true God by images or similitudes. Many heathen nations claimed that their images were mere figures or symbols by which the Deity was worshiped, but God has declared such worship to be sin. The attempt to represent the Eternal One by material objects would lower man's conception of God. The mind, turned away from the infinite perfection of Jehovah, would be attracted to the creature rather than to the Creator. And as his conceptions of God were lowered, so would man become degraded.

"I the Lord thy God am a jealous God." The close and sacred relation of God to His people is represented under the figure of marriage. Idolatry being spiritual adultery, the displeasure of God against it is fitly called jealousy.

"Visiting the iniquity of the fathers upon the children unto the third and fourth generation of them that hate Me." It is inevitable that children should suffer from the consequences of parental wrongdoing, but they are not punished for the parents' guilt, except as they participate in their sins. It is usually the case, however, that children walk in the steps of their parents. By inheritance and example the sons become partakers of the father's sin. Wrong tendencies, perverted appetites, and debased morals, as well as physical disease and degeneracy, are transmitted as a legacy from father to son, to the third and fourth generation. This fearful truth should have a solemn power to restrain men from following a course of sin.

"Showing mercy unto thousands of them that love Me, and keep My commandments." In prohibiting the worship of false gods, the second commandment by implication enjoins the worship of the true God. And to those who are faithful in His service, mercy is promised, not merely to the third and fourth generation as is the wrath threatened against those who hate Him, but to *thousands* of generations.

"Thou shalt not take the name of the Lord thy God in vain: for the Lord will not hold him guiltless that taketh His name in vain."

This commandment not only prohibits false oaths and common swearing, but it forbids us to use the name of God in a light or careless manner, without regard to its awful significance. By the thoughtless mention of God in common conversation, by appeals to Him in trivial matters, and by the frequent and thoughtless repetition of His name, we dishonor Him. "Holy and reverend is His name." Psalm 111:9. All should meditate upon His majesty, His purity and

[307]

holiness, that the heart may be impressed with a sense of His exalted character; and His holy name should be uttered with reverence and solemnity.

"Remember the Sabbath day, to keep it holy. Six days shalt thou labor, and do all thy work: but the seventh day is the Sabbath of the Lord thy God: in it thou shalt not do any work, thou, nor thy son, nor thy daughter, thy manservant, nor thy maidservant, nor thy cattle, nor thy stranger that is within thy gates: for in six days the Lord made heaven and earth, the sea, and all that in them is, and rested the seventh day: wherefore the Lord blessed the Sabbath day, and hallowed it."

The Sabbath is not introduced as a new institution but as having been founded at creation. It is to be remembered and observed as the memorial of the Creator's work. Pointing to God as the Maker of the heavens and the earth, it distinguishes the true God from all false gods. All who keep the seventh day signify by this act that they are worshipers of Jehovah. Thus the Sabbath is the sign of man's allegiance to God as long as there are any upon the earth to serve Him. The fourth commandment is the only one of all the ten in which are found both the name and the title of the Lawgiver. It is the only one that shows by whose authority the law is given. Thus it contains the seal of God, affixed to His law as evidence of its authenticity and binding force.

God has given men six days wherein to labor, and He requires that their own work be done in the six working days. Acts of necessity and mercy are permitted on the Sabbath, the sick and suffering are at all times to be cared for; but unnecessary labor is to be strictly avoided. "Turn away thy foot from the Sabbath, from doing thy pleasure on My holy day; and call the Sabbath a delight, the holy of the Lord, honorable; and ... honor Him, not doing thine own ways, nor finding thine own pleasure." Isaiah 58:13. Nor does the prohibition end here. "Nor speaking thine own words," says the prophet. Those who discuss business matters or lay plans on the Sabbath are regarded by God as though engaged in the actual transaction of business. To keep the Sabbath holy, we should not even allow our minds to dwell upon things of a worldly character. And the commandment includes all within our gates. The inmates of the house are to lay aside their worldly business during the sacred hours.

All should unite to honor God by willing service upon His holy day.

"Honor thy father and thy mother: that thy days may be long upon the land which the Lord thy God giveth thee."

Parents are entitled to a degree of love and respect which is due to no other person. God Himself, who has placed upon them a responsibility for the souls committed to their charge, has ordained that during the earlier years of life, parents shall stand in the place of God to their children. And he who rejects the rightful authority of his parents is rejecting the authority of God. The fifth commandment requires children not only to yield respect, submission, and obedience to their parents, but also to give them love and tenderness, to lighten their cares, to guard their reputation, and to succor and comfort them in old age. It also enjoins respect for ministers and rulers and for all others to whom God has delegated authority.

This, says the apostle, "is the first commandment with promise." Ephesians 6:2. To Israel, expecting soon to enter Canaan, it was a pledge to the obedient, of long life in that good land; but it has a wider meaning, including all the Israel of God, and promising eternal life upon the earth when it shall be freed from the curse of sin.

"Thou shalt not kill."

All acts of injustice that tend to shorten life; the spirit of hatred and revenge, or the indulgence of any passion that leads to injurious acts toward others, or causes us even to wish them harm (for "whosoever hateth his brother is a murderer"); a selfish neglect of caring for the needy or suffering; all self-indulgence or unnecessary deprivation or excessive labor that tends to injure health—all these are, to a greater or less degree, violations of the sixth commandment.

"Thou shalt not commit adultery."

This commandment forbids not only acts of impurity, but sensual thoughts and desires, or any practice that tends to excite them. Purity is demanded not only in the outward life but in the secret intents and emotions of the heart. Christ, who taught the far-reaching obligation of the law of God, declared the evil thought or look to be as truly sin as is the unlawful deed.

"Thou shalt not steal."

Both public and private sins are included in this prohibition. The eighth commandment condemns manstealing and slave dealing, and forbids wars of conquest. It condemns theft and robbery. It demands strict integrity in the minutest details of the affairs of life. It forbids overreaching in trade, and requires the payment of just debts or wages. It declares that every attempt to advantage oneself by the ignorance, weakness, or misfortune of another is registered as fraud in the books of heaven.

"Thou shalt not bear false witness against thy neighbor."

False speaking in any matter, every attempt or purpose to deceive our neighbor, is here included. An intention to deceive is what constitutes falsehood. By a glance of the eye, a motion of the hand, an expression of the countenance, a falsehood may be told as effectually as by words. All intentional overstatement, every hint or insinuation calculated to convey an erroneous or exaggerated impression, even the statement of facts in such a manner as to mislead, is falsehood. This precept forbids every effort to injure our neighbor's reputation by misrepresentation or evil surmising, by slander or tale bearing. Even the intentional suppression of truth, by which injury may result to others, is a violation of the ninth commandment.

"Thou shalt not covet thy neighbor's house, thou shalt not covet thy neighbor's wife, nor his manservant, nor his maidservant, nor his ox, nor his ass, nor anything that is thy neighbor's."

The tenth commandment strikes at the very root of all sins, prohibiting the selfish desire, from which springs the sinful act. He who in obedience to God's law refrains from indulging even a sinful desire for that which belongs to another will not be guilty of an act of wrong toward his fellow creatures.

Such were the sacred precepts of the Decalogue, spoken amid thunder and flame, and with a wonderful display of the power and majesty of the great Lawgiver. God accompanied the proclamation of His law with exhibitions of His power and glory, that His people might never forget the scene, and that they might be impressed with profound veneration for the Author of the law, the Creator of heaven and earth. He would also show to all men the sacredness, the importance, and the permanence of His law.

The people of Israel were overwhelmed with terror. The awful power of God's utterances seemed more than their trembling hearts could bear. For as God's great rule of right was presented before them, they realized as never before the offensive character of sin, and their own guilt in the sight of a holy God. They shrank away from the mountain in fear and awe. The multitude cried out to Moses, "Speak thou with us, and we will hear: but let not God speak with us, lest we die." The leader answered, "Fear not: for God is come to prove you, and that His fear may be before your faces, that ye sin not." The people, however, remained at a distance, gazing in terror upon the scene, while Moses "drew near unto the thick darkness where God was."

The minds of the people, blinded and debased by slavery and heathenism, were not prepared to appreciate fully the far-reaching principles of God's ten precepts. That the obligations of the Decalogue might be more fully understood and enforced, additional precepts were given, illustrating and applying the principles of the Ten Commandments. These laws were called judgments, both because they were framed in infinite wisdom and equity and because the magistrates were to give judgment according to them. Unlike the Ten Commandments, they were delivered privately to Moses, who was to communicate them to the people.

The first of these laws related to servants. In ancient times criminals were sometimes sold into slavery by the judges; in some cases, debtors were sold by their creditors; and poverty even led persons to sell themselves or their children. But a Hebrew could not be sold as a slave for life. His term of service was limited to six years; on the seventh he was to be set at liberty. Manstealing, deliberate murder, and rebellion against parental authority were to be punished with death. The holding of slaves not of Israelitish birth was permitted, but their life and person were strictly guarded. The murderer of a slave was to be punished; an injury inflicted upon one by his master, though no more than the loss of a tooth, entitled him to his freedom.

The Israelites had lately been servants themselves, and now that they were to have servants under them, they were to beware of indulging the spirit of cruelty and exaction from which they had suffered under their Egyptian taskmasters. The memory of their own bitter servitude should enable them to put themselves in the servant's place, leading them to be kind and compassionate, to deal with others as they would wish to be dealt with.

The rights of widows and orphans were especially guarded, and a tender regard for their helpless condition was enjoined. "If thou afflict them in any wise," the Lord declared, "and they cry at all unto Me, I will surely hear their cry; and My wrath shall wax hot, and I will kill you with the sword; and your wives shall be widows, and your children fatherless." Aliens who united themselves with Israel were to be protected from wrong or oppression. "Thou shalt not oppress a stranger: for ye know the heart of a stranger, seeing ye were strangers in the land of Egypt."

The taking of usury from the poor was forbidden. A poor man's raiment or blanket taken as a pledge, must be restored to him at nightfall. He who was guilty of theft was required to restore double. Respect for magistrates and rulers was enjoined, and judges were warned against perverting judgment, aiding a false cause, or receiving bribes. Calumny and slander were prohibited, and acts of kindness enjoined, even toward personal enemies.

Again the people were reminded of the sacred obligation of the Sabbath. Yearly feasts were appointed, at which all the men of the nation were to assemble before the Lord, bringing to Him their offerings of gratitude and the first fruits of His bounties. The object of all these regulations was stated: they proceeded from no exercise of mere arbitrary sovereignty; all were given for the good of Israel. The Lord said, "Ye shall be holy men unto Me"—worthy to be acknowledged by a holy God.

These laws were to be recorded by Moses, and carefully treasured as the foundation of the national law, and, with the ten precepts which they were given to illustrate, the condition of the fulfillment of God's promises to Israel.

The message was now given them from Jehovah: "Behold, I send an Angel before thee, to keep thee in the way, and to bring thee into the place which I have prepared. Beware of Him, and obey His voice, provoke Him not; for He will not pardon your transgressions: for My name is in Him. But if thou shalt indeed obey His voice, and do all that I speak; then I will be an enemy unto thine enemies, and an adversary unto thine adversaries." During all the wanderings of Israel, Christ, in the pillar of cloud and of fire, was their Leader. While there were types pointing to a Saviour to come, there was also a present Saviour, who gave commands to Moses for the people, and who was set forth before them as the only channel of blessing.

Upon descending from the mountain, "Moses came and told the people all the words of the Lord, and all the judgments: and all the people answered with one voice, and said, All the words which the Lord hath said will we do." This pledge, together with the words of the Lord which it bound them to obey, was written by Moses in a book.

[312]

Then followed the ratification of the covenant. An altar was built at the foot of the mountain, and beside it twelve pillars were set up, "according to the twelve tribes of Israel," as a testimony to their acceptance of the covenant. Sacrifices were then presented by young men chosen for the service.

Having sprinkled the altar with the blood of the offerings, Moses "took the book of the covenant, and read in the audience of the people." Thus the conditions of the covenant were solemnly repeated, and all were at liberty to choose whether or not they would comply with them. They had at the first promised to obey the voice of God; but they had since heard His law proclaimed; and its principles had been particularized, that they might know how much this covenant involved. Again the people answered with one accord, "All that the Lord hath said will we do, and be obedient." "When Moses had spoken every precept to all the people according to the law, he took the blood, ... and sprinkled both the book and all the people, saying, This is the blood of the testament which God hath enjoined unto you." Hebrews 9:19, 20.

Arrangements were now to be made for the full establishment of the chosen nation under Jehovah as their king. Moses had received the command, "Come up unto the Lord, thou, and Aaron, Nadab, and Abihu, and seventy of the elders of Israel; and worship ye afar off. And Moses alone shall come near the Lord." While the people worshiped at its foot, these chosen men were called up into the mount. The seventy elders were to assist Moses in the government of Israel, and God put upon them His Spirit, and honored them with a view of His power and greatness. "And they saw the God of Israel: and there was under His feet as it were a paved work of a sapphire stone, and as it were the body of heaven in his clearness." They did not behold the Deity, but they saw the glory of His presence. Before this they could not have endured such a scene; but the exhibition of God's power had awed them to repentance; they had been contemplating His glory, purity, and mercy, until they could approach nearer to Him who was the subject of their meditations.

[313] Moses and "his minister Joshua" were now summoned to meet with God. And as they were to be some time absent, the leader appointed Aaron and Hur, assisted by the elders, to act in his stead. "And Moses went up into the mount, and a cloud covered the mount. And the glory of the Lord abode upon Mount Sinai." For six days the cloud covered the mountain as a token of God's special presence; yet there was no revelation of Himself or communication of His will. During this time Moses remained in waiting for a summons to the presence chamber of the Most High. He had been directed, "Come up to Me into the mount, and be there," and though his patience and obedience were tested, he did not grow weary of watching, or forsake his post. This period of waiting was to him a time of preparation, of close self-examination. Even this favored servant of God could not at once approach into His presence and endure the exhibitions of His glory. Six days must be employed in devoting himself to God by searching of heart, meditation, and prayer before he could be prepared for direct communication with his Maker.

Upon the seventh day, which was the Sabbath, Moses was called up into the cloud. The thick cloud opened in the sight of all Israel, and the glory of the Lord broke forth like devouring fire. "And Moses went into the midst of the cloud, and gat him up into the mount; and Moses was in the mount forty days and forty nights." The forty days' tarry in the mount did not include the six days of preparation. During the six days Joshua was with Moses, and together they ate of the manna and drank of "the brook that descended out of the mount." But Joshua did not enter with Moses into the cloud. He remained without, and continued to eat and drink daily while awaiting the return of Moses, but Moses fasted during the entire forty days.

During his stay in the mount, Moses received directions for the building of a sanctuary in which the divine presence would be specially manifested. "Let them make Me a sanctuary; that I may dwell among them" (Exodus 25:8), was the command of God. For the third time the observance of the Sabbath was enjoined. "It is a sign between Me and the children of Israel forever," the Lord declared, "that ye may know that I am Jehovah that doth sanctify you. Ye shall keep the Sabbath therefore; for it is holy unto you.... Whosoever doeth any work therein, that soul shall be cut off from among his people." Exodus 31:17, 13, 14. Directions had just been given for the immediate erection of the tabernacle for the service of God; and now the people might conclude, because the object had in view was the glory of God, and also because of their great need of a place of worship, that they would be justified in working at the building upon the Sabbath. To guard them from this error, the warning was given. Even the sacredness and urgency of that special work for God must not lead them to infringe upon His holy rest day.

Henceforth the people were to be honored with the abiding presence of their King. "I will dwell among the children of Israel, and will be their God," "and the tabernacle shall be sanctified by My glory" (Exodus 29:45, 43), was the assurance given to Moses. As the symbol of God's authority and the embodiment of His will, there was delivered to Moses a copy of the Decalogue engraved by the finger of God Himself upon two tables of stone (Deuteronomy 9:10; Exodus 32:15, 16), to be sacredly enshrined in the sanctuary, which, when made, was to be the visible center of the nation's worship.

From a race of slaves the Israelites had been exalted above all peoples to be the peculiar treasure of the King of kings. God had separated them from the world, that He might commit to them a sacred trust. He had made them the depositaries of His law, and He purposed, through them, to preserve among men the knowledge of Himself. Thus the light of heaven was to shine out to a world enshrouded in darkness, and a voice was to be heard appealing to all peoples to turn from their idolatry to serve the living God. If the Israelites would be true to their trust, they would become a power in the world. God would be their defense, and He would exalt them above all other nations. His light and truth would be revealed through them, and they would stand forth under His wise and holy rule as an example of the superiority of His worship over every form of idolatry.

Chapter 28—Idolatry at Sinai

This chapter is based on Exodus 32 to 34.

While Moses was absent it was a time of waiting and suspense to Israel. The people knew that he had ascended the mount with Joshua, and had entered the cloud of thick darkness which could be seen from the plain below, resting on the mountain peak, illuminated from time to time with the lightnings of the divine Presence. They waited eagerly for his return. Accustomed as they had been in Egypt to material representations of deity, it had been hard for them to trust in an invisible being, and they had come to rely upon Moses to sustain their faith. Now he was taken from them. Day after day, week after week passed, and still he did not return. Notwithstanding the cloud was still in view, it seemed to many in the camp that their leader had deserted them, or that he had been consumed by the devouring fire.

During this period of waiting, there was time for them to meditate upon the law of God which they had heard, and to prepare their hearts to receive the further revelations that He might make to them. They had none too much time for this work; and had they been thus seeking a clearer understanding of God's requirements, and humbling their hearts before Him, they would have been shielded from temptation. But they did not do this, and they soon became careless, inattentive, and lawless. Especially was this the case with the mixed multitude. They were impatient to be on their way to the Land of Promise—the land flowing with milk and honey. It was only on condition of obedience that the goodly land was promised them, but they had lost sight of this. There were some who suggested a return to Egypt, but whether forward to Canaan or backward to Egypt, the masses of the people were determined to wait no longer for Moses.

Feeling their helplessness in the absence of their leader, they returned to their old superstitions. The "mixed multitude" had been the first to indulge murmuring and impatience, and they were the

Idolatry at Sinai

leaders in the apostasy that followed. Among the objects regarded by the Egyptians as symbols of deity was the ox or calf; and it was at the suggestion of those who had practiced this form of idolatry in Egypt that a calf was now made and worshiped. The people desired some image to represent God, and to go before them in the place of Moses. God had given no manner of similitude of Himself, and He had prohibited any material representation for such a purpose. The mighty miracles in Egypt and at the Red Sea were designed to establish faith in Him as the invisible, all-powerful Helper of Israel, the only true God. And the desire for some visible manifestation of His presence had been granted in the pillar of cloud and of fire that guided their hosts, and in the revealing of His glory upon Mount Sinai. But with the cloud of the Presence still before them, they turned back in their hearts to the idolatry of Egypt, and represented the glory of the invisible God by the similitude of an ox!

In the absence of Moses, the judicial authority had been delegated to Aaron, and a vast crowd gathered about his tent, with the demand, "Make us gods, which shall go before us; for as for this Moses, the man that brought us up out of the land of Egypt, we wot not what is become of him." [See Appendix, note 4.] The cloud, they said, that had heretofore led them, now rested permanently upon the mount; it would no longer direct their travels. They must have an image in its place; and if, as had been suggested, they should decide to return to Egypt, they would find favor with the Egyptians by bearing this image before them and acknowledging it as their god.

Such a crisis demanded a man of firmness, decision, and unflinching courage; one who held the honor of God above popular favor, personal safety, or life itself. But the present leader of Israel was not of this character. Aaron feebly remonstrated with the people, but his wavering and timidity at the critical moment only rendered them the more determined. The tumult increased. A blind, unreasoning frenzy seemed to take possession of the multitude. There were some who remained true to their covenant with God, but the greater part of the people joined in the apostasy. A few who ventured to denounce the proposed image making as idolatry, were set upon and roughly treated, and in the confusion and excitement they finally lost their lives.

Aaron feared for his own safety; and instead of nobly standing up for the honor of God, he yielded to the demands of the multitude. His first act was to direct that the golden earrings be collected from all the people and brought to him, hoping that pride would lead them to refuse such a sacrifice. But they willingly yielded up their ornaments; and from these he made a molten calf, in imitation of the gods of Egypt. The people proclaimed, "These be thy gods, O Israel, which brought thee up out of the land of Egypt." And Aaron basely permitted this insult to Jehovah. He did more. Seeing with what satisfaction the golden god was received, he built an altar before it, and made proclamation, "Tomorrow is a feast to the Lord." The announcement was heralded by trumpeters from company to company throughout the camp. "And they rose up early on the morrow, and offered burnt offerings, and brought peace offerings; and the people sat down to eat and to drink and rose up to play." Under the pretense of holding "a feast to the Lord," they gave themselves up to gluttony and licentious reveling.

How often, in our own day, is the love of pleasure disguised by a "form of godliness"! A religion that permits men, while observing the rites of worship, to devote themselves to selfish or sensual gratification, is as pleasing to the multitudes now as in the days of Israel. And there are still pliant Aarons, who, while holding positions of authority in the church, will yield to the desires of the unconsecrated, and thus encourage them in sin.

Only a few days had passed since the Hebrews had made a solemn covenant with God to obey His voice. They had stood trembling with terror before the mount, listening to the words of the Lord, "Thou shalt have no other gods before Me." The glory of God still hovered above Sinai in the sight of the congregation; but they turned away, and asked for other gods. "They made a calf in Horeb, and worshiped the molten image. Thus they changed their glory into the similitude of an ox." Psalm 106:19, 20. How could greater ingratitude have been shown, or more daring insult offered, to Him who had revealed Himself to them as a tender father and an all-powerful king!

Moses in the mount was warned of the apostasy in the camp and was directed to return without delay. "Go, get thee down," were the words of God; "thy people, which thou broughtest out of the land of

Egypt, have corrupted themselves: they have turned aside quickly out of the way which I commanded them. They have made them a molten calf, and have worshiped it." God might have checked the movement at the outset; but He suffered it to come to this height that He might teach all a lesson in His punishment of treason and apostasy.

God's covenant with His people had been disannulled, and He declared to Moses, "Let Me alone, that My wrath may wax hot against them, and that I may consume them: and I will make of thee a great nation." The people of Israel, especially the mixed multitude, would be constantly disposed to rebel against God. They would also murmur against their leader, and would grieve him by their unbelief and stubbornness, and it would be a laborious and soul-trying work to lead them through to the Promised Land. Their sins had already forfeited the favor of God, and justice called for their destruction. The Lord therefore proposed to destroy them, and make of Moses a mighty nation.

"Let Me alone, ... that I may consume them," were the words of God. If God had purposed to destroy Israel, who could plead for them? How few but would have left the sinners to their fate! How few but would have gladly exchanged a lot of toil and burden and sacrifice, repaid with ingratitude and murmuring, for a position of ease and honor, when it was God Himself that offered the release.

But Moses discerned ground for hope where there appeared only discouragement and wrath. The words of God, "Let Me alone," he understood not to forbid but to encourage intercession, implying that nothing but the prayers of Moses could save Israel, but that if thus entreated, God would spare His people. He "besought the Lord his God, and said, Lord, why doth Thy wrath wax hot against Thy people, which Thou hast brought forth out of the land of Egypt with great power, and with a mighty hand?"

God had signified that He disowned His people. He had spoken of them to Moses as "*thy* people, which *thou* broughtest out of Egypt." But Moses humbly disclaimed the leadership of Israel. They were not his, but God's—"*Thy* people, which *Thou* has brought forth ... with great power, and with a mighty hand. Wherefore," he urged, "should the Egyptians speak, and say, For mischief did He bring

[319]

them out, to slay them in the mountains, and to consume them from the face of the earth?"

During the few months since Israel left Egypt, the report of their wonderful deliverance had spread to all the surrounding nations. Fear and terrible foreboding rested upon the heathen. All were watching to see what the God of Israel would do for His people. Should they now be destroyed, their enemies would triumph, and God would be dishonored. The Egyptians would claim that their accusations were true—instead of leading His people into the wilderness to sacrifice, He had caused them to be sacrificed. They would not consider the sins of Israel; the destruction of the people whom He had so signally honored, would bring reproach upon His name. How great the responsibility resting upon those whom God has highly honored, to make His name a praise in the earth! With what care should they guard against committing sin, to call down His judgments and cause His name to be reproached by the ungodly!

As Moses interceded for Israel, his timidity was lost in his deep interest and love for those for whom he had, in the hands of God, been the means of doing so much. The Lord listened to his pleadings, and granted his unselfish prayer. God had proved His servant; He had tested his faithfulness and his love for that erring, ungrateful people, and nobly had Moses endured the trial. His interest in Israel sprang from no selfish motive. The prosperity of God's chosen people was dearer to him than personal honor, dearer than the privilege of becoming the father of a mighty nation. God was pleased with his faithfulness, his simplicity of heart, and his integrity, and He committed to him, as a faithful shepherd, the great charge of leading Israel to the Promised Land.

As Moses and Joshua came down from the mount, the former bearing the "tables of the testimony," they heard the shouts and outcries of the excited multitude, evidently in a state of wild uproar. To Joshua the soldier, the first thought was of an attack from their enemies. "There is a noise of war in the camp," he said. But Moses judged more truly the nature of the commotion. The sound was not that of combat, but of revelry. "It is not the voice of them that shout for mastery, neither is it the voice of them that cry for being overcome; but the noise of them that sing do I hear."

As they drew near the encampment, they beheld the people

shouting and dancing around their idol. It was a scene of heathen riot, an imitation of the idolatrous feasts of Egypt; but how unlike the solemn and reverent worship of God! Moses was overwhelmed. He had just come from the presence of God's glory, and though he had been warned of what was taking place, he was unprepared for that dreadful exhibition of the degradation of Israel. His anger was hot. To show his abhorrence of their crime, he threw down the tables of stone, and they were broken in the sight of all the people, thus signifying that as they had broken their covenant with God, so God had broken His covenant with them.

Entering the camp, Moses passed through the crowds of revelers, and seizing upon the idol, cast it into the fire. He afterward ground it to powder, and having strewed it upon the stream that descended from the mount, he made the people drink of it. Thus was shown the utter worthlessness of the god which they had been worshiping.

The great leader summoned his guilty brother and sternly demanded, "What did this people unto thee, that thou hast brought so great a sin upon them?" Aaron endeavored to shield himself by relating the clamors of the people; that if he had not complied with their wishes, he would have been put to death. "Let not the anger of my lord wax hot," he said; "thou knowest the people, that they are set on mischief. For they said unto me, Make us gods, which shall go before us: for as for this Moses, the man that brought us up out of the land of Egypt, we wot not what is become of him. And I said unto them, Whosoever hath any gold, let them break it off. So they gave it me: then I cast it into the fire, and there came out this calf." He would lead Moses to believe that a miracle had been wrought—that the gold had been cast into the fire, and by supernatural power changed to a calf. But his excuses and prevarications were of no avail. He was justly dealt with as the chief offender.

The fact that Aaron had been blessed and honored so far above the people was what made his sin so heinous. It was Aaron "the saint of the Lord" (Psalm 106:16), that had made the idol and announced the feast. It was he who had been appointed as spokesman for Moses, and concerning whom God Himself had testified, "I know that he can speak well" (Exodus 4:14), that had failed to check the idolaters in their heaven-daring purpose. He by whom God had wrought in bringing judgments both upon the Egyptians and upon their gods, had heard unmoved the proclamation before the molten image, "These be thy gods, O Israel, which brought thee up out of the land of Egypt." It was he who had been with Moses on the mount, and had there beheld the glory of the Lord, who had seen that in the manifestation of that glory there was nothing of which an image could be made—it was he who had changed that glory into the similitude of an ox. He to whom God had committed the government of the people in the absence of Moses, was found sanctioning their rebellion. "The Lord was very angry with Aaron to have destroyed him." Deuteronomy 9:20. But in answer to the earnest intercession of Moses, his life was spared; and in penitence and humiliation for his great sin, he was restored to the favor of God.

If Aaron had had courage to stand for the right, irrespective of consequences, he could have prevented that apostasy. If he had unswervingly maintained his own allegiance to God, if he had cited the people to the perils of Sinai, and had reminded them of their solemn covenant with God to obey His law, the evil would have been checked. But his compliance with the desires of the people and the calm assurance with which he proceeded to carry out their plans, emboldened them to go to greater lengths in sin than had before entered their minds.

When Moses, on returning to the camp, confronted the rebels, his severe rebukes and the indignation he displayed in breaking the sacred tables of the law were contrasted by the people with his brother's pleasant speech and dignified demeanor, and their sympathies were with Aaron. To justify himself, Aaron endeavored to make the people responsible for his weakness in yielding to their demand; but notwithstanding this, they were filled with admiration of his gentleness and patience. But God seeth not as man sees. Aaron's yielding spirit and his desire to please had blinded his eyes to the enormity of the crime he was sanctioning. His course in giving his influence to sin in Israel cost the life of thousands. In what contrast with this was the course of Moses, who, while faithfully executing God's judgments, showed that the welfare of Israel was dearer to him than prosperity or honor or life.

Of all the sins that God will punish, none are more grievous in His sight than those that encourage others to do evil. God would have His servants prove their loyalty by faithfully rebuking transgression, however painful the act may be. Those who are honored with a divine commission are not to be weak, pliant time-servers. They are not to aim at self-exaltation, or to shun disagreeable duties, but to perform God's work with unswerving fidelity.

Though God had granted the prayer of Moses in sparing Israel from destruction, their apostasy was to be signally punished. The lawlessness and insubordination into which Aaron had permitted them to fall, if not speedily crushed, would run riot in wickedness, and would involve the nation in irretrievable ruin. By terrible severity the evil must be put away. Standing in the gate of the camp, Moses called to the people, "Who is on the Lord's side? let him come unto me." Those who had not joined in the apostasy were to take their position at the right of Moses; those who were guilty but repentant, at the left. The command was obeyed. It was found that the tribe of Levi had taken no part in the idolatrous worship. From among other tribes there were great numbers who, although they had sinned, now signified their repentance. But a large company, mostly of the mixed multitude that instigated the making of the calf, stubbornly persisted in their rebellion. In the name of "the Lord God of Israel," Moses now commanded those upon his right hand, who had kept themselves clear of idolatry, to gird on their swords and slay all who persisted in rebellion. "And there fell of the people that day about three thousand men." Without regard to position, kindred, or friendship, the ringleaders in wickedness were cut off; but all who repented and humbled themselves were spared.

Those who performed this terrible work of judgment were acting by divine authority, executing the sentence of the King of heaven. Men are to beware how they, in their human blindness, judge and condemn their fellow men; but when God commands them to execute His sentence upon iniquity, He is to be obeyed. Those who performed this painful act, thus manifested their abhorrence of rebellion and idolatry, and consecrated themselves more fully to the service of the true God. The Lord honored their faithfulness by bestowing special distinction upon the tribe of Levi.

The Israelites had been guilty of treason, and that against a King who had loaded them with benefits and whose authority they had voluntarily pledged themselves to obey. That the divine government might be maintained justice must be visited upon the traitors. Yet even here God's mercy was displayed. While He maintained His law, He granted freedom of choice and opportunity for repentance to all. Only those were cut off who persisted in rebellion.

It was necessary that this sin should be punished, as a testimony to surrounding nations of God's displeasure against idolatry. By executing justice upon the guilty, Moses, as God's instrument, must leave on record a solemn and public protest against their crime. As the Israelites should hereafter condemn the idolatry of the neighboring tribes, their enemies would throw back upon them the charge that the people who claimed Jehovah as their God had made a calf and worshiped it in Horeb. Then though compelled to acknowledge the disgraceful truth, Israel could point to the terrible fate of the transgressors, as evidence that their sin had not been sanctioned or excused.

Love no less than justice demanded that for this sin judgment should be inflicted. God is the guardian as well as the sovereign of His people. He cuts off those who are determined upon rebellion, that they may not lead others to ruin. In sparing the life of Cain, God had demonstrated to the universe what would be the result of permitting sin to go unpunished. The influence exerted upon his descendants by his life and teaching led to the state of corruption that demanded the destruction of the whole world by a flood. The history of the antediluvians testifies that long life is not a blessing to the sinner; God's great forbearance did not repress their wickedness. The longer men lived, the more corrupt they became.

So with the apostasy at Sinai. Unless punishment had been speedily visited upon transgression, the same results would again have been seen. The earth would have become as corrupt as in the days of Noah. Had these transgressors been spared, evils would have followed, greater than resulted from sparing the life of Cain. It was the mercy of God that thousands should suffer, to prevent the necessity of visiting judgments upon millions. In order to save the many, He must punish the few. Furthermore, as the people had cast off their allegiance to God, they had forfeited the divine protection, and, deprived of their defense, the whole nation was exposed to the power of their enemies. Had not the evil been promptly put away, they would soon have fallen a prey to their numerous and powerful foes. It was necessary for the good of Israel, and also as a lesson to all succeeding generations, that crime should be promptly punished. And it was no less a mercy to the sinners themselves that they should be cut short in their evil course. Had their life been spared, the same spirit that led them to rebel against God would have been manifested in hatred and strife among themselves, and they would eventually have destroyed one another. It was in love to the world, in love to Israel, and even to the transgressors, that crime was punished with swift and terrible severity.

As the people were roused to see the enormity of their guilt, terror pervaded the entire encampment. It was feared that every offender was to be cut off. Pitying their distress, Moses promised to plead once more with God for them.

"Ye have sinned a great sin," he said, "and now I will go up unto the Lord; peradventure I shall make an atonement for your sin." He went, and in his confession before God he said, "Oh, this people have sinned a great sin, and have made them gods of gold. Yet now if Thou wilt forgive their sin—; and if not, blot me, I pray Thee, out of Thy book which Thou hast written." The answer was, "Whosoever hath sinned against Me, him will I blot out of My book. Therefore now go, lead the people into the place of which I have spoken unto thee: behold, Mine Angel shall go before thee: nevertheless, in the day when I visit, I will visit their sin upon them."

In the prayer of Moses our minds are directed to the heavenly records in which the names of all men are inscribed, and their deeds, whether good or evil, are faithfully registered. The book of life contains the names of all who have ever entered the service of God. If any of these depart from Him, and by stubborn persistence in sin become finally hardened against the influences of His Holy Spirit, their names will in the judgment be blotted from the book of life, and they themselves will be devoted to destruction. Moses realized how dreadful would be the fate of the sinner; yet if the people of Israel were to be rejected by the Lord, he desired his name to be blotted out with theirs; he could not endure to see the judgments of God fall upon those who had been so graciously delivered. The intercession of Moses in behalf of Israel illustrates the mediation of Christ for sinful men. But the Lord did not permit Moses to bear, as did Christ, the guilt of the transgressor. "Whosoever hath sinned against Me," He said, "him will I blot out of My book."

In deep sadness the people had buried their dead. Three thousand had fallen by the sword; a plague had soon after broken out in the encampment; and now the message came to them that the divine Presence would no longer accompany them in their journeyings. Jehovah had declared, "I will not go up in the midst of thee; for thou art a stiffnecked people: lest I consume thee in the way." And the command was given, "Put off thy ornaments from thee, that I may know what to do unto thee." Now there was mourning throughout the encampment. In penitence and humiliation "the children of Israel stripped themselves of their ornaments by the mount Horeb."

By the divine direction the tent that had served as a temporary place of worship was removed "afar off from the camp." This was still further evidence that God had withdrawn His presence from them. He would reveal Himself to Moses, but not to such a people. The rebuke was keenly felt, and to the conscience-smitten multitudes it seemed a foreboding of greater calamity. Had not the Lord separated Moses from the camp that He might utterly destroy them? But they were not left without hope. The tent was pitched without the encampment, but Moses called it "the tabernacle of the congregation." All who were truly penitent, and desired to return to the Lord, were directed to repair thither to confess their sins and seek His mercy. When they returned to their tents Moses entered the tabernacle. With agonizing interest the people watched for some token that his intercessions in their behalf were accepted. If God should condescend to meet with him, they might hope that they were not to be utterly consumed. When the cloudy pillar descended, and stood at the entrance of the tabernacle, the people wept for joy, and they "rose up and worshiped, every man in his tent door."

Moses knew well the perversity and blindness of those who were placed under his care; he knew the difficulties with which he must contend. But he had learned that in order to prevail with the people, he must have help from God. He pleaded for a clearer revelation of God's will and for an assurance of His presence: "See, Thou sayest unto me, Bring up this people: and Thou hast not let me know whom Thou wilt send with me. Yet Thou hast said, I know thee by name, and thou hast also found grace in My sight. Now therefore, I pray Thee, if I have found grace in Thy sight, show me now Thy way, that

I may know Thee, that I may find grace in Thy sight: and consider that this nation is Thy people."

The answer was, "My presence shall go with thee, and I will give thee rest." But Moses was not yet satisfied. There pressed upon his soul a sense of the terrible results should God leave Israel to hardness and impenitence. He could not endure that his interests should be separated from those of his brethren, and he prayed that the favor of God might be restored to His people, and that the token of His presence might continue to direct their journeyings: "If Thy presence go not with me, carry us not up hence. For wherein shall it be known here that I and Thy people have found grace in Thy sight? is it not in that Thou goest with us? So shall we be separated, I and Thy people, from all the people that are upon the face of the earth."

And the Lord said, "I will do this thing also that thou hast spoken: for thou hast found grace in My sight, and I know thee by name." Still the prophet did not cease pleading. Every prayer had been answered, but he thirsted for greater tokens of God's favor. He now made a request that no human being had ever made before: "I beseech Thee, show me Thy glory."

God did not rebuke his request as presumptuous; but the gracious words were spoken, "I will make all My goodness pass before thee." The unveiled glory of God, no man in this mortal state can look upon and live; but Moses was assured that he should behold as much of the divine glory as he could endure. Again he was summoned to the mountain summit; then the hand that made the world, that hand that "removeth the mountains, and they know not" (Job 9:5), took this creature of the dust, this mighty man of faith, and placed him in a cleft of the rock, while the glory of God and all His goodness passed before him.

This experience—above all else the promise that the divine Presence would attend him—was to Moses an assurance of success in the work before him; and he counted it of infinitely greater worth than all the learning of Egypt or all his attainments as a statesman or a military leader. No earthly power or skill or learning can supply the place of God's abiding presence.

To the transgressor it is a fearful thing to fall into the hands of the living God; but Moses stood alone in the presence of the Eternal One, and he was not afraid; for his soul was in harmony with the will of his Maker. Says the psalmist, "If I regard iniquity in my heart, the Lord will not hear me." Psalm 66:18. But "the secret of the Lord is with them that fear Him; and He will show them His covenant." Psalm 25:14.

The Deity proclaimed Himself, "The Lord, The Lord God, merciful and gracious, long-suffering, and abundant in goodness and truth, keeping mercy for thousands, forgiving iniquity and transgression and sin, and that will by no means clear the guilty."

"Moses made haste, and bowed his head toward the earth, and worshiped." Again he entreated that God would pardon the iniquity of His people, and take them for His inheritance. His prayer was granted. The Lord graciously promised to renew His favor to Israel, and in their behalf to do marvels such as had not been done "in all the earth, nor in any nation."

Forty days and nights Moses remained in the mount; and during all this time, as at the first, he was miraculously sustained. No man had been permitted to go up with him, nor during the time of his absence were any to approach the mount. At God's command he had prepared two tables of stone, and had taken them with him to the summit; and again the Lord "wrote upon the tables the words of the covenant, the Ten Commandments." [See Appendix, note 5.]

During that long time spent in communion with God, the face of Moses had reflected the glory of the divine Presence; unknown to himself his face shone with a dazzling light when he descended from the mountain. Such a light illumined the countenance of Stephen when brought before his judges; "and all that sat in the council, looking steadfastly on him, saw his face as it had been the face of an angel." Acts 6:15. Aaron as well as the people shrank away from Moses, and "they were afraid to come nigh him." Seeing their confusion and terror, but ignorant of the cause, he urged them to come near. He held out to them the pledge of God's reconciliation, and assured them of His restored favor. They perceived in his voice nothing but love and entreaty, and at last one ventured to approach him. Too awed to speak, he silently pointed to the countenance of Moses, and then toward heaven. The great leader understood his meaning. In their conscious guilt, feeling themselves still under the divine displeasure, they could not endure the heavenly light, which, had they been obedient to God, would have filled them with joy.

There is fear in guilt. The soul that is free from sin will not wish to hide from the light of heaven.

Moses had much to communicate to them; and compassionating their fear, he put a veil upon his face, and continued to do so thereafter whenever he returned to the camp from communion with God.

By this brightness God designed to impress upon Israel the sacred, exalted character of His law, and the glory of the gospel revealed through Christ. While Moses was in the mount, God presented to him, not only the tables of the law, but also the plan of salvation. He saw that the sacrifice of Christ was pre-figured by all the types and symbols of the Jewish age; and it was the heavenly light streaming from Calvary, no less than the glory of the law of God, that shed such a radiance upon the face of Moses. That divine illumination symbolized the glory of the dispensation of which Moses was the visible mediator, a representative of the one true Intercessor.

The glory reflected in the countenance of Moses illustrates the blessings to be received by God's commandment-keeping people through the mediation of Christ. It testifies that the closer our communion with God, and the clearer our knowledge of His requirements, the more fully shall we be conformed to the divine image, and the more readily do we become partakers of the divine nature.

Moses was a type of Christ. As Israel's intercessor veiled his countenance, because the people could not endure to look upon its glory, so Christ, the divine Mediator, veiled His divinity with humanity when He came to earth. Had He come clothed with the brightness of heaven, He could not have found access to men in their sinful state. They could not have endured the glory of His presence. Therefore He humbled Himself, and was made "in the likeness of sinful flesh" (Romans 8:3), that He might reach the fallen race, and lift them up.

Chapter 29—Satan's Enmity Against the Law

The very first effort of Satan to overthrow God's law—undertaken among the sinless inhabitants of heaven—seemed for a time to be crowned with success. A vast number of the angels were seduced; but Satan's apparent triumph resulted in defeat and loss, separation from God, and banishment from heaven.

When the conflict was renewed upon the earth, Satan again won a seeming advantage. By transgression, man became his captive, and man's kingdom also was betrayed into the hands of the archrebel. Now the way seemed open for Satan to establish an independent kingdom, and to defy the authority of God and His Son. But the plan of salvation made it possible for man again to be brought into harmony with God, and to render obedience to His law, and for both man and the earth to be finally redeemed from the power of the wicked one.

Again Satan was defeated, and again he resorted to deception, in the hope of converting his defeat into a victory. To stir up rebellion in the fallen race, he now represented God as unjust in having permitted man to transgress His law. "Why," said the artful tempter, "when God knew what would be the result, did He permit man to be placed on trial, to sin, and bring in misery and death?" And the children of Adam, forgetful of the long-suffering mercy that had granted man another trial, regardless of the amazing, the awful sacrifice which his rebellion had cost the King of heaven, gave ear to the tempter, and murmured against the only Being who could save them from the destructive power of Satan.

There are thousands today echoing the same rebellious complaint against God. They do not see that to deprive man of the freedom of choice would be to rob him of his prerogative as an intelligent being, and make him a mere automaton. It is not God's purpose to coerce the will. Man was created a free moral agent. Like the inhabitants of all other worlds, he must be subjected to the test of obedience; but he is never brought into such a position that yielding to evil becomes a matter of necessity. No temptation or trial is permitted to come to him which he is unable to resist. God made such ample provision that man need never have been defeated in the conflict with Satan.

As men increased upon the earth, almost the whole world joined the ranks of rebellion. Once more Satan seemed to have gained the victory. But omnipotent power again cut short the working of iniquity, and the earth was cleansed by the Flood from its moral pollution.

Says the prophet, "When Thy judgments are in the earth, the inhabitants of the world will learn righteousness. Let favor be showed to the wicked, yet will he not learn righteousness, ... and will not behold the majesty of Jehovah." Isaiah 26:9, 10. Thus it was after the Flood. Released from His judgments, the inhabitants of the earth again rebelled against the Lord. Twice God's covenant and His statutes had been rejected by the world. Both the people before the Flood and the descendants of Noah cast off the divine authority. Then God entered into covenant with Abraham, and took to Himself a people to become the depositaries of His law. To seduce and destroy this people, Satan began at once to lay his snares. The children of Jacob were tempted to contract marriages with the heathen and to worship their idols. But Joseph was faithful to God, and his fidelity was a constant testimony to the true faith. It was to quench this light that Satan worked through the envy of Joseph's brothers to cause him to be sold as a slave in a heathen land. God overruled events, however, so that the knowledge of Himself should be given to the people of Egypt. Both in the house of Potiphar and in the prison Joseph received an education and training that, with the fear of God, prepared him for his high position as prime minister of the nation. From the palace of the Pharaohs his influence was felt throughout the land, and the knowledge of God spread far and wide. The Israelites in Egypt also became prosperous and wealthy, and such as were true to God exerted a widespread influence. The idolatrous priests were filled with alarm as they saw the new religion finding favor. Inspired by Satan with his own enmity toward the God of heaven, they set themselves to quench the light. To the priests was committed the education of the heir to the throne, and it was this spirit of determined opposition to God and zeal for idolatry that molded the character of the future monarch, and led to cruelty and oppression toward the Hebrews.

During the forty years after the flight of Moses from Egypt, idolatry seemed to have conquered. Year by year the hopes of the Israelites grew fainter. Both king and people exulted in their power, and mocked the God of Israel. This grew until it culminated in the Pharaoh who was confronted by Moses. When the Hebrew leader came before the king with a message from "Jehovah, God of Israel," it was not ignorance of the true God, but defiance of His power, that prompted the answer, "Who is Jehovah, that I should obey His voice? ... I know not Jehovah." From first to last, Pharaoh's opposition to the divine command was not the result of ignorance, but of hatred and defiance.

Though the Egyptians had so long rejected the knowledge of God, the Lord still gave them opportunity for repentance. In the days of Joseph, Egypt had been an asylum for Israel; God had been honored in the kindness shown His people; and now the long-suffering One, slow to anger, and full of compassion, gave each judgment time to do its work; the Egyptians, cursed through the very objects they had worshiped, had evidence of the power of Jehovah, and all who would, might submit to God and escape His judgments. The bigotry and stubbornness of the king resulted in spreading the knowledge of God, and bringing many of the Egyptians to give themselves to His service.

It was because the Israelites were so disposed to connect themselves with the heathen and imitate their idolatry that God had permitted them to go down into Egypt, where the influence of Joseph was widely felt, and where circumstances were favorable for them to remain a distinct people. Here also the gross idolatry of the Egyptians and their cruelty and oppression during the latter part of the Hebrew sojourn should have inspired in them an abhorrence of idolatry, and should have led them to flee for refuge to the God of their fathers. This very providence Satan made a means to serve his purpose, darkening the minds of the Israelites and leading them to imitate the practices of their heathen masters. On account of the superstitious veneration in which animals were held by the Egyptians, the Hebrews were not permitted, during their bondage, to present the sacrificial offerings. Thus their minds were not directed by this service to the great Sacrifice, and their faith was weakened. When the time came for Israel's deliverance, Satan set himself to resist the purposes of God. It was his determination that that great people, numbering more than two million souls, should be held in ignorance and superstition. The people whom God had promised to bless and multiply, to make a power in the earth, and through whom He was to reveal the knowledge of His will—the people whom He was to make the keepers of His law—this very people Satan was seeking to keep in obscurity and bondage, that he might obliterate from their minds the remembrance of God.

When the miracles were wrought before the king, Satan was on the ground to counteract their influence and prevent Pharaoh from acknowledging the supremacy of God and obeying His mandate. Satan wrought to the utmost of his power to counterfeit the work of God and resist His will. The only result was to prepare the way for greater exhibitions of the divine power and glory, and to make more apparent, both to the Israelites and to all Egypt, the existence and sovereignty of the true and living God.

God delivered Israel with the mighty manifestations of His power, and with judgments upon all the gods of Egypt. "He brought forth His people with joy, and His chosen with gladness: ... that they might observe His statutes, and keep His laws." Psalm 105:43-45. He rescued them from their servile state, that He might bring them to a good land—a land which in His providence had been prepared for them as a refuge from their enemies, where they might dwell under the shadow of His wings. He would bring them to Himself, and encircle them in His everlasting arms; and in return for all His goodness and mercy to them they were required to have no other gods before Him, the living God, and to exalt His name and make it glorious in the earth.

During the bondage in Egypt many of the Israelites had, to a great extent, lost the knowledge of God's law, and had mingled its precepts with heathen customs and traditions. God brought them to Sinai, and there with His own voice declared His law.

Satan and evil angels were on the ground. Even while God was proclaiming His law to His people, Satan was plotting to tempt them to sin. This people whom God had chosen, he would wrench away, in the very face of Heaven. By leading them into idolatry, he would destroy the efficacy of all worship; for how can man be elevated by adoring what is no higher than himself and may be symbolized by his own handiwork? If men could become so blinded to the power, the majesty, and the glory of the infinite God as to represent Him by a graven image, or even by a beast or reptile; if they could so forget their own divine relationship, formed in the image of their Maker as to bow down to these revolting and senseless objects—then the way was open for foul license; the evil passions of the heart would be unrestrained, and Satan would have full sway.

At the very foot of Sinai, Satan began to execute his plans for overthrowing the law of God, thus carrying forward the same work he had begun in heaven. During the forty days while Moses was in the mount with God, Satan was busy exciting doubt, apostasy, and rebellion. While God was writing down His law, to be committed to His covenant people, the Israelites, denying their loyalty to Jehovah, were demanding gods of gold! When Moses came from the awful presence of the divine glory, with the precepts of the law which they had pledged themselves to obey, he found them, in open defiance of its commands, bowing in adoration before a golden image.

By leading Israel to this daring insult and blasphemy to Jehovah, Satan had planned to cause their ruin. Since they had proved themselves to be so utterly degraded, so lost to all sense of the privileges and blessings that God had offered them, and to their own solemn and repeated pledges of loyalty, the Lord would, he believed, divorce them from Himself and devote them to destruction. Thus would be secured the extinction of the seed of Abraham, that seed of promise that was to preserve the knowledge of the living God, and through whom He was to come—the true Seed, that was to conquer Satan. The great rebel had planned to destroy Israel, and thus thwart the purposes of God. But again he was defeated. Sinful as they were, the people of Israel were not destroyed. While those who stubbornly ranged themselves on the side of Satan were cut off, the people, humbled and repentant, were mercifully pardoned. The history of this sin was to stand as a perpetual testimony to the guilt and punishment of idolatry, and the justice and long-suffering mercy of God.

The whole universe had been witness to the scenes at Sinai. In the working out of the two administrations was seen the contrast between the government of God and that of Satan. Again the sinless inhabitants of other worlds beheld the results of Satan's apostasy, and the kind of government he would have established in heaven had he been permitted to bear sway.

By causing men to violate the second commandment, Satan aimed to degrade their conceptions of the Divine Being. By setting aside the fourth, he would cause them to forget God altogether. God's claim to reverence and worship, above the gods of the heathen, is based upon the fact that He is the Creator, and that to Him all other beings owe their existence. Thus it is presented in the Bible. Says the prophet Jeremiah: "The Lord is the true God, He is the living God, and an everlasting King.... The gods that have not made the heavens and the earth, even they shall perish from the earth, and from under these heavens. He hath made the earth by His power, He hath established the world by His wisdom, and hath stretched out the heavens by His discretion." "Every man is brutish in his knowledge: every founder is confounded by the graven image: for his molten image is falsehood, and there is no breath in them. They are vanity, and the work of errors: in the time of their visitation they shall perish. The portion of Jacob is not like them: for He is the former of all things." Jeremiah 10:10-12, 14-16. The Sabbath, as a memorial of God's creative power, points to Him as the maker of the heavens and the earth. Hence it is a constant witness to His existence and a reminder of His greatness, His wisdom, and His love. Had the Sabbath always been sacredly observed, there could never have been an atheist or an idolater.

The Sabbath institution, which originated in Eden, is as old as the world itself. It was observed by all the patriarchs, from creation down. During the bondage in Egypt, the Israelites were forced by their taskmasters to violate the Sabbath, and to a great extent they lost the knowledge of its sacredness. When the law was proclaimed at Sinai the very first words of the fourth commandment were, "Remember the Sabbath day, to keep it holy"—showing that the Sabbath was not then instituted; we are pointed back for its origin to creation. In order to obliterate God from the minds of men, Satan aimed to tear down this great memorial. If men could be led to forget their Creator, they would make no effort to resist the power of evil, and Satan would be sure of his prey.

Satan's enmity against God's law had impelled him to war against every precept of the Decalogue. To the great principle of love and loyalty to God, the Father of all, the principle of filial love and obedience is closely related. Contempt for parental authority will soon lead to contempt for the authority of God. Hence Satan's efforts to lessen the obligation of the fifth commandment. Among heathen peoples the principle enjoined in this precept was little heeded. In many nations parents were abandoned or put to death as soon as age had rendered them incapable of providing for themselves. In the family the mother was treated with little respect, and upon the death of her husband she was required to submit to the authority of her eldest son. Filial obedience was enjoined by Moses; but as the Israelites departed from the Lord, the fifth commandment, with others, came to be disregarded.

Satan was "a murderer from the beginning" (John 8:44); and as soon as he had obtained power over the human race, he not only prompted them to hate and slay one another, but, the more boldly to defy the authority of God, he made the violation of the sixth commandment a part of their religion.

By perverted conceptions of divine attributes, heathen nations were led to believe human sacrifices necessary to secure the favor of their deities; and the most horrible cruelties have been perpetrated under the various forms of idolatry. Among these was the practice of causing their children to pass through the fire before their idols. When one of them came through this ordeal unharmed, the people believed that their offerings were accepted; the one thus delivered was regarded as specially favored by the gods, was loaded with benefits, and ever afterward held in high esteem; and however aggravated his crimes, he was never punished. But should one be burned in passing through the fire, his fate was sealed; it was believed that the anger of the gods could be appeased only by taking the life of the victim, and he was accordingly offered as a sacrifice. In times of great apostasy these abominations prevailed, to some extent, among the Israelites.

The violation of the seventh commandment also was early practiced in the name of religion. The most licentious and abominable rites were made a part of the heathen worship. The gods themselves were represented as impure, and their worshipers gave the rein to the baser passions. Unnatural vices prevailed and the religious festivals were characterized by universal and open impurity.

Polygamy was practiced at an early date. It was one of the sins that brought the wrath of God upon the antediluvian world. Yet after the Flood it again became widespread. It was Satan's studied effort to pervert the marriage institution, to weaken its obligations and lessen its sacredness; for in no surer way could he deface the image of God in man and open the door to misery and vice.

From the opening of the great controversy it has been Satan's purpose to misrepresent God's character and to excite rebellion against His law, and this work appears to be crowned with success. The multitudes give ear to Satan's deceptions and set themselves against God. But amid the working of evil, God's purposes move steadily forward to their accomplishment; to all created intelligences He is making manifest His justice and benevolence. Through Satan's temptations the whole human race have become transgressors of God's law, but by the sacrifice of His Son a way is opened whereby they may return to God. Through the grace of Christ they may be enabled to render obedience to the Father's law. Thus in every age, from the midst of apostasy and rebellion, God gathers out a people that are true to Him—a people "in whose heart is His law." Isaiah 51:7.

It was by deception that Satan seduced angels; thus he has in all ages carried forward his work among men, and he will continue this policy to the last. Should he openly profess to be warring against God and His law, men would beware; but he disguises himself, and mixes truth with error. The most dangerous falsehoods are those that are mingled with truth. It is thus that errors are received that captivate and ruin the soul. By this means Satan carries the world with him. But a day is coming when his triumph will be forever ended.

God's dealings with rebellion will result in fully unmasking the work that has so long been carried on under cover. The results of Satan's rule, the fruits of setting aside the divine statutes, will be laid open to the view of all created intelligences. The law of God will stand fully vindicated. It will be seen that all the dealings of God have been conducted with reference to the eternal good of His people, and the good of all the worlds that He has created. Satan himself, in the presence of the witnessing universe, will confess the justice of God's government and the righteousness of His law.

The time is not far distant when God will arise to vindicate His insulted authority. "The Lord cometh out of His place to punish the inhabitants of the earth for their iniquity." Isaiah 26:21. "But who may abide the day of His coming? and who shall stand when He appeareth?" Malachi 3:2. The people of Israel, because of their sinfulness, were forbidden to approach the mount when God was about to descend upon it to proclaim His law, lest they should be consumed by the burning glory of His presence. If such manifestations of His power marked the place chosen for the proclamation of God's law, how terrible must be His tribunal when He comes for the execution of these sacred statutes. How will those who have trampled upon His authority endure His glory in the great day of final retribution? The terrors of Sinai were to represent to the people the scenes of the judgment. The sound of a trumpet summoned Israel to meet with God. The voice of the Archangel and the trump of God shall summon, from the whole earth, both the living and the dead to the presence of their Judge. The Father and the Son, attended by a multitude of angels, were present upon the mount. At the great judgment day Christ will come "in the glory of His Father with His angels." Matthew 16:27. He shall then sit upon the throne of His glory, and before Him shall be gathered all nations.

When the divine Presence was manifested upon Sinai, the glory of the Lord was like devouring fire in the sight of all Israel. But when Christ shall come in glory with His holy angels the whole earth shall be ablaze with the terrible light of His presence. "Our God shall come, and shall not keep silence: a fire shall devour before Him, and it shall be very tempestuous round about Him. He shall call to the heavens from above, and to the earth, that He may judge His people." Psalm 50:3, 4. A fiery stream shall issue and come forth from before Him, which shall cause the elements to melt with fervent heat, the earth also, and the works that are therein shall be burned up. "The Lord Jesus shall be revealed from heaven with His mighty angels, in flaming fire taking vengeance on them that know not God, and that obey not the gospel." 2 Thessalonians 1:7, 8.

Never since man was created had there been witnessed such a manifestation of divine power as when the law was proclaimed from

Sinai. "The earth shook, the heavens also dropped at the presence of God: even Sinai itself was moved at the presence of God, the God of Israel." Psalm 68:8. Amid the most terrific convulsions of nature the voice of God, like a trumpet, was heard from the cloud. The mountain was shaken from base to summit, and the hosts of Israel, pale and trembling with terror, lay upon their faces upon the earth. He whose voice then shook the earth has declared, "Yet once more I shake not the earth only, but also heaven." Hebrews 12:26. Says the Scripture, "The Lord shall roar from on high, and utter His voice from His holy habitation;" "and the heavens and the earth shall shake." Jeremiah 25:30; Joel 3:16. In that great coming day, the heaven itself shall depart "as a scroll when it is rolled together." Revelation 6:14. And every mountain and island shall be moved out of its place. "The earth shall reel to and fro like a drunkard, and shall be removed like a cottage; and the transgression thereof shall be heavy upon it; and it shall fall, and not rise again." Isaiah 24:20.

"Therefore shall all hands be faint," all faces shall be "turned into paleness," "and every man's heart shall melt. And they shall be afraid: pangs and sorrows shall take hold of them." "And I will punish the world for their evil," saith the Lord, "and I will cause the arrogancy of the proud to cease, and will lay low the haughtiness of the terrible." Isaiah 13:7, 8, 11; Jeremiah 30:6.

When Moses came from the divine Presence in the mount, where he had received the tables of the testimony, guilty Israel could not endure the light that glorified his countenance. How much less can transgressors look upon the Son of God when He shall appear in the glory of His Father, surrounded by all the heavenly host, to execute judgment upon the transgressors of His law and the rejecters of His atonement. Those who have disregarded the law of God and trodden under foot the blood of Christ, "the kings of the earth, and the great men, and the rich men, and the chief captains, and the mighty men," shall hide themselves "in the dens and in the rocks of the mountains," and they shall say to the mountains and rocks, "Fall on us, and hide us from the face of Him that sitteth on the throne, and from the wrath of the Lamb: for the great day of His wrath is come; and who shall be able to stand?" Revelation 6:15-17. "In that day a man shall cast his idols of silver, and his idols of gold, ... to the moles and to the bats; to go into the clefts of the rocks, and into the tops of the ragged rocks, for fear of the Lord, and for the glory of His majesty, when He ariseth to shake terribly the earth." Isaiah 2:20, 21.

Then it will be seen that Satan's rebellion against God has resulted in ruin to himself and to all that chose to become his subjects. He has represented that great good would result from transgression; but it will be seen that "the wages of sin is death." "For, behold, the day cometh, that shall burn as an oven; and all the proud, yea, and all that do wickedly, shall be stubble: and the day that cometh shall burn them up, saith the Lord of hosts, that it shall leave them neither root nor branch." Malachi 4:1. Satan, the root of every sin, and all evil workers, who are his branches, shall be utterly cut off. An end will be made of sin, with all the woe and ruin that have resulted from it. Says the psalmist, "Thou hast destroyed the wicked, thou hast put out their name forever and ever. O thou enemy, destructions are come to a perpetual end." Psalm 9:5, 6.

But amid the tempest of divine judgment the children of God will have no cause for fear. "The Lord will be the hope of His people, and the strength of the children of Israel." Joel 3:16. The day that brings terror and destruction to the transgressors of God's law will bring to the obedient "joy unspeakable and full of glory." "Gather My saints together unto Me," saith the Lord, "those that have made a covenant with Me by sacrifice. And the heavens shall declare His righteousness: for God is Judge Himself."

"Then shall ye return, and discern between the righteous and the wicked, between him that serveth God and him that serveth Him not." Malachi 3:18. "Hearken unto Me, ye that know righteousness, *the people in whose heart is My law*." "Behold, I have taken out of thine hand the cup of trembling, ... thou shalt no more drink it again." "I, even I, am He that comforteth you." Isaiah 51:7, 22, 12. "For the mountains shall depart, and the hills be removed; but My kindness shall not depart from thee, neither shall the covenant of My peace be removed, saith the Lord that hath mercy on thee." Isaiah 54:10.

The great plan of redemption results in fully bringing back the world into God's favor. All that was lost by sin is restored. Not only man but the earth is redeemed, to be the eternal abode of the obedient. For six thousand years Satan has struggled to maintain possession of the earth. Now God's original purpose in its creation is accomplished. "The saints of the Most High shall take the kingdom, and possess the kingdom forever, even forever and ever." Daniel 7:18.

"From the rising of the sun unto the going down of the same the Lord's name is to be praised." Psalm 113:3. "In that day shall there be one Lord, and His name one." "And Jehovah shall be king over all the earth." Zechariah 14:9. Says the Scripture, "Forever, O Lord, Thy word is settled in heaven." "All His commandments are sure. They stand fast forever and ever." Psalm 119:89; 111:7, 8. The sacred statutes which Satan has hated and sought to destroy, will be honored throughout a sinless universe. And "as the earth bringeth forth her bud, and as the garden causeth the things that are sown in it to spring forth; so the Lord God will cause righteousness and praise to spring forth before all nations." Isaiah 61:11.

Chapter 30—The Tabernacle and Its Services

This chapter is based on Exodus 25 to 40; Leviticus 4 and 16.

The command was communicated to Moses while in the mount with God, "Let them make Me a sanctuary; that I may dwell among them;" and full directions were given for the construction of the tabernacle. By their apostasy the Israelites forfeited the blessing of the divine Presence, and for the time rendered impossible the erection of a sanctuary for God among them. But after they were again taken into favor with Heaven, the great leader proceeded to execute the divine command.

Chosen men were especially endowed by God with skill and wisdom for the construction of the sacred building. God Himself gave to Moses the plan of that structure, with particular directions as to its size and form, the materials to be employed, and every article of furniture which it was to contain. The holy places made with hands were to be "figures of the true," "patterns of things in the heavens" (Hebrews 9:24, 23)—a miniature representation of the heavenly temple where Christ, our great High Priest, after offering His life as a sacrifice, was to minister in the sinner's behalf. God presented before Moses in the mount a view of the heavenly sanctuary, and commanded him to make all things according to the pattern shown him. All these directions were carefully recorded by Moses, who communicated them to the leaders of the people.

For the building of the sanctuary great and expensive preparations were necessary; a large amount of the most precious and costly material was required; yet the Lord accepted only freewill offerings. "Of every man that giveth it willingly with his heart ye shall take My offering" was the divine command repeated by Moses to the congregation. Devotion to God and a spirit of sacrifice were the first requisites in preparing a dwelling place for the Most High.

All the people responded with one accord. "They came, every one whose heart stirred him up, and every one whom his spirit made willing, and they brought the Lord's offering to the work of the tabernacle of the congregation, and for all His service, and for the holy garments. And they came, both men and women, as many as were willinghearted, and brought bracelets, and earrings, and rings, and tablets, all jewels of gold: and every man that offered, offered an offering of gold unto the Lord."

"And every man with whom was found blue, and purple, and scarlet, and fine linen, and goats' hair, and rams' skins dyed red, and sealskins, brought them. Everyone that did offer an offering of silver and brass brought the Lord's offering: and every man, with whom was found acacia wood for any work of the service, brought it.

"And all the women that were wisehearted did spin with their hands, and brought that which they had spun, the blue, and the purple, the scarlet, and the fine linen. And all the women whose heart stirred them up in wisdom spun the goats' hair.

"And the rulers brought the onyx stones, and the stones to be set, for the ephod, and for the breastplate; and the spice, and the oil; for the light, and for the anointing oil, and for the sweet incense." Exodus 35:23-28, R.V.

While the building of the sanctuary was in progress the people, old and young—men, women, and children—continued to bring their offerings, until those in charge of the work found that they had enough, and even more than could be used. And Moses caused to be proclaimed throughout the camp, "Let neither man nor woman make any more work for the offering of the sanctuary. So the people were restrained from bringing." The murmurings of the Israelites and the visitations of God's judgments because of their sins are recorded as a warning to after-generations. And their devotion, their zeal and liberality, are an example worthy of imitation. All who love the worship of God and prize the blessing of His sacred presence will manifest the same spirit of sacrifice in preparing a house where He may meet with them. They will desire to bring to the Lord an offering of the very best that they possess. A house built for God should not be left in debt, for He is thereby dishonored. An amount sufficient to accomplish the work should be freely given, that the workmen may be able to say, as did the builders of the tabernacle, "Bring no more offerings."

The tabernacle was so constructed that it could be taken apart and borne with the Israelites in all their journeyings. It was therefore small, being not more than fifty-five feet in length, and eighteen in breadth and height. Yet it was a magnificent structure. The wood employed for the building and its furniture was that of the acacia tree, which was less subject to decay than any other to be obtained at Sinai. The walls consisted of upright boards, set in silver sockets, and held firm by pillars and connecting bars; and all were overlaid with gold, giving to the building the appearance of solid gold. The roof was formed of four sets of curtains, the innermost of "fine twined linen, and blue, and purple, and scarlet: with cherubim of cunning work;" the other three respectively were of goats' hair, rams' skins dyed red, and sealskins, so arranged as to afford complete protection.

The building was divided into two apartments by a rich and beautiful curtain, or veil, suspended from gold-plated pillars; and a similar veil closed the entrance of the first apartment. These, like the inner covering, which formed the ceiling, were of the most gorgeous colors, blue, purple, and scarlet, beautifully arranged, while inwrought with threads of gold and silver were cherubim to represent the angelic host who are connected with the work of the heavenly sanctuary and who are ministering spirits to the people of God on earth.

The sacred tent was enclosed in an open space called the court, which was surrounded by hangings, or screens, of fine linen, suspended from pillars of brass. The entrance to this enclosure was at the eastern end. It was closed by curtains of costly material and beautiful workmanship, though inferior to those of the sanctuary. The hangings of the court being only about half as high as the walls of the tabernacle, the building could be plainly seen by the people without. In the court, and nearest the entrance, stood the brazen altar of burnt offering. Upon this altar were consumed all the sacrifices made by fire unto the Lord, and its horns were sprinkled with the atoning blood. Between the altar and the door of the tabernacle was the laver, which was also of brass, made from the mirrors that had been the freewill offering of the women of Israel. At the laver the priests were to wash their hands and their feet whenever they went into the sacred apartments, or approached the altar to offer a burnt offering unto the Lord.

In the first apartment, or holy place, were the table of showbread, the candlestick, or lampstand, and the altar of incense. The table of showbread stood on the north. With its ornamental crown, it was overlaid with pure gold. On this table the priests were each Sabbath to place twelve cakes, arranged in two piles, and sprinkled with frankincense. The loaves that were removed, being accounted holy, were to be eaten by the priests. On the south was the seven-branched candlestick, with its seven lamps. Its branches were ornamented with exquisitely wrought flowers, resembling lilies, and the whole was made from one solid piece of gold. There being no windows in the tabernacle, the lamps were never all extinguished at one time, but shed their light by day and by night. Just before the veil separating the holy place from the most holy and the immediate presence of God, stood the golden altar of incense. Upon this altar the priest was to burn incense every morning and evening; its horns were touched with the blood of the sin offering, and it was sprinkled with blood upon the great Day of Atonement. The fire upon this altar was kindled by God Himself and was sacredly cherished. Day and night the holy incense diffused its fragrance throughout the sacred apartments, and without, far around the tabernacle.

Beyond the inner veil was the holy of holies, where centered the symbolic service of atonement and intercession, and which formed the connecting link between heaven and earth. In this apartment was the ark, a chest of acacia wood, overlaid within and without with gold, and having a crown of gold about the top. It was made as a depository for the tables of stone, upon which God Himself had inscribed the Ten Commandments. Hence it was called the ark of God's testament, or the ark of the covenant, since the Ten Commandments were the basis of the covenant made between God and Israel.

The cover of the sacred chest was called the mercy seat. This was wrought of one solid piece of gold, and was surmounted by golden cherubim, one standing on each end. One wing of each angel was stretched forth on high, while the other was folded over the body (see Ezekiel 1:11) in token of reverence and humility. The position of the cherubim, with their faces turned toward each other, and looking reverently downward toward the ark, represented the reverence with which the heavenly host regard the law of God and their interest in the plan of redemption.

Above the mercy seat was the Shekinah, the manifestation of the divine Presence; and from between the cherubim, God made known His will. Divine messages were sometimes communicated to the high priest by a voice from the cloud. Sometimes a light fell upon the angel at the right, to signify approval or acceptance, or a shadow or cloud rested upon the one at the left to reveal disapproval or rejection.

The law of God, enshrined within the ark, was the great rule of righteousness and judgment. That law pronounced death upon the transgressor; but above the law was the mercy seat, upon which the presence of God was revealed, and from which, by virtue of the atonement, pardon was granted to the repentant sinner. Thus in the work of Christ for our redemption, symbolized by the sanctuary service, "mercy and truth are met together; righteousness and peace have kissed each other." Psalm 85:10.

No language can describe the glory of the scene presented within the sanctuary—the gold-plated walls reflecting the light from the golden candlestick, the brilliant hues of the richly embroidered curtains with their shining angels, the table, and the altar of incense, glittering with gold; beyond the second veil the sacred ark, with its mystic cherubim, and above it the holy Shekinah, the visible manifestation of Jehovah's presence; all but a dim reflection of the glories of the temple of God in heaven, the great center of the work for man's redemption.

A period of about half a year was occupied in the building of the tabernacle. When it was completed, Moses examined all the work of the builders, comparing it with the pattern shown him in the mount and the directions he had received from God. "As the Lord had commanded, even so had they done it: and Moses blessed them." With eager interest the multitudes of Israel crowded around to look upon the sacred structure. While they were contemplating the scene with reverent satisfaction, the pillar of cloud floated over the sanctuary and, descending, enveloped it. "And the glory of the Lord filled the tabernacle." There was a revealing of the divine majesty, and for a time even Moses could not enter. With deep emotion the people beheld the token that the work of their hands was accepted.

There were no loud demonstrations of rejoicing. A solemn awe rested upon all. But the gladness of their hearts welled up in tears of joy, and they murmured low, earnest words of gratitude that God had condescended to abide with them.

By divine direction the tribe of Levi was set apart for the service of the sanctuary. In the earliest times every man was the priest of his own household. In the days of Abraham the priesthood was regarded as the birthright of the eldest son. Now, instead of the first-born of all Israel, the Lord accepted the tribe of Levi for the work of the sanctuary. By this signal honor He manifested His approval of their fidelity, both in adhering to His service and in executing His judgments when Israel apostatized in the worship of the golden calf. The priesthood, however, was restricted to the family of Aaron. Aaron and his sons alone were permitted to minister before the Lord; the rest of the tribe were entrusted with the charge of the tabernacle and its furniture, and they were to attend upon the priests in their ministration, but they were not to sacrifice, to burn incense, or to see the holy things till they were covered.

In accordance with their office, a special dress was appointed for the priests. "Thou shalt make holy garments for Aaron thy brother, for glory and for beauty," was the divine direction to Moses. The robe of the common priest was of white linen, and woven in one piece. It extended nearly to the feet and was confined about the waist by a white linen girdle embroidered in blue, purple, and red. A linen turban, or miter, completed his outer costume. Moses at the burning bush was directed to put off his sandals, for the ground whereon he stood was holy. So the priests were not to enter the sanctuary with shoes upon their feet. Particles of dust cleaving to them would desecrate the holy place. They were to leave their shoes in the court before entering the sanctuary, and also to wash both their hands and their feet before ministering in the tabernacle or at the altar of burnt offering. Thus was constantly taught the lesson that all defilement must be put away from those who would approach into the presence of God.

The garments of the high priest were of costly material and beautiful workmanship, befitting his exalted station. In addition to the linen dress of the common priest, he wore a robe of blue, also woven in one piece. Around the skirt it was ornamented with golden

[351]

bells, and pomegranates of blue, purple, and scarlet. Outside of this was the ephod, a shorter garment of gold, blue, purple, scarlet, and white. It was confined by a girdle of the same colors, beautifully wrought. The ephod was sleeveless, and on its gold-embroidered shoulder pieces were set two onyx stones, bearing the names of the twelve tribes of Israel.

Over the ephod was the breastplate, the most sacred of the priestly vestments. This was of the same material as the ephod. It was in the form of a square, measuring a span, and was suspended from the shoulders by a cord of blue from golden rings. The border was formed of a variety of precious stones, the same that form the twelve foundations of the City of God. Within the border were twelve stones set in gold, arranged in rows of four, and, like those in the shoulder pieces, engraved with the names of the tribes. The Lord's direction was, "Aaron shall bear the names of the children of Israel in the breastplate of judgment upon his heart, when he goeth in unto the holy place, for a memorial before the Lord continually." Exodus 28:29. So Christ, the great High Priest, pleading His blood before the Father in the sinner's behalf, bears upon His heart the name of every repentant, believing soul. Says the psalmist, "I am poor and needy; yet the Lord thinketh upon me." Psalm 40:17.

At the right and left of the breastplate were two large stones of great brilliancy. These were known as the Urim and Thummim. By them the will of God was made known through the high priest. When questions were brought for decision before the Lord, a halo of light encircling the precious stone at the right was a token of the divine consent or approval, while a cloud shadowing the stone at the left was an evidence of denial or disapprobation.

The miter of the high priest consisted of the white linen turban, having attached to it by a lace of blue, a gold plate bearing the inscription, "Holiness to Jehovah." Everything connected with the apparel and deportment of the priests was to be such as to impress the beholder with a sense of the holiness of God, the sacredness of His worship, and the purity required of those who came into His presence.

Not only the sanctuary itself, but the ministration of the priests, was to "serve unto the example and shadow of heavenly things." Hebrews 8:5. Thus it was of great importance; and the Lord, through

Moses, gave the most definite and explicit instruction concerning every point of this typical service. The ministration of the sanctuary consisted of two divisions, a daily and a yearly service. The daily service was performed at the altar of burnt offering in the court of the tabernacle and in the holy place; while the yearly service was in the most holy.

No mortal eye but that of the high priest was to look upon the inner apartment of the sanctuary. Only once a year could the priest enter there, and that after the most careful and solemn preparation. With trembling he went in before God, and the people in reverent silence awaited his return, their hearts uplifted in earnest prayer for the divine blessing. Before the mercy seat the high priest made the atonement for Israel; and in the cloud of glory, God met with him. His stay here beyond the accustomed time filled them with fear, lest because of their sins or his own he had been slain by the glory of the Lord.

The daily service consisted of the morning and evening burnt offering, the offering of sweet incense on the golden altar, and the special offerings for individual sins. And there were also offerings for Sabbaths, new moons, and special feasts.

Every morning and evening a lamb of a year old was burned upon the altar, with its appropriate meat offering, thus symbolizing the daily consecration of the nation to Jehovah, and their constant dependence upon the atoning blood of Christ. God expressly directed that every offering presented for the service of the sanctuary should be "without blemish." Exodus 12:5. The priests were to examine all animals brought as a sacrifice, and were to reject every one in which a defect was discovered. Only an offering "without blemish" could be a symbol of His perfect purity who was to offer Himself as "a lamb without blemish and without spot." 1 Peter 1:19. The apostle Paul points to these sacrifices as an illustration of what the followers of Christ are to become. He says, "I beseech you therefore, brethren, by the mercies of God, that ye present your bodies a living sacrifice, holy, acceptable unto God, which is your reasonable service." Romans 12:1. We are to give ourselves to the service of God, and we should seek to make the offering as nearly perfect as possible. God will not be pleased with anything less than the best we can offer. Those who love Him with all the heart, will desire to give Him the best service of the life, and they will be constantly seeking to bring every power of their being into harmony with the laws that will promote their ability to do His will.

In the offering of incense the priest was brought more directly into the presence of God than in any other act of the daily ministration. As the inner veil of the sanctuary did not extend to the top of the building, the glory of God, which was manifested above the mercy seat, was partially visible from the first apartment. When the priest offered incense before the Lord, he looked toward the ark; and as the cloud of incense arose, the divine glory descended upon the mercy seat and filled the most holy place, and often so filled both apartments that the priest was obliged to retire to the door of the tabernacle. As in that typical service the priest looked by faith to the mercy seat which he could not see, so the people of God are now to direct their prayers to Christ, their great High Priest, who, unseen by human vision, is pleading in their behalf in the sanctuary above.

The incense, ascending with the prayers of Israel, represents the merits and intercession of Christ, His perfect righteousness, which through faith is imputed to His people, and which can alone make the worship of sinful beings acceptable to God. Before the veil of the most holy place was an altar of perpetual intercession, before the holy, an altar of continual atonement. By blood and by incense God was to be approached—symbols pointing to the great Mediator, through whom sinners may approach Jehovah, and through whom alone mercy and salvation can be granted to the repentant, believing soul.

As the priests morning and evening entered the holy place at the time of incense, the daily sacrifice was ready to be offered upon the altar in the court without. This was a time of intense interest to the worshipers who assembled at the tabernacle. Before entering into the presence of God through the ministration of the priest, they were to engage in earnest searching of heart and confession of sin. They united in silent prayer, with their faces toward the holy place. Thus their petitions ascended with the cloud of incense, while faith laid hold upon the merits of the promised Saviour prefigured by the atoning sacrifice. The hours appointed for the morning and the evening sacrifice were regarded as sacred, and they came to be observed as the set time for worship throughout the Jewish nation.

And when in later times the Jews were scattered as captives in distant lands, they still at the appointed hour turned their faces toward Jerusalem and offered up their petitions to the God of Israel. In this custom Christians have an example for morning and evening prayer. While God condemns a mere round of ceremonies, without the spirit of worship, He looks with great pleasure upon those who love Him, bowing morning and evening to seek pardon for sins committed and to present their requests for needed blessings.

The showbread was kept ever before the Lord as a perpetual offering. Thus it was a part of the daily sacrifice. It was called showbread, or "bread of the presence," because it was ever before the face of the Lord. It was an acknowledgment of man's dependence upon God for both temporal and spiritual food, and that it is received only through the mediation of Christ. God had fed Israel in the wilderness with bread from heaven, and they were still dependent upon His bounty, both for temporal food and spiritual blessings. Both the manna and the showbread pointed to Christ, the living Bread, who is ever in the presence of God for us. He Himself said, "I am the living Bread which came down from heaven." John 6:48-51. Frankincense was placed upon the loaves. When the bread was removed every Sabbath, to be replaced by fresh loaves, the frankincense was burned upon the altar as a memorial before God.

The most important part of the daily ministration was the service performed in behalf of individuals. The repentant sinner brought his offering to the door of the tabernacle, and, placing his hand upon the victim's head, confessed his sins, thus in figure transferring them from himself to the innocent sacrifice. By his own hand the animal was then slain, and the blood was carried by the priest into the holy place and sprinkled before the veil, behind which was the ark containing the law that the sinner had transgressed. By this ceremony the sin was, through the blood, transferred in figure to the sanctuary. In some cases the blood was not taken into the holy place; [See Appendix, note 6.] but the flesh was then to be eaten by the priest, as Moses directed the sons of Aaron, saying, "God hath given it you to bear the iniquity of the congregation." Leviticus 10:17. Both ceremonies alike symbolized the transfer of the sin from the penitent to the sanctuary.

Such was the work that went on day by day throughout the year. The sins of Israel being thus transferred to the sanctuary, the holy places were defiled, and a special work became necessary for the removal of the sins. God commanded that an atonement be made for each of the sacred apartments, as for the altar, to "cleanse it, and hallow it from the uncleanness of the children of Israel." Leviticus 16:19.

Once a year, on the great Day of Atonement, the priest entered the most holy place for the cleansing of the sanctuary. The work there performed completed the yearly round of ministration.

On the Day of Atonement two kids of the goats were brought to the door of the tabernacle, and lots were cast upon them, "one lot for the Lord, and the other lot for the scapegoat." The goat upon which the first lot fell was to be slain as a sin offering for the people. And the priest was to bring his blood within the veil, and sprinkle it upon the mercy seat. "And he shall make an atonement for the holy place, because of the uncleanness of the children of Israel, and because of their transgressions in all their sins; and so shall he do for the tabernacle of the congregation, that remaineth among them in the midst of their uncleanness."

"And Aaron shall lay both his hands upon the head of the live goat, and confess over him all the iniquities of the children of Israel, and all their transgressions in all their sins, putting them upon the head of the goat, and shall send him away by the hand of a fit man into the wilderness: and the goat shall bear upon him all their iniquities into a land not inhabited." Not until the goat had been thus sent away did the people regard themselves as freed from the burden of their sins. Every man was to afflict his soul while the work of atonement was going forward. All business was laid aside, and the whole congregation of Israel spent the day in solemn humiliation before God, with prayer, fasting, and deep searching of heart.

Important truths concerning the atonement were taught the people by this yearly service. In the sin offerings presented during the year, a substitute had been accepted in the sinner's stead; but the blood of the victim had not made full atonement for the sin. It had only provided a means by which the sin was transferred to the sanctuary. By the offering of blood, the sinner acknowledged the authority of the law, confessed the guilt of his transgression, and expressed his faith in Him who was to take away the sin of the world; but he was not entirely released from the condemnation of the law. On the Day of Atonement the high priest, having taken an offering for the congregation, went into the most holy place with the blood and sprinkled it upon the mercy seat, above the tables of the law. Thus the claims of the law, which demanded the life of the sinner, were satisfied. Then in his character of mediator the priest took the sins upon himself, and, leaving the sanctuary, he bore with him the burden of Israel's guilt. At the door of the tabernacle he laid his hands upon the head of the scapegoat and confessed over him "all the iniquities of the children of Israel, and all their transgressions in all their sins, putting them upon the head of the goat." And as the goat bearing these sins was sent away, they were, with him, regarded as forever separated from the people. Such was the service performed "unto the example and shadow of heavenly things." Hebrews 8:5.

As has been stated, the earthly sanctuary was built by Moses according to the pattern shown him in the mount. It was "a figure for the time then present, in which were offered both gifts and sacrifices;" its two holy places were "patterns of things in the heavens;" Christ, our great High Priest, is "a minister of the sanctuary, and of the true tabernacle, which the Lord pitched, and not man." Hebrews 9:9, 23; 8:2. As in vision the apostle John was granted a view of the temple of God in heaven, he beheld there "seven lamps of fire burning before the throne." He saw an angel "having a golden censer; and there was given unto him much incense, that he should offer it with the prayers of all saints upon the golden altar which was before the throne." Revelation 4:5; 8:3. Here the prophet was permitted to behold the first apartment of the sanctuary in heaven; and he saw there the "seven lamps of fire" and the "golden altar" represented by the golden candlestick and the altar of incense in the sanctuary on earth. Again, "the temple of God was opened" (Revelation 11:19), and he looked within the inner veil, upon the holy of holies. Here he beheld "the ark of His testament" (Revelation 11:19), represented by the sacred chest constructed by Moses to contain the law of God.

Moses made the earthly sanctuary, "according to the fashion that he had seen." Paul declares that "the tabernacle, and all the vessels of the ministry," when completed, were "the patterns of things in the heavens." Acts 7:44; Hebrews 9:21, 23. And John says that he saw the sanctuary in heaven. That sanctuary, in which Jesus ministers in our behalf, is the great original, of which the sanctuary built by Moses was a copy.

The heavenly temple, the abiding place of the King of kings, where "thousand thousands ministered unto Him, and ten thousand times ten thousand stood before Him" (Daniel 7:10), that temple filled with the glory of the eternal throne, where seraphim, its shining guardians, veil their faces in adoration—no earthly structure could represent its vastness and its glory. Yet important truths concerning the heavenly sanctuary and the great work there carried forward for man's redemption were to be taught by the earthly sanctuary and its services.

After His ascension, our Saviour was to begin His work as our High Priest. Says Paul, "Christ is not entered into the holy places made with hands, which are the figures of the true; but into heaven itself, now to appear in the presence of God for us." Hebrews 9:24. As Christ's ministration was to consist of two great divisions, each occupying a period of time and having a distinctive place in the heavenly sanctuary, so the typical ministration consisted of two divisions, the daily and the yearly service, and to each a department of the tabernacle was devoted.

As Christ at His ascension appeared in the presence of God to plead His blood in behalf of penitent believers, so the priest in the daily ministration sprinkled the blood of the sacrifice in the holy place in the sinner's behalf.

The blood of Christ, while it was to release the repentant sinner from the condemnation of the law, was not to cancel the sin; it would stand on record in the sanctuary until the final atonement; so in the type the blood of the sin offering removed the sin from the penitent, but it rested in the sanctuary until the Day of Atonement.

In the great day of final award, the dead are to be "judged out of those things which were written in the books, according to their works." Revelation 20:12. Then by virtue of the atoning blood of Christ, the sins of all the truly penitent will be blotted from the books of heaven. Thus the sanctuary will be freed, or cleansed, from the record of sin. In the type, this great work of atonement, or blotting out of sins, was represented by the services of the Day of Atonement—the cleansing of the earthly sanctuary, which was accomplished by the removal, by virtue of the blood of the sin offering, of the sins by which it had been polluted.

As in the final atonement the sins of the truly penitent are to be blotted from the records of heaven, no more to be remembered or come into mind, so in the type they were borne away into the wilderness, forever separated from the congregation.

Since Satan is the originator of sin, the direct instigator of all the sins that caused the death of the Son of God, justice demands that Satan shall suffer the final punishment. Christ's work for the redemption of men and the purification of the universe from sin will be closed by the removal of sin from the heavenly sanctuary and the placing of these sins upon Satan, who will bear the final penalty. So in the typical service, the yearly round of ministration closed with the purification of the sanctuary, and the confessing of the sins on the head of the scapegoat.

Thus in the ministration of the tabernacle, and of the temple that afterward took its place, the people were taught each day the great truths relative to Christ's death and ministration, and once each year their minds were carried forward to the closing events of the great controversy between Christ and Satan, the final purification of the universe from sin and sinners.

Chapter 31—The Sin of Nadab and Abihu

This chapter is based on Leviticus 10:1-11.

After the dedication of the tabernacle, the priests were consecrated to their sacred office. These services occupied seven days, each marked by special ceremonies. On the eighth day they entered upon their ministration. Assisted by his sons, Aaron offered the sacrifices that God required, and he lifted up his hands and blessed the people. All had been done as God commanded, and He accepted the sacrifice, and revealed His glory in a remarkable manner; fire came from the Lord and consumed the offering upon the altar. The people looked upon this wonderful manifestation of divine power with awe and intense interest. They saw in it a token of God's glory and favor, and they raised a universal shout of praise and adoration and fell on their faces as if in the immediate presence of Jehovah.

But soon afterward a sudden and terrible calamity fell upon the family of the high priest. At the hour of worship, as the prayers and praise of the people were ascending to God, two of the sons of Aaron took each his censer and burned fragrant incense thereon, to rise as a sweet odor before the Lord. But they transgressed His command by the use of "strange fire." For burning the incense they took common instead of the sacred fire which God Himself had kindled, and which He had commanded to be used for this purpose. For this sin a fire went out from the Lord and devoured them in the sight of the people.

Next to Moses and Aaron, Nadab and Abihu had stood highest in Israel. They had been especially honored by the Lord, having been permitted with the seventy elders to behold His glory in the mount. But their transgression was not therefore to be excused or lightly regarded. All this rendered their sin more grievous. Because men have received great light, because they have, like the princes of Israel, ascended to the mount, and been privileged to have communion with God, and to dwell in the light of His glory, let them not flatter themselves that they can afterward sin with impunity, that because they have been thus honored, God will not be strict to punish their iniquity. This is a fatal deception. The great light and privileges bestowed require returns of virtue and holiness corresponding to the light given. Anything short of this, God cannot accept. Great blessings or privileges should never lull to security or carelessness. They should never give license to sin or cause the recipients to feel that God will not be exact with them. All the advantages which God has given are His means to throw ardor into the spirit, zeal into effort, and vigor into the carrying out of His holy will.

Nadab and Abihu had not in their youth been trained to habits of self-control. The father's yielding disposition, his lack of firmness for right, had led him to neglect the discipline of his children. His sons had been permitted to follow inclination. Habits of self-indulgence, long cherished, obtained a hold upon them which even the responsibility of the most sacred office had not power to break. They had not been taught to respect the authority of their father, and they did not realize the necessity of exact obedience to the requirements of God. Aaron's mistaken indulgence of his sons prepared them to become the subjects of the divine judgments.

God designed to teach the people that they must approach Him with reverence and awe, and in His own appointed manner. He cannot accept partial obedience. It was not enough that in this solemn season of worship *nearly* everything was done as He had directed. God has pronounced a curse upon those who depart from His commandments, and put no difference between common and holy things. He declares by the prophet: "Woe unto them that call evil good, and good evil; that put darkness for light, and light for darkness! ... woe unto them that are wise in their own eyes, and prudent in their own sight! ... which justify the wicked for reward, and take away the righteousness of the righteous from him! ... They have cast away the law of the Lord of hosts, and despised the word of the Holy One of Israel." Isaiah 5:20-24. Let no one deceive himself with the belief that a part of God's commandments are nonessential, or that He will accept a substitute for that which He has required. Said the prophet Jeremiah, "Who is he that saith, and it cometh to pass, when the Lord commandeth it not?" Lamentations 3:37. God has placed in His word no command which men may obey or disobey at will and not suffer the consequences. If men choose any other path than that of strict obedience, they will find that "the end thereof are the ways of death." Proverbs 14:12.

"Moses said unto Aaron, and unto Eleazar and unto Ithamar, his sons, Uncover not your heads, neither rend your clothes; lest ye die, ... for the anointing oil of the Lord is upon you." The great leader reminded his brother of the words of God, "I will be sanctified in them that come nigh Me, and before all the people I will be glorified." Aaron was silent. The death of his sons, cut down without warning, in so terrible a sin—a sin which he now saw to be the result of his own neglect of duty—wrung the father's heart with anguish, but he gave his feelings no expression. By no manifestation of grief must he seem to sympathize with sin. The congregation must not be led to murmur against God.

The Lord would teach His people to acknowledge the justice of His corrections, that others may fear. There were those in Israel whom the warning of this terrible judgment might save from presuming upon God's forbearance until they, too, should seal their own destiny. The divine rebuke is upon that false sympathy for the sinner which endeavors to excuse his sin. It is the effect of sin to deaden the moral perceptions, so that the wrongdoer does not realize the enormity of transgression, and without the convicting power of the Holy Spirit he remains in partial blindness to his sin. It is the duty of Christ's servants to show these erring ones their peril. Those who destroy the effect of the warning by blinding the eyes of sinners to the real character and results of sin often flatter themselves that they thus give evidence of their charity; but they are working directly to oppose and hinder the work of God's Holy Spirit; they are lulling the sinner to rest on the brink of destruction; they are making themselves partakers in his guilt and incurring a fearful responsibility for his impenitence. Many, many, have gone down to ruin as the result of this false and deceptive sympathy.

Nadab and Abihu would never have committed that fatal sin had they not first become partially intoxicated by the free use of wine. They understood that the most careful and solemn preparation was necessary before presenting themselves in the sanctuary, where the divine Presence was manifested; but by intemperance they were disqualified for their holy office. Their minds became confused and their moral perceptions dulled so that they could not discern the difference between the sacred and the common. To Aaron and his surviving sons was given the warning: "Do not drink wine nor strong drink, thou, nor thy sons with thee, when ye go into the tabernacle of the congregation, lest ye die: it shall be a statute forever throughout your generations: and that ye may put difference between holy and unholy, and between unclean and clean; and that ye may teach the children of Israel all the statutes which the Lord hath spoken." The use of spirituous liquors has the effect to weaken the body, confuse the mind, and debase the morals. It prevents men from realizing the sacredness of holy things or the binding force of God's requirements. All who occupied positions of sacred responsibility were to be men of strict temperance, that their minds might be clear to discriminate between right and wrong, that they might possess firmness of principle, and wisdom to administer justice and to show mercy.

The same obligation rests upon every follower of Christ. The apostle Peter declares, "Ye are a chosen generation, a royal priesthood, an holy nation, a peculiar people." 1 Peter 2:9. We are required by God to preserve every power in the best possible condition, that we may render acceptable service to our Creator. When intoxicants are used, the same effects will follow as in the case of those priests of Israel. The conscience will lose its sensibility to sin, and a process of hardening to iniquity will most certainly take place, till the common and the sacred will lose all difference of significance. How can we then meet the standard of the divine requirements?" "Know ye not that your body is the temple of the Holy Ghost which is in you, which ye have of God, and ye are not your own? For ye are bought with a price: therefore glorify God in your body, and in your spirit, which are God's." 1 Corinthians 6:19, 20. "Whether therefore ye eat, or drink, or whatsoever ye do, do all to the glory of God." 1 Corinthians 10:31. To the church of Christ in all ages is addressed the solemn and fearful warning, "If any man defile the temple of God, him shall God destroy; for the temple of God is holy, which temple ye are." 1 Corinthians 3:17.

Chapter 32—The Law and the Covenants

Adam and Eve, at their creation, had a knowledge of the law of God; they were acquainted with its claims upon them; its precepts were written upon their hearts. When man fell by transgression the law was not changed, but a remedial system was established to bring him back to obedience. The promise of a Saviour was given, and sacrificial offerings pointing forward to the death of Christ as the great sin offering were established. But had the law of God never been transgressed, there would have been no death, and no need of a Saviour; consequently there would have been no need of sacrifices.

Adam taught his descendants the law of God, and it was handed down from father to son through successive generations. But notwithstanding the gracious provision for man's redemption, there were few who accepted it and rendered obedience. By transgression the world became so vile that it was necessary to cleanse it by the Flood from its corruption. The law was preserved by Noah and his family, and Noah taught his descendants the Ten Commandments. As men again departed from God, the Lord chose Abraham, of whom He declared, "Abraham obeyed My voice, and kept My charge, My commandments, My statutes, and My laws." Genesis 26:5. To him was given the rite of circumcision, which was a sign that those who received it were devoted to the service of God—a pledge that they would remain separate from idolatry, and would obey the law of God. The failure of Abraham's descendants to keep this pledge, as shown in their disposition to form alliances with the heathen and adopt their practices, was the cause of their sojourn and bondage in Egypt. But in their intercourse with idolaters, and their forced submission to the Egyptians, the divine precepts became still further corrupted with the vile and cruel teachings of heathenism. Therefore when the Lord brought them forth from Egypt, He came down upon Sinai, enshrouded in glory and surrounded by His angels, and in awful majesty spoke His law in the hearing of all the people.

He did not even then trust His precepts to the memory of a people who were prone to forget His requirements, but wrote them upon tables of stone. He would remove from Israel all possibility of mingling heathen traditions with His holy precepts, or of confounding His requirements with human ordinances or customs. But He did not stop with giving them the precepts of the Decalogue. The people had shown themselves so easily led astray that He would leave no door of temptation unguarded. Moses was commanded to write, as God should bid him, judgments and laws giving minute instruction as to what was required. These directions relating to the duty of the people to God, to one another, and to the stranger were only the principles of the Ten Commandments amplified and given in a specific manner, that none need err. They were designed to guard the sacredness of the ten precepts engraved on the tables of stone.

If man had kept the law of God, as given to Adam after his fall, preserved by Noah, and observed by Abraham, there would have been no necessity for the ordinance of circumcision. And if the descendants of Abraham had kept the covenant, of which circumcision was a sign, they would never have been seduced into idolatry, nor would it have been necessary for them to suffer a life of bondage in Egypt; they would have kept God's law in mind, and there would have been no necessity for it to be proclaimed from Sinai or engraved upon the tables of stone. And had the people practiced the principles of the Ten Commandments, there would have been no need of the additional directions given to Moses.

The sacrificial system, committed to Adam, was also perverted by his descendants. Superstition, idolatry, cruelty, and licentiousness corrupted the simple and significant service that God had appointed. Through long intercourse with idolaters the people of Israel had mingled many heathen customs with their worship; therefore the Lord gave them at Sinai definite instruction concerning the sacrificial service. After the completion of the tabernacle He communicated with Moses from the cloud of glory above the mercy seat, and gave him full directions concerning the system of offerings and the forms of worship to be maintained in the sanctuary. The ceremonial law was thus given to Moses, and by him written in a book. But the law of Ten Commandments spoken from Sinai had been written by God

[365]

Himself on the tables of stone, and was sacredly preserved in the ark.

There are many who try to blend these two systems, using the texts that speak of the ceremonial law to prove that the moral law has been abolished; but this is a perversion of the Scriptures. The distinction between the two systems is broad and clear. The ceremonial system was made up of symbols pointing to Christ, to His sacrifice and His priesthood. This ritual law, with its sacrifices and ordinances, was to be performed by the Hebrews until type met antitype in the death of Christ, the Lamb of God that taketh away the sin of the world. Then all the sacrificial offerings were to cease. It is this law that Christ "took ... out of the way, nailing it to His cross." Colossians 2:14. But concerning the law of Ten Commandments the psalmist declares, "Forever, O Lord, Thy word is settled in heaven." Psalm 119:89. And Christ Himself says, "Think not that I am come to destroy the law.... Verily I say unto you"—making the assertion as emphatic as possible—"Till heaven and earth pass, one jot or one tittle shall in no wise pass from the law, till all be fulfilled." Matthew 5:17, 18. Here He teaches, not merely what the claims of God's law had been, and were then, but that these claims should hold as long as the heavens and the earth remain. The law of God is as immutable as His throne. It will maintain its claims upon mankind in all ages.

Concerning the law proclaimed from Sinai, Nehemiah says, "Thou camest down also upon Mount Sinai, and spakest with them from heaven, and gavest them *right judgments, and true laws, good statutes and commandments.*" Nehemiah 9:13. And Paul, "the apostle to the Gentiles," declares, "The law is holy, and the commandment holy, and just, and good." Romans 7:12. This can be no other than the Decalogue; for it is the law that says, "Thou shalt not covet." Verse 7.

While the Saviour's death brought to an end the law of types and shadows, it did not in the least detract from the obligation of the moral law. On the contrary, the very fact that it was necessary for Christ to die in order to atone for the transgression of that law, proves it to be immutable.

Those who claim that Christ came to abrogate the law of God and to do away with the Old Testament, speak of the Jewish age as one of darkness, and represent the religion of the Hebrews as consisting of mere forms and ceremonies. But this is an error. All through the pages of sacred history, where the dealings of God with His chosen people are recorded, there are burning traces of the great I AM. Never has He given to the sons of men more open manifestations of His power and glory than when He alone was acknowledged as Israel's ruler, and gave the law to His people. Here was a scepter swayed by no human hand; and the stately goings forth of Israel's invisible King were unspeakably grand and awful.

In all these revelations of the divine presence the glory of God was manifested through Christ. Not alone at the Saviour's advent, but through all the ages after the Fall and the promise of redemption, "God was in Christ, reconciling the world unto Himself." 2 Corinthians 5:19. Christ was the foundation and center of the sacrificial system in both the patriarchal and the Jewish age. Since the sin of our first parents there has been no direct communication between God and man. The Father has given the world into the hands of Christ, that through His mediatorial work He may redeem man and vindicate the authority and holiness of the law of God. All the communion between heaven and the fallen race has been through Christ. It was the Son of God that gave to our first parents the promise of redemption. It was He who revealed Himself to the patriarchs. Adam, Noah, Abraham, Isaac, Jacob, and Moses understood the gospel. They looked for salvation through man's Substitute and Surety. These holy men of old held communion with the Saviour who was to come to our world in human flesh; and some of them talked with Christ and heavenly angels face to face.

Christ was not only the leader of the Hebrews in the wilderness—the Angel in whom was the name of Jehovah, and who, veiled in the cloudy pillar, went before the host—but it was He who gave the law to Israel. [See Appendix, note 7.] Amid the awful glory of Sinai, Christ declared in the hearing of all the people the ten precepts of His Father's law. It was He who gave to Moses the law engraved upon the tables of stone.

It was Christ that spoke to His people through the prophets. The apostle Peter, writing to the Christian church, says that the prophets "prophesied of the grace that should come unto you: searching what, or what manner of time the *Spirit of Christ* which was in them did signify, when it testified beforehand the sufferings of Christ and the glory that should follow." 1 Peter 1:10, 11. It is the voice of Christ that speaks to us through the Old Testament. "The testimony of Jesus is the spirit of prophecy." Revelation 19:10.

In His teachings while personally among men Jesus directed the minds of the people to the Old Testament. He said to the Jews, "Ye search the Scriptures, because ye think that in them ye have eternal life; and these are they which bear witness of Me." John 5:39, R.V. At this time the books of the Old Testament were the only part of the Bible in existence. Again the Son of God declared, "They have Moses and the prophets; let them hear them." And He added, "If they hear not Moses and the prophets, neither will they be persuaded, though one rose from the dead." Luke 16:29, 31.

The ceremonial law was given by Christ. Even after it was no longer to be observed, Paul presented it before the Jews in its true position and value, showing its place in the plan of redemption and its relation to the work of Christ; and the great apostle pronounces this law glorious, worthy of its divine Originator. The solemn service of the sanctuary typified the grand truths that were to be revealed through successive generations. The cloud of incense ascending with the prayers of Israel represents His righteousness that alone can make the sinner's prayer acceptable to God; the bleeding victim on the altar of sacrifice testified of a Redeemer to come; and from the holy of holies the visible token of the divine Presence shone forth. Thus through age after age of darkness and apostasy faith was kept alive in the hearts of men until the time came for the advent of the promised Messiah.

Jesus was the light of His people—the Light of the world—before He came to earth in the form of humanity. The first gleam of light that pierced the gloom in which sin had wrapped the world, came from Christ. And from Him has come every ray of heaven's brightness that has fallen upon the inhabitants of the earth. In the plan of redemption Christ is the Alpha and the Omega—the First and the Last.

Since the Saviour shed His blood for the remission of sins, and ascended to heaven "to appear in the presence of God for us" (Hebrews 9:24), light has been streaming from the cross of Calvary and from the holy places of the sanctuary above. But the clearer light granted us should not cause us to despise that which in earlier times was received through the types pointing to the coming Saviour. The gospel of Christ sheds light upon the Jewish economy and gives significance to the ceremonial law. As new truths are revealed, and that which has been known from the beginning is brought into clearer light, the character and purposes of God are made manifest in His dealings with His chosen people. Every additional ray of light that we receive gives us a clearer understanding of the plan of redemption, which is the working out of the divine will in the salvation of man. We see new beauty and force in the inspired word, and we study its pages with a deeper and more absorbing interest.

The opinion is held by many that God placed a separating wall between the Hebrews and the outside world; that His care and love, withdrawn to a great extent from the rest of mankind, were centered upon Israel. But God did not design that His people should build up a wall of partition between themselves and their fellow men. The heart of Infinite Love was reaching out toward all the inhabitants of the earth. Though they had rejected Him, He was constantly seeking to reveal Himself to them and make them partakers of His love and grace. His blessing was granted to the chosen people, that they might bless others.

God called Abraham, and prospered and honored him; and the patriarch's fidelity was a light to the people in all the countries of his sojourn. Abraham did not shut himself away from the people around him. He maintained friendly relations with the kings of the surrounding nations, by some of whom he was treated with great respect; and his integrity and unselfishness, his valor and benevolence, were representing the character of God. In Mesopotamia, in Canaan, in Egypt, and even to the inhabitants of Sodom, the God of heaven was revealed through His representative.

So to the people of Egypt and of all the nations connected with that powerful kingdom, God manifested Himself through Joseph. Why did the Lord choose to exalt Joseph so highly among the Egyptians? He might have provided some other way for the accomplishment of His purposes toward the children of Jacob; but He desired to make Joseph a light, and He placed him in the palace of the king, that the heavenly illumination might extend far and near. By his wisdom and justice, by the purity and benevolence of his daily life, by his devotion to the interests of the people—and that people a nation of idolaters—Joseph was a representative of Christ. In their benefactor, to whom all Egypt turned with gratitude and praise, that heathen people were to behold the love of their Creator and Redeemer. So in Moses also God placed a light beside the throne of the earth's greatest kingdom, that all who would, might learn of the true and living God. And all this light was given to the Egyptians before the hand of God was stretched out over them in judgments.

In the deliverance of Israel from Egypt a knowledge of the power of God spread far and wide. The warlike people of the stronghold of Jericho trembled. "As soon as we had heard these things," said Rahab, "our hearts did melt, neither did there remain any more courage in any man, because of you: for Jehovah your God, He is God in heaven above, and in earth beneath." Joshua 2:11. Centuries after the exodus the priests of the Philistines reminded their people of the plagues of Egypt, and warned them against resisting the God of Israel.

God called Israel, and blessed and exalted them, not that by obedience to His law they alone might receive His favor and become the exclusive recipients of His blessings, but in order to reveal Himself through them to all the inhabitants of the earth. It was for the accomplishment of this very purpose that He commanded them to keep themselves distinct from the idolatrous nations around them.

Idolatry and all the sins that followed in its train were abhorrent to God, and He commanded His people not to mingle with other nations, to "*do after their works*", and forget God. He forbade their marriage with idolaters, lest their hearts should be led away from Him. It was just as necessary then as it is now that God's people should be pure, "unspotted from the world." They must keep themselves free from its spirit, because it is opposed to truth and righteousness. But God did not intend that His people, in self-righteous exclusiveness, should shut themselves away from the world, so that they could have no influence upon it.

Like their Master, the followers of Christ in every age were to be the light of the world. The Saviour said, "A city that is set on an hill cannot be hid. Neither do men light a candle, and put it under a bushel, but on a candlestick; and it giveth light unto all that are in the house"—that is, in the world. And He adds, "Let your light so shine before men, that they may see your good works, and glorify your Father which is in heaven." Matthew 5:14-16. This is just what Enoch, and Noah, Abraham, Joseph, and Moses did. It is just what God designed that His people Israel should do.

It was their own evil heart of unbelief, controlled by Satan, that led them to hide their light, instead of shedding it upon surrounding peoples; it was that same bigoted spirit that caused them either to follow the iniquitous practices of the heathen or to shut themselves away in proud exclusiveness, as if God's love and care were over them alone.

As the Bible presents two laws, one changeless and eternal, the other provisional and temporary, so there are two covenants. The covenant of grace was first made with man in Eden, when after the Fall there was given a divine promise that the seed of the woman should bruise the serpent's head. To all men this covenant offered pardon and the assisting grace of God for future obedience through faith in Christ. It also promised them eternal life on condition of fidelity to God's law. Thus the patriarchs received the hope of salvation.

This same covenant was renewed to Abraham in the promise, "In thy seed shall all the nations of the earth be blessed." Genesis 22:18. This promise pointed to Christ. So Abraham understood it (see Galatians 3:8, 16), and he trusted in Christ for the forgiveness of sins. It was this faith that was accounted unto him for righteousness. The covenant with Abraham also maintained the authority of God's law. The Lord appeared unto Abraham, and said, "I am the Almighty God; walk before Me, and be thou perfect." Genesis 17:1. The testimony of God concerning His faithful servant was, "Abraham obeyed My voice, and kept My charge, My commandments, My statutes, and My laws." Genesis 26:5. And the Lord declared to him, "I will establish My covenant between Me and thee and thy seed after thee in their generations, for an *everlasting covenant*, to be a God unto thee and to thy seed after thee." Genesis 17:7.

Though this covenant was made with Adam and renewed to Abraham, it could not be ratified until the death of Christ. It had existed by the promise of God since the first intimation of redemption had been given; it had been accepted by faith; yet when ratified by Christ, it is called a *new* covenant. The law of God was the basis of this covenant, which was simply an arrangement for bringing men again into harmony with the divine will, placing them where they could obey God's law.

Another compact—called in Scripture the "old" covenant—was formed between God and Israel at Sinai, and was then ratified by the blood of a sacrifice. The Abrahamic covenant was ratified by the blood of Christ, and it is called the "second," or "new," covenant, because the blood by which it was sealed was shed after the blood of the first covenant. That the new covenant was valid in the days of Abraham is evident from the fact that it was then confirmed both by the promise and by the oath of God—the "two immutable things, in which it was impossible for God to lie." Hebrews 6:18.

But if the Abrahamic covenant contained the promise of redemption, why was another covenant formed at Sinai? In their bondage the people had to a great extent lost the knowledge of God and of the principles of the Abrahamic covenant. In delivering them from Egypt, God sought to reveal to them His power and His mercy, that they might be led to love and trust Him. He brought them down to the Red Sea—where, pursued by the Egyptians, escape seemed impossible—that they might realize their utter helplessness, their need of divine aid; and then He wrought deliverance for them. Thus they were filled with love and gratitude to God and with confidence in His power to help them. He had bound them to Himself as their deliverer from temporal bondage.

But there was a still greater truth to be impressed upon their minds. Living in the midst of idolatry and corruption, they had no true conception of the holiness of God, of the exceeding sinfulness of their own hearts, their utter inability, in themselves, to render obedience to God's law, and their need of a Saviour. All this they must be taught.

God brought them to Sinai; He manifested His glory; He gave them His law, with the promise of great blessings on condition of obedience: "If ye will obey My voice indeed, and keep My covenant, then ... ye shall be unto Me a kingdom of priests, and an holy nation." Exodus 19:5, 6. The people did not realize the sinfulness of their own hearts, and that without Christ it was impossible for them to keep God's law; and they readily entered into covenant with God. Feeling that they were able to establish their own righteousness, they declared, "All that the Lord hath said will we do, and be obedient."

Exodus 24:7. They had witnessed the proclamation of the law in awful majesty, and had trembled with terror before the mount; and yet only a few weeks passed before they broke their covenant with God, and bowed down to worship a graven image. They could not hope for the favor of God through a covenant which they had broken; and now, seeing their sinfulness and their need of pardon, they were brought to feel their need of the Saviour revealed in the Abrahamic covenant and shadowed forth in the sacrificial offerings. Now by faith and love they were bound to God as their deliverer from the bondage of sin. Now they were prepared to appreciate the blessings of the new covenant.

The terms of the "old covenant" were, Obey and live: "If a man do, he shall even live in them" (Ezekiel 20:11; Leviticus 18:5); but "cursed be he that confirmeth not all the words of this law to do them." Deuteronomy 27:26. The "new covenant" was established upon "better promises"—the promise of forgiveness of sins and of the grace of God to renew the heart and bring it into harmony with the principles of God's law. "This shall be the covenant that I will make with the house of Israel; After those days, saith the Lord, *I will put my law* in their inward parts, *and write it in their hearts....* I will *forgive* their iniquity, and will remember their sin no more." Jeremiah 31:33, 34.

The same law that was engraved upon the tables of stone is written by the Holy Spirit upon the tables of the heart. Instead of going about to establish our own righteousness we accept the righteousness of Christ. His blood atones for our sins. His obedience is accepted for us. Then the heart renewed by the Holy Spirit will bring forth "the fruits of the Spirit." Through the grace of Christ we shall live in obedience to the law of God written upon our hearts. Having the Spirit of Christ, we shall walk even as He walked. Through the prophet He declared of Himself, "I delight to do Thy will, O My God: yea, Thy law is within My heart." Psalm 40:8. And when among men He said, "The Father hath not left Me alone; for I do always those things that please Him." John 8:29.

The apostle Paul clearly presents the relation between faith and the law under the new covenant. He says: "Being *justified by faith*, we have peace with God through our Lord Jesus Christ." "Do we then make void the law through faith? God forbid: yea, we establish the law." "For what the law could not do, in that it was weak through the flesh"—it could not justify man, because in his sinful nature he could not keep the law—"God sending His own Son in the likeness of sinful flesh, and for sin, condemned sin in the flesh: that *the righteousness of the law* might be fulfilled in us, who walk not after the flesh, but after the Spirit." Romans 5:1; 3:31; 8:3, 4.

God's work is the same in all time, although there are different degrees of development and different manifestations of His power, to meet the wants of men in the different ages. Beginning with the first gospel promise, and coming down through the patriarchal and Jewish ages, and even to the present time, there has been a gradual unfolding of the purposes of God in the plan of redemption. The Saviour typified in the rites and ceremonies of the Jewish law is the very same that is revealed in the gospel. The clouds that enveloped His divine form have rolled back; the mists and shades have disappeared; and Jesus, the world's Redeemer, stands revealed. He who proclaimed the law from Sinai, and delivered to Moses the precepts of the ritual law, is the same that spoke the Sermon on the Mount. The great principles of love to God, which He set forth as the foundation of the law and the prophets, are only a reiteration of what He had spoken through Moses to the Hebrew people: "Hear, O Israel: The Lord our God is one Lord: and thou shalt love the Lord thy God with all thine heart, and with all thy soul, and with all thy might." Deuteronomy 6:4, 5. "Thou shalt love thy neighbor as thyself." Leviticus 19:18. The teacher is the same in both dispensations. God's claims are the same. The principles of His government are the same. For all proceed from Him "with whom is no variableness, neither shadow of turning." James 1:17.

Chapter 33—From Sinai to Kadesh [374]

This chapter is based on Numbers 11 and 12.

The building of the tabernacle was not begun for some time after Israel arrived at Sinai; and the sacred structure was first set up at the opening of the second year from the Exodus. This was followed by the consecration of the priests, the celebration of the Passover, the numbering of the people, and the completion of various arrangements essential to their civil or religious system, so that nearly a year was spent in the encampment at Sinai. Here their worship had taken a more definite form, the laws had been given for the government of the nation, and a more efficient organization had been effected preparatory to their entrance into the land of Canaan.

The government of Israel was characterized by the most thorough organization, wonderful alike for its completeness and its simplicity. The order so strikingly displayed in the perfection and arrangement of all God's created works was manifest in the Hebrew economy. God was the center of authority and government, the sovereign of Israel. Moses stood as their visible leader, by God's appointment, to administer the laws in His name. From the elders of the tribes a council of seventy was afterward chosen to assist Moses in the general affairs of the nation. Next came the priests, who consulted the Lord in the sanctuary. Chiefs, or princes, ruled over the tribes. Under these were "captains over thousands, and captains over hundreds, and captains over fifties, and captains over tens," and, lastly, officers who might be employed for special duties. Deuteronomy 1:15.

The Hebrew camp was arranged in exact order. It was separated into three great divisions, each having its appointed position in the encampment. In the center was the tabernacle, the abiding place of the invisible King. Around it were stationed the priests and Levites. [375] Beyond these were encamped all the other tribes.

To the Levites was committed the charge of the tabernacle and all that pertained thereto, both in the camp and on the journey. When the camp set forward they were to strike the sacred tent; when a halting place was reached they were to set it up. No person of another tribe was allowed to come near, on pain of death. The Levites were separated into three divisions, the descendants of the three sons of Levi, and each was assigned its special position and work. In front of the tabernacle, and nearest to it, were the tents of Moses and Aaron. On the south were the Kohathites, whose duty it was to care for the ark and the other furniture; on the north Merarites, who were placed in charge of the pillars, sockets, boards, etc.; in the rear the Gershonites, to whom the care of the curtains and hangings was committed.

The position of each tribe also was specified. Each was to march and to encamp beside its own standard, as the Lord had commanded: "Every man of the children of Israel shall pitch by his own standard, with the ensign of their father's house: far off about the tabernacle of the congregation shall they pitch." "As they encamp, so shall they set forward, every man in his place by their standards." Numbers 2:2, 17. The mixed multitude that had accompanied Israel from Egypt were not permitted to occupy the same quarters with the tribes, but were to abide upon the outskirts of the camp; and their offspring were to be excluded from the community until the third generation. Deuteronomy 23:7, 8.

Scrupulous cleanliness as well as strict order throughout the encampment and its environs was enjoined. Thorough sanitary regulations were enforced. Every person who was unclean from any cause was forbidden to enter the camp. These measures were indispensable to the preservation of health among so vast a multitude; and it was necessary also that perfect order and purity be maintained, that Israel might enjoy the presence of a holy God. Thus He declared: "The Lord thy God walketh in the midst of thy camp, to deliver thee, and to give up thine enemies before thee; therefore shall thy camp be holy."

In all the journeyings of Israel, "the ark of the covenant of the Lord went before them, ... to search out a resting place for them." Numbers 10:33. Borne by the sons of Kohath, the sacred chest containing God's holy law was to lead the van. Before it went Moses and Aaron; and the priests, bearing silver trumpets, were stationed near. These priests received directions from Moses, which they communicated to the people by the trumpets. It was the duty of the leaders of each company to give definite directions concerning all the movements to be made, as indicated by the trumpets. Whoever neglected to comply with the directions given was punished with death.

God is a God of order. Everything connected with heaven is in perfect order; subjection and thorough discipline mark the movements of the angelic host. Success can only attend order and harmonious action. God requires order and system in His work now no less than in the days of Israel. All who are working for Him are to labor intelligently, not in a careless, haphazard manner. He would have his work done with faith and exactness, that He may place the seal of His approval upon it.

God Himself directed the Israelites in all their travels. The place of their encampment was indicated by the descent of the pillar of cloud; and so long as they were to remain in camp, the cloud rested over the tabernacle. When they were to continue their journey it was lifted high above the sacred tent. A solemn invocation marked both the halt and the departure. "It came to pass, when the ark set forward, that Moses said, Rise up, Lord, and let Thine enemies be scattered; and let them that hate Thee flee before Thee. And when it rested, he said, Return, O Lord, unto the many thousands of Israel." Numbers 10:35, 36.

A distance of only eleven days' journey lay between Sinai and Kadesh, on the borders of Canaan; and it was with the prospect of speedily entering the goodly land that the hosts of Israel resumed their march when the cloud at last gave the signal for an onward movement. Jehovah had wrought wonders in bringing them from Egypt, and what blessings might they not expect now that they had formally covenanted to accept Him as their Sovereign, and had been acknowledged as the chosen people of the Most High?

Yet it was almost with reluctance that many left the place where they had so long encamped. They had come to regard it as their home. Within the shelter of those granite walls God had gathered His people, apart from all other nations, to repeat to them His holy law. They loved to look upon the sacred mount, on whose hoary peaks and barren ridges the divine glory had so often been displayed. The scene was so closely associated with the presence of God and holy angels that it seemed too sacred to be left thoughtlessly, or even gladly.

At the signal from the trumpeters, however, the entire camp set forward, the tabernacle borne in the midst, and each tribe in its appointed position, under its own standard. All eyes were turned anxiously to see in what direction the cloud would lead. As it moved toward the east, where were only mountain masses huddled together, black and desolate, a feeling of sadness and doubt arose in many hearts.

As they advanced, the way became more difficult. Their route lay through stony ravine and barren waste. All around them was the great wilderness—"a land of deserts and of pits," "a land of drought, and of the shadow of death," "a land that no man passed through, and where no man dwelt." Jeremiah 2:6. The rocky gorges, far and near, were thronged with men, women, and children, with beasts and wagons, and long lines of flocks and herds. Their progress was necessarily slow and toilsome; and the multitudes, after their long encampment, were not prepared to endure the perils and discomforts of the way.

After three days' journey open complaints were heard. These originated with the mixed multitude, many of whom were not fully united with Israel, and were continually watching for some cause of censure. The complainers were not pleased with the direction of the march, and they were continually finding fault with the way in which *Moses* was leading them, though they well knew that he, as well as they, was following the guiding cloud. Dissatisfaction is contagious, and it soon spread in the encampment.

Again they began to clamor for flesh to eat. Though abundantly supplied with manna, they were not satisfied. The Israelites, during their bondage in Egypt, had been compelled to subsist on the plainest and simplest food; but then keen appetite induced by privation and hard labor had made it palatable. Many of the Egyptians, however, who were now among them, had been accustomed to a luxurious diet; and these were the first to complain. At the giving of the manna, just before Israel reached Sinai, the Lord had granted them flesh in answer to their clamors; but it was furnished them for only one day.

God might as easily have provided them with flesh as with manna, but a restriction was placed upon them for their good. It was His purpose to supply them with food better suited to their wants than the feverish diet to which many had become accustomed in Egypt. The perverted appetite was to be brought into a more healthy state, that they might enjoy the food originally provided for man—the fruits of the earth, which God gave to Adam and Eve in Eden. It was for this reason that the Israelites had been deprived, in a great measure, of animal food.

Satan tempted them to regard this restriction as unjust and cruel. He caused them to lust after forbidden things, because he saw that the unrestrained indulgence of appetite would tend to produce sensuality, and by this means the people could be more easily brought under his control. The author of disease and misery will assail men where he can have the greatest success. Through temptations addressed to the appetite he has, to a large extent, led men into sin from the time when he induced Eve to eat of the forbidden fruit. It was by this same means that he led Israel to murmur against God. Intemperance in eating and drinking, leading as it does to the indulgence of the lower passions, prepares the way for men to disregard all moral obligations. When assailed by temptation, they have little power of resistance.

God brought the Israelites from Egypt, that He might establish them in the land of Canaan, a pure, holy, and happy people. In the accomplishment of this object He subjected them to a course of discipline, both for their own good and for the good of their posterity. Had they been willing to deny appetite, in obedience to His wise restrictions, feebleness and disease would have been unknown among them. Their descendants would have possessed both physical and mental strength. They would have had clear perceptions of truth and duty, keen discrimination, and sound judgment. But their unwillingness to submit to the restrictions and requirements of God, prevented them, to a great extent, from reaching the high standard which He desired them to attain, and from receiving the blessings which He was ready to bestow upon them.

Says the psalmist: "They tempted God in their heart by asking meat for their lust. Yea, they spake against God; they said, Can God furnish a table in the wilderness? Behold, He smote the rock, that the waters gushed out, and the streams overflowed; can He give bread also? can He provide flesh for His people? Therefore the Lord heard this, and was wroth." Psalm 78:18-21. Murmuring and tumults had been frequent during the journey from the Red Sea to Sinai, but in pity for their ignorance and blindness God had not then visited the sin with judgments. But since that time He had revealed Himself to them at Horeb. They had received great light, as they had been witnesses to the majesty, the power, and the mercy of God; and their unbelief and discontent incurred the greater guilt. Furthermore, they had covenanted to accept Jehovah as their king and to obey His authority. Their murmuring was now rebellion, and as such it must receive prompt and signal punishment, if Israel was to be preserved from anarchy and ruin. "The fire of Jehovah burnt among them, and consumed them that were in the uttermost parts of the camp." The most guilty of the complainers were slain by lightning from the cloud.

The people in terror besought Moses to entreat the Lord for them. He did so, and the fire was quenched. In memory of this judgment he called the name of the place Taberah, "a burning."

But the evil was soon worse than before. Instead of leading the survivors to humiliation and repentance, this fearful judgment seemed only to increase their murmurings. In all directions the people were gathered at the door of their tents, weeping and lamenting. "The mixed multitude that was among them fell a lusting: and the children of Israel also wept again, and said, Who shall give us flesh to eat? We remember the fish, which we did eat in Egypt freely; the cucumbers, and the melons, and the leeks, and the onions, and the garlic: but now our soul is dried away: there is nothing at all, beside this manna, before our eyes." Thus they manifested their discontent with the food provided for them by their Creator. Yet they had constant evidence that it was adapted to their wants; for notwithstanding the hardships they endured, there was not a feeble one in all their tribes.

The heart of Moses sank. He had pleaded that Israel should not be destroyed, even though his own posterity might then become a great nation. In his love for them he had prayed that his name might be blotted from the book of life rather than that they should be left to perish. He had imperiled all for them, and this was their response. All their hardships, even their imaginary sufferings, they charged upon him; and their wicked murmurings made doubly heavy the burden of care and responsibility under which he staggered. In his distress he was tempted even to distrust God. His prayer was almost a complaint. "Wherefore hast Thou afflicted Thy servant? and wherefore have I not found favor in Thy sight, that Thou layest the burden of all this people upon me? ... whence should I have flesh to give unto all this people? for they weep unto me, saying, Give us flesh, that we may eat. I am not able to bear all this people alone, because it is too heavy for me."

The Lord hearkened to his prayer, and directed him to summon seventy men of the elders of Israel—men not only advanced in years, but possessing dignity, sound judgment, and experience. "And bring them unto the tabernacle of the congregation," He said, "that they may stand there with thee. And I will come down and talk with thee there: and I will take of the spirit which is upon thee, and will put it upon them; and they shall bear the burden of the people with thee, that thou bear it not thyself alone."

The Lord permitted Moses to choose for himself the most faithful and efficient men to share the responsibility with him. Their influence would assist in holding in check the violence of the people, and quelling insurrection; yet serious evils would eventually result from their promotion. They would never have been chosen had Moses manifested faith corresponding to the evidences he had witnessed of God's power and goodness. But he had magnified his own burdens and services, almost losing sight of the fact that he was only the instrument by which God had wrought. He was not excusable in indulging, in the slightest degree, the spirit of murmuring that was the curse of Israel. Had he relied fully upon God, the Lord would have guided him continually and would have given him strength for every emergency.

Moses was directed to prepare the people for what God was about to do for them. "Sanctify yourselves against tomorrow, and ye shall eat flesh: for ye have wept in the ears of the Lord, saying, Who shall give us flesh to eat? for it was well with us in Egypt: therefore the Lord will give you flesh, and ye shall eat. Ye shall not eat one day, nor two days, nor five days, neither ten days, nor twenty days; but even a whole month, until it come out at your nostrils, and it be

[381]

loathsome unto you: because that ye have despised the Lord which is among you, and have wept before Him, saying, Why came we forth out of Egypt?"

"The people, among whom I am," exclaimed Moses, "are six hundred thousand footmen; and Thou has said, I will give them flesh, that they may eat a whole month. Shall the flocks and the herds be slain for them, to suffice them? or shall all the fish of the sea be gathered together for them?"

He was reproved for his distrust: "Is the Lord's hand waxed short? thou shalt see now whether My word shall come to pass unto thee or not."

Moses repeated to the congregation the words of the Lord, and announced the appointment of the seventy elders. The great leader's charge to these chosen men might well serve as a model of judicial integrity for the judges and legislators of modern times: "Hear the causes between your brethren, and judge righteously between every man and his brother, and the stranger that is with him. Ye shall not respect persons in judgment; but ye shall hear the small as well as the great; ye shall not be afraid of the face of man; for the judgment is God's." Deuteronomy 1:16, 17.

Moses now summoned the seventy to the tabernacle. "And the Lord came down in a cloud, and spake unto him, and took of the spirit that was upon him, and gave it unto the seventy elders: and it came to pass, that, when the spirit rested upon them, they prophesied, and did not cease." Like the disciples on the Day of Pentecost, they were endued with "power from on high." It pleased the Lord thus to prepare them for their work, and to honor them in the presence of the congregation, that confidence might be established in them as men divinely chosen to unite with Moses in the government of Israel.

Again evidence was given of the lofty, unselfish spirit of the great leader. Two of the seventy, humbly counting themselves unworthy of so responsible a position, had not joined their brethren at the tabernacle; but the Spirit of God came upon them where they were, and they, too, exercised the prophetic gift. On being informed of this, Joshua desired to check such irregularity, fearing that it might tend to division. Jealous for the honor of his master, "My lord Moses," he said, "forbid them." The answer was, "Enviest thou for my sake?

would God that all the Lord's people were prophets, and that the Lord would put His Spirit upon them."

A strong wind blowing from the sea now brought flocks of quails, "about a day's journey on this side, and a day's journey on the other side, round about the camp, and about two cubits above the face of the earth." Numbers 11:31, R.V. All that day and night, and the following day, the people labored in gathering the food miraculously provided. Immense quantities were secured. "He that gathered least gathered ten homers." All that was not needed for present use was preserved by drying, so that the supply, as promised, was sufficient for a whole month.

God gave the people that which was not for their highest good, because they persisted in desiring it; they would not be satisfied with those things that would prove a benefit to them. Their rebellious desires were gratified, but they were left to suffer the result. They feasted without restraint, and their excesses were speedily punished. "The Lord smote the people with a very great plague." Large numbers were cut down by burning fevers, while the most guilty among them were smitten as soon as they tasted the food for which they had lusted.

At Hazeroth, the next encampment after leaving Taberah, a still more bitter trial awaited Moses. Aaron and Miriam had occupied a position of high honor and leadership in Israel. Both were endowed with the prophetic gift, and both had been divinely associated with Moses in the deliverance of the Hebrews. "I sent before thee Moses, Aaron, and Miriam" (Micah 6:4), are the words of the Lord by the prophet Micah. Miriam's force of character had been early displayed when as a child she watched beside the Nile the little basket in which was hidden the infant Moses. Her self-control and tact God had made instrumental in preserving the deliverer of His people. Richly endowed with the gifts of poetry and music, Miriam had led the women of Israel in song and dance on the shore of the Red Sea. In the affections of the people and the honor of Heaven she stood second only to Moses and Aaron. But the same evil that first brought discord in heaven sprang up in the heart of this woman of Israel, and she did not fail to find a sympathizer in her dissatisfaction.

In the appointment of the seventy elders Miriam and Aaron had not been consulted, and their jealousy was excited against Moses.

At the time of Jethro's visit, while the Israelites were on the way to Sinai, the ready acceptance by Moses of the counsel of his father-in-law had aroused in Aaron and Miriam a fear that his influence with the great leader exceeded theirs. In the organization of the council of elders they felt that their position and authority had been ignored. Miriam and Aaron had never known the weight of care and responsibility which had rested upon Moses; yet because they had been chosen to aid him they regarded themselves as sharing equally with him the burden of leadership, and they regarded the appointment of further assistants as uncalled for.

Moses felt the importance of the great work committed to him as no other man had ever felt it. He realized his own weakness, and he made God his counselor. Aaron esteemed himself more highly, and trusted less in God. He had failed when entrusted with responsibility, giving evidence of the weakness of his character by his base compliance in the matter of the idolatrous worship at Sinai. But Miriam and Aaron, blinded by jealousy and ambition, lost sight of this. Aaron had been highly honored by God in the appointment of his family to the sacred office of the priesthood; yet even this now added to the desire for self-exaltation. "And they said, Hath the Lord indeed spoken only by Moses? hath He not spoken also by us?" Regarding themselves as equally favored by God, they felt that they were entitled to the same position and authority.

Yielding to the spirit of dissatisfaction, Miriam found cause of complaint in events that God had especially overruled. The marriage of Moses had been displeasing to her. That he should choose a woman of another nation, instead of taking a wife from among the Hebrews, was an offense to her family and national pride. Zipporah was treated with ill-disguised contempt.

Though called a "Cushite woman" (Numbers 12:1, R.V.), the wife of Moses was a Midianite, and thus a descendant of Abraham. In personal appearance she differed from the Hebrews in being of a somewhat darker complexion. Though not an Israelite, Zipporah was a worshiper of the true God. She was of a timid, retiring disposition, gentle and affectionate, and greatly distressed at the sight of suffering; and it was for this reason that Moses, when on the way to Egypt, had consented to her return to Midian. He desired to spare her the pain of witnessing the judgments that were to fall on the Egyptians.

When Zipporah rejoined her husband in the wilderness, she saw that his burdens were wearing away his strength, and she made known her fears to Jethro, who suggested measures for his relief. Here was the chief reason for Miriam's antipathy to Zipporah. Smarting under the supposed neglect shown to herself and Aaron, she regarded the wife of Moses as the cause, concluding that her influence had prevented him from taking them into his counsels as formerly. Had Aaron stood up firmly for the right, he might have checked the evil; but instead of showing Miriam the sinfulness of her conduct, he sympathized with her, listened to her words of complaint, and thus came to share her jealousy.

Their accusations were borne by Moses in uncomplaining silence. It was the experience gained during the years of toil and waiting in Midian—the spirit of humility and long-suffering there developed—that prepared Moses to meet with patience the unbelief and murmuring of the people and the pride and envy of those who should have been his unswerving helpers. Moses "was very meek, above all the men which were upon the face of the earth," and this is why he was granted divine wisdom and guidance above all others. Says the Scripture, "The meek will He guide in judgment: and the meek will He teach His way." Psalm 25:9. The meek are guided by the Lord, because they are teachable, willing to be instructed. They have a sincere desire to know and to do the will of God. The Saviour's promise is, "If any man will do His will, he shall know of the doctrine." John 7:17. And He declares by the apostle James, "If any of you lack wisdom, let him ask of God, that giveth to all men liberally, and upbraideth not; and it shall be given him." James 1:5. But His promise is only to those who are willing to follow the Lord wholly. God does not force the will of any; hence He cannot lead those who are too proud to be taught, who are bent upon having their own way. Of the double-minded man—he who seeks to follow his own will, while professing to do the will of God—it is written, "Let not that man think that he shall receive anything of the Lord." James 1:7.

God had chosen Moses, and had put His Spirit upon him; and Miriam and Aaron, by their murmurings, were guilty of disloyalty, not only to their appointed leader, but to God Himself. The seditious whisperers were summoned to the tabernacle, and brought face to face with Moses. "And Jehovah came down in the pillar of the cloud, and stood in the door of the tabernacle, and called Aaron and Miriam." Their claim to the prophetic gift was not denied; God might have spoken to them in visions and dreams. But to Moses, whom the Lord Himself declared "faithful in all Mine house," a nearer communion had been granted. With *him* God spake mouth to mouth. "Wherefore then were ye not afraid to speak against My servant Moses? And the anger of the Lord was kindled against them; and He departed." The cloud disappeared from the tabernacle in token of God's displeasure, and Miriam was smitten. She "became leprous, white as snow." Aaron was spared, but he was severely rebuked in Miriam's punishment. Now, their pride humbled in the dust, Aaron confessed their sin, and entreated that his sister might not be left to perish by that loathsome and deadly scourge. In answer to the prayers of Moses the leprosy was cleansed. Miriam was, however, shut out of the camp for seven days. Not until she was banished from the encampment did the symbol of God's favor again rest upon the tabernacle. In respect for her high position, and in grief at the blow that had fallen upon her, the whole company abode in Hazeroth, awaiting her return.

This manifestation of the Lord's displeasure was designed to be a warning to all Israel, to check the growing spirit of discontent and insubordination. If Miriam's envy and dissatisfaction had not been signally rebuked, it would have resulted in great evil. Envy is one of the most satanic traits that can exist in the human heart, and it is one of the most baleful in its effects. Says the wise man, "Wrath is cruel, and anger is outrageous; but who is able to stand before envy?" Proverbs 27:4. It was envy that first caused discord in heaven, and its indulgence has wrought untold evil among men. "Where envying and strife is, there is confusion and every evil work." James 3:16.

It should not be regarded as a light thing to speak evil of others or to make ourselves judges of their motives or actions. "He that speaketh evil of his brother, and judgeth his brother, speaketh evil of the law, and judgeth the law: but if thou judge the law, thou art not a doer of the law, but a judge." James 4:11. There is but one judge— He "who both will bring to light the hidden things of darkness, and will make manifest the counsels of the hearts." 1 Corinthians 4:5. And whoever takes it upon himself to judge and condemn his fellow men is usurping the prerogative of the Creator.

The Bible specially teaches us to beware of lightly bringing accusation against those whom God has called to act as His ambassadors. The apostle Peter, describing a class who are abandoned sinners, says, "Presumptuous are they, self-willed, they are not afraid to speak evil of dignities. Whereas angels, which are greater in power and might, bring not railing accusation against them before the Lord." 2 Peter 2:10, 11. And Paul, in his instruction for those who are placed over the church, says, "Against an elder receive not an accusation, but before two or three witnesses." 1 Timothy 5:19. He who has placed upon men the heavy responsibility of leaders and teachers of His people will hold the people accountable for the manner in which they treat His servants. We are to honor those whom God has honored. The judgment visited upon Miriam should be a rebuke to all who yield to jealousy, and murmur against those upon whom God lays the burden of His work.

Chapter 34—The Twelve Spies

This chapter is based on Numbers 13 and 14.

Eleven days after leaving Mount Horeb the Hebrew host encamped at Kadesh, in the wilderness of Paran, which was not far from the borders of the Promised Land. Here it was proposed by the people that spies be sent up to survey the country. The matter was presented before the Lord by Moses, and permission was granted, with the direction that one of the rulers of each tribe should be selected for this purpose. The men were chosen as had been directed, and Moses bade them go and see the country, what it was, its situation and natural advantages; and the people that dwelt therein, whether they were strong or weak, few or many; also to observe the nature of the soil and its productiveness and to bring of the fruit of the land.

They went, and surveyed the whole land, entering at the southern border and proceeding to the northern extremity. They returned after an absence of forty days. The people of Israel were cherishing high hopes and were waiting in eager expectancy. The news of the spies' return was carried from tribe to tribe and was hailed with rejoicing. The people rushed out to meet the messengers, who had safely escaped the dangers of their perilous undertaking. The spies brought specimens of the fruit, showing the fertility of the soil. It was in the time of ripe grapes, and they brought a cluster of grapes so large that it was carried between two men. They also brought of the figs and pomegranates which grew there in abundance.

The people rejoiced that they were to come into possession of so goodly a land, and they listened intently as the report was brought to Moses, that not a word should escape them. "We came unto the land whither thou sentest us," the spies began, "and surely it floweth with milk and honey; and this is the fruit of it." The people were enthusiastic; they would eagerly obey the voice of the Lord, and go up at once to possess the land. But after describing the beauty and fertility of the land, all but two of the spies enlarged upon the difficulties and dangers that lay before the Israelites should they undertake the conquest of Canaan. They enumerated the powerful nations located in various parts of the country, and said that the cities were walled and very great, and the people who dwelt therein were strong, and it would be impossible to conquer them. They also stated that they had seen giants, the sons of Anak, there, and it was useless to think of possessing the land.

Now the scene changed. Hope and courage gave place to cowardly despair, as the spies uttered the sentiments of their unbelieving hearts, which were filled with discouragement prompted by Satan. Their unbelief cast a gloomy shadow over the congregation, and the mighty power of God, so often manifested in behalf of the chosen nation, was forgotten. The people did not wait to reflect; they did not reason that He who had brought them thus far would certainly give them the land; they did not call to mind how wonderfully God had delivered them from their oppressors, cutting a path through the sea and destroying the pursuing hosts of Pharaoh. They left God out of the question, and acted as though they must depend solely on the power of arms.

In their unbelief they limited the power of God and distrusted the hand that had hitherto safely guided them. And they repeated their former error of murmuring against Moses and Aaron. "This, then, is the end of our high hopes," they said. "This is the land we have traveled all the way from Egypt to possess." They accused their leaders of deceiving the people and bringing trouble upon Israel.

The people were desperate in their disappointment and despair. A wail of agony arose and mingled with the confused murmur of voices. Caleb comprehended the situation, and, bold to stand in defense of the word of God, he did all in his power to counteract the evil influence of his unfaithful associates. For an instant the people were stilled to listen to his words of hope and courage respecting the goodly land. He did not contradict what had already been said; the walls were high and the Canaanites strong. But God had promised the land to Israel. "Let us go up at once and possess it," urged Caleb; "for we are well able to overcome it."

But the ten, interrupting him, pictured the obstacles in darker colors than at first. "We be not able to go up against the people," they declared; "for they are stronger than we.... All the people that we saw in it are men of a great stature. And there we saw the giants, the sons of Anak, which come of the giants: and we were in our own sight as grasshoppers, and so we were in their sight."

These men, having entered upon a wrong course, stubbornly set themselves against Caleb and Joshua, against Moses, and against God. Every advance step rendered them the more determined. They were resolved to discourage all effort to gain possession of Canaan. They distorted the truth in order to sustain their baleful influence. It "is a land that eateth up the inhabitants thereof," they said. This was not only an evil report, but it was also a lying one. It was inconsistent with itself. The spies had declared the country to be fruitful and prosperous, and the people of giant stature, all of which would be impossible if the climate were so unhealthful that the land could be said to "eat up the inhabitants." But when men yield their hearts to unbelief they place themselves under the control of Satan, and none can tell to what lengths he will lead them.

"And all the congregation lifted up their voice, and cried; and the people wept that night." Revolt and open mutiny quickly followed; for Satan had full sway, and the people seemed bereft of reason. They cursed Moses and Aaron, forgetting that God hearkened to their wicked speeches, and that, enshrouded in the cloudy pillar, the Angel of His presence was witnessing their terrible outburst of wrath. In bitterness they cried out, "Would God that we had died in the land of Egypt! or would God we had died in this wilderness!" Then their feelings rose against God: "Wherefore hath the Lord brought us unto this land, to fall by the sword, that our wives and our children should be a prey? were it not better for us to return into Egypt? And they said one to another, Let us make a captain, and let us return into Egypt." Thus they accused not only Moses, but God Himself, of deception, in promising them a land which they were not able to possess. And they went so far as to appoint a captain to lead them back to the land of their suffering and bondage, from which they had been delivered by the strong arm of Omnipotence.

In humiliation and distress "Moses and Aaron fell on their faces before all the assembly of the congregation of the children of Israel," not knowing what to do to turn them from their rash and passionate purpose. Caleb and Joshua attempted to quiet the tumult. With their garments rent in token of grief and indignation, they rushed in among the people, and their ringing voices were heard above the tempest of lamentation and rebellious grief: "The land, which we passed through to search it, is an exceeding good land. If the Lord delight in us, then He will bring us into this land, and give it us; a land which floweth with milk and honey. Only rebel not ye against the Lord, neither fear ye the people of the land; for they are bread for us: their defense is departed from them, and the Lord is with us: fear them not."

The Canaanites had filled up the measure of their iniquity, and the Lord would no longer bear with them. His protection being removed, they would be an easy prey. By the covenant of God the land was ensured to Israel. But the false report of the unfaithful spies was accepted, and through it the whole congregation were deluded. The traitors had done their work. If only the two men had brought the evil report, and all the ten had encouraged them to possess the land in the name of the Lord, they would still have taken the advice of the two in preference to the ten, because of their wicked unbelief. But there were only two advocating the right, while ten were on the side of rebellion.

The unfaithful spies were loud in denunciation of Caleb and Joshua, and the cry was raised to stone them. The insane mob seized missiles with which to slay those faithful men. They rushed forward with yells of madness, when suddenly the stones dropped from their hands, a hush fell upon them, and they shook with fear. God had interposed to check their murderous design. The glory of His presence, like a flaming light, illuminated the tabernacle. All the people beheld the signal of the Lord. A mightier one than they had revealed Himself, and none dared continue their resistance. The spies who brought the evil report crouched terror-stricken, and with bated breath sought their tents.

Moses now arose and entered the tabernacle. The Lord declared to him, "I will smite them with the pestilence, and disinherit them, and will make of thee a greater nation." But again Moses pleaded for his people. He could not consent to have them destroyed, and he himself made a mightier nation. Appealing to the mercy of God, he said: "I beseech Thee, let the power of my Lord be great according as Thou hast spoken, saying, The Lord is long-suffering, and of great mercy.... Pardon, I beseech Thee, the iniquity of this people according to the greatness of Thy mercy, and as Thou hast forgiven this people, from Egypt even until now."

The Lord promised to spare Israel from immediate destruction; but because of their unbelief and cowardice He could not manifest His power to subdue their enemies. Therefore in His mercy He bade them, as the only safe course, to turn back toward the Red Sea.

In their rebellion the people had exclaimed, "Would God we had died in this wilderness!" Now this prayer was to be granted. The Lord declared: "As ye have spoken in Mine ears, so will I do to you: your carcasses shall fall in this wilderness, and all that were numbered of you, according to your whole number, from twenty years old and upward.... But your little ones, which ye said should be a prey, them will I bring in, and they shall know the land which ye have despised." And of Caleb He said, "My servant Caleb, because he had another spirit with him, and hath followed Me fully, him will I bring into the land whereinto he went; and his seed shall possess it." As the spies had spent forty days in their journey, so the hosts of Israel were to wander in the wilderness forty years.

When Moses made known to the people the divine decision, their rage was changed to mourning. They knew that their punishment was just. The ten unfaithful spies, divinely smitten by the plague, perished before the eyes of all Israel; and in their fate the people read their own doom.

Now they seemed sincerely to repent of their sinful conduct; but they sorrowed because of the result of their evil course rather than from a sense of their ingratitude and disobedience. When they found that the Lord did not relent in His decree, their self-will again arose, and they declared that they would not return into the wilderness. In commanding them to retire from the land of their enemies, God tested their apparent submission and proved that it was not real. They knew that they had deeply sinned in allowing their rash feelings to control them and in seeking to slay the spies who had urged them to obey God; but they were only terrified to find that they had made a fearful mistake, the consequences of which would prove disastrous to themselves. Their hearts were unchanged, and they only needed an excuse to occasion a similar outbreak. This presented itself when

Moses, by the authority of God, commanded them to go back into the wilderness.

The decree that Israel was not to enter Canaan for forty years was a bitter disappointment to Moses and Aaron, Caleb and Joshua; yet without a murmur they accepted the divine decision. But those who had been complaining of God's dealings with them, and declaring that they would return to Egypt, wept and mourned greatly when the blessings which they had despised were taken from them. They had complained at nothing, and now God gave them cause to weep. Had they mourned for their sin when it was faithfully laid before them, this sentence would not have been pronounced; but they mourned for the judgment; their sorrow was not repentance, and could not secure a reversing of their sentence.

The night was spent in lamentation, but with the morning came a hope. They resolved to redeem their cowardice. When God had bidden them go up and take the land, they had refused; and now when He directed them to retreat they were equally rebellious. They determined to seize upon the land and possess it; it might be that God would accept their work and change His purpose toward them.

God had made it their privilege and their duty to enter the land at the time of His appointment, but through their willful neglect that permission had been withdrawn. Satan had gained his object in preventing them from entering Canaan; and now he urged them on to do the very thing, in the face of the divine prohibition, which they had refused to do when God required it. Thus the great deceiver gained the victory by leading them to rebellion the second time. They had distrusted the power of God to work with their efforts in gaining possession of Canaan; yet now they presumed upon their own strength to accomplish the work independent of divine aid. "We have sinned against the Lord," they cried; "we will go up and fight, according to all that the Lord our God commanded us." Deuteronomy 1:41. So terribly blinded had they become by transgression. The Lord had never commanded them to "go up and fight." It was not His purpose that they should gain the land by warfare, but by strict obedience to His commands.

Though their hearts were unchanged, the people had been brought to confess the sinfulness and folly of their rebellion at the report of the spies. They now saw the value of the blessing which they had so rashly cast away. They confessed that it was their own unbelief which had shut them out from Canaan. "We have sinned," they said, acknowledging that the fault was in themselves, and not in God, whom they had so wickedly charged with failing to fulfill His promises to them. Though their confession did not spring from true repentance, it served to vindicate the justice of God in His dealings with them.

The Lord still works in a similar manner to glorify His name by bringing men to acknowledge His justice. When those who profess to love Him complain of His providence, despise His promises, and, yielding to temptation, unite with evil angels to defeat the purposes of God, the Lord often so overrules circumstances as to bring these persons where, though they may have no real repentance, they will be convinced of their sin and will be constrained to acknowledge the wickedness of their course and the justice and goodness of God in His dealings with them. It is thus that God sets counteragencies at work to make manifest the works of darkness. And though the spirit which prompted to the evil course is not radically changed, confessions are made that vindicate the honor of God and justify His faithful reprovers, who have been opposed and misrepresented. Thus it will be when the wrath of God shall be finally poured out. When "the Lord cometh with ten thousand of His saints, to execute judgment upon all," He will also "convince all that are ungodly among them of all their ungodly deeds." Jude 14, 15. Every sinner will be brought to see and acknowledge the justice of his condemnation.

Regardless of the divine sentence, the Israelites prepared to undertake the conquest of Canaan. Equipped with armor and weapons of war, they were, in their own estimation, fully prepared for conflict; but they were sadly deficient in the sight of God and His sorrowful servants. When, nearly forty years later, the Lord directed Israel to go up and take Jericho, He promised to go with them. The ark containing His law was borne before their armies. His appointed leaders were to direct their movements, under the divine supervision. With such guidance, no harm could come to them. But now, contrary to the command of God and the solemn prohibition of their leaders, without the ark, and without Moses, they went out to meet the armies of the enemy.

The trumpet sounded an alarm, and Moses hastened after them with the warning, "Wherefore now do ye transgress the commandment of the Lord? but it shall not prosper. Go not up, for the Lord is not among you; that ye be not smitten before your enemies. For the Amalekites and the Canaanites are there before you, and ye shall fall by the sword."

The Canaanites had heard of the mysterious power that seemed to be guarding this people and of the wonders wrought in their behalf, and they now summoned a strong force to repel the invaders. The attacking army had no leader. No prayer was offered that God would give them the victory. They set forth with the desperate purpose to reverse their fate or to die in battle. Though untrained in war, they were a vast multitude of armed men, and they hoped by a sudden and fierce assault to bear down all opposition. They presumptuously challenged the foe that had not dared to attack them.

The Canaanites had stationed themselves upon a rocky tableland reached only by difficult passes and a steep and dangerous ascent. The immense numbers of the Hebrews could only render their defeat more terrible. They slowly threaded the mountain paths, exposed to the deadly missiles of their enemies above. Massive rocks came thundering down, marking their path with the blood of the slain. Those who reached the summit, exhausted with their ascent, were fiercely repulsed, and driven back with great loss. The field of carnage was strewn with the bodies of the dead. The army of Israel was utterly defeated. Destruction and death was the result of that rebellious experiment.

Forced to submission at last, the survivors "returned, and wept before the Lord;" but "the Lord would not hearken" to their voice. Deuteronomy 1:45. By their signal victory the enemies of Israel, who had before awaited with trembling the approach of that mighty host, were inspired with confidence to resist them. All the reports they had heard concerning the marvelous things that God had wrought for His people, they now regarded as false, and they felt that there was no cause for fear. That first defeat of Israel, by inspiring the Canaanites with courage and resolution, had greatly increased the difficulties of the conquest. Nothing remained for Israel but to fall back from the face of their victorious foes, into the wilderness, knowing that here must be the grave of a whole generation.

Chapter 35—The Rebellion of Korah

This chapter is based on Numbers 16 and 17.

The judgments visited upon the Israelites served for a time to restrain their murmuring and insubordination, but the spirit of rebellion was still in the heart and eventually brought forth the bitterest fruits. The former rebellions had been mere popular tumults, arising from the sudden impulse of the excited multitude; but now a deep-laid conspiracy was formed, the result of a determined purpose to overthrow the authority of the leaders appointed by God Himself.

Korah, the leading spirit in this movement, was a Levite, of the family of Kohath, and a cousin of Moses; he was a man of ability and influence. Though appointed to the service of the tabernacle, he had become dissatisfied with his position and aspired to the dignity of the priesthood. The bestowal upon Aaron and his house of the priestly office, which had formerly devolved upon the first-born son of every family, had given rise to jealousy and dissatisfaction, and for some time Korah had been secretly opposing the authority of Moses and Aaron, though he had not ventured upon any open act of rebellion. He finally conceived the bold design of overthrowing both the civil and the religious authority. He did not fail to find sympathizers. Close to the tents of Korah and the Kohathites, on the south side of the tabernacle, was the encampment of the tribe of Reuben, the tents of Dathan and Abiram, two princes of this tribe, being near that of Korah. These princes readily joined in his ambitious schemes. Being descendants from the eldest son of Jacob, they claimed that the civil authority belonged to them, and they determined to divide with Korah the honors of the priesthood.

The state of feeling among the people favored the designs of Korah. In the bitterness of their disappointment, their former doubts, jealousy, and hatred had returned, and again their complaints were directed against their patient leader. The Israelites were continually losing sight of the fact that they were under divine guidance. They forgot that the Angel of the covenant was their invisible leader, that, veiled by the cloudy pillar, the presence of Christ went before them, and that from Him Moses received all his directions.

They were unwilling to submit to the terrible sentence that they must all die in the wilderness, and hence they were ready to seize upon every pretext for believing that it was not God but Moses who was leading them and who had pronounced their doom. The best efforts of the meekest man upon the earth could not quell the insubordination of this people; and although the marks of God's displeasure at their former perverseness were still before them in their broken ranks and missing numbers, they did not take the lesson to heart. Again they were overcome by temptation.

The humble shepherd's life of Moses had been far more peaceful and happy than his present position as leader of that vast assembly of turbulent spirits. Yet Moses dared not choose. In place of a shepherd's crook a rod of power had been given him, which he could not lay down until God should release him.

He who reads the secrets of all hearts had marked the purposes of Korah and his companions and had given His people such warning and instruction as might have enabled them to escape the deception of these designing men. They had seen the judgment of God fall upon Miriam because of her jealousy and complaints against Moses. The Lord had declared that Moses was greater than a prophet. "With him will I speak mouth to mouth." "Wherefore, then," He added, "were ye not afraid to speak against My servant Moses?" Numbers 12:8. These instructions were not intended for Aaron and Miriam alone, but for all Israel.

Korah and his fellow conspirators were men who had been favored with special manifestations of God's power and greatness. They were of the number who went up with Moses into the mount and beheld the divine glory. But since that time a change had come. A temptation, slight at first, had been harbored, and had strengthened as it was encouraged, until their minds were controlled by Satan, and they ventured upon their work of disaffection. Professing great interest in the prosperity of the people, they first whispered their discontent to one another and then to leading men of Israel. Their insinuations were so readily received that they ventured still further, and at last they really believed themselves to be actuated by zeal for God.

They were successful in alienating two hundred and fifty princes, men of renown in the congregation. With these strong and influential supporters they felt confident of making a radical change in the government and greatly improving upon the administration of Moses and Aaron.

Jealousy had given rise to envy, and envy to rebellion. They had discussed the question of the right of Moses to so great authority and honor, until they had come to regard him as occupying a very enviable position, which any of them could fill as well as he. And they deceived themselves and one another into thinking that Moses and Aaron had themselves assumed the positions they held. The discontented ones said that these leaders had exalted themselves above the congregation of the Lord, in taking upon them the priesthood and government, but their house was not entitled to distinction above others in Israel; they were no more holy than the people, and it should be enough for them to be on a level with their brethren, who were equally favored with God's special presence and protection.

The next work of the conspirators was with the people. To those who are in the wrong, and deserving of reproof, there is nothing more pleasing than to receive sympathy and praise. And thus Korah and his associates gained the attention and enlisted the support of the congregation. The charge that the murmurings of the people had brought upon them the wrath of God was declared to be a mistake. They said that the congregation were not at fault, since they desired nothing more than their rights; but that Moses was an overbearing ruler; that he had reproved the people as sinners, when they were a holy people, and the Lord was among them.

Korah reviewed the history of their travels through the wilderness, where they had been brought into strait places, and many had perished because of their murmuring and disobedience. His hearers thought they saw clearly that their troubles might have been prevented if Moses had pursued a different course. They decided that all their disasters were chargeable to him, and that their exclusion from Canaan was in consequence of the mismanagement of Moses and Aaron; that if Korah would be their leader, and would encourage them by dwelling upon their good deeds, instead of reproving their sins, they would have a very peaceful, prosperous journey; instead of wandering to and fro in the wilderness, they would proceed directly to the Promised Land.

In this work of disaffection there was greater union and harmony among the discordant elements of the congregation than had ever before existed. Korah's success with the people increased his confidence and confirmed him in his belief that the usurpation of authority by Moses, if unchecked, would be fatal to the liberties of Israel; he also claimed that God had opened the matter to him, and had authorized him to make a change in the government before it should be too late. But many were not ready to accept Korah's accusations against Moses. The memory of his patient, self-sacrificing labors came up before them, and conscience was disturbed. It was therefore necessary to assign some selfish motive for his deep interest for Israel; and the old charge was reiterated, that he had led them out to perish in the wilderness, that he might seize upon their possessions.

For a time this work was carried on secretly. As soon, however, as the movement had gained sufficient strength to warrant an open rupture, Korah appeared at the head of the faction, and publicly accused Moses and Aaron of usurping authority which Korah and his associates were equally entitled to share. It was charged, further, that the people had been deprived of their liberty and independence. "Ye take too much upon you," said the conspirators, "seeing all the congregation are holy, every one of them, and the Lord is among them: wherefore then lift ye up yourselves above the congregation of the Lord?"

Moses had not suspected this deep-laid plot, and when its terrible significance burst upon him, he fell upon his face in silent appeal to God. He arose sorrowful indeed, but calm and strong. Divine guidance had been granted him. "Even tomorrow," he said, "the Lord will show who are His, and who is holy; and will cause him to come near unto Him: even him whom He hath chosen will He cause to come near unto Him." The test was to be deferred until the morrow, that all might have time for reflection. Then those who aspired to the priesthood were to come each with a censer, and offer incense at the tabernacle in the presence of the congregation. The law was very explicit that only those who had been ordained to the sacred office should minister in the sanctuary. And even the priests, Nadab and Abihu, had been destroyed for venturing to offer "strange fire," in disregard of a divine command. Yet Moses challenged his accusers, if they dared enter upon so perilous an appeal, to refer the matter to God.

Singling out Korah and his fellow Levites, Moses said, "Seemeth it but a small thing unto you, that the God of Israel hath separated you from the congregation of Israel, to bring you near to Himself to do the service of the tabernacle of the Lord, and to stand before the congregation to minister unto them? And He hath brought thee near to Him, and all thy brethren the sons of Levi with thee: and seek ye the priesthood also? for which cause both thou and all thy company are gathered together against the Lord. And what is Aaron, that ye murmur against him?"

Dathan and Abiram had not taken so bold a stand as had Korah; and Moses, hoping that they might have been drawn into the conspiracy without having become wholly corrupted, summoned them to appear before him, that he might hear their charges against him. But they would not come, and they insolently refused to acknowledge his authority. Their reply, uttered in the hearing of the congregation, was, "Is it a small thing that thou hast brought us up out of a land that floweth with milk and honey, to kill us in the wilderness, except thou make thyself altogether a prince over us? Moreover thou hast not brought us into a land that floweth with milk and honey, or given us inheritance of fields and vineyards: wilt thou put out the eyes of these men? We will not come up."

Thus they applied to the scene of their bondage the very language in which the Lord had described the promised inheritance. They accused Moses of pretending to act under divine guidance, as a means of establishing his authority; and they declared that they would no longer submit to be led about like blind men, now toward Canaan, and now toward the wilderness, as best suited his ambitious designs. Thus he who had been as a tender father, a patient shepherd, was represented in the blackest character of a tyrant and usurper. The exclusion from Canaan, in punishment of their own sins, was charged upon him.

It was evident that the sympathies of the people were with the disaffected party; but Moses made no effort at self-vindication. He solemnly appealed to God, in the presence of the congregation, as a witness to the purity of his motives and the uprightness of his conduct, and implored Him to be his judge.

On the morrow, the two hundred and fifty princes, with Korah at their head, presented themselves, with their censers. They were brought into the court of the tabernacle, while the people gathered without, to await the result. It was not Moses who assembled the congregation to behold the defeat of Korah and his company, but the rebels, in their blind presumption, had called them together to witness their victory. A large part of the congregation openly sided with Korah, whose hopes were high of carrying his point against Aaron. [400]

As they were thus assembled before God, "the glory of the Lord appeared unto all the congregation." The divine warning was communicated to Moses and Aaron, "Separate yourselves from among this congregation, that I may consume them in a moment." But they fell upon their faces, with the prayer, "O God, the God of the spirits of all flesh, shall one man sin, and wilt Thou be wroth with all the congregation?"

Korah had withdrawn from the assembly to join Dathan and Abiram when Moses, accompanied by the seventy elders, went down with a last warning to the men who had refused to come to him. The multitudes followed, and before delivering his message, Moses, by divine direction, bade the people, "Depart, I pray you, from the tents of these wicked men, and touch nothing of theirs, lest ye be consumed in all their sins." The warning was obeyed, for an apprehension of impending judgment rested upon all. The chief rebels saw themselves abandoned by those whom they had deceived, but their hardihood was unshaken. They stood with their families in the door of their tents, as if in defiance of the divine warning.

In the name of the God of Israel, Moses now declared, in the hearing of the congregation: "Hereby ye shall know that the Lord hath sent me to do all these works; for I have not done them of mine own mind. If these men die the common death of all men, or if they be visited after the visitation of all men, then the Lord hath not sent me. But if the Lord make a new thing, and the earth open her mouth, and swallow them up, with all that appertain unto them, and they go down quick into the pit, then ye shall understand that these men have provoked the Lord."

The eyes of all Israel were fixed upon Moses as they stood, in terror and expectation, awaiting the event. As he ceased speaking, the solid earth parted, and the rebels went down alive into the pit, with all that pertained to them, and "they perished from among the congregation." The people fled, self-condemned as partakers in the sin.

But the judgments were not ended. Fire flashing from the cloud consumed the two hundred and fifty princes who had offered incense. These men, not being the first in rebellion, were not destroyed with the chief conspirators. They were permitted to see their end, and to have an opportunity for repentance; but their sympathies were with the rebels, and they shared their fate.

When Moses was entreating Israel to flee from the coming destruction, the divine judgment might even then have been stayed, if Korah and his company had repented and sought forgiveness. But their stubborn persistence sealed their doom. The entire congregation were sharers in their guilt, for all had, to a greater or less degree, sympathized with them. Yet God in His great mercy made a distinction between the leaders in rebellion and those whom they had led. The people who had permitted themselves to be deceived were still granted space for repentance. Overwhelming evidence had been given that they were wrong, and that Moses was right. The signal manifestation of God's power had removed all uncertainty.

Jesus, the Angel who went before the Hebrews, sought to save them from destruction. Forgiveness was lingering for them. The judgment of God had come very near, and appealed to them to repent. A special, irresistible interference from heaven had arrested their rebellion. Now, if they would respond to the interposition of God's providence, they might be saved. But while they fled from the judgments, through fear of destruction, their rebellion was not cured. They returned to their tents that night terrified, but not repentant.

They had been flattered by Korah and his company until they really believed themselves to be very good people, and that they had been wronged and abused by Moses. Should they admit that Korah and his company were wrong, and Moses right, then they would be compelled to receive as the word of God the sentence that they must die in the wilderness. They were not willing to submit to this, and they tried to believe that Moses had deceived them. They had fondly cherished the hope that a new order of things was about to be established, in which praise would be substituted for reproof, and ease for anxiety and conflict. The men who had perished had spoken flattering words and had professed great interest and love for them, and the people concluded that Korah and his companions must have been good men, and that Moses had by some means been the cause of their destruction.

It is hardly possible for men to offer greater insult to God than to despise and reject the instrumentalities He would use for their salvation. The Israelites had not only done this, but had purposed to put both Moses and Aaron to death. Yet they did not realize the necessity of seeking pardon of God for their grievous sin. That night of probation was not passed in repentance and confession, but in devising some way to resist the evidences which showed them to be the greatest of sinners. They still cherished hatred of the men of God's appointment, and braced themselves to resist their authority. Satan was at hand to pervert their judgment and lead them blindfold to destruction.

All Israel had fled in alarm at the cry of the doomed sinners who went down into the pit, for they said, "Lest the earth swallow us up also." "But on the morrow all the congregation of the children of Israel murmured against Moses and against Aaron, saying, ye have killed the people of the Lord." And they were about to proceed to violence against their faithful, self-sacrificing leaders.

A manifestation of the divine glory was seen in the cloud above the tabernacle, and a voice from the cloud spoke to Moses and Aaron, "Get you up from among this congregation, that I may consume them as in a moment."

The guilt of sin did not rest upon Moses, and hence he did not fear and did not hasten away and leave the congregation to perish. Moses lingered, in this fearful crisis manifesting the true shepherd's interest for the flock of his care. He pleaded that the wrath of God might not utterly destroy the people of His choice. By his intercession he stayed the arm of vengeance, that a full end might not be made of disobedient, rebellious Israel.

But the minister of wrath had gone forth; the plague was doing its work of death. By his brother's direction, Aaron took a censer and hastened into the midst of the congregation to "make an atonement for them." "And he stood between the dead and the living." As the smoke of the incense ascended, the prayers of Moses in the tabernacle went up to God; and the plague was stayed; but not until fourteen thousand of Israel lay dead, an evidence of the guilt of murmuring and rebellion.

But further evidence was given that the priesthood had been established in the family of Aaron. By divine direction each tribe prepared a rod and wrote upon it the name of the tribe. The name of Aaron was upon that of Levi. The rods were laid up in the tabernacle, "before the testimony." The blossoming of any rod was to be a token that the Lord had chosen that tribe for the priesthood. On the morrow, "behold, the rod of Aaron for the house of Levi was budded, and brought forth buds, and bloomed blossoms, and yielded almonds." It was shown to the people, and afterward laid up in the tabernacle as a witness to succeeding generations. This miracle effectually settled the question of the priesthood.

It was now fully established that Moses and Aaron had spoken by divine authority, and the people were compelled to believe the unwelcome truth that they were to die in the wilderness. "Behold," they exclaimed, "we die, we perish, we all perish." They confessed that they had sinned in rebelling against their leaders, and that Korah and his company had suffered from the just judgment of God.

In the rebellion of Korah is seen the working out, upon a narrower stage, of the same spirit that led to the rebellion of Satan in heaven. It was pride and ambition that prompted Lucifer to complain of the government of God, and to seek the overthrow of the order which had been established in heaven. Since his fall it has been his object to infuse the same spirit of envy and discontent, the same ambition for position and honor, into the minds of men. He thus worked upon the minds of Korah, Dathan, and Abiram, to arouse the desire for self-exaltation and excite envy, distrust, and rebellion. Satan caused them to reject God as their leader, by rejecting the men of God's appointment. Yet while in their murmuring against Moses and Aaron they blasphemed God, they were so deluded as to think themselves righteous, and to regard those who had faithfully reproved their sins as actuated by Satan.

Do not the same evils still exist that lay at the foundation of Korah's ruin? Pride and ambition are widespread; and when these are cherished, they open the door to envy, and a striving for supremacy; the soul is alienated from God, and unconsciously drawn into the ranks of Satan. Like Korah and his companions, many, even of the professed followers of Christ, are thinking, planning, and working so eagerly for self-exaltation that in order to gain the sympathy and support of the people they are ready to pervert the truth, falsifying and misrepresenting the Lord's servants, and even charging them with the base and selfish motives that inspire their own hearts. By persistently reiterating falsehood, and that against all evidence, they at last come to believe it to be truth. While endeavoring to destroy the confidence of the people in the men of God's appointment, they really believe that they are engaged in a good work, verily doing God service.

The Hebrews were not willing to submit to the directions and restrictions of the Lord. They were restless under restraint, and unwilling to receive reproof. This was the secret of their murmuring against Moses. Had they been left free to do as they pleased, there would have been fewer complaints against their leader. All through the history of the church God's servants have had the same spirit to meet.

It is by sinful indulgence that men give Satan access to their minds, and they go from one stage of wickedness to another. The rejection of light darkens the mind and hardens the heart, so that it is easier for them to take the next step in sin and to reject still clearer light, until at last their habits of wrongdoing become fixed. Sin ceases to appear sinful to them. He who faithfully preaches God's word, thereby condemning their sins, too often incurs their hatred. Unwilling to endure the pain and sacrifice necessary to reform, they turn upon the Lord's servant and denounce his reproofs as uncalled for and severe. Like Korah, they declare that the people are not at fault; it is the reprover that causes all the trouble. And soothing their consciences with this deception, the jealous and disaffected combine to sow discord in the church and weaken the hands of those who would build it up.

Every advance made by those whom God has called to lead in His work has excited suspicion; every act has been misrepresented by the jealous and faultfinding. Thus it was in the time of Luther, of the Wesleys and other reformers. Thus it is today.

Korah would not have taken the course he did had he *known* that all the directions and reproofs communicated to Israel were from God. But he might have known this. God had given overwhelming evidence that He was leading Israel. But Korah and his companions rejected light until they became so blinded that the most striking manifestations of His power were not sufficient to convince them; they attributed them all to human or satanic agency. The same thing was done by the people, who the day after the destruction of Korah and his company came to Moses and Aaron, saying, "Ye have killed the people of the Lord." Notwithstanding they had had the most convincing evidence of God's displeasure at their course, in the destruction of the men who had deceived them, they dared to attribute His judgments to Satan, declaring that through the power of the evil one, Moses and Aaron had caused the death of good and holy men. It was this act that sealed their doom. They had committed the sin against the Holy Spirit, a sin by which man's heart is effectually hardened against the influence of divine grace. "Whosoever speaketh a word against the Son of man," said Christ, "it shall be forgiven him: but whosoever speaketh against the Holy Ghost, it shall not be forgiven him." Matthew 12:32. These words were spoken by our Saviour when the gracious works which He had performed through the power of God were attributed by the Jews to Beelzebub. It is through the agency of the Holy Spirit that God communicates with man; and those who deliberately reject this agency as satanic, have cut off the channel of communication between the soul and Heaven.

God works by the manifestation of His Spirit to reprove and convict the sinner; and if the Spirit's work is finally rejected, there is no more that God can do for the soul. The last resource of divine mercy has been employed. The transgressor has cut himself off from God, and sin has no remedy to cure itself. There is no reserved power by which God can work to convict and convert the sinner. "Let him alone" (Hosea 4:17) is the divine command. Then "there remaineth no more sacrifice for sins, but a certain fearful looking for of judgment and fiery indignation, which shall devour the adversaries." Hebrews 10:26, 27.

Chapter 36—In the Wilderness

For nearly forty years the children of Israel are lost to view in the obscurity of the desert. "The space," says Moses, "in which we came from Kadesh-barnea, until we were come over the brook Zered, was thirty and eight years; until all the generation of the men of war were wasted out from among the host, as the Lord sware unto them. For indeed the hand of the Lord was against them, to destroy them from among the host, until they were consumed." Deuteronomy 2:14, 15.

During these years the people were constantly reminded that they were under the divine rebuke. In the rebellion at Kadesh they had rejected God, and God had for the time rejected them. Since they had proved unfaithful to His covenant, they were not to receive the sign of the covenant, the rite of circumcision. Their desire to return to the land of slavery had shown them to be unworthy of freedom, and the ordinance of the Passover, instituted to commemorate the deliverance from bondage, was not to be observed.

Yet the continuance of the tabernacle service testified that God had not utterly forsaken His people. And His providence still supplied their wants. "The Lord thy God hath blessed thee in all the works of thy hand," said Moses, in rehearsing the history of their wanderings. "He knoweth thy walking through this great wilderness; these forty years the Lord thy God hath been with thee; thou hast lacked nothing." And the Levites' hymn, recorded by Nehemiah, vividly pictures God's care for Israel, even during these years of rejection and banishment: "Thou in Thy manifold mercies forsookest them not in the wilderness: the pillar of the cloud departed not from them by day, to lead them in the way; neither the pillar of fire by night, to show them light, and the way wherein they should go. Thou gavest also Thy good Spirit to instruct them, and withheldest not Thy manna from their mouth, and gavest them water for their thirst. Yea, forty years didst Thou sustain them in the wilderness; ... their clothes waxed not old, and their feet swelled not." Nehemiah 9:19-21.

The wilderness wandering was not only ordained as a judgment upon the rebels and murmurers, but it was to serve as a discipline for the rising generation, preparatory to their entrance into the Promised Land. Moses declared to them, "As a man chasteneth his son, so the Lord thy God chasteneth thee," "to humble thee, and to prove thee, to know what was in thine heart, whether thou wouldest keep His commandments, or no. And He ... suffered thee to hunger, and fed thee with manna, which thou knewest not, neither did thy fathers know; that He might make thee know that man doth not live by bread only, but by every word that proceedeth out of the mouth of the Lord doth man live." Deuteronomy 8:5, 2, 3.

"He found him in a desert land, and in the waste howling wilderness; He led him about, He instructed him, He kept him as the apple of His eye." "In all their affliction He was afflicted, and the Angel of His presence saved them; in His love and in His pity He redeemed them; and He bare them, and carried them all the days of old." Deuteronomy 32:10; Isaiah 63:9.

Yet the only records of their wilderness life are instances of rebellion against the Lord. The revolt of Korah had resulted in the destruction of fourteen thousand of Israel. And there were isolated cases that showed the same spirit of contempt for the divine authority.

On one occasion the son of an Israelitish woman and of an Egyptian, one of the mixed multitude that had come up with Israel from Egypt, left his own part of the camp, and entering that of the Israelites, claimed the right to pitch his tent there. This the divine law forbade him to do, the descendants of an Egyptian being excluded from the congregation until the third generation. A dispute arose between him and an Israelite, and the matter being referred to the judges was decided against the offender.

Enraged at this decision, he cursed the judge, and in the heat of passion blasphemed the name of God. He was immediately brought before Moses. The command had been given, "He that curseth his father, or his mother, shall surely be put to death" (Exodus 21:17); but no provision had been made to meet this case. So terrible was the crime that there was felt to be a necessity for special direction from God. The man was placed in ward until the will of the Lord could be ascertained. God Himself pronounced the sentence; by the divine direction the blasphemer was conducted outside the camp and stoned to death. Those who had been witness to the sin placed their hands upon his head, thus solemnly testifying to the truth of the charge against him. Then they threw the first stones, and the people who stood by afterward joined in executing the sentence.

This was followed by the announcement of a law to meet similar offenses: "Thou shalt speak unto the children of Israel, saying, Whosoever curseth his God shall bear his sin. And he that blasphemeth the name of the Lord, he shall surely be put to death, and all the congregation shall certainly stone him: as well the stranger, as he that is born in the land, when he blasphemeth the name of the Lord, shall be put to death." Leviticus 24:15, 16.

There are those who will question God's love and His justice in visiting so severe punishment for words spoken in the heat of passion. But both love and justice require it to be shown that utterances prompted by malice against God are a great sin. The retribution visited upon the first offender would be a warning to others, that God's name is to be held in reverence. But had this man's sin been permitted to pass unpunished, others would have been demoralized; and as the result many lives must eventually have been sacrificed.

The mixed multitude that came up with the Israelites from Egypt were a source of continual temptation and trouble. They professed to have renounced idolatry and to worship the true God; but their early education and training had molded their habits and character, and they were more or less corrupted with idolatry and with irreverence for God. They were oftenest the ones to stir up strife and were the first to complain, and they leavened the camp with their idolatrous practices and their murmurings against God.

Soon after the return into the wilderness, an instance of Sabbath violation occurred, under circumstances that rendered it a case of peculiar guilt. The Lord's announcement that He would disinherit Israel had roused a spirit of rebellion. One of the people, angry at being excluded from Canaan, and determined to show his defiance of God's law, ventured upon the open transgression of the fourth commandment by going out to gather sticks upon the Sabbath. During the sojourn in the wilderness the kindling of fires upon the seventh day had been strictly prohibited. The prohibition was not to extend to the land of Canaan, where the severity of the climate would often render fires a necessity; but in the wilderness, fire was not needed for warmth. The act of this man was a willful and deliberate violation of the fourth commandment—a sin, not of thoughtlessness or ignorance, but of presumption.

He was taken in the act and brought before Moses. It had already been declared that Sabbathbreaking should be punished with death, but it had not yet been revealed how the penalty was to be inflicted. The case was brought by Moses before the Lord, and the direction was given, "The man shall be surely put to death: all the congregation shall stone him with stones without the camp." Numbers 15:35. The sins of blasphemy and willful Sabbathbreaking received the same punishment, being equally an expression of contempt for the authority of God.

In our day there are many who reject the creation Sabbath as a Jewish institution and urge that if it is to be kept, the penalty of death must be inflicted for its violation; but we see that blasphemy received the same punishment as did Sabbathbreaking. Shall we therefore conclude that the third commandment also is to be set aside as applicable only to the Jews? Yet the argument drawn from the death penalty applies to the third, the fifth, and indeed to nearly all the ten precepts, equally with the fourth. Though God may not now punish the transgression of His law with temporal penalties, yet His word declares that the wages of sin is death; and in the final execution of the judgment it will be found that death is the portion of those who violate His sacred precepts.

During the entire forty years in the wilderness, the people were every week reminded of the sacred obligation of the Sabbath, by the miracle of the manna. Yet even this did not lead them to obedience. Though they did not venture upon so open and bold transgression as had received such signal punishment, yet there was great laxness in the observance of the fourth commandment. God declares through His prophet, "My Sabbaths they greatly polluted." Ezekiel 20:13-24. And this is enumerated among the reasons for the exclusion of the first generation from the Promised Land. Yet their children did not learn the lesson. Such was their neglect of the Sabbath during the forty years' wandering, that though God did not prevent them from entering Canaan, He declared that they should be scattered among the heathen after the settlement in the Land of Promise.

From Kadesh the children of Israel had turned back into the wilderness; and the period of their desert sojourn being ended, they came, "even the whole congregation, into the desert of Zin in the first month: and the people abode in Kadesh." Numbers 20:1.

Here Miriam died and was buried. From that scene of rejoicing on the shores of the Red Sea, when Israel went forth with song and dance to celebrate Jehovah's triumph, to the wilderness grave which ended a lifelong wandering—such had been the fate of millions who with high hopes had come forth from Egypt. Sin had dashed from their lips the cup of blessing. Would the next generation learn the lesson?

"For all this they sinned still, and believed not for His wondrous works.... When He slew them, then they sought Him: and they returned and inquired early after God. And they remembered that God was their Rock, and the high God their Redeemer." Psalm 78:32-35. Yet they did not turn to God with a sincere purpose. Though when afflicted by their enemies they sought help from Him who alone could deliver, yet "their heart was not right with Him, neither were they steadfast in His covenant. But He, being full of compassion, forgave their iniquity, and destroyed them not: yea, many a time turned He His anger away.... For He remembered that they were but flesh; a wind that passeth away, and cometh not again." Verses 37-39.

Chapter 37—The Smitten Rock

This chapter is based on Numbers 20:1-13.

From the smitten rock in Horeb first flowed the living stream that refreshed Israel in the desert. During all their wanderings, wherever the need existed, they were supplied with water by a miracle of God's mercy. The water did not, however, continue to flow from Horeb. Wherever in their journeyings they wanted water, there from the clefts of the rock it gushed out beside their encampment.

It was Christ, by the power of His word, that caused the refreshing stream to flow for Israel. "They drank of that spiritual Rock that followed them: and that Rock was Christ." 1 Corinthians 10:4. He was the source of all temporal as well as spiritual blessings. Christ, the true Rock, was with them in all their wanderings. "They thirsted not when He led them through the deserts: He caused the waters to flow out of the rock for them; He clave the rock also, and the waters gushed out." "They ran in the dry places like a river." Isaiah 48:21; Psalm 105:41.

The smitten rock was a figure of Christ, and through this symbol the most precious spiritual truths are taught. As the life-giving waters flowed from the smitten rock, so from Christ, "smitten of God," "wounded for our transgressions," "bruised for our iniquities" (Isaiah 53:4, 5), the stream of salvation flows for a lost race. As the rock had been once smitten, so Christ was to be "once offered to bear the sins of many." Hebrews 9:28. Our Saviour was not to be sacrificed a second time; and it is only necessary for those who seek the blessings of His grace to ask in the name of Jesus, pouring forth the heart's desire in penitential prayer. Such prayer will bring before the Lord of hosts the wounds of Jesus, and then will flow forth afresh the life-giving blood, symbolized by the flowing of the living water for Israel.

The flowing of the water from the rock in the desert was celebrated by the Israelites, after their establishment in Canaan, with demonstrations of great rejoicing. In the time of Christ this celebration had become a most impressive ceremony. It took place on the occasion of the Feast of Tabernacles, when the people from all the land were assembled at Jerusalem. On each of the seven days of the feast the priests went out with music and the choir of Levites to draw water in a golden vessel from the spring of Siloam. They were followed by multitudes of the worshipers, as many as could get near the stream drinking of it, while the jubilant strains arose, "With joy shall ye draw water out of the wells of salvation." Isaiah 12:3. Then the water drawn by the priests was borne to the temple amid the sounding of trumpets and the solemn chant, "Our feet shall stand within thy gates, O Jerusalem." Psalm 122:2. The water was poured out upon the altar of burnt offering, while songs of praise rang out, the multitudes joining in triumphant chorus with musical instruments and deep-toned trumpets.

The Saviour made use of this symbolic service to direct the minds of the people to the blessings that He had come to bring them. "In the last day, that great day of the feast," His voice was heard in tones that rang through the temple courts, "If any man thirst, let him come unto Me, and drink. He that believeth on Me, as the Scripture hath said, out of his belly shall flow rivers of living water." "This," said John, "spake He of the Spirit, which they that believe on Him should receive." John 7:37-39. The refreshing water, welling up in a parched and barren land, causing the desert place to blossom, and flowing out to give life to the perishing, is an emblem of the divine grace which Christ alone can bestow, and which is as the living water, purifying, refreshing, and invigorating the soul. He in whom Christ is abiding has within him a never-failing fountain of grace and strength. Jesus cheers the life and brightens the path of all who truly seek Him. His love, received into the heart, will spring up in good works unto eternal life. And not only does it bless the soul in which it springs, but the living stream will flow out in words and deeds of righteousness, to refresh the thirsting around him.

The same figure Christ had employed in His conversation with the woman of Samaria at Jacob's well: "Whosoever drinketh of the water that I shall give him shall never thirst; but the water that I shall give him shall be in him a well of water springing up into everlasting life." John 4:14. Christ combines the two types. He is the rock, He is the living water.

The same beautiful and expressive figures are carried throughout the Bible. Centuries before the advent of Christ, Moses pointed to Him as the rock of Israel's salvation (Deuteronomy 32:15); the psalmist sang of Him as "my Redeemer," "the rock of my strength," "the rock that is higher than I," "a rock of habitation," "rock of my heart," "rock of my refuge." In David's song His grace is pictured also as the cool, "still waters," amid green pastures, beside which the heavenly Shepherd leads His flock. Again, "Thou shalt make them," he says, "drink of the river of Thy pleasures. For with Thee is the fountain of life." Psalm 19:14; 62:7; Psalm 61:2; 71:3 (margin); 73:26 (margin); 94:22; 23:2; 36:8, 9. And the wise man declares, "The wellspring of wisdom [is] as a flowing brook." Proverbs 18:4. To Jeremiah, Christ is "the fountain of living waters;" to Zechariah, "a fountain opened ... for sin and for uncleanness." Jeremiah 2:13; Zechariah 13:1.

Isaiah describes Him as the "rock of ages," and "the shadow of a great rock in a weary land." Isaiah 26:4 (margin); 32:2. And he records the precious promise, bringing vividly to mind the living stream that flowed for Israel: "When the poor and needy seek water, and there is none, and their tongue faileth for thirst, I the Lord will hear them, I the God of Israel will not forsake them." "I will pour water upon him that is thirsty, and floods upon the dry ground;" "in the wilderness shall waters break out, and streams in the desert." The invitation is given, "Ho, every one that thirsteth, come ye to the waters." Isaiah 41:17; 44:3; Isaiah 35:6; 55:1. And in the closing pages of the Sacred Word this invitation is echoed. The river of the water of life, "clear as crystal," proceeds from the throne of God and the Lamb; and the gracious call is ringing down through the ages, "Whosoever will, let him take the water of life freely." Revelation 22:17.

Just before the Hebrew host reached Kadesh, the living stream ceased that for so many years had gushed out beside their encampment. It was the Lord's purpose again to test His people. He would prove whether they would trust His providence or imitate the unbelief of their fathers.

They were now in sight of the hills of Canaan. A few days' march would bring them to the borders of the Promised Land. They were but a little distance from Edom, which belonged to the descendants of Esau, and through which lay the appointed route to Canaan. The direction had been given to Moses, "Turn you northward. And command thou the people, saying, Ye are to pass through the coast of your brethren the children of Esau, which dwell in Seir; and they shall be afraid of you.... Ye shall buy meat of them for money, that ye may eat; and ye shall also buy water of them for money, that ye may drink." Deuteronomy 2:3-6. These directions should have been sufficient to explain why their supply of water had been cut off; they were about to pass through a well-watered, fertile country, in a direct course to the land of Canaan. God had promised them an unmolested passage through Edom, and an opportunity to purchase food, and also water sufficient to supply the host. The cessation of the miraculous flow of water should therefore have been a cause of rejoicing, a token that the wilderness wandering was ended. Had they not been blinded by their unbelief, they would have understood this. But that which should have been an evidence of the fulfillment of God's promise was made the occasion of doubt and murmuring. The people seemed to have given up all hope that God would bring them into possession of Canaan, and they clamored for the blessings of the wilderness.

Before God permitted them to enter Canaan, they must show that they believed His promise. The water ceased before they had reached Edom. Here was an opportunity for them, for a little time, to walk by faith instead of sight. But the first trial developed the same turbulent, unthankful spirit that had been manifested by their fathers. No sooner was the cry for water heard in the encampment than they forgot the hand that had for so many years supplied their wants, and instead of turning to God for help, they murmured against Him, in their desperation exclaiming, "Would God that we had died when our brethren died before the Lord!" (Numbers 20:1-13); that is, they wished they had been of the number who were destroyed in the rebellion of Korah.

Their cries were directed against Moses and Aaron: "Why have ye brought up the congregation of the Lord into this wilderness, that we and our cattle should die there? And wherefore have ye made us to come up out of Egypt, to bring us in unto this evil place? it is no place of seed, or of figs, or of vines, or of pomegranates; neither is there any water to drink."

The leaders went to the door of the tabernacle and fell upon their faces. Again "the glory of the Lord appeared," and Moses was directed, "Take the rod, and gather thou the assembly together, thou and Aaron thy brother, and speak ye unto the rock before their eyes; and it shall give forth his water, and thou shalt bring forth to them water out of the rock."

The two brothers went on before the multitude, Moses with the rod of God in his hand. They were now aged men. Long had they borne with the rebellion and obstinacy of Israel; but now, at last, even the patience of Moses gave way. "Hear now, ye rebels," he cried; "must we fetch you water out of this rock?" and instead of speaking to the rock, as God had commanded him, he smote it twice with the rod.

The water gushed forth in abundance to satisfy the host. But a great wrong had been done. Moses had spoken from irritated feeling; his words were an expression of human passion rather than of holy indignation because God had been dishonored. "Hear now, ye rebels," he said. This accusation was true, but even truth is not to be spoken in passion or impatience. When God had bidden Moses to charge upon Israel their rebellion, the words had been painful to him, and hard for them to bear, yet God had sustained him in delivering the message. But when he took it upon himself to accuse them, he grieved the Spirit of God and wrought only harm to the people. His lack of patience and self-control was evident. Thus the people were given occasion to question whether his past course had been under the direction of God, and to excuse their own sins. Moses, as well as they, had offended God. His course, they said, had from the first been open to criticism and censure. They had now found the pretext which they desired for rejecting all the reproofs that God had sent them through His servant.

Moses manifested distrust of God. "Shall we bring water?" he questioned, as if the Lord would not do what He promised. "Ye believed Me not," the Lord declared to the two brothers, "to sanctify Me in the eyes of the children of Israel." At the time when the water failed, their own faith in the fulfillment of God's promise had been shaken by the murmuring and rebellion of the people. The first generation had been condemned to perish in the wilderness because of their unbelief, yet the same spirit appeared in their children. Would these also fail of receiving the promise? Wearied and disheartened, Moses and Aaron had made no effort to stem the current of popular feeling. Had they themselves manifested unwavering faith in God, they might have set the matter before the people in such a light as would have enabled them to bear this test. By prompt, decisive exercise of the authority vested in them as magistrates, they might have quelled the murmuring. It was their duty to put forth every effort in their power to bring about a better state of things before asking God to do the work for them. Had the murmuring at Kadesh been promptly checked, what a train of evil might have been prevented!

By his rash act Moses took away the force of the lesson that God purposed to teach. The rock, being a symbol of Christ, had been once smitten, as Christ was to be once offered. The second time it was needful only to speak to the rock, as we have only to ask for blessings in the name of Jesus. By the second smiting of the rock the significance of this beautiful figure of Christ was destroyed.

More than this, Moses and Aaron had assumed power that belongs only to God. The necessity for divine interposition made the occasion one of great solemnity, and the leaders of Israel should have improved it to impress the people with reverence for God and to strengthen their faith in His power and goodness. When they angrily cried, "Must *we* fetch you water out of this rock?" they put themselves in God's place, as though the power lay with themselves, men possessing human frailties and passions. Wearied with the continual murmuring and rebellion of the people, Moses had lost sight of his Almighty Helper, and without the divine strength he had been left to mar his record by an exhibition of human weakness. The man who might have stood pure, firm, and unselfish to the close of his work had been overcome at last. God had been dishonored before the congregation of Israel, when He should have been magnified and exalted.

God did not on this occasion pronounce judgments upon those whose wicked course had so provoked Moses and Aaron. All the reproof fell upon the leaders. Those who stood as God's representatives had not honored Him. Moses and Aaron had felt themselves aggrieved, losing sight of the fact that the murmuring of the people was not against them but against God. It was by looking to themselves, appealing to their own sympathies, that they unconsciously fell into sin, and failed to set before the people their great guilt before God.

Bitter and deeply humiliating was the judgment immediately pronounced. "The Lord spake unto Moses and Aaron, Because ye believed Me not, to sanctify Me in the eyes of the children of Israel, therefore ye shall not bring this congregation into the land which I have given them." With rebellious Israel they must die before the crossing of the Jordan. Had Moses and Aaron been cherishing self-esteem or indulging a passionate spirit in the face of divine warning and reproof, their guilt would have been far greater. But they were not chargeable with willful or deliberate sin; they had been overcome by a sudden temptation, and their contrition was immediate and heartfelt. The Lord accepted their repentance, though because of the harm their sin might do among the people, He could not remit its punishment.

Moses did not conceal his sentence, but told the people that since he had failed to ascribe glory to God, he could not lead them into the Promised Land. He bade them mark the severe punishment visited upon him, and then consider how God must regard their murmurings in charging upon a mere man the judgments which they had by their sins brought upon themselves. He told them how he had pleaded with God for a remission of the sentence, and had been refused. "The Lord was wroth with me for your sakes," he said, "and would not hear me." Deuteronomy 3:26.

On every occasion of difficulty or trial the Israelites had been ready to charge Moses with having led them from Egypt, as though God had had no agency in the matter. Throughout their journeyings, as they had complained of the difficulties in the way, and murmured against their leaders, Moses had told them, "Your murmurings are against God. It is not I, but God, who has wrought in your deliverance." But his hasty words before the rock, "shall *we* bring water?" were a virtual admission of their charge, and would thus confirm them in their unbelief and justify their murmurings. The Lord would remove this impression forever from their minds, by forbidding Moses to enter the Promised Land. Here was unmistakable evidence that their leader was not Moses, but the mighty Angel of whom the

Lord had said, "Behold, I send an Angel before thee, to keep thee in the way, and to bring thee into the place which I have prepared. Beware of Him, and obey His voice: ... for My name is in Him." Exodus 23:20, 21.

[420] "The Lord was wroth with me for your sakes," said Moses. The eyes of all Israel were upon Moses, and his sin cast a reflection upon God, who had chosen him as the leader of His people. The transgression was known to the whole congregation; and had it been passed by lightly, the impression would have been given that unbelief and impatience under great provocation might be excused in those in responsible positions. But when it was declared that because of that one sin Moses and Aaron were not to enter Canaan, the people knew that God is no respecter of persons, and that He will surely punish the transgressor.

The history of Israel was to be placed on record for the instruction and warning of coming generations. Men of all future time must see the God of heaven as an impartial ruler, in no case justifying sin. But few realize the exceeding sinfulness of sin. Men flatter themselves that God is too good to punish the transgressor. But in the light of Bible history it is evident that God's goodness and His love engage Him to deal with sin as an evil fatal to the peace and happiness of the universe.

Not even the integrity and faithfulness of Moses could avert the retribution of his fault. God had forgiven the people greater transgressions, but He could not deal with sin in the leaders as in those who were led. He had honored Moses above every other man upon the earth. He had revealed to him His glory, and through him He had communicated His statutes to Israel. The fact that Moses had enjoyed so great light and knowledge made his sin more grievous. Past faithfulness will not atone for one wrong act. The greater the light and privileges granted to man, the greater is his responsibility, the more aggravated his failure, and the heavier his punishment.

Moses was not guilty of a great crime, as men would view the matter; his sin was one of common occurrence. The psalmist says that "he spake unadvisedly with his lips." Psalm 106:33. To human judgment this may seem a light thing; but if God dealt so severely with this sin in His most faithful and honored servant, He will not excuse it in others. The spirit of self-exaltation, the disposition to censure our brethren, is displeasing to God. Those who indulge in these evils cast doubt upon the work of God, and give the skeptical an excuse for their unbelief. The more important one's position, and the greater his influence, the greater is the necessity that he should cultivate patience and humility.

If the children of God, especially those who stand in positions of responsibility, can be led to take to themselves the glory that is due to God, Satan exults. He has gained a victory. It was thus that he fell. Thus he is most successful in tempting others to ruin. It is to place us on our guard against his devices that God has given in His word so many lessons teaching the danger of self-exaltation. There is not an impulse of our nature, not a faculty of the mind or an inclination of the heart, but needs to be, moment by moment, under the control of the Spirit of God. There is not a blessing which God bestows upon man, nor a trial which He permits to befall him, but Satan both can and will seize upon it to tempt, to harass and destroy the soul, if we give him the least advantage. Therefore however great one's spiritual light, however much he may enjoy of the divine favor and blessing, he should ever walk humbly before the Lord, pleading in faith that God will direct every thought and control every impulse.

All who profess godliness are under the most sacred obligation to guard the spirit, and to exercise self-control under the greatest provocation. The burdens placed upon Moses were very great; few men will ever be so severely tried as he was; yet this was not allowed to excuse his sin. God has made ample provision for His people; and if they rely upon His strength, they will never become the sport of circumstances. The strongest temptation cannot excuse sin. However great the pressure brought to bear upon the soul, transgression is our own act. It is not in the power of earth or hell to compel anyone to do evil. Satan attacks us at our weak points, but we need not be overcome. However severe or unexpected the assault, God has provided help for us, and in His strength we may conquer.

[421]

Chapter 38—The Journey Around Edom

This chapter is based on Numbers 20:14-29; 21:1-9.

The encampment of Israel at Kadesh was but a short distance from the borders of Edom, and both Moses and the people greatly desired to follow the route through this country to the Promised Land; accordingly they sent a message, as God had directed them, to the Edomite king—

"Thus saith thy brother Israel, Thou knowest all the travail that hath befallen us: how our fathers went down into Egypt, and we have dwelt in Egypt a long time; and the Egyptians vexed us, and our fathers: and when we cried unto the Lord, He heard our voice, and sent an Angel, and hath brought us forth out of Egypt: and, behold, we are in Kadesh, a city in the uttermost of thy border. Let us pass, I pray thee, through thy country: we will not pass through the fields, or through the vineyards, neither will we drink of the water of the wells: we will go by the king's highway, we will not turn to the right hand nor to the left, until we have passed thy borders."

To this courteous request a threatening refusal was returned: "Thou shalt not pass by me, lest I come out against thee with the sword."

Surprised at this repulse, the leaders of Israel sent a second appeal to the king, with the promise, "We will go by the highway: and if I and my cattle drink of thy water, then I will pay for it: I will only, without doing anything else, go through on my feet."

"Thou shalt not go through," was the answer. Armed bands of Edomites were already posted at the difficult passes, so that any peaceful advance in that direction was impossible, and the Hebrews were forbidden to resort to force. They must make the long journey around the land of Edom.

Had the people, when brought into trial, trusted in God, the Captain of the Lord's host would have led them through Edom, and the fear of them would have rested upon the inhabitants of the land, so that, instead of manifesting hostility, they would have shown them favor. But the Israelites did not act promptly upon God's word, and while they were complaining and murmuring, the golden opportunity passed. When they were at last ready to present their request to the king, it was refused. Ever since they left Egypt, Satan had been steadily at work to throw hindrances and temptations in their way, that they might not inherit Canaan. And by their own unbelief they had repeatedly opened the door for him to resist the purpose of God.

It is important to believe God's word and act upon it promptly, while His angels are waiting to work for us. Evil angels are ready to contest every step of advance. And when God's providence bids His children go forward, when He is ready to do great things for them, Satan tempts them to displease the Lord by hesitation and delay; he seeks to kindle a spirit of strife or to arouse murmuring or unbelief, and thus deprive them of the blessings that God desired to bestow. God's servants should be minutemen, ever ready to move as fast as His providence opens the way. And delay on their part gives time for Satan to work to defeat them.

In the directions first given to Moses concerning their passage through Edom, after declaring that the Edomites should be afraid of Israel, the Lord had forbidden His people to make use of this advantage against them. Because the power of God was engaged for Israel, and the fears of the Edomites would make them an easy prey, the Hebrews were not therefore to prey upon them. The command given them was, "Take ye good heed unto yourselves therefore: meddle not with them; for I will not give you of their land, no, not so much as a foot breadth; because I have given Mount Seir unto Esau for a possession." Deuteronomy 2:4, 5. The Edomites were descendants of Abraham and Isaac, and for the sake of these His servants, God had shown favor to the children of Esau. He had given them Mount Seir for a possession, and they were not to be disturbed unless by their sins they should place themselves beyond the reach of His mercy. The Hebrews were to dispossess and utterly destroy the inhabitants of Canaan, who had filled up the measure of their iniquity but the Edomites were still probationers, and as such were to be mercifully dealt with. God delights in mercy, and He manifests His compassion before He inflicts His judgments. He teaches Israel to spare the people of Edom, before requiring them to destroy the inhabitants of Canaan.

The ancestors of Edom and Israel were brothers, and brotherly kindness and courtesy should exist between them. The Israelites were forbidden, either then or at any future time, to revenge the affront given them in the refusal of passage through the land. They must not expect to possess any part of the land of Edom. While the Israelites were the chosen and favored people of God, they must heed the restrictions which He placed upon them. God had promised them a goodly inheritance; but they were not to feel that they alone had any rights in the earth, and seek to crowd out all others. They were directed, in all their intercourse with the Edomites, to beware of doing them injustice. They were to trade with them, buying such supplies as were needed, and promptly paying for all they received. As an encouragement to Israel to trust in God and obey His word they were reminded, "The Lord thy God hath blessed thee; ... thou hast lacked nothing." Deuteronomy 2:7. They were not dependent upon the Edomites, for they had a God rich in resources. They must not by force or fraud seek to obtain anything pertaining to them; but in all their intercourse they should exemplify the principle of the divine law, "Thou shalt love thy neighbor as thyself."

Had they in this manner passed through Edom, as God had purposed, the passage would have proved a blessing, not only to themselves, but to the inhabitants of the land; for it would have given them an opportunity to become acquainted with God's people and His worship and to witness how the God of Jacob prospered those who loved and feared Him . But all this the unbelief of Israel had prevented. God had given the people water in answer to their clamors, but He permitted their unbelief to work out its punishment. Again they must traverse the desert and quench their thirst from the miraculous spring, which, had they but trusted in Him , they would no longer have needed.

Accordingly the hosts of Israel again turned toward the south, and made their way over sterile wastes, that seemed even more dreary after a glimpse of the green spots among the hills and valleys of Edom. From the mountain range overlooking this gloomy desert, rises Mount Hor, whose summit was to be the place of Aaron's death and burial. When the Israelites came to this mountain, the divine command was addressed to Moses—

"Take Aaron and Eleazar his son, and bring them up unto Mount Hor: and strip Aaron of his garments, and put them upon Eleazar his son: and Aaron shall be gathered unto his people, and shall die there."

[425]

Together these two aged men and the younger one toiled up the mountain height. The heads of Moses and Aaron were white with the snows of sixscore winters. Their long and eventful lives had been marked with the deepest trials and the greatest honors that had ever fallen to the lot of man. They were men of great natural ability, and all their powers had been developed, exalted, and dignified by communion with the Infinite One. Their life had been spent in unselfish labor for God and their fellow men; their countenances gave evidence of great intellectual power, firmness and nobility of purpose, and strong affections.

Many years Moses and Aaron had stood side by side in their cares and labors. Together they had breasted unnumbered dangers, and had shared together the signal blessing of God; but the time was at hand when they must be separated. They moved on very slowly, for every moment in each other's society was precious. The ascent was steep and toilsome; and as they often paused to rest, they communed together of the past and the future. Before them, as far as the eye could reach, was spread out the scene of their desert wanderings. In the plain below were encamped the vast hosts of Israel, for whom these chosen men had spent the best portion of their lives; for whose welfare they had felt so deep an interest, and made so great sacrifices. Somewhere beyond the mountains of Edom was the path leading to the Promised Land—that land whose blessings Moses and Aaron were not to enjoy. No rebellious feelings found a place in their hearts, no expression of murmuring escaped their lips; yet a solemn sadness rested upon their countenances as they remembered what had debarred them from the inheritance of their fathers.

Aaron's work for Israel was done. Forty years before, at the age of eighty-three, God had called him to unite with Moses in his great and important mission. He had co-operated with his brother in leading the children of Israel from Egypt. He had held up the great leader's hands when the Hebrew hosts gave battle to Amalek. He had been permitted to ascend Mount Sinai, to approach into the presence of God, and to behold the divine glory. The Lord had conferred upon the family of Aaron the office of the priesthood, and had honored him with the sacred consecration of high priest. He had sustained him in the holy office by the terrible manifestations of divine judgment in the destruction of Korah and his company. It was through Aaron's intercession that the plague was stayed. When his two sons were slain for disregarding God's express command, he did not rebel or even murmur. Yet the record of his noble life had been marred. Aaron committed a grievous sin when he yielded to the clamors of the people and made the golden calf at Sinai; and again, when he united with Miriam in envy and murmuring against Moses. And he, with Moses, offended the Lord at Kadesh by disobeying the command to speak to the rock that it might give forth its water.

God intended that these great leaders of His people should be representatives of Christ. Aaron bore the names of Israel upon his breast. He communicated to the people the will of God. He entered the most holy place on the Day of Atonement, "not without blood," as a mediator for all Israel. He came forth from that work to bless the congregation, as Christ will come forth to bless His waiting people when His work of atonement in their behalf shall be ended. It was the exalted character of that sacred office as representative of our great High Priest that made Aaron's sin at Kadesh of so great magnitude.

With deep sorrow Moses removed from Aaron the holy vestments, and placed them upon Eleazar, who thus became his successor by divine appointment. For his sin at Kadesh, Aaron was denied the privilege of officiating as God's high priest in Canaan—of offering the first sacrifice in the goodly land, and thus consecrating the inheritance of Israel. Moses was to continue to bear his burden in leading the people to the very borders of Canaan. He was to come within sight of the Promised Land, but was not to enter it. Had these servants of God, when they stood before the rock at Kadesh, borne unmurmuringly the test there brought upon them, how different would have been their future! A wrong act can never be undone. It may be that the work of a lifetime will not recover what has been lost in a single moment of temptation or even thoughtlessness.

The absence from the camp of the two great leaders, and the fact that they had been accompanied by Eleazar, who, it was well known, was to be Aaron's successor in holy office, awakened a feeling of apprehension, and their return was anxiously awaited. As the people looked about them, upon their vast congregation, they saw that nearly all the adults who left Egypt had perished in the wilderness. All felt a foreboding of evil as they remembered the sentence pronounced against Moses and Aaron. Some were aware of the object of that mysterious journey to the summit of Mount Hor, and their solicitude for their leaders was heightened by bitter memories and self-accusings.

The forms of Moses and Eleazar were at last discerned, slowly descending the mountainside, but Aaron was not with them. Upon Eleazar were the sacerdotal garments, showing that he had succeeded his father in the sacred office. As the people with heavy hearts gathered about their leader, Moses told them that Aaron had died in his arms upon Mount Hor, and that they there buried him. The congregation broke forth in mourning and lamentation, for they all loved Aaron, though they had so often caused him sorrow. "They mourned for Aaron thirty days, even all the house of Israel."

Concerning the burial of Israel's high priest, the Scriptures give only the simple record, "There Aaron died, and there he was buried." Deuteronomy 10:6. In what striking contrast to the customs of the present day was this burial, conducted according to the express command of God. In modern times the funeral services of a man of high position are often made the occasion of ostentatious and extravagant display. When Aaron died, one of the most illustrious men that ever lived, there were only two of his nearest friends to witness his death and to attend his burial. And that lonely grave upon Mount Hor was forever hidden from the sight of Israel. God is not honored in the great display so often made over the dead, and the extravagant expense incurred in returning their bodies to the dust.

The whole congregation sorrowed for Aaron, yet they could not feel the loss so keenly as did Moses. The death of Aaron forcibly reminded Moses that his own end was near; but short as the time of his stay on earth must be, he deeply felt the loss of his constant companion—the one who had shared his joys and sorrows, his hopes and fears, for so many long years. Moses must now continue the work alone; but he knew that God was his friend, and upon Him he leaned more heavily.

[428] Soon after leaving Mount Hor the Israelites suffered defeat in an engagement with Arad, one of the Canaanite kings. But as they earnestly sought help from God, divine aid was granted them, and their enemies were routed. This victory, instead of inspiring gratitude and leading the people to feel their dependence upon God, made them boastful and self-confident. Soon they fell into the old habit of murmuring. They were now dissatisfied because the armies of Israel had not been permitted to advance upon Canaan immediately after their rebellion at the report of the spies nearly forty years before. They pronounced their long sojourn in the wilderness an unnecessary delay, reasoning that they might have conquered their enemies as easily heretofore as now.

As they continued their journey toward the south, their route lay through a hot, sandy valley, destitute of shade or vegetation. The way seemed long and difficult, and they suffered from weariness and thirst. Again they failed to endure the test of their faith and patience. By continually dwelling on the dark side of their experiences, they separated themselves farther and farther from God. They lost sight of the fact that but for their murmuring when the water ceased at Kadesh, they would have been spared the journey around Edom. God had purposed better things for them. Their hearts should have been filled with gratitude to Him that He had punished their sin so lightly. But instead of this, they flattered themselves that if God and Moses had not interfered, they might now have been in possession of the Promised Land. After bringing trouble upon themselves, making their lot altogether harder than God designed, they charged all their misfortunes upon Him. Thus they cherished bitter thoughts concerning His dealings with them, and finally they became discontented with everything. Egypt looked brighter and more desirable than liberty and the land to which God was leading them.

As the Israelites indulged the spirit of discontent, they were disposed to find fault even with their blessings. "And the people spake against God, and against Moses, Wherefore have ye brought us up out of Egypt to die in the wilderness? for there is no bread, neither is there any water; and our soul loatheth this light bread."

Moses faithfully set before the people their great sin. It was God's power alone that had preserved them in "that great and terrible wilderness, wherein were fiery serpents, and scorpions, and drought, where there was no water." Deuteronomy 8:15. Every day of their travels they had been kept by a miracle of divine mercy. In all the way of God's leading they had found water to refresh the thirsty, bread from heaven to satisfy their hunger, and peace and safety under the shadowy cloud by day and the pillar of fire by night. Angels had ministered to them as they climbed the rocky heights or threaded the rugged paths of the wilderness. Notwithstanding the hardships they had endured, there was not a feeble one in all their ranks. Their feet had not swollen in their long journeys, neither had their clothes grown old. God had subdued before them the fierce beasts of prey and the venomous reptiles of the forest and the desert. If with all these tokens of His love the people still continued to complain, the Lord would withdraw His protection until they should be led to appreciate His merciful care, and return to Him with repentance and humiliation.

Because they had been shielded by divine power they had not realized the countless dangers by which they were continually surrounded. In their ingratitude and unbelief they had anticipated death, and now the Lord permitted death to come upon them. The poisonous serpents that infested the wilderness were called fiery serpents, on account of the terrible effects produced by their sting, it causing violent inflammation and speedy death. As the protecting hand of God was removed from Israel, great numbers of the people were attacked by these venomous creatures.

Now there was terror and confusion throughout the encampment. In almost every tent were the dying or the dead. None were secure. Often the silence of night was broken by piercing cries that told of fresh victims. All were busy in ministering to the sufferers, or with agonizing care endeavoring to protect those who were not yet stricken. No murmuring now escaped their lips. When compared with the present suffering, their former difficulties and trials seemed unworthy of a thought.

The people now humbled themselves before God. They came to Moses with their confessions and entreaties. "We have sinned," they said, "for we have spoken against the Lord, and against thee." Only a little before, they had accused him of being their worst enemy, the cause of all their distress and afflictions. But even when the words were upon their lips, they knew that the charge was false; and as soon as real trouble came they fled to him as the only one who could intercede with God for them. "Pray unto the Lord," was their cry, "that He take away the serpents from us."

Moses was divinely commanded to make a serpent of brass resembling the living ones, and to elevate it among the people. To this, all who had been bitten were to look, and they would find relief. He did so, and the joyful news was sounded throughout the encampment that all who had been bitten might look upon the brazen serpent and live. Many had already died, and when Moses raised the serpent upon the pole, some would not believe that merely gazing upon that metallic image would heal them; these perished in their unbelief. Yet there were many who had faith in the provision which God had made. Fathers, mothers, brothers, and sisters were anxiously engaged in helping their suffering, dying friends to fix their languid eyes upon the serpent. If these, though faint and dying, could only once look, they were perfectly restored.

The people well knew that there was no power in the serpent of brass to cause such a change in those who looked upon it. The healing virtue was from God alone. In His wisdom He chose this way of displaying His power. By this simple means the people were made to realize that this affliction had been brought upon them by their sins. They were also assured that while obeying God they had no reason to fear, for He would preserve them.

The lifting up of the brazen serpent was to teach Israel an important lesson. They could not save themselves from the fatal effect of the poison in their wounds. God alone was able to heal them. Yet they were required to show their faith in the provision which He had made. They must look in order to live. It was their faith that was acceptable with God, and by looking upon the serpent their faith was shown. They knew that there was no virtue in the serpent itself, but it was a symbol of Christ; and the necessity of faith in His merits was thus presented to their minds. Heretofore many had brought their offerings to God, and had felt that in so doing they made ample atonement for their sins. They did not rely upon the Redeemer to come, of whom these offerings were only a type. The Lord would now teach them that their sacrifices, in themselves, had no more power or virtue than the serpent of brass, but were, like that, to lead their minds to Christ, the great sin offering.

"As Moses lifted up the serpent in the wilderness," even so was the Son of man "lifted up: that whosoever believeth in Him should not perish, but have eternal life." John 3:14, 15. All who have ever lived upon the earth have felt the deadly sting of "that old serpent, called the devil, and Satan." Revelation 12:9. The fatal effects of sin can be removed only by the provision that God has made. The Israelites saved their lives by looking upon the uplifted serpent. That look implied faith. They lived because they believed God's word, and trusted in the means provided for their recovery. So the sinner may look to Christ, and live. He receives pardon through faith in the atoning sacrifice. Unlike the inert and lifeless symbol, Christ has power and virtue in Himself to heal the repenting sinner.

[431]

While the sinner cannot save himself, he still has something to do to secure salvation. "Him that cometh to Me," says Christ, "I will in no wise cast out." John 6:37. But we must *come* to Him ; and when we repent of our sins, we must believe that He accepts and pardons us. Faith is the gift of God, but the power to exercise it is ours. Faith is the hand by which the soul takes hold upon the divine offers of grace and mercy.

Nothing but the righteousness of Christ can entitle us to one of the blessings of the covenant of grace. There are many who have long desired and tried to obtain these blessings, but have not received them, because they have cherished the idea that they could do something to make themselves worthy of them. They have not looked away from self, believing that Jesus is an all-sufficient Saviour. We must not think that our own merits will save us; Christ is our only hope of salvation. "For there is none other name under heaven given among men, whereby we must be saved." Acts 4:12.

When we trust God fully, when we rely upon the merits of Jesus as a sin-pardoning Saviour, we shall receive all the help that we can desire. Let none look to self, as though they had power to save themselves. Jesus died for us because we were helpless to do this. In Him is our hope, our justification, our righteousness. When we see our sinfulness we should not despond and fear that we have no Saviour, or that He has no thoughts of mercy toward us. At this very time He is inviting us to come to Him in our helplessness and be saved.

Many of the Israelites saw no help in the remedy which Heaven had appointed. The dead and dying were all around them, and they knew that, without divine aid, their own fate was certain; but they continued to lament their wounds, their pains, their sure death, until their strength was gone, and their eyes were glazed, when they might have had instant healing. If we are conscious of our needs, we should not devote all our powers to mourning over them. While we realize our helpless condition without Christ, we are not to yield to discouragement, but rely upon the merits of a crucified and risen Saviour. Look and live. Jesus has pledged His word; He will save all who come unto Him. Though millions who need to be healed will reject His offered mercy, not one who trusts in His merits will be left to perish.

Many are unwilling to accept of Christ until the whole mystery of the plan of salvation shall be made plain to them. They refuse the look of faith, although they see that thousands have looked, and have felt the efficacy of looking, to the cross of Christ. Many wander in the mazes of philosophy, in search of reasons and evidence which they will never find, while they reject the evidence which God has been pleased to give. They refuse to walk in the light of the Sun of Righteousness, until the reason of its shining shall be explained. All who persist in this course will fail to come to a knowledge of the truth. God will never remove every occasion for doubt. He gives sufficient evidence on which to base faith, and if this is not accepted, the mind is left in darkness. If those who were bitten by the serpents had stopped to doubt and question before they would consent to look, they would have perished. It is our duty, first, to look; and the look of faith will give us life.

Chapter 39—The Conquest of Bashan

This chapter is based on Deuteronomy 2; 3:1-11.

After passing to the south of Edom, the Israelites turned northward, and again set their faces toward the Promised Land. Their route now lay over a vast, elevated plain, swept by cool, fresh breezes from the hills. It was a welcome change from the parched valley through which they had been traveling, and they pressed forward, buoyant and hopeful. Having crossed the brook Zered, they passed to the east of the land of Moab; for the command had been given, "Distress not the Moabites, neither contend with them in battle: for I will not give thee of their land for a possession; because I have given Ar unto the children of Lot." And the same direction was repeated concerning the Ammonites, who were also descendants of Lot.

Still pushing northward, the hosts of Israel soon reached the country of the Amorites. This strong and warlike people originally occupied the southern part of the land of Canaan; but, increasing in numbers, they crossed the Jordan, made war upon the Moabites, and gained possession of a portion of their territory. Here they had settled, holding undisputed sway over all the land from the Arnon as far north as the Jabbok. The route to the Jordan which the Israelites desired to pursue lay directly through this territory, and Moses sent a friendly message to Sihon, the Amorite king, at his capital: "Let me pass through thy land: I will go along by the highway, I will neither turn unto the right hand nor to the left. Thou shalt sell me meat for money, that I may eat; and give me water for money, that I may drink: only I will pass through on my feet." The answer was a decided refusal, and all the hosts of the Amorites were summoned to oppose the progress of the invaders. This formidable army struck terror to the Israelites, who were poorly prepared for an encounter with well-armed and well-disciplined forces. So far as skill in warfare was concerned, their enemies had the advantage. To all human appearance, a speedy end would be made of Israel.

But Moses kept his gaze fixed upon the cloudy pillar, and encouraged the people with the thought that the token of God's presence was still with them. At the same time he directed them to do all that human power could do in preparing for war. Their enemies were eager for battle, and confident that they would blot out the unprepared Israelites from the land. But from the Possessor of all lands the mandate had gone forth to the leader of Israel: "Rise ye up, take your journey, and pass over the river Arnon: behold, I have given into thine hand Sihon the Amorite, king of Heshbon, and his land: begin to possess it, and contend with him in battle. This day will I begin to put the dread of thee and the fear of thee upon the nations that are under the whole heaven, who shall hear report of thee, and shall tremble, and be in anguish because of thee."

These nations on the borders of Canaan would have been spared, had they not stood, in defiance of God's word, to oppose the progress of Israel. The Lord had shown Himself to be long-suffering, of great kindness and tender pity, even to these heathen peoples. When Abraham was shown in vision that his seed, the children of Israel, should be strangers in a strange land four hundred years, the Lord gave him the promise, "In the fourth generation they shall come hither again: for the iniquity of the Amorites is not yet full." Genesis 15:16. Although the Amorites were idolaters, whose life was justly forfeited by their great wickedness, God spared them four hundred years to give them unmistakable evidence that He was the only true God, the Maker of heaven and earth. All His wonders in bringing Israel from Egypt were known to them. Sufficient evidence was given; they might have known the truth, had they been willing to turn from their idolatry and licentiousness. But they rejected the light and clung to their idols.

When the Lord brought His people a second time to the borders of Canaan, additional evidence of His power was granted to those heathen nations. They saw that God was with Israel in the victory gained over King Arad and the Canaanites, and in the miracle wrought to save those who were perishing from the sting of the serpents. Although the Israelites had been refused a passage through the land of Edom, thus being compelled to take the long and difficult route by the Red Sea, yet in all their journeyings and encampments, past the land of Edom, of Moab and Ammon, they had shown no hostility, and had done no injury to the people or their possessions. On reaching the border of the Amorites, Israel had asked permission only to travel directly through the country, promising to observe the same rules that had governed their intercourse with other nations. When the Amorite king refused this courteous solicitation, and defiantly gathered his hosts for battle, their cup of iniquity was full, and God would now exercise His power for their overthrow.

The Israelites crossed the river Arnon and advanced upon the foe. An engagement took place, in which the armies of Israel were victorious; and, following up the advantage gained, they were soon in possession of the country of the Amorites. It was the Captain of the Lord's host who vanquished the enemies of His people; and He would have done the same thirty-eight years before had Israel trusted in Him.

Filled with hope and courage, the army of Israel eagerly pressed forward, and, still journeying northward, they soon reached a country that might well test their courage and their faith in God. Before them lay the powerful and populous kingdom of Bashan, crowded with great stone cities that to this day excite the wonder of the world—"threescore cities ... with high walls, gates, and bars; besides unwalled towns a great many." Deuteronomy 3:1-11. The houses were constructed of huge black stones, of such stupendous size as to make the buildings absolutely impregnable to any force that in those times could have been brought against them. It was a country filled with wild caverns, lofty precipices, yawning gulfs, and rocky strongholds. The inhabitants of this land, descendants from a giant race, were themselves of marvelous size and strength, and so distinguished for violence and cruelty as to be the terror of all surrounding nations; while Og, the king of the country, was remarkable for size and prowess, even in a nation of giants.

But the cloudy pillar moved forward, and following its guidance the Hebrew hosts advanced to Edrei, where the giant king, with his forces, awaited their approach. Og had skillfully chosen the place of battle. The city of Edrei was situated upon the border of a tableland rising abruptly from the plain, and covered with jagged, volcanic rocks. It could be approached only by narrow pathways, steep and difficult of ascent. In case of defeat, his forces could find refuge in

[436]

that wilderness of rocks, where it would be impossible for strangers to follow them.

Confident of success, the king came forth with an immense army upon the open plain, while shouts of defiance were heard from the tableland above, where might be seen the spears of thousands, eager for the fray. When the Hebrews looked upon the lofty form of that giant of giants towering above the soldiers of his army; when they saw the hosts that surrounded him, and beheld the seemingly impregnable fortress, behind which unseen thousands were entrenched, the hearts of many in Israel quaked with fear. But Moses was calm and firm; the Lord had said concerning the king of Bashan, "Fear him not: for I will deliver him, and all his people, and his land, into thy hand; and thou shalt do unto him as thou didst unto Sihon king of the Amorites, which dwelt at Heshbon."

The calm faith of their leader inspired the people with confidence in God. They trusted all to His omnipotent arm, and He did not fail them. Not mighty giants nor walled cities, armed hosts nor rocky fortresses, could stand before the Captain of the Lord's host. The Lord led the army; the Lord discomfited the enemy; the Lord conquered in behalf of Israel. The giant king and his army were destroyed, and the Israelites soon took possession of the whole country. Thus was blotted from the earth that strange people who had given themselves up to iniquity and abominable idolatry.

In the conquest of Gilead and Bashan there were many who recalled the events which nearly forty years before had, in Kadesh, doomed Israel to the long desert wandering. They saw that the report of the spies concerning the Promised Land was in many respects correct. The cities were walled and very great, and were inhabited by giants, in comparison with whom the Hebrews were mere pygmies. But they could now see that the fatal mistake of their fathers had been in distrusting the power of God. This alone had prevented them from at once entering the goodly land.

When they were at the first preparing to enter Canaan, the undertaking was attended with far less difficulty than now. God had promised His people that if they would obey His voice He would go before them and fight for them; and He would also send hornets to drive out the inhabitants of the land. The fears of the nations had not been generally aroused, and little preparation had been made to oppose their progress. But when the Lord now bade Israel go forward, they must advance against alert and powerful foes, and must contend with large and well-trained armies that had been preparing to resist their approach.

In their contest with Og and Sihon the people were brought to the same test beneath which their fathers had so signally failed. But the trial was now far more severe than when God had commanded Israel to go forward. The difficulties in their way had greatly increased since they refused to advance when bidden to do so in the name of the Lord. It is thus that God still tests His people. And if they fail to endure the trial, He brings them again to the same point, and the second time the trial will come closer, and be more severe than the preceding. This is continued until they bear the test, or, if they are still rebellious, God withdraws His light from them and leaves them in darkness.

The Hebrews now remembered how once before, when their forces had gone to battle, they had been routed, and thousands slain. But they had then gone in direct opposition to the command of God. They had gone out without Moses, God's appointed leader, without the cloudy pillar, the symbol of the divine presence, and without the ark. But now Moses was with them, strengthening their hearts with words of hope and faith; the Son of God, enshrined in the cloudy pillar, led the way; and the sacred ark accompanied the host. This experience has a lesson for us. The mighty God of Israel is our God. In Him we may trust, and if we obey His requirements He will work for us in as signal a manner as He did for His ancient people. Everyone who seeks to follow the path of duty will at times be assailed by doubt and unbelief. The way will sometimes be so barred by obstacles, apparently insurmountable, as to dishearten those who will yield to discouragement; but God is saying to such, Go forward. Do your duty at any cost. The difficulties that seem so formidable, that fill your soul with dread, will vanish as you move forward in the path of obedience, humbly trusting in God.

[438] # Chapter 40—Balaam

This chapter is based on Numbers 22 to 24.

Returning to the Jordan from the conquest of Bashan, the Israelites, in preparation for the immediate invasion of Canaan, encamped beside the river, above its entrance into the Dead Sea, and just opposite the plain of Jericho. They were upon the very borders of Moab, and the Moabites were filled with terror at the close proximity of the invaders.

The people of Moab had not been molested by Israel, yet they had watched with troubled forebodings all that had taken place in the surrounding countries. The Amorites, before whom they had been forced to retreat, had been conquered by the Hebrews, and the territory which the Amorites had wrested from Moab was now in the possession of Israel. The hosts of Bashan had yielded before the mysterious power enshrouded in the cloudy pillar, and the giant strongholds were occupied by the Hebrews. The Moabites dared not risk an attack upon them; an appeal to arms was hopeless in face of the supernatural agencies that wrought in their behalf. But they determined, as Pharaoh had done, to enlist the power of sorcery to counteract the work of God. They would bring a curse upon Israel.

The people of Moab were closely connected with the Midianites, both by the ties of nationality and religion. And Balak, the king of Moab, aroused the fears of the kindred people, and secured their co-operation in his designs against Israel by the message, "Now shall this company lick up all that are round about us, as the ox licketh up the grass of the field." Balaam, an inhabitant of Mesopotamia, was reported to possess supernatural powers, and his fame had reached to the land of Moab. It was determined to call him to their aid. Accordingly, messengers of "the elders of Moab and the elders of Midian," were sent to secure his divinations and enchantments against Israel.

[439] The ambassadors at once set out on their long journey over the

mountains and across the deserts to Mesopotamia; and upon finding Balaam, they delivered to him the message of their king: "Behold, there is a people come out from Egypt: behold, they cover the face of the earth, and they abide over against me: come now therefore, I pray thee, curse me this people; for they are too mighty for me: peradventure I shall prevail, that we may smite them, and that I may drive them out of the land: for I wot that he whom thou blessest is blessed, and he whom thou cursest is cursed."

Balaam was once a good man and a prophet of God; but he had apostatized, and had given himself up to covetousness; yet he still professed to be a servant of the Most High. He was not ignorant of God's work in behalf of Israel; and when the messengers announced their errand, he well knew that it was his duty to refuse the rewards of Balak and to dismiss the ambassadors. But he ventured to dally with temptation, and urged the messengers to tarry with him that night, declaring that he could give no decided answer till he had asked counsel of the Lord. Balaam knew that his curse could not harm Israel. God was on their side, and so long as they were true to Him no adverse power of earth or hell could prevail against them. But his pride was flattered by the words of the ambassadors, "He whom thou blessest is blessed, and he whom thou cursest is cursed." The bribe of costly gifts and prospective exaltation excited his covetousness. He greedily accepted the offered treasures, and then, while professing strict obedience to the will of God, he tried to comply with the desires of Balak.

In the night season the angel of God came to Balaam with the message, "Thou shalt not go with them; thou shalt not curse the people: for they are blessed."

In the morning Balaam reluctantly dismissed the messengers, but he did not tell them what the Lord had said. Angry that his visions of gain and honor had been suddenly dispelled, he petulantly exclaimed, "Get you into your land: for the Lord refuseth to give me leave to go with you."

Balaam "loved the wages of unrighteousness." 2 Peter 2:15. The sin of covetousness, which God declares to be idolatry, had made him a timeserver, and through this one fault Satan gained entire control of him. It was this that caused his ruin. The tempter is ever presenting worldly gain and honor to entice men from the service of God. He tells them it is their overconscientiousness that keeps them from prosperity. Thus many are induced to venture out of the path of strict integrity. One wrong step makes the next easier, and they become more and more presumptuous. They will do and dare most terrible things when once they have given themselves to the control of avarice and a desire for power. Many flatter themselves that they can depart from strict integrity for a time, for the sake of some worldly advantage, and that having gained their object, they can change their course when they please. Such are entangling themselves in the snare of Satan, and it is seldom that they escape.

When the messengers reported to Balak the prophet's refusal to accompany them, they did not intimate that God had forbidden him. Supposing that Balaam's delay was merely to secure a richer reward, the king sent princes more in number and more honorable than the first, with promises of higher honors, and with authority to concede to any terms that Balaam might demand. Balak's urgent message to the prophet was, "Let nothing, I pray thee, hinder thee from coming unto me: for I will promote thee unto very great honor, and I will do whatsoever thou sayest unto me: come therefore, I pray thee, curse me this people."

A second time Balaam was tested. In response to the solicitations of the ambassadors he professed great conscientiousness and integrity, assuring them that no amount of gold and silver could induce him to go contrary to the will of God. But he longed to comply with the king's request; and although the will of God had already been definitely made known to him, he urged the messengers to tarry, that he might further inquire of God; as though the Infinite One were a man, to be persuaded.

In the night season the Lord appeared to Balaam and said, "If the men come to call thee, rise up, and go with them; but yet the word which I shall say unto thee, that shalt thou do." Thus far the Lord would permit Balaam to follow his own will, because he was determined upon it. He did not seek to do the will of God, but chose his own course, and then endeavored to secure the sanction of the Lord.

There are thousands at the present day who are pursuing a similar course. They would have no difficulty in understanding their duty if it were in harmony with their inclinations. It is plainly set before them in the Bible or is clearly indicated by circumstances and reason. But because these evidences are contrary to their desires and inclinations they frequently set them aside and presume to go to God to learn their duty. With great apparent conscientiousness they pray long and earnestly for light. But God will not be trifled with. He often permits such persons to follow their own desires and to suffer the result. "My people would not hearken to My voice.... So I gave them up unto their own hearts' lust: and they walked in their own counsels." Psalm 81:11, 12. When one clearly sees a duty, let him not presume to go to God with the prayer that he may be excused from performing it. He should rather, with a humble, submissive spirit, ask for divine strength and wisdom to meet its claims.

The Moabites were a degraded, idolatrous people; yet according to the light which they had received their guilt was not so great in the sight of heaven as was that of Balaam. As he professed to be God's prophet, however, all he should say would be supposed to be uttered by divine authority. Hence he was not to be permitted to speak as he chose, but must deliver the message which God should give him. "The word which I shall say unto thee, that shalt thou do," was the divine command.

Balaam had received permission to go with the messengers from Moab if they came in the morning to call him. But, annoyed at his delay, and expecting another refusal, they set out on their homeward journey without further consultation with him. Every excuse for complying with the request of Balak had now been removed. But Balaam was determined to secure the reward; and, taking the beast upon which he was accustomed to ride, he set out on the journey. He feared that even now the divine permission might be withdrawn, and he pressed eagerly forward, impatient lest he should by some means fail to gain the coveted reward.

But "the angel of the Lord stood in the way for an adversary against him." The animal saw the divine messenger, who was unperceived by the man, and turned aside from the highway into a field. With cruel blows Balaam brought the beast back into the path; but again, in a narrow place shut in by walls, the angel appeared, and the animal, trying to avoid the menacing figure, crushed her master's foot against the wall. Balaam was blinded to the heavenly interposition, and knew not that God was obstructing his path. The

[442]

man became exasperated, and beating the ass unmercifully, forced it to proceed.

Again, "in a narrow place, where was no way to turn either to the right hand or to the left," the angel appeared, as before, in a threatening attitude; and the poor beast, trembling with terror, made a full stop, and fell to the earth under its rider. Balaam's rage was unbounded, and with his staff he smote the animal more cruelly than before. God now opened its mouth, and by "the dumb ass speaking with man's voice," he "forbade the madness of the prophet." 2 Peter 2:16. "What have I done unto thee," it said, "that thou hast smitten me these three times?"

Furious at being thus hindered in his journey, Balaam answered the beast as he would have addressed an intelligent being—"Because thou hast mocked me: I would there were a sword in mine hand, for now would I kill thee." Here was a professed magician, on his way to pronounce a curse upon a whole people with the intent to paralyze their strength, while he had not power even to slay the animal upon which he rode!

The eyes of Balaam were now opened, and he beheld the angel of God standing with drawn sword ready to slay him. In terror "he bowed down his head, and fell flat on his face." The angel said to him, "Wherefore hast thou smitten thine ass these three times? Behold, I went out to withstand thee, because thy way is perverse before me: and the ass saw me, and turned from me these three times: unless she had turned from me surely now also I had slain thee, and saved her alive."

Balaam owed the preservation of his life to the poor animal that he had treated so cruelly. The man who claimed to be a prophet of the Lord, who declared that his eyes were open, and he saw the "vision of the Almighty," was so blinded by covetousness and ambition that he could not discern the angel of God visible to his beast. "The god of this world hath blinded the minds of them which believe not." 2 Corinthians 4:4. How many are thus blinded! They rush on in forbidden paths, transgressing the divine law, and cannot discern that God and His angels are against them. Like Balaam they are angry at those who would prevent their ruin.

Balaam had given evidence of the spirit that controlled him, by his treatment of his beast. "A righteous man regardeth the life of his beast: but the tender mercies of the wicked are cruel." Proverbs 12:10. Few realize as they should the sinfulness of abusing animals or leaving them to suffer from neglect. He who created man made the lower animals also, and "His tender mercies are over all His works." Psalm 145:9. The animals were created to serve man, but he has no right to cause them pain by harsh treatment or cruel exaction.

It is because of man's sin that "the whole creation groaneth and travaileth in pain together." Romans 8:22. Suffering and death were thus entailed, not only upon the human race, but upon the animals. Surely, then, it becomes man to seek to lighten, instead of increasing, the weight of suffering which his transgression has brought upon God's creatures. He who will abuse animals because he has them in his power is both a coward and a tyrant. A disposition to cause pain, whether to our fellow men or to the brute creation, is satanic. Many do not realize that their cruelty will ever be known, because the poor dumb animals cannot reveal it. But could the eyes of these men be opened, as were those of Balaam, they would see an angel of God standing as a witness, to testify against them in the courts above. A record goes up to heaven, and a day is coming when judgment will be pronounced against those who abuse God's creatures.

When he beheld the messenger of God, Balaam exclaimed in terror, "I have sinned; for I knew not that thou stoodest in the way against me: now therefore, if it displease thee, I will get me back again." The Lord suffered him to proceed on his journey, but gave him to understand that his words should be controlled by divine power. God would give evidence to Moab that the Hebrews were under the guardianship of Heaven, and this He did effectually when He showed them how powerless Balaam was even to utter a curse against them without divine permission.

The king of Moab, being informed of the approach of Balaam, went out with a large retinue to the borders of his kingdom, to receive him. When he expressed his astonishment at Balaam's delay, in view of the rich rewards awaiting him, the prophet's answer was, "Lo, I am come unto thee: have I now any power at all to say anything? the word that God putteth in my mouth, that shall I speak." Balaam greatly regretted this restriction; he feared that his purpose could not be carried out, because the Lord's controlling power was upon him.

With great pomp the king, with the chief dignitaries of his kingdom, escorted Balaam to "the high places of Baal," from which he could survey the Hebrew host. Behold the prophet as he stands upon the lofty height, looking down over the encampment of God's chosen people. How little do the Israelites know of what is taking place so near them! How little do they know of the care of God, extended over them by day and by night! How dull are the perceptions of God's people! How slow are they, in every age, to comprehend His great love and mercy! If they could discern the wonderful power of God constantly exerted in their behalf, would not their hearts be filled with gratitude for His love, and with awe at the thought of His majesty and power?

Balaam had some knowledge of the sacrificial offerings of the Hebrews, and he hoped that by surpassing them in costly gifts he might secure the blessing of God and ensure the accomplishment of his sinful projects. Thus the sentiments of the idolatrous Moabites were gaining control of his mind. His wisdom had become foolishness; his spiritual vision was beclouded; he had brought blindness upon himself by yielding to the power of Satan.

By Balaam's direction seven altars were erected, and he offered a sacrifice upon each. He then withdrew to a "high place," to meet with God, promising to make known to Balak whatever the Lord should reveal.

With the nobles and princes of Moab the king stood beside the sacrifice, while around them gathered the eager multitude, watching for the return of the prophet. He came at last, and the people waited for the words that should paralyze forever that strange power exerted in behalf of the hated Israelites. Balaam said:

> "The king of Moab hath brought me from Aram,
>   Out of the mountains of the east,
> Saying, Come, curse me Jacob,
>   And come, defy Israel.
> How shall I curse, whom God hath not cursed?
>   Or how shall I defy, whom the Lord hath not defied?
> For from the top of the rocks I see him,
>   And from the hills I behold him:
> Lo, the people shall dwell alone,

And shall not be reckoned among the nations.
Who can count the dust of Jacob,
And the number of the fourth part of Israel?
Let me die the death of the righteous,
And let my last end be like his!"

Balaam confessed that he came with the purpose of cursing Israel, but the words he uttered were directly contrary to the sentiments of his heart. He was constrained to pronounce blessings, while his soul was filled with curses.

As Balaam looked upon the encampment of Israel he beheld with astonishment the evidence of their prosperity. They had been represented to him as a rude, disorganized multitude, infesting the country in roving bands that were a pest and terror to the surrounding nations; but their appearance was the reverse of all this. He saw the vast extent and perfect arrangement of their camp, everything bearing the marks of thorough discipline and order. He was shown the favor with which God regarded Israel, and their distinctive character as His chosen people. They were not to stand upon a level with other nations, but to be exalted above them all. "The people shall dwell alone, and shall not be reckoned among the nations." At the time when these words were spoken the Israelites had no permanent settlement, and their peculiar character, their manners and customs, were not familiar to Balaam. But how strikingly was this prophecy fulfilled in the afterhistory of Israel! Through all the years of their captivity, through all the ages since they were dispersed among the nations, they have remained a distinct people. So the people of God—the true Israel—though scattered throughout all nations, are on earth but sojourners, whose citizenship is in heaven.

Not only was Balaam shown the history of the Hebrew people as a nation, but he beheld the increase and prosperity of the true Israel of God to the close of time. He saw the special favor of the Most High attending those who love and fear Him . He saw them supported by His arm as they enter the dark valley of the shadow of death. And he behold them coming forth from their graves, crowned with glory, honor, and immortality. He saw the redeemed rejoicing in the unfading glories of the earth made new. Gazing upon the scene, he exclaimed, "Who can count the dust of Jacob, and the number of the fourth part of Israel?" And as he saw the crown of glory on every brow, the joy beaming from every countenance, and looked forward to that endless life of unalloyed happiness, he uttered the solemn prayer, "Let me die the death of the righteous, and let my last end be like his!"

[448] If Balaam had had a disposition to accept the light that God had given, he would now have made true his words; he would at once have severed all connection with Moab. He would no longer have presumed upon the mercy of God, but would have returned to Him with deep repentance. But Balaam loved the wages of unrighteousness, and these he was determined to secure.

Balak had confidently expected a curse that would fall like a withering blight upon Israel; and at the words of the prophet he passionately exclaimed, "What hast thou done unto me? I took thee to curse mine enemies, and, behold, thou hast blessed them altogether." Balaam, seeking to make a virtue of necessity, professed to have spoken from a conscientious regard for the will of God the words that had been forced from his lips by divine power. His answer was, "Must I not take heed to speak that which the Lord hath put in my mouth?"

Balak could not even now relinquish his purpose. He decided that the imposing spectacle presented by the vast encampment of the Hebrews had so intimidated Balaam that he dared not practice his divinations against them. The king determined to take the prophet to some point where only a small part of the host might be seen. If Balaam could be induced to curse them in detached parties, the whole camp would soon be devoted to destruction. On the top of an elevation called Pisgah another trial was made. Again seven altars were erected, whereon were placed the same offerings as at the first. The king and his princes remained by the sacrifices, while Balaam retired to meet with God. Again the prophet was entrusted with a divine message, which he was powerless to alter or withhold.

When he appeared to the anxious, expectant company the question was put to him, "What hath the Lord spoken?" The answer, as before, struck terror to the heart of king and princes:

"God is not a man, that He should lie;
   Neither the son of man, that He should repent:

Hath He said, and shall He not do it?
> Or hath He spoken, and shall He not make it good?

Behold, I have received commandment to bless:
> And He hath blessed; and I cannot reverse it.

He hath not beheld iniquity in Jacob,
> Neither hath He seen perverseness in Israel:

The Lord his God is with him,
> And the shout of a king is among them."

Awed by these revelations, Balaam exclaimed, "Surely there is no enchantment against Jacob, neither is there any divination against Israel." The great magician had tried his power of enchantment, in accordance with the desire of the Moabites; but concerning this very occasion it should be said of Israel, "What hath God wrought!" While they were under the divine protection, no people or nation, though aided by all the power of Satan, should be able to prevail against them. All the world should wonder at the marvelous work of God in behalf of His people—that a man determined to pursue a sinful course should be so controlled by divine power as to utter, instead of imprecations, the richest and most precious promises, in the language of sublime and impassioned poetry. And the favor of God at this time manifested toward Israel was to be an assurance of His protecting care for His obedient, faithful children in all ages. When Satan should inspire evil men to misrepresent, harass, and destroy God's people, this very occurrence would be brought to their remembrance, and would strengthen their courage and their faith in God. [449]

The king of Moab, disheartened and distressed, exclaimed, "Neither curse them at all, nor bless them at all." Yet a faint hope still lingered in his heart, and he determined to make another trial. He now conducted Balaam to Mount Peor, where was a temple devoted to the licentious worship of Baal, their god. Here the same number of altars were erected as before, and the same number of sacrifices were offered; but Balaam went not alone, as at other times, to learn God's will. He made no pretense of sorcery, but standing beside the altars, he looked abroad upon the tents of Israel. Again the Spirit of God rested upon him, and the divine message came from his lips:

"How goodly are thy tents, O Jacob,
 And thy tabernacles, O Israel!
As the valleys are they spread forth, as gardens by the river's side,
 As the trees of lignaloes which the Lord hath planted, and as cedar
trees beside the waters.
 He shall pour the water out of his buckets, and his seed shall be in
many waters,
 And his King shall be higher than Agag, and his kingdom shall be
exalted....
 He couched, he lay down as a lion, and as a great lion: who shall
stir him up?
 Blessed is he that blesseth thee, and cursed is he that curseth thee."

[450] The prosperity of God's people is here represented by some of the most beautiful figures to be found in nature. The prophet likens Israel to fertile valleys covered with abundant harvests; to flourishing gardens watered by never-failing springs; to the fragrant sandal tree and the stately cedar. The figure last mentioned is one of the most strikingly beautiful and appropriate to be found in the inspired word. The cedar of Lebanon was honored by all the people of the East. The class of trees to which it belongs is found wherever man has gone throughout the earth. From the arctic regions to the tropic zone they flourish, rejoicing in the heat, yet braving the cold; springing in rich luxuriance by the riverside, yet towering aloft upon the parched and thirsty waste. They plant their roots deep among the rocks of the mountains and boldly stand in defiance of the tempest. Their leaves are fresh and green when all else has perished at the breath of winter. Above all other trees the cedar of Lebanon is distinguished for its strength, its firmness, its undecaying vigor; and this is used as a symbol of those whose life is "hid with Christ in God." Colossians 3:3. Says the Scripture, "The righteous ... shall grow like a cedar." Psalm 92:12. The divine hand has exalted the cedar as king over

the forest. "The fir trees were not like his boughs, and the chestnut trees were not like his branches" (Ezekiel 31:8); nor any tree in the garden of God. The cedar is repeatedly employed as an emblem of royalty, and its use in Scripture to represent the righteous shows how heaven regards those who do the will of God.

Balaam prophesied that Israel's King would be greater and more powerful than Agag. This was the name given to the kings of the Amalekites, who were at this time a very powerful nation; but Israel, if true to God, would subdue all her enemies. The King of Israel was the Son of God; and His throne was one day to be established in the earth, and His power to be exalted above all earthly kingdoms.

As he listened to the prophet's words Balak was overwhelmed with disappointed hope, with fear and rage. He was indignant that Balaam could have given him the least encouragement of a favorable response, when everything was determined against him. He regarded with scorn the prophet's compromising, deceptive course. The king exclaimed fiercely, "Therefore now flee thou to thy place: I thought to promote thee unto great honor; but, lo, the Lord hath kept thee back from honor." The answer was that the king had been forewarned that Balaam could speak only the message given him from God.

Before returning to his people, Balaam uttered a most beautiful and sublime prophecy of the world's Redeemer and the final destruction of the enemies of God: "I shall see Him , but not now: I shall behold Him , but not nigh:

There shall come a Star out of Jacob, and a Scepter shall rise out of
Israel,
And shall smite the corners of Moab, and destroy all the children of
Sheth."

And he closed by predicting the complete destruction of Moab and Edom, of Amalek and the Kenites, thus leaving to the Moabitish king no ray of hope.

Disappointed in his hopes of wealth and promotion, in disfavor with the king, and conscious that he had incurred the displeasure of God, Balaam returned from his self-chosen mission. After he had reached his home the controlling power of the Spirit of God left him, and his covetousness, which had been merely held in check, prevailed. He was ready to resort to any means to gain the reward promised by Balak. Balaam knew that the prosperity of Israel depended upon their obedience to God, and that there was no way to cause their overthrow but by seducing them into sin. He now decided to secure Balak's favor by advising the Moabites of the course to be pursued to bring a curse upon Israel.

He immediately returned to the land of Moab and laid his plans before the king. The Moabites themselves were convinced that so long as Israel remained true to God, He would be their shield. The plan proposed by Balaam was to separate them from God by enticing them into idolatry. If they could be led to engage in the licentious worship of Baal and Ashtaroth, their omnipotent Protector would become their enemy, and they would soon fall a prey to the fierce, warlike nations around them. This plan was readily accepted by the king, and Balaam himself remained to assist in carrying it into effect.

Balaam witnessed the success of his diabolical scheme. He saw the curse of God visited upon His people, and thousands falling under His judgments; but the divine justice that punished sin in Israel did not permit the tempters to escape. In the war of Israel against the Midianites, Balaam was slain. He had felt a presentiment that his own end was near when he exclaimed, "Let me die the death of the righteous, and let my last end be like his!" But he had not chosen to live the life of the righteous, and his destiny was fixed with the enemies of God.

The fate of Balaam was similar to that of Judas, and their characters bear a marked resemblance to each other. Both these men tried to unite the service of God and mammon, and met with signal failure. Balaam acknowledged the true God, and professed to serve Him ; Judas believed in Jesus as the Messiah, and united with His followers. But Balaam hoped to make the service of Jehovah the steppingstone to the acquirement of riches and worldly honor; and failing in this he stumbled and fell and was broken. Judas expected by his connection with Christ to secure wealth and promotion in that worldly kingdom which, as he believed, the Messiah was about to set up. The failure of his hopes drove him to apostasy and ruin.

Both Balaam and Judas had received great light and enjoyed special privileges, but a single cherished sin poisoned the entire character and caused their destruction.

It is a perilous thing to allow an unchristian trait to live in the heart. One cherished sin will, little by little, debase the character, bringing all its nobler powers into subjection to the evil desire. The removal of one safeguard from the conscience, the indulgence of one evil habit, one neglect of the high claims of duty, breaks down the defenses of the soul and opens the way for Satan to come in and lead us astray. The only safe course is to let our prayers go forth daily from a sincere heart, as did David, "Hold up my goings in Thy paths, that my footsteps slip not." Psalm 17:5.

Chapter 41—Apostasy at the Jordan

This chapter is based on Numbers 25.

With joyful hearts and renewed faith in God, the victorious armies of Israel had returned from Bashan. They had already gained possession of a valuable territory, and they were confident of the immediate conquest of Canaan. Only the river Jordan lay between them and the Promised Land. Just across the river was a rich plain, covered with verdure, watered with streams from copious fountains, and shaded by luxuriant palm trees. On the western border of the plain rose the towers and palaces of Jericho, so embosomed in its palm-tree groves that it was called "the city of palm trees."

On the eastern side of Jordan, between the river and the high tableland which they had been traversing, was also a plain, several miles in width and extending some distance along the river. This sheltered valley had the climate of the tropics; here flourished the shittim, or acacia, tree, giving to the plain the name, "Vale of Shittim." It was here that the Israelites encamped, and in the acacia groves by the riverside they found an agreeable retreat.

But amid these attractive surroundings they were to encounter an evil more deadly than mighty hosts of armed men or the wild beasts of the wilderness. That country, so rich in natural advantages, had been defiled by the inhabitants. In the public worship of Baal, the leading deity, the most degrading and iniquitous scenes were constantly enacted. On every side were places noted for idolatry and licentiousness, the very names being suggestive of the vileness and corruption of the people.

These surroundings exerted a polluting influence upon the Israelites. Their minds became familiar with the vile thoughts constantly suggested; their life of ease and inaction produced its demoralizing effect; and almost unconsciously to themselves they were departing from God and coming into a condition where they would fall an easy prey to temptation.

During the time of their encampment beside Jordan, Moses was preparing for the occupation of Canaan. In this work the great leader was fully employed; but to the people this time of suspense and expectation was most trying, and before many weeks had elapsed their history was marred by the most frightful departures from virtue and integrity.

At first there was little intercourse between the Israelites and their heathen neighbors, but after a time Midianitish women began to steal into the camp. Their appearance excited no alarm, and so quietly were their plans conducted that the attention of Moses was not called to the matter. It was the object of these women, in their association with the Hebrews, to seduce them into transgression of the law of God, to draw their attention to heathen rites and customs, and lead them into idolatry. These motives were studiously concealed under the garb of friendship, so that they were not suspected, even by the guardians of the people.

At Balaam's suggestion, a grand festival in honor of their gods was appointed by the king of Moab, and it was secretly arranged that Balaam should induce the Israelites to attend. He was regarded by them as a prophet of God, and hence had little difficulty in accomplishing his purpose. Great numbers of the people joined him in witnessing the festivities. They ventured upon the forbidden ground, and were entangled in the snare of Satan. Beguiled with music and dancing, and allured by the beauty of heathen vestals, they cast off their fealty to Jehovah. As they united in mirth and feasting, indulgence in wine beclouded their senses and broke down the barriers of self-control. Passion had full sway; and having defiled their consciences by lewdness, they were persuaded to bow down to idols. They offered sacrifice upon heathen altars and participated in the most degrading rites.

It was not long before the poison had spread, like a deadly infection, through the camp of Israel. Those who would have conquered their enemies in battle were overcome by the wiles of heathen women. The people seemed to be infatuated. The rulers and the leading men were among the first to transgress, and so many of the people were guilty that the apostasy became national. "Israel joined himself unto Baalpeor." When Moses was aroused to perceive the evil, the plots of their enemies had been so successful that not only were the Israelites participating in the licentious worship at Mount Peor, but the heathen rites were coming to be observed in the camp of Israel. The aged leader was filled with indignation, and the wrath of God was kindled.

Their iniquitous practices did that for Israel which all the enchantments of Balaam could not do—they separated them from God. By swift-coming judgments the people were awakened to the enormity of their sin. A terrible pestilence broke out in the camp, to which tens of thousands speedily fell a prey. God commanded that the leaders in this apostasy be put to death by the magistrates. This order was promptly obeyed. The offenders were slain, then their bodies were hung up in sight of all Israel that the congregation, seeing the leaders so severely dealt with, might have a deep sense of God's abhorrence of their sin and the terror of His wrath against them.

All felt that the punishment was just, and the people hastened to the tabernacle, and with tears and deep humiliation confessed their sin. While they were thus weeping before God, at the door of the tabernacle, while the plague was still doing its work of death, and the magistrates were executing their terrible commission, Zimri, one of the nobles of Israel, came boldly into the camp, accompanied by a Midianitish harlot, a princess "of a chief house in Midian," whom he escorted to his tent. Never was vice bolder or more stubborn. Inflamed with wine, Zimri declared his "sin as Sodom," and gloried in his shame. The priests and leaders had prostrated themselves in grief and humiliation, weeping "between the porch and the altar," and entreating the Lord to spare His people, and give not His heritage to reproach, when this prince in Israel flaunted his sin in the sight of the congregation, as if to defy the vengeance of God and mock the judges of the nation. Phinehas, the son of Eleazar the high priest, rose up from among the congregation, and seizing a javelin, "he went after the man of Israel into the tent," and slew them both. Thus the plague was stayed, while the priest who had executed the divine judgment was honored before all Israel, and the priesthood was confirmed to him and to his house forever.

Phinehas "hath turned My wrath away from the children of Israel," was the divine message; "wherefore say, Behold, I give unto him My covenant of peace: and he shall have it, and his seed after him, even the covenant of an everlasting priesthood; because he was zealous for his God, and made an atonement for the children of Israel."

The judgments visited upon Israel for their sin at Shittim, destroyed the survivors of that vast company, who, nearly forty years before, had incurred the sentence, "They shall surely die in the wilderness." The numbering of the people by divine direction, during their encampment on the plains of Jordan, showed that "of them whom Moses and Aaron the priest numbered, when they numbered the children of Israel in the wilderness of Sinai, ... there was not left a man of them, save Caleb the son of Jephunneh, and Joshua the son of Nun." Numbers 26:64, 65.

God had sent judgments upon Israel for yielding to the enticements of the Midianites; but the tempters were not to escape the wrath of divine justice. The Amalekites, who had attacked Israel at Rephidim, falling upon those who were faint and weary behind the host, were not punished till long after; but the Midianites who seduced them into sin were speedily made to feel God's judgments, as being the more dangerous enemies. "Avenge the children of Israel of the Midianites" (Numbers 31:2), was the command of God to Moses; "afterward shalt thou be gathered unto thy people." This mandate was immediately obeyed. One thousand men were chosen from each of the tribes and sent out under the leadership of Phinehas. "And they warred against the Midianites, as the Lord commanded Moses.... And they slew the kings of Midian, beside the rest of them that were slain; ... five kings of Midian: Balaam also the son of Beor they slew with the sword." Verses 7, 8. The women also, who had been made captives by the attacking army, were put to death at the command of Moses, as the most guilty and most dangerous of the foes of Israel.

Such was the end of them that devised mischief against God's people. Says the psalmist: "The heathen are sunk down in the pit that they made: in the net which they hid is their own foot taken." Psalm 9:15. "For the Lord will not cast off His people, neither will He forsake His inheritance. But judgment shall return unto righteousness." When men "gather themselves together against the soul of the righteous," the Lord "shall bring upon them their own iniquity, and shall cut them off in their own wickedness." Psalm 94:14, 15, 21, 23.

When Balaam was called to curse the Hebrews he could not, by all his enchantments, bring evil upon them; for the Lord had not "beheld iniquity in Jacob," neither had He "seen perverseness in Israel." Numbers 23:21, 23. But when through yielding to temptation they transgressed God's law, their defense departed from them. When the people of God are faithful to His commandments, "there is no enchantment against Jacob, neither is there any divination against Israel." Hence all the power and wily arts of Satan are exerted to seduce them into sin. If those who profess to be the depositaries of God's law become transgressors of its precepts, they separate themselves from God, and they will be unable to stand before their enemies.

The Israelites, who could not be overcome by the arms or by the enchantments of Midian, fell a prey to her harlots. Such is the power that woman, enlisted in the service of Satan, has exerted to entrap and destroy souls. "She hath cast down many wounded: yea, many strong men have been slain by her." Proverbs 7:26. It was thus that the children of Seth were seduced from their integrity, and the holy seed became corrupt. It was thus that Joseph was tempted. Thus Samson betrayed his strength, the defense of Israel, into the hands of the Philistines. Here David stumbled. And Solomon, the wisest of kings, who had thrice been called the beloved of his God, became a slave of passion, and sacrificed his integrity to the same bewitching power.

"Now all these things happened unto them for ensamples: and they are written for our admonition, upon whom the ends of the world are come. Wherefore let him that thinketh he standeth take heed lest he fall." 1 Corinthians 10:11, 12. Satan well knows the material with which he has to deal in the human heart. He knows—for he has studied with fiendish intensity for thousands of years—the points most easily assailed in every character; and through successive generations he has wrought to overthrow the strongest men, princes in Israel, by the same temptations that were so successful at Baalpeor. All along through the ages there are strewn wrecks of character that have been stranded upon the rocks of sensual indulgence. As we approach the close of time, as the people of God stand upon the borders of the heavenly Canaan, Satan will, as of old, redouble his efforts to prevent them from entering the goodly land. He lays his snares for every soul. It is not the ignorant and uncultured merely that need to be guarded; he will prepare his temptations for those in the highest positions, in the most holy office; if he can lead them to pollute their souls, he can through them destroy many. And he employs the same agents now as he employed three thousand years ago. By worldly friendships, by the charms of beauty, by pleasure seeking, mirth, feasting, or the wine cup, he tempts to the violation of the seventh commandment.

Satan seduced Israel into licentiousness before leading them to idolatry. Those who will dishonor God's image and defile His temple in their own persons will not scruple at any dishonor to God that will gratify the desire of their depraved hearts. Sensual indulgence weakens the mind and debases the soul. The moral and intellectual powers are benumbed and paralyzed by the gratification of the animal propensities; and it is impossible for the slave of passion to realize the sacred obligation of the law of God, to appreciate the atonement, or to place a right value upon the soul. Goodness, purity, and truth, reverence for God, and love for sacred things—all those holy affections and noble desires that link men with the heavenly world—are consumed in the fires of lust. The soul becomes a blackened and desolate waste, the habitation of the evil spirits, and the "cage of every unclean and hateful bird." Beings formed in the image of God are dragged down to a level with the brutes.

It was by associating with idolaters and joining in their festivities that the Hebrews were led to transgress God's law and bring His judgments upon the nation. So now it is by leading the followers of Christ to associate with the ungodly and unite in their amusements that Satan is most successful in alluring them into sin. "Come out from among them, and be ye separate, saith the Lord, and touch not the unclean." 2 Corinthians 6:17. God requires of His people now as great a distinction from the world, in customs, habits, and principles, as He required of Israel anciently. If they faithfully follow the teachings of His word, this distinction will exist; it cannot be otherwise. The warnings given to the Hebrews against assimilating with the heathen were not more direct or explicit than are those forbidding Christians to conform to the spirit and customs of the ungodly. Christ speaks to us, "Love not the world, neither the things that are in the world. If any man love the world, the love of the Father is not in him." 1 John 2:15. "The friendship of the world is enmity with God; whosoever therefore will be a friend of the world is the enemy of God." James 4:4. The followers of Christ are to separate themselves from sinners, choosing their society only when there is opportunity to do them good. We cannot be too decided in shunning the company of those who exert an influence to draw us away from God. While we pray, "Lead us not into temptation," we are to shun temptation, so far as possible.

It was when the Israelites were in a condition of outward ease and security that they were led into sin. They failed to keep God ever before them, they neglected prayer and cherished a spirit of self-confidence. Ease and self-indulgence left the citadel of the soul unguarded, and debasing thoughts found entrance. It was the traitors within the walls that overthrew the strongholds of principle and betrayed Israel into the power of Satan. It is thus that Satan still seeks to compass the ruin of the soul. A long preparatory process, unknown to the world, goes on in the heart before the Christian commits open sin. The mind does not come down at once from purity and holiness to depravity, corruption, and crime. It takes time to degrade those formed in the image of God to the brutal or the satanic. By beholding we become changed. By the indulgence of impure thoughts man can so educate his mind that sin which he once loathed will become pleasant to him.

Satan is using every means to make crime and debasing vice popular. We cannot walk the streets of our cities without encountering flaring notices of crime presented in some novel, or to be acted at some theater. The mind is educated to familiarity with sin. The course pursued by the base and vile is kept before the people in the periodicals of the day, and everything that can excite passion is brought before them in exciting stories. They hear and read so much of debasing crime that the once tender conscience, which would have recoiled with horror from such scenes, becomes hardened, and they dwell upon these things with greedy interest.

Many of the amusements popular in the world today, even with those who claim to be Christians, tend to the same end as did those of the heathen. There are indeed few among them that Satan does not turn to account in destroying souls. Through the drama he has worked for ages to excite passion and glorify vice. The opera, with its fascinating display and bewildering music, the masquerade, the dance, the card table, Satan employs to break down the barriers of principle and open the door to sensual indulgence. In every gathering for pleasure where pride is fostered or appetite indulged, where one is led to forget God and lose sight of eternal interests, there Satan is binding his chains about the soul.

"Keep thy heart with all diligence," is the counsel of the wise man; "for out of it are the issues of life." Proverbs 4:23. As man "thinketh in his heart, so is he." Proverbs 23:7. The heart must be renewed by divine grace, or it will be in vain to seek for purity of life. He who attempts to build up a noble, virtuous character independent of the grace of Christ is building his house upon the shifting sand. In the fierce storms of temptation it will surely be overthrown. David's prayer should be the petition of every soul: "Create in me a clean heart, O God; and renew a right spirit within me." Psalm 51:10. And having become partakers of the heavenly gift, we are to go on unto perfection, being "kept by the power of God through faith." 1 Peter 1:5.

Yet we have a work to do to resist temptation. Those who would not fall a prey to Satan's devices must guard well the avenues of the soul; they must avoid reading, seeing, or hearing that which will suggest impure thoughts. The mind should not be left to wander at random upon every subject that the adversary of souls may suggest. "Girding up the loins of your mind," says the apostle Peter, "Be sober, ... not fashioning yourselves according to your former lusts in ... your ignorance: but like as He which called you is holy, be ye yourselves also holy in all manner of living." 1 Peter 1:13-15, R.V. Says Paul, "Whatsoever things are true, whatsoever things are honest, whatsoever things are just, whatsoever things are pure, whatsoever things are lovely, whatsoever things are of good report; if there be any virtue, and if there be any praise, think on these things." Philippians 4:8. This will require earnest prayer and unceasing watchfulness. We must be aided by the abiding influence of the Holy Spirit, which will attract the mind upward, and habituate it to dwell on pure and holy things. And we must give diligent study to the word of God. "Wherewithal shall a young man cleanse his way?

by taking heed thereto according to Thy word." "Thy word," says the psalmist, "have I hid in mine heart, that I might not sin against Thee." Psalm 119:9, 11.

[461] Israel's sin at Beth-peor brought the judgments of God upon the nation, and though the same sins may not now be punished as speedily, they will as surely meet retribution. "If any man defile the temple of God, him shall God destroy." 1 Corinthians 3:17. Nature has affixed terrible penalties to these crimes—penalties which, sooner or later, will be inflicted upon every transgressor. It is these sins more than any other that have caused the fearful degeneracy of our race, and the weight of disease and misery with which the world is cursed. Men may succeed in concealing their transgression from their fellow men, but they will no less surely reap the result, in suffering, disease, imbecility, or death. And beyond this life stands the tribunal of the judgment, with its award of eternal penalties. "They which do such things shall not inherit the kingdom of God," but with Satan and evil angels shall have their part in that "lake of fire" which "is the second death." Galatians 5:21; Revelation 20:14.

"The lips of a strange woman drop as an honeycomb, and her mouth is smoother than oil: but her end is bitter as wormwood, sharp as a two-edged sword." Proverbs 5:3, 4. "Remove thy way far from her, and come not nigh the door of her house: lest thou give thine honor unto others, and thy years unto the cruel: lest strangers be filled with thy wealth; and thy labors be in the house of a stranger; and thou mourn at the last, when thy flesh and thy body are consumed." Verses 8-11. "Her house inclineth unto death." "None that go unto her return again." Proverbs 2:18, 19. "Her guests are in the depths of hell." Proverbs 9:18.

Chapter 42—The Law Repeated

This chapter is based on Deuteronomy 4 to 6; 28.

The Lord announced to Moses that the appointed time for the possession of Canaan was at hand; and as the aged prophet stood upon the heights overlooking the river Jordan and the Promised Land, he gazed with deep interest upon the inheritance of his people. Would it be possible that the sentence pronounced against him for his sin at Kadesh might be revoked? With deep earnestness he pleaded, "O Lord God, Thou hast begun to show Thy servant Thy greatness, and Thy mighty hand; for what god is there in heaven or in earth, that can do according to Thy works, and according to Thy might? I pray Thee, let me go over, and see the good land that is beyond Jordan, that goodly mountain, and Lebanon." Deuteronomy 3:24-27.

The answer was, "Let it suffice thee; speak no more unto Me of this matter. Get thee up into the top of Pisgah, and lift up thine eyes westward, and northward, and southward, and eastward, and behold it with thine eyes; for thou shalt not go over this Jordan."

Without a murmur Moses submitted to the decree of God. And now his great anxiety was for Israel. Who would feel the interest for their welfare that he had felt? From a full heart he poured forth the prayer, "Let the Lord, the God of the spirits of all flesh, set a man over the congregation, which may go out before them, and which may go in before them, and which may lead them out, and which may bring them in; that the congregation of the Lord be not as sheep which have no shepherd." Numbers 27:16, 17.

The Lord hearkened to the prayer of His servant; and the answer came, "Take thee Joshua, the son of Nun, a man in whom is the Spirit, and lay thine hand upon him; and set him before Eleazar the priest, and before all the congregation; and give him a charge in their sight. And thou shalt put some of thine honor upon him, that all the congregation of the people of Israel may be obedient." Verses 18-20. Joshua had long attended Moses; and being a man of wisdom, ability, and faith, he was chosen to succeed him.

Through the laying on of hands by Moses, accompanied by a most impressive charge, Joshua was solemnly set apart as the leader of Israel. He was also admitted to a present share in the government. The words of the Lord concerning Joshua came through Moses to the congregation, "He shall stand before Eleazar the priest, who shall ask counsel for him, after the judgment of Urim before the Lord. At his word shall they go out, and at his word they shall come in, both he, and all the children of Israel with him, even all the congregation." Verses 21-23.

Before relinquishing his position as the visible leader of Israel, Moses was directed to rehearse to them the history of their deliverance from Egypt and their journeyings in the wilderness, and also to recapitulate the law spoken from Sinai. When the law was given, but few of the present congregation were old enough to comprehend the awful solemnity of the occasion. As they were soon to pass over Jordan and take possession of the Promised Land, God would present before them the claims of His law and enjoin upon them obedience as the condition of prosperity.

Moses stood before the people to repeat his last warnings and admonitions. His face was illumined with a holy light. His hair was white with age; but his form was erect, his countenance expressed the unabated vigor of health, and his eye was clear and undimmed. It was an important occasion, and with deep feeling he portrayed the love and mercy of their Almighty Protector:

"Ask now of the days that are past, which were before thee, since the day that God created man upon the earth, and ask from the one side of heaven unto the other, whether there hath been any such thing as this great thing is, or hath been heard like it? Did ever people hear the voice of God speaking out of the midst of the fire, as thou hast heard, and live? or hath God assayed to go and take Him a nation from the midst of another nation, by temptations, by signs, and by wonders, and by war, and by a mighty hand, and by a stretched-out arm, and by great terrors, according to all that the Lord your God did for you in Egypt before your eyes? Unto thee it was showed, that thou mightest know that the Lord He is God; there is none else beside Him."

"The Lord did not set His love upon you, nor choose you, because ye were more in number than any people; for ye were the fewest of all people: but because the Lord loved you, and because He would keep the oath which He had sworn unto your fathers, hath the Lord brought you out with a mighty hand, and redeemed you out of the house of bondmen, from the hand of Pharaoh king of Egypt. Know therefore that Jehovah thy God, He is God, the faithful God, which keepeth covenant and mercy with them that love Him and keep His commandments to a thousand generations." Deuteronomy 7:7-9.

The people of Israel had been ready to ascribe their troubles to Moses; but now their suspicions that he was controlled by pride, ambition, or selfishness, were removed, and they listened with confidence to his words. Moses faithfully set before them their errors and the transgressions of their fathers. They had often felt impatient and rebellious because of their long wandering in the wilderness; but the Lord had not been chargeable with this delay in possessing Canaan; He was more grieved than they because He could not bring them into immediate possession of the Promised Land, and thus display before all nations His mighty power in the deliverance of His people. With their distrust of God, with their pride and unbelief, they had not been prepared to enter Canaan. They would in no way represent that people whose God is the Lord; for they did not bear His character of purity, goodness, and benevolence. Had their fathers yielded in faith to the direction of God, being governed by His judgments and walking in His ordinances, they would long before have been settled in Canaan, a prosperous, holy, happy people. Their delay to enter the goodly land dishonored God and detracted from His glory in the sight of surrounding nations.

Moses, who understood the character and value of the law of God, assured the people that no other nation had such wise, righteous, and merciful rules as had been given to the Hebrews. "Behold," he said, "I have taught you statutes and judgments, even as the Lord my God commanded me, that ye should do so in the land whither ye go to possess it. Keep therefore and do them; for this is your wisdom and your understanding in the sight of the nations, which shall hear all these statutes, and say, Surely this great nation is a wise and understanding people."

Moses called their attention to the "day that thou stoodest before the Lord thy God in Horeb." And he challenged the Hebrew host:

"What nation is there so great, who hath God so nigh unto them, as the Lord our God is in all things that we call upon Him for? And what nation is there so great, that hath statutes and judgments so righteous as all this law, which I set before you this day?" Today the challenge to Israel might be repeated. The laws which God gave His ancient people were wiser, better, and more humane than those of the most civilized nations of the earth. The laws of the nations bear marks of the infirmities and passions of the unrenewed heart; but God's law bears the stamp of the divine.

"The Lord hath taken you, and brought you forth out of the iron furnace," declared Moses, "to be unto Him a people of inheritance." The land which they were soon to enter, and which was to be theirs on condition of obedience to the law of God, was thus described to them—and how must these words have moved the hearts of Israel, as they remembered that he who so glowingly pictured the blessings of the goodly land had been, through their sin, shut out from sharing the inheritance of his people:

"The Lord thy God bringeth thee into a good land," "not as the land of Egypt, from whence ye came out, where thou sowedst thy seed, and wateredst it with thy foot, as a garden of herbs: but the land, whither ye go to possess it, is a land of hills and valleys, and drinketh water of the rain of heaven;" "a land of brooks of water, of fountains and depths that spring out of valleys and hills; a land of wheat, and barley, and vines, and fig trees, and pomegranates; a land of oil olive, and honey; a land wherein thou shalt eat bread without scarceness, thou shalt not lack anything in it; a land whose stones are iron, and out of whose hills thou mayest dig brass;" "a land which the Lord thy God careth for: the eyes of the Lord thy God are always upon it, from the beginning of the year even unto the end of the year." Deuteronomy 8:7-9; 11:10-12.

"And it shall be, when the Lord thy God shall have brought thee into the land which He sware unto thy fathers, to Abraham, to Isaac, and to Jacob, to give thee great and goodly cities, which thou buildedst not, and houses full of all good things, which thou filledst not, and wells digged, which thou diggedst not, vineyards and olive trees, which thou plantedst not; when thou shalt have eaten and be full; then beware lest thou forget the Lord." "Take heed unto yourselves, lest ye forget the covenant of the Lord your God.... For the Lord thy God is a consuming fire, even a jealous God." If they should do evil in the sight of the Lord, then, said Moses, "Ye shall soon utterly perish from off the land whereunto ye go over Jordan to possess it."

After the public rehearsal of the law, Moses completed the work of writing all the laws, the statutes, and the judgments which God had given him, and all the regulations concerning the sacrificial system. The book containing these was placed in charge of the proper officers, and was for safe keeping deposited in the side of the ark. Still the great leader was filled with fear that the people would depart from God. In a most sublime and thrilling address he set before them the blessings that would be theirs on condition of obedience, and the curses that would follow upon transgression:

"If thou shalt hearken diligently unto the voice of the Lord thy God, to observe and to do all His commandments which I command thee this day," "blessed shalt thou be in the city, and blessed shalt thou be in the field," in "the fruit of thy body, and the fruit of thy ground, and the fruit of thy cattle.... Blessed shall be thy basket and thy store. Blessed shalt thou be when thou comest in, and blessed shalt thou be when thou goest out. The Lord shall cause thine enemies that rise up against thee to be smitten before thy face.... The Lord shall command the blessing upon thee in thy storehouses, and in all that thou settest thine hand unto."

"But it shall come to pass, if thou wilt not hearken unto the voice of the Lord thy God, to observe to do all His commandments and His statutes which I command thee this day; that all these curses shall come upon thee," "and thou shalt become an astonishment, a proverb, and a byword, among all nations whither the Lord shall lead thee." "And the Lord shall scatter thee among all people, from the one end of the earth even unto the other; and there thou shalt serve other gods, which neither thou nor thy fathers have known, even wood and stone. And among these nations shalt thou find no ease, neither shall the sole of thy foot have rest: but the Lord shall give thee there a trembling heart, and failing of eyes, and sorrow of mind: and thy life shall hang in doubt before thee; and thou shalt fear day and night, and shalt have none assurance of thy life: in the morning thou shalt say, Would God it were even! and at even thou shalt say, Would God it were morning! for the fear of thine heart wherewith thou shalt fear, and for the sight of thine eyes which thou shalt see."

By the Spirit of Inspiration, looking far down the ages, Moses pictured the terrible scenes of Israel's final overthrow as a nation, and the destruction of Jerusalem by the armies of Rome: "The Lord shall bring a nation against thee from far, from the end of the earth, as swift as the eagle flieth; a nation whose tongue thou shalt not understand; a nation of fierce countenance, which shall not regard the person of the old, nor show favor to the young."

The utter wasting of the land and the horrible suffering of the people during the siege of Jerusalem under Titus centuries later, were vividly portrayed: "He shall eat the fruit of thy cattle, and the fruit of thy land, until thou be destroyed.... And he shall besiege thee in all thy gates, until thy high and fenced walls come down, wherein thou trustedst, throughout all thy land.... Thou shalt eat the fruit of thine own body, the flesh of thy sons and of thy daughters, which the Lord thy God hath given thee, in the siege, and in the straitness, wherewith thine enemies shall distress thee." "The tender and delicate woman among you, which would not adventure to set the sole of her foot upon the ground for delicateness and tenderness, her eye shall be evil toward the husband of her bosom, ... and toward her children which she shall bear: for she shall eat them for want of all things secretly in the siege and straitness, wherewith thine enemy shall distress thee in thy gates."

Moses closed with these impressive words: "I call heaven and earth to record this day against you, that I have set before you life and death, blessing and cursing: therefore choose life, that both thou and thy seed may live: that thou mayest love the Lord thy God, and that thou mayest obey His voice, and that thou mayest cleave unto Him : for He is thy life, and the length of thy days: that thou mayest dwell in the land which the Lord sware unto thy fathers, to Abraham, to Isaac, and to Jacob, to give them." Deuteronomy 30:19, 20.

The more deeply to impress these truths upon all minds, the great leader embodied them in sacred verse. This song was not only historical, but prophetic. While it recounted the wonderful dealings of God with His people in the past, it also foreshadowed the great events of the future, the final victory of the faithful when Christ shall come the second time in power and glory. The people were directed to commit to memory this poetic history, and to teach it to their children and children's children. It was to be chanted by the congregation when they assembled for worship, and to be repeated by the people as they went about their daily labors. It was the duty of parents to so impress these words upon the susceptible minds of their children that they might never be forgotten.

Since the Israelites were to be, in a special sense, the guardians and keepers of God's law, the significance of its precepts and the importance of obedience were especially to be impressed upon them, and through them, upon their children and children's children. The Lord commanded concerning His statutes: "Thou shalt teach them diligently unto thy children, and shalt talk of them when thou sittest in thine house, and when thou walkest by the way, and when thou liest down, and when thou risest up.... And thou shalt write them upon the posts of thy house, and on thy gates."

When their children should ask in time to come, "What mean the testimonies, and the statutes, and the judgments, which the Lord our God hath commanded you?" then the parents were to repeat the history of God's gracious dealings with them—how the Lord had wrought for their deliverance that they might obey His Law—and to declare to them, "The Lord commanded us to do all these statutes, to fear the Lord our God, for our good always, that He might preserve us alive, as it is at this day. And it shall be our righteousness, if we observe to do all these commandments before the Lord our God as He hath commanded us."

Chapter 43—The Death of Moses

This chapter is based on Deuteronomy 31 to 34.

In all the dealings of God with His people there is, mingled with His love and mercy, the most striking evidence of His strict and impartial justice. This is exemplified in the history of the Hebrew people. God had bestowed great blessings upon Israel. His lovingkindness toward them is touchingly portrayed: "As an eagle stirreth up her nest, fluttereth over her young, spreadeth abroad her wings, taketh them, beareth them on her wings: so the Lord alone did lead him." And yet what swift and severe retribution was visited upon them for their transgressions!

The infinite love of God has been manifested in the gift of His only-begotten Son to redeem a lost race. Christ came to the earth to reveal to men the character of His Father, and His life was filled with deeds of divine tenderness and compassion. And yet Christ Himself declares, "Till heaven and earth pass, one jot or one tittle shall in no wise pass from the law." Matthew 5:18. The same voice that with patient, loving entreaty invites the sinner to come to Him and find pardon and peace, will in the judgment bid the rejecters of His mercy, "Depart from Me, ye cursed." Matthew 25:41. In all the Bible, God is represented not only as a tender father but as a righteous judge. Though He delights in showing mercy, and "forgiving iniquity and transgression and sin," yet He "will by no means clear the guilty." Exodus 34:7.

The great Ruler of nations had declared that Moses was not to lead the congregation of Israel into the goodly land, and the earnest pleading of God's servant could not secure a reversing of His sentence. He knew that he must die. Yet he had not for a moment faltered in his care for Israel. He had faithfully sought to prepare the congregation to enter upon the promised inheritance. At the divine command Moses and Joshua repaired to the tabernacle, while the pillar of cloud came and stood over the door. Here the people were solemnly committed to the charge of Joshua. The work of Moses as leader of Israel was ended. Still he forgot himself in his interest for his people. In the presence of the assembled multitude Moses, in the name of God, addressed to his successor these words of holy cheer: "Be strong and of a good courage: for thou shalt bring the children of Israel into the land which I sware unto them: and I will be with thee." He then turned to the elders and officers of the people, giving them a solemn charge to obey faithfully the instructions he had communicated to them from God.

As the people gazed upon the aged man, so soon to be taken from them, they recalled, with a new and deeper appreciation, his parental tenderness, his wise counsels, and his untiring labors. How often, when their sins had invited the just judgments of God, the prayers of Moses had prevailed with Him to spare them! Their grief was heightened by remorse. They bitterly remembered that their own perversity had provoked Moses to the sin for which he must die.

The removal of their beloved leader would be a far stronger rebuke to Israel than any which they could have received had his life and mission been continued. God would lead them to feel that they were not to make the life of their future leader as trying as they had made that of Moses. God speaks to His people in blessings bestowed; and when these are not appreciated, He speaks to them in blessings removed, that they may be led to see their sins, and return to Him with all the heart.

That very day there came to Moses the command, "Get thee up ... unto Mount Nebo, ... and behold the land of Canaan, which I give unto the children of Israel for a possession: and die in the mount whither thou goest up, and be gathered unto thy people." Moses had often left the camp, in obedience to the divine summons, to commune with God; but he was now to depart on a new and mysterious errand. He must go forth to resign his life into the hands of his Creator. Moses knew that he was to die alone; no earthly friend would be permitted to minister to him in his last hours. There was a mystery and awfulness about the scene before him, from which his heart shrank. The severest trial was his separation from the people of his care and love—the people with whom his interest and his life had so long been united. But he had learned to trust in God, and with unquestioning faith he committed himself and his people to His love and mercy.

For the last time Moses stood in the assembly of his people. Again the Spirit of God rested upon him, and in the most sublime and touching language he pronounced a blessing upon each of the tribes, closing with a benediction upon them all:

> "There is none like unto God, O Jeshurun,
>   Who rideth upon the heaven for thy help,
> And in His excellency on the skies.
>   The eternal God is thy dwelling place,
> And underneath are the everlasting arms:
>   And He thrust out the enemy from before thee,
> And said, Destroy.
>   And Israel dwelleth in safety,
> The fountain of Jacob alone,
>   In a land of corn and wine;
> Yea, His heavens drop down dew.
>   Happy art thou, O Israel:
> Who is like unto thee, a people saved by Jehovah,
>   The shield of thy help."
>
>   Deuteronomy 33:26-29, R.V.

Moses turned from the congregation, and in silence and alone made his way up the mountainside. He went to "the mountain of Nebo, to the top of Pisgah." Upon that lonely height he stood, and gazed with undimmed eye upon the scene spread out before him. Far away to the west lay the blue waters of the Great Sea; in the north, Mount Hermon stood out against the sky; to the east was the tableland of Moab, and beyond lay Bashan, the scene of Israel's triumph; and away to the south stretched the desert of their long wanderings.

In solitude Moses reviewed his life of vicissitudes and hardships since he turned from courtly honors and from a prospective kingdom in Egypt, to cast in his lot with God's chosen people. He called to mind those long years in the desert with the flocks of Jethro, the appearance of the Angel in the burning bush, and his own call to deliver Israel. Again he beheld the mighty miracles of God's power displayed in behalf of the chosen people, and His long-suffering mercy during the years of their wandering and rebellion. Notwithstanding all that God had wrought for them, notwithstanding his own prayers and labors, only two of all the adults in the vast army that left Egypt had been found so faithful that they could enter the Promised Land. As Moses reviewed the result of his labors, his life of trial and sacrifice seemed to have been almost in vain.

[472]

Yet he did not regret the burdens he had borne. He knew that his mission and work were of God's own appointing. When first called to become the leader of Israel from bondage, he shrank from the responsibility; but since he had taken up the work he had not cast aside the burden. Even when the Lord had proposed to release him, and destroy rebellious Israel, Moses could not consent. Though his trials had been great, he had enjoyed special tokens of God's favor; he had obtained a rich experience during the sojourn in the wilderness, in witnessing the manifestations of God's power and glory, and in the communion of His love; he felt that he had made a wise decision in choosing to suffer affliction with the people of God, rather than to enjoy the pleasures of sin for a season.

As he looked back upon his experience as a leader of God's people, one wrong act marred the record. If that transgression could be blotted out, he felt that he would not shrink from death. He was assured that repentance, and faith in the promised Sacrifice, were all that God required, and again Moses confessed his sin and implored pardon in the name of Jesus.

And now a panoramic view of the Land of Promise was presented to him. Every part of the country was spread out before him, not faint and uncertain in the dim distance, but standing out clear, distinct, and beautiful to his delighted vision. In this scene it was presented, not as it then appeared, but as it would become, with God's blessing upon it, in the possession of Israel. He seemed to be looking upon a second Eden. There were mountains clothed with cedars of Lebanon, hills gray with olives and fragrant with the odor of the vine, wide green plains bright with flowers and rich in fruitfulness, here the palm trees of the tropics, there waving fields of wheat and barley, sunny valleys musical with the ripple of brooks and the song of birds, goodly cities and fair gardens, lakes rich in "the abundance of the seas," grazing flocks upon the hillsides, and even amid the rocks the wild bee's hoarded treasures. It was indeed such a land as Moses, inspired by the Spirit of God, had described to Israel: "Blessed of the Lord ... for the precious things of heaven, for the dew, and for the deep that coucheth beneath, and for the precious fruits brought forth by the sun, ... and for the chief things of the ancient mountains, ... and for the precious things of the earth and fullness thereof."

Moses saw the chosen people established in Canaan, each of the tribes in its own possession. He had a view of their history after the settlement of the Promised Land; the long, sad story of their apostasy and its punishment was spread out before him. He saw them, because of their sins, dispersed among the heathen, the glory departed from Israel, her beautiful city in ruins, and her people captives in strange lands. He saw them restored to the land of their fathers, and at last brought under the dominion of Rome.

He was permitted to look down the stream of time and behold the first advent of our Saviour. He saw Jesus as a babe in Bethlehem. He heard the voices of the angelic host break forth in the glad song of praise to God and peace on earth. He beheld in the heavens the star guiding the Wise Men of the East to Jesus, and a great light flooded his mind as he called those prophetic words, "There shall come a Star out of Jacob, and a Scepter shall rise out of Israel." Numbers 24:17. He beheld Christ's humble life in Nazareth, His ministry of love and sympathy and healing, His rejection by a proud, unbelieving nation. Amazed he listened to their boastful exaltation of the law of God, while they despised and rejected Him by whom the law was given. He saw Jesus upon Olivet as with weeping He bade farewell to the city of His love. As Moses beheld the final rejection of that people so highly blessed of Heaven—that people for whom he had toiled and prayed and sacrificed, for whom he had been willing that his own name should be blotted from the book of life; as he listened to those fearful words, "Behold your house is left unto you desolate" (Matthew 23:38), his heart was wrung with anguish, and bitter tears fell from his eyes, in sympathy with the sorrow of the Son of God.

He followed the Saviour to Gethsemane, and beheld the agony in the garden, the betrayal, the mockery and scourging—the crucifixion. Moses saw that as he had lifted up the serpent in the wilderness, so the Son of God must be lifted up, that whosoever would believe on Him "should not perish, but have eternal life." John 3:15. Grief, indignation, and horror filled the heart of Moses as he viewed the hypocrisy and satanic hatred manifested by the Jewish nation against their Redeemer, the mighty Angel who had gone before their fathers. He heard Christ's agonizing cry, "My God, My God, why hast Thou forsaken Me?" Mark 15:34. He saw Him lying in Joseph's new tomb. The darkness of hopeless despair seemed to enshroud the world. But he looked again, and beheld Him coming forth a conqueror, and ascending to heaven escorted by adoring angels and leading a multitude of captives. He saw the shining gates open to receive Him, and the host of heaven with songs of triumph welcoming their Commander. And it was there revealed to him that he himself would be one who should attend the Saviour, and open to Him the everlasting gates. As he looked upon the scene, his countenance shone with a holy radiance. How small appeared the trials and sacrifices of his life when compared with those of the Son of God! how light in contrast with the "far more exceeding and eternal weight of glory"! 2 Corinthians 4:17. He rejoiced that he had been permitted, even in a small measure, to be a partaker in the sufferings of Christ.

[476]

Moses beheld the disciples of Jesus as they went forth to carry His gospel to the world. He saw that though the people of Israel "according to the flesh" had failed of the high destiny to which God had called them, in their unbelief had failed to become the light of the world, though they had despised God's mercy and forfeited their blessings as His chosen people—yet God had not cast off the seed of Abraham; the glorious purposes which He had undertaken to accomplish through Israel were to be fulfilled. All who through Christ should become the children of faith were to be counted as Abraham's seed; they were inheritors of the covenant promises; like Abraham, they were called to guard and to make known to the world the law of God and the gospel of His Son. Moses saw the light of the gospel shining out through the disciples of Jesus to them "which sat in darkness" (Matthew 4:16), and thousands from the lands of the Gentiles flocking to the brightness of its rising. And beholding, he rejoiced in the increase and prosperity of Israel.

And now another scene passed before him. He had been shown the work of Satan in leading the Jews to reject Christ, while they professed to honor His Father's law. He now saw the Christian world under a similar deception in professing to accept Christ while they rejected God's law. He had heard from the priests and elders the frenzied cry, "Away with Him!" "Crucify Him, crucify Him!" and now he heard from professedly Christian teachers the cry, "Away with the law!" He saw the Sabbath trodden under foot, and a spurious institution established in its place. Again Moses was filled with astonishment and horror. How could those who believed in Christ reject the law spoken by His own voice upon the sacred mount? How could any that feared God set aside the law which is the foundation of His government in heaven and earth? With joy Moses saw the law of God still honored and exalted by a faithful few. He saw the last great struggle of earthly powers to destroy those who keep God's law. He looked forward to the time when God shall arise to punish the inhabitants of the earth for their iniquity, and those who have feared His name shall be covered and hid in the day of His anger. He heard God's covenant of peace with those who have kept His law, as He utters His voice from His holy habitation and the heavens and the earth do shake. He saw the second coming of Christ in glory, the righteous dead raised to immortal life, and the living saints translated without seeing death, and together ascending with songs of gladness to the City of God.

Still another scene opens to his view—the earth freed from the curse, lovelier than the fair Land of Promise so lately spread out before him. There is no sin, and death cannot enter. There the nations of the saved find their eternal home. With joy unutterable Moses looks upon the scene—the fulfillment of a more glorious deliverance than his brightest hopes have ever pictured. Their earthly wanderings forever past, the Israel of God have at last entered the goodly land.

Again the vision faded, and his eyes rested upon the land of Canaan as it spread out in the distance. Then, like a tired warrior, he lay down to rest. "So Moses the servant of the Lord died there in the land of Moab, according to the word of the Lord. And He buried him in a valley in the land of Moab, over against Beth-peor: but no man knoweth of his sepulcher." Many who had been unwilling to heed the counsels of Moses while he was with them would have been in danger of committing idolatry over his dead body had they known the place of his burial. For this reason it was concealed from men. But angels of God buried the body of His faithful servant and watched over the lonely grave.

"There arose not a prophet since in Israel like unto Moses, whom Jehovah knew face to face, in all the signs and the wonders which Jehovah sent him to do ... and in all that mighty hand, and in all the great terror which Moses showed in the sight of all Israel."

Had not the life of Moses been marred with that one sin, in failing to give God the glory of bringing water from the rock at Kadesh, he would have entered the Promised Land, and would have been translated to heaven without seeing death. But he was not long to remain in the tomb. Christ Himself, with the angels who had buried Moses, came down from heaven to call forth the sleeping saint. Satan had exulted at his success in causing Moses to sin against God, and thus come under the dominion of death. The great adversary declared that the divine sentence—"Dust thou art, and unto dust shalt thou return" (Genesis 3:19)—gave him possession of the dead. The power of the grave had never been broken, and all who were in the tomb he claimed as his captives, never to be released from his dark prison house.

For the first time Christ was about to give life to the dead. As the Prince of life and the shining ones approached the grave, Satan was alarmed for his supremacy. With his evil angels he stood to dispute an invasion of the territory that he claimed as his own. He boasted that the servant of God had become his prisoner. He declared that even Moses was not able to keep the law of God; that he had taken to himself the glory due to Jehovah—the very sin which had caused Satan's banishment from heaven—and by transgression had come under the dominion of Satan. The archtraitor reiterated the original charges that he had made against the divine government, and repeated his complaints of God's injustice toward him.

Christ did not stoop to enter into controversy with Satan. He might have brought against him the cruel work which his deceptions had wrought in heaven, causing the ruin of a vast number of its inhabitants. He might have pointed to the falsehoods told in Eden, that had led to Adam's sin and brought death upon the human race. He might have reminded Satan that it was his own work in tempting Israel to murmuring and rebellion, which had wearied the long-suffering patience of their leader, and in an unguarded moment had surprised him into the sin for which he had fallen under the power of death. But Christ referred all to His Father, saying, "The Lord rebuke thee." Jude 9. The Saviour entered into no dispute with His adversary, but He then and there began His work of breaking the power of the fallen foe, and bringing the dead to life. Here was an evidence that Satan could not controvert, of the supremacy of the Son of God. The resurrection was forever made certain. Satan was despoiled of his prey; the righteous dead would live again.

In consequence of sin Moses had come under the power of Satan. In his own merits he was death's lawful captive; but he was raised to immortal life, holding his title in the name of the Redeemer. Moses came forth from the tomb glorified, and ascended with his Deliverer to the City of God.

Never, till exemplified in the sacrifice of Christ, were the justice and the love of God more strikingly displayed than in His dealings with Moses. God shut Moses out of Canaan, to teach a lesson which should never be forgotten—that He requires exact obedience, and that men are to beware of taking to themselves the glory which is due to their Maker. He could not grant the prayer of Moses that he might share the inheritance of Israel, but He did not forget or forsake His servant. The God of heaven understood the suffering that Moses had endured; He had noted every act of faithful service through those long years of conflict and trial. On the top of Pisgah, God called Moses to an inheritance infinitely more glorious than the earthly Canaan.

Upon the mount of transfiguration Moses was present with Elijah, who had been translated. They were sent as bearers of light and glory from the Father to His Son. And thus the prayer of Moses, uttered so many centuries before, was at last fulfilled. He stood upon the "goodly mountain," within the heritage of his people, bearing witness to Him in whom all the promises to Israel centered. Such is the last scene revealed to mortal vision in the history of that man so highly honored of Heaven.

Moses was a type of Christ. He himself had declared to Israel, "The Lord thy God will raise up unto thee a Prophet from the midst of thee, of thy brethren, like unto me; unto Him ye shall hearken." Deuteronomy 18:15. God saw fit to discipline Moses in the school of affliction and poverty before he could be prepared to lead the hosts of Israel to the earthly Canaan. The Israel of God, journeying to the heavenly Canaan, have a Captain who needed no human teaching to prepare Him for His mission as a divine leader; yet He was made perfect through sufferings; and "in that He Himself hath suffered being tempted, He is able to succor them that are tempted." Hebrews 2:10, 18. Our Redeemer manifested no human weakness or imperfection; yet He died to obtain for us an entrance into the Promised Land.

"And Moses verily was faithful in all his house as a servant, for a testimony of those things which were to be spoken after; but Christ as a son over His own house; whose house are we, if we hold fast the confidence and the rejoicing of the hope firm unto the end." Hebrews 3:5, 6.

Chapter 44—Crossing the Jordan

This chapter is based on Joshua 1 to 5:12.

The Israelites deeply mourned for their departed leader, and thirty days were devoted to special services in honor of his memory. Never till he was taken from them had they so fully realized the value of his wise counsels, his parental tenderness, and his unswerving faith. With a new and deeper appreciation they recalled the precious lessons he had given while still with them.

Moses was dead, but his influence did not die with him. It was to live on, reproducing itself in the hearts of his people. The memory of that holy, unselfish life would long be cherished, with silent, persuasive power molding the lives even of those who had neglected his living words. As the glow of the descending sun lights up the mountain peaks long after the sun itself has sunk behind the hills, so the works of the pure, the holy, and the good shed light upon the world long after the actors themselves have passed away. Their works, their words, their example, will forever live. "The righteous shall be in everlasting remembrance." Psalm 112:6.

While they were filled with grief at their great loss, the people knew that they were not left alone. The pillar of cloud rested over the tabernacle by day, and the pillar of fire by night, an assurance that God would still be their guide and helper if they would walk in the way of His commandments.

Joshua was now the acknowledged leader of Israel. He had been known chiefly as a warrior, and his gifts and virtues were especially valuable at this stage in the history of his people. Courageous, resolute, and persevering, prompt, incorruptible, unmindful of selfish interests in his care for those committed to his charge, and, above all, inspired by a living faith in God—such was the character of the man divinely chosen to conduct the armies of Israel in their entrance upon the Promised Land. During the sojourn in the wilderness he had acted as prime minister to Moses, and by his quiet, unpretending

Crossing the Jordan

fidelity, his steadfastness when others wavered, his firmness to maintain the truth in the midst of danger, he had given evidence of his fitness to succeed Moses, even before he was called to the position by the voice of God.

It was with great anxiety and self-distrust that Joshua had looked forward to the work before him; but his fears were removed by the assurance of God, "As I was with Moses, so I will be with thee: I will not fail thee, nor forsake thee.... Unto this people shalt thou divide for an inheritance the land, which I sware unto their fathers to give them." "Every place that the sole of your foot shall tread upon, that have I given unto you, as I said unto Moses." To the heights of Lebanon in the far distance, to the shores of the Great Sea, and away to the banks of the Euphrates in the east—all was to be theirs.

To this promise was added the injunction, "Only be thou strong and very courageous, that thou mayest observe to do according to all the law, which Moses My servant commanded." The Lord's direction was, "This book of the law shall not depart out of thy mouth; but thou shalt meditate therein day and night;" "turn not from it to the right hand or to the left;" "for then thou shalt make thy way prosperous, and then thou shalt have good success."

The Israelites were still encamped on the east side of Jordan, which presented the first barrier to the occupation of Canaan. "Arise," had been the first message of God to Joshua, "go over this Jordan, thou, and all this people, unto the land which I do give to them." No instruction was given as to the way in which they were to make the passage. Joshua knew, however, that whatever God should command, He would make a way for His people to perform, and in this faith the intrepid leader at once began his arrangements for an advance.

A few miles beyond the river, just opposite the place where the Israelites were encamped, was the large and strongly fortified city of Jericho. This city was virtually the key to the whole country, and it would present a formidable obstacle to the success of Israel. Joshua therefore sent two young men as spies to visit this city and ascertain something as to its population, its resources, and the strength of its fortifications. The inhabitants of the city, terrified and suspicious, were constantly on the alert, and the messengers were in great danger. [483] They were, however, preserved by Rahab, a woman of Jericho, at the peril of her own life. In return for her kindness they gave her a promise of protection when the city should be taken.

The spies returned in safety with the tidings, "Truly the Lord hath delivered into our hands all the land; for even all the inhabitants of the country do faint because of us." It had been declared to them in Jericho, "We have heard how the Lord dried up the water of the Red Sea for you, when ye came out of Egypt; and what ye did unto the two kings of the Amorites, that were on the other side Jordan, Sihon and Og, whom ye utterly destroyed. And as soon as we had heard these things, our hearts did melt, neither did there remain any more courage in any man, because of you: for the Lord your God, He is God in heaven above, and in earth beneath."

Orders were now issued to make ready for an advance. The people were to prepare a three days' supply of food, and the army was to be put in readiness for battle. All heartily acquiesced in the plans of their leader and assured him of their confidence and support: "All that thou commandest us we will do, and whithersoever thou sendest us, we will go. According as we hearkened unto Moses in all things, so will we hearken unto thee: only the Lord thy God be with thee, as He was with Moses."

Leaving their encampment in the acacia groves of Shittim, the host descended to the border of the Jordan. All knew, however, that without divine aid they could not hope to make the passage. At this time of the year—in the spring season—the melting snows of the mountains had so raised the Jordan that the river overflowed its banks, making it impossible to cross at the usual fording places. God willed that the passage of Israel over Jordan should be miraculous. Joshua, by divine direction, commanded the people to sanctify themselves; they must put away their sins and free themselves from all outward impurity; "for tomorrow," he said, "the Lord will do wonders among you." The "ark of the covenant" was to lead the way before the host. When they should see the token of Jehovah's presence, borne by the priests, remove from its place in the center of the camp, and advance toward the river, then they were to remove from their place, "and go after it." The circumstances of the passage were minutely foretold; and said Joshua, "Hereby ye shall know that the living God is among you, and that He will without fail drive out from before you the Canaanites.... Behold, the ark of the covenant of the Lord of all the earth passeth over before you into Jordan."

At the appointed time began the onward movement, the ark, borne upon the shoulders of the priests, leading the van. The people had been directed to fall back, so that there was a vacant space of more than half a mile about the ark. All watched with deep interest as the priests advanced down the bank of the Jordan. They saw them with the sacred ark move steadily forward toward the angry, surging stream, till the feet of the bearers were dipped into the waters. Then suddenly the tide above was swept back, while the current below flowed on, and the bed of the river was laid bare.

At the divine command the priests advanced to the middle of the channel and stood there while the entire host descended and crossed to the farther side. Thus was impressed upon the minds of all Israel the fact that the power that stayed the waters of Jordan was the same that had opened the Red Sea to their fathers forty years before. When the people had all passed over, the ark itself was borne to the western shore. No sooner had it reached a place of security, and "the soles of the priests' feet were lifted up unto the dry land," than the imprisoned waters, being set free, rushed down, a resistless flood, in the natural channel of the stream.

Coming generations were not to be without a witness to this great miracle. While the priests bearing the ark were still in the midst of Jordan, twelve men previously chosen, one from each tribe, took up each a stone from the river bed where the priests were standing, and carried it over to the western side. These stones were to be set up as a monument in the first camping place beyond the river. The people were bidden to repeat to their children and children's children the story of the deliverance that God had wrought for them, as Joshua said, "That all the people of the earth might know the hand of the Lord, that it is mighty: that ye might fear the Lord your God forever."

The influence of this miracle, both upon the Hebrews and upon their enemies, was of great importance. It was an assurance to Israel of God's continued presence and protection—an evidence that He would work for them through Joshua as He had wrought through Moses. Such an assurance was needed to strengthen their hearts as they entered upon the conquest of the land—the stupendous task that had staggered the faith of their fathers forty years before. The Lord had declared to Joshua before the crossing, "This day will I begin to magnify thee in the sight of all Israel, that they may know that, as I was with Moses, so I will be with thee." And the result fulfilled the promise. "On that day the Lord magnified Joshua in the sight of all Israel; and they feared him, as they feared Moses, all the days of his life."

This exercise of divine power in behalf of Israel was designed also to increase the fear with which they were regarded by the surrounding nations, and thus prepare the way for their easier and complete triumph. When the tidings that God had stayed the waters of Jordan before the children of Israel, reached the kings of the Amorites and of the Canaanites, their hearts melted with fear. The Hebrews had already slain the five kings of Midian, the powerful Sihon, king of the Amorites, and Og of Bashan, and now the passage over the swollen and impetuous Jordan filled all the surrounding nations with terror. To the Canaanites, to all Israel, and to Joshua himself, unmistakable evidence had been given that the living God, the King of heaven and earth, was among His people, and that He would not fail them nor forsake them.

A short distance from Jordan the Hebrews made their first encampment in Canaan. Here Joshua "circumcised the children of Israel;" "and the children of Israel encamped in Gilgal, and kept the Passover." The suspension of the rite of circumcision since the rebellion at Kadesh had been a constant witness to Israel that their covenant with God, of which it was the appointed symbol, had been broken. And the discontinuance of the Passover, the memorial of their deliverance from Egypt, had been an evidence of the Lord's displeasure at their desire to return to the land of bondage. Now, however, the years of rejection were ended. Once more God acknowledged Israel as His people, and the sign of the covenant was restored. The rite of circumcision was performed upon all the people who had been born in the wilderness. And the Lord declared to Joshua, "This day have I rolled away the reproach of Egypt from off you," and in allusion to this the place of their encampment was called Gilgal, "a rolling away," or "rolling off."

Heathen nations had reproached the Lord and His people because the Hebrews had failed to take possession of Canaan, as they expected, soon after leaving Egypt. Their enemies had triumphed because Israel had wandered so long in the wilderness, and they had mockingly declared that the God of the Hebrews was not able to bring them into the Promised Land. The Lord had now signally manifested His power and favor in opening the Jordan before His people, and their enemies could no longer reproach them.

"On the fourteenth day of the month at even," the Passover was celebrated on the plains of Jericho. "And they did eat of the old corn of the land on the morrow after the Passover, unleavened cakes, and parched corn in the selfsame day. And the manna ceased on the morrow after they had eaten of the old corn of the land; neither had the children of Israel manna any more; but they did eat of the fruit of the land of Canaan." The long years of their desert wanderings were ended. The feet of Israel were at last treading the Promised Land.

Chapter 45—The Fall of Jericho

This chapter is based on Joshua 5:13-15; 6; 7.

The Hebrews had entered Canaan, but they had not subdued it; and to human appearance the struggle to gain possession of the land must be long and difficult. It was inhabited by a powerful race, who stood ready to oppose the invasion of their territory. The various tribes were bound together by the fear of a common danger. Their horses and iron battle chariots, their knowledge of the country, and their training in war, would give them great advantage. Furthermore, the country was guarded by fortresses—"cities great and fenced up to heaven." Deuteronomy 9:1. Only in the assurance of a strength not their own could the Israelites hope for success in the impending conflict.

One of the strongest fortresses in the land—the large and wealthy city of Jericho—lay just before them, but a little distance from their camp at Gilgal. On the border of a fertile plain abounding with the rich and varied productions of the tropics, its palaces and temples the abode of luxury and vice, this proud city, behind its massive battlements, offered defiance to the God of Israel. Jericho was one of the principal seats of idol worship, being especially devoted to Ashtaroth, the goddess of the moon. Here centered all that was vilest and most degrading in the religion of the Canaanites. The people of Israel, in whose minds were fresh the fearful results of their sin at Beth-peor, could look upon this heathen city only with disgust and horror.

To reduce Jericho was seen by Joshua to be the first step in the conquest of Canaan. But first of all he sought an assurance of divine guidance, and it was granted him. Withdrawing from the encampment to meditate and to pray that the God of Israel would go before His people, he beheld an armed warrior, of lofty stature and commanding presence, "with his sword drawn in his hand." To Joshua's challenge, "Art thou for us, or for our adversaries?" the answer was given, "As Captain of the host of the Lord am I now come." The same command given to Moses in Horeb, "Loose thy shoe from off thy foot; for the place whereon thou standest is holy," revealed the true character of the mysterious stranger. It was Christ, the Exalted One, who stood before the leader of Israel. Awe-stricken, Joshua fell upon his face and worshiped, and heard the assurance, "I have given into thine hand Jericho, and the king thereof, and the mighty men of valor," and he received instruction for the capture of the city.

In obedience to the divine command Joshua marshaled the armies of Israel. No assault was to be made. They were simply to make the circuit of the city, bearing the ark of God and blowing upon trumpets. First came the warriors, a body of chosen men, not now to conquer by their own skill and prowess, but by obedience to the directions given them from God. Seven priests with trumpets followed. Then the ark of God, surrounded by a halo of divine glory, was borne by priests clad in the dress denoting their sacred office. The army of Israel followed, each tribe under its standard. Such was the procession that compassed the doomed city. No sound was heard but the tread of that mighty host and the solemn peal of the trumpets, echoing among the hills and resounding through the streets of Jericho. The circuit completed, the army returned in silence to their tents, and the ark was restored to its place in the tabernacle.

With wonder and alarm the watchmen of the city marked every move, and reported to those in authority. They knew not the meaning of all this display; but when they beheld that mighty host marching around their city once each day, with the sacred ark and the attendant priests, the mystery of the scene struck terror to the hearts of priest and people. Again they would inspect their strong defenses, feeling certain they could successfully resist the most powerful attack. Many ridiculed the thought that any harm could come to them through these singular demonstrations. Others were awed as they beheld the procession that each day wound about the city. They remembered that the Red Sea had once parted before this people, and that a passage had just been opened for them through the river Jordan. They knew not what further wonders God might work for them.

For six days the host of Israel made the circuit of the city. The seventh day came, and with the first dawn of light, Joshua marshaled the armies of the Lord. Now they were directed to march seven times around Jericho, and at a mighty peal from the trumpets to shout with a loud voice, for God had given them the city.

The vast army marched solemnly around the devoted walls. All was silent, save the measured tread of many feet, and the occasional sound of the trumpet, breaking the stillness of the early morning. The massive walls of solid stone seemed to defy the siege of men. The watchers on the walls looked on with rising fear, as, the first circuit ended, there followed a second, then a third, a fourth, a fifth, a sixth. What could be the object of these mysterious movements? What mighty event was impending? They had not long to wait. As the seventh circuit was completed, the long procession paused, The trumpets, which for an interval had been silent, now broke forth in a blast that shook the very earth. The walls of solid stone, with their massive towers and battlements, tottered and heaved from their foundations, and with a crash fell in ruin to the earth. The inhabitants of Jericho were paralyzed with terror, and the hosts of Israel marched in and took possession of the city.

The Israelites had not gained the victory by their own power; the conquest had been wholly the Lord's; and as the first fruits of the land, the city, with all that it contained, was to be devoted as a sacrifice to God. It was to be impressed upon Israel that in the conquest of Canaan they were not to fight for themselves, but simply as instruments to execute the will of God; not to seek for riches or self-exaltation, but the glory of Jehovah their King. Before the capture the command had been given, "The city shall be accursed, even it, and all that are therein." "Keep yourselves from the accursed thing, lest ye make yourselves accursed ... and make the camp of Israel a curse, and trouble it."

All the inhabitants of the city, with every living thing that it contained, "both man and woman, young and old, and ox, and sheep, and ass," were put to the sword. Only faithful Rahab, with her household, was spared, in fulfillment of the promise of the spies. The city itself was burned; its palaces and temples, its magnificent dwellings with all their luxurious appointments, the rich draperies and the costly garments, were given to the flames. That which could not be destroyed by fire, "the silver, and the gold, and the vessels of brass and of iron," was to be devoted to the service of the tabernacle.

The very site of the city was accursed; Jericho was never to be rebuilt as a stronghold; judgments were threatened upon anyone who should presume to restore the walls that divine power had cast down. The solemn declaration was made in the presence of all Israel, "Cursed be the man before the Lord, that riseth up and buildeth this city Jericho: he shall lay the foundation thereof in his first-born, and in his youngest son shall he set up the gates of it."

The utter destruction of the people of Jericho was but a fulfillment of the commands previously given through Moses concerning the inhabitants of Canaan: "Thou shalt smite them, and utterly destroy them." Deuteronomy 7:2. "Of the cities of these people, ... thou shalt save alive nothing that breatheth." Deuteronomy 20:16. To many these commands seem to be contrary to the spirit of love and mercy enjoined in other portions of the Bible, but they were in truth the dictates of infinite wisdom and goodness. God was about to establish Israel in Canaan, to develop among them a nation and government that should be a manifestation of His kingdom upon the earth. They were not only to be inheritors of the true religion, but to disseminate its principles throughout the world. The Canaanites had abandoned themselves to the foulest and most debasing heathenism, and it was necessary that the land should be cleared of what would so surely prevent the fulfillment of God's gracious purposes.

The inhabitants of Canaan had been granted ample opportunity for repentance. Forty years before, the opening of the Red Sea and the judgments upon Egypt had testified to the supreme power of the God of Israel. And now the overthrow of the kings of Midian, of Gilead and Bashan, had further shown that Jehovah was above all gods. The holiness of His character and His abhorrence of impurity had been evinced in the judgments visited upon Israel for their participation in the abominable rites of Baalpeor. All these events were known to the inhabitants of Jericho, and there were many who shared Rahab's conviction, though they refused to obey it, that Jehovah, the God of Israel, "is God in heaven above, and upon the earth beneath." Like the men before the Flood, the Canaanites lived only to blaspheme Heaven and defile the earth. And both love and justice demanded the prompt execution of these rebels against God and foes to man.

How easily the armies of heaven brought down the walls of Jericho, that proud city whose bulwarks, forty years before, had struck terror to the unbelieving spies! The Mighty One of Israel had said, "I have given into thine hand Jericho." Against that word human strength was powerless.

"By faith the walls of Jericho fell down." Hebrews 11:30. The Captain of the Lord's host communicated only with Joshua; He did not reveal Himself to all the congregation, and it rested with them to believe or doubt the words of Joshua, to obey the commands given by him in the name of the Lord, or to deny his authority. *They* could not see the host of angels who attended them under the leadership of the Son of God. They might have reasoned: "What unmeaning movements are these, and how ridiculous the performance of marching daily around the walls of the city, blowing trumpets of rams' horns. This can have no effect upon those towering fortifications." But the very plan of continuing this ceremony through so long a time prior to the final overthrow of the walls afforded opportunity for the development of faith among the Israelites. It was to be impressed upon their minds that their strength was not in the wisdom of man, nor in his might, but only in the God of their salvation. They were thus to become accustomed to relying wholly upon their divine Leader.

God will do great things for those who trust in Him. The reason why His professed people have no greater strength is that they trust so much to their own wisdom, and do not give the Lord an opportunity to reveal His power in their behalf. He will help His believing children in every emergency if they will place their entire confidence in Him and faithfully obey Him.

Soon after the fall of Jericho, Joshua determined to attack Ai, a small town among the ravines a few miles to the west of the Jordan Valley. Spies sent to this place brought back the report that the inhabitants were but few, and that only a small force would be needed to overthrow it.

The great victory that God had gained for them had made the Israelites self-confident. Because He had promised them the land of Canaan they felt secure, and failed to realize that divine help alone could give them success. Even Joshua laid his plans for the conquest of Ai without seeking counsel from God.

The Israelites had begun to exalt their own strength and to look with contempt upon their foes. An easy victory was expected, and three thousand men were thought sufficient to take the place. These rushed to the attack without the assurance that God would be with them. They advanced nearly to the gate of the city, only to encounter the most determined resistance. Panic-stricken at the numbers and thorough preparation of their enemies, they fled in confusion down the steep descent. The Canaanites were in hot pursuit; "they chased them from before the gate, ... and smote them in the going down." Though the loss was small as to numbers—but thirty-six men being slain—the defeat was disheartening to the whole congregation. "The hearts of the people melted, and became as water." This was the first time they had met the Canaanites in actual battle, and if put to flight before the defenders of this little town, what would be the result in the greater conflicts before them? Joshua looked upon their ill success as an expression of God's displeasure, and in distress and apprehension he "rent his clothes, and fell to the earth upon his face before the ark of the Lord until the eventide, he and the elders of Israel, and put dust upon their heads."

"Alas, O Lord God," he cried, "wherefore hast Thou at all brought this people over Jordan, to deliver us into the hand of the Amorites, to destroy us? ... O Lord, what shall I say, when Israel turneth their backs before their enemies! For the Canaanites and all the inhabitants of the land shall hear of it, and shall environ us round, and cut off our name from the earth: and what wilt Thou do unto Thy great name?"

The answer from Jehovah was, "Get thee up; wherefore liest thou thus upon thy face? Israel hath ... transgressed My covenant which I commanded them." It was a time for prompt and decided action, and not for despair and lamentation. There was secret sin in the camp, and it must be searched out and put away before the presence and blessing of the Lord could be with His people. "Neither will I be with you any more, except ye destroy the accursed from among you."

God's command had been disregarded by one of those appointed to execute His judgments. And the nation was held accountable for the guilt of the transgressor: "*They* have even taken of the accursed thing, and have also stolen, and dissembled also." Instruction was given to Joshua for the discovery and punishment of the criminal. The lot was to be employed for the detection of the guilty. The sinner was not directly pointed out, the matter being left in doubt for a time, that the people might feel their responsibility for the sins existing among them, and thus be led to searching of heart and humiliation before God.

Early in the morning, Joshua gathered the people together by their tribes, and the solemn and impressive ceremony began. Step by step the investigation went on. Closer and still closer came the fearful test. First the tribe, then the family, then the household, then the man was taken, and Achan the son of Carmi, of the tribe of Judah, was pointed out by the finger of God as the troubler of Israel.

To establish his guilt beyond all question, leaving no ground for the charge that he had been unjustly condemned, Joshua solemnly adjured Achan to acknowledge the truth. The wretched man made full confession of his crime: "Indeed I have sinned against the Lord God of Israel.... When I saw among the spoils a goodly Babylonish garment, and two hundred shekels of silver, and a wedge of gold of fifty shekel's weight, then I coveted them, and took them; and, behold, they are hid in the earth in the midst of my tent." Messengers were immediately dispatched to the tent, where they removed the earth at the place specified, and "behold, it was hid in his tent, and the silver under it. And they took them out of the midst of the tent, and brought them unto Joshua, ... and laid them out before the Lord."

Sentence was pronounced and immediately executed. "Why hast thou troubled us?" said Joshua, "the Lord shall trouble thee this day." As the people had been held responsible for Achan's sin, and had suffered from its consequences, they were, through their representatives, to take part in its punishment. "All Israel stoned him with stones."

Then there was raised over him a great pile of stones—a witness to the sin and its punishment. "Wherefore the name of that place was called, The valley of Achor," that is, "trouble." In the book of Chronicles his memorial is written—"Achar, the troubler of Israel." 1 Chronicles 2:7.

Achan's sin was committed in defiance of the most direct and solemn warnings and the most mighty manifestations of God's power. "Keep yourselves from the accursed thing, lest ye make yourselves accursed," had been the proclamation to all Israel. The command was given immediately after the miraculous passage of the Jordan, and the recognition of God's covenant by the circumcision of the people—after the observance of the Passover, and the appearance of the Angel of the covenant, the Captain of the Lord's host. It had been followed by the overthrow of Jericho, giving evidence of the destruction which will surely overtake all transgressors of God's law. The fact that divine power alone had given the victory to Israel, that they had not come into possession of Jericho by their own strength, gave solemn weight to the command prohibiting them from partaking of the spoils. God, by the might of His own word, had overthrown this stronghold; the conquest was His, and to Him alone the city with all that it contained was to be devoted.

Of the millions of Israel there was but one man who, in that solemn hour of triumph and of judgment, had dared to transgress the command of God. Achan's covetousness was excited by the sight of that costly robe of Shinar; even when it had brought him face to face with death he called it "a *goodly* Babylonish garment." One sin had led to another, and he appropriated the gold and silver devoted to the treasury of the Lord—he robbed God of the first fruits of the land of Canaan.

The deadly sin that led to Achan's ruin had its root in covetousness, of all sins one of the most common and the most lightly regarded. While other offenses meet with detection and punishment, how rarely does the violation of the tenth commandment so much as call forth censure. The enormity of this sin, and its terrible results, are the lessons of Achan's history.

Covetousness is an evil of gradual development. Achan had cherished greed of gain until it became a habit, binding him in fetters well-nigh impossible to break. While fostering this evil, he would have been filled with horror at the thought of bringing disaster upon Israel; but his perceptions were deadened by sin, and when temptation came, he fell an easy prey.

Are not similar sins still committed, in the face of warnings as solemn and explicit? We are as directly forbidden to indulge covetousness as was Achan to appropriate the spoils of Jericho. God has declared it to be idolatry. We are warned, "Ye cannot serve God and mammon." Matthew 6:24. "Take heed, and beware of covetousness."

Luke 12:15. "Let it not be once named among you." Ephesians 5:3. We have before us the fearful doom of Achan, of Judas, of Ananias and Sapphira. Back of all these we have that of Lucifer, the "son of the morning," who, coveting a higher state, forfeited forever the brightness and bliss of heaven. And yet, notwithstanding all these warnings, covetousness abounds.

Everywhere its slimy track is seen. It creates discontent and dissension in families; it excites envy and hatred in the poor against the rich; it prompts the grinding oppression of the rich toward the poor. And this evil exists not in the world alone, but in the church. How common even here to find selfishness, avarice, overreaching, neglect of charities, and robbery of God "in tithes and offerings." Among church members "in good and regular standing" there are, alas! many Achans. Many a man comes stately to church, and sits at the table of the Lord, while among his possessions are hidden unlawful gains, the things that God has cursed. For a goodly Babylonish garment, multitudes sacrifice the approval of conscience and their hope of heaven. Multitudes barter their integrity, and their capabilities for usefulness, for a bag of silver shekels. The cries of the suffering poor are unheeded; the gospel light is hindered in its course; the scorn of worldlings is kindled by practices that give the lie to the Christian profession; and yet the covetous professor continues to heap up treasures. "Will a man rob God? Yet ye have robbed Me" (Malachi 3:8), saith the Lord.

Achan's sin brought disaster upon the whole nation. For one man's sin the displeasure of God will rest upon His church till the transgression is searched out and put away. The influence most to be feared by the church is not that of open opposers, infidels, and blasphemers, but of inconsistent professors of Christ. These are the ones that keep back the blessing of the God of Israel and bring weakness upon His people.

When the church is in difficulty, when coldness and spiritual declension exist, giving occasion for the enemies of God to triumph, then, instead of folding their hands and lamenting their unhappy state, let its members inquire if there is not an Achan in the camp. With humiliation and searching of heart, let each seek to discover the hidden sins that shut out God's presence.

Achan acknowledged his guilt, but when it was too late for the confession to benefit himself. He had seen the armies of Israel return from Ai defeated and disheartened; yet he did not come forward and confess his sin. He had seen Joshua and the elders of Israel bowed to the earth in grief too great for words. Had he then made confession, he would have given some proof of true penitence; but he still kept silence. He had listened to the proclamation that a great crime had been committed, and had even heard its character definitely stated. But his lips were sealed. Then came the solemn investigation. How his soul thrilled with terror as he saw his tribe pointed out, then his family and his household! But still he uttered no confession, until the finger of God was placed upon him. Then, when his sin could no longer be concealed, he admitted the truth. How often are similar confessions made. There is a vast difference between admitting facts after they have been proved and confessing sins known only to ourselves and to God. Achan would not have confessed had he not hoped by so doing to avert the consequences of his crime. But his confession only served to show that his punishment was just. There was no genuine repentance for sin, no contrition, no change of purpose, no abhorrence of evil.

So confessions will be made by the guilty when they stand before the bar of God, after every case has been decided for life or death. The consequences to result to himself will draw from each an acknowledgment of his sin. It will be forced from the soul by an awful sense of condemnation and a fearful looking for of judgment. But such confessions cannot save the sinner.

So long as they can conceal their transgressions from their fellow men, many, like Achan, feel secure, and flatter themselves that God will not be strict to mark iniquity. All too late their sins will find them out in that day when they shall not be purged with sacrifice or offering forever. When the records of heaven shall be opened, the Judge will not in words declare to man his guilt, but will cast one penetrating, convicting glance, and every deed, every transaction of life, will be vividly impressed upon the memory of the wrongdoer. The person will not, as in Joshua's day, need to be hunted out from tribe to family, but his own lips will confess his shame. The sins hidden from the knowledge of men will then be proclaimed to the whole world.

[498]

Chapter 46—The Blessings and the Curses

This chapter is based on Joshua 8.

After the execution of the sentence upon Achan, Joshua was commanded to marshal all the men of war and again advance against Ai. The power of God was with His people, and they were soon in possession of the city.

Military operations were now suspended, that all Israel might engage in a solemn religious service. The people were eager to obtain a settlement in Canaan; as yet they had not homes or lands for their families, and in order to gain these they must drive out the Canaanites; but this important work must be deferred, for a higher duty demanded their first attention.

Before taking possession of their inheritance, they must renew their covenant of loyalty to God. In the last instructions of Moses, direction had been twice given for a convocation of the tribes upon Mounts Ebal and Gerizim, at Shechem, for the solemn recognition of the law of God. In obedience to these injunctions the whole people, not only men, but "the women, and the little ones, and the strangers that were conversant among them" left their camp at Gilgal, and marched through the country of their enemies, to the vale of Shechem, near the center of the land. Though surrounded by unconquered foes, they were safe under the protection of God as long as they were faithful to Him. Now, as in the days of Jacob, "the terror of God was upon the cities that were round about them" (Genesis 35:5), and the Hebrews were unmolested.

The place appointed for this solemn service was one already sacred from its association with the history of their fathers. It was here that Abraham raised his first altar to Jehovah in the land of Canaan. Here both Abraham and Jacob had pitched their tents. Here the latter bought the field in which the tribes were to bury the body of Joseph. Here also was the well that Jacob had dug, and the oak under which he had buried the idolatrous images of his household.

The spot chosen was one of the most beautiful in all Palestine, and worthy to be the theater where this grand and impressive scene was to be enacted. The lovely valley, its green fields dotted with olive groves, watered with brooks from living fountains, and gemmed with wild flowers, spread out invitingly between the barren hills. Ebal and Gerizim, upon opposite sides of the valley, nearly approach each other, their lower spurs seeming to form a natural pulpit, every word spoken on one being distinctly audible on the other, while the mountainsides, receding, afford space for a vast assemblage.

According to the directions given by Moses, a monument of great stones was erected upon Mount Ebal. Upon these stones, previously prepared by a covering of plaster, the law was inscribed—not only the ten precepts spoken from Sinai and engraved on the tables of stone, but the laws communicated to Moses, and by him written in a book. Beside this monument was built an altar of unhewn stone, upon which sacrifices were offered unto the Lord. The fact that the altar was set up on Mount Ebal, the mountain upon which the curse was put, was significant, denoting that because of their transgressions of God's law, Israel had justly incurred His wrath, and that it would be at once visited, but for the atonement of Christ, represented by the altar of sacrifice.

Six of the tribes—all descended from Leah and Rachel—were stationed upon Mount Gerizim; while those that descended from the handmaids, together with Reuben and Zebulun, took their position on Ebal, the priests with the ark occupying the valley between them. Silence was proclaimed by the sound of the signal trumpet; and then in the deep stillness, and in the presence of this vast assembly, Joshua, standing beside the sacred ark, read the blessings that were to follow obedience to God's law. All the tribes on Gerizim responded by an Amen. He then read the curses, and the tribes on Ebal in like manner gave their assent, thousands upon thousands of voices uniting as the voice of one man in the solemn response. Following this came the reading of the law of God, together with the statutes and judgments that had been delivered to them by Moses.

Israel had received the law directly from the mouth of God at Sinai; and its sacred precepts, written by His own hand, were still preserved in the ark. Now it had been again written where all could read it. All had the privilege of seeing for themselves the conditions of the covenant under which they were to hold possession of Canaan. All were to signify their acceptance of the terms of the covenant and give their assent to the blessings or curses for its observance or neglect. The law was not only written upon the memorial stones, but was read by Joshua himself in the hearing of all Israel. It had not been many weeks since Moses gave the whole book of Deuteronomy in discourses to the people, yet now Joshua read the law again.

Not alone the men of Israel, but "all the women and the little ones" listened to the reading of the law; for it was important that they also should know and do their duty. God had commanded Israel concerning His statutes: "Therefore shall ye lay up these My words in your heart and in your soul, and bind them for a sign upon your hand, that they may be as frontlets between your eyes. And ye shall teach them your children, ... that your days may be multiplied, and the days of your children, in the land which the Lord sware unto your fathers to give them, as the days of heaven upon the earth." Deuteronomy 11:18-21.

Every seventh year the whole law was to be read in the assembly of all Israel, as Moses commanded: "At the end of every seven years, in the solemnity of the year of release, in the feast of tabernacles, when all Israel is come to appear before the Lord thy God in the place which he shall choose, thou shalt read this law before all Israel in their hearing. Gather the people together, men, and women, and children, and thy stranger that is within thy gates, that they may hear, and that they may learn, and fear the Lord your God, and observe to do all the words of this law: and that their children, which have not known anything, may hear, and learn to fear the Lord your God, as long as ye live in the land whither ye go over Jordan to possess it." Deuteronomy 31:10-13.

Satan is ever at work endeavoring to pervert what God has spoken, to blind the mind and darken the understanding, and thus lead men into sin. This is why the Lord is so explicit, making His requirements so very plain that none need err. God is constantly seeking to draw men close under His protection, that Satan may not practice his cruel, deceptive power upon them. He has condescended to speak to them with His own voice, to write with His own hand the living oracles. And these blessed words, all instinct with life and luminous with truth, are committed to men as a perfect guide. Because Satan is so ready to catch away the mind and divert the affections from the Lord's promises and requirements, the greater diligence is needed to fix them in the mind and impress them upon the heart.

Greater attention should be given by religious teachers to instructing the people in the facts and lessons of Bible history and the warnings and requirements of the Lord. These should be presented in simple language, adapted to the comprehension of children. It should be a part of the work both of ministers and parents to see that the young are instructed in the Scriptures.

Parents can and should interest their children in the varied knowledge found in the sacred pages. But if they would interest their sons and daughters in the word of God, they must be interested in it themselves. They must be familiar with its teachings, and, as God commanded Israel, speak of it, "when thou sittest in thine house, and when thou walkest by the way, when thou liest down, and when thou risest up." Deuteronomy 11:19. Those who desire their children to love and reverence God must talk of His goodness, His majesty, and His power, as revealed in His word and in the works of creation.

Every chapter and every verse of the Bible is a communication from God to men. We should bind its precepts as signs upon our hands and as frontlets between our eyes. If studied and obeyed, it would lead God's people, as the Israelites were led, by the pillar of cloud by day and the pillar of fire by night.

Chapter 47—League With the Gibeonites

This chapter is based on Joshua 9 and 10.

From Shechem the Israelites returned to their encampment at Gilgal. Here they were soon after visited by a strange deputation, who desired to enter into treaty with them. The ambassadors represented that they had come from a distant country, and this seemed to be confirmed by their appearance. Their clothing was old and worn, their sandals were patched, their provisions moldy, and the skins that served them for wine bottles were rent and bound up, as if hastily repaired on the journey.

In their far-off home—professedly beyond the limits of Palestine—their fellow countrymen, they said, had heard of the wonders which God had wrought for His people, and had sent them to make a league with Israel. The Hebrews had been specially warned against entering into any league with the idolaters of Canaan, and a doubt as to the truth of the strangers' words arose in the minds of the leaders. "Peradventure ye dwell among us," they said. To this the ambassadors only replied, "We are thy servants." But when Joshua directly demanded of them, "Who are ye? and from whence come ye?" they reiterated their former statement, and added, in proof of their sincerity, "This our bread we took hot for our provision out of our houses on the day we came forth to go unto you; but now, behold, it is dry, and it is moldy: and these bottles of wine, which we filled, were new; and, behold, they be rent: and these our garments and our shoes are become old by reason of the very long journey."

These representations prevailed. The Hebrews "asked not counsel at the mouth of the Lord. And Joshua made peace with them, and made a league with them, to let them live: and the princes of the congregation sware unto them." Thus the treaty was entered into. Three days afterward the truth was discovered. "They heard that they were their neighbors, and that they dwelt among them."

Knowing that it was impossible to resist the Hebrews, the Gibeonites had resorted to stratagem to preserve their lives.

Great was the indignation of the Israelites as they learned the deception that had been practiced upon them. And this was heightened when, after three days' journey, they reached the cities of the Gibeonites, near the center of the land. "All the congregation murmured against the princes;" but the latter refused to break the treaty, though secured by fraud, because they had "sworn unto them by the Lord God of Israel." "And the children of Israel smote them not." The Gibeonites had pledged themselves to renounce idolatry, and accept the worship of Jehovah; and the preservation of their lives was not a violation of God's command to destroy the idolatrous Canaanites. Hence the Hebrews had not by their oath pledged themselves to commit sin. And though the oath had been secured by deception, it was not to be disregarded. The obligation to which one's word is pledged—if it do not bind him to perform a wrong act—should be held sacred. No consideration of gain, of revenge, or of self-interest can in any way affect the inviolability of an oath or pledge. "Lying lips are abomination to the Lord." Proverbs 12:22. He that "shall ascend into the hill of the Lord," and "stand in His holy place," is "he that sweareth to his own hurt, and changeth not." Psalm 24:3; 15:4.

The Gibeonites were permitted to live, but were attached as bondmen to the sanctuary, to perform all menial services. "Joshua made them that day hewers of wood and drawers of water for the congregation, and for the altar of the Lord." These conditions they gratefully accepted, conscious that they had been at fault, and glad to purchase life on any terms. "Behold, we are in thine hand," they said to Joshua; "as it seemeth good and right unto thee to do unto us, do." For centuries their descendants were connected with the service of the sanctuary.

The territory of the Gibeonites comprised four cities. The people were not under the rule of a king, but were governed by elders, or senators. Gibeon, the most important of their towns, "was a great city, as one of the royal cities," "and all the men thereof were mighty." It is a striking evidence of the terror with which the Israelites had inspired the inhabitants of Canaan, that the people of such a city should have resorted to so humiliating an expedient to save their lives.

[507] But it would have fared better with the Gibeonites had they dealt honestly with Israel. While their submission to Jehovah secured the preservation of their lives, their deception brought them only disgrace and servitude. God had made provision that all who would renounce heathenism, and connect themselves with Israel, should share the blessings of the covenant. They were included under the term, "the stranger that sojourneth among you," and with few exceptions this class were to enjoy equal favors and privileges with Israel. The Lord's direction was—

"If a stranger sojourn with thee in your land, ye shall not vex him. But the stranger that dwelleth with you shall be unto you as one born among you, and thou shalt love him as thyself." Leviticus 19:33, 34. Concerning the Passover and the offering of sacrifices it was commanded, "One ordinance shall be both for you of the congregation, and also for the stranger that sojourneth with you: ... as ye are, so shall the stranger be before the Lord." Numbers 15:15.

Such was the footing on which the Gibeonites might have been received, but for the deception to which they had resorted. It was no light humiliation to those citizens of a "royal city," "all the men whereof were mighty," to be made hewers of wood and drawers of water throughout their generations. But they had adopted the garb of poverty for the purpose of deception, and it was fastened upon them as a badge of perpetual servitude. Thus through all their generations their servile condition would testify to God's hatred of falsehood.

The submission of Gibeon to the Israelites filled the kings of Canaan with dismay. Steps were at once taken for revenge upon those who had made peace with the invaders. Under the leadership of Adonizedek, king of Jerusalem, five of the Canaanite kings entered into a confederacy against Gibeon. Their movements were rapid. The Gibeonites were unprepared for defense, and they sent a message to Joshua at Gilgal: "Slack not thy hand from thy servants; come up to us quickly, and save us, and help us: for all the kings of the Amorites that dwell in the mountains are gathered together against us." The danger threatened not the people of Gibeon alone, but also Israel. This city commanded the passes to central and southern Palestine, and it must be held if the country was to be conquered.

Joshua prepared to go at once to the relief of Gibeon. The inhabitants of the besieged city had feared that he would reject their appeal, because of the fraud which they had practiced; but since they had submitted to the control of Israel, and had accepted the worship of God, he felt himself under obligation to protect them. He did not this time move without divine counsel, and the Lord encouraged him in the undertaking. "Fear them not," was the divine message; "for I have delivered them into thine hand; there shall not a man of them stand before thee." "So Joshua ascended from Gilgal, he, and all the people of war with him, and all the mighty men of valor."

[508]

By marching all night he brought his forces before Gibeon in the morning. Scarcely had the confederate princes mustered their armies about the city when Joshua was upon them. The attack resulted in the utter discomfiture of the assailants. The immense host fled before Joshua up the mountain pass to Beth-horon; and having gained the height, they rushed down the precipitous descent upon the other side. Here a fierce hailstorm burst upon them. "The Lord cast down great stones from heaven: ... they were more which died with hailstones than they whom the children of Israel slew with the sword."

While the Amorites were continuing their headlong flight, intent on finding refuge in the mountain strongholds, Joshua, looking down from the ridge above, saw that the day would be too short for the accomplishment of his work. If not fully routed, their enemies would again rally, and renew the struggle. "Then spake Joshua to the Lord, ... and he said in the sight of Israel, Sun, stand thou still upon Gibeon; and thou, Moon, in the valley of Ajalon. And the sun stood still, and the moon stayed, until the people had avenged themselves upon their enemies.... The sun stood still in the midst of heaven, and hasted not to go down about a whole day."

Before the evening fell, God's promise to Joshua had been fulfilled. The entire host of the enemy had been given into his hand. Long were the events of that day to remain in the memory of Israel. "There was no day like that before it or after it, that Jehovah hearkened unto the voice of a man: for the Lord fought for Israel." "The sun and moon stood still in their habitation: at the light of Thine arrows they went, and at the shining of Thy glittering spear. Thou didst march through the land in indignation, Thou didst thresh the heathen in anger. Thou wentest forth for the salvation of Thy people." Habakkuk 3:11-13.

The Spirit of God inspired Joshua's prayer, that evidence might again be given of the power of Israel's God. Hence the request did not show presumption on the part of the great leader. Joshua had received the promise that God would surely overthrow these enemies of Israel, yet he put forth as earnest effort as though success depended upon the armies of Israel alone. He did all that human energy could do, and then he cried in faith for divine aid. The secret of success is the union of divine power with human effort. Those who achieve the greatest results are those who rely most implicitly upon the Almighty Arm. The man who commanded, "Sun, stand thou still upon Gibeon; and thou, Moon, in the valley of Ajalon," is the man who for hours lay prostrate upon the earth in prayer in the camp of Gilgal. The men of prayer are the men of power.

This mighty miracle testifies that the creation is under the control of the Creator. Satan seeks to conceal from men the divine agency in the physical world—to keep out of sight the unwearied working of the first great cause. In this miracle all who exalt nature above the God of nature stand rebuked.

At His own will God summons the forces of nature to overthrow the might of His enemies—"fire, and hail; snow, and vapor; stormy wind fulfilling His word." Psalm 148:8. When the heathen Amorites had set themselves to resist His purposes, God interposed, casting down "great stones from heaven" upon the enemies of Israel. We are told of a greater battle to take place in the closing scenes of earth's history, when "Jehovah hath opened His armory, and hath brought forth the weapons of His indignation." Jeremiah 50:25. "Hast thou," he inquires, "entered into the treasures of the snow? or hast thou seen the treasures of the hail, which I have reserved against the time of trouble, against the day of battle and war?" Job 38:22, 23.

The revelator describes the destruction that is to take place when the "great voice out of the temple of heaven" announces, "It is done." He says, "There fell upon men a great hail out of heaven, every stone about the weight of a talent." Revelation 16:17, 21.

Chapter 48—The Division of Canaan

This chapter is based on Joshua 10:40-43; 11; 14-22.

The victory at Beth-horon was speedily followed by the conquest of southern Canaan. "Joshua smote all the country of the hills, and of the south, and of the vale.... And all these kings and their land did Joshua take at one time, because the Lord God of Israel fought for Israel. And Joshua returned, and all Israel with him, unto the camp at Gilgal."

The tribes of northern Palestine, terrified at the success which had attended the armies of Israel, now entered into a league against them. At the head of this confederacy was Jabin, king of Hazor, a territory to the west of Lake Merom. "And they went out, they and all their hosts with them." This army was much larger than any that the Israelites had before encountered in Canaan—"much people, even as the sand that is upon the seashore in multitude, with horses and chariots very many. And when all these kings were met together, they came and pitched together at the waters of Merom, to fight against Israel." Again a message of encouragement was given to Joshua: "Be not afraid because of them: for tomorrow about this time will I deliver them up all slain before Israel."

Near Lake Merom he fell upon the camp of the allies and utterly routed their forces. "The Lord delivered them into the hand of Israel, who smote them, and chased them ... until they left them none remaining." The chariots and horses that had been the pride and boast of the Canaanites were not to be appropriated by Israel. At the command of God the chariots were burned, and the horses lamed, and thus rendered unfit for use in battle. The Israelites were not to put their trust in chariots or horses, but "in the name of the Lord their God."

One by one the cities were taken, and Hazor, the stronghold of the confederacy, was burned. The war was continued for several years, but its close found Joshua master of Canaan. "And the land had rest from war."

But though the power of the Canaanites had been broken, they had not been fully dispossessed. On the west the Philistines still held a fertile plain along the seacoast, while north of them was the territory of the Sidonians. Lebanon also was in the possession of the latter people; and to the south, toward Egypt, the land was still occupied by the enemies of Israel.

Joshua was not, however, to continue the war. There was another work for the great leader to perform before he should relinquish the command of Israel. The whole land, both the parts already conquered and that which was yet unsubdued, was to be apportioned among the tribes. And it was the duty of each tribe to fully subdue its own inheritance. If the people should prove faithful to God, He would drive out their enemies from before them; and He promised to give them still greater possessions if they would but be true to His covenant.

To Joshua, with Eleazar the high priest, and the heads of the tribes, the distribution of the land was committed, the location of each tribe being determined by lot. Moses himself had fixed the bounds of the country as it was to be divided among the tribes when they should come in possession of Canaan, and had appointed a prince from each tribe to attend to the distribution. The tribe of Levi, being devoted to the sanctuary service, was not counted in this allotment; but forty-eight cities in different parts of the country were assigned the Levites as their inheritance.

Before the distribution of the land had been entered upon, Caleb, accompanied by the heads of his tribe, came forward with a special claim. Except Joshua, Caleb was now the oldest man in Israel. Caleb and Joshua were the only ones among the spies who had brought a good report of the Land of Promise, encouraging the people to go up and possess it in the name of the Lord. Caleb now reminded Joshua of the promise then made, as the reward of his faithfulness: "The land whereon thy feet have trodden shall be thine inheritance, and thy children's forever, because thou hast wholly followed the Lord." He therefore presented a request that Hebron be given him for a possession. Here had been for many years the home of Abraham, Isaac, and Jacob; and here, in the cave of Machpelah, they were buried. Hebron was the seat of the dreaded Anakim, whose formidable appearance had so terrified the spies, and through them destroyed the courage of all Israel. This, above all others, was the place which Caleb, trusting in the strength of God, chose for his inheritance.

"Behold, the Lord hath kept me alive," he said, "these forty and five years, even since the Lord spake this word unto Moses: ... and now, lo, I am this day fourscore and five years old. As yet I am as strong this day as I was in the day that Moses sent me: as my strength was then, even so is my strength now, for war, both to go out, and to come in. Now therefore give me this mountain, whereof the Lord spake in that day: for thou heardest in that day how the Anakim were there, and that the cities were great and fenced: if so be the Lord will be with me, then I shall be able to drive them out, as the Lord said." This request was supported by the chief men of Judah. Caleb himself being the one appointed from this tribe to apportion the land, he had chosen to unite these men with him in presenting his claim, that there might be no appearance of having employed his authority for selfish advantage.

His claim was immediately granted. To none could the conquest of this giant stronghold be more safely entrusted. "Joshua blessed him, and gave unto Caleb the son of Jephunneh Hebron for an inheritance," "because that he wholly followed the Lord God of Israel." Caleb's faith now was just what it was when his testimony had contradicted the evil report of the spies. He had believed God's promise that He would put His people in possession of Canaan, and in this he had followed the Lord fully. He had endured with his people the long wandering in the wilderness, thus sharing the disappointments and burdens of the guilty; yet he made no complaint of this, but exalted the mercy of God that had preserved him in the wilderness when his brethren were cut off. Amid all the hardships, perils, and plagues of the desert wanderings, and during the years of warfare since entering Canaan, the Lord had preserved him; and now at upwards of fourscore his vigor was unabated. He did not ask for himself a land already conquered, but the place which above all others the spies had thought it impossible to subdue. By the help of God he would wrest his stronghold from the very giants whose power had staggered the faith of Israel. It was no desire for honor

[512]

or aggrandizement that prompted Caleb's request. The brave old warrior was desirous of giving to the people an example that would honor God, and encourage the tribes fully to subdue the land which their fathers had deemed unconquerable.

Caleb obtained the inheritance upon which his heart had been set for forty years, and, trusting in God to be with him, he "drove thence the three sons of Anak." Having thus secured a possession for himself and his house, his zeal did not abate; he did not settle down to enjoy his inheritance, but pushed on to further conquests for the benefit of the nation and the glory of God.

The cowards and rebels had perished in the wilderness, but the righteous spies ate of the grapes of Eschol. To each was given according to his faith. The unbelieving had seen their fears fulfilled. Notwithstanding God's promise, they had declared that it was impossible to inherit Canaan, and they did not possess it. But those who trusted in God, looking not so much to the difficulties to be encountered as to the strength of their Almighty Helper, entered the goodly land. It was through faith that the ancient worthies "subdued kingdoms, ... escaped the edge of the sword, out of weakness were made strong, waxed valiant in fight, turned to flight the armies of the aliens." Hebrews 11:33, 34. "This is the victory that overcometh the world, even our faith." 1 John 5:4.

Another claim concerning the division of the land revealed a spirit widely different from that of Caleb. It was presented by the children of Joseph, the tribe of Ephraim with the half tribe of Manasseh. In consideration of their superior numbers, these tribes demanded a double portion of territory. The lot designated for them was the richest in the land, including the fertile plain of Sharon; but many of the principal towns in the valley were still in possession of the Canaanites, and the tribes shrank from the toil and danger of conquering their possessions, and desired an additional portion in territory already subdued. The tribe of Ephraim was one of the largest in Israel, as well as the one to which Joshua himself belonged, and its members naturally regarded themselves as entitled to special consideration. "Why hast thou given me but one lot and one portion to inherit," they said, "seeing I am a great people?" But no departure from strict justice could be won from the inflexible leader.

His answer was, "If thou be a great people, then get thee up to the wood country, and cut down for thyself there in the land of the Perizzites and of the giants, if Mount Ephraim be too narrow for thee."

Their reply showed the real cause of complaint. They lacked faith and courage to drive out the Canaanites. "The hill is not enough for us," they said; "and all the Canaanites that dwell in the land of the valley have chariots of iron."

The power of the God of Israel had been pledged to His people, and had the Ephraimites possessed the courage and faith of Caleb, no enemy could have stood before them. Their evident desire to shun hardship and danger was firmly met by Joshua. "Thou art a great people, and hast great power," he said; "thou shalt drive out the Canaanites, though they have iron chariots, and though they be strong." Thus their own arguments were turned against them. Being a great people, as they claimed, they were fully able to make their own way, as did their brethren. With the help of God they need not fear the chariots of iron.

Heretofore Gilgal had been the headquarters of the nation and the seat of the tabernacle. But now the tabernacle was to be removed to the place chosen for its permanent location. This was Shiloh, a little town in the lot of Ephraim. It was near the center of the land, and was easy of access to all the tribes. Here a portion of country had been thoroughly subdued, so that the worshipers would not be molested. "And the whole congregation of the children of Israel assembled together at Shiloh, and set up the tabernacle of the congregation there." The tribes that were still encamped when the tabernacle was removed from Gilgal followed it, and pitched near Shiloh. Here these tribes remained until they dispersed to their possessions.

The ark remained at Shiloh for three hundred years, until, because of the sins of Eli's house, it fell into the hands of the Philistines, and Shiloh was ruined. The ark was never returned to the tabernacle here, the sanctuary service was finally transferred to the temple at Jerusalem, and Shiloh fell into insignificance. There are only ruins to mark the spot where it once stood. Long afterward its fate was made use of as a warning to Jerusalem. "Go ye now unto My place which was in Shiloh," the Lord declared by the prophet Jeremiah, "where I set My name at the first, and see what I did to it for the wickedness of My people Israel.... Therefore will I do unto this house, which is called by My name, wherein ye trust, and unto the place which I gave to you and to your fathers, as I have done to Shiloh." Jeremiah 7:12-14.

"When they had made an end of dividing the land," and all the tribes had been allotted their inheritance. Joshua presented his claim. To him, as to Caleb, a special promise of inheritance had been given; yet he asked for no extensive province, but only a single city. "They gave him the city which he asked, ... and he built the city, and dwelt therein." The name given to the city was Timnath-serah, "the portion that remains"—a standing testimony to the noble character and unselfish spirit of the conqueror, who, instead of being the first to appropriate the spoils of conquest, deferred his claim until the humblest of his people had been served.

Six of the cities assigned to the Levites—three on each side the Jordan—were appointed as cities of refuge, to which the manslayer might flee for safety. The appointment of these cities had been commanded by Moses, "that the slayer may flee thither, which killeth any person at unawares. And they shall be unto you cities for refuge," he said, "that the manslayer die not, until he stand before the congregation in judgment." Numbers 35:11, 12. This merciful provision was rendered necessary by the ancient custom of private vengeance, by which the punishment of the murderer devolved on the nearest relative or the next heir of the deceased. In cases where guilt was clearly evident it was not necessary to wait for a trial by the magistrates. The avenger might pursue the criminal anywhere and put him to death wherever he should be found. The Lord did not see fit to abolish this custom at that time, but He made provision to ensure the safety of those who should take life unintentionally.

The cities of refuge were so distributed as to be within a half day's journey of every part of the land. The roads leading to them were always to be kept in good repair; all along the way signposts were to be erected bearing the word "Refuge" in plain, bold characters, that the fleeing one might not be delayed for a moment. Any person—Hebrew, stranger, or sojourner—might avail himself of this provision. But while the guiltless were not to be rashly slain, neither were the guilty to escape punishment. The case of the fugitive was to be fairly tried by the proper authorities, and only when found innocent of intentional murder was he to be protected in the city of refuge. The guilty were given up to the avenger. And those who were entitled to protection could receive it only on condition of remaining within the appointed refuge. Should one wander away beyond the prescribed limits, and be found by the avenger of blood, his life would pay the penalty of his disregard of the Lord's provision. At the death of the high priest, however, all who had sought shelter in the cities of refuge were at liberty to return to their possessions.

In a trial for murder the accused was not to be condemned on the testimony of one witness, even though circumstantial evidence might be strong against him. The Lord's direction was, "Whoso killeth any person, the murderer shall be put to death by the mouth of witnesses: but one witness shall not testify against any person to cause him to die." Numbers 35:30. It was Christ who gave to Moses these directions for Israel; and when personally with His disciples on earth, as He taught them how to treat the erring, the Great Teacher repeated the lesson that one man's testimony is not to acquit or condemn. One man's views and opinions are not to settle disputed questions. In all these matters two or more are to be associated, and together they are to bear the responsibility, "that in the mouth of two or three witnesses every word may be established." Matthew 18:16.

If the one tried for murder were proved guilty, no atonement or ransom could rescue him. "Whoso sheddeth man's blood, by man shall his blood be shed." Genesis 9:6. "Ye shall take no satisfaction for the life of a murderer, which is guilty of death: but he shall be surely put to death." "Thou shalt take him from Mine altar, that he may die," was the command of God; "the land cannot be cleansed of the blood that is shed therein, but by the blood of him that shed it." Numbers 35:31, 33; Exodus 21:14. The safety and purity of the nation demanded that the sin of murder be severely punished. Human life, which God alone could give, must be sacredly guarded.

The cities of refuge appointed for God's ancient people were a symbol of the refuge provided in Christ. The same merciful Saviour who appointed those temporal cities of refuge has by the shedding of His own blood provided for the transgressors of God's law a sure retreat, into which they may flee for safety from the second death.

No power can take out of His hands the souls that go to Him for pardon. "There is therefore now no condemnation to them which are in Christ Jesus." "Who is he that condemneth? It is Christ that died, yea rather, that is risen again, who is even at the right hand of God, who also maketh intercession for us;" that "we might have a strong consolation, who have fled for refuge to lay hold upon the hope set before us." Romans 8:1, 34; Hebrews 6:18.

He who fled to the city of refuge could make no delay. Family and employment were left behind. There was no time to say farewell to loved ones. His life was at stake, and every other interest must be sacrificed to the one purpose—to reach the place of safety. Weariness was forgotten, difficulties were unheeded. The fugitive dared not for one moment slacken his pace until he was within the wall of the city.

The sinner is exposed to eternal death, until he finds a hiding place in Christ; and as loitering and carelessness might rob the fugitive of his only chance for life, so delays and indifference may prove the ruin of the soul. Satan, the great adversary, is on the track of every transgressor of God's holy law, and he who is not sensible of his danger, and does not earnestly seek shelter in the eternal refuge, will fall a prey to the destroyer.

The prisoner who at any time went outside the city of refuge was abandoned to the avenger of blood. Thus the people were taught to adhere to the methods which infinite wisdom appointed for their security. Even so, it is not enough that the sinner *believe* in Christ for the pardon of sin; he must, by faith and obedience, *abide* in Him. "For if we sin willfully after that we have received the knowledge of the truth, there remaineth no more sacrifice for sins, but a certain fearful looking for of judgment and fiery indignation, which shall devour the adversaries." Hebrews 10:26, 27.

Two of the tribes of Israel, Gad and Reuben, with half the tribe of Manasseh, had received their inheritance before crossing the Jordan. To a pastoral people, the wide upland plains and rich forests of Gilead and Bashan, offering extensive grazing land for their flocks and herds, had attractions which were not to be found in Canaan itself, and the two and a half tribes, desiring to settle here, had pledged themselves to furnish their proportion of armed men to accompany their brethren across the Jordan and to share their battles till they also should enter upon their inheritance. The obligation had

Division of Canaan

been faithfully discharged. When the ten tribes entered Canaan forty thousand of "the children of Reuben, and the children of Gad, and half the tribe of Manasseh ... prepared for war passed over before the Lord unto battle, to the plains of Jericho." Joshua 4:12, 13. For years they had fought bravely by the side of their brethren. Now the time had come for them to get unto the land of their possession. As they had united with their brethren in the conflicts, so they had shared the spoils; and they returned "with much riches ... and with very much cattle, with silver, and with gold, and with brass, and with iron, and with very much raiment," all of which they were to share with those who had remained with the families and flocks.

They were now to dwell at a distance from the sanctuary of the Lord, and it was with an anxious heart that Joshua witnessed their departure, knowing how strong would be the temptations, in their isolated and wandering life, to fall into the customs of the heathen tribes that dwelt upon their borders.

While the minds of Joshua and other leaders were still oppressed with anxious forebodings, strange tidings reached them. Beside the Jordan, near the place of Israel's miraculous passage of the river, the two and a half tribes had erected a great altar, similar to the altar of burnt offering at Shiloh. The law of God prohibited, on pain of death, the establishment of another worship than that at the sanctuary. If such was the object of this altar, it would, if permitted to remain, lead the people away from the true faith.

The representatives of the people assembled at Shiloh, and in the heat of their excitement and indignation proposed to make war at once upon the offenders. Through the influence of the more cautious, however, it was decided to send first a delegation to obtain from the two and a half tribes an explanation of their conduct. Ten princes, one from each tribe, were chosen. At their head was Phinehas, who had distinguished himself by his zeal in the matter of Peor.

The two and a half tribes had been at fault in entering, without explanation, upon an act open to such grave suspicions. The ambassadors, taking it for granted that their brethren were guilty, met them with sharp rebuke. They accused them of rebelling against the Lord, and bade them remember how judgments had been visited upon Israel for joining themselves to Baalpeor. In behalf of all Israel, Phinehas stated to the children of Gad and Reuben that if they were unwilling to abide in that land without an altar for sacrifice, they would be welcome to a share in the possessions and privileges of their brethren on the other side.

In reply the accused explained that their altar was not intended for sacrifice, but simply as a witness that, although separated by the river, they were of the same faith as their brethren in Canaan. They had feared that in future years their children might be excluded from the tabernacle, as having no part in Israel. Then this altar, erected after the pattern of the altar of the Lord at Shiloh, would be a witness that its builders were also worshipers of the living God.

With great joy the ambassadors accepted this explanation, and immediately carried back the tidings to those who sent them. All thoughts of war were dismissed, and the people united in rejoicing, and praise to God.

The children of Gad and Reuben now placed upon their altar an inscription pointing out the purpose for which it was erected; and they said, "It shall be a witness between us that Jehovah is God." Thus they endeavored to prevent future misapprehension and to remove what might be a cause of temptation.

How often serious difficulties arise from a simple misunderstanding, even among those who are actuated by the worthiest motives; and without the exercise of courtesy and forbearance, what serious and even fatal results may follow. The ten tribes remembered how, in Achan's case, God had rebuked the lack of vigilance to discover the sins existing among them. Now they resolved to act promptly and earnestly; but in seeking to shun their first error, they had gone to the opposite extreme. Instead of making courteous inquiry to learn the facts in the case, they had met their brethren with censure and condemnation. Had the men of Gad and Reuben retorted in the same spirit, war would have been the result. While it is important on the one hand that laxness in dealing with sin be avoided, it is equally important on the other to shun harsh judgment and groundless suspicion.

While very sensitive to the least blame in regard to their own course, many are too severe in dealing with those whom they suppose to be in error. No one was ever reclaimed from a wrong position by censure and reproach; but many are thus driven further from the right path and led to harden their hearts against conviction. A spirit of kindness, a courteous, forbearing deportment may save the erring and hide a multitude of sins.

The wisdom displayed by the Reubenites and their companions is worthy of imitation. While honestly seeking to promote the cause of true religion, they were misjudged and severely censured; yet they manifested no resentment. They listened with courtesy and patience to the charges of their brethren before attempting to make their defense, and then fully explained their motives and showed their innocence. Thus the difficulty which had threatened such serious consequences was amicably settled.

Even under false accusation those who are in the right can afford to be calm and considerate. God is acquainted with all that is misunderstood and misinterpreted by men, and we can safely leave our case in His hands. He will as surely vindicate the cause of those who put their trust in Him as He searched out the guilt of Achan. Those who are actuated by the spirit of Christ will possess that charity which suffers long and is kind.

It is the will of God that union and brotherly love should exist among His people. The prayer of Christ just before His crucifixion was that His disciples might be one as He is one with the Father, that the world might believe that God had sent Him. This most touching and wonderful prayer reaches down the ages, even to our day; for His words were, "Neither pray I for these alone, but for them also which shall believe on Me through their word." John 17:20. While we are not to sacrifice one principle of truth, it should be our constant aim to reach this state of unity. This is the evidence of our discipleship. Said Jesus, "By this shall all men know that ye are My disciples, if ye have love one to another." John 13:35. The apostle Peter exhorts the church, "Be ye all of one mind, having compassion one of another; love as brethren, be pitiful, be courteous: not rendering evil for evil, or railing for railing: but contrariwise blessing; knowing that ye are thereunto called, that ye should inherit a blessing." 1 Peter 3:8, 9.

Chapter 49—The Last Words of Joshua

This chapter is based on Joshua 23 and 24.

The wars and conquest ended, Joshua had withdrawn to the peaceful retirement of his home at Timnath-serah. "And it came to pass, a long time after that the Lord had given rest unto Israel from all their enemies round about, that Joshua ... called for all Israel, and for their elders, and for their heads, and for their judges, and for their officers."

Some years had passed since the people had settled in their possessions, and already could be seen cropping out the same evils that had heretofore brought judgments upon Israel. As Joshua felt the infirmities of age stealing upon him, and realized that his work must soon close, he was filled with anxiety for the future of his people. It was with more than a father's interest that he addressed them, as they gathered once more about their aged chief. "Ye have seen," he said, "all that the Lord your God hath done unto all these nations because of you; for the Lord your God is He that hath fought for you." Although the Canaanites had been subdued, they still possessed a considerable portion of the land promised to Israel, and Joshua exhorted his people not to settle down at ease and forget the Lord's command to utterly dispossess these idolatrous nations.

The people in general were slow to complete the work of driving out the heathen. The tribes had dispersed to their possessions, the army had disbanded, and it was looked upon as a difficult and doubtful undertaking to renew the war. But Joshua declared: "The Lord your God, He shall expel them from before you, and drive them from out of your sight; and ye shall possess their land, as the Lord your God hath promised unto you. Be ye therefore very courageous to keep and to do all that is written in the book of the law of Moses, that ye turn not aside therefrom to the right hand or to the left."

Joshua appealed to the people themselves as witnesses that, so far as they had complied with the conditions, God had faithfully fulfilled His promises to them. "Ye know in all your hearts and in all your souls," he said, "that not one thing hath failed of all the good things which the Lord your God spake concerning you; all are come to pass unto you, and not one thing hath failed thereof." He declared to them that as the Lord had fulfilled His promises, so He would fulfill His threatenings. "It shall come to pass, that as all good things are come upon you, which the Lord your God promised you; so shall the Lord bring upon you all evil things.... When ye have transgressed the covenant of the Lord, ... then shall the anger of the Lord be kindled against you, and ye shall perish quickly from off the good land which He hath given unto you."

Satan deceives many with the plausible theory that God's love for His people is so great that He will excuse sin in them; he represents that while the threatenings of God's word are to serve a certain purpose in His moral government, they are never to be literally fulfilled. But in all His dealings with His creatures God has maintained the principles of righteousness by revealing sin in its true character—by demonstrating that its sure result is misery and death. The unconditional pardon of sin never has been, and never will be. Such pardon would show the abandonment of the principles of righteousness, which are the very foundation of the government of God. It would fill the unfallen universe with consternation. God has faithfully pointed out the results of sin, and if these warnings were not true, how could we be sure that His promises would be fulfilled? That so-called benevolence which would set aside justice is not benevolence but weakness.

God is the life-giver. From the beginning all His laws were ordained to life. But sin broke in upon the order that God had established, and discord followed. So long as sin exists, suffering and death are inevitable. It is only because the Redeemer has borne the curse of sin in our behalf that man can hope to escape, in his own person, its dire results.

Before the death of Joshua the heads and representatives of the tribes, obedient to his summons, again assembled at Shechem. No spot in all the land possessed so many sacred associations, carrying their minds back to God's covenant with Abraham and Jacob, and recalling also their own solemn vows upon their entrance into Canaan. Here were the mountains Ebal and Gerizim, the silent witnesses of those vows which now, in the presence of their dying leader, they had assembled to renew. On every side were evidences of what God had wrought for them; how He had given them a land for which they did not labor, and cities which they built not, vineyards and oliveyards which they planted not. Joshua reviewed once more the history of Israel, recounting the wonderful works of God, that all might have a sense of His love and mercy and might serve Him "in sincerity and in truth."

By Joshua's direction the ark had been brought from Shiloh. The occasion was one of great solemnity, and this symbol of God's presence would deepen the impression he wished to make upon the people. After presenting the goodness of God toward Israel, he called upon them, in the name of Jehovah, to choose whom they would serve. The worship of idols was still to some extent secretly practiced, and Joshua endeavored now to bring them to a decision that should banish this sin from Israel. "If it seem evil unto you to serve Jehovah," he said, "choose you this day whom ye will serve." Joshua desired to lead them to serve God, not by compulsion, but willingly. Love to God is the very foundation of religion. To engage in His service merely from hope of reward or fear of punishment would avail nothing. Open apostasy would not be more offensive to God than hypocrisy and mere formal worship.

The aged leader urged the people to consider, in all its bearings, what he had set before them, and to decide if they really desired to live as did the degraded idolatrous nations around them. If it seemed evil to them to serve Jehovah, the source of power, the fountain of blessing, let them that day choose whom they would serve— "the gods which your fathers served," from whom Abraham was called out, "or the gods of the Amorites, in whose land ye dwell." These last words were a keen rebuke to Israel. The gods of the Amorites had not been able to protect their worshipers. Because of their abominable and debasing sins, that wicked nation had been destroyed, and the good land which they once possessed had been given to God's people. What folly for Israel to choose the deities for whose worship the Amorites had been destroyed! "As for me and my house," said Joshua, "we will serve Jehovah." The same holy zeal that inspired the leader's heart was communicated to the people. His appeals called forth the unhesitating response, "God forbid that we should forsake Jehovah, to serve other gods."

"Ye cannot serve the Lord," said Joshua: "for He is a holy God; ... He will not forgive your transgressions nor your sins." Before there could be any permanent reformation the people must be led to feel their utter inability in themselves to render obedience to God. They had broken His law, it condemned them as transgressors, and it provided no way of escape. While they trusted in their own strength and righteousness, it was impossible for them to secure the pardon of their sins; they could not meet the claims of God's perfect law, and it was in vain that they pledged themselves to serve God. It was only by faith in Christ that they could secure pardon of sin and receive strength to obey God's law. They must cease to rely upon their own efforts for salvation, they must trust wholly in the merits of the promised Saviour, if they would be accepted of God.

Joshua endeavored to lead his hearers to weigh well their words, and refrain from vows which they would be unprepared to fulfill. With deep earnestness they repeated the declaration: "Nay; but we will serve the Lord." Solemnly consenting to the witness against themselves that they had chosen Jehovah, they once more reiterated their pledge of loyalty: "The Lord our God will we serve, and His voice will we obey.

"So Joshua made a covenant with the people that day, and set them a statute and an ordinance in Shechem." Having written an account of this solemn transaction, he placed it, with the book of the law, in the side of the ark. And he set up a pillar as a memorial, saying, "Behold, this stone shall be a witness unto us; for it hath heard all the words of the Lord which He spake unto us; it shall be therefore a witness unto you, lest ye deny your God. So Joshua let the people depart, every man unto his inheritance."

Joshua's work for Israel was done. He had "wholly followed the Lord;" and in the book of God he is written, "The servant of Jehovah." The noblest testimony to his character as a public leader is the history of the generation that had enjoyed his labors: "Israel served the Lord all the days of Joshua, and all the days of the elders that overlived Joshua."

Chapter 50—Tithes and Offerings

In the Hebrew economy one tenth of the income of the people was set apart to support the public worship of God. Thus Moses declared to Israel: "All the tithe of the land, whether of the seed of the land, or of the fruit of the tree, is the Lord's: it is holy unto the Lord." "And concerning the tithe of the herd, or of the flock, ... the tenth shall be holy unto the Lord." Leviticus 27:30, 32.

But the tithing system did not originate with the Hebrews. From the earliest times the Lord claimed a tithe as His, and this claim was recognized and honored. Abraham paid tithes to Melchizedek, the priest of the most high God. Genesis 14:20. Jacob, when at Bethel, an exile and a wanderer, promised the Lord, "Of all that Thou shalt give me I will surely give the tenth unto Thee." Genesis 28:22. As the Israelites were about to be established as a nation, the law of tithing was reaffirmed as one of the divinely ordained statutes upon obedience to which their prosperity depended.

The system of tithes and offerings was intended to impress the minds of men with a great truth—that God is the source of every blessing to His creatures, and that to Him man's gratitude is due for the good gifts of His providence.

"He giveth to all life, and breath, and all things." Acts 17:25. The Lord declares, "Every beast of the forest is Mine, and the cattle upon a thousand hills." Psalm 50:10. "The silver is Mine, and the gold is Mine." Haggai 2:8. And it is God who gives men power to get wealth. Deuteronomy 8:18. As an acknowledgment that all things came from Him, the Lord directed that a portion of His bounty should be returned to Him in gifts and offerings to sustain His worship.

"The tithe ... *is* the Lord's." Here the same form of expression is employed as in the law of the Sabbath. "The seventh day *is* the Sabbath of the Lord thy God." Exodus 20:10. God reserved to Himself a specified portion of man's time and of his means, and no man could, without guilt, appropriate either for his own interests.

The tithe was to be exclusively devoted to the use of the Levites, the tribe that had been set apart for the service of the sanctuary. But this was by no means the limit of the contributions for religious purposes. The tabernacle, as afterward the temple, was erected wholly by freewill offerings; and to provide for necessary repairs and other expenses, Moses directed that as often as the people were numbered, each should contribute a half shekel for "the service of the tabernacle." In the time of Nehemiah a contribution was made yearly for this purpose. See Exodus 30:12-16; 2 Kings 12:4, 5; 2 Chronicles 24:4-13; Nehemiah 10:32, 33. From time to time sin offerings and thank offerings were brought to God. These were presented in great numbers at the annual feasts. And the most liberal provision was made for the poor.

Even before the tithe could be reserved there had been an acknowledgment of the claims of God. The first that ripened of every product of the land was consecrated to Him. The first of the wool when the sheep were shorn, of the grain when the wheat was threshed, the first of the oil and the wine, was set apart for God. So also were the first-born of all animals; and a redemption price was paid for the first-born son. The first fruits were to be presented before the Lord at the sanctuary, and were then devoted to the use of the priests.

Thus the people were constantly reminded that God was the true proprietor of their fields, their flocks, and their herds; that He sent them sunshine and rain for their seedtime and harvest, and that everything they possessed was of His creation, and He had made them stewards of His goods.

As the men of Israel, laden with the first fruits of field and orchard and vineyard, gathered at the tabernacle, there was made a public acknowledgment of God's goodness. When the priest accepted the gift, the offerer, speaking as in the presence of Jehovah, said, "A Syrian ready to perish was my father;" and he described the sojourn in Egypt and the affliction from which God had delivered Israel "with an outstretched arm, and with great terribleness, and with signs, and with wonders." And he said, "He hath brought us into this place, and hath given us this land, even a land that floweth with milk and honey. And now, behold, I have brought the first fruits of the land, which Thou, Jehovah, hast given me." Deuteronomy 26:5, 8-11.

The contributions required of the Hebrews for religious and charitable purposes amounted to fully one fourth of their income. So heavy a tax upon the resources of the people might be expected to reduce them to poverty; but, on the contrary, the faithful observance of these regulations was one of the conditions of their prosperity. On condition of their obedience God made them this promise: "I will rebuke the devourer for your sakes, and he shall not destroy the fruits of your ground; neither shall your vine cast her fruit before the time in the field.... And all nations shall call you blessed: for ye shall be a delightsome land, saith the Lord of hosts." Malachi 3:11.

A striking illustration of the results of selfishly withholding even freewill offerings from the cause of God was given in the days of the prophet Haggai. After their return from the captivity in Babylon, the Jews undertook to rebuild the temple of the Lord; but meeting determined opposition from their enemies, they discontinued the work; and a severe drought, by which they were reduced to actual want, convinced them that it was impossible to complete the building of the temple. "The time is not come," they said, "the time that the Lord's house should be built." But a message was sent them by the Lord's prophet: "Is it time for you, O ye, to dwell in your ceiled houses, and this house lie waste? Now therefore thus saith the Lord of hosts; Consider your ways. Ye have sown much, and bring in little; ye eat, but ye have not enough; ye drink, but ye are not filled with drink; ye clothe you, but there is none warm; and he that earneth wages, earneth wages to put it into a bag with holes." Haggai 1:2-6. And then the reason is given: "Ye looked for much, and, lo, it came to little; and when ye brought it home, I did blow upon it. Why? saith the Lord of hosts. Because of Mine house that is waste, and ye run every man unto his own house. Therefore the heaven over you is stayed from dew, and the earth is stayed from her fruit. And I called for a drought upon the land, and upon the mountains, and upon the corn, and upon the new wine, and upon the oil, and upon that which the ground bringeth forth, and upon men, and upon cattle, and upon all the labor of the hands." Verses 9-11. "When one came to a heap of twenty measures, there were but ten: when one came to the pressfat for to draw out fifty vessels out of the press, there were

Tithes and Offerings 479

but twenty. I smote you with blasting and with mildew and with hail in all the labors of your hands." Haggai 2:16, 17.

Roused by these warnings, the people set themselves to build the house of God. Then the word of the Lord came to them: "Consider now from this day and upward, from the four and twentieth day of the ninth month, even from the day that the foundation of the Lord's temple was laid, ... from this day will I bless you." Verses 18, 19.

Says the wise man, "There is that scattereth, and yet increaseth; and there is that withholdeth more than is meet, but it tendeth to poverty." Proverbs 11:24. And the same lesson is taught in the New Testament by the apostle Paul: "He which soweth sparingly shall reap also sparingly; and he which soweth bountifully shall reap also bountifully." "God is able to make all grace abound toward you; that ye, always having all sufficiency in all things, may abound to every good work." 2 Corinthians 9:6, 8.

God intended that His people Israel should be light bearers to all the inhabitants of the earth. In maintaining His public worship they were bearing a testimony to the existence and sovereignty of the living God. And this worship it was their privilege to sustain, as an expression of their loyalty and their love to Him. The Lord has ordained that the diffusion of light and truth in the earth shall be dependent upon the efforts and offerings of those who are partakers of the heavenly gift. He might have made angels the ambassadors of His truth; He might have made known His will, as He proclaimed the law from Sinai, with His own voice; but in His infinite love and wisdom He called men to become colaborers with Himself, by choosing them to do this work.

In the days of Israel the tithe and freewill offerings were needed to maintain the ordinances of divine service. Should the people of God give less in this age? The principle laid down by Christ is that our offerings to God should be in proportion to the light and privileges enjoyed. "Unto whomsoever much is given, of him shall be much required." Luke 12:48. Said the Saviour to His disciples as He sent them forth, "Freely ye have received, freely give." Matthew 10:8. As our blessings and privileges are increased—above all, as we have before us the unparalleled sacrifice of the glorious Son of God—should not our gratitude find expression in more abundant gifts to extend to others the message of salvation? The work of the gospel, as it widens, requires greater provision to sustain it than was called for anciently; and this makes the law of tithes and offerings of even more urgent necessity now than under the Hebrew economy. If His people were liberally to sustain His cause by their voluntary gifts, instead of resorting to unchristian and unhallowed methods to fill the treasury, God would be honored, and many more souls would be won to Christ.

The plan of Moses to raise means for the building of the tabernacle was highly successful. No urging was necessary. Nor did he employ any of the devices to which churches in our day so often resort. He made no grand feast. He did not invite the people to scenes of gaiety, dancing, and general amusement; neither did he institute lotteries, nor anything of this profane order, to obtain means to erect the tabernacle for God. The Lord directed Moses to invite the children of Israel to bring their offerings. He was to accept gifts from everyone that gave willingly, from his heart. And the offerings came in so great abundance that Moses bade the people cease bringing, for they had supplied more than could be used.

God has made men His stewards. The property which He has placed in their hands is the means that He has provided for the spread of the gospel. To those who prove themselves faithful stewards He will commit greater trusts. Saith the Lord, "Them that honor Me I will honor." 1 Samuel 2:30. "God loveth a cheerful giver," and when His people, with grateful hearts, bring their gifts and offerings to Him, "not grudgingly, or of necessity," His blessing will attend them, as He has promised. "Bring ye all the tithes into the storehouse, that there may be meat in Mine house, and prove Me now herewith, saith the Lord of hosts, if I will not open you the windows of heaven, and pour you out a blessing, that there shall not be room enough to receive it." Malachi 3:10.

Chapter 51—God's Care for the Poor

To promote the assembling of the people for religious service, as well as to provide for the poor, a second tithe of all the increase was required. Concerning the first tithe, the Lord had declared, "I have given the children of Levi *all the tenth* in Israel." Numbers 18:21. But in regard to the second He commanded, "Thou shalt eat before the Lord thy God, in the place which He shall choose to place His name there, the tithe of thy corn, of thy wine, and of thine oil, and the firstlings of thy herds and of thy flocks; that thou mayest learn to fear the Lord thy God always." Deuteronomy 14:23, 29; 16:11-14. This tithe, or its equivalent in money, they were for two years to bring to the place where the sanctuary was established. After presenting a thank offering to God, and a specified portion to the priest, the offerers were to use the remainder for a religious feast, in which the Levite, the stranger, the fatherless, and the widow should participate. Thus provision was made for the thank offerings and feasts at the yearly festivals, and the people were drawn to the society of the priests and Levites, that they might receive instruction and encouragement in the service of God.

Every third year, however, this second tithe was to be used at home, in entertaining the Levite and the poor, as Moses said, "That they may eat within thy gates, and be filled." Deuteronomy 26:12. This tithe would provide a fund for the uses of charity and hospitality.

And further provision was made for the poor. There is nothing, after their recognition of the claims of God, that more distinguishes the laws given by Moses than the liberal, tender, and hospitable spirit enjoined toward the poor. Although God had promised greatly to bless His people, it was not His design that poverty should be wholly unknown among them. He declared that the poor should never cease out of the land. There would ever be those among His people who would call into exercise their sympathy, tenderness, and benevolence. Then, as now, persons were subject to misfortune, sickness, and loss of property; yet so long as they followed the instruction given by

God, there were no beggars among them, neither any who suffered for food.

The law of God gave the poor a right to a certain portion of the produce of the soil. When hungry, a man was at liberty to go to his neighbor's field or orchard or vineyard, and eat of the grain or fruit to satisfy his hunger. It was in accordance with this permission that the disciples of Jesus plucked and ate of the standing grain as they passed through a field upon the Sabbath day.

All the gleanings of harvest field, orchard, and vineyard, belonged to the poor. "When thou cuttest down thine harvest in thy field," said Moses, "and hast forgot a sheaf in the field, thou shalt not go again to fetch it.... When thou beatest thine olive tree, thou shalt not go over the boughs again.... When thou gatherest the grapes of thy vineyard, thou shalt not glean it afterward: it shall be for the stranger, for the fatherless, and for the widow. And thou shalt remember that thou wast a bondman in the land of Egypt." Deuteronomy 24:19-22; Leviticus 19:9, 10.

Every seventh year special provision was made for the poor. The sabbatical year, as it was called, began at the end of the harvest. At the seedtime, which followed the ingathering, the people were not to sow; they should not dress the vineyard in the spring; and they must expect neither harvest nor vintage. Of that which the land produced spontaneously they might eat while fresh, but they were not to lay up any portion of it in their storehouses. The yield of this year was to be free for the stranger, the fatherless, and the widow, and even for the creatures of the field. Exodus 23:10, 11; Leviticus 25:5.

But if the land ordinarily produced only enough to supply the wants of the people, how were they to subsist during the year when no crops were gathered? For this the promise of God made ample provision. "I will command My blessing upon you in the sixth year," He said, "and it shall bring forth fruit for three years. And ye shall sow the eighth year, and eat yet of old fruit until the ninth year; until her fruits come in ye shall eat of the old store." Leviticus 25:21, 22.

The observance of the sabbatical year was to be a benefit to both the land and the people. The soil, lying untilled for one season, would afterward produce more plentifully. The people were released from the pressing labors of the field; and while there were various branches of work that could be followed during this time, all enjoyed greater leisure, which afforded opportunity for the restoration of their physical powers for the exertions of the following years. They had more time for meditation and prayer, for acquainting themselves with the teachings and requirements of the Lord, and for the instruction of their households.

In the sabbatical year the Hebrew slaves were to be set at liberty, and they were not to be sent away portionless. The Lord's direction was: "When thou sendest him out free from thee, thou shalt not let him go away empty. Thou shalt furnish him liberally out of thy flock, and out of thy floor, and out of thy winepress: of that wherewith the Lord thy God hath blessed thee thou shalt give unto him." Deuteronomy 15:13, 14.

The hire of a laborer was to be promptly paid: "Thou shalt not oppress a hired servant that is poor and needy, whether he be of thy brethren, or of thy strangers that are in thy land: ... at his day thou shalt give him his hire, neither shall the sun go down upon it; for he is poor, and setteth his heart upon it." Deuteronomy 24:14, 15.

Special directions were also given concerning the treatment of fugitives from service: "Thou shalt not deliver unto his master the servant which is escaped from his master unto thee. He shall dwell with thee, even among you, in that place which he shall choose in one of thy gates, where it liketh him best: thou shalt not oppress him." Deuteronomy 23:15, 16.

To the poor, the seventh year was a year of release from debt. The Hebrews were enjoined at all times to assist their needy brethren by lending them money without interest. To take usury from a poor man was expressly forbidden: "If thy brother be waxen poor, and fallen in decay with thee; then thou shalt relieve him: yea, though he be a stranger, or a sojourner; that he may live with thee. Take thou no usury of him, or increase: but fear thy God; that thy brother may live with thee. Thou shalt not give him thy money upon usury, nor lend him thy victuals for increase." Leviticus 25:35-37. If the debt remained unpaid until the year of release, the principal itself could not be recovered. The people were expressly warned against withholding from their brethren needed assistance on account of this: "If there be among you a poor man of one of thy brethren, ... thou shalt not harden thine heart, nor shut thine hand from thy poor brother.... Beware that there be not a thought in thy wicked heart, saying, The seventh year, the year of release, is at hand; and thine eye be evil against thy poor brother, and thou givest him nought; and he cry unto the Lord against thee, and it be sin unto thee." "The poor shall never cease out of the land; therefore I command thee, saying, Thou shalt open thine hand wide unto thy brother, to thy poor, and to thy needy, in thy land," "and shalt surely lend him sufficient for his need, in that which he wanteth." Deuteronomy 15:7-9, 11, 8.

None need fear that their liberality would bring them to want. Obedience to God's commandments would surely result in prosperity. "Thou shalt lend unto many nations," He said, "but thou shalt not borrow; and thou shalt reign over many nations, but they shall not reign over thee." Deuteronomy 15:6.

After "seven sabbaths of years," "seven times seven years," came that great year of release—the jubilee. "Then shalt thou cause the trumpet of the jubilee to sound ... throughout all your land. And ye shall hallow the fiftieth year, and proclaim liberty throughout all the land unto all the inhabitants thereof: it shall be a jubilee unto you; and ye shall return every man unto his possession, and ye shall return every man unto his family." Leviticus 25:9, 10.

"On the tenth day of the seventh month, in the Day of Atonement," the trumpet of the jubilee was sounded. Throughout the land, wherever the Jewish people dwelt, the sound was heard, calling upon all the children of Jacob to welcome the year of release. On the great Day of Atonement satisfaction was made for the sins of Israel, and with gladness of heart the people would welcome the jubilee.

As in the sabbatical year, the land was not to be sown or reaped, and all that it produced was to be regarded as the rightful property of the poor. Certain classes of Hebrew slaves—all who did not receive their liberty in the sabbatical year—were now set free. But that which especially distinguished the year of jubilee was the reversion of all landed property to the family of the original possessor. By the special direction of God the land had been divided by lot. After the division was made no one was at liberty to trade his estate. Neither was he to sell his land unless poverty compelled him to do so, and then, whenever he or any of his kindred might desire to redeem it, the purchaser must not refuse to sell it; and if unredeemed, it would revert to its first possessor or his heirs in the year of jubilee.

The Lord declared to Israel: "The land shall not be sold forever: for the land is Mine; for ye are strangers and sojourners with Me." Leviticus 25:23. The people were to be impressed with the fact that it was God's land which they were permitted to possess for a time; that He was the rightful owner, the original proprietor, and that He would have special consideration made for the poor and unfortunate. It was to be impressed upon the minds of all that the poor have as much right to a place in God's world as have the more wealthy.

Such were the provisions made by our merciful Creator, to lessen suffering, to bring some ray of hope, to flash some gleam of sunshine, into the life of the destitute and distressed.

The Lord would place a check upon the inordinate love of property and power. Great evils would result from the continued accumulation of wealth by one class, and the poverty and degradation of another. Without some restraint the power of the wealthy would become a monopoly, and the poor, though in every respect fully as worthy in God's sight, would be regarded and treated as inferior to their more prosperous brethren. The sense of this oppression would arouse the passions of the poorer class. There would be a feeling of despair and desperation which would tend to demoralize society and open the door to crimes of every description. The regulations that God established were designed to promote social equality. The provisions of the sabbatical year and the jubilee would, in a great measure, set right that which during the interval had gone wrong in the social and political economy of the nation.

These regulations were designed to bless the rich no less than the poor. They would restrain avarice and a disposition for self-exaltation, and would cultivate a noble spirit of benevolence; and by fostering good will and confidence between all classes, they would promote social order, the stability of government. We are all woven together in the great web of humanity, and whatever we can do to benefit and uplift others will reflect in blessing upon ourselves. The law of mutual dependence runs through all classes of society. The poor are not more dependent upon the rich than are the rich upon the poor. While the one class ask a share in the blessings which God has bestowed upon their wealthier neighbors, the other need the faithful service, the strength of brain and bone and muscle, that are the capital of the poor.

Great blessings were promised to Israel on condition of obedience to the Lord's directions. "I will give you rain in due season," He declared, "and the land shall yield her increase, and the trees of the field shall yield their fruit. And your threshing shall reach unto the vintage, and the vintage shall reach unto the sowing time: and ye shall eat your bread to the full, and dwell in your land safely. And I will give peace in the land, and ye shall lie down, and none shall make you afraid: and I will rid evil beasts out of the land, neither shall the sword go through your land.... I will walk among you, and will be your God, and ye shall be My people.... But if ye will not hearken unto Me, and will not do all these commandments; and ... ye break My covenant: ... ye shall sow your seed in vain, for your enemies shall eat it. And I will set My face against you, and ye shall be slain before your enemies: they that hate you shall reign over you; and ye shall flee when none pursueth you." Leviticus 26:4-17.

There are many who urge with great enthusiasm that all men should have an equal share in the temporal blessings of God. But this was not the purpose of the Creator. A diversity of condition is one of the means by which God designs to prove and develop character. Yet He intends that those who have worldly possessions shall regard themselves merely as stewards of His goods, as entrusted with means to be employed for the benefit of the suffering and the needy.

Christ has said that we shall have the poor always with us, and He unites His interest with that of His suffering people. The heart of our Redeemer sympathizes with the poorest and lowliest of His earthly children. He tells us that they are His representatives on earth. He has placed them among us to awaken in our hearts the love that He feels toward the suffering and oppressed. Pity and benevolence shown to them are accepted by Christ as if shown to Himself. An act of cruelty or neglect toward them is regarded as though done to Him.

If the law given by God for the benefit of the poor had continued to be carried out, how different would be the present condition of the world, morally, spiritually, and temporally! Selfishness and self-importance would not be manifested as now, but each would cherish a kind regard for the happiness and welfare of others; and such widespread destitution as is now seen in many lands would not exist.

The principles which God has enjoined, would prevent the terrible evils that in all ages have resulted from the oppression of the rich toward the poor and the suspicion and hatred of the poor toward the rich. While they might hinder the amassing of great wealth and the indulgence of unbounded luxury, they would prevent the consequent ignorance and degradation of tens of thousands whose ill-paid servitude is required to build up these colossal fortunes. They would bring a peaceful solution of those problems that now threaten to fill the world with anarchy and bloodshed.

Chapter 52—The Annual Feasts

This chapter is based on Leviticus 23.

There were three annual assemblies of all Israel for worship at the sanctuary. Exodus 23:14-16. Shiloh was for a time the place of these gatherings; but Jerusalem afterward became the center of the nation's worship, and here the tribes convened for the solemn feasts.

The people were surrounded by fierce, warlike tribes, that were eager to seize upon their lands; yet three times every year all the able-bodied men and all the people who could make the journey were directed to leave their homes and repair to the place of assembly, near the center of the land. What was to hinder their enemies from sweeping down upon those unprotected households, to lay them waste with fire and sword? What was to prevent an invasion of the land, that would bring Israel into captivity to some foreign foe? God had promised to be the protector of His people. "The angel of Jehovah encampeth round about them that fear Him, and delivereth them." Psalm 34:7 [A.R.V.]. While the Israelites went up to worship, divine power would place a restraint upon their enemies. God's promise was, "I will cast out the nations before thee, and enlarge thy borders: neither shall any man desire thy land, when thou shalt go up to appear before the Lord thy God thrice in the year." Exodus 34:24.

The first of these festivals, the Passover, the feast of unleavened bread, occurred in Abib, the first month of the Jewish year, corresponding to the last of March and the beginning of April. The cold of winter was past, the latter rain had ended, and all nature rejoiced in the freshness and beauty of the springtime. The grass was green on the hills and valleys, and wild flowers everywhere brightened the fields. The moon, now approaching the full, made the evenings delightful. It was the season so beautifully pictured by the sacred singer:

"The winter is past,

> The rain is over and gone;
> The flowers appear on the earth;
>   The time of the singing of birds is come,
> And the voice of the turtle is heard in our land;
>   The fig tree ripeneth her green figs,
> And the vines are in blossom,
>   They give forth their fragrance." Song of Solomon 2:11-13, R.V.

Throughout the land bands of pilgrims were making their way toward Jerusalem. The shepherds from their flocks, the herdsmen from the mountains, fishers from the Sea of Galilee, the husbandmen from their fields, and sons of the prophets from the sacred schools—all turned their steps toward the place where God's presence was revealed. They journeyed by short stages, for many went on foot. The caravans were constantly receiving accessions, and often became very large before reaching the Holy City.

Nature's gladness awakened joy in the hearts of Israel and gratitude to the Giver of all good. The grand Hebrew psalms were chanted, exalting the glory and majesty of Jehovah. At the sound of the signal trumpet, with the music of cymbals, the chorus of thanksgiving arose, swelled by hundreds of voices:

> "I was glad when they said unto me,
>   Let us go unto the house of the Lord.
> Our feet are standing
>   Within thy gates, O Jerusalem....
> Whither the tribes go up, even the tribes of the Lord, ...
>   To give thanks unto the name of Jehovah....
> Pray for the peace of Jerusalem:
>   They shall prosper that love thee." Psalm 122:1-6, R.V.

As they saw around them the hills where the heathen had been wont to kindle their altar fires, the children of Israel sang:

> "Shall I lift up mine eyes to the hills?
>   Whence should my help come?
> My help cometh from Jehovah,
>   Which made heaven and earth." Psalm 121:1, 2 (margin).

"They that trust in the Lord
> Are as Mount Zion, which cannot be moved, but abideth forever.
>
> As the mountains are round about Jerusalem,
> So the Lord is round about His people,
>
> From this time forth and forevermore." Psalm 125:1, 2, R.V.

[539] Surmounting the hills in view of the Holy City, they looked with reverent awe upon the throngs of worshipers wending their way to the temple. They saw the smoke of the incense ascending, and as they heard the trumpets of the Levites heralding the sacred service, they caught the inspiration of the hour, and sang:

> "Great is the Lord, and greatly to be praised
> In the city of our God, in the mountain of His holiness.
>
> Beautiful for situation, the joy of the whole earth,
> Is Mount Zion, on the sides of the north,
>
> The city of the great King."
>
> Psalm 48:1, 2.

> "Peace be within thy walls,
> And prosperity within thy palaces."
>
> "Open to me the gates of righteousness:
> I will go into them, and I will praise the Lord."
>
> "I will pay my vows unto the Lord
> Now in the presence of all His people,
>
> In the courts of the Lord's house,
> In the midst of thee, O Jerusalem,
>
> Praise ye the Lord."
>
> Psalm 122:7; 118:19; Psalm 116:18, 19.

All the houses in Jerusalem were thrown open to the pilgrims, and rooms were furnished free; but this was not sufficient for the vast assembly, and tents were pitched in every available space in the city and upon the surrounding hills.

On the fourteenth day of the month, at even, the Passover was celebrated, its solemn, impressive ceremonies commemorating the deliverance from bondage in Egypt, and pointing forward to the sacrifice that should deliver from the bondage of sin. When the Saviour yielded up His life on Calvary, the significance of the Passover ceased, and the ordinance of the Lord's Supper was instituted as a memorial of the same event of which the Passover had been a type.

The Passover was followed by the seven day's feast of unleavened bread. The first and the seventh day were days of holy convocation, when no servile work was to be performed. On the second day of the feast, the first fruits of the year's harvest were presented before God. Barley was the earliest grain in Palestine, and at the opening of the feast it was beginning to ripen. A sheaf of this grain was waved by the priest before the altar of God, as an acknowledgment that all was His. Not until this ceremony had been performed was the harvest to be gathered.

Fifty days from the offering of first fruits, came the Pentecost, called also the feast of harvest and the feast of weeks. As an expression of gratitude for the grain prepared as food, two loaves baked with leaven were presented before God. The Pentecost occupied but one day, which was devoted to religious service.

In the seventh month came the Feast of Tabernacles, or of ingathering. This feast acknowledged God's bounty in the products of the orchard, the olive grove, and the vineyard. It was the crowning festal gathering of the year. The land had yielded its increase, the harvests had been gathered into the granaries, the fruits, the oil, and the wine had been stored, the first fruits had been reserved, and now the people came with their tributes of thanksgiving to God, who had thus richly blessed them.

This feast was to be pre-eminently an occasion of rejoicing. It occurred just after the great Day of Atonement, when the assurance had been given that their iniquity should be remembered no more. At peace with God, they now came before Him to acknowledge His goodness and to praise Him for His mercy. The labors of the harvest being ended, and the toils of the new year not yet begun, the people were free from care, and could give themselves up to the sacred, joyous influences of the hour. Though only the fathers and sons were commanded to appear at the feasts, yet, so far as possible, all the household were to attend them, and to their hospitality the servants, the Levites, the stranger, and the poor were made welcome.

Like the Passover, the Feast of Tabernacles was commemorative. In memory of their pilgrim life in the wilderness the people were now to leave their houses and dwell in booths, or arbors, formed from the green branches "of goodly trees, branches of palm trees, and the boughs of thick trees, and willows of the brook." Leviticus 23:40, 42, 43.

The first day was a holy convocation, and to the seven days of the feast an eighth day was added, which was observed in like manner.

At these yearly assemblies the hearts of old and young would be encouraged in the service of God, while the association of the people from the different quarters of the land would strengthen the ties that bound them to God and to one another. Well would it be for the people of God at the present time to have a Feast of Tabernacles—a joyous commemoration of the blessings of God to them. As the children of Israel celebrated the deliverance that God had wrought for their fathers, and His miraculous preservation of them during their journeyings from Egypt, so should we gratefully call to mind the various ways He has devised for bringing us out from the world, and from the darkness of error, into the precious light of His grace and truth.

With those who lived at a distance from the tabernacle, more than a month of every year must have been occupied in attendance upon the annual feasts. This example of devotion to God should emphasize the importance of religious worship and the necessity of subordinating our selfish, worldly interests to those that are spiritual and eternal. We sustain a loss when we neglect the privilege of associating together to strengthen and encourage one another in the service of God. The truths of His word lose their vividness and importance in our minds. Our hearts cease to be enlightened and aroused by the sanctifying influence, and we decline in spirituality. In our intercourse as Christians we lose much by lack of sympathy with one another. He who shuts himself up to himself is not filling the position that God designed he should. We are all children of one Father, dependent upon one another for happiness. The claims of God and of humanity are upon us. It is the proper cultivation of the social elements of our nature that brings us into sympathy with our brethren and affords us happiness in our efforts to bless others.

The Feast of Tabernacles was not only commemorative but typical. It not only pointed back to the wilderness sojourn, but, as the feast of harvest, it celebrated the ingathering of the fruits of the earth, and pointed forward to the great day of final ingathering, when the Lord of the harvest shall send forth His reapers to gather the tares together in bundles for the fire, and to gather the wheat into His garner. At that time the wicked will all be destroyed. They will become "as though they had not been." Obadiah 16. And every voice in the whole universe will unite in joyful praise to God. Says the revelator, "Every creature which is in heaven, and on the earth, and under the earth, and such as are in the sea, and all that are in them, heard I saying, Blessing, and honor, and glory, and power, be unto Him that sitteth upon the throne, and unto the Lamb forever and ever." Revelation 5:13.

The people of Israel praised God at the Feast of Tabernacles, as they called to mind His mercy in their deliverance from the bondage of Egypt and His tender care for them during their pilgrim life in the wilderness. They rejoiced also in the consciousness of pardon and acceptance, through the service of the day of atonement, just ended. But when the ransomed of the Lord shall have been safely gathered into the heavenly Canaan, forever delivered from the bondage of the curse, under which "the whole creation groaneth and travaileth in pain together until now" (Romans 8:22), they will rejoice with joy unspeakable and full of glory. Christ's great work of atonement for men will then have been completed, and their sins will have been forever blotted out.

> "The wilderness and the solitary place shall be glad for them;
>   And the desert shall rejoice, and blossom as the rose.
> It shall blossom abundantly, and rejoice even with joy and
>   singing:
> The glory of Lebanon shall be given unto it,
>   The excellency of Carmel and Sharon;
> They shall see the glory of the Lord, and the excellency of our
>   God.
>
> "Then the eyes of the blind shall be opened,
>   And the ears of the deaf shall be unstopped.

Then shall the lame man leap as an hart,
    And the tongue of the dumb sing:
"For in the wilderness shall waters break out,
    And streams in the desert.
And the parched ground shall become a pool,
    And the thirsty land springs of water: ...
"And an highway shall be there, and a way,
    And it shall be called The way of holiness;
The unclean shall not pass over it;
    But it shall be for those:
The wayfaring men, though fools, shall not err therein.

"No lion shall be there,
    Nor any ravenous beast shall go up thereon,
It shall not be found there;
    But the redeemed shall walk there:
"And the ransomed of the Lord shall return,
    And come to Zion with songs
And everlasting joy upon their heads:
    They shall obtain joy and gladness,
And sorrow and sighing shall flee away."

                        Isaiah 35:1, 2, 5-10.

Chapter 53—The Earlier Judges

This chapter is based on Judges 6 to 8; 10.

After the settlement in Canaan the tribes made no vigorous effort to complete the conquest of the land. Satisfied with the territory already gained, their zeal soon flagged, and the war was discontinued. "When Israel was strong, ... they put the Canaanites to tribute, and did not utterly drive them out." Judges 1:28.

The Lord had faithfully fulfilled, on His part, the promises made to Israel; Joshua had broken the power of the Canaanites, and had distributed the land to the tribes. It only remained for them, trusting in the assurance of divine aid, to complete the work of dispossessing the inhabitants of the land. But this they failed to do. By entering into league with the Canaanites they directly transgressed the command of God, and thus failed to fulfill the condition on which He had promised to place them in possession of Canaan.

From the very first communication of God with them at Sinai, they had been warned against idolatry. Immediately after the proclamation of the law the message was sent them by Moses concerning the nations of Canaan: "Thou shalt not bow down to their gods, nor serve them, nor do after their works: but thou shalt utterly overthrow them, and quite break down their images. And ye shall serve the Lord your God, and He shall bless thy bread, and thy water; and I will take sickness away from the midst of thee." Exodus 23:24, 25. The assurance was given that so long as they remained obedient, God would subdue their enemies before them: "I will send My fear before thee, and will destroy all the people to whom thou shalt come; and I will make all thine enemies turn their backs unto thee. And I will send hornets before thee, which shall drive out the Hivite, the Canaanite, and the Hittite, from before thee. I will not drive them out from before thee in one year; lest the land become desolate, and the beast of the field multiply against thee. By little and little I will drive them out from before thee, until thou be increased, and inherit the land.... I will deliver the inhabitants of the land into your hand; and thou shalt drive them out before thee. Thou shalt make no covenant with them, nor with their gods. They shall not dwell in thy land, lest they make thee sin against Me: for if thou serve their gods, it will surely be a snare unto thee." Exodus 23:27-33. These directions were reiterated in the most solemn manner by Moses before his death, and they were repeated by Joshua.

God had placed His people in Canaan as a mighty breastwork to stay the tide of moral evil, that it might not flood the world. If faithful to Him, God intended that Israel should go on conquering and to conquer. He would give into their hands nations greater and more powerful than the Canaanites. The promise was: "If ye shall diligently keep all these commandments which I command you, ... then will the Lord drive out all these nations from before you, and ye shall possess greater nations and mightier than yourselves. Every place whereon the soles of your feet shall tread shall be yours: from the wilderness and Lebanon, from the river, the river Euphrates, even unto the uttermost sea shall your coast be. There shall no man be able to stand before you: for the Lord your God shall lay the fear of you and the dread of you upon all the land that ye shall tread upon, as He hath said unto you." Deuteronomy 11:22-25.

But regardless of their high destiny, they chose the course of ease and self-indulgence; they let slip their opportunities for completing the conquest of the land; and for many generations they were afflicted by the remnant of these idolatrous peoples, that were, as the prophet had foretold, as "pricks" in their eyes, and as "thorns" in their sides. Numbers 33:55.

The Israelites were "mingled among the heathen, and learned their works." Psalm 106:35. They intermarried with the Canaanites, and idolatry spread like a plague throughout the land. "They served their idols: which were a snare unto them. Yea, they sacrificed their sons and their daughters unto devils: ... and the land was polluted with blood.... Therefore was the wrath of the Lord kindled against His people, insomuch that He abhorred His own inheritance." Psalm 106:36-40.

Until the generation that had received instruction from Joshua became extinct, idolatry made little headway; but the parents had prepared the way for the apostasy of their children. The disregard of the Lord's restrictions on the part of those who came in possession of Canaan sowed seed of evil that continued to bring forth bitter fruit for many generations. The simple habits of the Hebrews had secured them physical health; but association with the heathen led to the indulgence of appetite and passion, which gradually lessened physical strength and enfeebled the mental and moral powers. By their sins the Israelites were separated from God; His strength was removed from them, and they could no longer prevail against their enemies. Thus they were brought into subjection to the very nations that through God they might have subdued.

"They forsook the Lord God of their fathers, which brought them out of the land of Egypt," "and guided them in the wilderness like a flock." "They provoked Him to anger with their high places, and moved Him to jealousy with their graven images." Therefore the Lord "forsook the tabernacle of Shiloh, the tent which He placed among them; and delivered His strength into captivity, and His glory into the enemy's hand." Judges 2:12; Psalm 78:52, 58, 60, 61. Yet He did not utterly forsake His people. There was ever a remnant who were true to Jehovah; and from time to time the Lord raised up faithful and valiant men to put down idolatry and to deliver the Israelites from their enemies. But when the deliverer was dead, and the people were released from his authority, they would gradually return to their idols. And thus the story of backsliding and chastisement, of confession and deliverance, was repeated again and again.

The king of Mesopotamia, the king of Moab, and after them the Philistines, and the Canaanites of Hazor, led by Sisera, in turn became the oppressors of Israel. Othniel, Shamgar, and Ehud, Deborah and Barak, were raised up as deliverers of their people. But again "the children of Israel did evil in the sight of the Lord; and the Lord delivered them into the hand of Midian." Heretofore the hand of the oppressor had fallen but lightly on the tribes dwelling east of the Jordan, but in the present calamities they were the first sufferers.

The Amalekites on the south of Canaan, as well as the Midianites on its eastern border, and in the deserts beyond, were still the unrelenting enemies of Israel. The latter nation had been nearly destroyed by the Israelites in the days of Moses, but they had since increased greatly, and had become numerous and powerful. They had thirsted for revenge; and now that the protecting hand of God was withdrawn from Israel, the opportunity had come. Not alone the tribes east of Jordan, but the whole land suffered from their ravages. The wild, fierce inhabitants of the desert, "as locusts for multitude" (Judges 6:5, R.V.), came swarming into the land, with their flocks and herds. Like a devouring plague they spread over the country, from the river Jordan to the Philistine plain. They came as soon as the harvests began to ripen, and remained until the last fruits of the earth had been gathered. They stripped the fields of their increase and robbed and maltreated the inhabitants and then returned to the deserts. Thus the Israelites dwelling in the open country were forced to abandon their homes, and to congregate in walled towns, to seek refuge in fortresses, or even to find shelter in caves and rocky fastnesses among the mountains. For seven years this oppression continued, and then, as the people in their distress gave heed to the Lord's reproof, and confessed their sins, God again raised up a helper for them.

Gideon was the son of Joash, of the tribe of Manasseh. The division to which this family belonged held no leading position, but the household of Joash was distinguished for courage and integrity. Of his brave sons it is said, "Each one resembled the children of a king." All but one had fallen in the struggles against the Midianites, and he had caused his name to be feared by the invaders. To Gideon came the divine call to deliver his people. He was engaged at the time in threshing wheat. A small quantity of grain had been concealed, and not daring to beat it out on the ordinary threshing floor, he had resorted to a spot near the winepress; for the season of ripe grapes being still far off, little notice was now taken of the vineyards. As Gideon labored in secrecy and silence, he sadly pondered upon the condition of Israel and considered how the oppressor's yoke might be broken from off his people.

Suddenly the "Angel of the Lord" appeared and addressed him with the words, "Jehovah is with thee, thou mighty man of valor."

"O my Lord," was his answer, "if the Lord be with us, why then is all this befallen us? and where be all His miracles which our fathers told us of, saying, Did not the Lord bring us up from Egypt? but now the Lord hath forsaken us, and delivered us into the hands of the Midianites."

The Messenger of heaven replied, "Go in this thy might, and thou shalt save Israel from the hand of the Midianites: have not I sent thee?"

Gideon desired some token that the one now addressing him was the Covenant Angel, who in time past had wrought for Israel. Angels of God, who communed with Abraham, had once tarried to share his hospitality; and Gideon now entreated the divine Messenger to remain as his guest. Hastening to his tent, he prepared from his scanty store a kid and unleavened cakes, which he brought forth and set before Him. But the Angel bade him, "Take the flesh and the unleavened cakes, and lay them upon this rock, and pour out the broth." Gideon did so, and then the sign which he had desired was given: with the staff in His hand, the Angel touched the flesh and the unleavened cakes, and a flame bursting from the rock consumed the sacrifice. Then the Angel vanished from his sight.

Gideon's father, Joash, who shared in the apostasy of his countrymen, had erected at Ophrah, where he dwelt, a large altar to Baal, at which the people of the town worshiped. Gideon was commanded to destroy this altar and to erect an altar to Jehovah over the rock on which the offering had been consumed, and there to present a sacrifice to the Lord. The offering of sacrifice to God had been committed to the priests, and had been restricted to the altar at Shiloh; but He who had established the ritual service, and to whom all its offerings pointed, had power to change its requirements. The deliverance of Israel was to be preceded by a solemn protest against the worship of Baal. Gideon must declare war upon idolatry before going out to battle with the enemies of his people.

The divine direction was faithfully carried out. Knowing that he would be opposed if it were attempted openly, Gideon performed the work in secret; with the aid of his servants, accomplishing the whole in one night. Great was the rage of the men of Ophrah when they came next morning to pay their devotions to Baal. They would have taken Gideon's life had not Joash—who had been told of the Angel's visit—stood in defense of his son. "Will ye plead for Baal?" said Joash. "Will ye save him? he that will plead for him, let him be put to death whilst it is yet morning: if he be a god, let him plead for himself, because one hath cast down his altar." If Baal could not defend his own altar, how could he be trusted to protect his worshipers?

All thoughts of violence toward Gideon were dismissed; and when he sounded the trumpet of war, the men of Ophrah were among the first to gather to his standard. Heralds were dispatched to his own tribe of Manasseh, and also to Asher, Zebulum, and Naphtali, and all answered to the call.

Gideon dared not place himself at the head of the army without still further evidence that God had called him to his work, and that He would be with him. He prayed, "If Thou wilt save Israel by mine hand, as Thou hast said, behold, I will put a fleece of wool in the floor; and if the dew be on the fleece only, and it be dry upon all the earth besides, then shall I know that Thou wilt save Israel by mine hand, as Thou hast said." In the morning the fleece was wet, while the ground was dry. But now a doubt arose, since wool naturally absorbs moisture when there is any in the air; the test might not be decisive. Hence he asked that the sign be reversed, pleading that his extreme caution might not displease the Lord. His request was granted.

Thus encouraged, Gideon led out his forces to give battle to the invaders. "All the Midianites and the Amalekites and the children of the east were gathered together, and went over, and pitched in the valley of Jezreel." The entire force under Gideon's command numbered only thirty-two thousand men; but with the vast host of the enemy spread out before him, the word of the Lord came to him: "The people that are with thee are too many for Me to give the Midianites into their hands, lest Israel vaunt themselves against Me, saying, Mine own hand hath saved me. Now therefore go to, proclaim in the ears of the people, saying, Whosoever is fearful and afraid, let him return and depart early from Mount Gilead." Those who were unwilling to face danger and hardships, or whose worldly interests would draw their hearts from the work of God, would add no strength to the armies of Israel. Their presence would prove only a cause of weakness.

It had been made a law in Israel that before they went to battle the following proclamation should be made throughout the army: "What man is there that hath built a new house, and hath not dedicated it? let him go and return to his house, lest he die in the battle, and another man dedicate it. And what man is he that hath planted a vineyard, and hath not yet eaten of it? let him also go and return unto his house, lest he die in the battle, and another man eat of it. And what man is there that hath betrothed a wife, and hath not taken her? let him go and return unto his house, lest he die in the battle, and another man take her." And the officers were to speak further to the people, saying, "What man is there that is fearful and fainthearted? let him go and return unto his house, lest his brethren's heart faint as well as his heart." Deuteronomy 20:5-8.

Because his numbers were so few compared with those of the enemy, Gideon had refrained from making the usual proclamation. He was filled with astonishment at the declaration that his army was too large. But the Lord saw the pride and unbelief existing in the hearts of His people. Aroused by the stirring appeals of Gideon, they had readily enlisted; but many were filled with fear when they saw the multitudes of the Midianites. Yet, had Israel triumphed, those very ones would have taken the glory to themselves instead of ascribing the victory to God.

Gideon obeyed the Lord's direction, and with a heavy heart he saw twenty-two thousand, or more than two thirds of his entire force, depart for their homes. Again the word of the Lord came to him: "The people are yet too many; bring them down unto the water, and I will try them for thee there: and it shall be, that of whom I say unto thee, This shall go with thee, the same shall go with thee; and of whomsoever I say unto thee, This shall not go with thee, the same shall not go." The people were led down to the waterside, expecting to make an immediate advance upon the enemy. A few hastily took a little water in the hand and sucked it up as they went on; but nearly all bowed upon their knees, and leisurely drank from the surface of the stream. Those who took of the water in their hands were but three hundred out of ten thousand; yet these were selected; all the rest were permitted to return to their homes.

By the simplest means character is often tested. Those who in time of peril were intent upon supplying their own wants were not the men to be trusted in an emergency. The Lord has no place in His work for the indolent and self-indulgent. The men of His choice were the few who would not permit their own wants to delay them in the discharge of duty. The three hundred chosen men not only

[549]

[550] possessed courage and self-control, but they were men of faith. They had not defiled themselves with idolatry. God could direct them, and through them He could work deliverance for Israel. Success does not depend upon numbers. God can deliver by few as well as by many. He is honored not so much by the great numbers as by the character of those who serve Him.

The Israelites were stationed on the brow of a hill overlooking the valley where the hosts of the invaders lay encamped. "And the Midianites and the Amalekites and all the children of the east lay along in the valley like locusts for multitude; and their camels were without number, as the sand which is upon the seashore for multitude." Judges 7:12, R.V. Gideon trembled as he thought of the conflict of the morrow. But the Lord spoke to him in the night season and bade him, with Phurah his attendant, go down to the camp of the Midianites, intimating that he would there hear something for his encouragement. He went, and, waiting in the darkness and silence, he heard a soldier relating a dream to his companion: "Lo, a cake of barley bread tumbled into the host of Midian, and came unto a tent, and smote it that it fell, and overturned it, that the tent lay along." The other answered in words that stirred the heart of that unseen listener, "This is nothing else save the sword of Gideon the son of Joash, a man of Israel: for into his hand hath God delivered Midian, and all the host." Gideon recognized the voice of God speaking to him through those Midianitish strangers. Returning to the few men under his command, he said, "Arise; for the Lord hath delivered into your hand the host of Midian."

By divine direction a plan of attack was suggested to him, which he immediately set out to execute. The three hundred men were divided into three companies. To every man were given a trumpet, and a torch concealed in an earthen pitcher. The men were stationed in such a manner as to approach the Midianite camp from different directions. In the dead of night, at a signal from Gideon's war horn, the three companies sounded their trumpets; then, breaking their pitchers and displaying the blazing torches, they rushed upon the enemy with the terrible war cry, "The sword of the Lord, and of Gideon!"

The sleeping army was suddenly aroused. Upon every side was seen the light of the flaming torches. In every direction was heard the sound of trumpets, with the cry of the assailants. Believing themselves at the mercy of an overwhelming force, the Midianites were panic-stricken. With wild cries of alarm they fled for life, and, mistaking their own companions for enemies, they slew one another. As news of the victory spread, thousands of the men of Israel who had been dismissed to their homes returned and joined in pursuit of their fleeing enemies. The Midianites were making their way toward the Jordan, hoping to reach their own territory, beyond the river. Gideon sent messengers to the tribe of Ephraim, rousing them to intercept the fugitives at the southern fords. Meanwhile, with his three hundred, "faint, yet pursuing," Gideon crossed the stream hard after those who had already gained the farther side. The two princes, Zebah and Zalmunna, who had been over the entire host, and who had escaped with an army of fifteen thousand men, were overtaken by Gideon, their force completely scattered, and the leaders captured and slain.

In this signal defeat not less than one hundred and twenty thousand of the invaders perished. The power of the Midianites was broken, so that they were never again able to make war upon Israel. The tidings spread swiftly far and wide, that Israel's God had again fought for His people. No words can describe the terror of the surrounding nations when they learned what simple means had prevailed against the power of a bold, warlike people.

The leader whom God chose to overthrow the Midianites occupied no prominent position in Israel. He was not a ruler, a priest, or a Levite. He thought himself the least in his father's house. But God saw in him a man of courage and integrity. He was distrustful of himself and willing to follow the guidance of the Lord. God does not always choose for His work men of the greatest talents, but He selects those whom He can best use. "Before honor is humility." Proverbs 15:33. The Lord can work most effectually through those who are most sensible of their own insufficiency, and who will rely upon Him as their leader and source of strength. He will make them strong by uniting their weakness to His might, and wise by connecting their ignorance with His wisdom.

If they would cherish true humility, the Lord could do much more for His people; but there are few who can be trusted with any large measure of responsibility or success without becoming self-confident and forgetful of their dependence upon God. This is why, in choosing the instruments for His work, the Lord passes by those whom the world honors as great, talented, and brilliant. They are too often proud and self-sufficient. They feel competent to act without counsel from God.

The simple act of blowing a blast upon the trumpet by the army of Joshua around Jericho, and by Gideon's little band about the hosts of Midian, was made effectual, through the power of God, to overthrow the might of His enemies. The most complete system that men have ever devised, apart from the power and wisdom of God, will prove a failure, while the most unpromising methods will succeed when divinely appointed and entered upon with humility and faith. Trust in God and obedience to His will are as essential to the Christian in the spiritual warfare as to Gideon and Joshua in their battles with the Canaanites. By the repeated manifestations of His power in behalf of Israel, God would lead them to have faith in Him—with confidence to seek His help in every emergency. He is just as willing to work with the efforts of His people now and to accomplish great things through weak instrumentalities. All heaven awaits our demand upon its wisdom and strength. God is "able to do exceeding abundantly above all that we ask or think." Ephesians 3:20.

Gideon returned from pursuing the enemies of the nation, to meet censure and accusation from his own countrymen. When at his call the men of Israel had rallied against the Midianites, the tribe of Ephraim had remained behind. They looked upon the effort as a perilous undertaking; and as Gideon sent them no special summons, they availed themselves of this excuse not to join their brethren. But when the news of Israel's triumph reached them, the Ephraimites were envious because they had not shared it. After the rout of the Midianites, the men of Ephraim had, by Gideon's direction, seized the fords of the Jordan, thus preventing the escape of the fugitives. By this means a large number of the enemy were slain, among whom were two princes, Oreb and Zeeb. Thus the men of Ephraim followed up the battle, and helped complete the victory. Nevertheless, they were jealous and angry, as though Gideon had been led by his own will and judgment. They did not discern God's hand in the triumph of Israel, they did not appreciate His power and mercy in their deliverance; and this very fact showed them unworthy to be chosen as His special instruments.

Returning with the trophies of victory, they angrily reproached Gideon: "Why hast thou served us thus, that thou calledst us not, when thou wentest to fight with the Midianites?"

"What have I done now, in comparison of you?" said Gideon. "Is not the *gleaning* of the grapes of Ephraim better than the *vintage* of Abiezer? *God* hath delivered into your hands the princes of Midian, Oreb and Zeeb: and what was I able to do in comparison of you?"

The spirit of jealousy might easily have been fanned into a quarrel that would have caused strife and bloodshed; but Gideon's modest answer soothed the anger of the men of Ephraim, and they returned in peace to their homes. Firm and uncompromising where principle was concerned, and in war a "mighty man of valor," Gideon displayed also a spirit of courtesy that is rarely witnessed.

The people of Israel, in their gratitude at deliverance from the Midianites, proposed to Gideon that he should become their king, and that the throne should be confirmed to his descendants. This proposition was in direct violation of the principles of the theocracy. God was the king of Israel, and for them to place a man upon the throne would be a rejection of their Divine Sovereign. Gideon recognized this fact; his answer shows how true and noble were his motives. "I will not rule over you," he declared; "neither shall my son rule over you: the Lord shall rule over you."

But Gideon was betrayed into another error, which brought disaster upon his house and upon all Israel. The season of inactivity that succeeds a great struggle is often fraught with greater danger than is the period of conflict. To this danger Gideon was now exposed. A spirit of unrest was upon him. Hitherto he had been content to fulfill the directions given him from God; but now, instead of waiting for divine guidance, he began to plan for himself. When the armies of the Lord have gained a signal victory, Satan will redouble his efforts to overthrow the work of God. Thus thoughts and plans were suggested to the mind of Gideon, by which the people of Israel were led astray.

Because he had been commanded to offer sacrifice upon the rock where the Angel appeared to him, Gideon concluded that he had been appointed to officiate as a priest. Without waiting for the divine sanction, he determined to provide a suitable place, and to institute a system of worship similar to that carried on at the tabernacle. With the strong popular feeling in his favor he found no difficulty in carrying out his plan. At his request all the earrings of gold taken from the Midianites were given him as his share of the spoil. The people also collected many other costly materials, together with the richly adorned garments of the princes of Midian. From the material thus furnished, Gideon constructed an ephod and a breastplate, in imitation of those worn by the high priest. His course proved a snare to himself and his family, as well as to Israel. The unauthorized worship led many of the people finally to forsake the Lord altogether, to serve idols. After Gideon's death great numbers, among whom were his own family, joined in this apostasy. The people were led away from God by the very man who had once overthrown their idolatry.

There are few who realize how far-reaching is the influence of their words and acts. How often the errors of parents produce the most disastrous effects upon their children and children's children, long after the actors themselves have been laid in the grave. Everyone is exerting an influence upon others, and will be held accountable for the result of that influence. Words and actions have a telling power, and the long hereafter will show the effect of our life here. The impression made by our words and deeds will surely react upon ourselves in blessing or in cursing. This thought gives an awful solemnity to life, and should draw us to God in humble prayer that He will guide us by His wisdom.

Those who stand in the highest positions may lead astray. The wisest err; the strongest may falter and stumble. There is need that light from above should be constantly shed upon our pathway. Our only safety lies in trusting our way implicitly to Him who has said, "Follow Me."

After the death of Gideon "the children of Israel remembered not the Lord their God, who had delivered them out of the hands of all their enemies on every side: neither showed they kindness to the house of Jerubbaal, namely, Gideon, according to all the goodness which he had showed unto Israel." Forgetful of all that they owed to Gideon, their judge and deliverer, the people of Israel accepted his baseborn son Abimelech as their king, who, to sustain his power, murdered all but one of Gideon's lawful children. When men cast off the fear of God they are not long in departing from honor and integrity. An appreciation of the Lord's mercy will lead to an appreciation of those who, like Gideon, have been employed as instruments to bless His people. The cruel course of Israel toward the house of Gideon was what might be expected from a people who manifested so great ingratitude to God.

After the death of Abimelech the rule of judges who feared the Lord served for a time to put a check upon idolatry, but erelong the people returned to the practices of the heathen communities around them. Among the northern tribes the gods of Syria and Sidon had many worshipers. On the southwest the idols of the Philistines, and on the east those of Moab and Ammon, had turned the hearts of Israel from the God of their fathers. But apostasy speedily brought its punishment. The Ammonites subdued the eastern tribes and, crossing the Jordan, invaded the territory of Judah and Ephraim. On the west the Philistines came up from their plain beside the sea, burning and pillaging far and near. Again Israel seemed to be abandoned to the power of relentless foes.

Again the people sought help from Him whom they had so forsaken and insulted. "The children of Israel cried unto the Lord, saying, We have sinned against Thee, both because we have forsaken our God, and also served Baalim." But sorrow had not worked true repentance. The people mourned because their sins had brought suffering upon themselves, but not because they had dishonored God by transgression of His holy law. True repentance is more than sorrow for sin. It is a resolute turning away from evil.

The Lord answered them through one of His prophets: "Did I not deliver you from the Egyptians, and from the Amorites, from the children of Ammon, and from the Philistines? The Zidonians also, and the Amalekites, and the Maonites, did oppress you; and ye cried to Me, and I delivered you out of their hand. Yet ye have forsaken Me, and served other gods: wherefore I will deliver you no more. Go and cry unto the gods which ye have chosen; let them deliver you in the time of your tribulation."

These solemn and fearful words carry the mind forward to another scene—the great day of final judgment—when the rejecters of God's mercy and the despisers of His grace shall be brought face to face with His justice. At that tribunal must they render an account who have devoted their God-given talents of time, of means, or of intellect, to serving the gods of this world. They have forsaken their true and loving Friend, to follow the path of convenience and worldly pleasure. They intended at some time to return to God; but the world with its follies and deceptions absorbed the attention. Frivolous amusements, pride of dress, indulgence of appetite, hardened the heart and benumbed the conscience, so that the voice of truth was not heard. Duty was despised. Things of infinite value were lightly esteemed, until the heart lost all desire to sacrifice for Him who has given so much for man. But in the reaping time they will gather that which they have sown.

Saith the Lord: "I have called, and ye refused; I have stretched out My hand, and no man regarded; but ye have set at nought all My counsel, and would none of My reproof: ... when your fear cometh as desolation, and your destruction cometh as a whirlwind; when distress and anguish cometh upon you. Then shall they call upon Me, but I will not answer; they shall seek Me early, but they shall not find Me: for that they hated knowledge, and did not choose the fear of the Lord: they would none of My counsel: they despised all My reproof. Therefore shall they eat of the fruit of their own way, and be filled with their own devices." "But whoso hearkeneth unto Me shall dwell safely, and shall be quiet from fear of evil." Proverbs 1:24-31, 33.

The Israelites now humbled themselves before the Lord. "And they put away the strange gods from among them, and served Jehovah." And the Lord's heart of love was grieved—"*was grieved for the misery of Israel.*" Oh, the long-suffering mercy of our God! When His people put away the sins that had shut out His presence, He heard their prayers and at once began to work for them.

A deliverer was raised up in the person of Jephthah, a Gileadite, who made war upon the Ammonites and effectually destroyed their power. For eighteen years at this time Israel had suffered under the oppression of her foes, yet again the lesson taught by suffering was forgotten.

As His people returned to their evil ways, the Lord permitted them to be still oppressed by their powerful enemies, the Philistines. For many years they were constantly harassed, and at times completely subjugated, by this cruel and warlike nation. They had mingled with these idolaters, uniting with them in pleasure and in worship, until they seemed to be one with them in spirit and interest. Then these professed friends of Israel became their bitterest enemies and sought by every means to accomplish their destruction.

Like Israel, Christians too often yield to the influence of the world and conform to its principles and customs, in order to secure the friendship of the ungodly; but in the end it will be found that these professed friends are the most dangerous of foes. The Bible plainly teaches that there can be no harmony between the people of God and the world. "Marvel not, my brethren, if the world hate you." 1 John 3:13. Our Saviour says, "Ye know that it hated Me before it hated you." John 15:18. Satan works through the ungodly, under cover of a pretended friendship, to allure God's people into sin, that he may separate them from Him; and when their defense is removed, then he will lead his agents to turn against them and seek to accomplish their destruction.

Chapter 54—Samson

This chapter is based on Judges 13 to 16.

Amid the widespread apostasy the faithful worshipers of God continued to plead with Him for the deliverance of Israel. Though there was apparently no response, though year after year the power of the oppressor continued to rest more heavily upon the land, God's providence was preparing help for them. Even in the early years of the Philistine oppression a child was born through whom God designed to humble the power of these mighty foes.

On the border of the hill country overlooking the Philistine plain was the little town of Zorah. Here dwelt the family of Manoah, of the tribe of Dan, one of the few households that amid the general defection had remained true to Jehovah. To the childless wife of Manoah "the Angel of Jehovah" appeared with the message that she should have a son, through whom God would begin to deliver Israel. In view of this the Angel gave her instruction concerning her own habits, and also for the treatment of her child: "Now therefore beware, I pray thee, and drink not wine nor strong drink, and eat not any unclean thing." And the same prohibition was to be imposed, from the first, upon the child, with the addition that his hair should not be cut; for he was to be consecrated to God as a Nazarite from his birth.

The woman sought her husband, and, after describing the Angel, she repeated His message. Then, fearful that they should make some mistake in the important work committed to them, the husband prayed, "Let the Man of God which Thou didst send come again unto us, and teach us what we shall do unto the child that shall be born."

When the Angel again appeared, Manoah's anxious inquiry was, "How shall we order the child, and how shall we do unto him?" The previous instruction was repeated—"Of all that I said unto the woman let her beware. She may not eat of anything that cometh of the vine, neither let her drink wine or strong drink, nor eat any unclean thing: all that I commanded her let her observe."

God had an important work for the promised child of Manoah to do, and it was to secure for him the qualifications necessary for this work that the habits of both the mother and the child were to be carefully regulated. "Neither let her drink wine or strong drink," was the Angel's instruction for the wife of Manoah, "nor eat any unclean thing. All that I commanded her let her observe." The child will be affected for good or for evil by the habits of the mother. She must herself be controlled by principle and must practice temperance and self-denial, if she would seek the welfare of her child. Unwise advisers will urge upon the mother the necessity of gratifying every wish and impulse, but such teaching is false and mischievous. The mother is by the command of God Himself placed under the most solemn obligation to exercise self-control.

And fathers as well as mothers are involved in this responsibility. Both parents transmit their own characteristics, mental and physical, their dispositions and appetites, to their children. As the result of parental intemperance children often lack physical strength and mental and moral power. Liquor drinkers and tobacco users may, and do, transmit their insatiable craving, their inflamed blood and irritable nerves, to their children. The licentious often bequeath their unholy desires, and even loathsome diseases, as a legacy to their offspring. And as the children have less power to resist temptation than had the parents, the tendency is for each generation to fall lower and lower. To a great degree parents are responsible not only for the violent passions and perverted appetites of their children but for the infirmities of the thousands born deaf, blind, diseased, or idiotic.

The inquiry of every father and mother should be, "What shall we do unto the child that shall be born unto us?" The effect of prenatal influences has been by many lightly regarded; but the instruction sent from heaven to those Hebrew parents, and twice repeated in the most explicit and solemn manner, shows how this matter is looked upon by our Creator.

And it was not enough that the promised child should receive a good legacy from the parents. This must be followed by careful training and the formation of right habits. God directed that the future judge and deliverer of Israel should be trained to strict temperance from infancy. He was to be a Nazarite from his birth, thus being placed under a perpetual prohibition against the use of wine or strong drink. The lessons of temperance, self-denial, and self-control are to be taught to children even from babyhood.

The angel's prohibition included "every unclean thing." The distinction between articles of food as clean and unclean was not a merely ceremonial and arbitrary regulation, but was based upon sanitary principles. To the observance of this distinction may be traced, in a great degree, the marvelous vitality which for thousands of years has distinguished the Jewish people. The principles of temperance must be carried further than the mere use of spirituous liquors. The use of stimulating and indigestible food is often equally injurious to health, and in many cases sows the seeds of drunkenness. True temperance teaches us to dispense entirely with everything hurtful and to use judiciously that which is healthful. There are few who realize as they should how much their habits of diet have to do with their health, their character, their usefulness in this world, and their eternal destiny. The appetite should ever be in subjection to the moral and intellectual powers. The body should be servant to the mind, and not the mind to the body.

The divine promise to Manoah was in due time fulfilled in the birth of a son, to whom the name of Samson was given. As the boy grew up it became evident that he possessed extraordinary physical strength. This was not, however, as Samson and his parents well knew, dependent upon his well-knit sinews, but upon his condition as a Nazarite, of which his unshorn hair was a symbol. Had Samson obeyed the divine commands as faithfully as his parents had done, his would have been a nobler and happier destiny. But association with idolaters corrupted him. The town of Zorah being near the country of the Philistines, Samson came to mingle with them on friendly terms. Thus in his youth intimacies sprang up, the influence of which darkened his whole life. A young woman dwelling in the Philistine town of Timnath engaged Samson's affections, and he determined to make her his wife. To his God-fearing parents, who endeavored to dissuade him from his purpose, his only answer was, "She pleaseth me well." The parents at last yielded to his wishes, and the marriage took place.

Just as he was entering upon manhood, the time when he must execute his divine mission—the time above all others when he should have been true to God—Samson connected himself with the enemies of Israel. He did not ask whether he could better glorify God when united with the object of his choice, or whether he was placing himself in a position where he could not fulfill the purpose to be accomplished by his life. To all who seek first to honor Him, God has promised wisdom; but there is no promise to those who are bent upon self-pleasing.

How many are pursuing the same course as did Samson! How often marriages are formed between the godly and the ungodly, because inclination governs in the selection of husband or wife! The parties do not ask counsel of God, nor have His glory in view. Christianity ought to have a controlling influence upon the marriage relation, but it is too often the case that the motives which lead to this union are not in keeping with Christian principles. Satan is constantly seeking to strengthen his power over the people of God by inducing them to enter into alliance with his subjects; and in order to accomplish this he endeavors to arouse unsanctified passions in the heart. But the Lord has in His word plainly instructed His people not to unite themselves with those who have not His love abiding in them. "What concord hath Christ with Belial? or what part hath he that believeth with an infidel? and what agreement hath the temple of God with idols?" 2 Corinthians 6:15, 16.

At his marriage feast Samson was brought into familiar association with those who hated the God of Israel. Whoever voluntarily enters into such relations will feel it necessary to conform, to some degree, to the habits and customs of his companions. The time thus spent is worse than wasted. Thoughts are entertained and words are spoken that tend to break down the strongholds of principle and to weaken the citadel of the soul.

The wife, to obtain whom Samson had transgressed the command of God, proved treacherous to her husband before the close of the marriage feast. Incensed at her perfidy, Samson forsook her for the time, and went alone to his home at Zorah. When, afterward relenting, he returned for his bride, he found her the wife of another. His revenge, in the wasting of all the fields and vineyards of the Philistines, provoked them to murder her, although their threats had driven her to the deceit with which the trouble began. Samson had

[564]

already given evidence of his marvelous strength by slaying, single-handed, a young lion, and by killing thirty of the men of Askelon. Now, moved to anger by the barbarous murder of his wife, he attacked the Philistines and smote them "with a great slaughter." Then, wishing a safe retreat from his enemies, he withdrew to "the rock Etam," in the tribe of Judah.

To this place he was pursued by a strong force, and the inhabitants of Judah, in great alarm, basely agreed to deliver him to his enemies. Accordingly three thousand men of Judah went up to him. But even at such odds they would not have dared approach him had they not felt assured that he would not harm his own countrymen. Samson consented to be bound and delivered to the Philistines, but first exacted from the men of Judah a promise not to attack him themselves, and thus compel him to destroy them. He permitted them to bind him with two new ropes, and he was led into the camp of his enemies amid demonstrations of great joy. But while their shouts were waking the echoes of the hills, "the Spirit of Jehovah came mightily upon him." He burst asunder the strong new cords as if they had been flax burned in the fire. Then seizing the first weapon at hand, which, though only the jawbone of an ass, was rendered more effective than sword or spear, he smote the Philistines until they fled in terror, leaving a thousand men dead upon the field.

Had the Israelites been ready to unite with Samson and follow up the victory, they might at this time have freed themselves from the power of their oppressors. But they had become dispirited and cowardly. They had neglected the work which God commanded them to perform, in dispossessing the heathen, and had united with them in their degrading practices, tolerating their cruelty, and, so long as it was not directed against themselves, even countenancing their injustice. When themselves brought under the power of the oppressor, they tamely submitted to the degradation which they might have escaped, had they only obeyed God. Even when the Lord raised up a deliverer for them, they would, not infrequently, desert him and unite with their enemies.

After his victory the Israelites made Samson judge, and he ruled Israel for twenty years. But one wrong step prepares the way for another. Samson had transgressed the command of God by taking a wife from the Philistines, and again he ventured among them—

now his deadly enemies—in the indulgence of unlawful passion. Trusting to his great strength, which had inspired the Philistines with such terror, he went boldly to Gaza, to visit a harlot of that place. The inhabitants of the city learned of his presence, and they were eager for revenge. Their enemy was shut safely within the walls of the most strongly fortified of all their cities; they felt sure of their prey, and only waited till the morning to complete their triumph. At midnight Samson was aroused. The accusing voice of conscience filled him with remorse, as he remembered that he had broken his vow as a Nazarite. But notwithstanding his sin, God's mercy had not forsaken him. His prodigious strength again served to deliver him. Going to the city gate, he wrenched it from its place and carried it, with its posts and bars, to the top of a hill on the way to Hebron.

But even this narrow escape did not stay his evil course. He did not again venture among the Philistines, but he continued to seek those sensuous pleasures that were luring him to ruin. "He loved a woman in the valley of Sorek," not far from his own birthplace. Her name was Delilah, "the consumer." The vale of Sorek was celebrated for its vineyards; these also had a temptation for the wavering Nazarite, who had already indulged in the use of wine, thus breaking another tie that bound him to purity and to God. The Philistines kept a vigilant watch over the movements of their enemy, and when he degraded himself by this new attachment, they determined, through Delilah, to accomplish his ruin.

A deputation consisting of one leading man from each of the Philistine provinces was sent to the vale of Sorek. They dared not attempt to seize him while in possession of his great strength, but it was their purpose to learn, if possible, the secret of his power. They therefore bribed Delilah to discover and reveal it.

As the betrayer plied Samson with her questions, he deceived her by declaring that the weakness of other men would come upon him if certain processes were tried. When she put the matter to the test, the cheat was discovered. Then she accused him of falsehood, saying, "How canst thou say, I love thee, when thine heart is not with me? Thou hast mocked me these three times, and hast not told me wherein thy great strength lieth." Three times Samson had the clearest evidence that the Philistines had leagued with his charmer to destroy him; but when her purpose failed, she treated the matter as a jest, and he blindly banished fear.

Day by day Delilah urged him, until "his soul was vexed unto death;" yet a subtle power kept him by her side. Overcome at last, Samson made known the secret: "There hath not come a razor upon mine head; for I have been a Nazarite unto God from my mother's womb: if I be shaven, then my strength will go from me, and I shall become weak, and be like any other man." A messenger was immediately dispatched to the lords of the Philistines, urging them to come to her without delay. While the warrior slept, the heavy masses of his hair were severed from his head. Then, as she had done three times before, she called, "The Philistines be upon thee, Samson!" Suddenly awaking, he thought to exert his strength as before and destroy them; but his powerless arms refused to do his bidding, and he knew that "Jehovah was departed from him." When he had been shaven, Delilah began to annoy him and cause him pain, thus making a trial of his strength; for the Philistines dared not approach him till fully convinced that his power was gone. Then they seized him and, having put out both his eyes, they took him to Gaza. Here he was bound with fetters in their prison house and confined to hard labor.

What a change to him who had been the judge and champion of Israel!—now weak, blind, imprisoned, degraded to the most menial service! Little by little he had violated the conditions of his sacred calling. God had borne long with him; but when he had so yielded himself to the power of sin as to betray his secret, the Lord departed from him. There was no virtue in his long hair merely, but it was a token of his loyalty to God; and when the symbol was sacrificed in the indulgence of passion, the blessings of which it was a token were also forfeited.

In suffering and humiliation, a sport for the Philistines, Samson learned more of his own weakness than he had ever known before; and his afflictions led him to repentance. As his hair grew, his power gradually returned; but his enemies, regarding him as a fettered and helpless prisoner, felt no apprehensions.

The Philistines ascribed their victory to their gods; and, exulting, they defied the God of Israel. A feast was appointed in honor of Dagon, the fish god, "the protector of the sea." From town and country throughout the Philistine plain the people and their lords assembled. Throngs of worshipers filled the vast temple and crowded the galleries about the roof. It was a scene of festivity and rejoicing. There was the pomp of the sacrificial service, followed by music and feasting. Then, as the crowning trophy of Dagon's power, Samson was brought in. Shouts of exultation greeted his appearance. People and rulers mocked his misery and adored the god who had overthrown "the destroyer of their country." After a time, as if weary, Samson asked permission to rest against the two central pillars which supported the temple roof. Then he silently uttered the prayer, "O Lord God, remember me, I pray Thee, and strengthen me, I pray Thee, only this once, O God, that I may be at once avenged of the Philistines." With these words he encircled the pillars with his mighty arms; and crying, "Let me die with the Philistines!" he bowed himself, and the roof fell, destroying at one crash all that vast multitude. "So the dead which he slew at his death were more than they which he slew in his life."

The idol and its worshipers, priest and peasant, warrior and noble, were buried together beneath the ruins of Dagon's temple. And among them was the giant form of him whom God had chosen to be the deliverer of His people. Tidings of the terrible overthrow were carried to the land of Israel, and Samson's kinsmen came down from their hills, and, unopposed, rescued the body of the fallen hero. And they "brought him up, and buried him between Zorah and Eshtaol, in the burying place of Manoah his father."

God's promise that through Samson He would "begin to deliver Israel out of the hand of the Philistines" was fulfilled; but how dark and terrible the record of that life which might have been a praise to God and a glory to the nation! Had Samson been true to his divine calling, the purpose of God could have been accomplished in his honor and exaltation. But he yielded to temptation and proved untrue to his trust, and his mission was fulfilled in defeat, bondage, and death.

Physically, Samson was the strongest man upon the earth; but in self-control, integrity, and firmness, he was one of the weakest of men. Many mistake strong passions for a strong character, but the truth is that he who is mastered by his passions is a weak man. The real greatness of the man is measured by the power of the feelings that he controls, not by those that control him.

God's providential care had been over Samson, that he might be prepared to accomplish the work which he was called to do. At the very outset of life he was surrounded with favorable conditions for physical strength, intellectual vigor, and moral purity. But under the influence of wicked associates he let go that hold upon God which is man's only safeguard, and he was swept away by the tide of evil. Those who in the way of duty are brought into trial may be sure that God will preserve them; but if men willfully place themselves under the power of temptation, they will fall, sooner or later.

The very ones whom God purposes to use as His instruments for a special work, Satan employs his utmost power to lead astray. He attacks us at our weak points, working through defects in the character to gain control of the whole man; and he knows that if these defects are cherished, he will succeed. But none need be overcome. Man is not left alone to conquer the power of evil by his own feeble efforts. Help is at hand and will be given to every soul who really desires it. Angels of God, that ascend and descend the ladder which Jacob saw in vision, will help every soul who will, to climb even to the highest heaven.

Chapter 55—The Child Samuel

This chapter is based on 1 Samuel 1; 2:1-11.

Elkanah, a Levite of Mount Ephraim, was a man of wealth and influence, and one who loved and feared the Lord. His wife, Hannah, was a woman of fervent piety. Gentle and unassuming, her character was marked with deep earnestness and a lofty faith.

The blessing so earnestly sought by every Hebrew was denied this godly pair; their home was not gladdened by the voice of childhood; and the desire to perpetuate his name led the husband—as it had led many others—to contract a second marriage. But this step, prompted by a lack of faith in God, did not bring happiness. Sons and daughters were added to the household; but the joy and beauty of God's sacred institution had been marred and the peace of the family was broken. Peninnah, the new wife, was jealous and narrow-minded, and she bore herself with pride and insolence. To Hannah, hope seemed crushed and life a weary burden; yet she met the trial with uncomplaining meekness.

Elkanah faithfully observed the ordinances of God. The worship at Shiloh was still maintained, but on account of irregularities in the ministration his services were not required at the sanctuary, to which, being a Levite, he was to give attendance. Yet he went up with his family to worship and sacrifice at the appointed gatherings.

Even amid the sacred festivities connected with the service of God the evil spirit that had cursed his home intruded. After presenting the thank offerings, all the family, according to the established custom, united in a solemn yet joyous feast. Upon these occasions Elkanah gave the mother of his children a portion for herself and for each of her sons and daughters; and in token of regard for Hannah, he gave her a double portion, signifying that his affection for her was the same as if she had had a son. Then the second wife, fired with jealousy, claimed the precedence as one highly favored of God, and taunted Hannah with her childless state as evidence of the Lord's displeasure. This was repeated from year to year, until Hannah could endure it no longer. Unable to hide her grief, she wept without restraint, and withdrew from the feast. Her husband vainly sought to comfort her. "Why weepest thou? and why eatest thou not? and why is thy heart grieved?" he said; "am I not better to thee than ten sons?"

Hannah uttered no reproach. The burden which she could share with no earthly friend she cast upon God. Earnestly she pleaded that He would take away her reproach and grant her the precious gift of a son to nurture and train for Him. And she made a solemn vow that if her request were granted, she would dedicate her child to God, even from its birth. Hannah had drawn near to the entrance of the tabernacle, and in the anguish of her spirit she "prayed, ... and wept sore." Yet she communed with God in silence, uttering no sound. In those evil times such scenes of worship were rarely witnessed. Irreverent feasting and even drunkenness were not uncommon, even at the religious festivals; and Eli the high priest, observing Hannah, supposed that she was overcome with wine. Thinking to administer a deserved rebuke, he said sternly, "How long wilt thou be drunken? put away thy wine from thee."

Pained and startled, Hannah answered gently, "No, my lord, I am a woman of a sorrowful spirit: I have drunk neither wine nor strong drink, but have poured out my soul before the Lord. Count not thine handmaid for a daughter of Belial: for out of the abundance of my complaint and grief have I spoken hitherto."

The high priest was deeply moved, for he was a man of God; and in place of rebuke he uttered a blessing: "Go in peace: and the God of Israel grant thee thy petition that thou hast asked of Him."

Hannah's prayer was granted; she received the gift for which she had so earnestly entreated. As she looked upon the child, she called him Samuel—"asked of God." As soon as the little one was old enough to be separated from his mother, she fulfilled her vow. She loved her child with all the devotion of a mother's heart; day by day, as she watched his expanding powers and listened to his childish prattle, her affections entwined about him more closely. He was her only son, the special gift of Heaven; but she had received him as a treasure consecrated to God, and she would not withhold from the Giver His own.

Once more Hannah journeyed with her husband to Shiloh and presented to the priest, in the name of God, her precious gift, saying, "For this child I prayed; and the Lord hath given me my petition which I asked of Him: therefore also I have lent him to the Lord; as long as he liveth he shall be lent to the Lord." Eli was deeply impressed by the faith and devotion of this woman of Israel. Himself an overindulgent father, he was awed and humbled as he beheld this mother's great sacrifice in parting with her only child, that she might devote him to the service of God. He felt reproved for his own selfish love, and in humiliation and reverence he bowed before the Lord and worshiped.

The mother's heart was filled with joy and praise, and she longed to pour forth her gratitude to God. The Spirit of Inspiration came upon her; "and Hannah prayed, and said:

> "My heart rejoiceth in the Lord;
> > Mine horn is exalted in the Lord;
> My mouth is enlarged over mine enemies;
> > Because I rejoice in Thy salvation.
> There is none holy as the Lord:
> > For there is none beside Thee:
> Neither is there any rock like our God.
> > Talk no more so exceeding proudly;
> Let not arrogancy come out of your mouth;
> > For Jehovah is a God of knowledge,
> And by Him actions are weighed....
> > The Lord killeth, and maketh alive:
> He bringeth down to the grave, and bringeth up.
> > The Lord maketh poor, and maketh rich:
> He bringeth low, and lifteth up.
> > He raiseth up the poor out of the dust,
> And lifteth up the beggar from the dunghill,
> > To set them among princes,
> And to make them inherit the throne of glory:
> > For the pillars of the earth are the Lord's,
> And He hath set the world upon them.
> > He will keep the feet of His saints,
> And the wicked shall be silent in darkness;

>   For by strength shall no man prevail.
>   The adversaries of the Lord shall be broken to pieces;
>   Out of heaven shall He thunder upon them:
>   The Lord shall judge the ends of the earth;
>   And He shall give strength unto His king,
>   And exalt the horn of His anointed."

Hannah's words were prophetic, both of David, who should reign as king of Israel, and of the Messiah, the Lord's Anointed. Referring first to the boasting of an insolent and contentious woman, the song points to the destruction of the enemies of God and the final triumph of His redeemed people.

From Shiloh, Hannah quietly returned to her home at Ramah, leaving the child Samuel to be trained for service in the house of God, under the instruction of the high priest. From the earliest dawn of intellect she had taught her son to love and reverence God and to regard himself as the Lord's. By every familiar object surrounding him she had sought to lead his thoughts up to the Creator. When separated from her child, the faithful mother's solicitude did not cease. Every day he was the subject of her prayers. Every year she made, with her own hands, a robe of service for him; and as she went up with her husband to worship at Shiloh, she gave the child this reminder of her love. Every fiber of the little garment had been woven with a prayer that he might be pure, noble, and true. She did not ask for her son worldly greatness, but she earnestly pleaded that he might attain that greatness which Heaven values—that he might honor God and bless his fellow men.

What a reward was Hannah's! and what an encouragement to faithfulness is her example! There are opportunities of inestimable worth, interests infinitely precious, committed to every mother. The humble round of duties which women have come to regard as a wearisome task should be looked upon as a grand and noble work. It is the mother's privilege to bless the world by her influence, and in doing this she will bring joy to her own heart. She may make straight paths for the feet of her children, through sunshine and shadow, to the glorious heights above. But it is only when she seeks, in her own life, to follow the teachings of Christ that the mother can hope to form the character of her children after the divine pattern. The world teems with corrupting influences. Fashion and custom exert a strong power over the young. If the mother fails in her duty to instruct, guide, and restrain, her children will naturally accept the evil, and turn from the good. Let every mother go often to her Saviour with the prayer, "Teach us, how shall we order the child, and what shall we do unto him?" Let her heed the instruction which God has given in His word, and wisdom will be given her as she shall have need.

[573]

"The child Samuel grew on, and was in favor both with the Lord, and also with men." Though Samuel's youth was passed at the tabernacle devoted to the worship of God, he was not free from evil influences or sinful example. The sons of Eli feared not God, nor honored their father; but Samuel did not seek their company nor follow their evil ways. It was his constant endeavor to become what God would have him. This is the privilege of every youth. God is pleased when even little children give themselves to His service.

Samuel had been placed under the care of Eli, and the loveliness of his character drew forth the warm affection of the aged priest. He was kind, generous, obedient, and respectful. Eli, pained by the waywardness of his own sons, found rest and comfort and blessing in the presence of his charge. Samuel was helpful and affectionate, and no father ever loved his child more tenderly than did Eli this youth. It was a singular thing that between the chief magistrate of the nation and the simple child so warm an affection should exist. As the infirmities of age came upon Eli, and he was filled with anxiety and remorse by the profligate course of his own sons, he turned to Samuel for comfort.

It was not customary for the Levites to enter upon their peculiar services until they were twenty-five years of age, but Samuel had been an exception to this rule. Every year saw more important trusts committed to him; and while he was yet a child, a linen ephod was placed upon him as a token of his consecration to the work of the sanctuary. Young as he was when brought to minister in the tabernacle, Samuel had even then duties to perform in the service of God, according to his capacity. These were at first very humble, and not always pleasant; but they were performed to the best of his ability, and with a willing heart. His religion was carried into every duty of life. He regarded himself as God's servant, and his work as God's work. His efforts were accepted, because they were prompted by love to God and a sincere desire to do His will. It was thus that Samuel became a co-worker with the Lord of heaven and earth. And God fitted him to accomplish a great work for Israel.

If children were taught to regard the humble round of everyday duties as the course marked out for them by the Lord, as a school in which they were to be trained to render faithful and efficient service, how much more pleasant and honorable would their work appear. To perform every duty as unto the Lord, throws a charm around the humblest employment and links the workers on earth with the holy beings who do God's will in heaven.

Success in this life, success in gaining the future life, depends upon a faithful, conscientious attention to the little things. Perfection is seen in the least, no less than in the greatest, of the works of God. The hand that hung the worlds in space is the hand that wrought with delicate skill the lilies of the field. And as God is perfect in His sphere, so we are to be perfect in ours. The symmetrical structure of a strong, beautiful character is built up by individual acts of duty. And faithfulness should characterize our life in the least as well as in the greatest of its details. Integrity in little things, the performance of little acts of fidelity and little deeds of kindness, will gladden the path of life; and when our work on earth is ended, it will be found that every one of the little duties faithfully performed has exerted an influence for good—an influence that can never perish.

The youth of our time may become as precious in the sight of God as was Samuel. By faithfully maintaining their Christian integrity, they may exert a strong influence in the work of reform. Such men are needed at this time. God has a work for every one of them. Never did men achieve greater results for God and humanity than may be achieved in this our day by those who will be faithful to their God-given trust.

Chapter 56—Eli and His Sons

This chapter is based on 1 Samuel 2:12-36.

Eli was priest and judge in Israel. He held the highest and most responsible positions among the people of God. As a man divinely chosen for the sacred duties of the priesthood, and set over the land as the highest judicial authority, he was looked up to as an example, and he wielded a great influence over the tribes of Israel. But although he had been appointed to govern the people, he did not rule his own household. Eli was an indulgent father. Loving peace and ease, he did not exercise his authority to correct the evil habits and passions of his children. Rather than contend with them or punish them, he would submit to their will and give them their own way. Instead of regarding the education of his sons as one of the most important of his responsibilities, he treated the matter as of little consequence. The priest and judge of Israel had not been left in darkness as to the duty of restraining and governing the children that God had given to his care. But Eli shrank from this duty, because it involved crossing the will of his sons, and would make it necessary to punish and deny them. Without weighing the terrible consequences that would follow his course, he indulged his children in whatever they desired and neglected the work of fitting them for the service of God and the duties of life.

God had said of Abraham, "I know him, that he will *command* his children and his household after him, and they shall keep the way of the Lord, to do justice and judgment." Genesis 18:19. But Eli allowed his children to control him. The father became subject to the children. The curse of transgression was apparent in the corruption and evil that marked the course of his sons. They had no proper appreciation of the character of God or of the sacredness of His law. His service was to them a common thing. From childhood they had been accustomed to the sanctuary and its service; but instead of becoming more reverent, they had lost all sense of its holiness and significance. The father had not corrected their want of reverence for his authority, had not checked their disrespect for the solemn services of the sanctuary; and when they reached manhood, they were full of the deadly fruits of skepticism and rebellion.

Though wholly unfit for the office, they were placed as priests in the sanctuary to minister before God. The Lord had given the most specific directions in regard to offering sacrifices; but these wicked men carried their disregard of authority into the service of God, and did not give attention to the law of the offerings, which were to be made in the most solemn manner. The sacrifices, pointing forward to the death of Christ, were designed to preserve in the hearts of the people faith in the Redeemer to come; hence it was of the greatest importance that the Lord's directions concerning them should be strictly heeded. The peace offerings were especially an expression of thanksgiving to God. In these offerings the fat alone was to be burned upon the altar; a certain specified portion was reserved for the priests, but the greater part was returned to the offerer, to be eaten by him and his friends in a sacrificial feast. Thus all hearts were to be directed, in gratitude and faith, to the great Sacrifice that was to take away the sin of the world.

The sons of Eli, instead of realizing the solemnity of this symbolic service, only thought how they could make it a means of self-indulgence. Not content with the part of the peace offerings allotted them, they demanded an additional portion; and the great number of these sacrifices presented at the annual feasts gave the priests an opportunity to enrich themselves at the expense of the people. They not only demanded more than their right, but refused to wait even until the fat had been burned as an offering to God. They persisted in claiming whatever portion pleased them, and, if denied, threatened to take it by violence.

This irreverence on the part of the priests soon robbed the service of its holy and solemn significance, and the people "abhorred the offering of the Lord." The great antitypical sacrifice to which they were to look forward was no longer recognized. "Wherefore the sin of the young men was very great before the Lord."

These unfaithful priests also transgressed God's law and dishonored their sacred office by their vile and degrading practices; yet they continued to pollute by their presence the tabernacle of God.

Many of the people, filled with indignation at the corrupt course of Hophni and Phinehas, ceased to come up to the appointed place of worship. Thus the service which God had ordained was despised and neglected because associated with the sins of wicked men, while those whose hearts were inclined to evil were emboldened in sin. Ungodliness, profligacy, and even idolatry prevailed to a fearful extent.

Eli had greatly erred in permitting his sons to minister in holy office. By excusing their course, on one pretext and another, he became blinded to their sins; but at last they reached a pass where he could no longer hide his eyes from the crimes of his sons. The people complained of their violent deeds, and the high priest was grieved and distressed. He dared remain silent no longer. But his sons had been brought up to think of no one but themselves, and now they cared for no one else. They saw the grief of their father, but their hard hearts were not touched. They heard his mild admonitions, but they were not impressed, nor would they change their evil course though warned of the consequences of their sins. Had Eli dealt justly with his wicked sons, they would have been rejected from the priestly office and punished with death. Dreading thus to bring public disgrace and condemnation upon them, he sustained them in the most sacred positions of trust. He still permitted them to mingle their corruption with the holy service of God and to inflict upon the cause of truth an injury which years could not efface. But when the judge of Israel neglected his work, God took the matter in hand.

"There came a man of God unto Eli, and said unto him, Thus saith the Lord, Did I plainly appear unto the house of thy father, when they were in Egypt in Pharaoh's house? And did I choose him out of all the tribes of Israel to be My priest, to offer upon Mine altar, to burn incense, to wear an ephod before Me? and did I give unto the house of thy father all the offerings made by fire of the children of Israel? Wherefore kick ye at My sacrifice and at Mine offering, which I have commanded in My habitation; and honorest thy sons above Me, to make yourselves fat with the chiefest of all the offerings of Israel My people? Wherefore the Lord God of Israel saith, I said indeed that thy house, and the house of thy father, should walk before Me forever: but now the Lord saith, Be it far from Me; for them that honor Me I will honor, and they that despise Me shall be lightly esteemed.... And I will raise Me up a faithful priest, that shall do according to that which is in Mine heart and in My mind: and I will build him a sure house; and he shall walk before Mine anointed forever."

God charged Eli with honoring his sons above the Lord. Eli had permitted the offering appointed by God as a blessing to Israel to be made a thing of abhorrence, rather than bring his sons to shame for their impious and abominable practices. Those who follow their own inclination, in blind affection for their children, indulging them in the gratification of their selfish desires, and do not bring to bear the authority of God to rebuke sin and correct evil, make it manifest that they are honoring their wicked children more than they honor God. They are more anxious to shield their reputation than to glorify God; more desirous to please their children than to please the Lord and to keep His service from every appearance of evil.

God held Eli, as a priest and judge of Israel, accountable for the moral and religious standing of his people, and in a special sense for the character of his sons. He should first have attempted to restrain evil by mild measures; but if these did not avail, he should have subdued the wrong by the severest means. He incurred the Lord's displeasure by not reproving sin and executing justice upon the sinner. He could not be depended upon to keep Israel pure. Those who have too little courage to reprove wrong, or who through indolence or lack of interest make no earnest effort to purify the family or the church of God, are held accountable for the evil that may result from their neglect of duty. We are just as responsible for evils that we might have checked in others by exercise of parental or pastoral authority as if the acts had been our own.

Eli did not manage his household according to God's rules for family government. He followed his own judgment. The fond father overlooked the faults and sins of his sons in their childhood, flattering himself that after a time they would outgrow their evil tendencies. Many are now making a similar mistake. They think they know a better way of training their children than that which God has given in His word. They foster wrong tendencies in them, urging as an excuse, "They are too young to be punished. Wait till they become older, and can be reasoned with." Thus wrong habits are left to strengthen until they become second nature. The children grow up without restraint, with traits of character that are a lifelong curse to them and are liable to be reproduced in others.

There is no greater curse upon households than to allow the youth to have their own way. When parents regard every wish of their children and indulge them in what they know is not for their good, the children soon lose all respect for their parents, all regard for the authority of God or man, and are led captive at the will of Satan. The influence of an ill-regulated family is widespread and disastrous to all society. It accumulates in a tide of evil that affects families, communities, and governments.

Because of Eli's position, his influence was more extended than if he had been an ordinary man. His family life was imitated throughout Israel. The baleful results of his negligent, ease-loving ways were seen in thousands of homes that were molded by his example. If children are indulged in evil practices, while the parents make a profession of religion, the truth of God is brought into reproach. The best test of the Christianity of a home is the type of character begotten by its influence. Actions speak louder than the most positive profession of godliness. If professors of religion, instead of putting forth earnest, persistent, and painstaking effort to bring up a well-ordered household as a witness to the benefits of faith in God, are lax in their government and indulgent to the evil desires of their children, they are doing as did Eli, and are bringing disgrace on the cause of Christ and ruin upon themselves and their households. But great as are the evils of parental unfaithfulness under any circumstances, they are tenfold greater when they exist in the families of those appointed as teachers of the people. When these fail to control their own households, they are, by their wrong example, misleading many. Their guilt is as much greater than that of others as their position is more responsible.

The promise had been made that the house of Aaron should walk before God forever; but this promise had been made on condition that they should devote themselves to the work of the sanctuary with singleness of heart and honor God in all their ways, not serving self nor following their own perverse inclinations. Eli and his sons had been tested, and the Lord had found them wholly unworthy of the exalted position of priests in His service. And God declared, "Be it far from Me." He could not accomplish the good that He had meant to do them, because they failed to do their part.

The example of those who minister in holy things should be such as to impress the people with reverence for God and with fear to offend Him. When men, standing "in Christ's stead" (2 Corinthians 5:20) to speak to the people God's message of mercy and reconciliation, use their sacred calling as a cloak for selfish or sensual gratification, they make themselves the most effective agents of Satan. Like Hophni and Phinehas, they cause men to "abhor the offering of the Lord." They may pursue their evil course in secret for a time; but when at last their true character is exposed, the faith of the people receives a shock that often results in destroying their confidence in religion. There is left upon the mind a distrust of all who profess to teach the word of God. The message of the true servant of Christ is doubtfully received. The question constantly arises, "Will not this man prove to be like the one we thought so holy, and found so corrupt?" Thus the word of God loses its power upon the souls of men.

In Eli's reproof to his sons are words of solemn and fearful import—words that all who minister in sacred things would do well to ponder: "If one man sin against another, the judge shall judge him; but if a man sin against the Lord, who shall entreat for him?" Had their crimes injured only their fellow men, the judge might have made reconciliation by appointing a penalty and requiring restitution; and thus the offenders might have been pardoned. Or had they not been guilty of a presumptuous sin, a sin offering might have been presented for them. But their sins were so interwoven with their ministration as priests of the Most High, in offering sacrifice for sin, the work of God was so profaned and dishonored before the people, that no expiation could be accepted for them. Their own father, though himself high priest, dared not make intercession in their behalf; he could not shield them from the wrath of a holy God. Of all sinners, those are most guilty who cast contempt upon the means that Heaven has provided for man's redemption—who "crucify to themselves the Son of God afresh, and put Him to an open shame." Hebrews 6:6.

Chapter 57—The Ark Taken by the Philistines

This chapter is based on 1 Samuel 3 to 7.

Another warning was to be given to Eli's house. God could not communicate with the high priest and his sons; their sins, like a thick cloud, had shut out the presence of His Holy Spirit. But in the midst of evil the child Samuel remained true to Heaven, and the message of condemnation to the house of Eli was Samuel's commission as a prophet of the Most High.

"The word of the Lord was precious in those days; there was no open vision. And it came to pass at that time, when Eli was laid down in his place, and his eyes began to wax dim, that he could not see; and ere the lamp of God went out in the temple of the Lord, where the ark of God was, and Samuel was laid down to sleep; that the Lord called Samuel." Supposing the voice to be that of Eli, the child hastened to the bedside of the priest, saying, "Here am I; for thou calledst me." The answer was, "I called not, my son; lie down again." Three times Samuel was called, and thrice he responded in like manner. And then Eli was convinced that the mysterious call was the voice of God. The Lord had passed by His chosen servant, the man of hoary hairs, to commune with a child. This in itself was a bitter yet deserved rebuke to Eli and his house.

No feeling of envy or jealousy was awakened in Eli's heart. He directed Samuel to answer, if again called, "Speak, Lord; for Thy servant heareth." Once more the voice was heard, and the child answered, "Speak; for Thy servant heareth." So awed was he at the thought that the great God should speak to him that he could not remember the exact words which Eli bade him say.

"And the Lord said to Samuel, Behold, I will do a thing in Israel, at which both the ears of everyone that heareth it shall tingle. In that day I will perform against Eli all things which I have spoken concerning his house: when I begin, I will also make an end. For I have told him that I will judge his house forever for the iniquity which he knoweth; because his sons made themselves vile, and he restrained them not. And therefore I have sworn unto the house of Eli, that the iniquity of Eli's house shall not be purged with sacrifice nor offering forever."

Before receiving this message from God, "Samuel did not yet know the Lord, neither was the word of the Lord yet revealed unto him;" that is, he was not acquainted with such direct manifestations of God's presence as were granted to the prophets. It was the Lord's purpose to reveal Himself in an unexpected manner, that Eli might hear of it through the surprise and inquiry of the youth.

Samuel was filled with fear and amazement at the thought of having so terrible a message committed to him. In the morning he went about his duties as usual, but with a heavy burden upon his young heart. The Lord had not commanded him to reveal the fearful denunciation, hence he remained silent, avoiding, as far as possible, the presence of Eli. He trembled, lest some question should compel him to declare the divine judgments against one whom he loved and reverenced. Eli was confident that the message foretold some great calamity to him and his house. He called Samuel, and charged him to relate faithfully what the Lord had revealed. The youth obeyed, and the aged man bowed in humble submission to the appalling sentence. "It is the Lord," he said: "let Him do what seemeth Him good."

Yet Eli did not manifest the fruits of true repentance. He confessed his guilt, but failed to renounce the sin. Year after year the Lord delayed His threatened judgments. Much might have been done in those years to redeem the failures of the past, but the aged priest took no effective measures to correct the evils that were polluting the sanctuary of the Lord and leading thousands in Israel to ruin. The forbearance of God caused Hophni and Phinehas to harden their hearts and to become still bolder in transgression. The messages of warning and reproof to his house were made known by Eli to the whole nation. By this means he hoped to counteract, in some measure, the evil influence of his past neglect. But the warnings were disregarded by the people, as they had been by the priests. The people of surrounding nations also, who were not ignorant of the iniquities openly practiced in Israel, became still bolder in their idolatry and crime. They felt no sense of guilt for their sins, as they

Ark Taken by the Philistines

would have felt had the Israelites preserved their integrity. But a day of retribution was approaching. God's authority had been set aside, and His worship neglected and despised, and it became necessary for Him to interpose, that the honor of His name might be maintained.

"Now Israel went out against the Philistines to battle, and pitched beside Ebenezer: and the Philistines pitched in Aphek." This expedition was undertaken by the Israelites without counsel from God, without the concurrence of high priest or prophet. "And the Philistines put themselves in array against Israel: and when they joined battle, Israel was smitten before the Philistines: and they slew of the army in the field about four thousand men." As the shattered and disheartened force returned to their encampment, "the elders of Israel said, Wherefore hath the Lord smitten us today before the Philistines?" The nation was ripe for the judgments of God, yet they did not see that their own sins had been the cause of this terrible disaster. And they said, "Let us fetch the ark of the covenant of the Lord out of Shiloh unto us, that, when it cometh among us, it may save us out of the hand of our enemies." The Lord had given no command or permission that the ark should come into the army; yet the Israelites felt confident that victory would be theirs, and uttered a great shout when it was borne into the camp by the sons of Eli.

The Philistines looked upon the ark as the god of Israel. All the mighty works that Jehovah had wrought for His people were attributed to its power. As they heard the shouts of joy at its approach, they said, "What meaneth the noise of this great shout in the camp of the Hebrews? And they understood that the ark of the Lord was come into the camp. And the Philistines were afraid; for they said, God has come into the camp. And they said, Woe unto us! for there hath not been such a thing heretofore. Woe unto us! who shall deliver us out of the hand of these mighty Gods? These are the Gods that smote the Egyptians with all the plagues in the wilderness. Be strong, and quit yourselves like men, O ye Philistines, that ye be not servants unto the Hebrews, as they have been to you: quit yourselves like men, and fight."

The Philistines made a fierce assault, which resulted in the defeat of Israel, with great slaughter. Thirty thousand men lay dead upon the field, and the ark of God was taken, the two sons of Eli having fallen while fighting to defend it. Thus again was left upon the page of history a testimony for all future ages—that the iniquity of God's professed people will not go unpunished. The greater the knowledge of God's will, the greater the sin of those who disregard it.

The most terrifying calamity that could occur had befallen Israel. The ark of God had been captured, and was in the possession of the enemy. The glory had indeed departed from Israel when the symbol of the abiding presence and power of Jehovah was removed from the midst of them. With this sacred chest were associated the most wonderful revelations of God's truth and power. In former days miraculous victories had been achieved whenever it appeared. It was shadowed by the wings of the golden cherubim, and the unspeakable glory of the Shekinah, the visible symbol of the most high God, had rested over it in the holy of holies. But now it had brought no victory. It had not proved a defense on this occasion, and there was mourning throughout Israel.

They had not realized that their faith was only a nominal faith, and had lost its power to prevail with God. The law of God, contained in the ark, was also a symbol of His presence; but they had cast contempt upon the commandments, had despised their requirements, and had grieved the Spirit of the Lord from among them. When the people obeyed the holy precepts, the Lord was with them to work for them by His infinite power; but when they looked upon the ark, and did not associate it with God, nor honor His revealed will by obedience to His law, it could avail them little more than a common box. They looked to the ark as the idolatrous nations looked to their gods, as if it possessed in itself the elements of power and salvation. They transgressed the law it contained; for their very worship of the ark led to formalism, hypocrisy, and idolatry. Their sin had separated them from God, and He could not give them the victory until they had repented of and forsaken their iniquity.

It was not enough that the ark and the sanctuary were in the midst of Israel. It was not enough that the priests offered sacrifices, and that the people were called the children of God. The Lord does not regard the request of those who cherish iniquity in the heart; it is written that "he that turneth away his ear from hearing the law, even his prayer shall be abomination." Proverbs 28:9.

When the army went out to battle, Eli, blind and old, had tarried at Shiloh. It was with troubled forebodings that he awaited the result of the conflict; "for his heart trembled for the ark of God." Taking his position outside the gate of the tabernacle, he sat by the highway side day after day, anxiously expecting the arrival of a messenger from the battlefield.

At length a Benjamite from the army, "with his clothes rent, and with earth upon his head," came hurrying up the ascent leading to the city. Passing heedlessly the aged man beside the way, he rushed on to the town, and repeated to eager throngs the tidings of defeat and loss.

The sound of wailing and lamentation reached the watcher beside the tabernacle. The messenger was brought to him. And the man said unto Eli, "Israel is fled before the Philistines, and there hath been also a great slaughter among the people, and thy two sons also, Hophni and Phinehas, are dead." Eli could endure all this, terrible as it was, for he had expected it. But when the messenger added, "And the ark of God is taken," a look of unutterable anguish passed over his countenance. The thought that his sin had thus dishonored God and caused Him to withdraw His presence from Israel was more than he could bear; his strength was gone, he fell, "and his neck brake, and he died."

The wife of Phinehas, notwithstanding the impiety of her husband, was a woman who feared the Lord. The death of her father-in-law and her husband, and above all, the terrible tidings that the ark of God was taken, caused her death. She felt that the last hope of Israel was gone; and she named the child born in this hour of adversity, Ichabod, or "inglorious;" with her dying breath mournfully repeating the words, "The glory is departed from Israel: for the ark of God is taken."

But the Lord had not wholly cast aside His people, nor would He long suffer the exultation of the heathen. He had used the Philistines as the instrument to punish Israel, and He employed the ark to punish the Philistines. In time past the divine Presence had attended it, to be the strength and glory of His obedient people. That invisible Presence would still attend it, to bring terror and destruction to the transgressors of His holy law. The Lord often employs His bitterest enemies to punish the unfaithfulness of His professed people. The wicked may triumph for a time as they see Israel suffering chastisement, but the time will come when they, too, must meet the sentence of a holy, sin-hating God. Whenever iniquity is cherished, there, swift and unerring, the divine judgments will follow.

The Philistines removed the ark in triumph to Ashdod, one of their five principal cities, and placed it in the house of their god Dagon. They imagined that the power which had hitherto attended the ark would be theirs, and that this, united with the power of Dagon, would render them invincible. But upon entering the temple on the following day, they beheld a sight which filled them with consternation. Dagon had fallen upon his face to the earth before the ark of Jehovah. The priests reverently lifted the idol and restored it to its place. But the next morning they found it, strangely mutilated, again lying upon the earth before the ark. The upper part of this idol was like that of a man, and the lower part was in the likeness of a fish. Now every part that resembled the human form had been cut off, and only the body of the fish remained. Priests and people were horror-struck; they looked upon this mysterious event as an evil omen, foreboding destruction to themselves and their idols before the God of the Hebrews. They now removed the ark from their temple and placed it in a building by itself.

The inhabitants of Ashdod were smitten with a distressing and fatal disease. Remembering the plagues that were inflicted upon Egypt by the God of Israel, the people attributed their afflictions to the presence of the ark among them. It was decided to convey it to Gath. But the plague followed close upon its removal, and the men of that city sent it to Ekron. Here the people received it with terror, crying, "They have brought about the ark of the God of Israel to us, to slay us and our people." They turned to their gods for protection, as the people of Gath and Ashdod had done; but the work of the destroyer went on, until, in their distress, "the cry of the city went up to heaven." Fearing longer to retain the ark among the homes of men, the people next placed it in the open field. There followed a plague of mice, which infested the land, destroying the products of the soil, both in the storehouse and in the field. Utter destruction, by disease or famine, now threatened the nation.

For seven months the ark remained in Philistia, and during all this time the Israelites made no effort for its recovery. But the Philistines were now as anxious to free themselves from its presence as they had been to obtain it. Instead of being a source of strength to them, it was a great burden and a heavy curse. Yet they knew not what course to pursue; for wherever it went the judgments of God followed. The people called for the princes of the nation, with the priests and diviners, and eagerly inquired, "What shall we do to the ark of Jehovah? tell us wherewith we shall send it to his place?" They were advised to return it with a costly trespass offering. "Then," said the priests, "ye shall be healed, and it shall be known to you why His hand is not removed from you."

To ward off or to remove a plague, it was anciently the custom among the heathen to make an image in gold, silver, or other material, of that which caused the destruction, or of the object or part of the body specially affected. This was set up on a pillar or in some conspicuous place, and was supposed to be an effectual protection against the evils thus represented. A similar practice still exists among some heathen peoples. When a person suffering from disease goes for cure to the temple of his idol, he carries with him a figure of the part affected, which he presents as an offering to his god.

It was in accordance with the prevailing superstition that the Philistine lords directed the people to make representations of the plagues by which they had been afflicted—"five golden emerods, and five golden mice, according to the number of the lords of the Philistines: for," said they, "one plague was on you all, and on your lords."

These wise men acknowledged a mysterious power accompanying the ark—a power which they had no wisdom to meet. Yet they did not counsel the people to turn from their idolatry to serve the Lord. They still hated the God of Israel, though compelled by overwhelming judgments to submit to His authority. Thus sinners may be convinced by the judgments of God that it is in vain to contend against Him. They may be compelled to submit to His power, while at heart they rebel against His control. Such submission cannot save the sinner. The heart must be yielded to God—must be subdued by divine grace—before man's repentance can be accepted.

How great is the long-suffering of God toward the wicked! The idolatrous Philistines and backsliding Israel had alike enjoyed the gifts of His providence. Ten thousand unnoticed mercies were silently falling in the pathway of ungrateful, rebellious men. Every blessing spoke to them of the Giver, but they were indifferent to His love. The forbearance of God was very great toward the children of men; but when they stubbornly persisted in their impenitence, He removed from them His protecting hand. They refused to listen to the voice of God in His created works, and in the warnings, counsels, and reproofs of His word, and thus He was forced to speak to them through judgments.

There were some among the Philistines who stood ready to oppose the return of the ark to its own land. Such an acknowledgment of the power of Israel's God would be humiliating to the pride of Philistia. But "the priests and the diviners" admonished the people not to imitate the stubbornness of Pharaoh and the Egyptians, and thus bring upon themselves still greater afflictions. A plan which won the consent of all was now proposed, and immediately put in execution. The ark, with the golden trespass offering, was placed upon a new cart, thus precluding all danger of defilement; to this cart, or car, were attached two kine upon whose necks a yoke had never been placed. Their calves were shut up at home, and the cows were left free to go where they pleased. If the ark should thus be returned to the Israelites by the way of Beth-shemesh, the nearest city of the Levites, the Philistines would accept this as evidence that the God of Israel had done unto them this great evil; "but if not," they said, "then we shall know that it is not His hand that smote us; it was a chance that happened to us."

On being set free, the kine turned from their young and, lowing as they went, took the direct road to Beth-shemesh. Guided by no human hand, the patient animals kept on their way. The divine Presence accompanied the ark, and it passed on safely to the very place designated.

It was now the time of wheat harvest, and the men of Beth-shemesh were reaping in the valley. "And they lifted up their eyes, and saw the ark, and rejoiced to see it. And the cart came into the field of Joshua, a Beth-shemite, and stood there, where there was a great stone: and they clave the wood of the cart, and offered the kine of burnt-offering unto the Lord." The lords of the Philistines, who had followed the ark "unto the border of Beth-shemesh," and had witnessed its reception, now returned to Ekron. The plague had ceased, and they were convinced that their calamities had been a judgment from the God of Israel.

The men of Beth-shemesh quickly spread the tidings that the ark was in their possession, and the people from the surrounding country flocked to welcome its return. The ark had been placed upon the stone that first served for an altar, and before it additional sacrifices were offered unto the Lord. Had the worshipers repented of their sins, God's blessing would have attended them. But they were not faithfully obeying His law; and while they rejoiced at the return of the ark as a harbinger of good, they had no true sense of its sacredness. Instead of preparing a suitable place for its reception, they permitted it to remain in the harvest field. As they continued to gaze upon the sacred chest and to talk of the wonderful manner in which it had been restored, they began to conjecture wherein lay its peculiar power. At last, overcome by curiosity, they removed the coverings and ventured to open it.

All Israel had been taught to regard the ark with awe and reverence. When required to remove it from place to place the Levites were not so much as to look upon it. Only once a year was the high priest permitted to behold the ark of God. Even the heathen Philistines had not dared to remove its coverings. Angels of heaven, unseen, ever attended it in all its journeyings. The irreverent daring of the people at Beth-shemesh was speedily punished. Many were smitten with sudden death.

The survivors were not led by this judgment to repent of their sin, but only to regard the ark with superstitious fear. Eager to be free from its presence, yet not daring to remove it, the Beth-shemites sent a message to the inhabitants of Kirjath-jearim, inviting them to take it away. With great joy the men of this place welcomed the sacred chest. They knew that it was the pledge of divine favor to the obedient and faithful. With solemn gladness they brought it to their city and placed it in the house of Abinadab, a Levite. This man appointed his son Eleazar to take charge of it, and it remained there for many years.

During the years since the Lord first manifested Himself to the son of Hannah, Samuel's call to the prophetic office had come to be acknowledged by the whole nation. By faithfully delivering the divine warning to the house of Eli, painful and trying as the duty had been, Samuel had given proof of his fidelity as Jehovah's messenger; "and the Lord was with him, and did let none of his words fall to the ground. And all Israel from Dan even to Beersheba knew that Samuel was established to be a prophet of the Lord."

The Israelites as a nation still continued in a state of irreligion and idolatry, and as a punishment they remained in subjection to the Philistines. During this time Samuel visited the cities and villages throughout the land, seeking to turn the hearts of the people to the God of their fathers; and his efforts were not without good results. After suffering the oppression of their enemies for twenty years, the Israelites "mourned after the Lord." Samuel counseled them, "If ye do return unto the Lord with all your hearts, then put away the strange gods and Ashtaroth from among you, and prepare your hearts unto the Lord, and serve Him only." Here we see that practical piety, heart religion, was taught in the days of Samuel as taught by Christ when He was upon the earth. Without the grace of Christ the outward forms of religion were valueless to ancient Israel. They are the same to modern Israel.

There is need today of such a revival of true heart religion as was experienced by ancient Israel. Repentance is the first step that must be taken by all who would return to God. No one can do this work for another. We must individually humble our souls before God and put away our idols. When we have done all that we can do, the Lord will manifest to us His salvation.

With the co-operation of the heads of the tribes, a large assembly was gathered at Mizpeh. Here a solemn fast was held. With deep humiliation the people confessed their sins; and as an evidence of their determination to obey the instructions they had heard, they invested Samuel with the authority of judge.

The Philistines interpreted this gathering to be a council of war, and with a strong force set out to disperse the Israelites before their plans could be matured. The tidings of their approach caused great terror in Israel. The people entreated Samuel, "Cease not to cry unto the Lord our God for us, that He will save us out of the hand of the Philistines."

While Samuel was in the act of presenting a lamb as a burnt offering, the Philistines drew near for battle. Then the Mighty One who had descended upon Sinai amid fire and smoke and thunder, who had parted the Red Sea and made a way through Jordan for the children of Israel, again manifested His power. A terrible storm burst upon the advancing host, and the earth was strewn with the dead bodies of mighty warriors.

The Israelites had stood in silent awe, trembling with hope and fear. When they beheld the slaughter of their enemies, they knew that God had accepted their repentance. Though unprepared for battle, they seized the weapons of the slaughtered Philistines and pursued the fleeing host to Beth-car. This signal victory was gained upon the very field where, twenty years before, Israel had been smitten before the Philistines, the priests slain, and the ark of God taken. For nations as well as for individuals, the path of obedience to God is the path of safety and happiness, while that of transgression leads only to disaster and defeat. The Philistines were now so completely subdued that they surrendered the strongholds which had been taken from Israel and refrained from acts of hostility for many years. Other nations followed this example, and the Israelites enjoyed peace until the close of Samuel's sole administration.

That the occasion might never be forgotten, Samuel set up, between Mizpeh and Shen, a great stone as a memorial. He called the name of it Ebenezer, "the stone of help," saying to the people, "hitherto hath Jehovah helped us."

Chapter 58—The Schools of the Prophets

The Lord Himself directed the education of Israel. His care was not restricted to their religious interests; whatever affected their mental or physical well-being was also the subject of divine providence, and came within the sphere of divine law.

God had commanded the Hebrews to teach their children His requirements and to make them acquainted with all His dealings with their fathers. This was one of the special duties of every parent—one that was not to be delegated to another. In the place of stranger lips the loving hearts of the father and mother were to give instruction to their children. Thoughts of God were to be associated with all the events of daily life. The mighty works of God in the deliverance of His people and the promises of the Redeemer to come were to be often recounted in the homes of Israel; and the use of figures and symbols caused the lessons given to be more firmly fixed in the memory. The great truths of God's providence and of the future life were impressed on the young mind. It was trained to see God alike in the scenes of nature and the words of revelation. The stars of heaven, the trees and flowers of the field, the lofty mountains, the rippling brooks—all spoke of the Creator. The solemn service of sacrifice and worship at the sanctuary and the utterances of the prophets were a revelation of God.

Such was the training of Moses in the lowly cabin home in Goshen; of Samuel, by the faithful Hannah; of David, in the hill dwelling at Bethlehem; of Daniel, before the scenes of the captivity separated him from the home of his fathers. Such, too, was the early life of Christ at Nazareth; such the training by which the child Timothy learned from the lips of his grandmother Lois, and his mother Eunice (2 Timothy 1:5; 3:15), the truths of Holy Writ.

Further provision was made for the instruction of the young, by the establishment of the schools of the prophets. If a youth desired to search deeper into the truths of the word of God and to seek wisdom from above, that he might become a teacher in Israel, these schools were open to him. The schools of the prophets were founded by Samuel to serve as a barrier against the widespread corruption, to provide for the moral and spiritual welfare of the youth, and to promote the future prosperity of the nation by furnishing it with men qualified to act in the fear of God as leaders and counselors. In the accomplishment of this object Samuel gathered companies of young men who were pious, intelligent, and studious. These were called the sons of the prophets. As they communed with God and studied His word and His works, wisdom from above was added to their natural endowments. The instructors were men not only well versed in divine truth, but those who had themselves enjoyed communion with God and had received the special endowment of His Spirit. They enjoyed the respect and confidence of the people, both for learning and piety.

In Samuel's day there were two of these schools—one at Ramah, the home of the prophet, and the other at Kirjath-jearim, where the ark then was. Others were established in later times.

The pupils of these schools sustained themselves by their own labor in tilling the soil or in some mechanical employment. In Israel this was not thought strange or degrading; indeed, it was regarded a crime to allow children to grow up in ignorance of useful labor. By the command of God every child was taught some trade, even though he was to be educated for holy office. Many of the religious teachers supported themselves by manual labor. Even so late as the time of the apostles, Paul and Aquila were no less honored because they earned a livelihood by their trade of tentmaking.

The chief subjects of study in these schools were the law of God, with the instructions given to Moses, sacred history, sacred music, and poetry. The manner of instruction was far different from that in the theological schools of the present day, from which many students graduate with less real knowledge of God and religious truth than when they entered. In those schools of the olden time it was the grand object of all study to learn the will of God and man's duty toward Him. In the records of sacred history were traced the footsteps of Jehovah. The great truths set forth by the types were brought to view, and faith grasped the central object of all that system—the Lamb of God that was to take away the sin of the world.

A spirit of devotion was cherished. Not only were students taught the duty of prayer, but they were taught how to pray, how to approach their Creator, how to exercise faith in Him, and how to understand and obey the teachings of His Spirit. Sanctified intellects brought forth from the treasure house of God things new and old, and the Spirit of God was manifested in prophecy and sacred song.

Music was made to serve a holy purpose, to lift the thoughts to that which is pure, noble, and elevating, and to awaken in the soul devotion and gratitude to God. What a contrast between the ancient custom and the uses to which music is now too often devoted! How many employ this gift to exalt self, instead of using it to Glorify God! A love for music leads the unwary to unite with world lovers in pleasure gatherings where God has forbidden His children to go. Thus that which is a great blessing when rightly used, becomes one of the most successful agencies by which Satan allures the mind from duty and from the contemplation of eternal things.

Music forms a part of God's worship in the courts above, and we should endeavor, in our songs of praise, to approach as nearly as possible to the harmony of the heavenly choirs. The proper training of the voice is an important feature in education and should not be neglected. Singing, as a part of religious service, is as much an act of worship as is prayer. The heart must feel the spirit of the song to give it right expression.

How wide the difference between those schools taught by the prophets of God and our modern institutions of learning! How few schools are to be found that are not governed by the maxims and customs of the world! There is a deplorable lack of proper restraint and judicious discipline. The existing ignorance of God's word among a people professedly Christian is alarming. Superficial talk, mere sentimentalism, passes for instruction in morals and religion. The justice and mercy of God, the beauty of holiness and the sure reward of rightdoing, the heinous character of sin and the certainty of its terrible results, are not impressed upon the minds of the young. Evil associates are instructing the youth in the ways of crime, dissipation, and licentiousness.

Are there not some lessons which the educators of our day might learn with profit from the ancient schools of the Hebrews? He who created man has provided for his development in body and mind and soul. Hence, real success in education depends upon the fidelity with which men carry out the Creator's plan.

The true object of education is to restore the image of God in the soul. In the beginning God created man in His own likeness. He endowed him with noble qualities. His mind was well balanced, and all the powers of his being were harmonious. But the Fall and its effects have perverted these gifts. Sin has marred and well-nigh obliterated the image of God in man. It was to restore this that the plan of salvation was devised, and a life of probation was granted to man. To bring him back to the perfection in which he was first created is the great object of life—the object that underlies every other. It is the work of parents and teachers, in the education of the youth, to co-operate with the divine purpose; and in so doing they are "laborers together with God." 1 Corinthians 3:9.

All the varied capabilities that men possess—of mind and soul and body—are given them by God, to be so employed as to reach the highest possible degree of excellence. But this cannot be a selfish and exclusive culture; for the character of God, whose likeness we are to receive, is benevolence and love. Every faculty, every attribute, with which the Creator has endowed us is to be employed for His glory and for the uplifting of our fellow men. And in this employment is found its purest, noblest, and happiest exercise.

Were this principle given the attention which its importance demands, there would be a radical change in some of the current methods of education. Instead of appealing to pride and selfish ambition, kindling a spirit of emulation, teachers would endeavor to awaken the love for goodness and truth and beauty—to arouse the desire for excellence. The student would seek the development of God's gifts in himself, not to excel others, but to fulfill the purpose of the Creator and to receive His likeness. Instead of being directed to mere earthly standards, or being actuated by the desire for self-exaltation, which in itself dwarfs and belittles, the mind would be directed to the Creator, to know Him and to become like Him.

"The fear of the Lord is the beginning of wisdom: and *the knowledge of the Holy* is understanding." Proverbs 9:10. The great work of life is character building, and a knowledge of God is the foundation of all true education. To impart this knowledge and to mold the character in harmony with it should be the object of the teacher's work.

The law of God is a reflection of His character. Hence the psalmist says, "All Thy commandments are righteousness;" and "through Thy precepts I get understanding." Psalm 119:172, 104. God has revealed Himself to us in His word and in the works of creation. Through the volume of inspiration and the book of nature we are to obtain a knowledge of God.

It is a law of the mind that it gradually adapts itself to the subjects upon which it is trained to dwell. If occupied with commonplace matters only, it will become dwarfed and enfeebled. If never required to grapple with difficult problems, it will after a time almost lose the power of growth. As an educating power the Bible is without a rival. In the word of God the mind finds subject for the deepest thought, the loftiest aspiration. The Bible is the most instructive history that men possess. It came fresh from the fountain of eternal truth, and a divine hand has preserved its purity through all the ages. It lights up the far-distant past, where human research seeks vainly to penetrate. In God's word we behold the power that laid the foundation of the earth and that stretched out the heavens. Here only can we find a history of our race unsullied by human prejudice or human pride. Here are recorded the struggles, the defeats, and the victories of the greatest men this world has ever known. Here the great problems of duty and destiny are unfolded. The curtain that separates the visible from the invisible world is lifted, and we behold the conflict of the opposing forces of good and evil, from the first entrance of sin to the final triumph of righteousness and truth; and all is but a revelation of the character of God. In the reverent contemplation of the truths presented in His word the mind of the student is brought into communion with the infinite mind. Such a study will not only refine and ennoble the character, but it cannot fail to expand and invigorate the mental powers.

The teaching of the Bible has a vital bearing upon man's prosperity in all the relations of this life. It unfolds the principles that are the cornerstone of a nation's prosperity—principles with which is bound up the well-being of society, and which are the safeguard of the family—principles without which no man can attain usefulness, happiness, and honor in this life, or can hope to secure the future, immortal life. There is no position in life, no phase of human experience, for which the teaching of the Bible is not an essential preparation. Studied and obeyed, the word of God would give to the world men of stronger and more active intellect than will the closest application to all the subjects that human philosophy embraces. It would give men of strength and solidity of character, of keen perception and sound judgment—men who would be an honor to God and a blessing to the world.

In the study of the sciences also we are to obtain a knowledge of the Creator. All true science is but an interpretation of the handwriting of God in the material world. Science brings from her research only fresh evidences of the wisdom and power of God. Rightly understood, both the book of nature and the written word make us acquainted with God by teaching us something of the wise and beneficent laws through which He works.

The student should be led to see God in all the works of creation. Teachers should copy the example of the Great Teacher, who from the familiar scenes of nature drew illustrations that simplified His teachings and impressed them more deeply upon the minds of His hearers. The birds caroling in the leafy branches, the flowers of the valley, the lofty trees, the fruitful lands, the springing grain, the barren soil, the setting sun gilding the heavens with its golden beams—all served as means of instruction. He connected the visible works of the Creator with the words of life which He spoke, that whenever these objects should be presented to the eyes of His hearers, their thoughts might revert to the lessons of truth He had linked with them.

The impress of Deity, manifest in the pages of revelation, is seen upon the lofty mountains, the fruitful valleys, the broad, deep ocean. The things of nature speak to man of his Creator's love. He has linked us to Himself by unnumbered tokens in heaven and in earth. This world is not all sorrow and misery. "God is love," is written upon every opening bud, upon the petals of every flower, and upon every spire of grass. Though the curse of sin has caused the earth to bring forth thorns and thistles, there are flowers upon the thistles and the thorns are hidden by roses. All things in nature testify to the tender, fatherly care of our God and to His desire to make His children happy. His prohibitions and injunctions are not intended merely to display His authority, but in all that He does He has the

[600]

well-being of His children in view. He does not require them to give up anything that it would be for their best interest to retain.

The opinion which prevails in some classes of society, that religion is not conducive to health or to happiness in this life, is one of the most mischievous of errors. The Scripture says: "The fear of the Lord tendeth to life: and he that hath it shall abide satisfied." Proverbs 19:23. "What man is he that desireth life, and loveth many days, that he may see good? Keep thy tongue from evil, and thy lips from speaking guile. Depart from evil, and do good; seek peace, and pursue it." Psalm 34:12-14. The words of wisdom "are life unto those that find them, and health to all their flesh." Proverbs 4:22.

True religion brings man into harmony with the laws of God, physical, mental, and moral. It teaches self-control, serenity, temperance. Religion ennobles the mind, refines the taste, and sanctifies the judgment. It makes the soul a partaker of the purity of heaven. Faith in God's love and overruling providence lightens the burdens of anxiety and care. It fills the heart with joy and contentment in the highest or the lowliest lot. Religion tends directly to promote health, to lengthen life, and to heighten our enjoyment of all its blessings. It opens to the soul a never-failing fountain of happiness. Would that all who have not chosen Christ might realize that He has something vastly better to offer them that they are seeking for themselves. Man is doing the greatest injury and injustice to his own soul when he thinks and acts contrary to the will of God. No real joy can be found in the path forbidden by Him who knows what is best, and who plans for the good of His creatures. The path of transgression leads to misery and destruction; but wisdom's "ways are ways of pleasantness, and all her paths are peace." Proverbs 3:17.

The physical as well as the religious training practiced in the schools of the Hebrews may be profitably studied. The worth of such training is not appreciated. There is an intimate relation between the mind and the body, and in order to reach a high standard of moral and intellectual attainment the laws that control our physical being must be heeded. To secure a strong, well-balanced character, both the mental and the physical powers must be exercised and developed. What study can be more important for the young than that which treats of this wonderful organism that God has committed to us, and of the laws by which it may be preserved in health?

And now, as in the days of Israel, every youth should be instructed in the duties of practical life. Each should acquire a knowledge of some branch of manual labor by which, if need be, he may obtain a livelihood. This is essential, not only as a safeguard against the vicissitudes of life, but from its bearing upon physical, mental, and moral development. Even if it were certain that one would never need to resort to manual labor for his support, still he should be taught to work. Without physical exercise, no one can have a sound constitution and vigorous health; and the discipline of well-regulated labor is no less essential to the securing of a strong and active mind and a noble character.

Every student should devote a portion of each day to active labor. Thus habits of industry would be formed and a spirit of self-reliance encouraged, while the youth would be shielded from many evil and degrading practices that are so often the result of idleness. And this is all in keeping with the primary object of education, for in encouraging activity, diligence, and purity we are coming into harmony with the Creator.

Let the youth be led to understand the object of their creation, to honor God and bless their fellow men; let them see the tender love which the Father in heaven has manifested toward them, and the high destiny for which the discipline of this life is to prepare them, the dignity and honor to which they are called, even to become the sons of God, and thousands would turn with contempt and loathing from the low and selfish aims and the frivolous pleasures that have hitherto engrossed them. They would learn to hate sin and to shun it, not merely from hope of reward or fear of punishment, but from a sense of its inherent baseness, because it would be a degrading of their God-given powers, a stain upon their Godlike manhood.

God does not bid the youth to be less aspiring. The elements of character that make a man successful and honored among men—the irrepressible desire for some greater good, the indomitable will, the strenuous exertion, the untiring perseverance—are not to be crushed out. By the grace of God they are to be directed to objects as much higher than mere selfish and temporal interests as the heavens are higher than the earth. And the education begun in this life will be continued in the life to come. Day by day the wonderful works of God, the evidences of His wisdom and power in creating and sustaining the universe, the infinite mystery of love and wisdom in the plan of redemption, will open to the mind in new beauty. "Eye hath not seen, nor ear heard, neither have entered into the heart of man, the things which God hath prepared for them that love Him." 1 Corinthians 2:9. Even in this life we may catch glimpses of His presence and may taste the joy of communion with Heaven, but the fullness of its joy and blessing will be reached in the hereafter. Eternity alone can reveal the glorious destiny to which man, restored to God's image, may attain.

Chapter 59—The First King of Israel

This chapter is based on 1 Samuel 8 to 12.

The government of Israel was administered in the name and by the authority of God. The work of Moses, of the seventy elders, of the rulers and judges, was simply to enforce the laws that God had given; they had no authority to legislate for the nation. This was, and continued to be, the condition of Israel's existence as a nation. From age to age men inspired by God were sent to instruct the people and to direct in the enforcement of the laws.

The Lord foresaw that Israel would desire a king, but He did not consent to a change in the principles upon which the state was founded. The king was to be the vicegerent of the Most High. God was to be recognized as the Head of the nation, and His law was to be enforced as the supreme law of the land. [See Appendix, note 8.]

When the Israelites first settled in Canaan they acknowledged the principles of the theocracy, and the nation prospered under the rule of Joshua. But increase of population and intercourse with other nations brought a change. The people adopted many of the customs of their heathen neighbors and thus sacrificed to a great degree their own peculiar, holy character. Gradually they lost their reverence for God and ceased to prize the honor of being His chosen people. Attracted by the pomp and display of heathen monarchs, they tired of their own simplicity. Jealousy and envy sprang up between the tribes. Internal dissensions made them weak; they were continually exposed to the invasion of their heathen foes, and the people were coming to believe that in order to maintain their standing among the nations, the tribes must be united under a strong central government. As they departed from obedience to God's law, they desired to be freed from the rule of their divine Sovereign; and thus the demand for a monarchy became widespread throughout Israel.

Since the days of Joshua the government had never been conducted with so great wisdom and success as under Samuel's administration. Divinely invested with the threefold office of judge, prophet, and priest, he had labored with untiring and disinterested zeal for the welfare of his people, and the nation had prospered under his wise control. Order had been restored, and godliness promoted, and the spirit of discontent was checked for the time. But with advancing years the prophet was forced to share with others the cares of government, and he appointed his two sons to act as his assistants. While Samuel continued the duties of his office at Ramah, the young men were stationed at Beersheba, to administer justice among the people near the southern border of the land.

It was with the full assent of the nation that Samuel had appointed his sons to office, but they did not prove themselves worthy of their father's choice. The Lord had, through Moses, given special directions to His people that the rulers of Israel should judge righteously, deal justly with the widow and the fatherless, and receive no bribes. But the sons of Samuel "turned aside after lucre, and took bribes, and perverted judgment." The sons of the prophet had not heeded the precepts which he had sought to impress upon their minds. They had not copied the pure, unselfish life of their father. The warning given to Eli had not exerted the influence upon the mind of Samuel that it should have done. He had been to some extent too indulgent with his sons, and the result was apparent in their character and life.

The injustice of these judges caused much dissatisfaction, and a pretext was thus furnished for urging the change that had long been secretly desired. "All the elders of Israel gathered themselves together, and came to Samuel unto Ramah, and said unto him, Behold, thou art old, and thy sons walk not in thy ways: now make us a king to judge us like all the nations." The cases of abuse among the people had not been referred to Samuel. Had the evil course of his sons been known to him, he would have removed them without delay; but this was not what the petitioners desired. Samuel saw that their real motive was discontent and pride, and that their demand was the result of a deliberate and determined purpose. No complaint had been made against Samuel. All acknowledged the integrity and wisdom of his administration; but the aged prophet looked upon the request as a censure upon himself, and a direct effort to set him aside. He did not, however, reveal his feelings; he uttered no reproach, but carried the matter to the Lord in prayer and sought counsel from Him alone.

And the Lord said unto Samuel: "Hearken unto the voice of the people in all that they say unto thee: for they have not rejected thee, but they have rejected Me, that I should not reign over them. According to all the works which they have done since the day that I brought them up out of Egypt even unto this day, wherewith they have forsaken Me, and served other gods, so do they also unto thee." The prophet was reproved for grieving at the conduct of the people toward himself as an individual. They had not manifested disrespect for him, but for the authority of God, who had appointed the rulers of His people. Those who despise and reject the faithful servant of God show contempt, not merely for the man, but for the Master who sent him. It is God's words, His reproofs and counsel, that are set at nought; it is His authority that is rejected.

The days of Israel's greatest prosperity had been those in which they acknowledged Jehovah as their King—when the laws and the government which He had established were regarded as superior to those of all other nations. Moses had declared to Israel concerning the commandments of the Lord: "This is your wisdom and your understanding in the sight of the nations, which shall hear all these statutes, and say, Surely this great nation is a wise and understanding people." Deuteronomy 4:6. But by departing from God's law the Hebrews had failed to become the people that God desired to make them, and then all the evils which were the result of their own sin and folly they charged upon the government of God. So completely had they become blinded by sin.

The Lord had, through His prophets, foretold that Israel would be governed by a king; but it does not follow that this form of government was best for them or according to His will. He permitted the people to follow their own choice, because they refused to be guided by His counsel. Hosea declares that God gave them a king in His anger. Hosea 13:11. When men choose to have their own way, without seeking counsel from God, or in opposition to His revealed will, He often grants their desires, in order that, through the bitter experience that follows, they may be led to realize their folly and to repent of their sin. Human pride and wisdom will prove a dangerous guide. That which the heart desires contrary to the will of God will in the end be found a curse rather than a blessing.

God desired His people to look to Him alone as their Law-giver and their Source of strength. Feeling their dependence upon God, they would be constantly drawn nearer to Him. They would become elevated and ennobled, fitted for the high destiny to which He had called them as His chosen people. But when a man was placed upon the throne, it would tend to turn the minds of the people from God. They would trust more to human strength, and less to divine power, and the errors of their king would lead them into sin and separate the nation from God.

Samuel was instructed to grant the request of the people, but to warn them of the Lord's disapproval, and also make known what would be the result of their course. "And Samuel told all the words of the Lord unto the people that asked of him a king." He faithfully set before them the burdens that would be laid upon them, and showed the contrast between such a state of oppression and their present comparatively free and prosperous condition. Their king would imitate the pomp and luxury of other monarchs, to support which, grievous exactions upon their persons and property would be necessary. The goodliest of their young men he would require for his service. They would be made charioteers and horsemen and runners before him. They must fill the ranks of his army, and they would be required to till *his* fields, to reap *his* harvests, and to manufacture implements of war for *his* service. The daughters of Israel would be for confectioners and bakers for the royal household. To support his kingly state he would seize upon the best of their lands, bestowed upon the people by Jehovah Himself. The most valuable of their servants also, and of their cattle, he would take, and "put them to his work." Besides all this, the king would require a tenth of all their income, the profits of their labor, or the products of the soil. "Ye shall be his servants," concluded the prophet. "And ye shall cry out in that day because of your king which ye shall have chosen you; and the Lord will not hear you in that day." However burdensome its exactions should be found, when once a monarchy was established, they could not set it aside at pleasure.

But the people returned the answer, "Nay; but we will have a king over us; that we also may be like all the nations; and that our king may judge us, and go out before us, and fight our battles."

"Like all the nations." The Israelites did not realize that to be in this respect unlike other nations was a special privilege and blessing. God had separated the Israelites from every other people, to make them His own peculiar treasure. But they, disregarding this high honor, eagerly desired to imitate the example of the heathen! And still the longing to conform to worldly practices and customs exists among the professed people of God. As they depart from the Lord they become ambitious for the gains and honors of the world. Christians are constantly seeking to imitate the practices of those who worship the god of this world. Many urge that by uniting with worldlings and conforming to their customs they might exert a stronger influence over the ungodly. But all who pursue this course thereby separate from the Source of their strength. Becoming the friends of the world, they are the enemies of God. For the sake of earthly distinction they sacrifice the unspeakable honor to which God has called them, of showing forth the praises of Him who hath called us out of darkness into His marvelous light. 1 Peter 2:9.

With deep sadness Samuel listened to the words of the people; but the Lord said unto him, "Hearken unto their voice, and make them a king." The prophet had done his duty. He had faithfully presented the warning, and it had been rejected. With a heavy heart he dismissed the people, and himself departed to prepare for the great change in the government.

Samuel's life of purity and unselfish devotion was a perpetual rebuke both to self-serving priests and elders and to the proud, sensual congregation of Israel. Although he assumed no pomp and made no display, his labors bore the signet of Heaven. He was honored by the world's Redeemer, under whose guidance he ruled the Hebrew nation. But the people had become weary of his piety and devotion; they despised his humble authority and rejected him for a man who should rule them as a king.

In the character of Samuel we see reflected the likeness of Christ. It was the purity of our Saviour's life that provoked the wrath of Satan. That life was the light of the world, and revealed the hidden depravity in the hearts of men. It was the holiness of Christ that stirred up against Him the fiercest passions of falsehearted professors of godliness. Christ came not with the wealth and honors of earth, yet the works which He wrought showed Him to possess power greater than that of any human prince. The Jews looked for the Messiah to break the oppressor's yoke, yet they cherished the sins that had bound it upon their necks. Had Christ cloaked their sins and applauded their piety, they would have accepted Him as their king; but they would not bear His fearless rebuke of their vices. The loveliness of a character in which benevolence, purity, and holiness reigned supreme, which entertained no hatred except for sin, they despised. Thus it has been in every age of the world. The light from heaven brings condemnation on all who refuse to walk in it. When rebuked by the example of those who hate sin, hypocrites will become agents of Satan to harass and persecute the faithful. "All that will live godly in Christ Jesus shall suffer persecution." 2 Timothy 3:12.

Though a monarchical form of government for Israel had been foretold in prophecy, God had reserved to Himself the right to choose their king. The Hebrews so far respected the authority of God as to leave the selection entirely to Him. The choice fell upon Saul, a son of Kish, of the tribe of Benjamin.

The personal qualities of the future monarch were such as to gratify that pride of heart which prompted the desire for a king. "There was not among the children of Israel a goodlier person than he." 1 Samuel 9:2. Of noble and dignified bearing, in the prime of life, comely and tall, he appeared like one born to command. Yet with these external attractions, Saul was destitute of those higher qualities that constitute true wisdom. He had not in youth learned to control his rash, impetuous passions; he had never felt the renewing power of divine grace.

Saul was the son of a powerful and wealthy chief, yet in accordance with the simplicity of the times he was engaged with his father in the humble duties of a husbandman. Some of his father's animals having strayed upon the mountains, Saul went with a servant to seek for them. For three days they searched in vain, when, as they were not far from Ramah, [See Appendix, note 9.] the home of Samuel, the servant proposed that they should inquire of the prophet concerning the missing property. "I have here at hand the fourth part of a shekel of silver," he said: "that will I give to the man of God, to tell us our way." This was in accordance with the custom of the times. A person approaching a superior in rank or office made him a small present, as an expression of respect.

As they drew near to the city they met some young maidens who had come out to draw water, and inquired of them for the seer. In reply they were told that a religious service was about to take place, that the prophet had already arrived, there was to be an offering upon "the high place," and after that a sacrificial feast. A great change had taken place under Samuel's administration. When the call of God first came to him the services of the sanctuary were held in contempt. "Men abhorred the offering of the Lord." 1 Samuel 2:17. But the worship of God was now maintained throughout the land, and the people manifested an interest in religious services. There being no ministration in the tabernacle, sacrifices were for the time offered elsewhere; and the cities of the priests and Levites, where the people resorted for instruction, were chosen for this purpose. The highest points in these cities were usually selected as the place of sacrifice, and hence were called "the high places."

At the gate of the city Saul was met by the prophet himself. God had revealed to Samuel that at that time the chosen king of Israel would present himself before him. As they now stood face to face, the Lord said to Samuel, "Behold the man whom I spake to thee of! this same shall reign over My people."

To the request of Saul, "Tell me, I pray thee, where the seer's house is," Samuel replied, "I am the seer." Assuring him also that the lost animals had been found, he urged him to tarry and attend the feast, at the same time giving some intimation of the great destiny before him: "On whom is all the desire of Israel? Is it not on thee, and on all thy father's house?" The listener's heart thrilled at the prophet's words. He could not but perceive something of their significance, for the demand for a king had become a matter of absorbing interest to the whole nation. Yet with modest self-depreciation Saul replied, "Am not I a Benjamite, of the smallest of the tribes of Israel? and my family the least of all the families of the tribe of Benjamin? wherefore then speakest thou so to me?"

Samuel conducted the stranger to the place of assembly, where the principal men of the town were gathered. Among them, at the prophet's direction, the place of honor was given to Saul, and at the

[610]

feast the choicest portion was set before him. The services over, Samuel took his guest to his own home, and there upon the housetop he communed with him, setting forth the great principles on which the government of Israel had been established, and thus seeking to prepare him, in some measure, for his high station.

When Saul departed, early next morning, the prophet went forth with him. Having passed through the town, he directed the servant to go forward. Then he bade Saul stand still to receive a message sent him from God. "Then Samuel took a vial of oil, and poured it upon his head, and kissed him, and said, Is it not because Jehovah hath anointed thee to be captain over His inheritance?" As evidence that this was done by divine authority, he foretold the incidents that would occur on the homeward journey and assured Saul that he would be qualified by the Spirit of God for the station awaiting him. "The Spirit of Jehovah will come upon thee," said the prophet, and thou "shalt be turned into another man. And let it be, when these signs are come unto thee, that thou do as occasion serve thee; for God is with thee."

As Saul went on his way, all came to pass as the prophet had said. Near the border of Benjamin he was informed that the lost animals had been found. In the plain of Tabor he met three men who were going to worship God at Bethel. One of them carried three kids for sacrifice, another three loaves of bread, and the third a bottle of wine, for the sacrificial feast. They gave Saul the usual salutation and also presented him with two of the three loaves of bread. At Gibeah, his own city, a band of prophets returning from "the high place" were singing the praise of God to the music of the pipe and the harp, the psaltery and the tabret. As Saul approached them the Spirit of the Lord came upon him also, and he joined in their song of praise, and prophesied with them. He spoke with so great fluency and wisdom, and joined so earnestly in the service, that those who had known him exclaimed in astonishment, "What is this that is come unto the son of Kish? Is Saul also among the prophets?"

As Saul united with the prophets in their worship, a great change was wrought in him by the Holy Spirit. The light of divine purity and holiness shone in upon the darkness of the natural heart. He saw himself as he was before God. He saw the beauty of holiness. He was now called to begin the warfare against sin and Satan, and he was made to feel that in this conflict his strength must come wholly from God. The plan of salvation, which had before seemed dim and uncertain, was opened to his understanding. The Lord endowed him with courage and wisdom for his high station. He revealed to him the Source of strength and grace, and enlightened his understanding as to the divine claims and his own duty.

The anointing of Saul as king had not been made known to the nation. The choice of God was to be publicly manifested by lot. For this purpose Samuel convoked the people at Mizpeh. Prayer was offered for divine guidance; then followed the solemn ceremony of casting the lot. In silence the assembled multitude awaited the issue. The tribe, the family, and the household were successively designated, and then Saul, the son of Kish, was pointed out as the individual chosen. But Saul was not in the assembly. Burdened with a sense of the great responsibility about to fall upon him, he had secretly withdrawn. He was brought back to the congregation, who observed with pride and satisfaction that he was of kingly bearing and noble form, being "higher than any of the people from his shoulders and upward." Even Samuel, when presenting him to the assembly, exclaimed, "See ye him whom the Lord hath chosen, that there is none like him among all the people?" And in response arose from the vast throng one long, loud shout of joy, "God save the king!"

Samuel then set before the people "the manner of the kingdom," stating the principles upon which the monarchial government was based, and by which it should be controlled. The king was not to be an absolute monarch, but was to hold his power in subjection to the will of the Most High. This address was recorded in a book, wherein were set forth the prerogatives of the prince and the rights and privileges of the people. Though the nation had despised Samuel's warning, the faithful prophet, while forced to yield to their desires, still endeavored, as far as possible, to guard their liberties.

While the people in general were ready to acknowledge Saul as their king, there was a large party in opposition. For a monarch to be chosen from Benjamin, the smallest of the tribes of Israel—and that to the neglect of both Judah and Ephraim, the largest and most powerful—was a slight which they could not brook. They refused to profess allegiance to Saul or to bring him the customary presents.

Those who had been most urgent in their demand for a king were the very ones that refused to accept with gratitude the man of God's appointment. The members of each faction had their favorite, whom they wished to see placed on the throne, and several among the leaders had desired the honor for themselves. Envy and jealousy burned in the hearts of many. The efforts of pride and ambition had resulted in disappointment and discontent.

In this condition of affairs Saul did not see fit to assume the royal dignity. Leaving Samuel to administer the government as formerly, he returned to Gibeah. He was honorably escorted thither by a company, who, seeing the divine choice in his selection, were determined to sustain him. But he made no attempt to maintain by force his right to the throne. In his home among the uplands of Benjamin he quietly occupied himself in the duties of a husbandman, leaving the establishment of his authority entirely to God.

Soon after Saul's appointment the Ammonites, under their king, Nahash, invaded the territory of the tribes east of Jordan and threatened the city of Jabesh-gilead. The inhabitants tried to secure terms of peace by offering to become tributary to the Ammonites. To this the cruel king would not consent but on condition that he might put out the right eye of every one of them, thus making them abiding witnesses to his power.

The people of the besieged city begged a respite of seven days. To this the Ammonites consented, thinking thus to heighten the honor of their expected triumph. Messengers were at once dispatched from Jabesh, to seek help from the tribes west of Jordan. They carried the tidings to Gibeah, creating widespread terror. Saul, returning at night from following the oxen in the field, heard the loud wail that told of some great calamity. He said, "What aileth the people that they weep?" When the shameful story was repeated, all his dormant powers were roused. "The Spirit of God came upon Saul.... And he took a yoke of oxen, and hewed them in pieces, and sent them throughout all the coasts of Israel by the hands of messengers, saying, Whosoever cometh not forth after Saul and after Samuel, so shall it be done unto his oxen."

Three hundred and thirty thousand men gathered on the plain of Bezek, under the command of Saul. Messengers were immediately sent to the besieged city with the assurance that they might expect help on the morrow, the very day on which they were to submit to the Ammonites. By a rapid night march Saul and his army crossed the Jordan and arrived before Jabesh in "the morning watch." Like Gideon, dividing his force into three companies, he fell upon the Ammonite camp at that early hour, when, not suspecting danger, they were least secure. In the panic that followed they were routed with great slaughter. And "they which remained were scattered, so that two of them were not left together."

The promptness and bravery of Saul, as well as the generalship shown in the successful conduct of so large a force, were qualities which the people of Israel had desired in a monarch, that they might be able to cope with other nations. They now greeted him as their king, attributing the honor of the victory to human agencies and forgetting that without God's special blessing all their efforts would have been in vain. In their enthusiasm some proposed to put to death those who had at first refused to acknowledge the authority of Saul. But the king interfered, saying, "There shall not a man be put to death this day: for today the Lord hath wrought salvation in Israel." Here Saul gave evidence of the change that had taken place in his character. Instead of taking honor to himself, he gave the glory to God. Instead of showing a desire for revenge, he manifested a spirit of compassion and forgiveness. This is unmistakable evidence that the grace of God dwells in the heart.

Samuel now proposed that a national assembly should be convoked at Gilgal, that the kingdom might there be publicly confirmed to Saul. It was done; "and there they sacrificed sacrifices of peace offerings before the Lord; and there Saul and all the men of Israel rejoiced greatly."

Gilgal had been the place of Israel's first encampment in the Promised Land. It was here that Joshua, by divine direction, set up the pillar of twelve stones to commemorate the miraculous passage of the Jordan. Here circumcision had been renewed. Here they had kept the first Passover after the sin at Kadesh and the desert sojourn. Here the manna ceased. Here the Captain of the Lord's host had revealed Himself as chief in command of the armies of Israel. From this place they marched to the overthrow of Jericho and the conquest of Ai. Here Achan met the penalty of his sin, and here was made that treaty with the Gibeonites which punished Israel's

[614]

neglect to ask counsel of God. Upon this plain, linked with so many thrilling associations, stood Samuel and Saul; and when the shouts of welcome to the king had died away, the aged prophet gave his parting words as ruler of the nation.

"Behold," he said, "I have hearkened unto your voice in all that ye said unto me, and have made a king over you. And now, behold, the king walketh before you: and I am old and gray-headed; ... and I have walked before you from my childhood unto this day. Behold, here I am: witness against me before the Lord, and before His anointed: whose ox have I taken? or whose ass have I taken? or whom have I defrauded? whom have I oppressed? or of whose hand have I received any bribe to blind mine eyes therewith? and I will restore it you."

With one voice the people answered, "Thou hast not defrauded us, nor oppressed us, neither hast thou taken ought of any man's hand."

Samuel was not seeking merely to justify his own course. He had previously set forth the principles that should govern both the king and the people, and he desired to add to his words the weight of his own example. From childhood he had been connected with the work of God, and during his long life one object had been ever before him—the glory of God and the highest good of Israel.

Before there could be any hope of prosperity for Israel they must be led to repentance before God. In consequence of sin they had lost their faith in God and their discernment of His power and wisdom to rule the nation—lost their confidence in His ability to vindicate His cause. Before they could find true peace they must be led to see and confess the very sin of which they had been guilty. They had declared the object of the demand for a king to be, "That our king may judge us, and go out before us, and fight our battles." Samuel recounted the history of Israel, from the day when God brought them from Egypt. Jehovah, the King of kings, had gone out before them and had fought their battles. Often their sins had sold them into the power of their enemies, but no sooner did they turn from their evil ways than God's mercy raised up a deliverer. The Lord sent Gideon and Barak, and "Jephthah, and Samuel, and delivered you out of the hand of your enemies on every side, and ye dwelt safe." Yet when threatened with danger they had declared, "A king shall reign over us," when, said the prophet, "Jehovah your God was your King."

"Now therefore," continued Samuel, "stand and see this great thing, which the Lord will do before your eyes. Is it not wheat harvest today? I will call unto the Lord, and He shall send thunder and rain; that ye may perceive and see that your wickedness is great, which ye have done in the sight of the Lord, in asking you a king. So Samuel called unto the Lord; and the Lord sent thunder and rain that day." At the time of wheat harvest, in May and June, no rain fell in the East. The sky was cloudless, and the air serene and mild. So violent a storm at this season filled all hearts with fear. In humiliation the people now confessed their sin—the very sin of which they had been guilty: "Pray for thy servants unto the Lord thy God, that we die not: for we have added unto all our sins this evil, to ask us a king."

Samuel did not leave the people in a state of discouragement, for this would have prevented all effort for a better life. Satan would lead them to look upon God as severe and unforgiving, and they would thus be exposed to manifold temptations. God is merciful and forgiving, ever desiring to show favor to His people when they will obey His voice. "Fear not," was the message of God by His servant: "ye have done all this wickedness: yet turn not aside from following the Lord, but serve the Lord with all your heart; and turn ye not aside: for then should ye go after vain things, which cannot profit nor deliver; for they are vain. For the Lord will not forsake His people."

Samuel said nothing of the slight which had been put upon himself; he uttered no reproach for the ingratitude with which Israel had repaid his lifelong devotion; but he assured them of his unceasing interest for them: "God forbid that I should sin against the Lord in ceasing to pray for you: but I will teach you the good and the right way: only fear the Lord, and serve Him in truth with all your heart: for consider how great things He hath done for you. But if ye shall still do wickedly, ye shall be consumed, both ye and your king."

Chapter 60—The Presumption of Saul

This chapter is based on 1 Samuel 13; 1 Samuel 14.

After the assembly at Gilgal, Saul disbanded the army that had at his call arisen to overthrow the Ammonites, reserving only two thousand men to be stationed under his command at Michmash and one thousand to attend his son Jonathan at Gibeah. Here was a serious error. His army was filled with hope and courage by the recent victory; and had he proceeded at once against other enemies of Israel, a telling blow might have been struck for the liberties of the nation.

Meanwhile their warlike neighbors, the Philistines, were active. After the defeat at Ebenezer they had still retained possession of some hill fortresses in the land of Israel, and now they established themselves in the very heart of the country. In facilities, arms, and equipments the Philistines had great advantage over Israel. During the long period of their oppressive rule they had endeavored to strengthen their power by forbidding the Israelites to practice the trade of smiths, lest they should make weapons of war. After the conclusion of peace the Hebrews had still resorted to the Philistine garrisons for such work as needed to be done. Controlled by love of ease and the abject spirit induced by long oppression, the men of Israel had, to a great extent, neglected to provide themselves with weapons of war. Bows and slings were used in warfare, and these the Israelites could obtain; but there were none among them, except Saul and his son Jonathan, who possessed a spear or a sword.

It was not until the second year of Saul's reign that an attempt was made to subdue the Philistines. The first blow was struck by Jonathan, the king's son, who attacked and overcame their garrison at Geba. The Philistines, exasperated by this defeat, made ready for a speedy attack upon Israel. Saul now caused war to be proclaimed by the sound of the trumpet throughout the land, calling upon all the men of war, including the tribes across the Jordan, to assemble at Gilgal. This summons was obeyed.

The Philistines had gathered an immense force at Michmash—"thirty thousand chariots, and six thousand horsemen, and people as the sand which is on the seashore in multitude." When the tidings reached Saul and his army at Gilgal, the people were appalled at thought of the mighty forces they would have to encounter in battle. They were not prepared to meet the enemy, and many were so terrified that they dared not come to the test of an encounter. Some crossed the Jordan, while others hid themselves in caves and pits and amid the rocks that abounded in that region. As the time for the encounter drew near, the number of desertions rapidly increased, and those who did not withdraw from the ranks were filled with foreboding and terror.

When Saul was first anointed king of Israel, he had received from Samuel explicit directions concerning the course to be pursued at this time. "Thou shalt go down before me to Gilgal," said the prophet; "and, behold, I will come down unto thee, to offer burnt offerings, and to sacrifice sacrifices of peace offerings: seven days shalt thou tarry, till I come to thee, and show thee what thou shalt do." 1 Samuel 10:8.

Day after day Saul tarried, but without making decided efforts toward encouraging the people and inspiring confidence in God. Before the time appointed by the prophet had fully expired, he became impatient at the delay and allowed himself to be discouraged by the trying circumstances that surrounded him. Instead of faithfully seeking to prepare the people for the service that Samuel was coming to perform, he indulged in unbelief and foreboding. The work of seeking God by sacrifice was a most solemn and important work; and God required that His people should search their hearts and repent of their sins, that the offering might be made with acceptance before Him, and that His blessing might attend their efforts to conquer the enemy. But Saul had grown restless; and the people, instead of trusting in God for help, were looking to the king whom they had chosen, to lead and direct them.

Yet the Lord still cared for them and did not give them up to the disasters that would have come upon them if the frail arm of flesh had become their only support. He brought them into close places, that they might be convicted of the folly of depending on man, and that they might turn to Him as their only help. The time for the proving of Saul had come. He was now to show whether or not he would depend on God and patiently wait according to His command, thus revealing himself as one whom God could trust in trying places as the ruler of His people, or whether he would be vacillating and unworthy of the sacred responsibility that had devolved upon him. Would the king whom Israel had chosen, listen to the Ruler of all kings? Would he turn the attention of his fainthearted soldiers to the One in whom is everlasting strength and deliverance?

With growing impatience he awaited the arrival of Samuel and attributed the confusion and distress and desertion of his army to the absence of the prophet. The appointed time came, but the man of God did not immediately appear. God's providence had detained His servant. But Saul's restless, impulsive spirit would no longer be restrained. Feeling that something must be done to calm the fears of the people, he determined to summon an assembly for religious service, and by sacrifice entreat the divine aid. God had directed that only those consecrated to the office should present sacrifices before Him. But Saul commanded, "Bring hither a burnt offering;" and, equipped as he was with armor and weapons of war, he approached the altar and offered sacrifice before God.

"And it came to pass, that as soon as he had made an end of offering the burnt offering, behold, Samuel came; and Saul went out to meet him, that he might salute him." Samuel saw at once that Saul had gone contrary to the express directions that had been given him. The Lord had spoken by His prophet that at this time He would reveal what Israel must do in this crisis. If Saul had fulfilled the conditions upon which divine help was promised, the Lord would have wrought a marvelous deliverance for Israel, with the few who were loyal to the king. But Saul was so well satisfied with himself and his work that he went out to meet the prophet as one who should be commended rather than disapproved.

Samuel's countenance was full of anxiety and trouble; but to his inquiry, "What hast thou done?" Saul offered excuses for his presumptuous act. He said: "I saw that the people were scattered from me, and that thou camest not within the days appointed, and that the Philistines gathered themselves together at Michmash; therefore said I, The Philistines will come down now upon me to Gilgal, and I have not made supplication unto the Lord: I forced myself therefore, and offered a burnt offering.

"And Samuel said to Saul, Thou hast done foolishly: thou hast not kept the commandment of the Lord thy God, which He commanded thee: for now would the Lord have established thy kingdom upon Israel forever. But now thy kingdom shall not continue: the Lord hath sought Him a man after His own heart, and the Lord hath commanded him to be captain over His people.... And Samuel arose, and gat him up from Gilgal unto Gibeah of Benjamin."

Either Israel must cease to be the people of God, or the principle upon which the monarchy was founded must be maintained, and the nation must be governed by a divine power. If Israel would be wholly the Lord's, if the will of the human and earthly were held in subjection to the will of God, He would continue to be the Ruler of Israel. So long as the king and the people would conduct themselves as subordinate to God, so long He could be their defense. But in Israel no monarchy could prosper that did not in all things acknowledge the supreme authority of God.

If Saul had shown a regard for the requirements of God in this time of trial, God could have worked His will through him. His failure now proved him unfit to be the vicegerent of God to His people. He would mislead Israel. His will, rather than the will of God, would be the controlling power. If Saul had been faithful, his kingdom would have been established forever; but since he had failed, the purpose of God must be accomplished by another. The government of Israel must be committed to one who would rule the people according to the will of Heaven.

We do not know what great interests may be at stake in the proving of God. There is no safety except in strict obedience to the word of God. All His promises are made upon condition of faith and obedience, and a failure to comply with His commands cuts off the fulfillment to us of the rich provisions of the Scriptures. We should not follow impulse, nor rely on the judgment of men; we should look to the revealed will of God and walk according to His definite commandment, no matter what circumstances may surround us. God will take care of the results; by faithfulness to His word we may in time of trial prove before men and angels that the Lord can

[622]

trust us in difficult places to carry out His will, honor His name, and bless His people.

Saul was in disfavor with God, and yet unwilling to humble his heart in penitence. What he lacked in real piety he would try to make up by his zeal in the forms of religion. Saul was not ignorant of Israel's defeat when the ark of God was brought into the camp by Hophni and Phinehas; and yet, knowing all this, he determined to send for the sacred chest and its attendant priest. Could he by this means inspire confidence in the people, he hoped to reassemble his scattered army and give battle to the Philistines. He would now dispense with Samuel's presence and support, and thus free himself from the prophet's unwelcome criticisms and reproofs.

The Holy Spirit had been granted to Saul to enlighten his understanding and soften his heart. He had received faithful instruction and reproof from the prophet of God. And yet how great was his perversity! The history of Israel's first king presents a sad example of the power of early wrong habits. In his youth Saul did not love and fear God; and that impetuous spirit, not early trained to submission, was ever ready to rebel against divine authority. Those who in their youth cherish a sacred regard for the will of God, and who faithfully perform the duties of their position, will be prepared for higher service in afterlife. But men cannot for years pervert the powers that God has given them, and then, when they choose to change, find these powers fresh and free for an entirely opposite course.

Saul's efforts to arouse the people proved unavailing. Finding his force reduced to six hundred men, he left Gilgal and retired to the fortress at Geba, lately taken from the Philistines. This stronghold was on the south side of a deep, rugged valley, or gorge, a few miles north of the site of Jerusalem. On the north side of the same valley, at Michmash, the Philistine force lay encamped while detachments of troops went out in different directions to ravage the country.

God had permitted matters to be thus brought to a crisis that He might rebuke the perversity of Saul and teach His people a lesson of humility and faith. Because of Saul's sin in his presumptuous offering, the Lord would not give him the honor of vanquishing the Philistines. Jonathan, the king's son, a man who feared the Lord, was chosen as the instrument to deliver Israel. Moved by a divine impulse, he proposed to his armor-bearer that they should make a secret attack upon the enemy's camp. "It may be," he urged, "that the Lord will work for us: for there is no restraint to the Lord to save by many or by few."

The armor-bearer, who also was a man of faith and prayer, encouraged the design, and together they withdrew from the camp, secretly, lest their purpose should be opposed. With earnest prayer to the Guide of their fathers, they agreed upon a sign by which they might determine how to proceed. Then passing down into the gorge separating the two armies, they silently threaded their way, under the shadow of the cliff, and partially concealed by the mounds and ridges of the valley. Approaching the Philistine fortress, they were revealed to the view of their enemies, who said, tauntingly, "Behold, the Hebrews come forth out of the holes where they had hid themselves," then challenged them, "Come up to us, and we will show you a thing," meaning that they would punish the two Israelites for their daring. This challenge was the token that Jonathan and his companion had agreed to accept as evidence that the Lord would prosper their undertaking. Passing now from the sight of the Philistines, and choosing a secret and difficult path, the warriors made their way to the summit of a cliff that had been deemed inaccessible, and was not very strongly guarded. Thus they penetrated the enemy's camp and slew the sentinels, who, overcome with surprise and fear, offered no resistance.

Angels of heaven shielded Jonathan and his attendant, angels fought by their side, and the Philistines fell before them. The earth trembled as though a great multitude with horsemen and chariots were approaching. Jonathan recognized the tokens of divine aid, and even the Philistines knew that God was working for the deliverance of Israel. Great fear seized upon the host, both in the field and in the garrison. In the confusion, mistaking their own soldiers for enemies, the Philistines began to slay one another.

Soon the noise of the battle was heard in the camp of Israel. The king's sentinels reported that there was great confusion among the Philistines, and that their numbers were decreasing. Yet it was not known that any part of the Hebrew army had left the camp. Upon inquiry it was found that none were absent except Jonathan and his armor-bearer. But seeing that the Philistines were meeting with a repulse, Saul led his army to join the assault. The Hebrews who had deserted to the enemy now turned against them; great numbers also came out of their hiding places, and as the Philistines fled, discomfited, Saul's army committed terrible havoc upon the fugitives.

Determined to make the most of his advantage, the king rashly forbade his soldiers to partake of food for the entire day, enforcing his command by the solemn imprecation, "Cursed be the man that eateth any food until evening, that I may be avenged on mine enemies." The victory had already been gained, without Saul's knowledge or co-operation, but he hoped to distinguish himself by the utter destruction of the vanquished army. The command to refrain from food was prompted by selfish ambition, and it showed the king to be indifferent to the needs of his people when these conflicted with his desire for self-exaltation. To confirm his prohibition by a solemn oath showed Saul to be both rash and profane. The very words of the curse give evidence that Saul's zeal was for himself, and not for the honor of God. He declared his object to be, not "that the Lord may be avenged on *His* enemies," but "that *I* may be avenged on *mine* enemies."

The prohibition resulted in leading the people to transgress the command of God. They had been engaged in warfare all day, and were faint for want of food; and as soon as the hours of restriction were over, they fell upon the spoil and devoured the flesh with the blood, thus violating the law that forbade the eating of blood.

During the day's battle Jonathan, who had not heard of the king's command, unwittingly offended by eating a little honey as he passed through a wood. Saul learned of this at evening. He had declared that the violation of his edict should be punished with death; and though Jonathan had not been guilty of a willful sin, though God had miraculously preserved his life and had wrought deliverance through him, the king declared that the sentence must be executed. To spare the life of his son would have been an acknowledgment on the part of Saul that he had sinned in making so rash a vow. This would have been humiliating to his pride. "God do so, and more also," was his terrible sentence: "thou shalt surely die, Jonathan."

Saul could not claim the honor of the victory, but he hoped to be honored for his zeal in maintaining the sacredness of his oath.

Even at the sacrifice of his son, he would impress upon his subjects the fact that the royal authority must be maintained. At Gilgal, but a short time before, Saul had presumed to officiate as priest, contrary to the command of God. When reproved by Samuel, he had stubbornly justified himself. Now, when his own command was disobeyed—though the command was unreasonable and had been violated through ignorance—the king and father sentenced his son to death.

The people refused to allow the sentence to be executed. Braving the anger of the king, they declared, "Shall Jonathan die, who hath wrought this great salvation in Israel? God forbid: as the Lord liveth, there shall not one hair of his head fall to the ground; for he hath wrought with God this day." The proud monarch dared not disregard this unanimous verdict, and the life of Jonathan was preserved.

Saul could not but feel that his son was preferred before him, both by the people and by the Lord. Jonathan's deliverance was a severe reproof to the king's rashness. He felt a presentiment that his curses would return upon his own head. He did not longer continue the war with the Philistines, but returned to his home, moody and dissatisfied.

Those who are most ready to excuse or justify themselves in sin are often most severe in judging and condemning others. Many, like Saul, bring upon themselves the displeasure of God, but they reject counsel and despise reproof. Even when convinced that the Lord is not with them, they refuse to see in themselves the cause of their trouble. They cherish a proud, boastful spirit, while they indulge in cruel judgment or severe rebuke of others who are better than they. Well would it be for such self-constituted judges to ponder those words of Christ: "With what judgment ye judge, ye shall be judged: and with what measure ye mete, it shall be measured to you again." Matthew 7:2.

Often those who are seeking to exalt themselves are brought into positions where their true character is revealed. So it was in the case of Saul. His own course convinced the people that kingly honor and authority were dearer to him than justice, mercy, or benevolence. Thus the people were led to see their error in rejecting the government that God had given them. They had exchanged the pious prophet, whose prayers had brought down blessings, for a king who in his blind zeal had prayed for a curse upon them.

Had not the men of Israel interposed to save the life of Jonathan, their deliverer would have perished by the king's decree. With what misgivings must that people afterward have followed Saul's guidance! How bitter the thought that he had been placed upon the throne by their own act! The Lord bears long with the waywardness of men, and to all He grants opportunity to see and forsake their sins; but while He may seem to prosper those who disregard His will and despise His warnings, He will, in His own time, surely make manifest their folly.

Chapter 61—Saul Rejected

This chapter is based on 1 Samuel 15.

Saul had failed to bear the test of faith in the trying situation at Gilgal, and had brought dishonor upon the service of God; but his errors were not yet irretrievable, and the Lord would grant him another opportunity to learn the lesson of unquestioning faith in His word and obedience to His commands.

When reproved by the prophet at Gilgal, Saul saw no great sin in the course he had pursued. He felt that he had been treated unjustly, and endeavored to vindicate his actions and offered excuses for his error. From that time he had little intercourse with the prophet. Samuel loved Saul as his own son, while Saul, bold and ardent in temper, had held the prophet in high regard; but he resented Samuel's rebuke, and thenceforth avoided him so far as possible.

But the Lord sent His servant with another message to Saul. By obedience he might still prove his fidelity to God and his worthiness to walk before Israel. Samuel came to the king and delivered the word of the Lord. That the monarch might realize the importance of heeding the command, Samuel expressly declared that he spoke by divine direction, by the same authority that had called Saul to the throne. The prophet said, "Thus saith the Lord of hosts, I remember that which Amalek did to Israel, how he laid wait for him in the way, when he came up from Egypt. Now go and smite Amalek, and utterly destroy all that they have, and spare them not; but slay both man and woman, infant and suckling, ox and sheep, camel and ass." The Amalekites had been the first to make war upon Israel in the wilderness; and for this sin, together with their defiance of God and their debasing idolatry, the Lord, through Moses, had pronounced sentence upon them. By divine direction the history of their cruelty toward Israel had been recorded, with the command, "Thou shalt blot out the remembrance of Amalek from under heaven; thou shalt not forget it." Deuteronomy 25:19. For four hundred years the execution of this sentence had been deferred; but the Amalekites had not turned from their sins. The Lord knew that this wicked people would, if it were possible, blot out His people and His worship from the earth. Now the time had come for the sentence, so long delayed, to be executed.

The forbearance that God has exercised toward the wicked, emboldens men in transgression; but their punishment will be none the less certain and terrible for being long delayed. "The Lord shall rise up as in Mount Perazim, He shall be wroth as in the valley of Gibeon, that He may do His work, His strange work; and bring to pass His act, His strange act." Isaiah 28:21. To our merciful God the act of punishment is a strange act. "As I live, saith the Lord God, I have no pleasure in the death of the wicked; but that the wicked turn from his way and live." Ezekiel 33:11. The Lord is "merciful and gracious, long-suffering, and abundant in goodness and truth, ... forgiving iniquity and transgression and sin." Yet He will "by no means clear the guilty." Exodus 34:6, 7. While He does not delight in vengeance, He will execute judgment upon the transgressors of His law. He is forced to do this, to preserve the inhabitants of the earth from utter depravity and ruin. In order to save some He must cut off those who have become hardened in sin. "The Lord is slow to anger, and great in power, and will not at all acquit the wicked." Nahum 1:3. By terrible things in righteousness He will vindicate the authority of His downtrodden law. And the very fact of His reluctance to execute justice testifies to the enormity of the sins that call forth His judgments and to the severity of the retribution awaiting the transgressor.

But while inflicting judgment, God remembered mercy. The Amalekites were to be destroyed, but the Kenites, who dwelt among them, were spared. This people, though not wholly free from idolatry, were worshipers of God and were friendly to Israel. Of this tribe was the brother-in-law of Moses, Hobab, who had accompanied the Israelites in their travels through the wilderness, and by his knowledge of the country had rendered them valuable assistance.

Since the defeat of the Philistines at Michmash, Saul had made war against Moab, Ammon, and Edom, and against the Amalekites and the Philistines; and wherever he turned his arms, he gained fresh victories. On receiving the commission against the Amalekites, he at once proclaimed war. To his own authority was added that of the prophet, and at the call to battle the men of Israel flocked to his standard. The expedition was not to be entered upon for the purpose of self-aggrandizement; the Israelites were not to receive either the honor of the conquest or the spoils of their enemies. They were to engage in the war solely as an act of obedience to God, for the purpose of executing His judgment upon the Amalekites. God intended that all nations should behold the doom of that people that had defied His sovereignty, and should mark that they were destroyed by the very people whom they had despised.

"Saul smote the Amalekites from Havilah until thou comest to Shur, that is over against Egypt. And he took Agag the king of the Amalekites alive, and utterly destroyed all the people with the edge of the sword. But Saul and the people spared Agag, and the best of the sheep, and of the oxen, and of the fatlings, and the lambs, and all that was good, and would not utterly destroy them: but everything that was vile and refuse, that they destroyed utterly."

This victory over the Amalekites was the most brilliant victory that Saul had ever gained, and it served to rekindle the pride of heart that was his greatest peril. The divine edict devoting the enemies of God to utter destruction was but partially fulfilled. Ambitious to heighten the honor of his triumphal return by the presence of a royal captive, Saul ventured to imitate the customs of the nations around him and spared Agag, the fierce and warlike king of the Amalekites. The people reserved for themselves the finest of the flocks, herds, and beasts of burden, excusing their sin on the ground that the cattle were reserved to be offered as sacrifices to the Lord. It was their purpose, however, to use these merely as a substitute, to save their own cattle.

Saul had now been subjected to the final test. His presumptuous disregard of the will of God, showing his determination to rule as an independent monarch, proved that he could not be trusted with royal power as the vicegerent of the Lord. While Saul and his army were marching home in the flush of victory, there was deep anguish in the home of Samuel the prophet. He had received a message from the Lord denouncing the course of the king: "It repenteth Me that I have set up Saul to be king: for he is turned back from following Me, and hath not performed My commandments." The prophet was deeply grieved over the course of the rebellious king, and he wept and prayed all night for a reversing of the terrible sentence.

God's repentance is not like man's repentance. "The Strength of Israel will not lie nor repent: for He is not a man, that He should repent." Man's repentance implies a change of mind. God's repentance implies a change of circumstances and relations. Man may change his relation to God by complying with the conditions upon which he may be brought into the divine favor, or he may, by his own action, place himself outside the favoring condition; but the Lord is the same "yesterday, and today, and forever." Hebrews 13:8. Saul's disobedience changed his relation to God; but the conditions of acceptance with God were unaltered—God's requirements were still the same, for with Him there "is no variableness, neither shadow of turning." James 1:17.

With an aching heart the prophet set forth the next morning to meet the erring king. Samuel cherished a hope that, upon reflection, Saul might become conscious of his sin, and by repentance and humiliation be again restored to the divine favor. But when the first step is taken in the path of transgression the way becomes easy. Saul, debased by his disobedience, came to meet Samuel with a lie upon his lips. He exclaimed, "Blessed be thou of the Lord: I have performed the commandment of the Lord."

The sounds that fell on the prophet's ears disproved the statement of the disobedient king. To the pointed question, "What meaneth then this bleating of the sheep in mine ears, and the lowing of the oxen which I hear?" Saul made answer, "They have brought them from the Amalekites: for the people spared the best of the sheep and of the oxen, to sacrifice unto the Lord thy God; and the rest we have utterly destroyed." The people had obeyed Saul's directions; but in order to shield himself, he was willing to charge upon them the sin of his disobedience.

The message of Saul's rejection brought unspeakable grief to the heart of Samuel. It had to be delivered before the whole army of Israel, when they were filled with pride and triumphal rejoicing over a victory that was accredited to the valor and generalship of their king, for Saul had not associated God with the success of Israel in this conflict; but when the prophet saw the evidence of Saul's rebellion, he was stirred with indignation that he, who had been so highly favored of God, should transgress the commandment of Heaven and lead Israel into sin. Samuel was not deceived by the subterfuge of the king. With mingled grief and indignation he declared, "Stay, and I will tell thee what the Lord hath said to me this night.... When thou wast little in thine own sight, wast thou not made the head of the tribes of Israel, and the Lord anointed thee king over Israel?" He repeated the command of the Lord concerning Amalek, and demanded the reason of the king's disobedience.

Saul persisted in self-justification: "Yea, I have obeyed the voice of the Lord, and have gone the way which the Lord sent me, and have brought Agag the king of Amalek, and have utterly destroyed the Amalekites. But the people took of the spoil, sheep and oxen, the chief of the things which should have been utterly destroyed, to sacrifice unto the Lord thy God in Gilgal."

In stern and solemn words the prophet swept away the refuge of lies and pronounced the irrevocable sentence: "Hath the Lord as great delight in burnt offerings and sacrifices, as in obeying the voice of the Lord? Behold, to obey is better than sacrifice, and to hearken than the fat of rams. For rebellion is as the sin of witchcraft, and stubbornness is as iniquity and idolatry. Because thou hast rejected the word of the Lord, He hath also rejected thee from being king."

As the king heard this fearful sentence he cried out, "I have sinned: for I have transgressed the commandment of the Lord, and thy words: because I feared the people, and obeyed their voice." Terrified by the denunciation of the prophet, Saul acknowledged his guilt, which he had before stubbornly denied; but he still persisted in casting blame upon the people, declaring that he had sinned through fear of them.

It was not sorrow for sin, but fear of its penalty, that actuated the king of Israel as he entreated Samuel, "I pray thee, pardon my sin, and turn again with me, that I may worship the Lord." If Saul had had true repentance, he would have made public confession of his sin; but it was his chief anxiety to maintain his authority and retain the allegiance of the people. He desired the honor of Samuel's presence in order to strengthen his own influence with the nation.

"I will not return with thee," was the answer of the prophet: "for thou hast rejected the word of the Lord, and the Lord hath rejected thee from being king over Israel." As Samuel turned to depart, the king, in an agony of fear, laid hold of his mantle to hold him back, but it rent in his hands. Upon this, the prophet declared, "The Lord hath rent the kingdom of Israel from thee this day, and hath given it to a neighbor of thine, that is better than thou."

Saul was more disturbed by the alienation of Samuel than by the displeasure of God. He knew that the people had greater confidence in the prophet than in himself. Should another by divine command be now anointed king, Saul felt that it would be impossible to maintain his own authority. He feared an immediate revolt should Samuel utterly forsake him. Saul entreated the prophet to honor him before the elders and the people by publicly uniting with him in a religious service. By divine direction Samuel yielded to the king's request, that no occasion might be given for a revolt. But he remained only as a silent witness of the service.

An act of justice, stern and terrible, was yet to be performed. Samuel must publicly vindicate the honor of God and rebuke the course of Saul. He commanded that the king of the Amalekites be brought before him. Above all who had fallen by the sword of Israel, Agag was the most guilty and merciless; one who had hated and sought to destroy the people of God, and whose influence had been strongest to promote idolatry. He came at the prophet's command, flattering himself that the danger of death was past. Samuel declared: "As thy sword hath made women childless, so shall thy mother be childless among women. And Samuel hewed Agag in pieces before the Lord." This done, Samuel returned to his home at Ramah, Saul to his at Gibeah. Only once thereafter did the prophet and the king ever meet each other.

When called to the throne, Saul had a humble opinion of his own capabilities, and was willing to be instructed. He was deficient in knowledge and experience and had serious defects of character. But the Lord granted him the Holy Spirit as a guide and helper, and placed him in a position where he could develop the qualities requisite for a ruler of Israel. Had he remained humble, seeking constantly to be guided by divine wisdom, he would have been enabled to discharge the duties of his high position with success and honor. Under the influence of divine grace every good quality would have been gaining strength, while evil tendencies would have lost their power. This is the work which the Lord proposes to do for all who consecrate themselves to Him. There are many whom He has called to positions in His work because they have a humble and teachable spirit. In His providence He places them where they may learn of Him. He will reveal to them their defects of character, and to all who seek His aid He will give strength to correct their errors.

But Saul presumed upon his exaltation, and dishonored God by unbelief and disobedience. Though when first called to the throne he was humble and self-distrustful, success made him self-confident. The very first victory of his reign had kindled that pride of heart which was his greatest danger. The valor and military skill displayed in the deliverance of Jabesh-gilead had roused the enthusiasm of the whole nation. The people honored their king, forgetting that he was but the agent by whom God had wrought; and though at first Saul ascribed the glory to God, he afterward took honor to himself. He lost sight of his dependence upon God, and in heart departed from the Lord. Thus the way was prepared for his sin of presumption and sacrilege at Gilgal. The same blind self-confidence led him to reject Samuel's reproof. Saul acknowledged Samuel to be a prophet sent from God; hence he should have accepted the reproof, though he could not himself see that he had sinned. Had he been willing to see and confess his error, this bitter experience would have proved a safeguard for the future.

If the Lord had then separated Himself entirely from Saul, He would not have again spoken to him through His prophet, entrusting him with a definite work to perform, that he might correct the errors of the past. When one who professes to be a child of God becomes careless in doing His will, thereby influencing others to be irreverent and unmindful of the Lord's injunctions, it is still possible for his failures to be turned into victories if he will but accept reproof with true contrition of soul and return to God in humility and faith. The humiliation of defeat often proves a blessing by showing us our inability to do the will of God without His aid.

When Saul turned away from the reproof sent him by God's Holy Spirit, and persisted in his stubborn self-justification, he rejected the only means by which God could work to save him from himself. He had willfully separated himself from God. He could not receive divine help or guidance until he should return to God by confession of his sin.

At Gilgal, Saul had made an appearance of great conscientiousness, as he stood before the army of Israel offering up a sacrifice to God. But his piety was not genuine. A religious service performed in direct opposition to the command of God only served to weaken Saul's hands, placing him beyond the help that God was so willing to grant him.

In his expedition against Amalek, Saul thought he had done all that was essential of that which the Lord had commanded him; but the Lord was not pleased with partial obedience, nor willing to pass over what had been neglected through so plausible a motive. God has given men no liberty to depart from His requirements. The Lord had declared to Israel, "Ye shall not do ... every man whatsoever is right in his own eyes;" but ye shall "observe and hear all these words which I command thee." Deuteronomy 12:8, 28. In deciding upon any course of action we are not to ask whether we can see that harm will result from it, but whether it is in keeping with the will of God. "There is a way which seemeth right unto a man; but the end thereof are the ways of death." Proverbs 14:12.

"To obey is better than sacrifice." The sacrificial offerings were in themselves of no value in the sight of God. They were designed to express on the part of the offerer penitence for sin and faith in Christ and to pledge future obedience to the law of God. But without penitence, faith, and an obedient heart, the offerings were worthless. When, in direct violation of God's command, Saul proposed to present a sacrifice of that which God had devoted to destruction, open contempt was shown for the divine authority. The service would have been an insult to Heaven. Yet with the sin of Saul and its result before us, how many are pursuing a similar course. While they refuse to believe and obey some requirement of the Lord, they persevere in offering up to God their formal services of religion. There is no response of the Spirit of God to such service. No matter how zealous men may be in their observance of religious ceremonies, the Lord cannot accept them if they persist in willful violation of one of His commands.

"Rebellion is as the sin of witchcraft, and stubbornness is as iniquity and idolatry." Rebellion originated with Satan, and all rebellion against God is directly due to satanic influence. Those who set themselves against the government of God have entered into an alliance with the archapostate, and he will exercise his power and cunning to captivate the senses and mislead the understanding. He will cause everything to appear in a false light. Like our first parents, those who are under his bewitching spell see only the great benefits to be received by transgression.

No stronger evidence can be given of Satan's delusive power than that many who are thus led by him deceive themselves with the belief that they are in the service of God. When Korah, Dathan, and Abiram rebelled against the authority of Moses, they thought they were opposing only a human leader, a man like themselves; and they came to believe that they were verily doing God service. But in rejecting God's chosen instrument they rejected Christ; they insulted the Spirit of God. So, in the days of Christ, the Jewish scribes and elders, who professed great zeal for the honor of God, crucified His Son. The same spirit still exists in the hearts of those who set themselves to follow their own will in opposition to the will of God.

Saul had had the most ample proof that Samuel was divinely inspired. His venturing to disregard the command of God through the prophet was against the dictates of reason and sound judgment. His fatal presumption must be attributed to satanic sorcery. Saul had manifested great zeal in suppressing idolatry and witchcraft; yet in his disobedience to the divine command he had been actuated by the same spirit of opposition to God and had been as really inspired by Satan as are those who practice sorcery; and when reproved, he had added stubbornness to rebellion. He could have offered no greater insult to the Spirit of God had he openly united with idolaters.

It is a perilous step to slight the reproofs and warnings of God's word or of His Spirit. Many, like Saul, yield to temptation until they become blind to the true character of sin. They flatter themselves that they have had some good object in view, and have done no wrong in departing from the Lord's requirements. Thus they do despite to the Spirit of grace, until its voice is no longer heard, and they are left to the delusions which they have chosen.

In Saul, God had given to Israel a king after their own heart, as Samuel said when the kingdom was confirmed to Saul at Gilgal, "Behold the king *whom ye have chosen, and whom ye have desired.*" 1 Samuel 12:13. Comely in person, of noble stature and princely bearing, his appearance accorded with their conceptions of royal dignity; and his personal valor and his ability in the conduct of armies were the qualities which they regarded as best calculated to secure respect and honor from other nations. They felt little solicitude that their king should possess those higher qualities which alone could fit him to rule with justice and equity. They did not ask for one who had true nobility of character, who possessed the love and fear of God. They had not sought counsel from God as to the qualities a ruler should possess, in order to preserve their distinctive, holy character as His chosen people. They were not seeking God's way, but their own way. Therefore God gave them such a king as they desired—one whose character was a reflection of their own. Their hearts were not in submission to God, and their king also was unsubdued by divine grace. Under the rule of this king they would obtain the experience necessary in order that they might see their error, and return to their allegiance to God.

Yet the Lord, having placed on Saul the responsibility of the kingdom, did not leave him to himself. He caused the Holy Spirit to rest upon Saul to reveal to him his own weakness and his need of divine grace; and had Saul relied upon God, God would have been with him. So long as his will was controlled by the will of God, so long as he yielded to the discipline of His Spirit, God could crown his efforts with success. But when Saul chose to act independently of God, the Lord could no longer be his guide, and was forced to set him aside. Then He called to the throne "a man after His own heart" (1 Samuel 13:14)—not one who was faultless in character, but who, instead of trusting to himself, would rely upon God, and be guided by His Spirit; who, when he sinned, would submit to reproof and correction.

Chapter 62—The Anointing of David

This chapter is based on 1 Samuel 16:1-13.

A few miles south of Jerusalem, "the city of the great King," is Bethlehem, where David, the son of Jesse, was born more than a thousand years before the infant Jesus was cradled in the manger and worshiped by the Wise Men from the East. Centuries before the advent of the Saviour, David, in the freshness of boyhood, kept watch of his flocks as they grazed on the hills surrounding Bethlehem. The simple shepherd boy sang the songs of his own composing, and the music of his harp made a sweet accompaniment to the melody of his fresh young voice. The Lord had chosen David, and was preparing him, in his solitary life with his flocks, for the work He designed to commit to his trust in after years.

While David was thus living in the retirement of his humble shepherd's life, the Lord God was speaking about him to the prophet Samuel. "And the Lord said unto Samuel, How long wilt thou mourn for Saul, seeing I have rejected him from reigning over Israel? fill thine horn with oil, and go, I will send thee to Jesse the Bethlehemite: for I have provided Me a king among his sons.... Take an heifer with thee, and say, I am come to sacrifice to the Lord. And call Jesse to the sacrifice, and I will show thee what thou shalt do: and thou shalt anoint unto Me him whom I name unto thee. And Samuel did that which the Lord spake, and came to Bethlehem. And the elders of the town trembled at his coming, and said, Comest thou peaceably? And he said, Peaceably." The elders accepted an invitation to the sacrifice, and Samuel called also Jesse and his sons. The altar was built and the sacrifice was ready. All the household of Jesse were present, with the exception of David, the youngest son, who had been left to guard the sheep, for it was not safe to leave the flocks unprotected.

When the sacrifice was ended, and before partaking of the offering feast, Samuel began his prophetic inspection of the noble-appearing sons of Jesse. Eliab was the eldest, and more nearly resembled Saul for stature and beauty than the others. His comely features and finely developed form attracted the attention of the prophet. As Samuel looked upon his princely bearing, he thought, "This is indeed the man whom God has chosen as successor to Saul," and he waited for the divine sanction that he might anoint him. But Jehovah did not look upon the outward appearance. Eliab did not fear the Lord. Had he been called to the throne, he would have been a proud, exacting ruler. The Lord's word to Samuel was, "Look not on his countenance, or on the height of his stature; because I have refused him: for the Lord seeth not as man seeth; for man looketh on the outward appearance, but the Lord looketh on the heart." No outward beauty can recommend the soul to God. The wisdom and excellence revealed in the character and deportment, express the true beauty of the man; and it is the inner worth, the excellency of the heart, that determines our acceptance with the Lord of hosts. How deeply should we feel this truth in the judgment of ourselves and others. We may learn from the mistake of Samuel how vain is the estimation that rests on beauty of face or nobility of stature. We may see how incapable is man's wisdom of understanding the secrets of the heart or of comprehending the counsels of God without special enlightenment from heaven. The thoughts and ways of God in relation to His creatures are above our finite minds; but we may be assured that His children will be brought to fill the very place for which they are qualified, and will be enabled to accomplish the very work committed to their hands, if they will but submit their will to God, that His beneficent plans may not be frustrated by the perversity of man.

Eliab passed from the inspection of Samuel, and the six brothers who were in attendance at the service followed in succession to be observed by the prophet; but the Lord did not signify His choice of any one of them. With painful suspense Samuel had looked upon the last of the young men; the prophet was perplexed and bewildered. He inquired of Jesse, "Are here all thy children?" The father answered, "There remaineth yet the youngest, and behold, he keepeth the sheep." Samuel directed that he should be summoned, saying, "We will not sit down till he come hither."

The lonely shepherd was startled by the unexpected call of the

Anointing of David

messenger, who announced that the prophet had come to Bethlehem and had sent for him. With surprise he questioned why the prophet and judge of Israel should desire to see him; but without delay he obeyed the call. "Now he was ruddy, and withal of a beautiful countenance, and goodly to look to." As Samuel beheld with pleasure the handsome, manly, modest shepherd boy, the voice of the Lord spoke to the prophet, saying, "Arise, anoint him: for this is he." David had proved himself brave and faithful in the humble office of a shepherd, and now God had chosen him to be captain of His people. "Then Samuel took the horn of oil, and anointed him in the midst of [from among] his brethren: and the Spirit of the Lord came upon David from that day forward." The prophet had accomplished his appointed work, and with a relieved heart he returned to Ramah.

Samuel had not made known his errand, even to the family of Jesse, and the ceremony of anointing David had been performed in secret. It was an intimation to the youth of the high destiny awaiting him, that amid all the varied experiences and perils of his coming years, this knowledge might inspire him to be true to the purpose of God to be accomplished by his life.

The great honor conferred upon David did not serve to elate him. Notwithstanding the high position which he was to occupy, he quietly continued his employment, content to await the development of the Lord's plans in His own time and way. As humble and modest as before his anointing, the shepherd boy returned to the hills and watched and guarded his flocks as tenderly as ever. But with new inspiration he composed his melodies and played upon his harp. Before him spread a landscape of rich and varied beauty. The vines, with their clustering fruit, brightened in the sunshine. The forest trees, with their green foliage, swayed in the breeze. He beheld the sun flooding the heavens with light, coming forth as a bridegroom out of his chamber and rejoicing as a strong man to run a race. There were the bold summits of the hills reaching toward the sky; in the faraway distance rose the barren cliffs of the mountain wall of Moab; above all spread the tender blue of the overarching heavens. And beyond was God. He could not see Him, but His works were full of His praise. The light of day, gilding forest and mountain, meadow and stream, carried the mind up to behold the Father of lights, the Author of every good and perfect gift. Daily revelations of the character and majesty of his Creator filled the young poet's heart with adoration and rejoicing. In contemplation of God and His works the faculties of David's mind and heart were developing and strengthening for the work of his afterlife. He was daily coming into a more intimate communion with God. His mind was constantly penetrating into new depths for fresh themes to inspire his song and to wake the music of his harp. The rich melody of his voice poured out upon the air, echoed from the hills as if responsive to the rejoicing of the angels' songs in heaven.

Who can measure the results of those years of toil and wandering among the lonely hills? The communion with nature and with God, the care of his flocks, the perils and deliverances, the griefs and joys, of his lowly lot, were not only to mold the character of David and to influence his future life, but through the psalms of Israel's sweet singer they were in all coming ages to kindle love and faith in the hearts of God's people, bringing them nearer to the ever-loving heart of Him in whom all His creatures live.

David, in the beauty and vigor of his young manhood, was preparing to take a high position with the noblest of the earth. His talents, as precious gifts from God, were employed to extol the glory of the divine Giver. His opportunities of contemplation and meditation served to enrich him with that wisdom and piety that made him beloved of God and angels. As he contemplated the perfections of his Creator, clearer conceptions of God opened before his soul. Obscure themes were illuminated, difficulties were made plain, perplexities were harmonized, and each ray of new light called forth fresh bursts of rapture, and sweeter anthems of devotion, to the glory of God and the Redeemer. The love that moved him, the sorrows that beset him, the triumphs that attended him, were all themes for his active thought; and as he beheld the love of God in all the providences of his life, his heart throbbed with more fervent adoration and gratitude, his voice rang out in a richer melody, his harp was swept with more exultant joy; and the shepherd boy proceeded from strength to strength, from knowledge to knowledge; for the Spirit of the Lord was upon him.

Chapter 63—David and Goliath

This chapter is based on 1 Samuel 16:14-23; 17.

When King Saul realized that he had been rejected by God, and when he felt the force of the words of denunciation that had been addressed to him by the prophet, he was filled with bitter rebellion and despair. It was not true repentance that had bowed the proud head of the king. He had no clear perception of the offensive character of his sin, and did not arouse to the work of reforming his life, but brooded over what he thought was the injustice of God in depriving him of the throne of Israel and in taking the succession away from his posterity. He was ever occupied in anticipating the ruin that had been brought upon his house. He felt that the valor which he had displayed in encountering his enemies should offset his sin of disobedience. He did not accept with meekness the chastisement of God; but his haughty spirit became desperate, until he was on the verge of losing his reason. His counselors advised him to seek for the services of a skillful musician, in the hope that the soothing notes of a sweet instrument might calm his troubled spirit. In the providence of God, David, as a skillful performer upon the harp, was brought before the king. His lofty and heaven-inspired strains had the desired effect. The brooding melancholy that had settled like a dark cloud over the mind of Saul was charmed away.

When his services were not required at the court of Saul, David returned to his flocks among the hills and continued to maintain his simplicity of spirit and demeanor. Whenever it was necessary, he was recalled to minister before the king, to soothe the mind of the troubled monarch till the evil spirit should depart from him. But although Saul expressed delight in David and his music, the young shepherd went from the king's house to the fields and hills of his pasture with a sense of relief and gladness.

David was growing in favor with God and man. He had been instructed in the way of the Lord, and he now set his heart more fully to do the will of God than ever before. He had new themes for thought. He had been in the court of the king and had seen the responsibilities of royalty. He had discovered some of the temptations that beset the soul of Saul and had penetrated some of the mysteries in the character and dealings of Israel's first king. He had seen the glory of royalty shadowed with a dark cloud of sorrow, and he knew that the household of Saul, in their private life, were far from happy. All these things served to bring troubled thoughts to him who had been anointed to be king over Israel. But while he was absorbed in deep meditation, and harassed by thoughts of anxiety, he turned to his harp, and called forth strains that elevated his mind to the Author of every good, and the dark clouds that seemed to shadow the horizon of the future were dispelled.

God was teaching David lessons of trust. As Moses was trained for his work, so the Lord was fitting the son of Jesse to become the guide of His chosen people. In his watchcare for his flocks, he was gaining an appreciation of the care that the Great Shepherd has for the sheep of His pasture.

The lonely hills and the wild ravines where David wandered with his flocks were the lurking place of beasts of prey. Not infrequently the lion from the thickets by the Jordan, or the bear from his lair among the hills, came, fierce with hunger, to attack the flocks. According to the custom of his time, David was armed only with his sling and shepherd's staff; yet he early gave proof of his strength and courage in protecting his charge. Afterward describing these encounters, he said: "When there came a lion, or a bear, and took a lamb out of the flock, I went out after him, and smote him, and delivered it out of his mouth: and when he arose against me, I caught him by his beard, and smote him, and slew him." 1 Samuel 17:34, 35, R.V. His experience in these matters proved the heart of David and developed in him courage and fortitude and faith.

Even before he was summoned to the court of Saul, David had distinguished himself by deeds of valor. The officer who brought him to the notice of the king declared him to be "a mighty valiant man, and a man of war, and prudent in matters," and he said, "The Lord is with him."

When war was declared by Israel against the Philistines, three of the sons of Jesse joined the army under Saul; but David remained at home. After a time, however, he went to visit the camp of Saul. By his father's direction he was to carry a message and a gift to his elder brothers and to learn if they were still in safety and health. But, unknown to Jesse, the youthful shepherd had been entrusted with a higher mission. The armies of Israel were in peril, and David had been directed by an angel to save his people.

As David drew near to the army, he heard the sound of commotion, as if an engagement was about to begin. And "the host was going forth to the fight, and shouted for the battle." Israel and the Philistines were drawn up in array, army against army. David ran to the army, and came and saluted his brothers. While he was talking with them, Goliath, the champion of the Philistines, came forth, and with insulting language defied Israel and challenged them to provide a man from their ranks who would meet him in single combat. He repeated his challenge, and when David saw that all Israel were filled with fear, and learned that the Philistine's defiance was hurled at them day after day, without arousing a champion to silence the boaster, his spirit was stirred within him. He was fired with zeal to preserve the honor of the living God and the credit of His people.

The armies of Israel were depressed. Their courage failed. They said one to another, "Have ye seen this man that is come up? surely to defy Israel is he come up." In shame and indignation, David exclaimed, "Who is this uncircumcised Philistine, that he should defy the armies of the living God?"

Eliab, David's eldest brother, when he heard these words, knew well the feelings that were stirring the young man's soul. Even as a shepherd, David had manifested daring, courage, and strength but rarely witnessed; and the mysterious visit of Samuel to their father's house, and his silent departure, had awakened in the minds of the brothers suspicions of the real object of his visit. Their jealousy had been aroused as they saw David honored above them, and they did not regard him with the respect and love due to his integrity and brotherly tenderness. They looked upon him as merely a stripling shepherd, and now the question which he asked was regarded by Eliab as a censure upon his own cowardice in making no attempt to silence the giant of the Philistines. The elder brother exclaimed angrily, "Why camest thou down hither? and with whom hast thou left those few sheep in the wilderness? I know thy pride, and the naughtiness of thine heart; for thou art come down that thou mightest see the battle." David's answer was respectful but decided: "What have I now done? Is there not a cause?"

The words of David were repeated to the king, who summoned the youth before him. Saul listened with astonishment to the words of the shepherd, as he said, "Let no man's heart fail because of him; thy servant will go and fight with this Philistine." Saul strove to turn David from his purpose, but the young man was not to be moved. He replied in a simple, unassuming way, relating his experiences while guarding his father's flocks. And he said, "The Lord that delivered me out of the paw of the lion, and out of the paw of the bear, He will deliver me out of the hand of this Philistine. And Saul said unto David, Go, and the Lord be with thee."

For forty days the host of Israel had trembled before the haughty challenge of the Philistine giant. Their hearts failed within them as they looked upon his massive form, in height measuring six cubits and a span. Upon his head was a helmet of brass, he was clothed with a coat of mail that weighed five thousand shekels, and he had greaves of brass upon his legs. The coat was made of plates of brass that overlaid one another, like the scales of a fish, and they were so closely joined that no dart or arrow could possibly penetrate the armor. At his back the giant bore a huge javelin, or lance, also of brass. "The staff of his spear was like a weaver's beam; and his spear's head weighed six hundred shekels of iron; and one bearing a shield went before him."

Morning and evening Goliath had approached the camp of Israel, saying with a loud voice, "Why are ye come out to set your battle in array? am not I a Philistine, and ye servants to Saul? choose you a man for you, and let him come down to me. If he be able to fight with me, and to kill me, then will we be your servants: but if I prevail against him, and kill him, then shall ye be our servants, and serve us. And the Philistine said, I defy the armies of Israel this day; give me a man, that we may fight together."

Though Saul had given David permission to accept Goliath's challenge, the king had small hope that David would be successful in his courageous undertaking. Command was given to clothe the youth in the king's own armor. The heavy helmet of brass was put upon his head, and the coat of mail was placed upon his body; the monarch's sword was at his side. Thus equipped, he started upon his errand, but erelong began to retrace his steps. The first thought in the minds of the anxious spectators was that David had decided not to risk his life in meeting an antagonist in so unequal an encounter. But this was far from the thought of the brave young man. When he returned to Saul he begged permission to lay aside the heavy armor, saying, "I cannot go with these; for I have not proved them." He laid off the king's armor, and in its stead took only his staff in his hand, with his shepherd's scrip and a simple sling. Choosing five smooth stones out of the brook, he put them in his bag, and, with his sling in his hand, drew near to the Philistine. The giant strode boldly forward, expecting to meet the mightiest of the warriors of Israel. His armor-bearer walked before him, and he looked as if nothing could withstand him. As he came nearer to David he saw but a stripling, called a boy because of his youth. David's countenance was ruddy with health, and his well-knit form, unprotected by armor, was displayed to advantage; yet between its youthful outline and the massive proportions of the Philistine, there was a marked contrast.

Goliath was filled with amazement and anger. "Am I a dog," he exclaimed, "that thou comest to me with staves?" Then he poured upon David the most terrible curses by all the gods of his knowledge. He cried in derision, "Come to me, and I will give thy flesh unto the fowls of the air, and to the beasts of the field."

David did not weaken before the champion of the Philistines. Stepping forward, he said to his antagonist: "Thou comest to me with a sword, and with a spear, and with a shield: but I come to thee in the name of the Lord of hosts, the God of the armies of Israel, whom thou hast defied. This day will the Lord deliver thee into mine hand; and I will smite thee, and take thine head from thee; and I will give the carcasses of the host of the Philistines this day unto the fowls of the air, and to the wild beasts of the earth; that all the earth may know that there is a God in Israel. And all this assembly shall know that the Lord saveth not with sword and spear: for the battle is the Lord's, and He will give you into our hands."

There was a ring of fearlessness in his tone, a look of triumph and rejoicing upon his fair countenance. This speech, given in a clear, musical voice, rang out on the air, and was distinctly heard by

[648]

the listening thousands marshaled for war. The anger of Goliath was roused to the very highest heat. In his rage he pushed up the helmet that protected his forehead and rushed forward to wreak vengeance upon his opponent. The son of Jesse was preparing for his foe. "And it came to pass, when the Philistine arose, and came and drew nigh to meet David, that David hasted, and ran toward the army to meet the Philistine. And David put his hand in his bag, and took thence a stone, and slang it, and smote the Philistine in the forehead, that the stone sunk into his forehead; and he fell upon his face to the earth."

Amazement spread along the lines of the two armies. They had been confident that David would be slain; but when the stone went whizzing through the air, straight to the mark, they saw the mighty warrior tremble, and reach forth his hands, as if he were struck with sudden blindness. The giant reeled, and staggered, and like a smitten oak, fell to the ground. David did not wait an instant. He sprang upon the prostrate form of the Philistine, and with both hands laid hold of Goliath's heavy sword. A moment before, the giant had boasted that with it he would sever the youth's head from his shoulders and give his body to the fowls of the air. Now it was lifted in the air, and then the head of the boaster rolled from his trunk, and a shout of exultation went up from the camp of Israel.

The Philistines were smitten with terror, and the confusion which ensued resulted in a precipitate retreat. The shouts of the triumphant Hebrews echoed along the summits of the mountains, as they rushed after their fleeing enemies; and they "pursued the Philistines, until thou come to the valley, and to the gates of Ekron. And the wounded of the Philistines fell down by the way to Shaaraim, even unto Gath, and unto Ekron. And the children of Israel returned from chasing after the Philistines, and they spoiled their tents. And David took the head of the Philistine, and brought it to Jerusalem; but he put his armor in his tent."

Chapter 64—David a Fugitive

This chapter is based on 1 Samuel 18 to 22.

After the slaying of Goliath, Saul kept David with him, and would not permit him to return to his father's house. And it came to pass that "the soul of Jonathan was knit with the soul of David, and Jonathan loved him as his own soul." Jonathan and David made a covenant to be united as brethren, and the king's son "stripped himself of the robe that was upon him, and gave it to David, and his garments, even to his sword, and to his bow, and to his girdle." David was entrusted with important responsibilities, yet he preserved his modesty, and won the affection of the people as well as the royal household.

"David went out whithersoever Saul sent him, and behaved himself wisely: and Saul set him over the men of war." David was prudent and faithful, and it was evident that the blessing of God was with him. Saul at times realized his own unfitness for the government of Israel, and he felt that the kingdom would be more secure if there could be connected with him one who received instruction from the Lord. Saul hoped also that his connection with David would be a safeguard to himself. Since David was favored and shielded by the Lord, his presence might be a protection to Saul when he went out with him to war.

It was the providence of God that had connected David with Saul. David's position at court would give him a knowledge of affairs, in preparation for his future greatness. It would enable him to gain the confidence of the nation. The vicissitudes and hardships which befell him, through the enmity of Saul, would lead him to feel his dependence upon God, and to put his whole trust in Him. And the friendship of Jonathan for David was also of God's providence, to preserve the life of the future ruler of Israel. In all these things God was working out His gracious purposes, both for David and for the people of Israel.

Saul, however, did not long remain friendly to David. When Saul and David were returning from battle with the Philistines, "the women came out of all cities of Israel, singing and dancing, to meet King Saul, with tabrets, with joy, and with instruments of music." One company sang, "Saul hath slain his thousands," while another company took up the strain, and responded, "And David his ten thousands." The demon of jealousy entered the heart of the king. He was angry because David was exalted above himself in the song of the women of Israel. In place of subduing these envious feelings, he displayed the weakness of his character, and exclaimed. "They have ascribed unto David ten thousands, and to me they have ascribed but thousands: and what can he have more but the kingdom?"

One great defect in the character of Saul was his love of approbation. This trait had had a controlling influence over his actions and thoughts; everything was marked by his desire for praise and self-exaltation. His standard of right and wrong was the low standard of popular applause. No man is safe who lives that he may please men, and does not seek first for the approbation of God. It was the ambition of Saul to be first in the estimation of men; and when this song of praise was sung, a settled conviction entered the mind of the king that David would obtain the hearts of the people and reign in his stead.

Saul opened his heart to the spirit of jealousy by which his soul was poisoned. Notwithstanding the lessons which he had received from the prophet Samuel, instructing him that God would accomplish whatsoever He chose, and that no one could hinder it, the king made it evident that he had no true knowledge of the plans or power of God. The monarch of Israel was opposing his will to the will of the Infinite One. Saul had not learned, while ruling the kingdom of Israel, that he should rule his own spirit. He allowed his impulses to control his judgment, until he was plunged into a fury of passion. He had paroxysms of rage, when he was ready to take the life of any who dared oppose his will. From this frenzy he would pass into a state of despondency and self-contempt, and remorse would take possession of his soul.

He loved to hear David play upon his harp, and the evil spirit seemed to be charmed away for the time; but one day when the youth was ministering before him, and bringing sweet music from his instrument, accompanying his voice as he sang the praises of God, Saul suddenly threw his spear at the musician, for the purpose of putting an end to his life. David was preserved by the interposition of God, and without injury fled from the rage of the maddened king.

As Saul's hatred of David increased, he became more and more watchful to find an opportunity to take his life; but none of his plans against the anointed of the Lord were successful. Saul gave himself up to the control of the wicked spirit that ruled over him; while David trusted in Him who is mighty in counsel, and strong to deliver. "The fear of the Lord is the beginning of wisdom" (Proverbs 9:10), and David's prayer was continually directed to God, that he might walk before Him in a perfect way.

Desiring to be freed from the presence of his rival, the king "removed him from him, and made him his captain over a thousand.... But all Israel and Judah loved David." The people were not slow to see that David was a competent person, and that the affairs entrusted to his hands were managed with wisdom and skill. The counsels of the young man were of a wise and discreet character, and proved to be safe to follow; while the judgment of Saul was at times unreliable, and his decisions were not wise.

Though Saul was ever on the alert for an opportunity to destroy David, he stood in fear of him, since it was evident that the Lord was with him. David's blameless character aroused the wrath of the king; he deemed that the very life and presence of David cast a reproach upon him, since by contrast it presented his own character to disadvantage. It was envy that made Saul miserable and put the humble subject of his throne in jeopardy. What untold mischief has this evil trait of character worked in our world! The same enmity existed in the heart of Saul that stirred the heart of Cain against his brother Abel, because Abel's works were righteous, and God honored him, and his own works were evil, and the Lord could not bless him. Envy is the offspring of pride, and if it is entertained in the heart, it will lead to hatred, and eventually to revenge and murder. Satan displayed his own character in exciting the fury of Saul against him who had never done him harm.

The king kept a strict watch upon David, hoping to find some occasion of indiscretion or rashness that might serve as an excuse to bring him into disgrace. He felt that he could not be satisfied until he could take the young man's life and still be justified before the nation for his evil act. He laid a snare for the feet of David, urging him to conduct the war against the Philistines with still greater vigor, and promising, as a reward of his valor, an alliance with the eldest daughter of the royal house. To this proposal David's modest answer was, "Who am I? and what is my life, or my father's family in Israel, that I should be son-in-law to the king?" The monarch manifested his insincerity by wedding the princess to another.

An attachment for David on the part of Michal, Saul's youngest daughter, afforded the king another opportunity to plot against his rival. Michal's hand was offered the young man on condition that evidence should be given of the defeat and slaughter of a specified number of their national foes. "Saul thought to make David fall by the hand of the Philistines," but God shielded His servant. David returned a victor from the battle, to become the king's son-in-law. "Michal Saul's daughter loved him," and the monarch, enraged, saw that his plots had resulted in the elevation of him whom he sought to destroy. He was still more assured that this was the man whom the Lord had said was better than he, and who should reign on the throne of Israel in his place. Throwing off all disguise, he issued a command to Jonathan and to the officers of the court to take the life of the one he hated.

Jonathan revealed the king's intention to David and bade him conceal himself while he would plead with his father to spare the life of the deliverer of Israel. He presented before the king what David had done to preserve the honor and even the life of the nation, and what terrible guilt would rest upon the murderer of the one whom God had used to scatter their enemies. The conscience of the king was touched, and his heart was softened. "And Saul sware, As the Lord liveth, he shall not be slain." David was brought to Saul, and he ministered in his presence, as he had done in the past.

Again war was declared between the Israelites and the Philistines, and David led the army against their enemies. A great victory was gained by the Hebrews, and the people of the realm praised his wisdom and heroism. This served to stir up the former bitterness of Saul against him. While the young man was playing before the king, filling the palace with sweet harmony, Saul's passion overcame him, and he hurled a javelin at David, thinking to pin the musician to

David a Fugitive

the wall; but the angel of the Lord turned aside the deadly weapon. David escaped and fled to his own house. Saul sent spies that they might take him as he should come out in the morning, and put an end to his life.

Michal informed David of the purpose of her father. She urged him to flee for his life, and let him down from the window, thus enabling him to make his escape. He fled to Samuel at Ramah, and the prophet, fearless of the king's displeasure, welcomed the fugitive. The home of Samuel was a peaceful place in contrast with the royal palace. It was here, amid the hills, that the honored servant of the Lord continued his work. A company of seers was with him, and they studied closely the will of God and listened reverently to the words of instruction that fell from the lips of Samuel. Precious were the lessons that David learned from the teacher of Israel. David believed that the troops of Saul would not be ordered to invade this sacred place, but no place seemed to be sacred to the darkened mind of the desperate king. David's connection with Samuel aroused the jealousy of the king, lest he who was revered as a prophet of God throughout all Israel should lend his influence to the advancement of Saul's rival. When the king learned where David was, he sent officers to bring him to Gibeah, where he intended to carry out his murderous design.

The messengers went on their way, intent upon taking David's life; but One greater than Saul controlled them. They were met by unseen angels, as was Balaam when he was on his way to curse Israel. They began to utter prophetic sayings of what would occur in the future, and proclaimed the glory and majesty of Jehovah. Thus God overruled the wrath of man and manifested His power to restrain evil, while He walled in His servant by a guard of angels.

The tidings reached Saul as he eagerly waited to have David in his power; but instead of feeling the rebuke of God, he was still more exasperated, and sent other messengers. These also were overpowered by the Spirit of God, and united with the first in prophesying. The third embassage was sent by the king; but when they came into the company of the prophets, the divine influence fell upon them also, and they prophesied. Saul then decided that he himself would go, for his fierce enmity had become uncontrollable. He was determined to wait for no further chance to kill David; as soon as he should come within reach of him, he intended with his own hand to slay him, whatever might be the consequences.

But an angel of God met him on the way and controlled him. The Spirit of God held him in Its power, and he went forward uttering prayers to God, interspersed with predictions and sacred melodies. He prophesied of the coming Messiah as the world's Redeemer. When he came to the prophet's home in Ramah, he laid aside the outer garments that betokened his rank, and all day and all night he lay before Samuel and his pupils, under the influence of the divine Spirit. The people were drawn together to witness this strange scene, and the experience of the king was reported far and wide. Thus again, near the close of his reign, it became a proverb in Israel that Saul also was among the prophets.

Again the persecutor was defeated in his purpose. He assured David that he was at peace with him, but David had little confidence in the king's repentance. He took this opportunity to escape, lest the mood of the king should change, as formerly. His heart was wounded within him, and he longed to see his friend Jonathan once more. Conscious of his innocence, he sought the king's son and made a most touching appeal. "What have I done?" he asked, "what is mine iniquity? and what is my sin before thy father, that he seeketh my life?" Jonathan believed that his father had changed his purpose and no longer intended to take the life of David. And Jonathan said unto him, "God forbid; thou shalt not die: behold, my father will do nothing either great or small, but that he will show it me: and why should my father hide this thing from me? It is not so." After the remarkable exhibition of the power of God, Jonathan could not believe that his father would still harm David, since this would be manifest rebellion against God. But David was not convinced. With intense earnestness he declared to Jonathan, "As the Lord liveth, and as thy soul liveth, there is but a step between me and death."

At the time of the new moon a sacred festival was celebrated in Israel. This festival recurred upon the day following the interview between David and Jonathan. At this feast it was expected that both the young men would appear at the king's table; but David feared to be present, and it was arranged that he should visit his brothers in Bethlehem. On his return he was to hide himself in a field not far from the banqueting hall, for three days absenting himself from the presence of the king; and Jonathan would note the effect upon Saul. If inquiry should be made as to the whereabouts of the son of Jesse, Jonathan was to say that he had gone home to attend the sacrifice offered by his father's household. If no angry demonstrations were made by the king, but he should answer, "It is well," then it would be safe for David to return to the court. But if he should become enraged at his absence, it would decide the matter of David's flight.

On the first day of the feast the king made no inquiry concerning the absence of David; but when his place was vacant the second day, he questioned, "Wherefore cometh not the son of Jesse to meat, neither yesterday nor today? And Jonathan answered Saul, David earnestly asked leave of me to go to Bethlehem: and he said, Let me go, I pray thee; for our family hath a sacrifice in the city; and my brother, he hath commanded me to be there: and now, if I have found favor in thine eyes, let me get away, I pray thee, and see my brethren. Therefore he cometh not unto the king's table." When Saul heard these words, his anger was ungovernable. He declared that as long as David lived, Jonathan could not come to the throne of Israel, and he demanded that David should be sent for immediately, that he might be put to death. Jonathan again made intercession for his friend, pleading, "Wherefore shall he be slain? what hath he done?" This appeal to the king only made him more satanic in his fury, and the spear which he had intended for David he now hurled at his own son.

The prince was grieved and indignant, and leaving the royal presence, he was no more a guest at the feast. His soul was bowed down with sorrow as he repaired at the appointed time to the spot where David was to learn the king's intentions toward him. Each fell upon the other's neck, and they wept bitterly. The dark passion of the king cast its shadow upon the life of the young men, and their grief was too intense for expression. Jonathan's last words fell upon the ear of David as they separated to pursue their different paths, "Go in peace, forasmuch as we have sworn both of us in the name of the Lord, saying, The Lord be between me and thee, and between my seed and thy seed forever."

The king's son returned to Gibeah, and David hastened to reach Nob, a city but a few miles distant, and also belonging to the tribe of Benjamin. The tabernacle had been taken to this place from

[656]

Shiloh, and here Ahimelech the high priest ministered. David knew not whither to flee for refuge, except to the servant of God. The priest looked upon him with astonishment, as he came in haste and apparently alone, with a countenance marked by anxiety and sorrow. He inquired what had brought him there. The young man was in constant fear of discovery, and in his extremity he resorted to deception. David told the priest that he had been sent by the king on a secret errand, one which required the utmost expedition. Here he manifested a want of faith in God, and his sin resulted in causing the death of the high priest. Had the facts been plainly stated, Ahimelech would have known what course to pursue to preserve his life. God requires that truthfulness shall mark His people, even in the greatest peril. David asked the priest for five loaves of bread. There was nothing but hallowed bread in the possession of the man of God, but David succeeded in removing his scruples, and obtained the bread to satisfy his hunger.

A new danger now presented itself. Doeg, the chief of Saul's herdsmen, who had professed the faith of the Hebrews, was now paying his vows in the place of worship. At sight of this man David determined to make haste to secure another place of refuge, and to obtain some weapon with which to defend himself if defense should become necessary. He asked Ahimelech for a sword, and was told that he had none except the sword of Goliath, which had been kept as a relic in the tabernacle. David replied, "There is none like that; give it me." His courage revived as he grasped the sword that he had once used in destroying the champion of the Philistines.

David fled to Achish, the king of Gath; for he felt that there was more safety in the midst of the enemies of his people than in the dominions of Saul. But it was reported to Achish that David was the man who had slain the Philistine champion years before; and now he who had sought refuge with the foes of Israel found himself in great peril. But, feigning madness, he deceived his enemies and thus made his escape.

The first error of David was his distrust of God at Nob, and his second mistake was his deception before Achish. David had displayed noble traits of character, and his moral worth had won him favor with the people; but as trial came upon him, his faith was shaken, and human weakness appeared. He saw in every man a spy and a betrayer. In a great emergency David had looked up to God with a steady eye of faith, and had vanquished the Philistine giant. He believed in God, he went in His name. But as he had been hunted and persecuted, perplexity and distress had nearly hidden his heavenly Father from his sight.

Yet this experience was serving to teach David wisdom; for it led him to realize his weakness and the necessity of constant dependence upon God. Oh, how precious is the sweet influence of the Spirit of God as it comes to depressed or despairing souls, encouraging the fainthearted, strengthening the feeble, and imparting courage and help to the tried servants of the Lord! Oh, what a God is ours, who deals gently with the erring and manifests His patience and tenderness in adversity, and when we are overwhelmed with some great sorrow!

Every failure on the part of the children of God is due to their lack of faith. When shadows encompass the soul, when we want light and guidance, we must look up; there is light beyond the darkness. David ought not to have distrusted God for one moment. He had cause for trusting in Him: he was the Lord's anointed, and in the midst of danger he had been protected by the angels of God; he had been armed with courage to do wonderful things; and if he had but removed his mind from the distressing situation in which he was placed, and had thought of God's power and majesty, he would have been at peace even in the midst of the shadows of death; he could with confidence have repeated the promise of the Lord, "The mountains shall depart, and the hills be removed; but My kindness shall not depart from thee, neither shall the covenant of My peace be removed." Isaiah 54:10.

Among the mountains of Judah, David sought refuge from the pursuit of Saul. He made good his escape to the cave of Adullam, a place that, with a small force, could be held against a large army. "And when his brethren and all his father's house heard it, they went down thither to him." The family of David could not feel secure, knowing that at any time the unreasonable suspicions of Saul might be directed against them on account of their relation to David. They had now learned—what was coming to be generally known in Israel—that God had chosen David as the future ruler of His people; and they believed that they would be safer with him, even though he was a fugitive in a lonely cave, than they could be while exposed to the insane madness of a jealous king.

In the cave of Adullam the family were united in sympathy and affection. The son of Jesse could make melody with voice and harp as he sang, "Behold, how good and how pleasant it is for brethren to dwell together in unity!" Psalm 133:1. He had tasted the bitterness of distrust on the part of his own brothers; and the harmony that had taken the place of discord brought joy to the exile's heart. It was here that David composed the fifty-seventh psalm.

It was not long before David's company was joined by others who desired to escape the exactions of the king. There were many who had lost confidence in the ruler of Israel, for they could see that he was no longer guided by the Spirit of the Lord. "And everyone that was in distress, and everyone that was in debt, and everyone that was discontented," resorted to David, "and he became a captain over them: and there were with him about four hundred men." Here David had a little kingdom of his own, and in it order and discipline prevailed. But even in his retreat in the mountains he was far from feeling secure, for he received continual evidence that the king had not relinquished his murderous purpose.

He found a refuge for his parents with the king of Moab, and then, at a warning of danger from a prophet of the Lord, he fled from his hiding place to the forest of Hareth. The experience through which David was passing was not unnecessary or fruitless. God was giving him a course of discipline to fit him to become a wise general as well as a just and merciful king. With his band of fugitives he was gaining a preparation to take up the work that Saul, because of his murderous passion and blind indiscretion, was becoming wholly unfitted to do. Men cannot depart from the counsel of God and still retain that calmness and wisdom which will enable them to act with justice and discretion. There is no insanity so dreadful, so hopeless, as that of following human wisdom, unguided by the wisdom of God.

Saul had been preparing to ensnare and capture David in the cave of Adullam, and when it was discovered that David had left this place of refuge, the king was greatly enraged. The flight of David was a mystery to Saul. He could account for it only by the belief that there had been traitors in his camp, who had informed the son of Jesse of his proximity and design.

He affirmed to his counselors that a conspiracy had been formed against him, and with the offer of rich gifts and positions of honor he bribed them to reveal who among his people had befriended David. Doeg the Edomite turned informer. Moved by ambition and avarice, and by hatred of the priest, who had reproved his sins, Doeg reported David's visit to Ahimelech, representing the matter in such a light as to kindle Saul's anger against the man of God. The words of that mischievous tongue, set on fire of hell, stirred up the worst passions in Saul's heart. Maddened with rage, he declared that the whole family of the priest should perish. And the terrible decree was executed. Not only Ahimelech, but the members of his father's house—"four-score and five persons that did wear a linen ephod"—were slain at the king's command, by the murderous hand of Doeg.

"And Nob, the city of the priests, smote he with the edge of the sword, both men and women, children and sucklings, and oxen, and asses, and sheep." This is what Saul could do under the control of Satan. When God had said that the iniquity of the Amalekites was full, and had commanded him to destroy them utterly, he thought himself too compassionate to execute the divine sentence, and he spared that which was devoted to destruction; but now, without a command from God, under the guidance of Satan, he could slay the priests of the Lord and bring ruin upon the inhabitants of Nob. Such is the perversity of the human heart that has refused the guidance of God.

This deed filled all Israel with horror. It was the king whom they had chosen that had committed this outrage, and he had only done after the manner of the kings of other nations that feared not God. The ark was with them, but the priests of whom they had inquired were slain with the sword. What would come next?

Chapter 65—The Magnanimity of David

This chapter is based on 1 Samuel 22:20- 23; 23-27.

After Saul's atrocious slaughter of the priests of the Lord, "one of the sons of Ahimelech the son of Ahitub, named Abiathar, escaped, and fled after David. And Abiathar showed David that Saul had slain the Lord's priests. And David said unto Abiathar, I knew it that day, when Doeg the Edomite was there, that he would surely tell Saul: I have occasioned the death of all the persons of thy father's house. Abide thou with me, fear not: for he that seeketh my life seeketh thy life: but with me thou shalt be in safeguard."

Still hunted by the king, David found no place of rest or security. At Keilah his brave band saved the town from capture by the Philistines, but they were not safe, even among the people whom they had delivered. From Keilah they repaired to the wilderness of Ziph.

At this time, when there were so few bright spots in the path of David, he was rejoiced to receive an unexpected visit from Jonathan, who had learned the place of his refuge. Precious were the moments which these two friends passed in each other's society. They related their varied experiences, and Jonathan strengthened the heart of David, saying, "Fear not: for the hand of Saul my father shall not find thee; and thou shalt be king over Israel, and I shall be next unto thee; and that also Saul my father knoweth." As they talked of the wonderful dealings of God with David, the hunted fugitive was greatly encouraged. "And they two made a covenant before the Lord: and David abode in the wood, and Jonathan went to his house."

After the visit of Jonathan, David encouraged his soul with songs of praise, accompanying his voice with his harp as he sang:

"In the Lord put I my trust:
How say ye to my soul,

Flee as a bird to your mountain?
    For, lo, the wicked bend their bow,
They make ready their arrow upon the string,
    That they may privily shoot at the upright in heart.
If the foundations be destroyed,
    What can the righteous do?
The Lord is in His holy temple,
    The Lord's throne is in heaven:
His eyes behold, His eyelids try, the children of men.
    The Lord trieth the righteous:
But the wicked and him that loveth violence His soul
    hateth." Psalm 11:1-5.

The Ziphites, into whose wild regions David went from Keilah, sent word to Saul in Gibeah that they knew where David was hiding, and that they would guide the king to his retreat. But David, warned of their intentions, changed his position, seeking refuge in the mountains between Maon and the Dead Sea.

Again word was sent to Saul, "Behold, David is in the wilderness of Engedi. Then Saul took three thousand chosen men out of all Israel, and went to seek David and his men upon the rocks of the wild goats." David had only six hundred men in his company, while Saul advanced against him with an army of three thousand. In a secluded cave the son of Jesse and his men waited for the guidance of God as to what should be done. As Saul was pressing his way up the mountains, he turned aside, and entered, alone, the very cavern in which David and his band were hidden. When David's men saw this they urged their leader to kill Saul. The fact that the king was now in their power was interpreted by them as certain evidence that God Himself had delivered the enemy into their hand, that they might destroy him. David was tempted to take this view of the matter; but the voice of conscience spoke to him, saying, "Touch not the anointed of the Lord."

David's men were still unwilling to leave Saul in peace, and they reminded their commander of the words of God, "Behold, I will deliver thine enemy into thine hand, that thou mayest do to him as it shall seem good unto thee. Then David arose, and cut off the skirt of Saul's robe privily." But his conscience smote him afterward, because he had even marred the garment of the king.

[662] Saul rose up and went out of the cave to continue his search, when a voice fell upon his startled ears, saying, "My lord the king." He turned to see who was addressing him, and lo! it was the son of Jesse, the man whom he had so long desired to have in his power that he might kill him. David bowed himself to the king, acknowledging him as his master. Then he addressed Saul in these words: "Wherefore hearest thou men's words, saying, Behold, David seeketh thy hurt? Behold, this day thine eyes have seen how that the Lord hath delivered thee today into mine hand in the cave: and some bade me kill thee; but mine eye spared thee; and I said, I will not put forth mine hand against my lord; for he is the Lord's anointed. Moreover, my father, see, yea, see the skirt of thy robe in my hand: for in that I cut off the skirt of thy robe, and killed thee not, know thou and see that there is neither evil nor transgression in mine hand, and I have not sinned against thee; yet thou huntest my soul to take it."

When Saul heard the words of David he was humbled, and could not but admit their truthfulness. His feelings were deeply moved as he realized how completely he had been in the power of the man whose life he sought. David stood before him in conscious innocence. With a softened spirit, Saul exclaimed, "Is this thy voice, my son David? And Saul lifted up his voice, and wept." Then he declared to David: "Thou art more righteous than I: for thou hast rewarded me good, whereas I have rewarded thee evil.... For if a man find his enemy, will he let him go well away? wherefore the Lord reward thee good for that thou hast done unto me this day. And now, behold, I know well that thou shalt surely be king, and that the kingdom of Israel shall be established in thine hand." And David made a covenant with Saul that when this should take place he would favorably regard the house of Saul, and not cut off his name.

Knowing what he did of Saul's past course, David could put no confidence in the assurances of the king, nor hope that his penitent condition would long continue. So when Saul returned to his home David remained in the strongholds of the mountains.

The enmity that is cherished toward the servants of God by those who have yielded to the power of Satan changes at times to a feeling of reconciliation and favor, but the change does not always prove to be lasting. After evil-minded men have engaged in doing and saying wicked things against the Lord's servants, the conviction that they have been in the wrong sometimes takes deep hold upon their minds. The Spirit of the Lord strives with them, and they humble their hearts before God, and before those whose influence they have sought to destroy, and they may change their course toward them. But as they again open the door to the suggestions of the evil one, the old doubts are revived, the old enmity is awakened, and they return to engage in the same work which they repented of, and for a time abandoned. Again they speak evil, accusing and condemning in the bitterest manner the very ones to whom they made most humble confession. Satan can use such souls with far greater power after such a course has been pursued than he could before, because they have sinned against greater light.

"And Samuel died; and all the Israelites were gathered together, and lamented him, and buried him in his house at Ramah." The death of Samuel was regarded as an irreparable loss by the nation of Israel. A great and good prophet and an eminent judge had fallen in death, and the grief of the people was deep and heartfelt. From his youth up Samuel had walked before Israel in the integrity of his heart; although Saul had been the acknowledged king, Samuel had wielded a more powerful influence than he, because his record was one of faithfulness, obedience, and devotion. We read that he judged Israel all the days of his life.

As the people contrasted the course of Saul with that of Samuel, they saw what a mistake they had made in desiring a king that they might not be different from the nations around them. Many looked with alarm at the condition of society, fast becoming leavened with irreligion and godlessness. The example of their ruler was exerting a widespread influence, and well might Israel mourn that Samuel, the prophet of the Lord, was dead.

The nation had lost the founder and president of its sacred schools, but that was not all. It had lost him to whom the people had been accustomed to go with their great troubles—lost one who had constantly interceded with God in behalf of the best interests of its people. The intercession of Samuel had given a feeling of security; for "the effectual fervent prayer of a righteous man availeth much." James 5:16. The people felt now that God was forsaking them. The king seemed little less than a madman. Justice was perverted, and order was turned to confusion.

It was when the nation was racked with internal strife, when the calm, God-fearing counsel of Samuel seemed to be most needed, that God gave His aged servant rest. Bitter were the reflections of the people as they looked upon his quiet resting place, and remembered their folly in rejecting him as their ruler; for he had had so close a connection with Heaven that he seemed to bind all Israel to the throne of Jehovah. It was Samuel who had taught them to love and obey God; but now that he was dead, the people felt that they were left to the mercies of a king who was joined to Satan, and who would divorce the people from God and heaven.

David could not be present at the burial of Samuel, but he mourned for him as deeply and tenderly as a faithful son could mourn for a devoted father. He knew that Samuel's death had broken another bond of restraint from the actions of Saul, and he felt less secure than when the prophet lived. While the attention of Saul was engaged in mourning for the death of Samuel, David took the opportunity to seek a place of greater security; so he fled to the wilderness of Paran. It was here that he composed the one hundred and twentieth and twenty-first psalms. In these desolate wilds, realizing that the prophet was dead, and the king was his enemy, he sang:

> "My help cometh from the Lord,
>   Which made heaven and earth.
> He will not suffer thy foot to be moved:
>   He that keepeth thee will not slumber.
> Behold, He that keepeth Israel
>   Shall neither slumber nor sleep....
> The Lord shall preserve thee from all evil:
>   He shall preserve thy soul.
> The Lord shall preserve thy going out and thy
>   coming in
> From this time forth, and even forevermore."
>
> Psalm 121:2-8.

While David and his men were in the wilderness of Paran, they protected from the depredations of marauders the flocks and herds of a wealthy man named Nabal, who had vast possessions in that region. Nabal was a descendant of Caleb, but his character was churlish and niggardly.

It was the time of sheepshearing, a season of hospitality. David and his men were in sore need of provisions; and in accordance with the custom of the times, the son of Jesse sent ten young men to Nabal, bidding them greet him in their master's name; and he added: "Thus shall ye say to him that liveth in prosperity, Peace be both to thee, and peace be to thine house, and peace be unto all that thou hast. And now I have heard that thou hast shearers: now thy shepherds which were with us, we hurt them not, neither was there aught missing unto them, all the while they were in Carmel. [Not Mount Carmel, but a place in the territory of Judah, near the hill town of Maon.] Ask thy young men, and they will show thee. Wherefore let the young men find favor in thine eyes; for we come in a good day: give, I pray thee, whatsoever cometh to thine hand unto thy servants, and to thy son David."

David and his men had been like a wall of protection to the shepherds and flocks of Nabal; and now this rich man was asked to furnish from his abundance some relief to the necessities of those who had done him such valuable service. David and his men might have helped themselves from the flocks and herds, but they did not. They behaved themselves in an honest way. Their kindness, however, was lost upon Nabal. The answer he returned to David was indicative of his character: "Who is David? and who is the son of Jesse? There be many servants nowadays that break away every man from his master. Shall I then take my bread, and my water, and my flesh that I have killed for my shearers, and give it unto men, whom I know not whence they be?"

When the young men returned empty-handed and related the affair to David, he was filled with indignation. He commanded his men to equip themselves for an encounter; for he had determined to punish the man who had denied him what was his right, and had added insult to injury. This impulsive movement was more in harmony with the character of Saul than with that of David, but the son of Jesse had yet to learn of patience in the school of affliction.

One of Nabal's servants hastened to Abigail, the wife of Nabal, after he had dismissed David's young men, and told her what had happened. "Behold," he said, "David sent messengers out of the wilderness to salute our master; and he railed on them. But the men were very good unto us, and we were not hurt, neither missed we anything, as long as we were conversant with them, when we were in the fields. They were a wall unto us both by night and day, all the while we were with them keeping the sheep. Now therefore know and consider what thou wilt do; for evil is determined against our master, and against all his household."

Without consulting her husband or telling him of her intention, Abigail made up an ample supply of provisions, which, laded upon asses, she sent forward in the charge of servants, and herself started out to meet the band of David. She met them in a covert of a hill. "And when Abigail saw David, she hasted, and lighted off the ass, and fell before David on her face, and bowed herself to the ground, and fell at his feet, and said, Upon me, my lord, upon me let this iniquity be: and let thine handmaid, I pray thee, speak in thine audience." Abigail addressed David with as much reverence as though speaking to a crowned monarch. Nabal had scornfully exclaimed, "Who is David?" but Abigail called him, "my lord." With kind words she sought to soothe his irritated feelings, and she pleaded with him in behalf of her husband. With nothing of ostentation or pride, but full of the wisdom and love of God, Abigail revealed the strength of her devotion to her household; and she made it plain to David that the unkind course of her husband was in no wise premeditated against him as a personal affront, but was simply the outburst of an unhappy and selfish nature.

"Now therefore, my lord, as the Lord liveth, and as thy soul liveth, seeing the Lord hath withholden thee from coming to shed blood, and from avenging thyself with thine own hand, now let thine enemies, and they that seek evil to my lord, be as Nabal." Abigail did not take to herself the credit of this reasoning to turn David from his hasty purpose, but gave to God the honor and the praise. She then offered her rich provision as a peace offering to the men of David, and still pleaded as if she herself were the one who had so excited the resentment of the chief.

"I pray thee," she said, "forgive the trespass of thine handmaid: for the Lord will certainly make my lord a sure house; because my lord fighteth the battles of the Lord, and evil hath not been found in thee all thy days." Abigail presented by implication the course that David ought to pursue. He should fight the battles of the Lord. He was not to seek revenge for personal wrongs, even though persecuted as a traitor. She continued: "Though man be risen up to pursue thee, and to seek thy soul, yet the soul of my lord shall be bound in the bundle of life with the Lord thy God.... And it shall come to pass, when the Lord shall have done to my lord according to all the good that He hath spoken concerning thee, and shall have appointed thee prince over Israel; that this shall be no grief unto thee, nor offense of heart unto my lord, either that thou hast shed blood causeless, or that my lord hath avenged himself: and when the Lord shall have dealt well with my lord, then remember thine handmaid." 1 Samuel 25:29-31, R. V.

These words could have come only from the lips of one who had partaken of the wisdom from above. The piety of Abigail, like the fragrance of a flower, breathed out all unconsciously in face and word and action. The Spirit of the Son of God was abiding in her soul. Her speech, seasoned with grace, and full of kindness and peace, shed a heavenly influence. Better impulses came to David, and he trembled as he thought what might have been the consequences of his rash purpose. "Blessed are the peacemakers: for they shall be called the children of God." Matthew 5:9. Would that there were many more like this woman of Israel, who would soothe the irritated feelings, prevent rash impulses, and quell great evils by words of calm and well-directed wisdom.

A consecrated Christian life is ever shedding light and comfort and peace. It is characterized by purity, tact, simplicity, and usefulness. It is controlled by that unselfish love that sanctifies the influence. It is full of Christ, and leaves a track of light wherever its possessor may go. Abigail was a wise reprover and counselor. David's passion died away under the power of her influence and reasoning. He was convinced that he had taken an unwise course and had lost control of his own spirit.

With a humble heart he received the rebuke, in harmony with his own words, "Let the righteous smite me; it shall be a kindness:

and let him reprove me; it shall be an excellent oil." Psalm 141:5. He gave thanks and blessings because she advised him righteously. There are many who, when they are reproved, think it praiseworthy if they receive the rebuke without becoming impatient; but how few take reproof with gratitude of heart and bless those who seek to save them from pursuing an evil course.

[668] When Abigail returned home she found Nabal and his guests in the enjoyment of a great feast, which they had converted into a scene of drunken revelry. Not until the next morning did she relate to her husband what had occurred in her interview with David. Nabal was a coward at heart; and when he realized how near his folly had brought him to a sudden death, he seemed smitten with paralysis. Fearful that David would still pursue his purpose of revenge, he was filled with horror, and sank down in a condition of helpless insensibility. After ten days he died. The life that God had given him had been only a curse to the world. In the midst of his rejoicing and making merry, God had said to him, as He said to the rich man of the parable, "This night thy soul shall be required of thee." Luke 12:20.

David afterward married Abigail. He was already the husband of one wife, but the custom of the nations of his time had perverted his judgment and influenced his actions. Even great and good men have erred in following the practices of the world. The bitter result of marrying many wives was sorely felt throughout all the life of David.

After the death of Samuel, David was left in peace for a few months. Again he repaired to the solitude of the Ziphites; but these enemies, hoping to secure the favor of the king, informed him of David's hiding place. This intelligence aroused the demon of passion that had been slumbering in Saul's breast. Once more he summoned his men of arms and led them out in pursuit of David. But friendly spies brought tidings to the son of Jesse that Saul was again pursuing him; and with a few of his men, David started out to learn the location of his enemy. It was night when, cautiously advancing, they came upon the encampment, and saw before them the tents of the king and his attendants. They were unobserved, for the camp was quiet in slumber. David called upon his friends to go with him into the very midst of the foe. In answer to his question, "Who will go down with me to Saul to the camp?" Abishai promptly responded, "I will go down with thee."

Hidden by the deep shadows of the hills, David and his attendant entered the encampment of the enemy. As they sought to ascertain the exact number of their foes, they came upon Saul sleeping, his spear stuck in the ground, and a cruse of water at his head. Beside him lay Abner, his chief commander, and all around them were the soldiers, locked in slumber. Abishai raised his spear, and said to David, "God hath delivered thine enemy into thine hand this day: now therefore let me smite him, I pray thee, with the spear even to the earth at once, and I will not smite him the second time." He waited for the word of permission; but there fell upon his ear the whispered words: "Destroy him not: for who can stretch forth his hand against the Lord's anointed, and be guiltless? ... As the Lord liveth, the Lord shall smite him; or his day shall come to die; or he shall descend into battle, and perish. The Lord forbid that I should stretch forth mine hand against the Lord's anointed: but, I pray thee, take thou now the spear that is at his bolster, and the cruse of water, and let us go. So David took the spear and the cruse of water from Saul's bolster; and they gat them away, and no man saw it, nor knew it, neither awaked: for they were all asleep; because a deep sleep from the Lord was fallen upon them." How easily the Lord can weaken the strongest, remove prudence from the wisest, and baffle the skill of the most watchful!

When David was at a safe distance from the camp he stood on the top of a hill and cried with a loud voice to the people and to Abner, saying, "Art not thou a valiant man? and who is like to thee in Israel? wherefore then hast thou not kept thy lord the king? for there came one of the people in to destroy the king thy lord. This thing is not good that thou hast done. As the Lord liveth, ye are worthy to die, because ye have not kept your master the Lord's anointed. And now see where the king's spear is, and the cruse of water that was at his bolster. And Saul knew David's voice, and said, Is this thy voice, my son David? And David said, It is my voice, my lord, O king. And he said, Wherefore doth my lord thus pursue after his servant? for what have I done? or what evil is in mine hand? Now therefore, I pray thee, let my lord the king hear the words of his servant." Again the acknowledgment fell from the lips of the king, "I have sinned:

return, my son David; for I will no more do thee harm, because my soul was precious in thine eyes this day: behold, I have played the fool, and have erred exceedingly. And David answered and said, Behold the king's spear! and let one of the young men come over and fetch it." Although Saul had made the promise, "I will no more do thee harm," David did not place himself in his power.

The second instance of David's respect for his sovereign's life made a still deeper impression upon the mind of Saul and brought from him a more humble acknowledgment of his fault. He was astonished and subdued at the manifestation of such kindness. In parting from David, Saul exclaimed, "Blessed be thou, my son David: thou shalt both do great things, and also shalt still prevail." But the son of Jesse had no hope that the king would long continue in this frame of mind.

David despaired of a reconciliation with Saul. It seemed inevitable that he should at last fall a victim to the malice of the king, and he determined again to seek refuge in the land of the Philistines. With the six hundred men under his command, he passed over to Achish, the king of Gath.

David's conclusion that Saul would certainly accomplish his murderous purpose was formed without the counsel of God. Even while Saul was plotting and seeking to accomplish his destruction, the Lord was working to secure David the kingdom. God works out His plans, though to human eyes they are veiled in mystery. Men cannot understand the ways of God; and, looking at appearances, they interpret the trials and tests and provings that God permits to come upon them as things that are against them, and that will only work their ruin. Thus David looked on appearances, and not at the promises of God. He doubted that he would ever come to the throne. Long trials had wearied his faith and exhausted his patience.

The Lord did not send David for protection to the Philistines, the most bitter foes of Israel. This very nation would be among his worst enemies to the last, and yet he had fled to them for help in his time of need. Having lost all confidence in Saul and in those who served him, he threw himself upon the mercies of the enemies of his people. David was a brave general, and had proved himself a wise and successful warrior; but he was working directly against his own interests when he went to the Philistines. God had appointed him to set up his standard in the land of Judah, and it was want of faith that led him to forsake his post of duty without a command from the Lord.

God was dishonored by David's unbelief. The Philistines had feared David more than they had feared Saul and his armies; and by placing himself under the protection of the Philistines, David discovered to them the weakness of his own people. Thus he encouraged these relentless foes to oppress Israel. David had been anointed to stand in defense of the people of God; and the Lord would not have His servants give encouragement to the wicked by disclosing the weakness of His people or by an appearance of indifference to their welfare. Furthermore, the impression was received by his brethren that he had gone to the heathen to serve their gods. By this act he gave occasion for misconstruing his motives, and many were led to hold prejudice against him. The very thing that Satan desired to have him do he was led to do; for, in seeking refuge among the Philistines, David caused great exultation to the enemies of God and His people. David did not renounce his worship of God nor cease his devotion to His cause; but he sacrificed his trust in Him to his personal safety, and thus tarnished the upright and faithful character that God requires His servants to possess.

David was cordially received by the king of the Philistines. The warmth of this reception was partly due to the fact that the king admired him and partly to the fact that it was flattering to his vanity to have a Hebrew seek his protection. David felt secure from betrayal in the dominions of Achish. He brought his family, his household, and his possessions, as did also his men; and to all appearance he had come to settle permanently in the land of Philistia. All this was gratifying to Achish, who promised to protect the fugitive Israelites.

At David's request for a residence in the country, removed from the royal city, the king graciously granted Ziklag as a possession. David realized that it would be dangerous for himself and his men to be under the influence of idolaters. In a town wholly separated for their use they might worship God with more freedom than they could if they remained in Gath, where the heathen rites could not but prove a source of evil and annoyance.

While dwelling in this isolated town David made war upon the Geshurites, the Gezrites, and the Amalekites, and he left none alive to bring tidings to Gath. When he returned from battle he gave Achish to understand that he had been warring against those of his own nation, the men of Judah. By this dissembling he was the means of strengthening the hand of the Philistines; for the king said, "He hath made his people Israel utterly to abhor him; therefore he shall be my servant forever." David knew that it was the will of God that those heathen tribes should be destroyed, and he knew that he was appointed to do this work; but he was not walking in the counsel of God when he practiced deception.

"And it came to pass in those days, that the Philistines gathered their armies together for warfare, to fight with Israel. And Achish said unto David, Know thou assuredly, that thou shalt go out with me to battle, thou and thy men." David had no intention of lifting his hand against his people; but he was not certain as to what course he would pursue, until circumstances should indicate his duty. He answered the king evasively, and said, "Surely thou shalt know what thy servant can do." Achish understood these words as a promise of assistance in the approaching war, and pledged his word to bestow upon David great honor, and give him a high position at the Philistine court.

But although David's faith had staggered somewhat at the promises of God, he still remembered that Samuel had anointed him king of Israel. He recalled the victories that God had given him over his enemies in the past. He reviewed the great mercy of God in preserving him from the hand of Saul, and determined not to betray a sacred trust. Even though the king of Israel had sought his life, he would not join his forces with the enemies of his people.

Chapter 66—The Death of Saul

Again war was declared between Israel and the Philistines. "The Philistines gathered themselves together, and came and pitched in Shunem," on the northern edge of the plain of Jezreel; while Saul and his forces encamped but a few miles distant, at the foot of Mount Gilboa, on the southern border of the plain. It was on this plain that Gideon, with three hundred men, had put to flight the hosts of Midian. But the spirit that inspired Israel's deliverer was widely different from that which now stirred the heart of the king. Gideon went forth strong in faith in the mighty God of Jacob; but Saul felt himself to be alone and defenseless, because God had forsaken him. As he looked abroad upon the Philistine host, "he was afraid, and his heart greatly trembled."

Saul had learned that David and his force were with the Philistines, and he expected that the son of Jesse would take this opportunity to revenge the wrongs he had suffered. The king was in sore distress. It was his own unreasoning passion, spurring him on to destroy the chosen of God, that had involved the nation in so great peril. While he had been engrossed in pursuing David he had neglected the defense of his kingdom. The Philistines, taking advantage of its unguarded condition, had penetrated into the very heart of the country. Thus while Satan had been urging Saul to employ every energy in hunting David, that he might destroy him, the same malignant spirit had inspired the Philistines to seize their opportunity to work Saul's ruin and overthrow the people of God. How often is the same policy still employed by the archenemy! He moves upon some unconsecrated heart to kindle envy and strife in the church, and then, taking advantage of the divided condition of God's people, he stirs up his agents to work their ruin.

On the morrow Saul must engage the Philistines in battle. The shadows of impending doom gathered dark about him; he longed for help and guidance. But it was in vain that he sought counsel from God. "The Lord answered him not, neither by dreams, nor by Urim, nor by prophets." The Lord never turned away a soul that came to Him in sincerity and humility. Why did he turn Saul away unanswered? The king had by his own act forfeited the benefits of all the methods of inquiring of God. He had rejected the counsel of Samuel the prophet; he had exiled David, the chosen of God; he had slain the priests of the Lord. Could he expect to be answered by God when he had cut off the channels of communication that Heaven had ordained? He had sinned away the Spirit of grace, and could he be answered by dreams and revelations from the Lord? Saul did not turn to God with humility and repentance. It was not pardon for sin and reconciliation with God, that he sought, but deliverance from his foes. By his own stubbornness and rebellion he had cut himself off from God. There could be no return but by the way of penitence and contrition; but the proud monarch, in his anguish and despair, determined to seek help from another source.

"Then said Saul unto his servants, Seek me a woman that hath a familiar spirit, that I may go to her, and inquire of her." Saul had a full knowledge of the character of necromancy. It had been expressly forbidden by the Lord, and the sentence of death was pronounced against all who practiced its unholy arts. During the life of Samuel, Saul had commanded that all wizards and those that had familiar spirits should be put to death; but now, in the rashness of desperation, he had recourse to that oracle which he had condemned as an abomination.

It was told the king that a woman who had a familiar spirit was living in concealment at Endor. This woman had entered into covenant with Satan to yield herself to his control, to fulfill his purposes; and in return, the prince of evil wrought wonders for her and revealed secret things to her.

Disguising himself, Saul went forth by night with but two attendants, to seek the retreat of the sorceress. Oh, pitiable sight! the king of Israel led captive by Satan at his will! What path so dark for human feet to tread as that chosen by one who has persisted in having his own way, resisting the holy influences of the Spirit of God! What bondage so terrible as that of him who is given over to the control of the worst of tyrants—himself! Trust in God and obedience to His will were the only conditions upon which Saul could be king of Israel. Had he complied with these conditions throughout his reign, his kingdom would have been secure; God would have been his guide, the Omnipotent his shield. God had borne long with Saul; and although his rebellion and obstinacy had well-nigh silenced the divine voice in the soul, there was still opportunity for repentance. But when in his peril he turned from God to obtain light from a confederate of Satan, he had cut the last tie that bound him to his Maker; he had placed himself fully under the control of that demoniac power which for years had been exercised upon him, and which had brought him to the verge of destruction.

Under the cover of darkness Saul and his attendants made their way across the plain, and, safely passing the Philistine host, they crossed the mountain ridge, to the lonely home of the sorceress of Endor. Here the woman with a familiar spirit had hidden herself away that she might secretly continue her profane incantations. Disguised as he was, Saul's lofty stature and kingly port declared that he was no common soldier. The woman suspected that her visitor was Saul, and his rich gifts strengthened her suspicions. To his request, "I pray thee, divine unto me by the familiar spirit, and bring me him up, whom I shall name unto thee," the woman answered, "Behold, thou knowest what Saul hath done, how he hath cut off those that have familiar spirits, and the wizards, out of the land: wherefore then layest thou a snare for my life, to cause me to die?" Then "Saul sware to her by the Lord, saying, As the Lord liveth, there shall no punishment happen to thee for this thing." And when she said, "Whom shall I bring up unto thee?" he answered, "Samuel."

After practicing her incantations, she said, "I saw gods ascending out of the earth.... An old man cometh up; and he is covered with a mantle. And Saul perceived that it was Samuel, and he stooped with his face to the ground, and bowed himself."

It was not God's holy prophet that came forth at the spell of a sorcerer's incantation. Samuel was not present in that haunt of evil spirits. That supernatural appearance was produced solely by the power of Satan. He could as easily assume the form of Samuel as he could assume that of an angel of light, when he tempted Christ in the wilderness.

The woman's first words under the spell of her incantation had been addressed to the king, "Why hast thou deceived me? for thou art Saul." Thus the first act of the evil spirit which personated the

[680]

prophet was to communicate secretly with this wicked woman, to warn her of the deception that had been practiced upon her. The message to Saul from the pretended prophet was, "Why hast thou disquieted me, to bring me up? And Saul answered, I am sore distressed; for the Philistines make war against me, and God is departed from me, and answereth me no more, neither by prophets, nor by dreams: therefore I have called thee, that thou mayest make known unto me what I shall do."

When Samuel was living, Saul had despised his counsel and had resented his reproofs. But now, in the hour of his distress and calamity, he felt that the prophet's guidance was his only hope, and in order to communicate with Heaven's ambassador he vainly had recourse to the messenger of hell! Saul had placed himself fully in the power of Satan; and now he whose only delight is in causing misery and destruction, made the most of his advantage, to work the ruin of the unhappy king. In answer to Saul's agonized entreaty came the terrible message, professedly from the lips of Samuel:

"Wherefore then dost thou ask of me, seeing the Lord is departed from thee, and is become thine enemy? And the Lord hath done to him, as he spake by me: for the Lord hath rent the kingdom out of thine hand, and given it to thy neighbor, even to David: because thou obeyedst not the voice of the Lord, nor executedst His fierce wrath upon Amalek, therefore hath the Lord done this thing unto thee this day. Moreover the Lord will also deliver Israel with thee into the hand of the Philistines."

All through his course of rebellion Saul had been flattered and deceived by Satan. It is the tempter's work to belittle sin, to make the path of transgression easy and inviting, to blind the mind to the warnings and threatenings of the Lord. Satan, by his bewitching power, had led Saul to justify himself in defiance of Samuel's reproofs and warning. But now, in his extremity, he turned upon him, presenting the enormity of his sin and the hopelessness of pardon, that he might goad him to desperation. Nothing could have been better chosen to destroy his courage and confuse his judgment, or to drive him to despair and self-destruction.

Saul was faint with weariness and fasting; he was terrified and conscience-stricken. As the fearful prediction fell upon his ear, his form swayed like an oak before the tempest, and he fell prostrate to the earth.

The sorceress was filled with alarm. The king of Israel lay before her like one dead. Should he perish in her retreat, what would be the consequences to herself? She besought him to arise and partake of food, urging that since she had imperiled her life in granting his desire, he should yield to her request for the preservation of his own. His servants joining their entreaties, Saul yielded at last, and the woman set before him the fatted calf and unleavened bread hastily prepared. What a scene!—In the wild cave of the sorceress, which but a little before had echoed with the words of doom—in the presence of Satan's messenger—he who had been anointed of God as king over Israel sat down to eat, in preparation for the day's deadly strife.

Before the break of day he returned with his attendants to the camp of Israel to make ready for the conflict. By consulting that spirit of darkness Saul had destroyed himself. Oppressed by the horror of despair, it would be impossible for him to inspire his army with courage. Separated from the Source of strength, he could not lead the minds of Israel to look to God as their helper. Thus the prediction of evil would work its own accomplishment.

On the plain of Shunem and the slopes of Mount Gilboa the armies of Israel and the hosts of the Philistines closed in mortal combat. Though the fearful scene in the cave of Endor had driven all hope from his heart, Saul fought with desperate valor for his throne and his kingdom. But it was in vain. "The men of Israel fled from before the Philistines, and fell down slain in Mount Gilboa." Three brave sons of the king died at his side. The archers pressed upon Saul. He had seen his soldiers falling around him and his princely sons cut down by the sword. Himself wounded, he could neither fight nor fly. Escape was impossible, and determined not to be taken alive by the Philistines, he bade his armor-bearer, "Draw thy sword, and thrust me through therewith." When the man refused to lift his hand against the Lord's anointed, Saul took his own life by falling upon his sword.

Thus the first king of Israel perished, with the guilt of self-murder upon his soul. His life had been a failure, and he went down in dishonor and despair, because he had set up his own perverse will against the will of God.

The tidings of defeat spread far and wide, carrying terror to all Israel. The people fled from the cities, and the Philistines took undisturbed possession. Saul's reign, independent of God, had well-nigh proved the ruin of his people.

On the day following the engagement, the Philistines, searching the battlefield to rob the slain, discovered the bodies of Saul and his three sons. To complete their triumph, they cut off the head of Saul and stripped him of his armor; then the head and the armor, reeking with blood, were sent to the country of the Philistines as a trophy of victory, "to publish it in the house of their idols, and among the people." The armor was finally put in "the house of Ashtaroth," while the head was fastened in the temple of Dagon. Thus the glory of the victory was ascribed to the power of these false gods, and the name of Jehovah was dishonored.

The dead bodies of Saul and his sons were dragged to Beth-shan, a city not far from Gilboa, and near the river Jordan. Here they were hung up in chains, to be devoured by birds of prey. But the brave men of Jabesh-gilead, remembering Saul's deliverance of their city in his earlier and happier years, now manifested their gratitude by rescuing the bodies of the king and princes, and giving them honorable burial. Crossing the Jordan by night, they "took the body of Saul and the bodies of his sons from the wall of Beth-shan, and came to Jabesh, and burnt them there, and they took their bones, and buried them under a tree at Jabesh, and fasted seven days." Thus the noble deed performed forty years before, secured for Saul and his sons burial by tender and pitying hands in that dark hour of defeat and dishonor.

Chapter 67—Ancient and Modern Sorcery

The Scripture account of Saul's visit to the woman of Endor has been a source of perplexity to many students of the Bible. There are some who take the position that Samuel was actually present at the interview with Saul, but the Bible itself furnishes sufficient ground for a contrary conclusion. If, as claimed by some, Samuel was in heaven, he must have been summoned thence, either by the power of God or by that of Satan. None can believe for a moment that Satan had power to call the holy prophet of God from heaven to honor the incantations of an abandoned woman. Nor can we conclude that God summoned him to the witch's cave; for the Lord had already refused to communicate with Saul, by dreams, by Urim, or by prophets. 1 Samuel 28:6. These were God's own appointed mediums of communication, and He did not pass them by to deliver the message through the agent of Satan.

The message itself is sufficient evidence of its origin. Its object was not to lead Saul to repentance, but to urge him on to ruin; and this is not the work of God, but of Satan. Furthermore, the act of Saul in consulting a sorceress is cited in Scripture as one reason why he was rejected by God and abandoned to destruction: "Saul died for his transgression which he committed against the Lord, even against the word of the Lord, which he kept not, and also for asking counsel of one that had a familiar spirit, *to inquire of it;* and inquired not of the Lord: therefore He slew him, and turned the kingdom unto David the son of Jesse." 1 Chronicles 10:13, 14. Here it is distinctly stated that Saul inquired of the familiar spirit, not of the Lord. He did not communicate with Samuel, the prophet of God; but through the sorceress he held intercourse with Satan. Satan could not present the real Samuel, but he did present a counterfeit, that served his purpose of deception.

Nearly all forms of ancient sorcery and witchcraft were founded upon a belief in communion with the dead. Those who practiced the arts of necromancy claimed to have intercourse with departed spirits, and to obtain through them a knowledge of future events. This custom of consulting the dead is referred to in the prophecy of Isaiah: "When they shall say unto you, Seek unto them that have familiar spirits, and unto wizards that peep and that mutter: should not a people seek unto their God? *for the living to the dead?*" Isaiah 8:19.

This same belief in communion with the dead formed the cornerstone of heathen idolatry. The gods of the heathen were believed to be the deified spirits of departed heroes. Thus the religion of the heathen was a worship of the dead. This is evident from the Scriptures. In the account of the sin of Israel at Bethpeor, it is stated: "Israel abode in Shittim, and the people began to commit whoredom with the daughters of Moab. And they called the people unto the sacrifices of their gods: and the people did eat, and bowed down to their gods. And Israel joined himself unto Baalpeor." Numbers 25:1-3. The psalmist tells us to what kind of gods these sacrifices were offered. Speaking of the same apostasy of the Israelites, he says, "They joined themselves also unto Baalpeor, and *ate the sacrifices of the dead*" (Psalm 106:28); that is, sacrifices that had been offered to the dead.

The deification of the dead has held a prominent place in nearly every system of heathenism, as has also the supposed communion with the dead. The gods were believed to communicate their will to men, and also, when consulted, to give them counsel. Of this character were the famous oracles of Greece and Rome.

The belief in communion with the dead is still held, even in professedly Christian lands. Under the name of spiritualism the practice of communicating with beings claiming to be the spirits of the departed has become widespread. It is calculated to take hold of the sympathies of those who have laid their loved ones in the grave. Spiritual beings sometimes appear to persons in the form of their deceased friends, and relate incidents connected with their lives and perform acts which they performed while living. In this way they lead men to believe that their dead friends are angels, hovering over them and communicating with them. Those who thus assume to be the spirits of the departed are regarded with a certain idolatry, and with many their word has greater weight than the word of God.

There are many, however, who regard spiritualism as a mere imposture. The manifestations by which it supports its claims to a supernatural character are attributed to fraud on the part of the medium. But while it is true that the results of trickery have often been palmed off as genuine manifestations, there have also been marked evidences of supernatural power. And many who reject spiritualism as the result of human skill or cunning will, when confronted with manifestations which they cannot account for upon this ground, be led to acknowledge its claims.

Modern spiritualism and the forms of ancient witchcraft and idol worship—all having communion with the dead as their vital principle—are founded upon that first lie by which Satan beguiled Eve in Eden: "Ye shall not surely die: for God doth know that in the day ye eat thereof, ... ye shall be as gods." Genesis 3:4, 5. Alike based upon falsehood and perpetuating the same, they are alike from the father of lies.

The Hebrews were expressly forbidden to engage in any manner in pretended communion with the dead. God closed this door effectually when He said: "The dead know not anything.... Neither have they any more a portion forever in anything that is done under the sun." Ecclesiastes 9:5, 6. "His breath goeth forth, he returneth to his earth; in that very day his thoughts perish." Psalm 146:4. And the Lord declared to Israel: "The soul that turneth after such as have familiar spirits, and after wizards, to go a whoring after them, I will even set My face against that soul, and will cut him off from among his people." Leviticus 20:6.

The "familiar spirits" were not the spirits of the dead, but evil angels, the messengers of Satan. Ancient idolatry, which, as we have seen, comprises both worship of the dead and pretended communion with them, is declared by the Bible to have been demon worship. The apostle Paul, in warning his brethren against participating, in any manner, in the idolatry of their heathen neighbors, says, "The things which the Gentiles sacrifice, they sacrifice to devils, and not to God, and I would not that ye should have fellowship with devils." 1 Corinthians 10:20. The psalmist, speaking of Israel, says that "they sacrificed their sons and their daughters unto devils," and in the next verse he explains that they sacrificed them "unto the idols of Canaan." Psalm 106:37, 38. In their supposed worship of dead men they were in reality worshiping demons.

Modern spiritualism, resting upon the same foundation, is but a revival in a new form of the witchcraft and demon worship that God condemned and prohibited of old. It is foretold in the Scriptures, which declare that "in the latter times some shall depart from the faith, giving heed to seducing spirits, and doctrines of devils." 1 Timothy 4:1. Paul, in his second letter to the Thessalonians, points to the special working of Satan in spiritualism as an event to take place immediately before the second advent of Christ. Speaking of Christ's second coming, he declares that it is "after the working of Satan with all power and signs and lying wonders." 2 Thessalonians 2:9. And Peter, describing the dangers to which the church was to be exposed in the last days, says that as there were false prophets who led Israel into sin, so there will be false teachers, "who privily shall bring in damnable heresies, even denying the Lord that bought them.... And many shall follow their pernicious ways." 2 Peter 2:1, 2. Here the apostle has pointed out one of the marked characteristics of spiritualist teachers. They refuse to acknowledge Christ as the Son of God. Concerning such teachers the beloved John declares: "Who is a liar but he that denieth that Jesus is the Christ? He is antichrist, that denieth the Father and the Son. Whosoever denieth the Son, the same hath not the Father." 1 John 2:22, 23. Spiritualism, by denying Christ, denies both the Father and the Son, and the Bible pronounces it the manifestation of antichrist.

By the prediction of Saul's doom, given through the woman of Endor, Satan planned to ensnare the people of Israel. He hoped that they would be inspired with confidence in the sorceress, and would be led to consult her. Thus they would turn from God as their counselor and would place themselves under the guidance of Satan. The lure by which spiritualism attracts the multitudes is its pretended power to draw aside the veil from the future and reveal to men what God has hidden. God has in His word opened before us the great events of the future—all that it is essential for us to know—and He has given us a safe guide for our feet amid all its perils; but it is Satan's purpose to destroy men's confidence in God, to make them dissatisfied with their condition in life, and to lead them to seek a knowledge of what God has wisely veiled from them, and to despise what He has revealed in His Holy Word.

There are many who become restless when they cannot know the definite outcome of affairs. They cannot endure uncertainty, and in their impatience they refuse to wait to see the salvation of God. Apprehended evils drive them nearly distracted. They give way to their rebellious feelings, and run hither and thither in passionate grief, seeking intelligence concerning that which has not been revealed. If they would but trust in God, and watch unto prayer, they would find divine consolation. Their spirit would be calmed by communion with God. The weary and the heavy-laden would find rest unto their souls if they would only go to Jesus; but when they neglect the means that God has ordained for their comfort, and resort to other sources, hoping to learn what God has withheld, they commit the error of Saul, and thereby gain only a knowledge of evil.

God is not pleased with this course, and has expressed it in the most explicit terms. This impatient haste to tear away the veil from the future reveals a lack of faith in God and leaves the soul open to the suggestions of the master deceiver. Satan leads men to consult those that have familiar spirits; and by revealing hidden things of the past, he inspires confidence in his power to foretell things to come. By experience gained through the long ages he can reason from cause to effect and often forecast, with a degree of accuracy, some of the future events of man's life. Thus he is enabled to deceive poor, misguided souls and bring them under his power and lead them captive at his will.

God has given us the warning by His prophet: "When they shall say unto you, Seek unto them that have familiar spirits, and unto wizards that peep and that mutter: should not a people seek unto their God? for the living to the dead? To the law and to the testimony: if they speak not according to this word, it is because there is no light in them." Isaiah 8:19, 20.

Shall those who have a holy God, infinite in wisdom and power, go unto wizards, whose knowledge comes from intimacy with the enemy of our Lord? God Himself is the light of His people; He bids them fix their eyes by faith upon the glories that are veiled from human sight. The Sun of Righteousness sends its bright beams into their hearts; they have light from the throne of heaven, and they have no desire to turn away from the source of light to the messengers of Satan.

The demon's message to Saul, although it was a denunciation of sin and a prophecy of retribution, was not meant to reform him, but to goad him to despair and ruin. Oftener, however, it serves the tempter's purpose best to lure men to destruction by flattery. The teaching of the demon gods in ancient times fostered the vilest license. The divine precepts condemning sin and enforcing righteousness were set aside; truth was lightly regarded, and impurity was not only permitted but enjoined. Spiritualism declares that there is no death, no sin, no judgment, no retribution; that "men are unfallen demigods;" that desire is the highest law; and that man is accountable only to himself. The barriers that God has erected to guard truth, purity, and reverence are broken down, and many are thus emboldened in sin. Does not such teaching suggest an origin similar to that of demon worship?

The Lord presented before Israel the results of holding communion with evil spirits, in the abominations of the Canaanites: they were without natural affection, idolaters, adulterers, murderers, and abominable by every corrupt thought and revolting practice. Men do not know their own hearts; for "the heart is deceitful above all things, and desperately wicked." Jeremiah 17:9. But God understands the tendencies of the depraved nature of man. Then, as now, Satan was watching to bring about conditions favorable to rebellion, that the people of Israel might make themselves as abhorrent to God as were the Canaanites. The adversary of souls is ever on the alert to open channels for the unrestrained flow of evil in us; for he desires that we may be ruined, and be condemned before God.

Satan was determined to keep his hold on the land of Canaan, and when it was made the habitation of the children of Israel, and the law of God was made the law of the land, he hated Israel with a cruel and malignant hatred and plotted their destruction. Through the agency of evil spirits strange gods were introduced; and because of transgression, the chosen people were finally scattered from the Land of Promise. This history Satan is striving to repeat in our day. God is leading His people out from the abominations of the world, that they may keep His law; and because of this, the rage of "the accuser of our brethren" knows no bounds. "The devil is come down unto you, having great wrath, because he knoweth that he hath but a short time." Revelation 12:10, 12. The antitypical land of promise is just before us, and Satan is determined to destroy the people of God and cut them off from their inheritance. The admonition, "Watch ye and pray, lest ye enter into temptation" (Mark 14:38), was never more needed than now.

The word of the Lord to ancient Israel is addressed also to His people in this age: "Regard not them that have familiar spirits, neither seek after wizards, to be defiled by them;" "for all that do these things are an abomination unto the Lord." Leviticus 19:31; Deuteronomy 18:12.

Chapter 68—David at Ziklag

This chapter is based on 1 Samuel 29; 30; 2 Samuel 1.

David and his men had not taken part in the battle between Saul and the Philistines, though they had marched with the Philistines to the field of conflict. As the two armies prepared to join battle the son of Jesse found himself in a situation of great perplexity. It was expected that he would fight for the Philistines. Should he in the engagement quit the post assigned him and retire from the field, he would not only brand himself with cowardice, but with ingratitude and treachery to Achish, who had protected him and confided in him. Such an act would cover his name with infamy, and would expose him to the wrath of enemies more to be feared than Saul. Yet he could not for a moment consent to fight against Israel. Should he do this, he would become a traitor to his country—the enemy of God and of His people. It would forever bar his way to the throne of Israel; and should Saul be slain in the engagement, his death would be charged upon David.

David was caused to feel that he had missed his path. Far better would it have been for him to find refuge in God's strong fortresses of the mountains than with the avowed enemies of Jehovah and His people. But the Lord in His great mercy did not punish this error of His servant by leaving him to himself in his distress and perplexity; for though David, losing his grasp on divine power, had faltered and turned aside from the path of strict integrity, it was still the purpose of his heart to be true to God. While Satan and his host were busy helping the adversaries of God and of Israel to plan against a king who had forsaken God, the angels of the Lord were working to deliver David from the peril into which he had fallen. Heavenly messengers moved upon the Philistine princes to protest against the presence of David and his force with the army in the approaching conflict.

"What do these Hebrews here?" cried the Philistine lords, pressing about Achish. The latter, unwilling to part with so important an ally, answered, "Is not this David, the servant of Saul the king of Israel, which hath been with me these days, or these years, and I have found no fault in him since he fell unto me unto this day?"

But the princes angrily persisted in their demand: "Make this fellow return, that he may go again to his place which thou hast appointed him, and let him not go down with us to battle, lest in the battle he be an adversary to us: for wherewith should he reconcile himself unto his master? should it not be with the heads of these men? Is not this David, of whom they sang one to another in dances, saying, Saul slew his thousands, and David his ten thousands?" The slaughter of their famed champion and the triumph of Israel upon that occasion were still fresh in the memory of the Philistine lords. They did not believe that David would fight against his own people; and should he, in the heat of battle, take sides with them, he could inflict greater harm on the Philistines than would the whole of Saul's army.

Thus Achish was forced to yield, and calling David, said unto him, "Surely as Jehovah liveth, thou hast been upright, and thy going out and thy coming in with me in the host is good in my sight: for I have not found evil in thee since the day of thy coming unto me unto this day. Nevertheless the lords favor thee not. Wherefore now return, and go in peace, that thou displease not the lords of the Philistines."

David, fearing to betray his real feelings, answered, "But what have I done? and what hast thou found in thy servant so long as I have been with thee unto this day, that I may not go fight against the enemies of my lord the king?"

The reply of Achish must have sent a thrill of shame and remorse through David's heart, as he thought how unworthy of a servant of Jehovah were the deceptions to which he had stooped. "I know that thou art good in my sight, as an angel of God," said the king: "notwithstanding, the princes of the Philistines have said, He shall not go up with us to the battle. Wherefore now rise up early in the morning with thy master's servants that are come with thee: and as soon as ye be up early in the morning, and have light, depart." Thus the snare in which David had become entangled was broken, and he was set free.

After three days' travel David and his band of six hundred men reached Ziklag, their Philistine home. But a scene of desolation met their view. The Amalekites, taking advantage of David's absence, with his force, had avenged themselves for his incursions into their territory. They had surprised the city while it was left unguarded, and having sacked and burned it, had departed, taking all the women and children as captives, with much spoil.

Dumb with horror and amazement, David and his men for a little time gazed in silence upon the blackened and smoldering ruins. Then as a sense of their terrible desolation burst upon them, those battle-scarred warriors "lifted up their voice and wept, until they had no more power to weep."

Here again David was chastened for the lack of faith that had led him to place himself among the Philistines. He had opportunity to see how much safety could be found among the foes of God and His people. David's followers turned upon him as the cause of their calamities. He had provoked the vengeance of the Amalekites by his attack upon them; yet, too confident of security in the midst of his enemies, he had left the city unguarded. Maddened with grief and rage, his soldiers were now ready for any desperate measures, and they threatened even to stone their leader.

David seemed to be cut off from every human support. All that he held dear on earth had been swept from him. Saul had driven him from his country; the Philistines had driven him from the camp; the Amalekites had plundered his city; his wives and children had been made prisoners; and his own familiar friends had banded against him, and threatened him even with death. In this hour of utmost extremity David, instead of permitting his mind to dwell upon these painful circumstances, looked earnestly to God for help. He "encouraged himself in the Lord." He reviewed his past eventful life. Wherein had the Lord ever forsaken him? His soul was refreshed in recalling the many evidences of God's favor. The followers of David, by their discontent and impatience, made their affliction doubly grievous; but the man of God, having even greater cause for grief, bore himself with fortitude. "What time I am afraid, I will trust in Thee" (Psalm 56:3), was the language of his heart. Though he himself could not discern a way out of the difficulty, God could see it, and would teach him what to do.

Sending for Abiathar the priest, the son of Ahimelech, "David inquired of the Lord, saying, If I pursue after this troop, shall I overtake them?" The answer was, "Pursue: for thou shalt surely overtake them, and shalt without fail recover all." 1 Samuel 30:8, R.V.

At these words the tumult of grief and passion ceased. David and his soldiers at once set out in pursuit of their fleeing foe. So rapid was their march, that upon reaching the brook Besor, which empties near Gaza into the Mediterranean Sea, two hundred of the band were compelled by exhaustion to remain behind. But David with the remaining four hundred pressed forward, nothing daunted.

Advancing, they came upon an Egyptian slave apparently about to perish from weariness and hunger. Upon receiving food and drink, however, he revived, and they learned that he had been left to die by his cruel master, an Amalekite belonging to the invading force. He told the story of the raid and pillage; and then, having exacted a promise that he should not be slain or delivered to his master, he consented to lead David's company to the camp of their enemies.

As they came in sight of the encampment a scene of revelry met their gaze. The victorious host were holding high festival. "They were spread abroad upon all the earth, eating and drinking, and dancing, because of all the great spoil that they had taken out of the land of the Philistines, and out of the land of Judah." An immediate attack was ordered, and the pursuers rushed fiercely upon their prey. The Amalekites were surprised and thrown into confusion. The battle was continued all that night and the following day, until nearly the entire host was slain. Only a band of four hundred men, mounted upon camels, succeeded in making their escape. The word of the Lord was fulfilled. "David recovered all that the Amalekites had carried away: and David rescued his two wives. And there was nothing lacking to them, neither small nor great, neither sons nor daughters, neither spoil, nor anything that they had taken to them: David recovered all."

When David had invaded the territory of the Amalekites, he had put to the sword all the inhabitants that fell into his hands. But for the restraining power of God the Amalekites would have retaliated by destroying the people of Ziklag. They decided to spare the captives, desiring to heighten the honor of the triumph by leading home a large number of prisoners, and intending afterward to sell them as slaves. Thus, unwittingly, they fulfilled God's purpose, keeping the prisoners unharmed, to be restored to their husbands and fathers.

All earthly powers are under the control of the Infinite One. To the mightiest ruler, to the most cruel oppressor, He says, "Hitherto shalt thou come, but no further." Job 38:11. God's power is constantly exercised to counteract the agencies of evil; He is ever at work among men, not for their destruction, but for their correction and preservation.

With great rejoicing the victors took up their homeward march. Upon reaching their companions who had remained behind, the more selfish and unruly of the four hundred urged that those who had had no part in the battle should not share the spoils; that it was enough for them to recover each his wife and children. But David would permit no such arrangement. "Ye shall not do so, my brethren," he said, "with that which the Lord hath given us.... As his part is that goeth down to the battle, so shall his part be that tarrieth by the stuff; they shall part alike." Thus the matter was settled, and it afterward became a statute in Israel that all who were honorably connected with a military campaign should share the spoils equally with those who engaged in actual combat.

Besides recovering all the spoil that had been taken from Ziklag, David and his band had captured extensive flocks and herds belonging to the Amalekites. These were called "David's spoil;" and upon returning to Ziklag, he sent from this spoil presents to the elders of his own tribe of Judah. In this distribution all those were remembered who had befriended him and his followers in the mountain fastnesses, when he had been forced to flee from place to place for his life. Their kindness and sympathy, so precious to the hunted fugitive, were thus gratefully acknowledged.

It was the third day since David and his warriors returned to Ziklag. As they labored to restore their ruined homes, they watched with anxious hearts for tidings of the battle which they knew must have been fought between Israel and the Philistines. Suddenly a messenger entered the town, "with his clothes rent, and earth upon his head." He was at once brought to David, before whom he bowed with reverence, expressing recognition of him as a powerful prince, whose favor he desired. David eagerly inquired how the battle had gone. The fugitive reported Saul's defeat and death, and the death of Jonathan. But he went beyond a simple statement of facts. Evidently supposing that David must cherish enmity toward his relentless persecutor, the stranger hoped to secure honor to himself as the slayer of the king. With an air of boasting the man went on to relate that during the battle he found the monarch of Israel wounded, and sore pressed by his foes, and that at his own request the messenger had slain him. The crown from his head and the golden bracelets from his arm he had brought to David. He confidently expected that these tidings would be hailed with joy, and that a rich reward would be his for the part that he had acted.

But "David took hold on his clothes, and rent them; and likewise all the men that were with him: and they mourned, and wept, and fasted until even, for Saul, and for Jonathan his son, and for the people of the Lord, and for the house of Israel; because they were fallen by the sword."

The first shock of the fearful tidings past, David's thoughts returned to the stranger herald, and the crime of which, according to his own statement, he was guilty. The chief demanded of the young man, "Whence art thou?" And he answered, "I am the son of a stranger, an Amalekite. And David said unto him, How wast thou not afraid to stretch forth thine hand to destroy the Lord's anointed?" Twice David had had Saul in his power; but when urged to slay him, he had refused to lift his hand against him who had been consecrated by the command of God to rule over Israel. Yet the Amalekite feared not to boast that he had slain the king of Israel. He had accused himself of a crime worthy of death, and the penalty was inflicted at once. David said, "Thy blood be upon thy head; for thy mouth hath testified against thee, saying, I have slain the Lord's anointed."

David's grief at the death of Saul was sincere and deep, evincing the generosity of a noble nature. He did not exult in the fall of his enemy. The obstacle that had barred his access to the throne of Israel was removed, but at this he did not rejoice. Death had obliterated the remembrance of Saul's distrust and cruelty, and now nothing in his history was thought of but that which was noble and kingly. The name of Saul was linked with that of Jonathan, whose friendship had been so true and so unselfish.

The song in which David gave utterance to the feelings of his heart became a treasure to his nation, and to the people of God in all subsequent ages:

"Thy glory, O Israel, is slain upon thy high places!
    How are the mighty fallen!
Tell it not in Gath,
    Publish it not in the streets of Ashkelon;
Lest the daughters of the Philistines rejoice,
    Lest the daughters of the uncircumcised triumph.
Ye mountains of Gilboa, Let there be no dew nor rain upon you,
      neither fields of
    offerings:
For there the shield of the mighty was vilely cast away,
    The shield of Saul as of one not anointed with oil....
Saul and Jonathan were lovely and pleasant in their lives,
    And in their death they were not divided;
They were swifter than eagles,
    They were stronger than lions.
Ye daughters of Israel, weep over Saul,
    Who clothed you in scarlet delicately,
Who put ornaments of gold upon your apparel.
    How are the mighty fallen in the midst of the battle!
Jonathan is slain upon thy high places.
    I am distressed for thee, my brother Jonathan:
Very pleasant hast thou been unto me:
    Thy love to me was wonderful,
Passing the love of women.
    How are the mighty fallen,
And the weapons of war perished!"

2 Samuel 1:19-27, R.V.

Chapter 69—David Called to the Throne

This chapter is based on 2 Samuel 2 to 5:5.

The death of Saul removed the dangers that had made David an exile. The way was now open for him to return to his own land. When the days of mourning for Saul and Jonathan were ended, "David inquired of the Lord, saying, Shall I go up into any of the cities of Judah? And the Lord said unto him, Go up. And David said, Whither shall I go up? And He said, Unto Hebron."

Hebron was twenty miles north from Beersheba, and about midway between that city and the future site of Jerusalem. It was originally called Kirjath-arba, the city of Arba, the father of Anak. Later it was called Mamre, and here was the burial place of the patriarchs, "the cave of Machpelah." Hebron had been the possession of Caleb and was now the chief city of Judah. It lies in a valley surrounded by fertile hill country and fruitful lands. The most beautiful vineyards of Palestine were on its borders, together with numerous plantations of olive and other fruit trees.

David and his followers immediately prepared to obey the instruction which they had received from God. The six hundred armed men, with their wives and children, their flocks and herds, were soon on the way to Hebron. As the caravan entered the city the men of Judah were waiting to welcome David as the future king of Israel. Arrangements were at once made for his coronation. "And there they anointed David king over the house of Judah." But no effort was made to establish his authority by force over the other tribes.

One of the first acts of the new-crowned monarch was to express his tender regard for the memory of Saul and Jonathan. Upon learning of the brave deed of the men of Jabesh-gilead in rescuing the bodies of the fallen leaders and giving them honorable burial, David sent an embassy to Jabesh with the message, "Blessed be ye of the Lord, that ye have showed this kindness unto your lord, even unto Saul, and have buried him. And now the Lord show kindness and truth unto you: and I also will requite you this kindness." And he announced his own accession to the throne of Judah and invited the allegiance of those who had proved themselves so truehearted.

The Philistines did not oppose the action of Judah in making David king. They had befriended him in his exile, in order to harass and weaken the kingdom of Saul, and now they hoped that because of their former kindness to David the extension of his power would, in the end, work to their advantage. But David's reign was not to be free from trouble. With his coronation began the dark record of conspiracy and rebellion. David did not sit upon a traitor's throne; God had chosen him to be king of Israel, and there had been no occasion for distrust or opposition. Yet hardly had his authority been acknowledged by the men of Judah, when through the influence of Abner, Ishbosheth, the son of Saul, was proclaimed king, and set upon a rival throne in Israel.

Ishbosheth was but a weak and incompetent representative of the house of Saul, while David was pre-eminently qualified to bear the responsibilities of the kingdom. Abner, the chief agent in raising Ishbosheth to kingly power, had been commander-in-chief of Saul's army, and was the most distinguished man in Israel. Abner knew that David had been appointed by the Lord to the throne of Israel, but having so long hunted and pursued him, he was not now willing that the son of Jesse should succeed to the kingdom over which Saul had reigned.

The circumstances under which Abner was placed served to develop his real character and showed him to be ambitious and unprincipled. He had been intimately associated with Saul and had been influenced by the spirit of the king to despise the man whom God had chosen to reign over Israel. His hatred had been increased by the cutting rebuke that David had given him at the time when the cruse of water and the spear of the king had been taken from the side of Saul as he slept in the camp. He remembered how David had cried in the hearing of the king and the people of Israel, "Art not thou a valiant man? and who is like to thee in Israel? wherefore then hast thou not kept thy lord the king? ... This thing is not good that thou hast done. As the Lord liveth, ye are worthy to die, because ye have not kept your master, the Lord's anointed." This reproof had rankled in his breast, and he determined to carry out his revengeful purpose and create division in Israel, whereby he himself might be exalted. He employed the representative of departed royalty to advance his own selfish ambitions and purposes. He knew that the people loved Jonathan. His memory was cherished, and Saul's first successful campaigns had not been forgotten by the army. With determination worthy a better cause, this rebellious leader went forward to carry out his plans.

Mahanaim, on the farther side of Jordan, was chosen as the royal residence, since it offered the greatest security against attack, either from David or from the Philistines. Here the coronation of Ishbosheth took place. His reign was first accepted by the tribes east of Jordan, and was finally extended over all Israel except Judah. For two years the son of Saul enjoyed his honors in his secluded capital. But Abner, intent upon extending his power over all Israel, prepared for aggressive warfare. And "there was long war between the house of Saul and the house of David: but David waxed stronger and stronger, and the house of Saul waxed weaker and weaker."

At last treachery overthrew the throne that malice and ambition had established. Abner, becoming incensed against the weak and incompetent Ishbosheth, deserted to David, with the offer to bring over to him all the tribes of Israel. His proposals were accepted by the king, and he was dismissed with honor to accomplish his purpose. But the favorable reception of so valiant and famed a warrior excited the jealousy of Joab, the commander-in-chief of David's army. There was a blood feud between Abner and Joab, the former having slain Asahel, Joab's brother, during the war between Israel and Judah. Now Joab, seeing an opportunity to avenge his brother's death and rid himself of a prospective rival, basely took occasion to waylay and murder Abner.

David, upon hearing of this treacherous assault, exclaimed, "I and my kingdom are guiltless before the Lord forever from the blood of Abner the son of Ner. Let it rest on the head of Joab; and on all his father's house." In view of the unsettled state of the kingdom, and the power and position of the murderers—for Joab's brother Abishai had been united with him—David could not visit the crime with just retribution, yet he publicly manifested his abhorrence of the bloody deed. The burial of Abner was attended with public honors. The army, with Joab at their head, were required to take part in the services of mourning, with rent garments and clothed in sackcloth. The king manifested his grief by keeping a fast upon the day of burial; he followed the bier as chief mourner; and at the grave he pronounced an elegy which was a cutting rebuke of the murderers. "The king lamented over Abner, and said:

> "Died Abner as a fool dieth?
>   Thy hands were not bound,
> Nor thy feet put into fetters:
>   As a man falleth before wicked men,
> So fellest thou."

David's magnanimous recognition of one who had been his bitter enemy won the confidence and admiration of all Israel. "All the people took notice of it, and it pleased them: as whatsoever the king did pleased all the people. For all the people and all Israel understood that day that it was not of the king to slay Abner the son of Ner." In the private circle of his trusted counselors and attendants the king spoke of the crime, and recognizing his own inability to punish the murderers as he desired, he left them to the justice of God: "Know ye not that there is a prince and a great man fallen this day in Israel? And I am this day weak, though anointed king; and these men the sons of Zeruiah be too hard for me: the Lord shall reward the doer of evil according to his wickedness."

Abner had been sincere in his offers and representations to David, yet his motives were base and selfish. He had persistently opposed the king of God's appointment, in the expectation of securing honor to himself. It was resentment, wounded pride, and passion that led him to forsake the cause he had so long served; and in deserting to David he hoped to receive the highest position of honor in his service. Had he succeeded in his purpose, his talents and ambition, his great influence and want of godliness, would have endangered the throne of David and the peace and prosperity of the nation.

"When Saul's son heard that Abner was dead in Hebron, his hands were feeble, and all the Israelites were troubled." It was evident that the kingdom could not long be maintained. Soon another act of treachery completed the downfall of the waning power. Ishbosheth was foully murdered by two of his captains, who, cutting off his head, hastened with it to the king of Judah, hoping thus to ingratiate themselves in his favor.

They appeared before David with the gory witness to their crime, saying, "Behold the head of Ishbosheth the son of Saul thine enemy, which sought thy life; and the Lord hath avenged my lord the king this day of Saul, and of his seed." But David, whose throne God Himself had established, and whom God had delivered from his adversaries, did not desire the aid of treachery to establish his power. He told these murderers of the doom visited upon him who boasted of slaying Saul. "How much more," he added, "when wicked men have slain a righteous person in his own house upon his bed? shall I not therefore now require his blood of your hand, and take you away from the earth? And David commanded his young men, and they slew them.... But they took the head of Ishbosheth and buried it in the sepulchre of Abner in Hebron."

After the death of Ishbosheth there was a general desire among the leading men of Israel that David should become king of all the tribes. "Then came all the tribes of Israel to David unto Hebron, and spake, saying, Behold, we are thy bone and thy flesh." They declared, "Thou wast he that leddest out and broughtest in Israel: and the Lord said to thee, Thou shalt feed My people Israel, and thou shalt be a captain over Israel. So all the elders of Israel came to the king to Hebron; and King David made a league with them in Hebron before the Lord." Thus through the providence of God the way had been opened for him to come to the throne. He had no personal ambition to gratify, for he had not sought the honor to which he had been brought.

More than eight thousand of the descendants of Aaron and of the Levites waited upon David. The change in the sentiments of the people was marked and decisive. The revolution was quiet and dignified, befitting the great work they were doing. Nearly half a million souls, the former subjects of Saul, thronged Hebron and its environs. The very hills and valleys were alive with the multitudes. The hour for the coronation was appointed; the man who had been expelled from the court of Saul, who had fled to the mountains and hills and to the caves of the earth to preserve his life, was about to receive the highest honor that can be conferred upon man by his fellow man. Priests and elders, clothed in the garments of their sacred office, officers and soldiers with glittering spear and helmet, and strangers from long distances, stood to witness the coronation of the chosen king. David was arrayed in the royal robe. The sacred oil was put upon his brow by the high priest, for the anointing by Samuel had been prophetic of what would take place at the inauguration of the king. The time had come, and David, by solemn rite, was consecrated to his office as God's vicegerent. The scepter was placed in his hands. The covenant of his righteous sovereignty was written, and the people gave their pledges of loyalty. The diadem was placed upon his brow, and the coronation ceremony was over. Israel had a king by divine appointment. He who had waited patiently for the Lord, beheld the promise of God fulfilled. "And David went on, and grew great, and the Lord God of hosts was with him." 2 Samuel 5:10.

Chapter 70—The Reign of David

This chapter is based on 2 Samuel 5:6-25; 6; 7; 9; 10.

As soon as David was established on the throne of Israel he began to seek a more appropriate location for the capital of his realm. Twenty miles from Hebron a place was selected as the future metropolis of the kingdom. Before Joshua had led the armies of Israel over Jordan it had been called Salem. Near this place Abraham had proved his loyalty to God. Eight hundred years before the coronation of David it had been the home of Melchizedek, the priest of the most high God. It held a central and elevated position in the country and was protected by an environment of hills. Being on the border between Benjamin and Judah, it was in close proximity to Ephraim and was easy of access to the other tribes.

In order to secure this location the Hebrews must dispossess a remnant of the Canaanites, who held a fortified position on the mountains of Zion and Moriah. This stronghold was called Jebus, and its inhabitants were known as Jebusites. For centuries Jebus had been looked upon as impregnable; but it was besieged and taken by the Hebrews under the command of Joab, who, as the reward of his valor, was made commander-in-chief of the armies of Israel. Jebus now became the national capital, and its heathen name was changed to Jerusalem.

Hiram, king of the wealthy city of Tyre, on the Mediterranean Sea, now sought an alliance with the king of Israel, and lent his aid to David in the work of erecting a palace at Jerusalem. Ambassadors were sent from Tyre, accompanied by architects and workmen and long trains laden with costly wood, cedar trees, and other valuable material.

The increasing strength of Israel in its union under David, the acquisition of the stronghold of Jebus, and the alliance with Hiram, king of Tyre, excited the hostility of the Philistines, and they again invaded the country with a strong force, taking up their position in the valley of Rephaim, but a short distance from Jerusalem. David with his men of war retired to the stronghold of Zion, to await divine direction. "And David inquired of the Lord, saying, Shall I go up to the Philistines? wilt thou deliver them into mine hand? And the Lord said unto David, Go up: for I will doubtless deliver the Philistines into thine hand."

David advanced upon the enemy at once, defeated and destroyed them, and took from them the gods which they had brought with them to ensure their victory. Exasperated by the humiliation of their defeat, the Philistines gathered a still larger force, and returned to the conflict. And again they "spread themselves in the valley of Rephaim." Again David sought the Lord and the great I AM took the direction of the armies of Israel.

God instructed David, saying, "Thou shalt not go up; but fetch a compass behind them, and come upon them over against the mulberry trees. And let it be, when thou hearest the sound of a going in the tops of the mulberry trees, that then thou shalt bestir thyself: for then shall the Lord go out before thee, to smite the host of the Philistines." If David, like Saul, had chosen his own way, success would not have attended him. But he did as the Lord had commanded, and he "smote the host of the Philistines from Gibeon even to Gazer. And the fame of David went out into all lands; and the Lord brought the fear of him upon all nations." 1 Chronicles 14:16, 17.

Now that David was firmly established upon the throne and free from the invasions of foreign foes, he turned to the accomplishment of a cherished purpose—to bring up the ark of God to Jerusalem. For many years the ark had remained at Kirjath-jearim, nine miles distant; but it was fitting that the capital of the nation should be honored with the token of the divine Presence.

David summoned thirty thousand of the leading men of Israel, for it was his purpose to make the occasion a scene of great rejoicing and imposing display. The people responded gladly to the call. The high priest, with his brethren in sacred office and the princes and leading men of the tribes, assembled at Kirjath-jearim. David was aglow with holy zeal. The ark was brought out from the house of Abinadab and placed upon a new cart drawn by oxen, while two of the sons of Abinadab attended it.

The men of Israel followed with exultant shouts and songs of rejoicing, a multitude of voices joining in melody with the sound of musical instruments; "David and all the house of Israel played before the Lord ... on harps, and on psalteries, and on timbrels, and on cornets, and on cymbals." It had been long since Israel had witnessed such a scene of triumph. With solemn gladness the vast procession wound its way along the hills and valleys toward the Holy City.

But "when they came to Nachon's threshing floor, Uzzah put forth his hand to the ark of God, and took hold of it; for the oxen shook it. And the anger of the Lord was kindled against Uzzah, and God smote him there for his rashness; [marginal reading] and there he died by the ark of God." A sudden terror fell upon the rejoicing throng. David was astonished and greatly alarmed, and in his heart he questioned the justice of God. He had been seeking to honor the ark as the symbol of the divine presence. Why, then, had that fearful judgment been sent to turn the season of gladness into an occasion of grief and mourning? Feeling that it would be unsafe to have the ark near him, David determined to let it remain where it was. A place was found for it nearby, at the house of Obed-edom the Gittite.

The fate of Uzzah was a divine judgment upon the violation of a most explicit command. Through Moses the Lord had given special instruction concerning the transportation of the ark. None but the priests, the descendants of Aaron, were to touch it, or even to look upon it uncovered. The divine direction was, "The sons of Kohath shall come to bear it: but they shall not touch any holy thing, lest they die." Numbers 4:15. The priests were to cover the ark, and then the Kohathites must lift it by the staves, which were placed in rings upon each side of the ark and were never removed. To the Gershonites and Merarites, who had in charge the curtains and boards and pillars of the tabernacle, Moses gave carts and oxen for the transportation of that which was committed to them. "But unto the sons of Kohath he gave none: because the service of the sanctuary belonging unto them was that they should bear *upon their shoulders*." Numbers 7:9. Thus in the bringing of the ark from Kirjath-jearim there had been a direct and inexcusable disregard of the Lord's directions.

David and his people had assembled to perform a sacred work, and they had engaged in it with glad and willing hearts; but the

Lord could not accept the service, because it was not performed in accordance with His directions. The Philistines, who had not a knowledge of God's law, had placed the ark upon a cart when they returned it to Israel, and the Lord accepted the effort which they made. But the Israelites had in their hands a plain statement of the will of God in all these matters, and their neglect of these instructions was dishonoring to God. Upon Uzzah rested the greater guilt of presumption. Transgression of God's law had lessened his sense of its sacredness, and with unconfessed sins upon him he had, in face of the divine prohibition, presumed to touch the symbol of God's presence. God can accept no partial obedience, no lax way of treating His commandments. By the judgment upon Uzzah He designed to impress upon all Israel the importance of giving strict heed to His requirements. Thus the death of that one man, by leading the people to repentance, might prevent the necessity of inflicting judgments upon thousands.

Feeling that his own heart was not wholly right with God, David, seeing the stroke upon Uzzah, had feared the ark, lest some sin on his part should bring judgments upon him. But Obed-edom, though he rejoiced with trembling, welcomed the sacred symbol as the pledge of God's favor to the obedient. The attention of all Israel was now directed to the Gittite and his household; all watched to see how it would fare with them. "And the Lord blessed Obed-edom, and all his household."

Upon David the divine rebuke accomplished its work. He was led to realize as he had never realized before the sacredness of the law of God and the necessity of strict obedience. The favor shown to the house of Obed-edom led David again to hope that the ark might bring a blessing to him and to his people.

At the end of three months he resolved to make another attempt to remove the ark, and he now gave earnest heed to carry out in every particular the directions of the Lord. Again the chief men of the nation were summoned, and a vast assemblage gathered about the dwelling place of the Gittite. With reverent care the ark was now placed upon the shoulders of men of divine appointment, the multitude fell into line, and with trembling hearts the vast procession again set forth. After advancing six paces the trumpet sounded a halt. By David's direction sacrifices of "oxen and fatlings" were to be offered. Rejoicing now took the place of trembling and terror. The king had laid aside his royal robes and had attired himself in a plain linen ephod, such as was worn by the priests. He did not by this act signify that he assumed priestly functions, for the ephod was sometimes worn by others besides the priests. But in this holy service he would take his place as, before God, on an equality with his subjects. Upon that day Jehovah was to be adored. He was to be the sole object of reverence.

Again the long train was in motion, and the music of harp and cornet, trumpet and cymbal, floated heavenward, blended with the melody of many voices. "And David danced before the Lord," in his gladness keeping time to the measure of the song.

David's dancing in reverent joy before God has been cited by pleasure lovers in justification of the fashionable modern dance, but there is no ground for such an argument. In our day dancing is associated with folly and midnight reveling. Health and morals are sacrificed to pleasure. By the frequenters of the ballroom God is not an object of thought and reverence; prayer or the song of praise would be felt to be out of place in their assemblies. This test should be decisive. Amusements that have a tendency to weaken the love for sacred things and lessen our joy in the service of God are not to be sought by Christians. The music and dancing in joyful praise to God at the removal of the ark had not the faintest resemblance to the dissipation of modern dancing. The one tended to the remembrance of God and exalted His holy name. The other is a device of Satan to cause men to forget God and to dishonor Him.

The triumphal procession approached the capital, following the sacred symbol of their invisible King. Then a burst of song demanded of the watchers upon the walls that the gates of the Holy City should be thrown open:

> "Lift up your heads, O ye gates;
> And be ye lift up, ye everlasting doors;
> And the King of glory shall come in."

A band of singers and players answered:

> "Who is this King of glory?"

From another company came the response:

"The Lord strong and mighty,
　The Lord mighty in battle."

Then hundreds of voices, uniting, swelled the triumphal chorus:

"Lift up your heads, O ye gates;
　Even lift them up, ye everlasting doors;
And the King of glory shall come in."

Again the joyful interrogation was heard, "Who is this King of glory?" And the voice of the great multitude, like "the sound of many waters," was heard in the rapturous reply:

"The Lord of hosts,
　He is the King of glory." Psalm 24:7-10.

Then the gates were opened wide, the procession entered, and with reverent awe the ark was deposited in the tent that had been prepared for its reception. Before the sacred enclosure altars for sacrifice were erected; the smoke of peace offerings and burnt offerings, and the clouds of incense, with the praises and supplications of Israel, ascended to heaven. The service ended, the king himself pronounced a benediction upon his people. Then with regal bounty he caused gifts of food and wine to be distributed for their refreshment.

All the tribes had been represented in this service, the celebration of the most sacred event that had yet marked the reign of David. The Spirit of divine inspiration had rested upon the king, and now as the last beams of the setting sun bathed the tabernacle in a hallowed light, his heart was uplifted in gratitude to God that the blessed symbol of His presence was now so near the throne of Israel.

Thus musing, David turned toward his palace, "to bless his household." But there was one who had witnessed the scene of rejoicing with a spirit widely different from that which moved the heart of David. "As the ark of the Lord came into the city of David, Michal Saul's daughter looked through a window, and saw King David leaping and dancing before the Lord; and she despised him in her heart." In the bitterness of her passion she could not await

David's return to the palace, but went out to meet him, and to his kindly greeting poured forth a torrent of bitter words. Keen and cutting was the irony of her speech:

"How glorious was the king of Israel today, who uncovered himself today in the eyes of the handmaids of his servants, as one of the vain fellows shamelessly uncovereth himself!"

David felt that it was the service of God which Michal had despised and dishonored, and he sternly answered: "It was before the Lord, which chose me before thy father, and before all his house, to appoint me ruler over the people of the Lord, over Israel: therefore will I play before the Lord. And I will yet be more vile than thus, and will be base in mine own sight: and of the maidservants which thou hast spoken of, of them shall I be had in honor." To David's rebuke was added that of the Lord: because of her pride and arrogance, Michal "had no child unto the day of her death."

The solemn ceremonies attending the removal of the ark had made a lasting impression upon the people of Israel, arousing a deeper interest in the sanctuary service and kindling anew their zeal for Jehovah. David endeavored by every means in his power to deepen these impressions. The service of song was made a regular part of religious worship, and David composed psalms, not only for the use of the priests in the sanctuary service, but also to be sung by the people in their journeys to the national altar at the annual feasts. The influence thus exerted was far-reaching, and it resulted in freeing the nation from idolatry. Many of the surrounding peoples, beholding the prosperity of Israel, were led to think favorably of Israel's God, who had done such great things for His people.

The tabernacle built by Moses, with all that appertained to the sanctuary service, except the ark, was still at Gibeah. It was David's purpose to make Jerusalem the religious center of the nation. He had erected a palace for himself, and he felt that it was not fitting for the ark of God to rest within a tent. He determined to build for it a temple of such magnificence as should express Israel's appreciation of the honor granted the nation in the abiding presence of Jehovah their King. Communicating his purpose to the prophet Nathan, he received the encouraging response, "Do all that is in thine heart; for the Lord is with thee."

But that same night the word of the Lord came to Nathan, giving him a message for the king. David was to be deprived of the privilege of building a house for God, but he was granted an assurance of the divine favor to him, to his posterity, and to the kingdom of Israel: "Thus saith Jehovah of hosts; I took thee from the sheepcote, from following the sheep, to be ruler over My people, over Israel; and I was with thee whithersoever thou wentest, and have cut off all thine enemies out of thy sight, and have made thee a great name, like unto the name of the great men that are in the earth. Moreover I will appoint a place for My people Israel, and will plant them, that they may dwell in a place of their own, and move no more; neither shall the children of wickedness afflict them any more, as beforetime."

As David had desired to build a house for God, the promise was given. "The Lord telleth thee that He will make thee a house.... I will set up thy seed after thee.... He shall build a house for My name, and I will stablish the throne of his kingdom forever."

The reason why David was not to build the temple was declared: "Thou hast shed blood abundantly, and hast made great wars: thou shalt not build a house unto My name.... Behold, a son shall be born to thee, who shall be a man of rest; and I will give him rest from all his enemies: ... his name shall be Solomon [peaceable], and I will give peace and quietness unto Israel in his days. He shall build a house for My name." 1 Chronicles 22:8-10.

Though the cherished purpose of his heart had been denied, David received the message with gratitude. "Who am I, O Lord God?" he exclaimed, "and what is my house, that Thou hast brought me hitherto? And this was yet a small thing in Thy sight, O Lord God; but Thou hast spoken also of Thy servant's house for a great while to come;" and he then renewed his covenant with God.

David knew that it would be an honor to his name and would bring glory to his government to perform the work that he had purposed in his heart to do, but he was ready to submit his will to the will of God. The grateful resignation thus manifested is rarely seen, even among Christians. How often do those who have passed the strength of manhood cling to the hope of accomplishing some great work upon which their hearts are set, but which they are unfitted to perform! God's providence may speak to them, as did His prophet to David, declaring that the work which they so much desire is not committed to them. It is theirs to prepare the way for another to accomplish it. But instead of gratefully submitting to the divine direction, many fall back as if slighted and rejected, feeling that if they cannot do the one thing which they desire to do, they will do nothing. Many cling with desperate energy to responsibilities which they are incapable of bearing, and vainly endeavor to accomplish a work for which they are insufficient, while that which they might do, lies neglected. And because of this lack of co-operation on their part the greater work is hindered or frustrated.

David, in his covenant with Jonathan, had promised that when he should have rest from his enemies he would show kindness to the house of Saul. In his prosperity, mindful of this covenant, the king made inquiry, "Is there yet any that is left of the house of Saul, that I may show him kindness for Jonathan's sake?" He was told of a son of Jonathan, Mephibosheth, who had been lame from childhood. At the time of Saul's defeat by the Philistines at Jezreel, the nurse of this child, attempting to flee with him, had let him fall, thus making him a lifelong cripple. David now summoned the young man to court and received him with great kindness. The private possessions of Saul were restored to him for the support of his household; but the son of Jonathan was himself to be the constant guest of the king, sitting daily at the royal table. Through reports from the enemies of David, Mephibosheth had been led to cherish a strong prejudice against him as a usurper; but the monarch's generous and courteous reception of him and his continued kindness won the heart of the young man; he became strongly attached to David, and, like his father Jonathan, he felt that his interest was one with that of the king whom God had chosen.

After David's establishment upon the throne of Israel the nation enjoyed a long interval of peace. The surrounding peoples, seeing the strength and unity of the kingdom, soon thought it prudent to desist from open hostilities; and David, occupied with the organization and upbuilding of his kingdom, refrained from aggressive war. At last, however, he made war upon Israel's old enemies, the Philistines, and upon the Moabites, and succeeded in overcoming both and making them tributary.

Then there was formed against the kingdom of David a vast coalition of the surrounding nations, out of which grew the greatest wars and victories of his reign and the most extensive accessions to his power. This hostile alliance, which really sprang from jealousy of David's increasing power, had been wholly unprovoked by him. The circumstances that led to its rise were these:

Tidings were received at Jerusalem announcing the death of Nahash, king of the Ammonites—a monarch who had shown kindness to David when he was a fugitive from the rage of Saul. Now, desiring to express his grateful appreciation of the favor shown him in his distress, David sent ambassadors with a message of sympathy to Hanun, the son and successor of the Ammonite king. "Said David, I will show kindness unto Hanun the son of Nahash, as his father showed kindness unto me."

But his courteous act was misinterpreted. The Ammonites hated the true God and were the bitter enemies of Israel. The apparent kindness of Nahash to David had been prompted wholly by hostility to Saul as king of Israel. The message of David was misconstrued by Hanun's counselors. They "said unto Hanun their lord, Thinkest thou that David doth honor thy father, that he hath sent comforters unto thee? hath not David rather sent his servants unto thee, to search the city, and to spy it out, and to overthrow it?" It was by the advice of his counselors that Nahash, half a century before, had been led to make the cruel condition required of the people of Jabesh-gilead, when, besieged by the Ammonites, they sued for a covenant of peace. Nahash had demanded the privilege of thrusting out all their right eyes. The Ammonites still vividly remembered how the king of Israel had foiled their cruel design, and had rescued the people whom they would have humbled and mutilated. The same hatred of Israel still prompted them. They could have no conception of the generous spirit that had inspired David's message. When Satan controls the minds of men he will excite envy and suspicion which will misconstrue the very best intentions. Listening to his counselors, Hanun regarded David's messengers as spies, and loaded them with scorn and insult.

The Ammonites had been permitted to carry out the evil purposes of their hearts without restraint, that their real character might be revealed to David. It was not God's will that Israel should enter into a league with this treacherous heathen people.

In ancient times, as now, the office of ambassador was held sacred. By the universal law of nations it ensured protection from personal violence or insult. The ambassador standing as a representative of his sovereign, any indignity offered to him demanded prompt retaliation. The Ammonites, knowing that the insult offered to Israel would surely be avenged, made preparation for war. "When the children of Ammon saw that they had made themselves odious to David, Hanun and the children of Ammon sent a thousand talents of silver to hire them chariots and horsemen out of Mesopotamia, and out of Syria-maachah, and out of Zobah. So they hired thirty and two thousand chariots.... And the children of Ammon gathered themselves together from their cities, and came to battle." 1 Chronicles 19:6, 7.

[715]

It was indeed a formidable alliance. The inhabitants of the region lying between the river Euphrates and the Mediterranean Sea had leagued with the Ammonites. The north and east of Canaan was encircled with armed foes, banded together to crush the kingdom of Israel.

The Hebrews did not wait for the invasion of their country. Their forces, under Joab, crossed the Jordan and advanced toward the Ammonite capital. As the Hebrew captain led his army to the field he sought to inspire them for the conflict, saying, "Be of good courage, and let us behave ourselves valiantly for our people, and for the cities of our God: and let the Lord do that which is good in His sight." 1 Chronicles 19:13. The united forces of the allies were overcome in the first engagement. But they were not yet willing to give over the contest, and the next year renewed the war. The king of Syria gathered his forces, threatening Israel with an immense army. David, realizing how much dependent upon the result of this contest, took the field in person, and by the blessing of God inflicted upon the allies a defeat so disastrous that the Syrians, from Lebanon to the Euphrates, not only gave up the war, but became tributary to Israel. Against the Ammonites David pushed the war with vigor, until their strongholds fell and the whole region came under the dominion of Israel.

The dangers which had threatened the nation with utter destruction proved, through the providence of God, to be the very means by which it rose to unprecedented greatness. In commemorating his remarkable deliverances, David sings:

"The Lord liveth; and blessed be my rock; and exalted be the
    God of my salvation:
Even the God that executeth vengeance for me, and subdueth
    peoples under me.
He rescueth me from mine enemies:
    Yea, Thou liftest me up above them that rise up against me:
Thou deliverest me from the violent man.
    Therefore I will give thanks unto Thee, O Lord, among the
nations,
    And will sing praises unto Thy name.
Great deliverance giveth He to His king;
    And sheweth loving-kindness to His anointed,
To David and to his seed, forevermore."

Psalm 18:46-50, R.V.

And throughout the songs of David the thought was impressed on his people that Jehovah was their strength and deliverer:

"There is no king saved by the multitude of a host:
    A mighty man is not delivered by much strength.
A horse is a vain thing for safety:
    Neither shall he deliver any by his great strength."

Psalm 33:16, 17.

"Thou art my King, O God:
    Command deliverances for Jacob.
Through Thee will we push down our enemies:
    Through Thy name will we tread them under that rise up
against us.
    For I will not trust in my bow,
Neither shall my sword save me.
    But Thou hast saved us from our enemies,
And hast put them to shame that hated us." Psalm 44:4-7.

"Some trust in chariots, and some in horses:
But we will remember the name of Jehovah our God."

Psalm 20:7.

The kingdom of Israel had now reached in extent the fulfillment of the promise given to Abraham, and afterward repeated to Moses: "Unto thy seed have I given this land, from the river of Egypt unto the great river, the river Euphrates." Genesis 15:18. Israel had become a mighty nation, respected and feared by surrounding peoples. In his own realm David's power had become very great. He commanded, as few sovereigns in any age have been able to command, the affections and allegiance of his people. He had honored God, and God was now honoring him.

But in the midst of prosperity lurked danger. In the time of his greatest outward triumph David was in the greatest peril, and met his most humiliating defeat.

Chapter 71—David's Sin and Repentance

This chapter is based on 2 Samuel 11; 12.

The Bible has little to say in praise of men. Little space is given to recounting the virtues of even the best men who have ever lived. This silence is not without purpose; it is not without a lesson. All the good qualities that men possess are the gift of God; their good deeds are performed by the grace of God through Christ. Since they owe all to God the glory of whatever they are or do belongs to Him alone; they are but instruments in His hands. More than this—as all the lessons of Bible history teach—it is a perilous thing to praise or exalt men; for if one comes to lose sight of his entire dependence on God, and to trust to his own strength, he is sure to fall. Man is contending with foes who are stronger than he. "We wrestle not against flesh and blood, but against principalities, against powers, against the rulers of the darkness of this world, against wicked spirits in high places." Ephesians 6:12, margin. It is impossible for us in our own strength to maintain the conflict; and whatever diverts the mind from God, whatever leads to self-exaltation or to self-dependence, is surely preparing the way for our overthrow. The tenor of the Bible is to inculcate distrust of human power and to encourage trust in divine power.

It was the spirit of self-confidence and self-exaltation that prepared the way for David's fall. Flattery and the subtle allurements of power and luxury were not without effect upon him. Intercourse with surrounding nations also exerted an influence for evil. According to the customs prevailing among Eastern rulers, crimes not to be tolerated in subjects were uncondemned in the king; the monarch was not under obligation to exercise the same self-restraint as the subject. All this tended to lessen David's sense of the exceeding sinfulness of sin. And instead of relying in humility upon the power of Jehovah, he began to trust to his own wisdom and might. As soon as Satan can separate the soul from God, the only Source of strength, he will seek to arouse the unholy desires of man's carnal nature. The work of the enemy is not abrupt; it is not, at the outset, sudden and startling; it is a secret undermining of the strongholds of principle. It begins in apparently small things—the neglect to be true to God and to rely upon Him wholly, the disposition to follow the customs and practices of the world.

Before the conclusion of the war with the Ammonites, David, leaving the conduct of the army to Joab, returned to Jerusalem. The Syrians had already submitted to Israel, and the complete overthrow of the Ammonites appeared certain. David was surrounded by the fruits of victory and the honors of his wise and able rule. It was now, while he was at ease and unguarded, that the tempter seized the opportunity to occupy his mind. The fact that God had taken David into so close connection with Himself and had manifested so great favor toward him, should have been to him the strongest of incentives to preserve his character unblemished. But when in ease and self-security he let go his hold upon God, David yielded to Satan and brought upon his soul the stain of guilt. He, the Heaven-appointed leader of the nation, chosen by God to execute His law, himself trampled upon its precepts. He who should have been a terror to evildoers, by his own act strengthened their hands.

Amid the perils of his earlier life David in conscious integrity could trust his case with God. The Lord's hand had guided him safely past the unnumbered snares that had been laid for his feet. But now, guilty and unrepentant, he did not ask help and guidance from Heaven, but sought to extricate himself from the dangers in which sin had involved him. Bathsheba, whose fatal beauty had proved a snare to the king, was the wife of Uriah the Hittite, one of David's bravest and most faithful officers. None could foresee what would be the result should the crime become known. The law of God pronounced the adulterer guilty of death, and the proud-spirited soldier, so shamefully wronged, might avenge himself by taking the life of the king or by exciting the nation to revolt.

Every effort which David made to conceal his guilt proved unavailing. He had betrayed himself into the power of Satan; danger surrounded him, dishonor more bitter than death was before him. There appeared but one way of escape, and in his desperation he was hurried on to add murder to adultery. He who had compassed the destruction of Saul was seeking to lead David also to ruin. Though the temptations were different, they were alike in leading to transgression of God's law. David reasoned that if Uriah were slain by the hand of enemies in battle, the guilt of his death could not be traced home to the king, Bathsheba would be free to become David's wife, suspicion could be averted, and the royal honor would be maintained.

Uriah was made the bearer of his own death warrant. A letter sent by his hand to Joab from the king commanded, "Set ye Uriah in the forefront of the hottest battle, and retire ye from him, that he may be smitten, and die." Joab, already stained with the guilt of one wanton murder, did not hesitate to obey the king's instructions, and Uriah fell by the sword of the children of Ammon.

Heretofore David's record as a ruler had been such as few monarchs have ever equaled. It is written of him that he "executed judgment and justice unto all his people." 2 Samuel 8:15. His integrity had won the confidence and fealty of the nation. But as he departed from God and yielded himself to the wicked one, he became for the time the agent of Satan; yet he still held the position and authority that God had given him, and because of this, claimed obedience that would imperil the soul of him who should yield it. And Joab, whose allegiance had been given to the king rather than to God, transgressed God's law because the king commanded it.

David's power had been given him by God, but to be exercised only in harmony with the divine law. When he commanded that which was contrary to God's law, it became sin to obey. "The powers that be are ordained of God" (Romans 13:1), but we are not to obey them contrary to God's law. The apostle Paul, writing to the Corinthians, sets forth the principle by which we should be governed. He says, "Be ye followers of me, even as I also am of Christ." 1 Corinthians 11:1.

An account of the execution of his order was sent to David, but so carefully worded as not to implicate either Joab or the king. Joab "charged the messenger saying, When thou hast made an end of telling the matters of the war unto the king, and if so be that the king's wrath arise, ... then say thou, Thy servant Uriah the Hittite is dead also. So the messenger went, and came and showed David all that Joab had sent him for."

The king's answer was, "Thus shalt thou say unto Joab, Let not this thing displease thee, for the sword devoureth one as well as another: make thy battle more strong against the city, and overthrow it: and encourage thou him."

Bathsheba observed the customary days of mourning for her husband; and at their close "David sent and fetched her to his house, and she became his wife." He whose tender conscience and high sense of honor would not permit him, even when in peril of his life, to put forth his hand against the Lord's anointed, had so fallen that he could wrong and murder one of his most faithful and most valiant soldiers, and hope to enjoy undisturbed the reward of his sin. Alas! how had the fine gold become dim! how had the most fine gold changed!

From the beginning Satan has portrayed to men the gains to be won by transgression. Thus he seduced angels. Thus he tempted Adam and Eve to sin. And thus he is still leading multitudes away from obedience to God. The path of transgression is made to appear desirable; "but the end thereof are the ways of death." Proverbs 14:12. Happy they who, having ventured in this way, learn how bitter are the fruits of sin, and turn from it betimes. God in His mercy did not leave David to be lured to utter ruin by the deceitful rewards of sin.

For the sake of Israel also there was a necessity for God to interpose. As time passed on, David's sin toward Bathsheba became known, and suspicion was excited that he had planned the death of Uriah. The Lord was dishonored. He had favored and exalted David, and David's sin misrepresented the character of God and cast reproach upon His name. It tended to lower the standard of godliness in Israel, to lessen in many minds the abhorrence of sin; while those who did not love and fear God were by it emboldened in transgression.

Nathan the prophet was bidden to bear a message of reproof to David. It was a message terrible in its severity. To few sovereigns could such a reproof be given but at the price of certain death to the reprover. Nathan delivered the divine sentence unflinchingly, yet with such heaven-born wisdom as to engage the sympathies of the king, to arouse his conscience, and to call from his lips the sentence of death upon himself. Appealing to David as the divinely appointed guardian of his people's rights, the prophet repeated a story of wrong and oppression that demanded redress.

"There were two men in one city," he said, "the one rich, and the other poor. The rich man had exceeding many flocks and herds: but the poor man had nothing, save one little ewe lamb, which he had bought and nourished up: and it grew up together with him, and with his children; it did eat of his own meat, and drank of his own cup, and lay in his bosom, and was unto him as a daughter. And there came a traveler unto the rich man, and he spared to take of his own flock and of his own herd, to dress for the wayfaring man that was come unto him; but took the poor man's lamb, and dressed it for the man that was come to him."

The anger of the king was roused, and he exclaimed, "As the Lord liveth, the man that hath done this thing is worthy to die. And he shall restore the lamb fourfold, because he did this thing, and because he had no pity." 2 Samuel 12:5, 6, margin.

Nathan fixed his eyes upon the king; then, lifting his right hand to heaven, he solemnly declared, "Thou art the man." "Wherefore," he continued, "hast thou despised the commandment of the Lord, to do evil in His sight?" The guilty may attempt, as David had done, to conceal their crime from men; they may seek to bury the evil deed forever from human sight or knowledge; but "all things are naked and opened unto the eyes of Him with whom we have to do." Hebrews 4:13. "There is nothing covered, that shall not be revealed; and hid, that shall not be known." Matthew 10:26.

Nathan declared: "Thus saith the Lord God of Israel, I anointed thee king over Israel, and I delivered thee out of the hand of Saul.... Wherefore hast thou despised the commandment of the Lord, to do evil in His sight? thou hast killed Uriah the Hittite with the sword, and hast taken his wife to be thy wife, and hast slain him with the sword of the children of Ammon. Now therefore the sword shall never depart from thine house.... Behold, I will raise up evil against thee out of thine own house, and I will take thy wives before thine eyes, and give them unto thy neighbor.... For thou didst it secretly; but I will do this thing before all Israel, and before the sun."

The prophet's rebuke touched the heart of David; conscience was aroused; his guilt appeared in all its enormity. His soul was bowed in penitence before God. With trembling lips he said, "I have sinned against the Lord." All wrong done to others reaches back from the injured one to God. David had committed a grievous sin, toward both Uriah and Bathsheba, and he keenly felt this. But infinitely greater was his sin against God.

Though there would be found none in Israel to execute the sentence of death upon the anointed of the Lord, David trembled, lest, guilty and unforgiven, he should be cut down by the swift judgment of God. But the message was sent him by the prophet, "The Lord also hath put away thy sin; thou shalt not die." Yet justice must be maintained. The sentence of death was transferred from David to the child of his sin. Thus the king was given opportunity for repentance; while to him the suffering and death of the child, as a part of his punishment, was far more bitter than his own death could have been. The prophet said, "Because by this deed thou hast given great occasion to the enemies of the Lord to blaspheme, the child also that is born unto thee shall surely die."

When his child was stricken, David, with fasting and deep humiliation, pleaded for its life. He put off his royal robes, he laid aside his crown, and night after night he lay upon the earth, in heartbroken grief interceding for the innocent one suffering for his guilt. "The elders of his house arose, and went to him, to raise him up from the earth: but he would not." Often when judgments had been pronounced upon persons or cities, humiliation and repentance had turned aside the blow, and the Ever-Merciful, swift to pardon, had sent messengers of peace. Encouraged by this thought, David persevered in his supplication so long as the child was spared. Upon learning that it was dead, he quietly submitted to the decree of God. The first stroke had fallen of that retribution which he himself had declared just; but David, trusting in God's mercy, was not without comfort.

Very many, reading the history of David's fall, have inquired, "Why has this record been made public? Why did God see fit to throw open to the world this dark passage in the life of one so highly honored of Heaven?" The prophet, in his reproof to David, had declared concerning his sin, "By this deed thou hast given great occasion to the enemies of the Lord to blaspheme." Through successive generations infidels have pointed to the character of David, bearing this dark stain, and have exclaimed in triumph and derision,

[723]

"This is the man after God's own heart!" Thus a reproach has been brought upon religion, God and His word have been blasphemed, souls have been hardened in unbelief, and many, under a cloak of piety, have become bold in sin.

But the history of David furnishes no countenance to sin. It was when he was walking in the counsel of God that he was called a man after God's own heart. When he sinned, this ceased to be true of him until by repentance he had returned to the Lord. The word of God plainly declares, "The thing that David had done was evil in the eyes of the Lord." 2 Samuel 11:27, margin. And the Lord said to David by the prophet, "Wherefore hast thou despised the commandment of the Lord, to do evil in His sight? ... Now therefore the sword shall never depart from thine house; because thou hast despised Me." Though David repented of his sin and was forgiven and accepted by the Lord, he reaped the baleful harvest of the seed he himself had sown. The judgments upon him and upon his house testify to God's abhorrence of the sin.

Heretofore God's providence had preserved David against all the plottings of his enemies, and had been directly exercised to restrain Saul. But David's transgression had changed his relation to God. The Lord could not in any wise sanction iniquity. He could not exercise His power to protect David from the results of his sin as He had protected him from the enmity of Saul.

There was a great change in David himself. He was broken in spirit by the consciousness of his sin and its far-reaching results. He felt humbled in the eyes of his subjects. His influence was weakened. Hitherto his prosperity had been attributed to his conscientious obedience to the commandments of the Lord. But now his subjects, having a knowledge of his sin, would be led to sin more freely. His authority in his own household, his claim to respect and obedience from his sons, was weakened. A sense of his guilt kept him silent when he should have condemned sin; it made his arm feeble to execute justice in his house. His evil example exerted its influence upon his sons, and God would not interpose to prevent the result. He would permit things to take their natural course, and thus David was severely chastised.

For a whole year after his fall David lived in apparent security; there was no outward evidence of God's displeasure. But the divine sentence was hanging over him. Swiftly and surely a day of judgment and retribution was approaching, which no repentance could avert, agony and shame that would darken his whole earthly life. Those who, by pointing to the example of David, try to lessen the guilt of their own sins, should learn from the Bible record that the way of transgression is hard. Though like David they should turn from their evil course, the results of sin, even in this life, will be found bitter and hard to bear.

God intended the history of David's fall to serve as a warning that even those whom He has greatly blessed and favored are not to feel secure and neglect watchfulness and prayer. And thus it has proved to those who in humility have sought to learn the lesson that God designed to teach. From generation to generation thousands have thus been led to realize their own danger from the tempter's power. The fall of David, one so greatly honored by the Lord, has awakened in them distrust of self. They have felt that God alone could keep them by His power through faith. Knowing that in Him was their strength and safety, they have feared to take the first step on Satan's ground.

Even before the divine sentence was pronounced against David he had begun to reap the fruit of transgression. His conscience was not at rest. The agony of spirit which he then endured is brought to view in the thirty-second psalm. He says:

> "Blessed is he whose transgression is forgiven, whose sin is covered.
> Blessed is the man unto whom the Lord imputeth not iniquity,
> And in whose spirit there is no guile.
> When I kept silence, my bones waxed old
> Through my roaring all the day long.
> For day and night Thy hand was heavy upon me:
> My moisture was changed as with the drought of summer."
>
> Psalm 32:1-4, R.V.

And the fifty-first psalm is an expression of David's repentance, when the message of reproof came to him from God:

> "Have mercy upon me, O God, according to Thy loving-kindness:

According unto the multitude of Thy tender mercies blot out my transgressions.

Wash me throughly from mine iniquity, and cleanse me from my sin.

For I acknowledge my transgressions: and my sin is ever before me....

Purge me with hyssop, and I shall be clean: wash me, and I shall be whiter than snow.

Make me to hear joy and gladness;
That the bones which Thou hast broken may rejoice.

Hide Thy face from my sins,
And blot out all mine iniquities.

Create in me a clean heart, O God;
And renew a right spirit within me.

Cast me not away from Thy presence;
And take not Thy Holy Spirit from me.

Restore unto me the joy of Thy salvation;
And uphold me with Thy free Spirit.

Then will I teach transgressors Thy ways;
And sinners shall be converted unto Thee.

Deliver me from bloodguiltiness, O God, Thou God of my salvation:

And my tongue shall sing aloud of Thy righteousness."

Psalm 51:1-14.

Thus in a sacred song to be sung in the public assemblies of his people, in the presence of the court—priests and judges, princes and men of war—and which would preserve to the latest generation the knowledge of his fall, the king of Israel recounted his sin, his repentance, and his hope of pardon through the mercy of God. Instead of endeavoring to conceal his guilt he desired that others might be instructed by the sad history of his fall.

David's repentance was sincere and deep. There was no effort to palliate his crime. No desire to escape the judgments threatened, inspired his prayer. But he saw the enormity of his transgression against God; he saw the defilement of his soul; he loathed his sin. It was not for pardon only that he prayed, but for purity of heart. David did not in despair give over the struggle. In the promises of God to repentant sinners he saw the evidence of his pardon and acceptance.

> "For Thou desirest not sacrifice; else would I give it:
>   Thou delightest not in burnt offering.
> The sacrifices of God are a broken spirit:
>   A broken and a contrite heart, O God, Thou wilt not despise."
>
> Psalm 51:16, 17.

Though David had fallen, the Lord lifted him up. He was now more fully in harmony with God and in sympathy with his fellow men than before he fell. In the joy of his release he sang:

> "I acknowledged my sin unto Thee, and mine iniquity have I not hid.
> I said, I will confess my transgressions unto the Lord;
>   And Thou forgavest the iniquity of my sin....
> Thou art my hiding place; Thou shalt preserve me from trouble;
> Thou shalt compass me about with songs of deliverance."
>
> Psalm 32:5-7.

Many have murmured at what they called God's injustice in sparing David, whose guilt was so great, after having rejected Saul for what appear to them to be far less flagrant sins. But David humbled himself and confessed his sin, while Saul despised reproof and hardened his heart in impenitence.

This passage in David's history is full of significance to the repenting sinner. It is one of the most forcible illustrations given us of the struggles and temptations of humanity, and of genuine repentance toward God and faith in our Lord Jesus Christ. Through all the ages it has proved a source of encouragement to souls that, having fallen into sin, were struggling under the burden of their guilt. Thousands of the children of God, who have been betrayed into sin, when ready to give up to despair have remembered how David's sincere repentance and confession were accepted by God, notwithstanding he suffered for his transgression; and they also have taken courage to repent and try again to walk in the way of God's commandments.

Whoever under the reproof of God will humble the soul with confession and repentance, as did David, may be sure that there is hope for him. Whoever will in faith accept God's promises, will find pardon. The Lord will never cast away one truly repentant soul. He has given this promise: "Let him take hold of My strength, that he may make peace with Me; and he shall make peace with Me." Isaiah 27:5. "Let the wicked forsake his way, and the unrighteous man his thoughts: and let him return unto the Lord, and He will have mercy upon him; and to our God, for He will *abundantly* pardon." Isaiah 55:7.

Chapter 72—The Rebellion of Absalom

This chapter is based on 2 Samuel 13-19.

"He shall restore fourfold," had been David's unwitting sentence upon himself, on listening to the prophet Nathan's parable; and according to his own sentence he was to be judged. Four of his sons must fall, and the loss of each would be a result of the father's sin.

The shameful crime of Amnon, the first-born, was permitted by David to pass unpunished and unrebuked. The law pronounced death upon the adulterer, and the unnatural crime of Amnon made him doubly guilty. But David, self-condemned for his own sin, failed to bring the offender to justice. For two full years Absalom, the natural protector of the sister so foully wronged, concealed his purpose of revenge, but only to strike more surely at the last. At a feast of the king's sons the drunken, incestuous Amnon was slain by his brother's command.

Twofold judgment had been meted out to David. The terrible message was carried to him, "Absalom hath slain all the king's sons, and there is not one of them left. Then the king arose, and tare his garments, and lay on the earth; and all his servants stood by with their clothes rent." The king's sons, returning in alarm to Jerusalem, revealed to their father the truth; Amnon alone had been slain; and they "lifted up their voice and wept: and the king also and all his servants wept very sore." But Absalom fled to Talmai, the king of Geshur, his mother's father.

Like other sons of David, Amnon had been left to selfish indulgence. He had sought to gratify every thought of his heart, regardless of the requirements of God. Notwithstanding his great sin, God had borne long with him. For two years he had been granted opportunity for repentance; but he continued in sin, and with his guilt upon him, he was cut down by death, to await the awful tribunal of the judgment.

David had neglected the duty of punishing the crime of Amnon, and because of the unfaithfulness of the king and father and the impenitence of the son, the Lord permitted events to take their natural course, and did not restrain Absalom. When parents or rulers neglect the duty of punishing iniquity, God Himself will take the case in hand. His restraining power will be in a measure removed from the agencies of evil, so that a train of circumstances will arise which will punish sin with sin.

The evil results of David's unjust indulgence toward Amnon were not ended, for it was here that Absalom's alienation from his father began. After he fled to Geshur, David, feeling that the crime of his son demanded some punishment, refused him permission to return. And this had a tendency to increase rather than to lessen the inextricable evils in which the king had come to be involved. Absalom, energetic, ambitious, and unprincipled, shut out by his exile from participation in the affairs of the kingdom, soon gave himself up to dangerous scheming.

At the close of two years Joab determined to effect a reconciliation between the father and his son. And with this object in view he secured the services of a woman of Tekoah, reputed for wisdom. Instructed by Joab, the woman represented herself to David as a widow whose two sons had been her only comfort and support. In a quarrel one of these had slain the other, and now all the relatives of the family demanded that the survivor should be given up to the avenger of blood. "And so," said the mother, "they shall quench my coal which is left, and shall not leave to my husband neither name nor remainder upon the earth." The king's feelings were touched by this appeal, and he assured the woman of the royal protection for her son.

After drawing from him repeated promises for the young man's safety, she entreated the king's forbearance, declaring that he had spoken as one at fault, in that he did not fetch home again his banished. "For," she said, "we must needs die, and are as water spilt on the ground, which cannot be gathered up again; neither doth God respect any person; yet doth *He devise means, that His banished be not expelled from Him.*" This tender and touching portrayal of the love of God toward the sinner—coming as it did from Joab, the rude soldier—is a striking evidence of the familiarity of the Israelites with the great truths of redemption. The king, feeling his own need of God's mercy, could not resist this appeal. To Joab the command was given, "Go therefore, bring the young man Absalom again."

Absalom was permitted to return to Jerusalem, but not to appear at court or to meet his father. David had begun to see the evil effects of his indulgence toward his children; and tenderly as he loved this beautiful and gifted son, he felt it necessary, as a lesson both to Absalom and to the people, that abhorrence for such a crime should be manifested. Absalom lived two years in his own house, but banished from the court. His sister dwelt with him, and her presence kept alive the memory of the irreparable wrong she had suffered. In the popular estimation the prince was a hero rather than an offender. And having this advantage, he set himself to gain the hearts of the people. His personal appearance was such as to win the admiration of all beholders. "In all Israel there was none to be so much praised as Absalom for his beauty: from the sole of his foot even to the crown of his head there was no blemish in him." It was not wise for the king to leave a man of Absalom's character—ambitious, impulsive, and passionate—to brood for two years over supposed grievances. And David's action in permitting him to return to Jerusalem, and yet refusing to admit him to his presence, enlisted in his behalf the sympathies of the people.

With the memory ever before him of his own transgression of the law of God, David seemed morally paralyzed; he was weak and irresolute, when before his sin he had been courageous and decided. His influence with the people had been weakened. And all this favored the designs of his unnatural son.

Through the influence of Joab, Absalom was again admitted to his father's presence; but though there was an outward reconciliation, he continued his ambitious scheming. He now assumed an almost royal state, having chariots and horses, and fifty men to run before him. And while the king was more and more inclined to desire retirement and solitude, Absalom sedulously courted the popular favor.

The influence of David's listlessness and irresolution extended to his subordinates; negligence and delay characterized the administration of justice. Absalom artfully turned every cause of dissatisfaction to his own advantage. Day by day this man of noble mien might be seen at the gate of the city, where a crowd of suppliants waited to present their wrongs for redress. Absalom mingled with them and listened to their grievances, expressing sympathy with their sufferings and regret at the inefficiency of the government. Having thus listened to the story of a man of Israel, the prince would reply, "Thy matters are good and right; but there is no man deputed of the king to hear thee;" adding, "O that I were made judge in the land, that every man which hath any suit or cause might come unto me, and I would do him justice! And it was so, that when any man came nigh to him to do him obeisance, he put forth his hand, and took him, and kissed him."

Fomented by the artful insinuations of the prince, discontent with the government was fast spreading. The praise of Absalom was on the lips of all. He was generally regarded as heir to the kingdom; the people looked upon him with pride as worthy of this high station, and a desire was kindled that he might occupy the throne. "So Absalom stole the hearts of the men of Israel." Yet the king, blinded by affection for his son, suspected nothing. The princely state which Absalom had assumed, was regarded by David as intended to do honor to his court—as an expression of joy at the reconciliation.

The minds of the people being prepared for what was to follow, Absalom secretly sent picked men throughout the tribes, to concert measures for a revolt. And now the cloak of religious devotion was assumed to conceal his traitorous designs. A vow made long before while he was in exile must be paid in Hebron. Absalom said to the king, "I pray thee, let me go and pay my vow, which I have vowed unto the Lord, in Hebron. For thy servant vowed a vow while I abode at Geshur in Syria, saying, If the Lord shall bring me again indeed to Jerusalem, then I will serve the Lord." The fond father, comforted with this evidence of piety in his son, dismissed him with his blessing. The conspiracy was now fully matured. Absalom's crowning act of hypocrisy was designed not only to blind the king but to establish the confidence of the people, and thus to lead them on to rebellion against the king whom God had chosen.

Absalom set forth for Hebron, and there went with him "two hundred men out of Jerusalem, that were called; and they went in their simplicity, and they knew not anything." These men went with Absalom, little thinking that their love for the son was leading them into rebellion against the father. Upon arriving at Hebron, Absalom immediately summoned Ahithophel, one of the chief counselors of David, a man in high repute for wisdom, whose opinion was thought to be as safe and wise as that of an oracle. Ahithophel joined the conspirators, and his support made the cause of Absalom appear certain of success, attracting to his standard many influential men from all parts of the land. As the trumpet of revolt was sounded, the prince's spies throughout the country spread the tidings that Absalom was king, and many of the people gathered to him.

Meanwhile the alarm was carried to Jerusalem, to the king. David was suddenly aroused, to see rebellion breaking out close beside his throne. His own son—the son whom he had loved and trusted—had been planning to seize his crown and doubtless to take his life. In his great peril David shook off the depression that had so long rested upon him, and with the spirit of his earlier years he prepared to meet this terrible emergency. Absalom was mustering his forces at Hebron, only twenty miles away. The rebels would soon be at the gates of Jerusalem.

From his palace David looked out upon his capital—"beautiful for situation, the joy of the whole earth, ... the city of the great King." Psalm 48:2. He shuddered at the thought of exposing it to carnage and devastation. Should he call to his help the subjects still loyal to his throne, and make a stand to hold his capital? Should he permit Jerusalem to be deluged with blood? His decision was taken. The horrors of war should not fall upon the chosen city. He would leave Jerusalem, and then test the fidelity of his people, giving them an opportunity to rally to his support. In this great crisis it was his duty to God and to his people to maintain the authority with which Heaven had invested him. The issue of the conflict he would trust with God.

In humility and sorrow David passed out of the gate of Jerusalem—driven from his throne, from his palace, from the ark of God, by the insurrection of his cherished son. The people followed in long, sad procession, like a funeral train. David's bodyguard of Cherethites, Pelethites, and six hundred Gittites from Gath, under the command of Ittai, accompanied the king. But David, with characteristic unselfishness, could not consent that these strangers who had sought his protection should be involved in his calamity. He expressed surprise that they should be ready to make this sacrifice

[731]

for him. Then said the king to Ittai the Gittite, "Wherefore goest thou also with us? return to thy place, and abide with the king: for thou art a stranger, and also an exile. Whereas thou camest but yesterday, should I this day make thee go up and down with us? seeing I go whither I may, return thou, and take back thy brethren: mercy and truth be with thee."

Ittai answered, "As the Lord liveth, and as my lord the king liveth, surely in what place my lord the king shall be, whether in death or life, even there also will thy servant be." These men had been converted from paganism to the worship of Jehovah, and nobly they now proved their fidelity to their God and their king. David, with grateful heart, accepted their devotion to his apparently sinking cause, and all passed over the brook Kidron on the way toward the wilderness.

Again the procession halted. A company clad in holy vestments was approaching. "And lo Zadok also, and all the Levites were with him, bearing the ark of the covenant of God." The followers of David looked upon this as a happy omen. The presence of that sacred symbol was to them a pledge of their deliverance and ultimate victory. It would inspire the people with courage to rally to the king. Its absence from Jerusalem would bring terror to the adherents of Absalom.

At sight of the ark joy and hope for a brief moment thrilled the heart of David. But soon other thoughts came to him. As the appointed ruler of God's heritage he was under solemn responsibility. Not personal interests, but the glory of God and the good of his people, were to be uppermost in the mind of Israel's king. God, who dwelt between the cherubim, had said of Jerusalem, "This is My rest" (Psalm 132:14); and without divine authority neither priest nor king had a right to remove therefrom the symbol of His presence. And David knew that his heart and life must be in harmony with the divine precepts, else the ark would be the means of disaster rather than of success. His great sin was ever before him. He recognized in this conspiracy the just judgment of God. The sword that was not to depart from his house had been unsheathed. He knew not what the result of the struggle might be. It was not for him to remove from the capital of the nation the sacred statutes which embodied the will of their divine Sovereign, which were the constitution of the realm and the foundation of its prosperity.

He commanded Zadok, "Carry back the ark of God into the city: if I shall find favor in the eyes of the Lord, He will bring me again, and show me both it and His habitation: but if He thus say, I have no delight in thee; behold, here am I, let Him do to me as seemeth good unto Him."

David added, "Art not thou a seer?"—a man appointed of God to instruct the people. "Return into the city in peace, and your two sons with you, Ahimaaz thy son, and Jonathan the son of Abiathar. See, I will tarry in the plain of the wilderness, until there come word from you to certify me." In the city the priests might do him good service by learning the movements and purposes of the rebels, and secretly communicating them to the king by their sons, Ahimaaz and Jonathan.

As the priests turned back toward Jerusalem a deeper shadow fell upon the departing throng. Their king a fugitive, themselves outcasts, forsaken even by the ark of God—the future was dark with terror and foreboding. "And David went up by the ascent of Mount Olivet, and wept as he went up, and had his head covered, and he went barefoot: and all the people that was with him covered every man his head, and they went up, weeping as they went up. And one told David, saying, Ahithophel is among the conspirators with Absalom." Again David was forced to recognize in his calamities the results of his own sin. The defection of Ahithophel, the ablest and most wily of political leaders, was prompted by revenge for the family disgrace involved in the wrong to Bathsheba, who was his granddaughter.

"And David said, O Lord, I pray Thee, turn the counsel of Ahithophel into foolishness." Upon reaching the top of the mount, the king bowed in prayer, casting upon God the burden of his soul and humbly supplicating divine mercy. His prayer seemed to be at once answered. Hushai the Archite, a wise and able counselor, who had proved himself a faithful friend to David, now came to him with his robes rent and with earth upon his head, to cast in his fortunes with the dethroned and fugitive king. David saw, as by a divine enlightenment, that this man, faithful and truehearted, was the one needed to serve the interests of the king in the councils at the capital.

At David's request Hushai returned to Jerusalem to offer his services to Absalom and defeat the crafty counsel of Ahithophel.

[736] With this gleam of light in the darkness, the king and his followers pursued their way down the eastern slope of Olivet, through a rocky and desolate waste, through wild ravines, and along stony and precipitous paths, toward the Jordan. "And when King David came to Bahurim, behold, thence came out a man of the family of the house of Saul, whose name was Shimei, the son of Gera: he came forth, and cursed still as he came. And he cast stones at David, and at all the servants of King David: and all the people and all the mighty men were on his right hand and on his left. And thus said Shimei when he cursed, Come out, come out, thou bloody man, and thou man of Belial. The Lord hath returned upon thee all the blood of the house of Saul, in whose stead thou hast reigned; and the Lord hath delivered the kingdom into the hand of Absalom thy son: and, behold, thou art taken in thy mischief, because thou art a bloody man."

In David's prosperity Shimei had not shown by word or act that he was not a loyal subject. But in the affliction of the king this Benjamite revealed his true character. He had honored David upon his throne, but he cursed him in his humiliation. Base and selfish, he looked upon others as of the same character as himself, and, inspired by Satan, he wreaked his hatred upon him whom God had chastened. The spirit that leads man to triumph over, to revile or distress, one who is in affliction is the spirit of Satan.

Shimei's accusations against David were utterly false—a baseless and malignant slander. David had not been guilty of wrong toward Saul or his house. When Saul was wholly in his power, and he could have slain him, he merely cut the skirt of his robe, and he reproached himself for showing even this disrespect for the Lord's anointed.

Of David's sacred regard for human life, striking evidence had been given, even while he himself was hunted like a beast of prey. One day while he was hidden in the cave of Adullam, his thoughts turning back to the untroubled freedom of his boyhood life, the fugitive exclaimed, "Oh that one would give me drink of the water of the well of Bethlehem, which is by the gate!" 2 Samuel 23:13-17. Bethlehem was at that time in the hands of the Philistines; but three mighty men of David's band broke through the guard, and brought of the water of Bethlehem to their master. David could not drink it. "Be it far from me," he cried; "is not this the blood of the men that went in jeopardy of their lives?" And he reverently poured out the water as an offering to God. David had been a man of war, much of his life had been spent amid scenes of violence; but of all who have passed through such an ordeal, few indeed have been so little affected by its hardening, demoralizing influence as was David.

[737]

David's nephew, Abishai, one of the bravest of his captains, could not listen patiently to Shimei's insulting words. "Why," he exclaimed, "should this dead dog curse my lord the king? let me go over, I pray thee, and take off his head." But the king forbade him. "Behold," he said, "my son ... seeketh my life: how much more now may this Benjamite do it? let him alone, and let him curse; for the Lord hath bidden him. It may be that the Lord will look on mine affliction, and that the Lord will requite me good for his cursing this day."

Conscience was uttering bitter and humiliating truths to David. While his faithful subjects wondered at his sudden reverse of fortune, it was no mystery to the king. He had often had forebodings of an hour like this. He had wondered that God had so long borne with his sins, and had delayed the merited retribution. And now in his hurried and sorrowful flight, his feet bare, his royal robes changed for sackcloth, the lamentations of his followers awaking the echoes of the hills, he thought of his loved capital—of the place which had been the scene of his sin—and as he remembered the goodness and long-suffering of God, he was not altogether without hope. He felt that the Lord would still deal with him in mercy.

Many a wrongdoer has excused his own sin by pointing to David's fall, but how few there are who manifest David's penitence and humility. How few would bear reproof and retribution with the patience and fortitude that he manifested. He had confessed his sin, and for years had sought to do his duty as a faithful servant of God; he had labored for the upbuilding of his kingdom, and under his rule it had attained to strength and prosperity never reached before. He had gathered rich stores of material for the building of the house of God, and now was all the labor of his life to be swept away? Must the results of years of consecrated toil, the work of genius and devotion and statesmanship, pass into the hands of his reckless and traitorous son, who regarded not the honor of God nor the prosperity of Israel? How natural it would have seemed for David to murmur against God in this great affliction!

But he saw in his own sin the cause of his trouble. The words of the prophet Micah breathe the spirit that inspired David's heart. "When I sit in darkness, the Lord shall be a light unto me. I will bear the indignation of the Lord, because I have sinned against Him, until He plead my cause, and execute judgment for me." Micah 7:8, 9. And the Lord did not forsake David. This chapter in his experience, when, under cruelest wrong and insult, he shows himself to be humble, unselfish, generous, and submissive, is one of the noblest in his whole experience. Never was the ruler of Israel more truly great in the sight of heaven than at this hour of his deepest outward humiliation.

Had God permitted David to go on unrebuked in sin, and while transgressing the divine precepts, to remain in peace and prosperity upon his throne, the skeptic and infidel might have had some excuse for citing the history of David as a reproach to the religion of the Bible. But in the experience through which He caused David to pass, the Lord shows that He cannot tolerate or excuse sin. And David's history enables us to see also the great ends which God has in view in His dealings with sin; it enables us to trace, even through darkest judgments, the working out of His purposes of mercy and beneficence. He caused David to pass under the rod, but He did not destroy him; the furnace is to purify, but not to consume. The Lord says, "If they break My statutes, and keep not My commandments; then will I visit their transgression with the rod, and their iniquity with stripes. Nevertheless My loving-kindness will I not utterly take from him, nor suffer My faithfulness to fail." Psalm 89:31-33.

Soon after David left Jerusalem, Absalom and his army entered, and without a struggle took possession of the stronghold of Israel. Hushai was among the first to greet the new-crowned monarch, and the prince was surprised and gratified at the accession of his father's old friend and counselor. Absalom was confident of success. Thus far his schemes had prospered, and eager to strengthen his throne and secure the confidence of the nation, he welcomed Hushai to his court.

Absalom was now surrounded by a large force, but it was mostly composed of men untrained for war. As yet they had not been brought into conflict. Ahithophel well knew that David's situation was far from hopeless. A large part of the nation were still true to him; he was surrounded by tried warriors, who were faithful to their king, and his army was commanded by able and experienced generals. Ahithophel knew that after the first burst of enthusiasm in favor of the new king, a reaction would come. Should the rebellion fail, Absalom might be able to secure a reconciliation with his father; then Ahithophel, as his chief counselor, would be held most guilty for the rebellion; upon him the heaviest punishment would fall. To prevent Absalom from retracing his steps, Ahithophel counseled him to an act that in the eyes of the whole nation would make reconciliation impossible. With hellish cunning this wily and unprincipled statesman urged Absalom to add the crime of incest to that of rebellion. In the sight of all Israel he was to take to himself his father's concubines, according to the custom of oriental nations, thus declaring that he succeeded to his father's throne. And Absalom carried out the vile suggestion. Thus was fulfilled the word of God to David by the prophet, "Behold, I will raise up evil against thee out of thine own house, and I will take thy wives before thine eyes, and give them unto thy neighbor.... For thou didst it secretly: but I will do this thing before all Israel, and before the sun." 2 Samuel 12:11, 12. Not that God prompted these acts of wickedness, but because of David's sin He did not exercise His power to prevent them.

Ahithophel had been held in high esteem for his wisdom, but he was destitute of the enlightenment which comes from God. "The fear of the Lord is the beginning of wisdom" (Proverbs 9:10); and this, Ahithophel did not possess, or he could hardly have based the success of treason upon the crime of incest. Men of corrupt hearts plot wickedness, as if there were no overruling Providence to cross their designs; but "He that sitteth in the heavens shall laugh: the Lord shall have them in derision." Psalm 2:4. The Lord declares: "They would none of My counsel: they despised all My reproof. Therefore shall they eat of the fruit of their own way, and be filled with their own devices. For the turning away of the simple shall slay them, and the prosperity of fools shall destroy them." Proverbs 1:30-32.

Having succeeded in the plot for securing his own safety, Ahithophel urged upon Absalom the necessity of immediate action against David. "Let me now choose out twelve thousand men," he said, "and I will arise and pursue after David this night: and I will come upon him while he is weary and weak-handed, and will make him afraid: and all the people that are with him shall flee; and I will smite the king only: and I will bring back all the people unto thee." This plan was approved by the king's counselors. Had it been followed, David would surely have been slain, unless the Lord had directly interposed to save him. But a wisdom higher than that of the renowned Ahithophel was directing events. "The Lord had appointed to defeat the good counsel of Ahithophel, to the intent that the Lord might bring evil upon Absalom."

Hushai had not been called to the council, and he would not intrude himself unasked, lest suspicion should be drawn upon him as a spy; but after the assembly had dispersed, Absalom, who had a high regard for the judgment of his father's counselor, submitted to him the plan of Ahithophel. Hushai saw that if the proposed plan were followed, David would be lost. And he said, "The counsel that Ahithophel hath given is not good at this time. For, said Hushai, thou knowest thy father and his men, that they be mighty men, and they be chafed in their minds, as a bear robbed of her whelps in the field: and thy father is a man of war, and will not lodge with the people. Behold, he is hid now in some pit, or in some other place;" he argued that, if Absalom's forces should pursue David, they would not capture the king; and should they suffer a reverse, it would tend to dishearten them and work great harm to Absalom's cause. "For," he said, "all Israel knoweth that thy father is a mighty man, and they which be with him are valiant men." And he suggested a plan attractive to a vain and selfish nature, fond of the show of power: "I counsel that all Israel be generally gathered unto thee, from Dan even to Beer-sheba, as the sand that is by the sea for multitude; and that thou go to battle in thine own person. So shall we come upon him in some place where he shall be found, and we will light upon him as the dew falleth on the ground: and of him and of all the men that are with him there shall not be left so much as one. Moreover, if he be gotten into a city, then shall all Israel bring ropes to that city, and we will draw it into the river, until there be not one small stone found there.

"And Absalom and all the men of Israel said, The counsel of Hushai the Archite is better than the counsel of Ahithophel." But there was one who was not deceived—one who clearly foresaw the result of this fatal mistake of Absalom's. Ahithophel knew that the cause of the rebels was lost. And he knew that whatever might be the fate of the prince, there was no hope for the counselor who had instigated his greatest crimes. Ahithophel had encouraged Absalom in rebellion; he had counseled him to the most abominable wickedness, to the dishonor of his father; he had advised the slaying of David and had planned its accomplishment; he had cut off the last possibility of his own reconciliation with the king; and now another was preferred before him, even by Absalom. Jealous, angry, and desperate, Ahithophel "gat him home to his house, to his city, and put his household in order, and hanged himself, and died." Such was the result of the wisdom of one, who, with all his high endowments, did not make God his counselor. Satan allures men with flattering promises, but in the end it will be found by every soul, that the "wages of sin is death." Romans 6:23.

Hushai, not certain that his counsel would be followed by the fickle king, lost no time in warning David to escape beyond Jordan without delay. To the priests, who were to forward it by their sons, Hushai sent the message: "Thus and thus did Ahithophel counsel Absalom and the elders of Israel; and thus and thus have I counseled. Now therefore ... lodge not this night in the plains of the wilderness, but speedily pass over; lest the king be swallowed up, and all the people that are with him."

The young men were suspected and pursued, yet they succeeded in performing their perilous mission. David, spent with toil and grief after that first day of flight, received the message that he must cross the Jordan that night, for his son was seeking his life.

What were the feelings of the father and king, so cruelly wronged, in this terrible peril? "A mighty valiant man," a man of war, a king, whose word was law, betrayed by his son whom he had loved and indulged and unwisely trusted, wronged and deserted by subjects bound to him by the strongest ties of honor and fealty—in what words did David pour out the feelings of his soul? In the hour of his darkest trial David's heart was stayed upon God, and he sang:

> "Lord, how are they increased that trouble me!
>   Many are they that rise up against me.
> Many there be which say of my soul,
>   There is no help for him in God.
> But Thou, O Lord, art a shield for me;
>   My glory, and the lifter up of mine head.
> I cried unto the Lord with my voice,
>   And He heard me out of His holy hill.
> I laid me down and slept;
>   I awaked; for the Lord sustained me.
> I will not be afraid of ten thousands of people,
>   That have set themselves against me round about....
> Salvation belongeth unto the Lord:
>   Thy blessing is upon Thy people." Psalm 3:1-8.

David and all his company—warriors and statesmen, old men and youth, the women and the little children—in the darkness of night crossed the deep and swift-flowing river. "By the morning light there lacked not one of them that was not gone over Jordan."

David and his forces fell back to Mahanaim, which had been the royal seat of Ishbosheth. This was a strongly fortified city, surrounded by a mountainous district favorable for retreat in case of war. The country was well-provisioned, and the people were friendly to the cause of David. Here many adherents joined him, while wealthy tribesmen brought abundant gifts of provision, and other needed supplies.

Hushai's counsel had achieved its object, gaining for David opportunity for escape; but the rash and impetuous prince could not be long restrained, and he soon set out in pursuit of his father. "And Absalom passed over Jordan, he and all the men of Israel with him." Absalom made Amasa, the son of David's sister Abigail, commander-in-chief of his forces. His army was large, but it was undisciplined and poorly prepared to cope with the tried soldiers of his father.

Rebellion of Absalom

David divided his forces into three battalions under the command of Joab, Abishai, and Ittai the Gittite. It had been his purpose himself to lead his army in the field; but against this the officers of the army, the counselors, and the people vehemently protested. "Thou shalt not go forth," they said: "for if we flee away, they will not care for us; neither if half of us die, will they care for us: but thou art worth ten thousand of us: therefore now it is better that thou be ready to succour us out of the city. And the king said unto them, What seemeth you best I will do." 2 Samuel 18:3, 4, R.V.

[743]

From the walls of the city the long lines of the rebel army were in full view. The usurper was accompanied by a vast host, in comparison with which David's force seemed but a handful. But as the king looked upon the opposing forces, the thought uppermost in his mind was not of the crown and the kingdom, nor of his own life, that depended upon the wage of battle. The father's heart was filled with love and pity for his rebellious son. As the army filed out from the city gates David encouraged his faithful soldiers, bidding them go forth trusting that the God of Israel would give them the victory. But even here he could not repress his love for Absalom. As Joab, leading the first column, passed his king, the conqueror of a hundred battlefields stooped his proud head to hear the monarch's last message, as with trembling voice he said, "Deal gently *for my sake* with the young man, even with Absalom." And Abishai and Ittai received the same charge—"Deal gently *for my sake* with the young man, even with Absalom." But the king's solicitude, seeming to declare that Absalom was dearer to him than his kingdom, dearer even than the subjects faithful to his throne, only increased the indignation of the soldiers against the unnatural son.

The place of battle was a wood near the Jordan, in which the great numbers of Absalom's army were only a disadvantage to him. Among the thickets and marshes of the forest these undisciplined troops became confused and unmanageable. And "the people of Israel were slain before the servants of David, and there was there a great slaughter that day of twenty thousand men." Absalom, seeing that the day was lost, had turned to flee, when his head was caught between the branches of a widespreading tree, and his mule going out from under him, he was left helplessly suspended, a prey to his enemies. In this condition he was found by a soldier, who, for fear of displeasing the king, spared Absalom, but reported to Joab what he had seen. Joab was restrained by no scruples. He had befriended Absalom, having twice secured his reconciliation with David, and the trust had been shamelessly betrayed. But for the advantages gained by Absalom through Joab's intercession, this rebellion, with all its horrors, could never have occurred. Now it was in Joab's power at one blow to destroy the instigator of all this evil. "And he took three darts in his hand, and thrust them through the heart of Absalom.... And they took Absalom, and cast him into a great pit in the wood, and laid a very great heap of stones upon him."

Thus perished the instigators of rebellion in Israel. Ahithophel had died by his own hand. The princely Absalom, whose glorious beauty had been the pride of Israel, had been cut down in the vigor of his youth, his dead body thrust into a pit, and covered with a heap of stones, in token of everlasting reproach. During his lifetime Absalom had reared for himself a costly monument in the king's dale, but the only memorial which marked his grave was that heap of stones in the wilderness.

The leader of the rebellion being slain, Joab by the sound of the trumpet recalled his army from the pursuit of the fleeing host, and messengers were at once dispatched to bear the tidings to the king.

The watchman upon the city wall, looking out toward the battlefield, discovered a man running alone. Soon a second came in sight. As the first drew nearer, the watchman said to the king, who was waiting beside the gate, "Me thinketh the running of the foremost is like the running of Ahimaaz the son of Zadok. And the king said, He is a good man, and cometh with good tidings. And Ahimaaz called, and said unto the king, All is well. And he fell down to the earth upon his face before the king, and said, Blessed be the Lord thy God, which hath delivered up the men that lifted up their hand against my lord the king." To the king's eager inquiry, "Is the young man Absalom safe?" Ahimaaz returned an evasive answer.

The second messenger came, crying, "Tidings, my lord the king: for the Lord hath avenged thee this day of all them that rose up against thee." Again from the father's lips came the absorbing question, "Is the young man Absalom safe?" Unable to conceal the heavy tidings, the herald answered, "The enemies of my lord the king, and all that rise against thee to do thee hurt, be as that young man is." It was enough. David questioned no further, but with bowed head he "went up to the chamber over the gate, and wept: and as he went, thus he said, O my son Absalom! my son, my son Absalom! would God I had died for thee, O Absalom, my son, my son!"

The victorious army, returning from the field, approached the city, their shouts of triumph awaking the echoes of the hills. But as they entered the city gate the shout died away, their banners drooped in their hands, and with downcast gaze they advanced more like those who had suffered defeat than like conquerors. For the king was not waiting to bid them welcome, but from the chamber above the gate his wailing cry was heard, "O my son Absalom! my son, my son Absalom! would God I had died for thee, O Absalom, my son, my son!" [745]

"The victory that day was turned into mourning unto all the people; for the people heard say that day how the king was grieved for his son. And the people gat them by stealth that day into the city, as people being ashamed steal away when they flee in battle."

Joab was filled with indignation. God had given them reason for triumph and gladness; the greatest rebellion that had ever been known in Israel had been crushed; and yet this great victory was turned to mourning for him whose crime had cost the blood of thousands of brave men. The rude, blunt captain pushed his way into the presence of the king, and boldly said, "Thou hast shamed this day the faces of all thy servants, which this day have saved thy life, and the lives of thy sons and of thy daughters; ... in that thou lovest thine enemies, and hatest thy friends. For thou hast declared this day, that thou regardest neither princes nor servants: for this day I perceive, that if Absalom had lived, and all we had died this day, then it had pleased thee well. Now therefore arise, go forth, and speak comfortably unto thy servants: for I swear by the Lord, if thou go not forth, there will not tarry one with thee this night: and that will be worse unto thee than all the evil that befell thee from thy youth until now."

Harsh and even cruel as was the reproof to the heart-stricken king, David did not resent it. Seeing that his general was right, he went down to the gate, and with words of courage and commendation greeted his brave soldiers as they marched past him.

Chapter 73—The Last Years of David

This chapter is based on 2 Samuel 24; 1 Kings 1; 1 Chronicles 21; 28; 29.

The overthrow of Absalom did not at once bring peace to the kingdom. So large a part of the nation had joined in revolt that David would not return to his capital and resume his authority without an invitation from the tribes. In the confusion that followed Absalom's defeat there was no prompt and decided action to recall the king, and when at last Judah undertook to bring back David, the jealousy of the other tribes was roused, and a counter-revolution followed. This, however, was speedily quelled, and peace returned to Israel.

The history of David affords one of the most impressive testimonies ever given to the dangers that threaten the soul from power and riches and worldly honor—those things that are most eagerly desired among men. Few have ever passed through an experience better adapted to prepare them for enduring such a test. David's early life as a shepherd, with its lessons of humility, of patient toil, and of tender care for his flocks; the communion with nature in the solitude of the hills, developing his genius for music and poetry, and directing his thoughts to the Creator; the long discipline of his wilderness life, calling into exercise courage, fortitude, patience, and faith in God, had been appointed by the Lord as a preparation for the throne of Israel. David had enjoyed precious experiences of the love of God, and had been richly endowed with His Spirit; in the history of Saul he had seen the utter worthlessness of mere human wisdom. And yet worldly success and honor so weakened the character of David that he was repeatedly overcome by the tempter.

Intercourse with heathen peoples led to a desire to follow their national customs and kindled ambition for worldly greatness. As the people of Jehovah, Israel was to be honored; but as pride and self-confidence increased, the Israelites were not content with this pre-eminence. They cared rather for their standing among other nations. This spirit could not fail to invite temptation. With a view to extending his conquests among foreign nations, David determined to increase his army by requiring military service from all who were of proper age. To effect this, it became necessary to take a census of the population. It was pride and ambition that prompted this action of the king. The numbering of the people would show the contrast between the weakness of the kingdom when David ascended the throne and its strength and prosperity under his rule. This would tend still further to foster the already too great self-confidence of both king and people. The Scripture says, "Satan stood up against Israel, and provoked David to number Israel." The prosperity of Israel under David had been due to the blessing of God rather than to the ability of her king or the strength of her armies. But the increasing of the military resources of the kingdom would give the impression to surrounding nations that Israel's trust was in her armies, and not in the power of Jehovah.

Though the people of Israel were proud of their national greatness, they did not look with favor upon David's plan for so greatly extending the military service. The proposed enrollment caused much dissatisfaction; consequently it was thought necessary to employ the military officers in place of the priests and magistrates, who had formerly taken the census. The object of the undertaking was directly contrary to the principles of a theocracy. Even Joab remonstrated, unscrupulous as he had heretofore shown himself. He said, "The Lord make His people a hundred times so many more as they be: but, my lord the king, are they not all my lord's servants? why then doth my lord require this thing? why will he be a cause of trespass to Israel? Nevertheless the king's word prevailed against Joab. Wherefore Joab departed, and went throughout all Israel, and came to Jerusalem." The numbering was not finished when David was convicted of his sin. Self-condemned, he "said unto God, I have sinned greatly, because I have done this thing: but now, I beseech Thee, do away the iniquity of Thy servant; for I have done very foolishly." The next morning a message was brought to David by the prophet Gad: "Thus saith the Lord, Choose thee either three years' famine; or three months to be destroyed before thy foes, while that the sword of thine enemies overtaketh thee; or else three days the sword of the Lord, even the pestilence, in the land, and the angel of the Lord destroying throughout all the coasts of Israel. Now therefore," said the prophet, "advise thyself what word I shall bring again to Him that sent me."

The king's answer was, "I am in a great strait: let us fall now into the hand of the Lord; for His mercies are great: and let me not fall into the hand of man."

The land was smitten with pestilence, which destroyed seventy thousand in Israel. The scourge had not yet entered the capital, when "David lifted up his eyes, and saw the angel of the Lord stand between the earth and the heaven, having a drawn sword in his hand stretched out over Jerusalem. Then David and the elders of Israel, who were clothed in sackcloth, fell upon their faces." The king pleaded with God in behalf of Israel: "Is it not I that commanded the people to be numbered? even I it is that have sinned and done evil indeed; but as for these sheep, what have they done? let Thine hand, I pray Thee, O Lord my God, be on me, and on my father's house; but not on Thy people, that they should be plagued."

The taking of the census had caused disaffection among the people; yet they had themselves cherished the same sins that prompted David's action. As the Lord through Absalom's sin visited judgment upon David, so through David's error he punished the sins of Israel.

The destroying angel had stayed his course outside Jerusalem. He stood upon Mount Moriah, "in the threshing floor of Ornan the Jebusite." Directed by the prophet, David went to the mountain, and there built an altar to the Lord, "and offered burnt offerings and peace offerings, and called upon the Lord; and He answered him from heaven by fire upon the altar of burnt offering." "So the Lord was entreated for the land, and the plague was stayed from Israel."

The spot upon which the altar was erected, henceforth ever to be regarded as holy ground, was tendered to the king by Ornan as a gift. But the king declined thus to receive it. "I will verily buy it for the full price," he said; "for I will not take that which is thine for the Lord, nor offer burnt offerings without cost. So David gave to Ornan for the place six hundred shekels of gold by weight." This spot, memorable as the place where Abraham had built the altar to offer up his son, and now hallowed by this great deliverance, was afterward chosen as the site of the temple erected by Solomon.

Still another shadow was to gather over the last years of David. He had reached the age of threescore and ten. The hardships and exposures of his early wanderings, his many wars, the cares and afflictions of his later years, had sapped the fountain of life. Though his mind retained its clearness and strength, feebleness and age, with their desire for seclusion, prevented a quick apprehension of what was passing in the kingdom, and again rebellion sprang up in the very shadow of the throne. Again the fruit of David's parental indulgence was manifest. The one who now aspired to the throne was Adonijah, "a very goodly man" in person and bearing, but unprincipled and reckless. In his youth he had been subjected to but little restraint; for "his father had not displeased him at any time in saying, Why hast thou done so?" He now rebelled against the authority of God, who had appointed Solomon to the throne. Both by natural endowments and religious character Solomon was better qualified than his elder brother to become ruler of Israel; yet although the choice of God had been clearly indicated, Adonijah did not fail to find sympathizers. Joab, though guilty of many crimes, had heretofore been loyal to the throne; but he now joined the conspiracy against Solomon, as did also Abiathar the priest.

The rebellion was ripe; the conspirators had assembled at a great feast just without the city to proclaim Adonijah king, when their plans were thwarted by the prompt action of a few faithful persons, chief among whom were Zadok the priest, Nathan the prophet, and Bathsheba the mother of Solomon. They represented the state of affairs to the king, reminding him of the divine direction that Solomon should succeed to the throne. David at once abdicated in favor of Solomon, who was immediately anointed and proclaimed king. The conspiracy was crushed. Its chief actors had incurred the penalty of death. Abiathar's life was spared, out of respect to his office and his former fidelity to David; but he was degraded from the office of high priest, which passed to the line of Zadok. Joab and Adonijah were spared for the time, but after the death of David they suffered the penalty of their crime. The execution of the sentence upon the son of David completed the fourfold judgment that testified to God's abhorrence of the father's sin.

From the very opening of David's reign one of his most cherished plans had been that of erecting a temple to the Lord. Though he had not been permitted to execute this design, he had manifested no less zeal and earnestness in its behalf. He had provided an abundance of the most costly material—gold, silver, onyx stones, and stones of divers colors; marble, and the most precious woods. And now these valuable treasures that he had collected must be committed to others; for other hands must build the house for the ark, the symbol of God's presence.

Seeing that his end was near, the king summoned the princes of Israel, with representative men from all parts of the kingdom, to receive this legacy in trust. He desired to commit to them his dying charge and secure their concurrence and support in the great work to be accomplished. Because of his physical weakness, it had not been expected that he would attend to this transfer in person; but the inspiration of God came upon him, and with more than his wonted fervor and power, he was able, for the last time, to address his people. He told them of his own desire to build the temple, and of the Lord's command that the work should be committed to Solomon his son. The divine assurance was, "Solomon thy son, he shall build My house and My courts; for I have chosen him to be My son, and I will be his Father. Moreover I will establish his kingdom forever, if he be constant to do My commandments and My judgments, as at this day." "Now therefore," David said, "in the sight of all Israel the congregation of the Lord, and in the audience of our God, keep and seek for all the commandments of the Lord your God: that ye may possess this good land, and leave it for an inheritance for your children after you forever."

David had learned by his own experience how hard is the path of him who departs from God. He had felt the condemnation of the broken law, and had reaped the fruits of transgression; and his whole soul was moved with solicitude that the leaders of Israel should be true to God, and that Solomon should obey God's law, shunning the sins that had weakened his father's authority, embittered his life, and dishonored God. David knew that it would require humility of heart, a constant trust in God, and unceasing watchfulness to withstand the temptations that would surely beset Solomon in his exalted station; for such prominent characters are a special mark for the shafts of Satan. Turning to his son, already acknowledged as his successor on the throne, David said: "And thou, Solomon my son, know thou the God of thy father, and serve Him with a perfect heart and with a willing mind: for the Lord searcheth all hearts, and understandeth all the imaginations of the thoughts: if thou seek Him, He will be found of thee; but if thou forsake Him, He will cast thee off forever. Take heed now; for the Lord hath chosen thee to build a house for the sanctuary: be strong, and do it."

David gave Solomon minute directions for building the temple, with patterns of every part, and of all its instruments of service, as had been revealed to him by divine inspiration. Solomon was still young, and shrank from the weighty responsibilities that would devolve upon him in the erection of the temple and in the government of God's people. David said to his son, "Be strong and of good courage, and do it: fear not, nor be dismayed, for the Lord God, even my God, will be with thee; He will not fail thee, nor forsake thee."

Again David appealed to the congregation: "Solomon my son, whom alone God hath chosen, is yet young and tender, and the work is great: for the palace is not for man, but for the Lord God." He said, "I have prepared with all my might for the house of my God," and he went on to enumerate the materials he had gathered. More than this, he said, "I have set my affection to the house of my God, I have of mine own proper good, of gold and silver, which I have given to the house of my God, over and above all that I have prepared for the holy house, even three thousand talents of gold, of the gold of Ophir, and seven thousand talents of refined silver, to overlay the walls of the houses withal." "Who then," he asked of the assembled multitude that had brought their liberal gifts—"who then is willing to consecrate his *service* this day unto the Lord?"

There was a ready response from the assembly. "The chief of the fathers and princes of the tribes of Israel, and the captains of thousands and of hundreds, with the rulers of the king's work, offered willingly, and gave, for the service of the house of God, of gold five thousand talents and ten thousand drams, and of silver ten thousand talents, and of brass eighteen thousand talents, and one hundred thousand talents of iron. And they with whom precious stones were found gave them to the treasure of the house of the Lord.... Then the people rejoiced, for that they offered willingly, because with perfect heart they offered willingly to the Lord: and David the king also rejoiced with great joy.

[752]

"Wherefore David blessed the Lord before all the congregation: and David said, Blessed be Thou, Lord God of Israel our father, forever and ever. Thine, O Lord, is the greatness, and the power, and the glory, and the victory, and the majesty: for all that is in the heaven and in the earth is Thine; Thine is the kingdom, O Lord, and Thou art exalted as head above all. Both riches and honor come of Thee, and Thou reignest over all; and in Thine hand is power and might; and in Thine hand it is to make great, and to give strength unto all. Now therefore, our God, we thank Thee, and praise Thy glorious name. But who am I, and what is my people, that we should be able to offer so willingly after this sort? for all things come of Thee, and of Thine own have we given Thee. For we are strangers before Thee, and sojourners, as were all our fathers: our days on the earth are as a shadow, and there is none abiding. O Lord our God, all this store that we have prepared to build Thee an house for Thine holy name cometh of Thine hand, and is all Thine own. I know also, my God, that Thou triest the heart, and hast pleasure in uprightness.

"As for me, in the uprightness of mine heart I have willingly offered all these things: and now have I seen with joy Thy people, which are present here, to offer willingly unto Thee. O Lord God of Abraham, Isaac and of Israel, our fathers, keep this forever in the imagination of the thoughts of the heart of Thy people, and prepare their heart unto Thee: and give unto Solomon my son a perfect heart, to keep Thy commandments, Thy testimonies, and Thy statutes, and to do all these things, and to build the palace, for the which I have made provision. And David said to all the congregation, Now bless the Lord your God. And all the congregation blessed the Lord God of their fathers, and bowed down their heads, and worshiped the Lord."

With deepest interest the king had gathered the rich material for building and beautifying the temple. He had composed the glorious anthems that in afteryears should echo through its courts. Now his heart was made glad in God, as the chief of the fathers and the princes of Israel so nobly responded to his appeal, and offered themselves to the important work before them. And as they gave their service, they were disposed to do more. They swelled the offerings, giving of their own possessions into the treasury. David had felt deeply his own unworthiness in gathering the material for the house of God, and the expression of loyalty in the ready response of the nobles of his kingdom, as with willing hearts they dedicated their treasures to Jehovah and devoted themselves to His service, filled him with joy. But it was God alone who had imparted this disposition to His people. He, not man, must be glorified. It was He who had provided the people with the riches of earth, and His Spirit had made them willing to bring their precious things for the temple. It was all of the Lord; if His love had not moved upon the hearts of the people, the king's efforts would have been vain, and the temple would never have been erected.

All that man receives of God's bounty still belongs to God. Whatever God has bestowed in the valuable and beautiful things of earth is placed in the hands of men to test them—to sound the depths of their love for Him and their appreciation of His favors. Whether it be the treasures of wealth or of intellect, they are to be laid, a willing offering, at the feet of Jesus; the giver saying, meanwhile, with David, "All things come of Thee, and of Thine own have we given Thee."

When he felt that death was approaching, the burden of David's heart was still for Solomon and for the kingdom of Israel, whose prosperity must so largely depend upon the fidelity of her king. "And he charged Solomon his son, saying, I go the way of all the earth: be thou strong therefore, and show thyself a man; and keep the charge of the Lord thy God, to walk in His ways, to keep His statutes, and His commandments, and His judgments, and His testimonies, ... that thou mayest prosper in all that thou doest, and whithersoever thou turnest thyself: that the Lord may continue His word which He spake concerning me, saying, If thy children take heed to their way, to walk before Me in truth with all their heart and with all their soul, there shall not fail thee (said He) a man on the throne of Israel." 1 Kings 2:1-4.

David's "last words," as recorded, are a song—a song of trust, of loftiest principle, and undying faith:

[754]

"David the son of Jesse saith,
    And the man who was raised on high saith,
The anointed of the God of Jacob,
    And the sweet psalmist of Israel:

>   The Spirit of Jehovah spake by me: ...
>   One that ruleth over men righteously,
>   That ruleth in the fear of God,
>   He shall be as the light of the morning, when the sun riseth,
>   A morning without clouds;
>   When the tender grass springeth out of the earth,
>   Through clear shining after rain.
>   Verily my house is not so with God;
>   Yet He hath made me an everlasting covenant,
>   Ordered in all things, and sure:
>   For it is all my salvation, and all my desire."
>
>   2 Samuel 23:1-5, R.V.

Great had been David's fall, but deep was his repentance, ardent was his love, and strong his faith. He had been forgiven much, and therefore he loved much. Luke 7:47.

The psalms of David pass through the whole range of experience, from the depths of conscious guilt and self-condemnation to the loftiest faith and the most exalted communing with God. His life record declares that sin can bring only shame and woe, but that God's love and mercy can reach to the deepest depths, that faith will lift up the repenting soul to share the adoption of the sons of God. Of all the assurances which His word contains, it is one of the strongest testimonies to the faithfulness, the justice, and the covenant mercy of God.

Man "fleeth also as a shadow, and continueth not," "but the word of our God shall stand forever." "The mercy of Jehovah is from everlasting to everlasting upon them that fear Him, and His righteousness unto children's children; to such as keep His covenant, and to those that remember His commandments to do them." Job 14:2; Isaiah 40:8; Psalm 103:17, 18.

"Whatsoever God doeth, it shall be forever." Ecclesiastes 3:14.

Glorious are the promises made to David and his house, promises that look forward to the eternal ages, and find their complete fulfillment in Christ. The Lord declared:

"I have sworn unto David My servant ... with whom My hand shall be established: Mine arm also shall strengthen him.... My faithfulness and My mercy shall be with him: and in My name shall his horn be exalted. I will set his hand also in the sea, and his right hand in the rivers. He shall cry unto Me, Thou art my Father, my God, and the Rock of my salvation. Also I will make him My firstborn, higher than the kings of the earth. My mercy will I keep for him forevermore, and My covenant shall stand fast with him." Psalm 89:3-28.

> "His seed also will I make to endure forever,
>   And his throne as the days of heaven." Psalm 89:29.

> "He shall judge the poor of the people,
>   He shall save the children of the needy,
> And shall break in pieces the oppressor.
>   They shall fear thee while the sun endureth,
> And so long as the moon, throughout all generations....
>   In his days shall the righteous flourish;
> And abundance of peace, till the moon be no more.
>   He shall have dominion also from sea to sea,
> And from the river unto the ends of the earth."
>   "His name shall endure forever:
> His name shall be continued as long as the sun:
>   And men shall be blessed in him:
> All nations shall call him blessed."
>   Psalm 72:4-8, R.V., 17.

"For unto us a Child is born, unto us a Son is given: and the government shall be upon His shoulder: and His name shall be called Wonderful, Counselor, The mighty God, The everlasting Father, The Prince of Peace." "He shall be great, and shall be called the Son of the Highest; and the Lord God shall give unto Him the throne of His father David: and He shall reign over the house of Jacob forever; and of His kingdom there shall be no end." Isaiah 9:6; Luke 1:32, 33(757).

Appendix

[756]
[757]

Note 1. Page 258. In the command for Israel's release, the Lord said to Pharaoh, "Israel is my son, even my first-born.... Let my son go, that he may serve Me." Exodus 4:22, 23. The psalmist tells us why God delivered Israel from Egypt: "He brought forth His people with joy, and His chosen with gladness: And gave them the lands of the heathen: And they inherited the labor of the people; that they might observe His statutes, and keep His laws." Psalm 105:43-45. Here we learn that the Hebrews could not serve God in Egypt.

In Deuteronomy 5:14, 15 we find special emphasis given to that portion of the fourth commandment which requires the manservant and the maidservant to rest, and the Israelite was told to remember that he had been a servant in the land of Egypt. The Lord said, "the seventh day is the Sabbath of the Lord thy God: In it thou shalt not do any work, thou, nor thy son, nor thy daughter, nor thy manservant, nor thy maidservant, nor thine ox, nor thine ass, nor any of thy cattle, nor thy stranger that is within thy gates; that thy manservant and thy maidservant may rest as well as thou. And remember that thou wast a servant in the land of Egypt, and that the Lord thy God brought thee out thence through a mighty hand and by a stretched-out arm: Therefore the Lord thy God commanded thee to keep the Sabbath day." In Exodus 5:5 we learn that Moses and Aaron made the people "*rest* from their burdens."

From these facts we may conclude that the Sabbath was one of the things in which they could not serve the Lord in Egypt; and when Moses and Aaron came with the message of God (Exodus 4:29-31), they attempted a reform, which only increased the oppression. The Israelites were delivered that they might observe the statutes of the Lord, including the fourth commandment, and this placed upon them an additional obligation to keep the Sabbath strictly, as well as to keep all the commandments. Thus in Deuteronomy 24:17, 18 the fact of their deliverance from Egypt is cited as placing them under special obligation to show kindness to the widow and the fatherless:

"Thou shalt not pervert the judgment of the stranger, nor of the fatherless; nor take a widow's raiment to pledge: But thou shalt remember that thou wast a bondman in Egypt, and the Lord thy God redeemed thee thence: Therefore I command thee to do this thing."

Note 2. Page 272. That the plagues were designed to destroy the confidence of the Egyptians in the power and protection of their idols, and even made their gods to appear as cruel tormentors of their worshipers, can be seen from a study of the Egyptian religion. A few examples may serve to illustrate this fact. [758]

The first plague, turning the water of the river Nile and of all canals into blood (Exodus 7:19), was directed against the source of Egypt's very existence. The river Nile was regarded with religious reverence, and at several places sacrifices were offered to the Nile as to a god.

The second plague brought frogs over Egypt. Exodus 8:6. Frogs were held sacred by the Egyptians, and one of their deities, Heqa, was a frog-headed goddess thought to possess creative power. When the frogs, as the result of Moses' command, multiplied to the extent that they filled the land from one end to the other, the Egyptians may have wondered why Heqa was tormenting her ardent worshipers instead of protecting them. In this way the Egyptians were not only punished by the second plague, but witnessed also contempt heaped upon them, as they supposed, by one of their gods (Exodus 9:3), of which many represented powerful gods in the Egyptians pantheon. To mention only a few, we find that the Apis bull was dedicated to Ptah, the father of all the gods, the cow was sacred to Hathor, one of the most widely worshiped of all female deities of the Nile country, while the ram represented several gods like Khnemu, and the ram-headed Amen, who was Egypt's chief god in the New Empire period. Hence, the disease which slew the animals dedicated to their deities revealed to the Egyptians the impotence of their gods in the presence of the God of the despised Hebrews.

The ninth plague (Exodus 10:21) dealt a heavy blow to one of the greatest gods of Egypt, the sun god Ra, who had been continuously worshiped from the earliest times of that country's known history. In a land which hardly ever saw clouds in the sky, the sun was recognized as a never-failing power which provided warmth, light, life, and growth to the whole world. Every Egyptian king considered himself as a "son of Ra," and carried this expression in his titulary. When Amen of Thebes became chief god of Egypt during the eighteenth dynasty, the power of the sun god Ra was recognized as so great that a compromise was made by combining Amen and Ra to make one god—Amen-Ra. A few years after the Exodus, when Ikhnaton introduced a short-lived monotheism, the only god retained was Aton, the sun disk. Seeing how entrenched sun worship was in the religious life of the Egyptians, and how highly the sun god Ra, Amen-Ra, or Aton was revered, we can understand why the plague directed against the god was brought upon Egypt toward the culmination of the fight between the God of the Hebrews and His Egyptian adversaries.

[759] Also the tenth plague, the slaughtering of the first-born (Exodus 12:29), was striking at least one god, and that was the king, who was considered to be Horus, the son of Osiris. As the ruler of the Nile country, he was addressed by his subjects as "the good god." Hence, the last plague crowned the actions wrought by the miracle-working power of the Hebrew God. So far gods controlling the forces of nature or animals had been disgraced, but now a god living in a visible form among the Egyptians was also humiliated by the despised God of the Hebrew slaves, of whom the proud Pharaoh once had said, "Who is the Lord, that I should obey His voice to let Israel go? I know not the Lord, neither will I let Israel go." Exodus 5:2.

Note 3. Page 282. In Genesis 15:13 we read that the Lord said to Abraham, "Know of a surety that thy seed shall be a stranger in a land that is not theirs, and shall serve them: And they shall afflict them four hundred years." This text raises the questions whether the 400 years refer to the time of affliction or sojourning, or both, and what the relation of the 400 years is to the 430 years of Exodus 12:40, 41, and Galatians 3:16, 17.

The statement in Exodus 12:40, that "the sojourning of the children of Israel, who dwelt in Egypt, was four hundred and thirty years," gives the impression that the Israelites, from Jacob's entry into Egypt to the Exodus, actually spent 430 years in the country of the Nile. That this impression cannot be correct is obvious from Paul's inspired interpretation presented in Galatians 3:16, 17, where the 430 years are said to cover the period beginning when God made

His covenant with Abraham until the law was promulgated at Sinai. Paul seems to refer to the first promise made by God to Abraham when he was called to leave Haran. Genesis 12:1-3. At that time the 430 years began, when Abraham was seventy-five years old (chapter 12:4), while the 400 years of the prophecy of Genesis 15:13 began thirty years later, when Abraham was 105 and his son Isaac five years old (Chapter 21:5). At that time Ishmael, who "was born after the flesh persecuted him [Isaac] that was born after the Spirit" (Galatians 4:29; Genesis 21:9-11), beginning a time of affliction of Abraham's seed which intermittently would be continued until the time of the Exodus. Isaac had not only troubles with his half brother Ishmael, but also with the Philistines (Genesis 26:15, 20, 21); Jacob fled for his life from Esau (Genesis 27:41-43), and later from Laban (Genesis 31:21), and then was again in jeopardy from Esau (Genesis 32:8); Joseph was sold into slavery by his brethren (Genesis 37:28), and the children of Israel were oppressed by the Egyptians for many decades (Exodus 1:14).

The time from Abraham's call to Jacob's entry into Egypt was 215 years, being the total of (1) twenty-five years lying between Abraham's call and the birth of Isaac (Genesis 12:4; Genesis 21:5), (2) sixty years lying between Isaac's birth and Jacob's birth (Genesis 25:26), and (3) the age of Jacob at the time of his migration into Egypt (Genesis 47:9). This leaves the remaining 215 years of the 430 as the actual time the Hebrews spent in Egypt. Hence the 430 years of Exodus 12:40 includes the sojourn of the patriarchs in Canaan as well as their stay in Egypt. Since in the time of Moses, Palestine was part of the Egyptian empire, it is not strange to find an author of that period including Canaan in the term "Egypt." The translators of the Septuagint, knowing that the 430 years included the sojourn of the patriarchs in Canaan, made this point clear in their rendering of this passage: "And the sojourning of the children of Israel, while they sojourned in the land of Egypt and the land of Canaan, was four hundred and thirty years." An additional corroboration of the interpretation of the 430 years given above is found in the prophecy that the fourth generation of those who had entered Egypt would leave it (Genesis 15:16), and its recorded fulfillment in Exodus 6:16-20.

Note 4. Page 316. The Israelites, in their adoration of the golden calf, *professed* to be worshiping God. Thus Aaron, when inaugurating the worship of the idol, proclaimed, "Tomorrow is a feast unto Jehovah." They proposed to worship God, as the Egyptians worshiped Osiris, under the semblance of the image. But God could not accept the service. Though offered in His name, the sun god, and not Jehovah, was the real object of their adoration.

The worship of Apis was accompanied with the grossest licentiousness, and the Scripture record indicates that the calf worship by the Israelites was attended with all the license usual in heathen worship. We read: "They rose up early on the morrow, and offered burnt offerings, and brought peace offerings; and the people sat down to eat and to drink, and rose up to play." Exodus 32:6. The Hebrew word rendered "to play" signifies playing with leaping, singing, and dancing. This dancing, especially among the Egyptians, was sensual and indecent. The word rendered "corrupted" in the next verse, where it is said, "thy people, which thou broughtest out of the land of Egypt, have corrupted themselves," is the same that is used in Genesis 6:11, 12, where we read that the earth was corrupt, "for all flesh had corrupted his way upon the earth." This explains the terrible anger of the Lord, and why He desired to consume the people at once.

Note 5. Page 329. The Ten Commandments were the "covenant" to which the Lord referred when, in proposing a covenant with Israel, He said, "If ye will obey My voice indeed, and keep *My* covenant," etc. Exodus 19:5. The ten commandments were termed God's "covenant" before the covenant was made with Israel. They were *not an agreement* made, but something which God *commanded them to perform*. Thus the Ten Commandments—God's covenant—became the *basis* of the covenant made between Him and Israel. The Ten Commandments in all their details are "all these words," *concerning which* the covenant was made. See Exodus 24:8.

Note 6. Page 354. When a sin offering was presented for a priest or for the whole congregation, the blood was carried into the holy place and sprinkled before the veil and placed upon the horns of the Golden Altar. The fat was consumed upon the altar of burnt offering in the court, but the body of the victim was burned without the camp. See Leviticus 4:1-21.

When, however, the offering was for a ruler or for one of the people, the blood was not taken into the holy place, but the flesh was to be eaten by the priest, as the Lord directed Moses: "The priest that offereth it for sin shall eat it: In a holy place shall it be eaten, in the court of the tent of meeting." Leviticus 6:26, R.V. See also Leviticus 4:22-35.

Note 7. Page 366. That the One who spoke the law, who called Moses into the mount and talked with him, was our Lord Jesus Christ, is evident from the following considerations:

Christ is the One through whom God has at all times revealed Himself to man. "But to us there is but one God, the Father, of whom are all things, and we in Him; and one Lord Jesus Christ, *by whom are all things*, and we by Him." 1 Corinthians 8:6. "This is he [Moses], that was in the church in the wilderness with the Angel which spake to him in the Mount Sinai, and with our fathers: who received the lively oracles to give unto us." Acts 7:38. This Angel was the Angel of God's presence (Isaiah 63:9), the Angel in whom was the name of the great Jehovah (Exodus 23:20-23). The expression can refer to no other than the Son of God.

Again: Christ is called the Word of God. John 1:1-3. He is so called because God gave His revelations to man in all ages through Christ. It was His Spirit that inspired the prophets. 1 Peter 1:10, 11. He was revealed to them as the Angel of Jehovah, the Captain of the Lord's host, Michael the Archangel.

Note 8. Page 603. The question has been raised, and is now much agitated, if a theocracy was good in the time of Israel, why would not a theocratical form of government be equally good for this time? The answer is easy:

A theocracy is a government which derives its power immediately from God. The government of Israel was a true theocracy. That was really a government of God. At the burning bush, God commissioned Moses to lead His people out of Egypt. By signs and wonders and mighty miracles multiplied, God delivered Israel from Egypt and led them through the wilderness and finally into the Promised Land. There He ruled them by judges "until Samuel the prophet," to whom, when he was a child, God spoke, and by whom He made known His will. In the days of Samuel the people asked that they might have a king. This was allowed, and God chose Saul, and Samuel anointed him king of Israel. Saul failed to do the will of God; and as he rejected the word of the Lord, the Lord rejected him from being king and sent Samuel to anoint David king of Israel; and David's throne God established forevermore. When Solomon succeeded to the kingdom in the place of David his father, the record is: "Then Solomon sat on the *throne of the Lord* as king instead of David his father." 1 Chronicles 29:23. David's throne was the throne of the Lord, and Solomon sat on the throne of the Lord as king over the earthly kingdom of God. The succession to the throne descended in David's line to Zedekiah, who was made subject to the king of Babylon, and who entered into a solemn covenant before God that he would loyally render allegiance to the king of Babylon. But Zedekiah broke his covenant, and then God said to him:

"Thou, profane wicked prince of Israel, whose day is come, when iniquity shall have an end, thus saith the Lord God; remove the diadem, and take off the crown: This shall not be the same: Exalt him that is low, and abase him that is high. I will overturn, overturn, overturn, it: And it shall be no more, until He come whose right it is; and I will give it him." Ezekiel 21:25-27. See also chapter 17:1-21.

The kingdom was then subject to Babylon. When Babylon fell, and Medo-Persia succeeded, it was overturned the first time. When Medo-Persia fell and was succeeded by Greece, it was overturned the second time. When the Greek empire gave way to Rome, it was overturned the third time. And then says the word, "It shall be no more, until He come whose right it is; and I will give it Him." Who is He whose right it is? "Thou ... Shalt call His name Jesus. He shall be great, and shall be called the Son of the Highest: and the Lord God shall give unto Him the throne of His father David: And He shall reign over the house of Jacob forever; and of His kingdom there shall be no end." Luke 1:31-33. And while He was here as "that Prophet," a Man of Sorrows and acquainted with grief, the night in which He was betrayed He Himself declared, "My kingdom is not of this world." Thus the throne of the Lord has been removed from this world and will "be no more, until He come whose right it is," and then it will be given Him. And *that time* is the end of this world, and the beginning of "the world to come."

To the twelve apostles the Saviour said, "I appoint unto you a kingdom, as My Father hath appointed unto Me; that ye may eat and drink at My table in My kingdom, and sit on thrones, judging the twelve tribes of Israel." Luke 22:29, 30. From Matthew's account of Christ's promise to the twelve we learn when it will be fulfilled; "in the regeneration when the Son of man shall sit on the throne of His glory, ye also shall sit upon twelve thrones, judging the twelve tribes of Israel." Matthew 19:28. In the parable of the talents, Christ represents Himself under the figure of a nobleman who "went into a far country to receive for himself a kingdom, and to return." Luke 19:12. And He Himself has told us when He will sit upon the throne of His glory: "When the Son of man shall come in His glory, and all the holy angels with Him, *then* shall He sit upon the throne of His glory: And before Him shall be gathered all nations." Matthew 25:31, 32.

To this time the revelator looks forward when he says, "The kingdoms of this world *are become* the kingdoms of our Lord, and of His Christ; and He shall reign forever and ever." Revelation 11:15. The context clearly shows when this will take place: "The nations were angry, and Thy wrath is come, and the time of the dead, that they should be judged, and that Thou shouldest give reward unto Thy servants the prophets, and to the saints, and them that fear Thy name, small and great; and shouldest destroy them which destroy the earth." Verse 18. It is at the time of the final judgment, the reward of the righteous, and the punishment of the wicked that the kingdom of Christ will be set up. When all who oppose the sovereignty of Christ have been destroyed, the kingdoms of this world become the kingdoms of our Lord and of His Christ.

Then Christ will reign, "King of kings, and Lord of lords." Revelation 19:16. "And the kingdom and dominion, and the greatness of the kingdom under the whole heaven, shall be given to the people of the saints of the Most High." And "the saints of the Most High shall take the kingdom, and possess the kingdom forever, even forever and ever." Daniel 7:27, 18.

Until that time the kingdom of Christ cannot be established on the earth. His kingdom is not of this world. His followers are to account themselves "strangers and pilgrims on the earth." Paul says, "Our citizenship is in heaven; from whence also we wait for a Saviour, the Lord Jesus Christ." Hebrews 11:13; Philippians 3:20, R.V.

[763]

Since the kingdom of Israel passed away, God has never delegated authority to any man or body of men to execute His laws as such. "Vengeance is mine; I will repay, saith the Lord." Romans 12:19. Civil governments have to do with the relations of man with man; but they have nothing whatever to do with the duties that grow out of man's relation to God.

Except the kingdom of Israel, no government has ever existed on the earth in which God by inspired men directed the affairs of state. Whenever men have endeavored to form such a government as that of Israel, they have, of necessity, taken it upon themselves to interpret and enforce the law of God. They have assumed the right to control the conscience, and thus have usurped the prerogative of God.

In the former dispensation, while sins against God were visited with temporal penalties, the judgments executed were not only by divine sanction, but under His direct control, and by His command. Sorcerers were to be put to death. Idolaters were to be slain. Profanity and sacrilege were punished with death. Whole nations of idolaters were to be exterminated. But the infliction of these penalties was directed by Him who reads the hearts of men, who knows the measure of their guilt, and who deals with His creatures in wisdom and mercy. When men, with human frailties and passions, undertake to do this work, it needs no argument to show that the door is opened to unrestrained injustice and cruelty. The most inhuman crimes will be perpetrated, and all in the sacred name of Christ.

From the laws of Israel, which punished offenses against God, arguments have been drawn to prove the duty of punishing similar sins in this age. All persecutors have employed them to justify their deeds. The principle that God has delegated to human authority the right to control the conscience is the very foundation of religious tyranny and persecution. But all who reason thus lose sight of the fact that we are now living in a different dispensation, under conditions wholly different from those of Israel; that the kingdom of Israel was a type of the kingdom of Christ, which will not be set up until His second coming; and that the duties which pertain to man's relation to God are not to be regulated or enforced by human authority.

Note 9. Page 608. Concerning the identity of the Ramah of Samuel with the Ramah of Benjamin, Dr. Edersheim says: "These two points seem established: Saul's residence was at Gibeah, and he first met Samuel in Ramah. But if so, it seems impossible, in view of 1 Samuel 10:2, to identify the Ramah of Samuel with the Ramah of Benjamin, or to regard it as the modern *Neby Samuel*, four miles northwest of Jerusalem."

www.ingramcontent.com/pod-product-compliance
Lightning Source LLC
Chambersburg PA
CBHW080857010526
44118CB00015B/2177